TWENTIETH-CENTURY WORLD

TWENTIETH-CENTURY WORLD

CARTER VAUGHN FINDLEY
The Ohio State University

JOHN ALEXANDER MURRAY ROTHNEY
The Ohio State University

Houghton Mifflin Company
Boston

Dallas / Geneva, Illinois / Lawrenceville, New Jersey / Palo Alto

Library of Congress Catalog Card Number:
85-71109

ISBN: 0-395-35037-9

ABCDEFGHIJ-A-898765

Contents

List of Maps xii
Preface xiii
The Twentieth Century: A Time Chart xvi–xix
The World, 1980s xx–xxi

Part 1
Introduction

Chapter 1
Twentieth-Century Themes 2

Global Interrelatedness and Its Shifting
Patterns 4
  The Global Pattern of 1914 6
  The Rise of the West 7
  From the Global Pattern of 1914 to That of
  the 1980s 10
Cultural Conservatism versus the Search
for New Ways 12
  Culturally Conservative Societies 13
  Change-oriented Societies 16
  Confrontation Between Conservative and
  Change-oriented Ways 20
The Rise of the Mass-oriented Society 20
  Pluralistic Mass Societies 22
  Authoritarian Mass Societies 22
Technological Triumph over Nature 23
Values for Survival 26
Conclusion 27
  Suggestions for Further Reading 27

Chapter 2
European and Colonial Horizons in
the Early Twentieth Century: A
Photographic Essay 28

Imperial Berlin: European Metropolis 30
  Capital of the German Nation 30
  The City as Crucible of Change 33
  The Social Classes 36
  Germany in the Age of Mass Politics 39
  Berlin and the Coming Century 41
Dinshawai: An Egyptian Village 41
  The Dinshawai Incident of 1906 42
  The Village as Setting of the Rustic
  Drama 44
  Village Society 47
  The Kinship Society and the World
  Outside 49
  Economic Life of the Village 50
  The Life of the Spirit 52
Conclusion: Berlin and Dinshawai 54
  Notes 54
  Suggestions for Further Reading 54

Part 2
Crisis in the European-dominated
World Order

Chapter 3
World War I: The Turning Point of
European Ascendancy 56

Causes of World War I 58
  Aggression or Accident? 58

The Multinational Empire 59
Alliances and Mobilization 60
Nationalism and Interdependence 63
An Age of Militarism 64
Battlefronts, 1914–1918 65
The Entente versus the Central Powers 65
Stalemate in the West 66
1917: The Turning Point 69
Home Fronts, 1914–1918 70
War and Government 71
War, Economics, and Society 72
War's Psychological Impact 74
Peacemaking, 1919 and After 75
The Wilsonian Agenda 75
Colonial Issues in 1919 76
The Peace Treaties 77
Conclusion 84
Suggestions for Further Reading 85

Chapter 4
Restructuring the Social and Political Order: The Bolshevik Revolution in World Perspective 86

The End of Tsarist Russia 89
Society and Politics 89
The Western Challenge 89
Lenin's Russia, 1917–1924 91
The Provisional Government 91
Second Revolution, 1917 92
Invasion, Civil War, and New Economic Policy 94
Stalin's Soviet Union, 1924–1939 95
Socialism in One Country 95
Assessing the Soviet Experience Under Lenin and Stalin 96
Contrasts in Revolution and Mass Mobilization 97
The Mexican Revolution 98
Gandhi's Nonviolence—a Means to Revolution? 101
Marxism as a Challenge to Imperialism: Mao Zedong 103

Conclusion: Revolutions Compared 107
Notes 108
Suggestions for Further Reading 108

Chapter 5
Global Economic Crisis and Restructuring of the Social and Political Order 109

Prelude to Depression 111
From Wall Street Crash to World Depression 113
Origins of the Crisis 115
Stock Market Collapse 115
Mass Production and Underconsumption: Basic U.S. Economic Flaws 116
The Spread of the Depression 117
The Depression in the Developing World 118
Britain, France, and the Dilemma of Democratic Socialism 120
The Failure of Economic Liberalism 120
The Socialist Alternative 122
Britain 123
France 123
The New Deal in Global Perspective 125
The "Roosevelt Revolution" 126
Evaluating the New Deal 127
Conclusion: The Global Trend Toward the Guarantor State 128
Notes 129
Suggestions for Further Reading 129

Chapter 6
Restructuring the Social and Political Order: Fascism 130

The Varieties of Authoritarianism After 1918 132
Borrowings from Left and Right 132
Economic and Social Change and the Growth of Fascism 133

The Original Fascism: The Italian
Model   135
  The Rise of Fascism   136
  Fascist Myth versus Fascist Reality   137
From Weimar Republic to Third Reich   140
  Weakness of the Weimar Republic   140
  From Hindenburg to Hitler   142
  The Nazi State   143
  Nazi Society and Economy   143
The Road to War   145
  Design for Aggression   145
  *Hitler's Destruction of the Versailles
  System   146*
  *The Record of the 1930s and the Lessons of
  History   149*
Fascism Around the World   150
  Other European Fascist Movements   150
  The Brazilian Integralistas   151
  The Lebanese Phalange   152
Conclusion: The Permanent Temptation of
Fascism   152
  Notes   153
  Suggestions for Further Reading   153

Chapter 7
Western Intellectual and Artistic Life Between the World Wars   154

The Optimistic Vision Shattered   156
  *The Nineteenth-Century World of Certainty
  and Uniformity   156*
  *The Discovery of Relativity and the
  Unconscious   157*
Einstein's Universe: Curved Space and
Subatomic Particles   158
  *The Theory of Special Relativity and
  E = mc² 158*
  *From Atomic Physics to Atomic
  Weapons   159*
Freud: The Path into the Unconscious   161
  The Founding of Psychoanalysis   161
  Freud's Influence   163
Cultural Relativism: Non-Western Societies
and European Global Dominance   164
Modern Art and Architecture: Mind versus
Eye   166

The Emergence of Mass Culture   171
Conclusion: An Age of Uncertainty   172
  Notes   174
  Suggestions for Further Reading   175

Part 3
Latin America, Africa, and Asia Through World War II

Chapter 8
Latin America's Struggle for Development   178

Continental Overview: The Illusion of
Independence   180
  Latin American Societies   180
  Latin American Economies   181
  Politics and International Relations   184
  *Context of the Struggle for Independence
  and Development   186*
The Amazing Argentine   186
  The Radical Period   188
  *The Depression and the "Infamous
  Decade"   189*
  The Rise of Perón   190
Brazil from Empire to New State   190
  The Old Republic   191
  *The Depression Destroys the Old
  Republic   192*
  Vargas and the New State   192
Mexico and the Legacy of the Great
Rebellion   195
  The End of the Díaz Regime   195
  The Great Rebellion   195
  Reconstruction and Depression   197
  *Cárdenas and the Revolutionary Legacy
  198*
Conclusion: Charismatic Leaders
Compared   199
  Notes   201
  Suggestions for Further Reading   201

Chapter 9
Sub-Saharan Africa Under European Sway   202

Continental Overview: African Diversity, European Domination   204
  African Diversity   204
  Common Traits   207
  Integration into the Europe-centered Global Pattern   208
  Impact of Colonial Rule   212
  African Responses to Imperialism   213
Nigeria Under the British   214
  Unification Under British Rule   214
  Nigeria's Development Under the British   216
  Rise of Nigerian Nationalism   218
South Africa: A History of Two Struggles   219
  The Union of South Africa: Politics and Economy   221
  Nonwhite Responses to Consolidation of White Supremacy   224
Conclusion: South Africa in the Perspective of World History   225
  Suggestions for Further Reading   226

Chapter 10
Asian Struggles for Independence and Development   227

India Under the British   229
  From Company Rule to Crown Rule   229
  Gradual Progress Toward Self-rule   230
  Gandhi and Nonviolence   231
The Middle East and North Africa in the Era of European Expansionism   234
  Dimensions of European Dominance   235
  Political Fragmentation and the Drive for National Independence   236
China and Japan: Contrasts in Development   243
  China's Crisis of Authority   244
  Japan's First Rise to Great Power Status   249

Conclusion: China, India, Turkey, and Japan Compared   254
  Notes   256
  Suggestions for Further Reading   256

Part 4
World War II and the Period of Superpower Rivalry

Chapter 11
World War II: The Final Crisis of European Global Dominance   258

From Phony War to Operation Barbarossa, 1939–1941   261
  The Phony War and the Fall of France   261
  "Their Finest Hour"   262
  Mediterranean Campaigns   263
  Operation Barbarossa   264
The Japanese Bid for Empire and the U.S. Reaction, 1941–1942   264
  Pearl Harbor   265
  The End of U.S. Isolation   265
The Turning Points, 1942   267
The Home Fronts   268
  Allied Mobilization   268
  Hitler's European Empire   270
  The Holocaust   271
The Defeat of the Axis, 1943–1945   272
A World Divided into Three   276
  The Yalta Conference   277
  The End of the European Empires   280
The Revolutionary Impact of World War II   281
  The War and Postwar Society   281
  The War and Postwar Technology   282
Conclusion: The High Point of U.S. Power   282
  Notes   283
  Suggestions for Further Reading   284

Chapter 12
Emergence and Decline of Superpower Bipolarity 285

Interpreting Post-1945 International Relations 287
The Cold War to 1953 289
The Containment of Khrushchev, 1953–1962 293
   The Soviet Union in Eastern Europe 294
   The Soviet Union and Berlin 296
   The Cuban Missile Crisis 296
Challenges to Bipolarity, 1962–1973 298
   The Integration of Europe 298
   The Gaullist Challenge to U.S. Leadership 299
   Playing the China Card 300
   The American Misadventure in Vietnam 300
Multipolar Détente versus Renewed Confrontation, 1973–1984 305
   The Making of Détente 305
   The Soviet Dilemma 306
   The United States in the World Economy 308
   Détente for Europeans 308
   The Carter Years: Détente Dissolved 309
   The OPEC Challenge and the Iranian Revolution 310
   The Return to Confrontation 311
Conclusion 312
   Notes 314
   Suggestions for Further Reading 314

Chapter 13
Postindustrial Society in the Postwar Decades 315

The United States and Western Europe in the Cold War Era 319
   The Acceleration of Change 320
   The Computer Revolution and the Knowledge Explosion 321
   The Flight to the Suburbs 322
   Television: The Electronic World View 323

The Collapse of Authority in the 1960s 325
   The Black Rebellion 325
   The Rebellion of the Young 327
   The Postwar Welfare State in Europe and the United States 330
The Struggle in the 1970s to Re-establish Authority 331
   The Women's Liberation Movement 331
   Stagflation and the Search for Political Direction 333
Continuing Problems and Old Slogans in the 1980s 337
   France Under Mitterrand 337
   The United States Under Reagan 339
Conclusion 340
   Notes 342
   Suggestions for Further Reading 342

Part 5
Independence for the Third World?

Chapter 14
Latin America: Mobilization and Development, or Neocolonial Militarism? 344

Continental Overview: The Shark and the Sardines 346
   Mounting Social Pressures 346
   The Uncertain Course of Economic Development 347
   Political Reflections of Socioeconomic Stress 350
   U.S.–Latin American Relations, with a Chilean Example 352
Argentina: The Perils of Authoritarianism, with Charisma and Without 355
   Toward Democracy and Development 355
   Neocolonial Militarism in Argentina 358

*Again Toward Democracy and
Development?* *359*
Brazil: Political and Economic
Vacillations 360
   The Second Republic 360
   Brazil's Military Phase 362
   The Return to Civilian Rule 363
Mexico Drifts Away from Its
"Revolutionary" Legacy 364
   The Single-Party Regime 364
   Economic Shifts 365
Cuba: Social Revolution Without an End to
Dependence 367
   Whence the Cuban Revolution? 367
   Castro and the Revolution 369
Nicaragua and the Sandinista
Revolution 373
Conclusion 375
   Notes 376
   Suggestions for Further Reading 376

Chapter 15
Sub-Saharan Africa: Development or
Collapse? 377

Continental Overview: The Hungry South
par Excellence 378
   The Spread of Independence 379
   Africa's Population Explosion 382
   Economic Development in Reverse? 383
   *Political Evolution: Common Phases and
   Themes 387*
   Africa and Outside Powers 391
Nigeria: Independence plus Oil
Dependency 392
   Rise and Fall of the First Republic 392
   *From the Biafran Civil War Through the
   Second Republic 394*
South Africa: Inequality, Exploitation, and
Isolation 398
   *White Domination, Economic and
   Political 398*
   Apartheid in Action 400
   African Responses to Apartheid 403
Conclusion 406
   Notes 406
   Suggestions for Further Reading 406

Chapter 16
Asian Resurgence 407

The Middle East and North Africa: The
Struggle for Unity and Development 409
   *Iran from Empire to Islamic
   Revolution 412*
   Egypt Struggles to Escape Its Poverty 415
   *The State of Israel and Its Search for
   Security 420*
India: Combination of Developed North and
Hungry South 426
   India Under Nehru 426
   India Under Indira Gandhi 429
China Under the Communists 432
   *The First Phase of Communist Rule,
   1949–1953 432*
   *The Socialist Transformation,
   1953–1961 434*
   The Second Revolution, 1962–1976 435
   Socialist Modernization 437
Japan: Re-emergence of the East Asian
Challenger 439
   *Reconstruction Under U.S.
   Occupation 440*
   *The Emergence of an Economic
   Superpower 440*
   Major Factors in Japan's Success 443
   *Japanese Society and Economic
   Growth 444*
   Consensual Politics amid Affluence 446
Conclusion: Asian Challenges 447
   Notes 448
   Suggestions for Further Reading 448

Part 6
The World Today

Chapter 17
Affluent North and Hungry South: A
Contemporary Photographic
Essay 450

Los Angeles: Modern Megalopolis 452
   Technology and the LA Economy 453

A Society of Immigrants   454
*Politics: Home Base of Nixon and
Reagan   456*
Watts, 1965   457
*Frontier of the Hungry South in
the 1980s   458*
Cairo: The Urbanization of Poverty   462
Cairo, Third World Megalopolis   462
Social Fabric of the City   466
Economic Life of the City   469
*Political Mobilization Without
Participation?   470*
*Cairo as a Center of Intellectual and
Spiritual Life   472*
Conclusion   473
Notes   474
Suggestions for Further Reading   474

Chapter 18
A World of Interdependence amid
Scarcity   475

Population   476
Food and Energy   478
Food for the Billions?   479
Energy, Nonrenewable and Renewable   481

Alternative Strategies of Economic
Development   484
*Developmental Strategies of the Affluent
North   484*
*Developmental Strategies of the Hungry
South   488*
Transnational Integration and Economic
Relations   490
*Existing Forms of Transnational
Integration, with Economic Examples   490*
*Transnational Economic Integration as It
Might Be   491*
Science and Security for the Nuclear
Civilization   492
Global Militarization   493
Effects of a Nuclear Explosion   494
*Nuclear Weapons and Their Uses—or
Nonuses   495*
Defense Against Nuclear Attack   499
Peacemaking and Arms Control   500
Proliferation   502
Conclusion: Sustainability or Self-
destruction—Toward a New World
Order?   504
Notes   504
Suggestions for Further Reading   505

Index   507

List of Maps

The World, 1980s   xx–xxi
1.1 The World, 1914   5
2.1 Berlin, 1911, and Population Growth Since 1800   32
2.2 Egypt, 1911, Showing Location of Dinshawai and al-Agami   42
3.1 Ethnic Groups in Germany, the Austro-Hungarian Empire, and the Balkans Before World War I   61
3.2 World War I in Europe, 1914–1918   67
3.3 Post–World War I Boundary Changes   83
5.1 Percentage of Unemployment in European Countries During the Depression   121
6.1 German and Italian Aggressions, 1935–1939   139
8.1 Latin America, 1910   185
9.1 Africa, 1914   211
10.1 The Partition of British India, 1947   233
10.2 The Middle East, Post–World War I   237
10.3 China and Japan in the 1930s   249
11.1 World War II: The European Theater   269
11.2 World War II: The Pacific Theater   275
11.3 USSR Western Border Changes, 1914 to the Present   279
12.1 NATO, the Soviet Bloc, and the Third World   291
14.1 The Contemporary Caribbean   369
15.1 Political Independence in Africa and Asia   381
15.2 Nigeria's Three Regions (1960), Twelve States (1967), and Nineteen States (1976)   393
15.3 South Africa, with the Homelands and Surrounding States   399
16.1 The Islamic World, c. 1980   410
16.2 Israel and Its Neighbors, 1947–1985   421
16.3 South Asia and Southeast Asia, 1980s   436
17.1 Contemporary Los Angeles and Surrounding Communities   453
17.2 Contemporary Cairo   463
18.1 and 18.2   Alternative Maps of the World, by Population and Wealth   486–487

Preface

The goal of *Twentieth-Century World* is to help students understand how our world has evolved since World War I. The authors believe that history, of all scholarly disciplines, provides the most effective means for understanding the state of the world because history studies society as a whole. Economic, social, political, military, intellectual, scientific, and other forces all play important parts in shaping human societies. Ultimately, however, we need to put these forces together and to see how their patterns of interaction have evolved over time. The study of world history offers us the best way to understand this interaction.

No study of a subject as large as twentieth-century world history is intelligible unless it is organized according to clear principles. Those principles that have guided the authors are as follows:

Global Integration

The world forms a tightly integrated whole. Responsible citizenship in this increasingly interdependent world requires understanding global interrelationships. To explain these interrelationships, *Twentieth-Century World* emphasizes global patterns of integration and presents major issues and events, not as unique occurrences, but in terms of their global impact. For example, the Bolshevik Revolution is discussed not just as a turning point in Russian history, but as the most influential revolutionary experience of the twentieth century.

Balanced and Selective Coverage

The authors have explicitly rejected an approach centered on Europe or the United States. This book provides balanced coverage of both developed and developing societies, of both the Western and the non-Western worlds. At the same time, the "incremental" method of writing world history, which assumes that adding together national histories will produce a history of the world, has been avoided. The approach has been selective and thematic, not encyclopedic, and aims at ensuring that students see world history as more than a jumble of facts.

A Multifaceted Conception of History

Twentieth-Century World discusses a broad range of subjects—economic, social, political, artistic, scientific, and military—to convey a fully rounded understanding of the contemporary world. Every chapter addresses several of these subjects. Certain chapters perform special functions, however. Chapter 1 states and defines the book's interpretive themes. Chapters 2 and 17 illuminate these themes by both photographs and descriptions of representative environments of the early and late twentieth-century world. Chapter 2 contrasts life in a European capital with that in a colonial village as seen at the beginning of the century. Similarly, Chapter 17 compares a supermetropolis of the 1980s in an affluent country with another in a Third World country. The narrative chapters beginning with Chapter 3 emphasize mainly political, economic, and social developments. Chapter 7, however, explores the most influential intellectual and artistic developments of the century. Chapter 18 completes the book with a discussion of such vital future-oriented issues as the population crisis and the nuclear arms race.

Clearly Stated Themes

To provide interpretive continuity, the authors have organized this book around the five themes defined in Chapter 1.

1. The shift in the pattern of *global interrelatedness* from the 1914 world of great powers and colonies to the 1980s world of interdependence amid scarcity.
2. The *contrast between change-oriented and culturally conservative societies*, a clash that has occurred around the world with the expansion of European and U.S. influence.
3. The *rise of the mass society*, sometimes in the form of pluralistic democracy, more often in the form of mass-based dictatorship.
4. The *triumph of technology over nature*, culminating in humankind's power to destroy the earth.
5. The *search for appropriate values*, prompted by doubt whether those values that have shaped the dominant societies of the twentieth-century are conducive to the future welfare of humanity.

Twentieth-Century World meets many needs of students and teachers. The book's global emphasis and clearly stated interpretive themes put the spotlight on what is most essential for understanding world history. Selective coverage permits meaningful discussion of specific examples of general developments in the text. Also it allows instructors to present other examples of their own choosing in class. Other aids to understanding include division of the text into clearly titled parts, chapters, sections, and subsections. Key terms are italicized. Maps, illustrations, and a time chart enhance the text, as do the suggestions for further reading at the end of each chapter.

The writing of *Twentieth-Century World* has been a collaborative venture in the profoundest sense. The authors have tried hard, from their first days in the team-teaching of world history, to achieve a community of views about major themes and interpretations. They have been their own first and most persistent critics, always with an eye to maintaining the thematic integrity of the book. Within this symbiotic working relationship, Carter Findley wrote Chapter 1 (with contributions from John Rothney), the section on Dinshawai in Chapter 2, Chapters 8–10 and 14–16, the section on Cairo in Chapter 17, and Chapter 18. John Rothney wrote the section on Berlin in Chapter 2, Chapters 3–7 (with contributions from Carter Findley in Chapter 4), Chapters 11–13, and the section on Los Angeles in Chapter 17. The authors are indebted to the following scholars for their critical reading of the entire manuscript and for their helpful comments:

Michael C. Batinski, *Southern Illinois University*

Robert E. Burton, *California Polytechnic State University, San Luis Obispo*
Robert F. Byrnes, *Indiana University*
Catherine Ann Cline, *The Catholic University of America*
William B. Cohen, *Indiana University*
C. Stewart Doty, *University of Maine*
Kenneth O. Hall, *State University of New York at Albany*
Jonathan K. Ocko, *North Carolina State University*
Edward J. O'Day, *Southern Illinois University*
K. David Patterson, *The University of North Carolina, Charlotte*
Johannes Postma, *Mankato State University*
James R. Roebuck, Jr., *Drexel University*
Alan Schaffer, *Clemson University*

Others who have provided valuable comments and assistance are Professors Carl Brown of Princeton University, Philip Curtin of Johns Hopkins University, Don Peretz of the State University of New York at Binghamton, Iliya Harik of Indiana University, Carl Petry of Northwestern University, James K. Baird of the University of Alabama at Huntsville, Muhammad Hasan Abdel-Al and Rafet al-Nabarawi of the University of Cairo, Çiğdem Kâğitçibaşi and Metin Heper of Bosphorus University (Istanbul), and Müge Göçek of Princeton University. At Ohio State University, the following faculty members and graduate students have kindly provided advice and assistance, some of them very substantially: Reuben Ahroni, Chadwick Al-ger, Kenneth Andrien, James Bartholomew, Alan Beyerchen, Chang Hao, Samuel Chu, Donald Cooper, Michael Curran, Stephen Dale, June Fullmer, M. Eugene Gilliom, Barbara Welling Hall, Allan R. Millett, Isaac Mowoe, Saad Nagi, Bruce Nardulli, Norman Rask, Claire Robertson, Donald Sylvan, and Warren Van Tine. With so many debts, the authors will inevitably owe apologies to some whose names they have neglected to mention.

At an earlier stage of our work, the Exxon Education Foundation provided funding to the authors in developing their team-taught course. The authors are also especially indebted to the Houghton Mifflin staff. For word processing at Ohio State, thanks are due to Chris Burton, Belinda Warner, Jo White, Maria Mazon, and Janice Gulker. Over the years, by what they understood, what they showed was not understandable, and what they contributed of their own, hundreds of our Ohio State students have also contributed to the making of this book.

Carter Findley wishes to acknowledge the encouragement of four generations of family members: Inez Vaughn Oliver; Elizabeth S. and John C. Findley; Lucia B. Findley, Clay M. Findley, and Carol Barden; and Madeleine and Benjamin Findley. John Rothney is grateful for the enduring friendship of Malcolm and Dolores Baroway, Ronald E. Coons, Sheila Porter, and Richard E. Rogers.

C.V.F.
J.A.M.R.

The Twentieth Century: A Time Chart

	Events and Issues of Global Significance	Scientific-Technical-Intellectual	North America
Pre-1900	Heyday of European world dominance	19th-century materialism, rationalism, and political liberalism increasingly challenged in the 1890s	Spanish-American War (1898) is first assertion of U.S. world power
1900		Freud's *On the Interpretation of Dreams*, 1900 Wright brothers make first powered aircraft flight, 1903 Einstein's "On the Electrodynamics of Moving Bodies," 1905 Picasso's *Demoiselles d'Avignon*, 1907	Presidency of Theodore Roosevelt, 1901–1909 Presidency of William Howard Taft, 1909–1913
1910	World War I, 1914–1918 Paris Peace Conference, 1919		Presidency of Woodrow Wilson, 1913–1921 U.S. declares war on Germany, 1917
1920	League of Nations founded, 1920 First Fascists in power with Mussolini's March on Rome, 1922 Great Depression, 1929–	Franz Kafka's *The Trial*, 1924 First nonstop trans-Atlantic solo flight, 1925	Constitutional amendment gives women the vote, 1920 Presidency of Warren G. Harding, 1921–1923 Presidency of Calvin Coolidge, 1923–1929 Presidency of Herbert Hoover, 1929–1933 Wall Street crash, 1929
1930	Global population explosion since 1930 World War II, 1939–1945	Ortega y Gasset's *The Revolt of the Masses*, 1930	Smoot-Hawley Tariff, 1930 Presidency of Franklin D. Roosevelt, 1933–1945 Social Security Act, 1935

Europe	Latin America	Africa	Asia
Franco-Russian alliance, 1894, first step in forming a rival bloc to the Triple Alliance of Germany, Austria-Hungary, and Italy (1879)	Brazil's "Old Republic," 1889–1930	"Scramble" for Africa begins, 1880s Gandhi in South Africa, 1893–1914 Anglo-Boer War, 1899–1902	Meiji Restoration, Japan, 1868 British occupation of Egypt, 1882 Boxer Uprising, China, 1899–1901
Beginning of Anglo-German naval race, 1900 Anglo-French Entente, 1904 First Moroccan Crisis, 1905 Anglo-Russian Entente, 1907 Bosnian Crisis, 1908			Japanese-British alliance, 1902 Russo-Japanese War, 1904–1905
Second Moroccan Crisis, 1911 Italy enters World War I, 1915 Abdication of the Tsar and establishment of the Provisional Government in Russia, March 1917 Bolshevik Revolution, November 1917 Treaty of Brest-Litovsk, 1918 Establishment of the Weimar Republic in Germany, 1919	Mexico's "Great Rebellion," 1910–1920 Radical period in Argentina, 1916–1930	Creation of Union of South Africa, 1910 Unification of Nigeria under British Rule, 1914 French and British seize German colonies, 1914–1915; East Africa campaign, through 1918 France recruits African troops for Western Front	Revolution of 1911, China Gandhi returns to India, 1915 Japan participates in World War I and Paris Peace Conference, 1914–1919 Egyptian "revolution" of 1919 Amritsar Massacre, India, 1919 May Fourth Movement, China, 1919
Russian New Economic Policy, 1921 French occupation of the Ruhr, 1923 Runaway German inflation, 1923 First Labour Government in Britain, 1924 First Soviet Five-Year Plan, 1928 Second British Labour Government, 1929–1931	Growth of artistic interest in developing distinctly national culture in Brazil and Mexico	African National Congress founded, South Africa, 1923	Founding of Chinese Communist Party, 1921 Government of India Acts, 1921, 1935 Mandate system in Syria, Iraq, Palestine, 1922–1923 Turkish Republic founded, 1923 GMD gains control of all China, 1928
"National" government in Britain, 1931–1935 Adolf Hitler named German chancellor, 1933 Popular Front in France, 1936–1937 Munich Agreement, 1938	Getúlio Vargas in power, Brazil, 1930–1945 Presidency of Lázaro Cárdenas, Mexico, 1934–1940	Boom in South Africa, 1933–late 1970s Italy conquers Ethiopia, 1935–1936	Japanese aggression against China, 1931– Japan and China at war, 1937–1940s

(Continued on next page)

	Events and Issues of Global Significance	Scientific-Technical-Intellectual	North America
1940	United Nations founded, 1945 Nuclear era begins with bombing of Hiroshima and Nagasaki, 1945	Germans launch first guided missile, the V-2, 1942	Presidency of Harry S Truman, 1945–1953 Truman Doctrine, 1947 Taft-Hartley Act, 1947
1950	Era of global economic growth, petroleum based, 1950–1973	Explosion of first U.S. hydrogen bomb, 1952 Explosion of first Soviet hydrogen bomb, 1953 Watson and Crick describe the double-helix structure of DNA, 1953 Soviets launch first orbiting satellite, Sputnik, 1957	Korean War, 1950–1953 Presidency of Dwight D. Eisenhower, 1953–1961 U.S. Supreme Court strikes down racial segregation in schools, 1953
1960	Population growth and superurbanization become major Third World issues. Cuban Missile Crisis, 1962 Global wave of protest by the young and disadvantaged, mid-1960s–early 1970s	United States lands first astronauts on the moon, 1969	Presidency of John F. Kennedy, 1961–1963 Presidency of Lyndon B. Johnson, 1963–1969 Tonkin Gulf Resolution, 1964 Assassination of Martin Luther King, Jr., 1968 Presidency of Richard M. Nixon, 1969–1974
1970	OPEC oil price increases (1973,1979) symbolize opening of era of interdependence amid scarcity	SALT I Treaty, 1972 SALT II Treaty, 1979 (not ratified by U.S. Senate)	Watergate scandal, 1972–1974 U.S. Supreme Court strikes down anti-abortion laws, 1973 Presidency of Gerald R. Ford, 1974–1977 Presidency of Jimmy Carter, 1977–1981
1980		President Reagan calls for U.S. Strategic Defense Initiative ("Star Wars"), 1983	Presidency of Ronald Reagan, 1981–

Europe	Latin America	Africa	Asia
Winston Churchill, British prime minister, 1940–1945 Yalta Conference, 1945 Labour Government in Britain, 1945–1950 Fourth French Republic, 1946–1958 Marshall Plan, 1947 Berlin crisis, 1948 Foundation of German Federal Republic (West) and German Democratic Republic (East), 1949 North Atlantic Treaty Organization Founded, 1949	Presidency of Juan Perón, Argentina, 1946–1955 Second Republic in Brazil, 1946–1964	North African Campaigns, 1941–1943 National Council of Nigeria and Cameroons, 1944 Apartheid becomes policy in South Africa, 1948	Japanese alliance with Germany and Italy, 1940 Japanese bomb Pearl Harbor, 1941 Muhammad Reza Shah, Iran, 1941–1979 U.S. occupation of Japan, 1945–1952 China's civil war, 1946–1949 India's independence, 1947; Jawaharlal Nehru, premier, 1947–1964 Israel's statehood, 1948
Hungarian Revolt, 1956 Khrushchev in sole leadership of the USSR, 1957–1964 Foundation of the European Common Market, 1958 Establishment of the Fifth French Republic, 1958	Fidel Castro's regime in Cuba, 1959–	Freedom Charter, South Africa, 1955	Iran's oil nationalization crisis, 1951–1954 Gamal Nasser's regime in Egypt, 1952–1970; Pan-Arabism Collectivization in China, 1955 Japan's GNP regains pre-war level, 1955 Suez Campaign, 1956 China's Great Leap Forward, 1958–1962
Soviets crush Czech revolt, 1968 "Days of May" in France, 1968	Period of military authoritarianism and economic neocolonialism, mid-1960s–1980s Military rule in Brazil, 1964–1985 Military dominance of Argentine politics, 1966–1983	Decolonization, 1960s; drift toward military rule. South Africa declared a republic, 1960 Military overthrow of first Nigerian republic, 1966 Biafran civil war, 1967–1970	China acquires nuclear weapons, 1964 China's Cultural Revolution begins, 1965 Indira Gandhi, premier of India, 1966–1977, 1980–1984 Six-Day War, 1967 (third Arab-Israeli war)
Nixon visits USSR, 1972 Helsinki Agreements, 1975, climax "Era of Detente"	Presidency of Salvador Allende, Chile, 1973 Presidency of Juan Perón, Argentina, 1973–1974 Major oil discoveries, Mexico, 1974 End of Brazil's economic "miracle," late 1970s Sandinista government in Nicaragua, 1979	Nigeria becomes large oil exporter, 1970s Widespread drought and famine, early 1970s Ethiopian revolution, 1974 South Africa begins giving "independence" to homelands; Soweto incident, 1976 Nigeria returns to civilian government, 1979	Japanese-U.S. trade tensions, 1971–1980s October War, 1973 (fourth Arab-Israeli war) Indian nuclear explosion, 1974; self-sufficiency in grain, 1978 Death of Mao Zedong, 1976 Menachem Begin government in Israel, 1977–1983 Iranian revolution, 1979
Solidarity, independent Polish trade union movement, 1980–1983	Alfonsín presidency, civilian rule restored, Argentina, 1983– Return to civilian rule in Brazil, 1985	Widespread drought and famine, environmental erosion, c. 1982– Military coup in Nigeria, 1983 South African Constitution of 1984; mounting anti-apartheid protests	Deng Xiaoping in power in China, 1980–1981 Israeli invasion of Lebanon, 1982 (fifth Arab-Israeli war)

The World, 1980 s

Part 1

INTRODUCTION

Chapter *1*

TWENTIETH-CENTURY THEMES

To understand the problems of the present and foreseeable future, we must discern the historical processes at work in the world around us. All of us—especially young people, who have the largest stake in the future—need this understanding, for the number of issues that affect our well being seems to grow steadily. We encounter shifts in values that widen our freedom but leave us uncertain about what we can expect from others. We confront problems that affect our environment, the supply of vital resources, and our economic security. The destructiveness of modern weaponry makes us worry about the very survival of our species. People alive in 1900 could scarcely have comprehended some of the challenges we face.

How can we understand something as vast as the world we live in? Can we recognize significant patterns in the mass of information before us?

This chapter identifies five interrelated themes that the events and problems of the twentieth century have illustrated repeatedly. With these themes in mind, we can work toward an understanding of the twentieth-century world in a selective way, without trying to survey every example of every issue. Chapter 2 begins this selective study of the twentieth-century experience by showing how the five themes expressed themselves in two representative environments, one European and one colonial, at the start of this century. In that chapter and the rest of the book the goal is not to compile facts exhaustively, but rather to illustrate the large patterns that run through the history of this century and help explain the specific cases discussed in these pages, and many others.

The first of our five themes, and the most important single fact about world history, is that the world forms an interconnected whole, far greater than the sum of its parts. The history of the world is more than just an accumulation of the histories of all parts of the world. Rather, there is a pattern of global interconnectedness, which changes over time. To understand global history, we must first define this pattern of integration, which has changed and tightened in this century more than ever before. From the tightening of global integration emerges our second theme, the contrast between two approaches to life—one culturally conservative, the other oriented toward change—that characterize different cultures. This century has brought these two approaches into sharp confrontation. Out of the political implications of this confrontation, our third theme emerges: the rise of the mass society. Scientific and technological implications of accelerating change raise, as our fourth theme, questions about humanity's triumph over nature. The fifth theme emerges as a question implied in the first four: will the values that have made the world what it is prove well adapted to human survival in future? The remainder of this chapter will define these themes more fully.

Global Interrelatedness and Its Shifting Patterns

To define the global pattern of interrelatedness, we must classify the world's societies into categories with common traits, then define the relationships among the categories. Like any effort at simplification, this process risks some distortion. Yet the need for such categorizations frequently makes itself felt. Many have been produced in this century. All of us are familiar with one or more of them: great powers and colonies; developed and underdeveloped (or developing) countries; East and West; first, second, and third worlds (or, in the terminology of the 1950s, the free world, the communist bloc, and the nonaligned countries); Affluent North and Hungry South; core and periphery. Different terms have seemed useful at different times.

The changing global pattern makes it difficult to find one set of terms that is applicable to the entire twentieth century. Therefore, our usage will vary. The various sets of terms also present other problems. For example, categorizations like *developed* and *underdeveloped* divide the world into just two parts. But the world's societies have many differences that we need to recognize, even though sorting these societies into a few large categories defined by criteria like wealth

▶

Map 1.1   The World, 1914

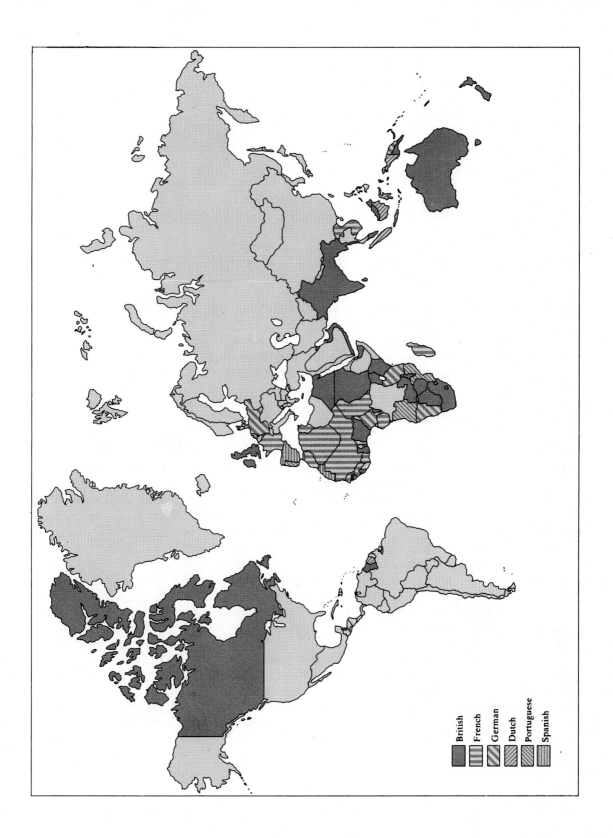

British
French
German
Dutch
Portuguese
Spanish

or power may be useful for some purposes. Some classifications are also objectionable because they assume that the vantage point of some people should be that of all. This is especially true of the designations *East* and *West*, and their derivatives *Middle East* or *Far East*, which reflect a European viewpoint. Finding unobjectionable substitutes is not always easy. When debatable terms are used, we shall explain what we mean by them.

The realities that the terms symbolize are more important than the terms themselves. We shall, therefore, concentrate here on defining the pattern of global interrelatedness as it had come to be in 1914, and as it is today. Also, we shall summarize the processes that governed the evolution of the global pattern.

The Global Pattern of 1914

The world pattern of 1914 was sharply defined. Europeans, especially, tended to think of the world as divided into great powers and colonies, although close inspection also shows some states of intermediate status.

The dominant concept of a *great power* was a nation-state with an industrial economy and a colonial empire. We can define a *nation-state* as an independent political entity that rules over, and in a sense represents, a single nationality. A *nationality* normally consists of people who share a common language, culture, history, and sense of identity. Ideally, the territory that the nationality inhabits is the territory of the state. Creation of an independent nation-state meant fulfillment for the political nationalisms that were so strong in nineteenth-century Eu-

rope and have since appeared all over the world.

In the European view, the great powers of 1914 were Great Britain, France, Germany, Austria-Hungary, and Russia. Some of these powers were not nation-states at all, and none fulfilled the ideal perfectly. Austria-Hungary and Russia represented an older political form, the multinational empire, which the spread of nationalism threatened. Germany, unified only in 1871, did not include all speakers of German. The United Kingdom consisted officially of the "four kingdoms" of England, Wales, Scotland, and Ireland; the name Great Britain properly refers to the first three of these. There was a separatist nationalist movement in Ireland; in the twentieth century, local nationalisms have been an issue in Wales and Scotland also. France came closest to the nation-state ideal, although it too included unassimilated minorities, such as the Bretons.

Similarly, the great powers were not all fully endowed with industrial economies or colonial empires. Austria and Russia were late starters in industrialization and acquired no overseas colonies, though they continued to expand their rule over adjacent territories. During the nineteenth century, for example, Russia acquired huge tracts in Asia, mostly peopled by Muslims. Germany was unified too late to acquire many colonies, but had a few by 1914. It had certainly built up the military and industrial might of a great colonial power. France had long enjoyed national integration. It had a developed industrial economy and the second-largest colonial empire. Great Britain, the original homeland of the Industrial Revolution and still the leading maritime power, possessed the largest colonial empire of all, on which—the British proudly said—the sun never set.

The colonial lands included all of Latin America, Africa, and Asia. Most of the Latin American countries, and a few in Africa and Asia, were officially independent. Yet even those were dependent on the great powers in economic and other senses. Economic dependence took the form of the "colonial economy," in which the dependent country produced one or a few agricultural products or minerals for export to the dominant country, which processed these raw materials and exported industrial products back to the dependent country. Political dependence took a variety of forms, with even supposedly independent countries subject to chronic interference by the great powers. In colonial countries that had lost nominal independence, internal political arrangements varied, from direct military rule to what the British idealized as indirect rule. In the latter case a small staff of Europeans worked through survivors of the precolonial leadership. Everywhere, too, cultural dependence was a major reality. This might result from direct initiatives, especially those of missionaries, in evangelization or public health. Or it might simply reflect local fascination with, and dread of, the European powers, and a desire to know what made them work.

Some nations in the world of 1914 fell into an intermediate group between the great powers and the colonies. The category includes some small European countries with overseas empires, such as Belgium, Holland, and Italy, as well as the fallen leaders of the first age of European expansion, Portugal and Spain. Though regarded as great powers, Austria-Hungary and Russia perhaps fit this category better. Japan too was beginning to command recognition as a power. So were the nations of the English-speaking world outside Europe. Most important of these, the United States had already become the world's most productive nation in both industry and agriculture, and had begun to play an assertive role in Latin America and the Pacific, though not yet in European affairs.

The Rise of the West

The processes that created the European-dominated world of 1914 operated over long centuries. The result is what historians refer to as "the rise of the West," in the sense of Western Europe and its overseas extensions in the Americas and Australasia. The rise of the West illustrates that European societies possessed, from early times, a potential for self-transformation that was exceptional on a world scale. This potential no doubt derived from the dual origins—Judeo-Christian and Greco-Roman—of European civilization. But other factors reinforced the readiness to change. When the ancient Roman Empire fell, for example, it was not replaced by another monolithic empire, as would have been normal in the other old world centers of civilization, but by a multiplicity of power centers. This multiplicity suggests a competitive dynamism, and a pluralism of authorities, that helped confirm the potential for change.

In the Middle Ages, European civilization also began to acquire an outwardly expansive momentum. The militarism of the era of knighthood expressed itself in domination of outlying parts of Europe and in overseas expansion with the Crusades, campaigns that started at the end of the eleventh century and aimed at recapturing Jerusalem from the Muslims. By the thirteenth century, competitive national monarchies, with distinct languages and cultures, were emerging. Significant innovations also occurred in economic life. These included the iron-pointed plow, which made it possible to cultivate the heavy soils of northern Europe, and the gradual clearing of the forests, which increased agricultural productivity. This productivity contributed to population growth, which reinforced the expansive momentum and stimulated technological innovation in fields, such as metallurgy and navigation, that had direct applications in warfare and exploration.

Population growth gave an important stimulus to the development of towns and trade. At first focused on luxuries, trade gradually expanded into such basics as woolens, iron, and timber. Europe had good natural facilities for water transport of bulky commodities, and towns grew up to handle the trade. In the politically fragmented environment, townsmen banded together to press kings and feudal lords for privileges. Thus emerged autonomous municipalities, guilds, even leagues of commercial cities. European merchants acquired higher status and greater power than their counterparts elsewhere. New forms of business organization began to emerge, along with new attitudes about practices such as loaning money at interest. The rise of Western capitalism was under way.

Awareness of the world outside Europe soon drew capitalist interest toward overseas expansion. Europeans knew of the existence of other contemporary civilizations, starting with that of Islam, centered just across the Mediterranean in what is now commonly called the Middle East (Southwest Asia plus Egypt) and North Africa. Parts of Europe—Sicily and the Iberian Peninsula (Spain and Portugal)—had long been under Islamic rule. The Crusades, in particular, exposed Europeans to the higher civilization of the Islamic world and spread tastes for luxury goods produced in the Middle East or brought there from farther east. Italians, especially Venetians, became rich from trade in these goods. The desire of other Europeans to undercut them played a critical role in opening the age of exploration.

The key events occurred in the Iberian Peninsula. The Portuguese, after inching their way down the African coast for many years, reached the Cape of Good Hope at the southern tip of the continent in 1488. Under Vasco da Gama, they reached India in 1498. Meanwhile, from Spain, Columbus set sail to the west, seeking the Indies of the east, but finding a "new world." His voyage of 1492 coincided with the fall of the last Muslim bastion in Spain, a fact suggesting that the Spanish drive against the Muslims led directly into the age of overseas expansion. In this way two of Europe's fledgling national states began tying the world into a European-dominated configuration.

Many more changes had to occur before this configuration assumed its form of 1914. Spain and Portugal were replaced as the dominant powers by countries with better-developed economies, and with a larger population than Portugal's. The Netherlands contended for dominance in the seventeenth century, establishing its hold over the Dutch East Indies (now Indonesia). By the eighteenth century, France and Great Britain were the leading contenders.

Before the struggle could be decided, the combination of nation-state and capitalist economy had to develop into an efficient mechanism for creating and maintaining a world-embracing empire. Politically, the medieval fragmentation of authority was replaced by centralized states with enhanced capabilities for administration, taxation, and warfare. Through the eighteenth century, the characteristic form of such states was the absolute monarchy, as illustrated by the France of Louis XIV. The two main exceptions were England, where the Parliament emerged as the real center of power in the seventeenth century, and the Netherlands, which created a federal union after winning independence in 1609. Other major changes included improvements in navigation and shipbuilding, and new forms of commercial organization, such as the joint-stock company.

Meanwhile, European pluralism entered a new phase with the Renaissance, which began in Italy in the fourteenth century and aimed to revive the intellectual and artistic culture of ancient Greece and Rome. The Renaissance overlapped with the Reformation, launched by Martin Luther in 1517, an attempt to purify Christian faith and practice. Nothing better illustrates the exceptional European capacity for self-transformation than the simultaneous flourishing of these two cultural movements, one attempting to revive a pagan culture, the other to revitalize Christianity. The Reformation produced a multiplicity of sects and religious authorities, decisively advancing the development of European pluralism. By challenging inherited practices and worldviews, both the Renaissance and the Reformation also contributed to other changes that helped consolidate the emerging global pattern. In particular, the Scientific Revolution of the seventeenth century, by upsetting views of the universe that had enjoyed religious sanction, provided the basis for ongoing development in science and technology.

Among the greatest proofs of the self-transformative potential of European civilization, however, were the dual revolutions—industrial and democratic—of the late eighteenth and nineteenth centuries. The Industrial Revolution, beginning in England, opened a new phase in Europe's struggle to dominate the globe. The first breakthroughs in mechanization launched an unprecedented expansion in productivity. More importantly, technological breakthroughs continued not just for a time—as had happened in earlier cases—but indefinitely, in a self-compounding and accelerating way. Nineteenth-century European imperialism grew out of all that had preceded, since Columbus and da Gama. Yet its impact was raised to an entirely new order, as the leading colonial powers developed industrial economies with which nonindustrial economies could not compete.

Meanwhile the Democratic Revolution, starting—as far as the old world is concerned—in France in 1789, began to transform the ideal political structure for the nation-state from absolute monarchy to some form of democracy, in which ultimate authority rests with the people. To justify this political reorientation, a major political philosophy emerged in the shape of nineteenth-century liberalism. Politically, this emphasized parliamentary-constitutional government with guaranteed individual rights. Such a political system might be either a constitutional monarchy, as in Great Britain, or a republic, as in France or the United States. Economically, nineteenth-century liberalism expressed the mentality of the Industrial Revolution. Government was not to interfere in business, and trade was to be free across international borders, with no tariff restrictions. By 1914, competition had created doubt about the economics of the early liberals. Doubt gave rise, in time, to a new liberalism demanding regulation of the economy to protect the disadvantaged. In contemporary U.S. terms, the old liberalism has become the conservatism of the Republican party, while the new is the ideology of the Democrats.

As industrial societies developed, some nineteenth-century thinkers shifted their emphasis from the rights that preoccupied affluent liberals to the economic relationships that made them affluent. The key figure here was Karl Marx (1818–1883). For him, politics depended on economic forces and class relationships. The middle class, with its liberalism, had destroyed absolutism in a few countries, but its ascendancy meant industrial capitalism and exploitation of the workers. Exploitation was bound to become steadily worse, until the workers rose, destroyed liberalism and private property, and created a classless communist society. Moreover, since industrialization created the same problems everywhere, Marx believed that the revolution would not be limited to any one country. The "workers of the world" would unite to throw off their chains.

Marx's revolutionary vision remains influential. But it also gave rise to a reformist trend, aiming to achieve a more egalitarian order without revolution. This school of thought is usually referred to as socialist, rather than communist. Socialism is the background of the Social Democratic parties found in many countries today; it is commonly no more "radical" than twentieth-century U.S. liberalism. *Democratic socialism* is perhaps the best name for nonrevolutionary socialism, because Marxists committed to revolution also sometimes refer to themselves as socialists.

By 1914, then, processes of accelerating change had created a Europe-centered pattern of world domination. A handful of Western economies controlled an unprecedented share of the world's wealth and resources. These were capitalist economies, oriented toward growth. Yet experience showed that even in an industrial economy, growth could not continue indefinitely without crises, in which much of the accumulated wealth would be lost. Added threats emerged from the fact that the great, and would-be great, powers saw themselves in competition with one another. Each sought to protect itself by acquiring colonies and forming alliances with others, until the European powers became divided into two opposing alignments. Even a small crisis between these alignments could set off a chain reaction that might be felt all over the world.

From the Global Pattern of 1914 to That of the 1980s

The economic and political weaknesses of the Europe-centered global configuration produced a series of catastrophes—World Wars I and II, and the Great Depression of 1929—that ultimately destroyed the pattern of 1914. Parts 2 and 4 of this book will examine these crises, which undermined the European powers' ability to maintain their former position, while new powers of larger scale emerged elsewhere. Today Western Europeans cannot figure prominently among the world's power centers except by acting together. To the extent that the new global pattern has assumed clear form, the main powers are now the

An American ship delivers U.S. wheat to the Soviet port of Odessa. World trade is marked by interdependency. In 1964, as part of the U.S.-Soviet trade deal, the *Exilona* brought 23,000 tons of grain grown by American farmers to the USSR.
AP/Wide World Photos

United States, the Soviet Union, Japan, and perhaps Western Europe as a whole. Observing that these powerful—and mostly wealthy—states are all in the northern hemisphere, some analysts now characterize the global pattern in terms of Affluent North and Hungry South. In the Hungry South, the end of the old European dominance brought decolonization and formal independence, so that the world of the mid-1980s has almost 170 independent states. Most of them are not fully viable as nation-states, either economically or socially. As in 1914, some states fall somewhere between the dominant and the dependent. In this intermediate category are countries—such as Brazil or South Korea—that have become far more industrialized than other developing countries, yet are not on a par with the strongest economies.

The relationship between the dominant powers and the rest of the world has altered in complex ways. In some respects, the gap between strong and weak states now seems wider than ever. For example, the ability of the most heavily armed powers to exert force has increased dramatically. Although the colonialism of the nineteenth century has all but disappeared, huge inequalities remain in relations between great and small states. In addition to the governments of the great powers, an increasing range of nongovernmental entities, particularly multinational corporations, are major forces in what some critics now call "neoimperialism." Because the great powers continue to be the main centers of technological advance, the economic development gap between them and the poorer countries has tended to widen with time. Finally, though improvements in transportation and communication have tied the world together more closely than ever before, the great powers, especially the United States, usually dominate the means of transport and communication and create the messages conveyed through the media. Television series created purely for entertainment have become a large part of the message the United States conveys to the world.

Other factors have undercut the dominance of the great powers. The immense power of nuclear weapons makes them virtually useless for many purposes—assuming sanity on the part of decision makers. Nonetheless, nuclear technologies are widespread and continue to proliferate. The nuclear issue aside, poor peoples the world over have learned how to rise in their own defense in ways that great powers may find impossible to control at acceptable cost. This results partly from the spread of new ideologies of resistance, as seen in Vietnam. But perhaps the most important factor in narrowing the gap between great and small powers is that the age of exploration has ended on this planet. We have no more new continents to open up, and fewer and fewer untapped natural resources. Yet population increases steadily. As a result, competition for natural resources has become much keener, while the number of needed resources has grown. The dispersion of these resources about the globe makes the idea of national self-sufficiency an illusion.

Economically, the opposite of colonial dependency is not independence, but a relative ability to determine, or at least influence, the terms of a nation's integration into the world economy.

In the case of petroleum, resource competition led in the 1970s to the creation of a new power concentration in the Middle East, and to a greater and more rapid transfer of wealth to a few countries—Saudi Arabia, Iran, Iraq, Libya, Algeria, and the small states of the Arabo-Persian Gulf—than had ever occurred before. It remains to be seen whether countries producing other raw materials can exert equivalent leverage. For now, it is clear that if the gap between great and small powers has widened in some respects, it has narrowed in others. The best characterization of the global pattern in the nuclear age is: interdependence amid scarcity.

The changing form of the global configuration is the most important point to watch in world history. As we move from the pattern of European great powers and overseas colonies to that of Affluent North and Hungry South in the nuclear age, several related issues claim our attention.

Cultural Conservatism versus the Search for New Ways

Europe's expanding influence over the globe brought the exceptional self-transformative potential of Western civilization face to face with the more conservative outlooks that then characterized all other cultures. In fact, cultural conservatism once pervaded the world, for the further back we look in European history, the more we find such a spirit there too. For many Latin American,

Asian, and African peoples discussed in Parts 3 and 5 of this book, the twentieth-century tightening of global integration has meant a confrontation between these two approaches to life. Many believe this will eventually produce a homogenized world civilization. Whatever the outcome, the confrontation can be extremely painful to live through. A comparison of culturally conservative and change-oriented approaches to life will help us understand this key part of the human experience in our time.

Culturally Conservative Societies

Culturally conservative societies have covered a vast range, from small tribal bands living under Stone Age conditions, to huge empires with highly sophisticated literary traditions. Yet all have displayed important traits in common.

The most distinctive trait of conservative cultures is that their way of life centers on maintenance of inherited patterns. Custom or the practice of one's ancestors is an important sanction for these patterns. But most often, the patterns are regarded as divinely instituted when God either created the world or intervened in it—for example, through revelation to a prophet—to set the pattern by which the society should live. An exception was ancient China, where Confucius took little interest in "the spirits," yet created an ethical system that survived as the ancestral practice of millions of Chinese until this century.

The patterns to which a society became committed did not remain changeless ever after. Members of some cultures thought that subsequent divine interventions altered their original religious tradition. Everywhere, the meaning of the central tradition was elaborated through

ongoing study. Members of each generation had to react to one another, to strangers, to ideas from other traditions, and to a changeable environment. These confrontations necessarily brought change. Conservative cultures could also be extremely creative. In the eleventh century, for example, China came close to launching an industrial revolution. In China and elsewhere, the core traditions of the great civilizations also included their own concepts of change. Sometimes, as in the case of revival movements, exponents of these traditions would use change to reassert traditional values. Alternatively, innovators might attempt to mask change as the reassertion of traditional values in their "original" form.

What culturally conservative world views did not appreciate, however, was change for its own sake. If anything, the contrary attitude prevailed: change meant decline. Some people term this an "old person's view of history": each new generation will go to the dogs unless kept in check. The historic fact that most societies have been predominantly agrarian, have depended economically on the forces of nature, and have had difficulty accumulating surplus resources to support experimentation, has reinforced this conservatism.

If the primary characteristic of conservative cultures is commitment to inherited, sacrosanct patterns, there are many secondary characteristics. The one that manifests itself in the most numerous ways, and becomes especially obvious in comparison with change-oriented societies, is relative lack of the specialization and differentiation that we are so conscious of today. Since tradition-oriented societies have covered a wide spectrum, there is much variation in this regard. In the simplest case, that of an isolated kin group living under primitive conditions, all valued functions—social, artistic, political, economic, religious, military, medical—are performed by members of the kin group. The main factors differentiating roles are sex and age. By contrast, in a premodern empire with a highly developed intellectual tradition and complex political institutions, additional forms of specialization and differentiation appear. The intellectual tradition develops different fields, each with its own specialists; a government with different agencies arises; trade and handicrafts become divided into guilds. But the scope of these processes remains limited by twentieth-century standards. Even in China, probably the greatest example of such an empire, the dominant reality for the vast majority remained membership in, really subordination to, a family unit that made its living in agriculture.

The nondifferentiation of culturally conservative societies expresses itself in political, economic, and social life, to the extent that these become distinct. Politically, the idea that authority and legitimacy come from on high through maintenance of a divinely appointed order encourages authoritarian forms of rule. Small societies may run their affairs as participatory democracies or have chiefs who function mainly as consensus-makers and leaders by example. But in larger states, the usual pattern has been authoritarian monarchy. The ruler's authority stems from a mixture of political and religious functions. Such sovereigns have been said to rule by the grace of God (England), to be the shadow of God on earth (Islamic sultanates), or to be the son of heaven (China). Where the pattern is fully intact, political authority flows from the top down. Participation in government means being a servant of the ruler. Commitment to established patterns restricts argument about policy. Court and bureaucracy monopolize politics, and the people usually have no part in it. The individual is not a citizen, but a subject, of the state. One compensation for this condition is that such states, despite the authoritarian claims of the rulers, have lacked the means to interfere in their subjects' lives as extensively as even the freest of present-day states can.

In economic terms, the large-scale integration that characterizes the world today was unknown until recent times. Two hundred years ago—even as a world-embracing system of economic linkages was forming—most countries did not have a single national economy, but many local ones. Rural people had to know how to produce most of what they used, as was still true in parts of the nineteenth-century United States. Before such improvements as railroads and steamships, problems of transportation and communication were enough to limit large-scale integration. The main exceptions were for places with outstanding natural facilities for transport by water, and for goods whose value was high in proportion to their weight or volume. The first of these exceptions helps explain the rise of capitalism in Europe; the second helps explain the importance of spices and other luxuries in stimulating the voyages of exploration.

With such limits to economic integration, people generally assumed that their local economy was fixed in size and could not grow in any lasting way. Except perhaps in the liveliest trade centers, ideas about economic life centered on questions of supply and distribution within an economy considered stable in size. Rulers sought ways to assure the provisioning of their subjects, especially in the capital city, where famine could mean political upheaval. Craftsmen were often organized into guilds, which distributed raw materials, controlled prices, and limited competition to assure that every member made a living and no one made more than his fair share. Shops of a given type were likely to be located together, rather than separately, and a craftsman who had already made his first sale of the day might be expected to pass the next customer on to a neighbor who had not. In the countryside, peasants and herdsmen yielded part of their produce to landlords or tax collectors, consumed part of it, bartered part of it for other things they needed, perhaps sold some, and redistributed part in hospitality, which their neighbors reciprocated. However strange the idea seems to Europeans or Americans today, social status often depended on what one gave away, not on what one accumulated. That notion still prevails in settings as far apart as the tent of the bedouin *shaykh* in Arabia and the long houses of the Indians of British Columbia. This kind of economic life can be described as *communalism*. Peoples of communalistic heritage often see their economic values as far preferable to those of capitalism.

In social life, the most distinctive trait of conservative cultures has been the submersion of the individual in larger groups that perform a variety of functions. In some civilizations, the sense of common membership in a religious community—that of Muslims or, in the Middle Ages, that of Christians—has been an important identifier. But the group identification that affects the individual most intimately is membership in a kin group. Poverty or early death could keep kin groups from being large. Yet societies around the world tended to idealize groupings larger than the nuclear family

A militiaman from Lebanon's Shii community performs afternoon prayers while helping guard a hijacked jetliner, Beirut, summer 1985. Among the disadvantaged, the struggle to reassert traditional values in a fast-changing world can produce violence. *The New York Times/Ingeborg Lippman*

(parents and children) as meaningful social entities—such groupings as the extended family, clan, tribe, or even tribal confederation.

In such contexts, kinship functions more as a principle of social organization than as a set of facts about genealogy. There are usually ways of adopting non-kin into the kin group, and kin groups may split over conflicts they cannot resolve. Still, the idea that society should be organized around kinship, and the genealogies that explain it, provides a clear example of cultural conservatism at the grassroots level. Everyone must know his or her place in the kin group and its genealogy, and would be lost without this continuity. Typically the kin group is the economically productive unit. It plays a vital role in religious life and education of the young. It polices morals. It perpetuates itself by arranging marriages, often within its own circle. It provides care in sickness and age. It arbitrates disputes, provides protection, and may even function as a military unit. One or more senior members—king, chief, or council of elders—make the major decisions for the group. Historically, many kinship societies never acknowledged any political authority above their own leadership, and few would do so without at least the threat of force.

Life in such settings has many important consequences for the individual. One is that his or her obligations to the kin group, like its roles, tend to be seen as total and undifferentiated. There is little sense that one has different obligations to family, work place, or society in general. Unless larger entities like the state interfere with the kinship society, most social obligations are to the kin group itself, and most social relations are personal ones within it. There is none of the impersonality that so characterizes social relations for most Americans. Although great cohesion exists within the kin group, there is also great potential for conflict between groups. Feuds can go on for generations. Because primary loyalty remains with the kin group, integration of these entities into larger units, such as states, is difficult.

The kinship mentality also restricts the sense of individual freedom. Of course, individuals who have been reared within a kinship society and know little of alternative social forms tend to find their accustomed social patterns reassuring, or at least to accept them passively. Unless these patterns are challenged, members of the kinship society are less likely to feel alienated, or to initiate movements of protest, than are individuals in much freer, change-oriented environments. For example, children in the Arab world who grew up knowing they would marry a certain cousin seldom balked at the idea—until they learned that other societies permit young people to choose their own spouses.

Change-oriented Societies

The most central point in distinguishing the change-oriented from the conservative approach to life is that change comes to be valued, even when it disrupts ways sanctioned by traditional values. The "old person's view of history" has to yield to the idea that change can produce improvement. Although the new idea is not exclusively a "young person's view," it expresses the dynamism of youth. Over time, change becomes identified with the present-day concept of progress—this had happened in Europe by roughly the eighteenth century—and the scope for experimentation enlarges. Experimentation leads to the creation of new domains of endeavor—through exploration of previously unknown parts of the world, or through creation of new branches of science, technology, art, or literature—about which the wisdom of earlier generations had little to say. If experimentation begins to produce a steady stream of benefits, as it did in the rise of the West, questions about the legitimacy of change decrease, and innovation may become self-compounding.

In the rise of the West, the first change-oriented civilization, innovation was particularly associated with science and technology. Some have dismissed the resulting modern Western civilization as "materialistic," in contrast to something vaguely termed the "spiritual East." But although materialism is a problem in Western civilization (and others), the modern West has also produced nonmaterial benefits of immense significance. It has created the political systems that most effectively guarantee individual rights, including religious freedom. Its educational and cultural institutions have flourished by any standard. Indeed, the distinction of material and spiritual proves shallow, for many material achievements of the modern West are of great spiritual benefit. Well-developed systems of public libraries make ideas freely available to people who cannot afford books. In countless instances, the sick return to the enjoyment of life, in both material and spiritual senses, because modern medicine has restored their health. To dismiss Western civilization as materialistic is to underestimate its accomplishments.

What happens to inherited beliefs and values as a new way of life, oriented to change in pursuit of progress, emerges? This question is important for both religion and politics. Secularization does occur as a society develops new fields of thought not directly linked to religious tradition. Historically, many Western men and women have become absorbed in these processes, have assumed positions that conflicted with religious authority, or have even lost interest in religion. Some scholars have assumed that the societies of the future would be completely secular. This outcome now seems unlikely. Religion no longer pervades all phases of thought and endeavor in the West—or many other parts of the world—as thoroughly as it did centuries ago. Yet it remains a vital force in contemporary life and will continue to do so. Religion offers believers a way to orient their lives, not only to the here and now, but to values that transcend the immediate. The appeal of such beliefs has been increased, if anything, by the moral questions raised by some modern secular innovations. Are there limits to the proper applications of genetic engineering? What about the uses of technology for military destruction? In our rapidly changing societies, all of us seek focal points around which to integrate our lives.

If individuals have this need, whole societies also require basic principles as they attempt to organize their political life. To survive, political systems must be able to accommodate demands for change. Yet they must also be based on constitutional principles that are essentially beyond contest. Policies and politicians come and go. But if such fundamentals as the definition of national identity, or basic rules for the exercise of power, are matters of widespread controversy, then the nation may fall into the kind of chaos seen in Lebanon since 1975. The point here is that consensus about constitutional principles seems to be partly a matter of how long they have been in effect, and even of how much they are rooted in traditional belief systems. Among the strongest and oldest constitutional ideas and symbols are the "self-evident truths" on which the U.S. political system rests, and the British and Japanese monarchies. Just as the change-oriented society is not entirely secular, then, its political life needs to be oriented as much to unquestioned, long-established principles as to originating new policies.

If the primary characteristic of change-oriented societies is the positive value attached to change, they also have many distinctive secondary traits. These result primarily from processes of specialization and differentiation that affect many phases of life—political, economic, and social.

In political terms, the rise of the change-oriented society has revolutionary implications for traditional institutions. Above all, the idea that reason can be applied in new ways to produce progress, even at the expense of inherited patterns, undermines the old concept of authoritarian rule by divine right. No political order can both pursue innovative policies based on free use of reason and maintain a divinely appointed pattern that goes back to the origins of the tradition on which the state is based. Before long, the innovations that reason suggests disrupt the patterns that tradition sanctions. How, too, can one determine which of the many possible innovations to pursue? When a political system moves beyond the maintenance of patterns sanctioned by long-established custom, or by the will of God as historically understood, the range of policy choices begins to assume the breadth with which we are familiar today. Political ideologies—general philosophies, like liberalism or Marxism, about which policies are best—emerge. When new concepts seem to promise greater freedom or efficiency, the fundamental principles of the old political order come into question. Movements grow up to promote the new ideas and compete for popular support. Almost without fail, a coup or revolution occurs before the new demands for mass political participation and ongoing policy change can be accommodated. The danger of violence is greatest where political change begins late and abruptly, as in Russia or China. Then, revolution may transform not only

political institutions, but also social and economic relations and even cultural life. For the new regime to achieve stability, its basic constitutional principles must gain acceptance as essentially beyond dispute, and it must develop structural capabilities for absorbing demands for policy change, which are bound to continue indefinitely.

Once the transformation of political life has begun, the only satisfactory way to legitimate the new policies is to seek the approval of the people whom they affect. The old idea that sovereignty, meaning ultimate authority in government, belongs to God, or to a ruler regarded as his earthly representative, must give way to the characteristically modern idea that sovereignty belongs to the people, or perhaps to their elected representatives: thence nationalism and the revolution. So far, Iran is probably unique among revolutionary regimes in affirming that sovereignty belongs to God—but even the Iranian constitution of 1979 attempts to combine this idea with popular sovereignty.

Even in the most democratic societies, the revolutionaries who speak of popular sovereignty often understand the term in a limited sense. In the United States, for example, there has been a lengthy struggle to expand the politically participatory "people" from propertied white males to the entire adult populace. Not all political systems in which sovereignty "belongs to the people" turn out to be democratic in any profound sense. The survival of authoritarianism in the age of mass politics is a problem to which we shall return in the next section. In one sense or another, however, the rise of change-oriented society means a shift to a mass-oriented political system.

In economic life, equally important changes occur. Although nations share the benefits of technological change unequally, its effects are felt everywhere. Old forms of economic production, like hand weaving, become obsolete, and new ones, like power looms, take their place. Improvements in transportation and communication, from steamships to communications satellites, integrate local economies into networks of larger, ultimately global, scale. As innovation comes to be taken for granted, the concept of ongoing economic growth becomes established, even though economic crises continue to occur.

In the twentieth century, a major government policy concern has been how to stimulate and maintain economic growth. In the Western world, with its capitalist tradition, the response to this growth orientation has been especially enthusiastic. Even in parts of the world where historical forms of economic life have little in common with capitalism, the desire for economic growth and for the productive capabilities of modern industry has expressed itself in the creation of centralized planning agencies and the adoption of development programs—five-year plans and the like. Late in the twentieth century, however, most poor countries remain in an essentially colonial economic position. Though the industrial productivity of the Third World has increased sharply in this century, most Third World countries fall far short of Japan's success in becoming competitive on the world scale in commerce and industry. Explanations for this lack of success vary. Some emphasize the neo-imperial domination of Third World economies by the highly developed nations. Others blame policy choices made in the Third World countries. Later chapters will consider both approaches to this complicated problem.

In social life, the rise of the change-oriented society has put increasing emphasis on the individual, and on his or her freedom of action. In the West, where liberation of the individual has gone furthest, even the nuclear family has seemed threatened in recent years. In the United States of the 1980s, a quarter of all households contained only one person. To some degree, this freeing of the individual has been accompanied by his or her integration into a variety of social groups, often of much larger scale than the old kin groups. Such groupings include voluntary associations, interest groups, the personnel of business firms, and the citizenry of the modern nation. The differentiation and specialization that accompanied the rise of change-oriented societies have greatly increased the variety of group forms.

For the individual, membership in these groups differs in important ways from membership in a kinship society. Increasingly, social relations are with nonrelatives and strangers, and the old personalization of relationships gives way to impersonality. In contrast to total obligation within the kin group, an individual's obligations become segmented and limited. The types of service and loyalty due to nuclear family, employer, club, church, and nation are all different. Usually, they are defined within a narrow range. If obligations are especially important, they may be defined in a written contract, enforceable by the impersonal procedures of the law, or in the law itself. Even the freest modern states have much greater means of controlling their citizens where they wish to—particularly in tax collection and military conscription—than had the earlier authoritarian monarchies.

Small wonder that we feel our societies to be increasingly complex, bureaucratic, and bewildering. With the liberation of the individual has come a heightened sense of alienation, psychic distress, and a growing readiness to protest—often by joining political or religious movements. The decline of familial authority over the young has also brought out a degree of intergenerational conflict that would not exist, or find open expression, in a kinship society. The varied forms of protest are especially evident in Western societies, where the orientation to change has been established longest. Under conditions of poverty or repression, such protests may be muted for a time, but they will burst forth when given the chance.

Confrontation Between Conservative and Change-oriented Ways

The differences between culturally conservative and change-oriented societies go far beyond the ideas that those terms directly evoke. Not surprisingly, the transition from one way of life to the other, or any confrontation between the two, causes conflict. People who have grown up in modern Western societies usually have little sense of this conflict, for the transition from the culturally conservative to the change-oriented outlook was spread out over generations for their forebears and did not represent a clash of alien civilizations. In other parts of the world, depending on how a given culture reacts to alien ideas, things have been quite different. In many cases, the clash of outlooks has seemed like a collision between alien worlds, in which one would triumph and the other lose, or be destroyed. To be committed in one's heart to a civilization that appears vitally threatened by another creates, for a thoughtful person, an intolerable dilemma of how to respond. Only if many

like-minded individuals work together can a problem of this magnitude be addressed. No single approach is correct in all cases, as the examples discussed in later chapters will illustrate, nor is success guaranteed.

A survey of the world today suggests that the sense of conflict between civilizations will eventually fade, as people in different parts of the world decide which elements of the two approaches to life fit together for them. To the extent that westerners experienced the culture clash, this is what they have done. It is what the Japanese have done, too. Obviously the outcome will depend very much on each culture's openness to ideas of foreign origin—and the openness of the Japanese is exceptional. In time, something nearer to a homogenized world civilization may emerge. But it will never be completely homogenized. The fact that the sense of civilizational conflict remains keen in some places suggests the determination of those societies to preserve key elements of their own tradition in a world of accelerating change. The fact that the Japan of kimonos and tea ceremonies is just as alive as that of cameras and computers makes the same point in a different way.

The Rise of the Mass-oriented Society

How is it that the concept of popular sovereignty leads in some cases to relatively democratic, libertarian political systems and in others to authoritarian, repressive systems? To answer that question, we have to look at the processes of mobilization that shape the mass-oriented society, and at an ambiguity at the heart of those processes.

Indian villagers watch an educational television program. A mass medium like television—here being used as an educational tool—can serve to mobilize public opinion.
Raghu Rai/Magnum

The confrontation between cultural conservatism and change-oriented outlooks tends to "free" the individual from social groups into which he or she was previously integrated. This opens the way for mobilizing the individual into larger collectivities, of which the nation is politically most important. Mobilization has many dimensions. The spread of literacy and the rise of compulsory education help draw the young into the national culture and train them for citizenship. National economic integration creates demands for mobilizing the work force—for example, when a developing industrial sector first draws labor out of the agricultural workforce. Improvements in transportation and communication activate the populace by expanding their range of movement and their awareness of events outside their local communities. In particular, the rise of the mass media stimulates the development of public opinion and political awareness. As the scope of political controversy increases, activist movements mobilize the populace by competing for their support. Where the political transformation leads to revolution or war, mass military mobilization also occurs. Mass conscription was seldom attempted in old-fashioned monarchies, in which the individual was only a subject and might have no deep loyalty to the state. But mass politics usually carries with it the idea of citizen obligation, at least for males, to join in defense of the nation. The sovereign people are their own defenders.

Pluralistic Mass Societies

The results of mobilization depend on the underlying concept of "the people." In some societies, mass mobilization proves compatible with political pluralism. Here, the "masses" are seen as consisting of individuals, who are entitled to differences and have rights that society must protect. Not surprisingly, the clearest examples of such political systems have emerged in the pluralistic societies of Western Europe and their overseas extensions.

In these societies, the concern for rights and freedoms has grown slowly and remains imperfectly realized. But on world scale, the accomplishments of these societies are extraordinary. For example, proclamations of basic rights began early with the English Bill of Rights (1688), the French Declaration of the Rights of Man and the Citizen (1789), and the U.S. Bill of Rights (1791). The British abolished slavery in their colonies in 1833, and the United States abolished it in the 1860s. Universal manhood suffrage became the law in the United States by the 1830s, in France in 1848, in Britain (with some exceptions) in 1884, in Germany in 1871, and in

Italy in 1912. By then, movements had emerged to demand the vote for women in Britain and the United States. The kind of competitive political party system that we assume in the United States today began to emerge in Britain in the first half of the nineteenth century. Of key importance in making it possible to change leaders and policies without having to resort to revolution, such a system is an embodiment of political pluralism.

The pluralistic political systems have not concerned themselves only with political rights. Legislation for protection of workers began in England in the 1840s. Social insurance legislation first emerged in the authoritarian Germany of Bismarck in the 1880s. England passed a national insurance act in 1911. To pay for social benefits, among other things, every major power had begun to collect an income tax by the end of World War I. As the twentieth century opened, great economic inequity persisted in the more democratic societies. In 1914, the wealthiest 5 percent of the population received about a quarter of the national income in the United States, and almost half the national income in Great Britain. Yet these and similar countries were committed to pluralistic democratic principles that would achieve fuller realization in the future, and would combine individual freedom with social justice in a way not matched elsewhere.

Authoritarian Mass Societies

In contrast to the pluralistic political systems, other mass societies of the twentieth century have treated the masses as just that: an undifferentiated totality not entitled to individual differences, but required to maintain unity under its leadership. Most such nations lack the pluralistic heritage of Western Europe and have traditions of authoritarian rule. Examples include the Soviet Union, China, and Iran, as discussed in Chapters 4 and 16. Some European states that went through a phase of totalitarian mass mobilization experienced great difficulty in achieving national unity or independence, and so tended at a stage in their history to emphasize the nation at the expense of its members. The obvious examples are Fascist Italy and Nazi Germany, as we shall see in Chapter 6.

Authoritarian states of either type must respond to the forces that gave rise to the modern idea of popular sovereignty. Many of them emerged out of revolutions that destroyed authoritarian monarchies and advanced apparently democratic ideologies in place of traditional values. As a result, "democracy" and "the people" are prominent concepts in the political symbolism of such regimes. Yet if the new regimes represent government "for the people," it is not government "by the people." Elections in these societies typically allow the voters only to express approval or disapproval of a single official candidate. There is normally only one political party, which is more the government's way of regimenting the populace than their way of expressing their demands. Individual rights have no protection. And no one is at greater risk than minorities who do not or—like the Jews in Nazi Germany—cannot conform to official expectations.

No one can justify such injustices. But we must acknowledge that the more effective of the authoritarian mass-oriented regimes have used their vast power to produce improvements in living conditions for the masses—not counting dissenters and vulnerable minorities, to be sure. In nations like the Soviet Union and the People's Republic of China, this has been possible partly because living conditions for the masses were initially so poor, partly because the new regimes have not hesitated to carry through programs that imposed extremely heavy human costs. Just as ancient emperors used slave labor to build temples, their present-day successors use inhumane methods to build dams and steel mills for the masses—and for the consolidation of state power in the age of mass politics.

A terrible irony of the twentieth century has been the ability of authoritarian politics to survive the collapse of the old monarchies and the transition to the mass society. In later chapters, we shall see how much the persistence of authoritarian politics has cost the world in recent times, and how it continues to divide societies today.

Technological Triumph over Nature

The modern love of change has long been linked to the technical achievements that made possible the age of exploration, the Scientific Revolution, the Industrial Revolution, and today's high technology. These achievements have drastically altered societies and their relationship to their natural environment. Before the rise of modern science and technology, most human beings lived close to nature, having little control over it and taking little from it in the way of nonrenewable resources. People were extremely vulnerable to the forces of nature. Disease and famine carried off vast numbers and kept population within rather narrow limits. Over long periods, people caused environmental damage through deforestation or overexploitation of agricultural lands, usually without realizing what they were doing. The integration of the human and natural worlds was deeply imprinted on the thoughts and values of most members of culturally conservative societies, however. The next chapter will show how turn-of-the-century Egyptian villagers experienced this integration.

The technical advances that accompanied the rise of change-oriented societies have almost destroyed this close relationship. Today we are oppressively conscious of this fact. But for a full comprehension of the twentieth-century experience with technology, we must note some other facts as well.

The first is that the concerns about science and technology that most of us feel today were largely unknown in the most advanced Western societies at the beginning of this century. People were dazzled by new achievements that seemed to come forth in steady succession, and had little sense that technical advances posed environmental or other dangers. The age of the automobile and the airplane was just dawning. Though the first long-distance, high-tension electrical line had been erected only in 1891 in Germany, electrification was spreading through the urban centers of the major nations. Governments, led by Germany, increasingly realized that scientific talent was a national resource and joined with prominent businesses to found research institutes. The pre-1914 sense of optimism about science and technology is something that we now feel only intermittently, for example with the astronauts' moon landing in 1969 or more recently with the extraordinary development of microelectronics.

The second major fact that requires note is the inequality in the worldwide availability of modern technology and the determination of disadvantaged peoples to get access to its benefits, whatever the cost. Before World War I, Russia was just beginning to industrialize. In 1908, for example, when the tsar's government encouraged the construction of a giant farm machinery factory at Kharkov, the project required borrowing German capital to buy American machine tools to be operated under a British manager—facts that reflect growing global integration, as well as Russia's underdevelopment. At the time, a third of Russia's peasants still tilled their fields with homemade wooden plows, as the Romans had two thousand years earlier. If that situation prevailed in a great European power, we can imagine how little the masses of Asia and Africa or Latin America had been touched by European technology. These colonial peoples had experienced the latest improvements in military technology from the wrong side of the firing line, and had seen railways and steamships come to transport their products to faraway markets where Europeans reaped most of the profits.

It is not hard to understand, then, why the drive for independence in the colonial world has been accompanied by eagerness to acquire modern technology. When the Nasser regime came to power in Egypt with the 1952 revolution, one of its goals was to build the Aswan High Dam, completed in 1971. Historically, Egyptian agriculture had depended on the annual Nile River flood. Since the nineteenth century, Egypt's rulers had sought ways to dam the river so as to permit year-round irrigation and multiple cropping. In the twentieth century, the desire to produce hydroelectric power emerged as an added motive. From the 1890s on, a series of low dams was built, and electrification eventually began. But a reservoir was still needed to even out year-to-year differences between high and low floods and to make year-round irrigation possible throughout Egypt's agricultural area. The Aswan High Dam was to provide that reservoir. It was also to provide water for reclaiming large tracts of desert and for generating electric power for both household and industrial use.

Like a modern pyramid, but one intended for the good of the people and not just the ruler, the high dam became a symbol of the new regime and its drive for development. But the dam's planners gave too little attention to its social and ecological effects. Its completion made it possible to bring more than a million new acres under cultivation, an increase of 15 percent in Egypt's cultivated area. The dam also produced as much electric power as Egypt needed in the 1960s. But in regions to which the dam brought year-round irrigation for the first time, peasants found their lives to be much changed. Public health risks from the water-borne *Bilharzia* parasite increased with the shift to year-round irrigation. Inadequate drainage of the fields created another problem: increased salinity of the soil, which reduced productivity and required costly repair work. Because of its high birth rate, Egypt became a net importer of food again within a few years after completing the dam. For many reasons, including the characteristics of the desert soils, the reclamation projects failed. The state-sponsored enterprises, like steel and fertilizer plants built to use Aswan electricity, proved inefficient.

The Nile itself was no longer the same. Behind the dam, there was now a vast lake, into which the silt that had created Egypt's fertile delta slowly settled. Downstream, changes in the flow and quality of the river affected even the fish catch in the Mediterranean off Egypt's coast.

Although the record of the Aswan Dam was hardly all good, outsiders should not criticize too freely. Egyptians had realized some of their goals. And the entire project reflects an attitude historically much stronger in the West than in Egypt: that human beings are not parts of the natural world, but its masters, who can tame it and shape it to their will.

For Egyptians, the Aswan Dam symbolized hopes of independence and development as bright as those that the motorcar and the airplane roused in European hearts in the early twentieth century. Yet the social and environmental impact of the dam makes clear that the dark side of scientific and technological advance, of which Westerners are now so conscious, has appeared in the developing countries too. Today the air of U.S. cities is far less polluted than that of Cairo or Mexico City, where local governments lack the resources that the United States invests in environmental protection, and local residents—if conscious of the problem at all—most often think that development comes first.

Our ability to dominate the natural environment has become so great in this century that we have to ask whether we have overdone it. Many people today believe that we have. The exploitation of nonrenewable resources cannot proceed blindly ahead without catastrophe. If nothing else, we must learn to rely more on renewable energy sources. Unless population growth is checked, it will threaten obliteration of the natural environment, a danger already visible in some industrial centers of the developed countries and around some fast-growing supermetropolises of the Third World. A more immediate danger is the existence of more than enough nuclear weapons to destroy the world—and we continue to build more.

Never before the second half of the twentieth century have human beings held such power, or such responsibility for its use. Since our mastery of the material world now seems almost too great for our own good, our emphasis must shift to custodianship of the environment, and to cooperation with others for that purpose. The historical record does not inspire great confidence that we can make this adjustment. On the other hand, we have never before played for such a high stake: survival.

In time, space exploration may open new vistas for humanity and create new outlets for the competitiveness that threatens us on earth. So far, however, this prospect seems more dream than reality—probably a desirable situation until we learn to cope with the problems that we have so far failed to solve on earth.

Values for Survival

The fascinating but frightening questions at the heart of contemporary world history have implications extending far beyond the realms of science and technology. Ultimately they raise questions about the values that have guided the development of the societies that are now most influential, and about how these values will affect the future of humanity.

Considering these value questions, we have to ask: is there a need to redirect the overall development of our contemporary societies? Many people now think that there is such a need. The processes of differentiation and specialization that have accompanied accelerating change have created a world so complex and fragmented that many people feel dangerously isolated and bewildered. In the world of knowledge, for example, the multiplication of fields and subfields has created serious problems of communication. The result is a great need for efforts at reintegration—including the study of world history. It may well be that the push for economic growth, so central to the dynamics of Western society, cannot go on unrestrained in a world so tightly integrated, yet so plagued by economic inequalities. Nor can processes of secularization go much further without aggravating an already serious sense of moral drift. Finally, in the midst of the nuclear arms race discussed in Chapter 18, the very meaning of security no longer seems as clear as it once was.

In many respects, we live at a turning point in history. If we negotiate it successfully, a reformulation of values seems likely to be a major part of our future. The values at the heart of the old culturally conservative approaches to life may have much to contribute to this reformulation. There is already a widespread desire for greater emphasis on social solidarity, on the symbiosis of human beings and nature, on social and cultural reintegration, and on religious values and beliefs. We sense that these ancient ideals should perhaps moderate the search for individual fulfillment, the thrust for mastery of nature, the emphasis on growth and profit, and the competitiveness in commerce and international relations.

Conclusion

We cannot simply return to the past, but it may help us face the future. Young people who grew up in the optimistic atmosphere of the late nineteenth century were caught unawares by the horrors of World War I. Young people of today, oppressed by their consciousness of the world's problems, may turn their awareness to good account. The philosopher George Santayana warned that those who will not learn from history are condemned to repeat it. In the nuclear age, they could be condemned to something far worse. Guided by the five themes discussed in this chapter—global integration, the clash between cultural conservatism and the search for new ways, the rise of the mass society, the problems of technology, and the question of values for survival—we shall now set out to learn from the history of the twentieth-century world.

Suggestions for Further Reading

Braudel, Fernand, *Civilization and Capitalism, 15th–18th Centuries*, trans. Siân Reynolds, 3 vols. (1981–1984).

McKay, John P., Bennett D. Hill, and John Buckler, *A History of World Societies*, 2 vols. (1983).

McNeill, William H. *The Rise of the West: A History of the Human Community* (1970).

———, *A World History* (1979).

Roberts, J. M. *History of the World*, 2 vols. (1976).

Stavrianos, L. S., *Global Rift: The Third World Comes of Age* (1981).

Wallerstein, Immanuel, *The Modern World-System*, 2 vols. (1976, 1980).

Chapter 2

EUROPEAN AND COLONIAL HORIZONS IN THE EARLY TWENTIETH CENTURY: A PHOTOGRAPHIC ESSAY

The world of 1914 was an integrated whole in which the rapidly changing societies of Europe and North America dominated the culturally conservative societies of the rest of the globe. This domination reflected the growing ability of modern technology to break down obstacles to the exploitation of natural resources. By radically increasing the speed of travel, railways and steamships in effect brought all parts of the globe closer together. In this way, improvements in transportation undermined the old local bases of political authority and, by involving everyone in national or even international relationships, enhanced demands for political rights for all. Even in the villages of the non-Western world, the presence of Europeans was beginning to stimulate this kind of change.

To illustrate the nature of the 1914 world system and the difference between change-oriented and tradition-oriented societies, it is helpful to look closely at two dramatically contrasting environments: a great European city and a non-Western village. Of course each city and village was unique in many respects, but our illustrative discussion focuses on the general characteristics distinguishing these two environments.

Imperial Berlin: European Metropolis

Capital of the German Nation

To understand Europe's world dominance in 1914, we must visit one of its great metropolises, for it was the economic and intellectual creativity of its urban population that made European dominance possible. Berlin may seem an obvious choice to examine, because it was the capital of the newest and most powerful of the continental great powers, the German Empire, or Reich. But a more important reason for choosing Berlin over London, Paris, or Vienna is that it had only recently achieved worldwide prominence. Until the unification of Germany in 1871, Berlin was merely the capital of Prussia, the largest of the thirty-nine German states. Berlin's tremendous growth in size and influence came in the half-century before 1914, coinciding with the consolidation of European world domination. Thus the characteristics of the new century can be seen particularly clearly in Berlin.

An American visitor of 1914 might have felt more at home in Berlin than in the older European capitals. Europeans were invariably struck by Berlin's stark newness. To meet the demand for housing, the city was expanding into the open countryside; streets and apartment buildings were being constructed practically overnight. "You would think yourself in America at the moment a new city was being founded," wrote one astonished French visitor. "In twenty years Berlin will have four million inhabitants and it will be Chicago."

Both Berlin and Chicago had grown to giant size at unprecedented speed. Chicago had doubled its population within fifteen years and by 1914 was the world's fourth-largest city. Its development reflected the tremendous growth of the American economy after the Civil War. In 1914, however, the United States was only beginning to assert a worldwide influence corresponding to its economic power. Otherwise we might well have chosen Chicago as our representative Western urban environment.

Berlin's growth also reflected the consolidation of a national state through war. Many of its monuments commemorated the battles of the Franco-Prussian War of 1870, in which Prussia had defeated France and created a united Germany under Prussian leadership. Glittering cavalry and goose-stepping infantry were on parade everywhere. Berlin's monuments were intended not only to impress the foreign visitor, but also to enhance Germans' own identification with their nation. Half a century after German unification, many non-Prussian Germans still identified with their local state or city. But as accelerating economic and social change uprooted more and more people from local backgrounds, Germans, like other Europeans, inevitably came to think of themselves as belonging above all to a national state.

From identification with a unique national group, it was only a short step to the belief that the world was divided among biologically differing races. In the United States in 1914, there was much talk of the virtues of the "Anglo-Saxon race." Many Germans believed themselves to be especially valuable members

Guards cavalry returning to their Berlin barracks. The elite Guards regiments, officered for generations by the same landowning aristocratic families, were a reminder of Prussia's warlike past.
Album von Berlin (Berlin, Parnassus, c. 1900)

of the white "race" that had so easily and quickly seized dominion of the world. Latecomers to the colonial contest, the Germans had only a tiny empire in tropical Africa and the South Pacific, far smaller than the holdings of their British and French rivals. Most Germans took tremendous pride in ruling over some 15 million "natives." It seemed unimportant that their colonies attracted few settlers and cost the German government

more than they benefited the German economy. By conquering Africans, Germans felt, they were giving savages the opportunity to benefit from a superior civilization. Africans were exhibited at carnivals like sideshow freaks, with no recognition that their civilization was as old and in subtle ways as complex as any in Europe. Indeed, African resistance to colonization was regarded as perverse, and the German army had punished

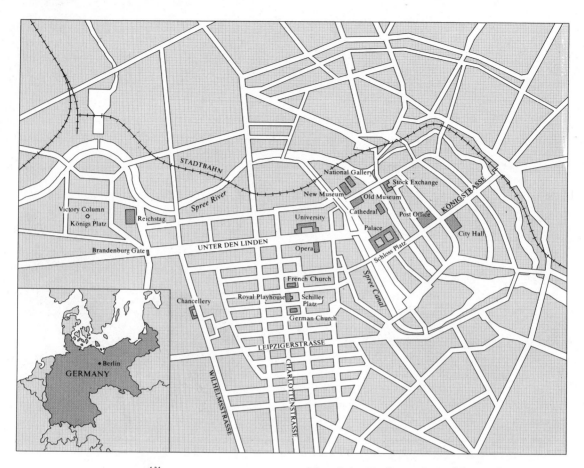

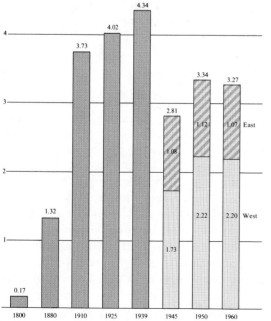

Map 2.1 Berlin, 1911, and Population Growth Since 1800 (in millions).

After 1945, Berlin became two cities: East Berlin and West Berlin.

such resistance by systematic massacres.

German militarism was not focused on the colonial lands, however. Instead, Berlin's monuments and parades advertised Germany's preparedness for the "real" war, the one among the great powers. Berliners disagreed as to whether such a war was coming, but all were confident that if it did, Germany would win it.

The City as Crucible of Change

Their role in preparing for war sustained the prestige of the Prussian aristocracy, the top 1 percent of Berlin's society. Titled landowners continued to dominate the army officer corps, in prestige if not in numbers. Observing their arrogant demeanor on the sidewalks of Berlin, foreigners might well have wondered why these relics of Prussia's past remained influential in a giant modern city. In culturally conservative societies the caste of warriors has often been pre-eminent. But Berlin by 1914 was far more than the garrison city for the Prussian Guards. It had become a laboratory and work place of the change-oriented society, like the other great cities of Europe and North America. Though titled officers might still elbow civilians aside, it was bankers, chemists, and lathe operators, not generals and colonels, that had made Berlin a world city.

The transformation had taken only two generations. Germany had not joined the world's headlong rush to urbanization and industrialization until after the unification of 1871. As late as 1870, almost half of Germany's people were still employed, as most human beings have been throughout history, in farming the countryside. By the early 1900s, that proportion had dropped to a third. During roughly the same period, the number of German cities with a population over 100,000 rose from eight to forty-eight. Berlin's population doubled.

Today we take for granted the near-miracles of technology and hygiene that enabled people to find a better life in the city. In the late twentieth century we expect pure drinking water, adequate sanitation and fire protection, safe and dependable transportation systems. In 1914, however, these triumphs of human organization were so new that they seemed remarkable. Electric trains swept into their stations in quick succession, each disgorging hundreds of hurrying passengers, who might push the visitor aside without even a glance of apology. Each morning the streets were washed by a disciplined brigade of boys. Police ordered litterers to pick their trash up again.

Perhaps half of 1914's Berliners had come from the very different environment of villages and farms. Urban life offered in one day a greater variety of new experiences than their former homes could provide in a lifetime. Even a poor Berliner could see the world's great art in a museum, borrow a book on any subject from a branch library, and marvel at the world's most exotic animals collected in the zoo. At a store on the corner one could buy the inventions of faraway countries, like the Kodak camera George Eastman had first produced in Rochester, New York, in 1888.

In many ways, Berliners' lives were far freer than those of their rural ancestors. But paradoxically, the complexity of urban life also required the authorities to maintain more control over the individual. The law compelled every child in Berlin to attend school, for example, and hygiene demanded an annual physical

Four levels of traffic in Berlin. The different economic activities of a modern metropolis required varied transport: the canal with barges and boats; the street traffic; the freight railway above these; and the electric passenger train taking the fastest route, through a building.
Album von Berlin (Berlin, Parnassus, c. 1900)

examination for each school child. By 1914 such measures had largely eliminated the danger of epidemics in the closely packed population. Detailed records were kept for every child—and for the investigations of meat inspectors, factory inspectors, and building inspectors. More and more government officials were employed in maintaining these records. Watching them at work, a visitor might have admired their efficiency, but worried about the potential for bureaucratic interference in individual lives.

The space and time of Berlin were quite unlike those of the village and the farm. Berliners might commute twenty miles to work. To catch their trains, they had to know the time exactly, and so they carried watches. As they rode, most commuters glanced through one of Berlin's cheap newspapers, whose numbers had grown even faster than the city's population.

The large metropolitan newspaper was the first of the twentieth-century mass media. The telegraph and radio enabled it to involve its readers with events

Friedrichstrasse and Unter den Linden. The Victoria Hotel at this busy
Berlin crossroads honors Kaiser William's mother, oldest daughter of Britain's Queen Victoria and her namesake. This close relationship between
the two royal families did not prevent war in 1914.
Album von Berlin (Berlin, Parnassus, c. 1900)

on the other side of the world and encourage them to hold opinions, informed
or not, about distant happenings. Not
that Berliners lingered long over their
newspapers. Like Americans, they were
usually in a hurry, often munching a
quick lunch standing up at one of a chain
of identical restaurants. The Berliner's
rapid-fire slang, in which words were
often abbreviated to initials, was regarded as very "American" by other
Germans.

Like Chicagoans, Berliners in 1914
lived in a highly organized, fast-moving
world of strangers. Their horizons extended around the world. Their entirely
man-made environment—an "ocean of
buildings"—could hardly have been
more different from the environment of
village and farm, where people still
walked most places, recognized most of
the people they saw, and told time by
watching the sun move across the sky.

Its pace made Berlin exciting. It welcomed four times as many tourists in
1914 as it had two generations earlier.
Some thoughtful people, however, were
worried by the growth of the giant twen-

tieth-century metropolis. The German philosopher Oswald Spengler, for example, lamented that urban populations would soon outnumber rural people bound to traditions—"live people born of and grown in the soil." To Spengler, "the parasitical city dweller" was "tradition-less, utterly matter of fact, religionless, clever, unfruitful, deeply contemptuous of rural people."

Conservatives in Germany and elsewhere have continued to criticize the great metropolis, the most visible symbol of twentieth-century change. But the very qualities of the metropolis that Spengler disliked—the impersonal crowding together of millions, each person responsible for the speedy performance of a specialized job—made possible the change-oriented society, and with it European global dominance.

A city like Berlin or Chicago was a great human beehive. What might seem a confused swarming of people was actually the intricate interaction of millions of individuals. Together, their efforts yielded the city's products. Berlin was a world leader in such modern industries as electrical equipment, chemicals, and machine tools. Their profits helped supply capital to the city's big banks, which invested around the world from Turkey to Argentina to China.

The collective efforts of Berliners also created innovation: an intangible product just as real as machinery and investment capital. Many of Berlin's huge factories had begun as small workshops in which entrepreneurs perfected their discovery of an industrial process like the making of a synthetic dyestuff. More recently the kaiser had supported the creation of research institutes, backed by both industry and government, to institutionalize the business of discovery. Scientists working in Berlin laboratories had discovered both the bacillus that causes tuberculosis and the x ray that could detect the deadly disease. A government-sponsored researcher won a Nobel Prize for discovering a cure for syphilis. Such discoveries had made Germany the world leader in science and medicine. Emerging U.S. research universities were designed to follow German models.

Berlin provided the human critical mass for an explosion of creativity felt around the world. The contribution of its millions of workers was as essential as that of the industrialists and scientists.

The Social Classes

Not every contribution, of course, received equal reward. Berlin in 1914 was a society of layers. Each social class differed sharply from those above and below it in income, lifestyle, and even appearance.

Far outnumbering the aristocrats who represented the top 1 percent of this social pyramid, the middle classes may have represented almost 40 percent of the population. Wealth varied widely within this group. The richest members of the middle class included many of the three hundred or so powerful company directors who controlled most of German industry. Such men would have been among the few Berliners who could afford a Mercedes or another early automobile. They lived in mansions rivaling those of the imperial family.

Hardly less comfortable were the homes of doctors, senior civil servants, and university professors: ten- or twelve-room apartments overlooking fashionable streets and squares. Guests could confirm their invitation by telephone, ride up in an elevator, announce themselves to a uniformed maid, and await their hosts in a room lit by electricity and warmed by central heating. The lower middle class did not enjoy all these comforts, but even a young journalist could find a comfortable apartment by following the building boom out into the suburbs.

Jews occupied a special place in Berlin society. This community numbered nearly 160,000, four times more than in 1871. Because of their successful careers in banking, journalism, manufacturing, and entertainment, most Jews would have qualified as middle class. Yet partly because their success had coincided with accelerating change in Germany, they met hostility from many who regretted change and wished to blame it upon someone. Prejudice excluded Jews from much of high society and from government employment down to the level of postman. Though its strength seemed to be waning by 1914, an anti-Semitic party had elected members to parliament on a platform of expelling Jews from Germany. But few Berlin Jews doubted that their future lay in that city

Bayrischerplatz, Berlin. Nursemaids and children from nearby apartment buildings crowd this square in an upper middle-class neighborhood.
Album von Berlin (Berlin, Parnassus, c. 1900)

Moving day. Even in a prosperous metropolis like Berlin, a majority of people had few possessions. Still their standard of living was much higher than that of most people in the non-Western world.
Heinrich Zille/Schirmer/Mosel Munich

or sympathized with the Zionist movement's aspiration to found a Jewish state in Palestine.

The base of Berlin's social pyramid was formed by the working classes, about 60 percent of the population. They lived much as American workers did. Though Berlin was too new to have extensive slums, the typical working-class couple inhabited a one- or two-room walkup apartment in a cheaply constructed tenement. Often the family took in a lodger, who would occupy a bed in one corner of the kitchen. Landlords were harsh, and evictions were frequent. Moving was relatively easy, for most of

a couple's possessions could be loaded onto a small cart. Most workers spent long hours on the job six days a week. Significantly, the workingmen's cut-rate streetcar tickets were good only before 7:00 A.M. and after 5:00 P.M.

The life of a Berlin worker was far from desperate, however. Most ate meat—only recently a rare luxury—once a day, with perhaps even a roast goose on Sunday. The family might spend Sunday at the shore of some suburban lake or working in their garden. To attract workers away from the bars, the city rented them suburban garden plots.

German and American workingmen

in 1914 differed in two important respects. Berlin's workers were protected by the world's first comprehensive welfare state, and they were virtually all committed Socialists. Beginning in the 1880s, the German government had insured workingmen against the risks of sickness, accidents, and disability. Government benefits also provided "social security" in old age. These benefit plans, which required contributions from both employer and employee, violated the basic principles of nineteenth-century liberal economics, which held that the government should not tamper with the operation of a free-market economy by interfering with employment conditions. Germany's welfare state had actually been constructed in defiance of these liberal ideas by conservative politicians, who hoped to wean Germany's workers from Marxism.

Germany in the Age of Mass Politics

By 1914 this conservative hope appeared to have been disappointed. Five of "Red Berlin's" six representatives to the German parliament, or Reichstag, were members of the Socialist party, the nation's largest. In the 1912 elections, a third of the electorate had voted for this party, which still officially followed Marx in advocating revolution to overthrow the bourgeoisie, give power to the workers, and abolish private property.

The typical Berlin Socialist voter, however, was probably not wholly committed to his party's official program. Workingmen wanted to eliminate some relics of Prussia's oppressive past, like systematic brutalizing of army recruits, and sought economic benefits like the eight-hour day. They were not so sure that abolishing private property was a

good idea, or that Marx's idea of class warfare still made sense in a modern society where trade unions were becoming stronger and workingmen had the right to vote.

Some workers undoubtedly felt that if the kaiser and his regime continued to

Social classes in Berlin. The class to which persons belonged could easily be identified by their dress and bearing. The two gentlemen in the background clearly belong to the middle class.
Heinrich Zille/Schirmer/Mosel Munich

The Reichstag, or Parliament. Completed in 1894, the building was a pompous monument to the national pride of newly united Germany.
Album von Berlin (Berlin, Parnassus, c. 1900)

obstruct reform, the working class would simply sweep them away. Under the German constitution of 1871, the kaiser continued to play a political role that seemed strangely out of date. He still claimed authority as God's delegate on earth. His "divine right" to rule was not derived from the consent of the people but from heaven itself. Just as in the Middle Ages, crowds of petitioners gathered daily outside the royal castle—significantly situated close to the cathedral—hoping to win a moment's attention from the monarch. Thus Berlin retained a medieval model of kingship that other Western European nations had abandoned for a limited constitutional monarchy. Kaiser Wilhelm II boasted that he had never read the constitution. But it was he, not the Reichstag, who appointed and dismissed the cabinet members who formed Germany's executive branch of government.

Despite universal manhood suffrage, Germany was not a real democracy in 1914. The Reichstag had little power. Because its proceedings were not decisive, they were dominated by the petty quarrels and cynical deals of special-interest parties and well-organized lobbies. Germany's first experience with the age of mass politics was one of corruption and frustration, rather than a lesson in self-government.

Berlin and the Coming Century

Even in a European society accustomed to welcoming change as progress, tradition died hard. In Germany, the global power of a modern urban and industrial economy was entrusted to a backward political system that left power in the hands of one man, the kaiser, who was known to be unstable. Most Berliners, however, were optimistic about their city's future. Berlin spent a quarter of its budget to provide an elementary education for every child. Like most other Europeans and North Americans, Berliners believed that common schooling would break down whatever cultural differences lingered among the young, and would inspire continuing innovation to improve the quality of life.

A newspaper poll showed that the two historical figures Berliners most admired early in the twentieth century were Joseph Lister, discoverer of antiseptics, and James Watt, inventor of the steam engine (both Englishmen). The control of disease had raised German life expectancy from thirty-five to forty-seven years within a few decades, and the new source of energy had revolutionized the German economy. It seemed likely that the talent and energy of Berliners would produce equally miraculous changes in the next half-century. In such an era of change, how long could traditional ideas and practices survive? Already the practice of religion was dwindling, so that only a quarter of the babies born in Berlin in 1914 were baptized. Now that science was unravelling the secrets of the universe, many Berliners thought, this legacy of the superstitious past could be discarded.

Only thirty years later, devastated by the bombing of World War II, Berlin would lie in ruins. But in 1914 only the most pessimistic of people recognized the dangers that lurked in the very characteristics that had enabled European civilization to conquer the world. The rivalries of national pride would prove disastrous when Europeans turned on one another the ferocity that they had already shown against Africans and Asians. The advances of science, reinforced by the methods of administrative control that had made Berlin so efficient, would make war far more deadly. War's unequal stress on social classes would bring revolution. The domination of the masses in politics would help give power to leaders with ideas far more dangerous than the kaiser's vague dream of extending German influence everywhere.

In twenty years, these developments would fatally undermine the global pattern of European domination. In 1914, however, it still stood triumphant. To see that system from the perspective of non-Europeans is our next task.

Dinshawai: An Egyptian Village

If a great metropolis like Berlin was the pre-eminent European environment of 1914, the characteristic setting for life in the colonial world was the village. No single village can typify the colonial countries as well as Berlin did the Western powers. But Dinshawai, in Egypt,

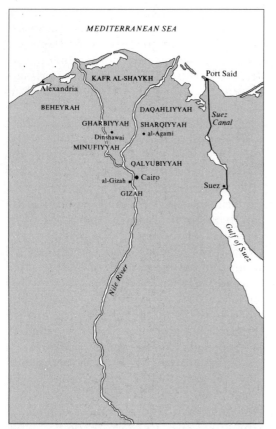

MEDITERRANEAN SEA

Port Said

KAFR AL-SHAYKH

Alexandria

BEHEYRAH

DAQAHLIYYAH

Suez
Canal

GHARBIYYAH SHARQIYYAH

Dinshawai • al-Agami

MINUFIYYAH

QALYUBIYYAH

al-Gizah • • Cairo

Suez •

GIZAH

Nile River

Gulf of Suez

Map 2.2 Egypt, 1911, Showing Location of Dinshawai and al-Agami

The Dinshawai Incident of 1906

The Egypt of 1906 had been brought under European domination in an unusual way. There was more to the matter economically, as we shall see. But politically, Egypt was still a province of the Ottoman Empire, which was ruled by the sultan at Istanbul, and included part of southeastern Europe, together with Turkey, the Arab countries of southwestern Asia (including what later became Israel), and Libya. Yet Egypt was no ordinary province. The same family had governed it since 1805, as they would until 1952, and they had acquired powers that made them little less than independent. When the British occupied Egypt in 1882, they did not bother to remove the family of hereditary governors, then known as khedives, or to deny—until World War I—the sovereignty of the Ottoman sultan. The British left outward forms unchanged, but they took charge.

It has never been entirely clear what happened at Dinshawai, perhaps because of differences in perception by people of different cultures. The incident began when British officers, on march through Minufiyyah Province, northwest of Cairo, went pigeon shooting. Western accounts of the incident usually fail to mention that pigeons in Egypt are not wild birds. The peasants raise them for food and build towerlike houses, atop their own houses, for pigeons to nest in. At Dinshawai, a British shot apparently started a fire in some grain on the threshing grounds at the edge of the village. Another shot hit a woman. The villagers sought vengeance, as their code demanded. In the ensuing fracas, two officers were wounded, and the others opened fire on the villagers. One of the wounded officers attempted to go for

not only offers a vivid picture of village life, but also illustrates how European power made itself felt in far parts of the world. An ugly incident that occurred in Dinshawai in 1906 provides a good starting point for a discussion of village life in the Egyptian Delta at the beginning of this century.

Many features of the village's physical appearance, its social composition, and its political, economic, and spiritual life are specific to the Nile Delta. But in important respects Dinshawai resembled villages all over the colonial world of the early twentieth century.

Pigeon tower, said to be atop the house of Zahran, one of the heroes of Dinshawai, Minufiyyah Province, 1983.
(C. V. Findley)

help, but died on the way. Another officer managed to bring in more troops. More shooting followed, and another villager was killed.

The annals of imperialism include many similar episodes. In a sense, they were part of the costs of the game, and it was not always possible for the dominant power to avoid losing. But this time, Lord Cromer, the highest British official in Egypt from 1883 to 1907, decided to exact punishment. He had fifty-two villagers arrested and tried under a regulation against attacks on British army personnel. In keeping with the pre-tense that the khedive ruled Egypt, prominent officials from Cairo were sent out to serve as judge and lawyers. Thus, Egyptians prosecuted Egyptians for attacking foreigners who had inflicted the first injury. Four men were sentenced to death, others to hard labor, others to public flogging. The hangings and floggings were carried out on the threshing grounds at the village edge, while the victims' families looked on helplessly.

Egyptians have never forgotten these events. Village bards immortalized them in folk ballads. As a boy, Anwar al-Sadat, who became president of Egypt from

Prisoner No. 48—perhaps Muhammad Zahran himself—leaves the court at Dinshawai after being condemned to death. The British press denounced the condemned men as murderers.
(Illustrated London News, July 14, 1906)

1970 to 1981, heard his grandmother sing about Zahran, the villagers' hero and one of those hanged. Sadat and others grew up wanting to overthrow those responsible for what had happened—a dream that the 1952 revolution fulfilled.[1] In the Cairo of 1906, intellectuals poured forth their outrage in verse and newspaper articles. In terms of political mobilization, this was a great moment: the first time educated Egyptians had supported peasant violence. Critics of British policy as far away as France and England wrote about the incident. Cromer had to retire a year later, and his successor arranged for the pardon and release of the villagers still in prison.

The Village as Setting of the Rustic Drama

Passing by a village in the Nile Delta in 1906, one would ordinarily have seen little sign of events as dramatic as those that led to the trials. From the distance, the village looked like an indistinct mass of low houses, with a few trees, surrounded by fields. Unlike the United States, where farmhouses are normally isolated, the pattern in the Middle East, and most other parts of the world, is for those who till the soil to live together in a village and go out each day to their fields. Very likely, the only structure in the village that differed from others very

Skyline of al-Agami Village, Sharqiyyah Province, 1983. The painted domed building is the shrine of a local saint. Al-Agami is a Delta village with many resemblances to Dinshawai.
(C. V. Findley)

noticeably was the domed and painted shrine of the local saint. The village might have a small mosque, or simply an open space to use for prayers, at the edge of the fields. If some villagers belonged to Egypt's Coptic Christian community, there would be a church. The village would also have displayed few signs of occupational specialization. There might be one or two religious functionaries, a barber who also served the villagers' medical needs, and a grocer selling sugar, tea, soap, oil, kerosene, tobacco, and matches. To find other shops or to market their own surplus produce, villagers went to a larger market town down the road.

Many villages lacked streets that cut through them. Often, there were only one or two lanes, muddy and littered with wastes—Egyptian villagers had none of the amenities that enabled Berliners to live at close quarters in cleanliness and comfort. Often, the lanes penetrated only part way through the mass of buildings, only far enough to give access to the various quarters. Ordinarily the households of a kinship group were clustered together in a particular quarter of the village. In such a case, the main thoroughfare was a circular route around the village. Threshing grounds and open spaces for prayers or festivals lay near this route.

Within the village, the crowded, flat-roofed houses were much like those of ancient times. The villagers still built with the same kind of unbaked mud-and-straw bricks mentioned in the Bible. The sparsely furnished interiors were still lit by oil-burning Roman-style lamps of baked clay and heated by braziers of clay or copper. The houses themselves expressed the cultural conservatism of the society.

The thick mud-brick walls kept the interior of the house cool. Inside, one would usually find chickens, cows, even a camel, as well as people. On the rooftop, there might be a pigeon tower, crops drying in the sun, or a stack of dung cakes for use as fuel. Mud and dung in the lane outside, livestock and people inside, dung cakes or drying crops on the roof—the human and natural worlds were not separate. The French sociologist Jacques Berque, who studied a village near Dinshawai, likened its life to a rustic drama with earth, water, plants, animals, and human beings as its heroes.[2] At any moment, the drama may be unfolding only slowly, but over time,

Brickyard at al-Agami Village, Sharqiyyah Province, 1983. Villagers mix mud and straw (foreground) to make unbaked mud brick, the traditional building material of the village. Newer building techniques are also now in use.
(C. V. Findley)

considerable action can occur, sometimes violently.

Village Society

The greatest difference between social
life in the village and in the United
States or Europe was in the role of the
individual. In the village, the extended
kin group was all-important; the individual counted for much less. Death
claimed more than a quarter of all in-
fants within their first year, and—partly
for that reason—average life expectancy
for the entire population barely exceeded
twenty years. Most people had little time
to make a mark of their own. While life
lasted, its quality was not good. Tuberculosis and hereditary syphilis were endemic, as were parasitic diseases like bil-
harziasis, hookworm, and malaria. In
particular, men of the village almost all
contracted parasitic diseases from long
work in water and mud.

Social roles also limited the individual. They were highly standardized and
little differentiated, except in terms of
sex and age. The normal routine for the
men was field work, including irrigation.
Women were in charge of housework,
child care, and the milking and feeding
of livestock. They also helped in the
fields and took produce to sell in the
market town. Men had a very limited
range of occupational choices. After their
years at the village Qur'an school, a few
of the brightest boys would go elsewhere
for advanced study and become religious
scholars. Some would take up barbering,
building, or singing in addition to their
field work. Choice was almost nonexistent for the women. Uncontrolled fertility dominated their lives. Their standard
dress, the long black *gallabiyah* (the same
term used for the nightshirt-like outfit of

**Sabiha, a woman in Dinshawai, with a
child from the village, 1983.**
(C. V. Findley)

the men) was always full enough to accommodate pregnancy and had two slits
at the side of either breast for nursing.

Villagers often married during their
teens. A young couple normally remained in the groom's father's household and shared in its work. Even after
they had children, the young couple ac-

quired little autonomy as long as the older generation lived. The closest thing to independence came with age, for males who became heads of extended-family households, and for their wives, who thus acquired charge of their daughters-in-law and grandchildren.

To the extent that the short average life expectancy allowed the pattern to be maintained, a villager lived much of his or her life in an extended household that included not only parents and children, but also grandparents, uncles, aunts, and cousins. For some purposes, such as farming its own land, this three-generation household was the meaningful social unit. But in many respects, even more extended kin groups were the fundamental social units of the village. A village like Dinshawai might have only five or six such kin groups. But each kin group might have up to one thousand or two thousand members at the start of this century, and might have several times that many today. Members of a large kin group were united by their common name, the given name of the group's founder.

The feelings of solidarity associated with common descent were the strongest loyalties that village society knew. Often the founder of the kin group was regarded as a saint. Nothing, except the claim to descent from the Prophet Muhammad, could enhance family prestige more than for one of the domed shrines that dominated the village skyline to be the tomb of the family founder. The kin group preserved its integrity by arranging marriages, usually within its own circle. The group had a male head, whose functions included dispensing hospitality, solving disputes within the group, and handling relations with the outside world, especially the government. The

elders who traditionally ran the village were kin group heads. When the government created the office of village headman ('umdah), it was usually filled by the leading kin group head, with the others still grouped around him as elders. The unofficial institutions of kin group leadership thus became the first link in an official chain that extended to Cairo and on to London.

The kin group expressed its solidarity through several physical institutions. The most important was the "big house" (duwwar), which served as headquarters for the kin group head, guest house, meeting place for the leading members of the kin group, and scene for the celebration of marriages, circumcisions, healings, or returns from journeys, especially the pilgrimage to Mecca. So frequent were the meetings, and the shared meals that accompanied them, that the big house played a major economic role in redistributing goods within the kin group. One of the many burdens on the women was the requirement to help with the chores there.

The legendary image of Middle Eastern hospitality was no doubt formed in settings like the big house. A visitor who had an introduction to a village kin group could rely on this hospitality for accommodation. When used by the village headman and elders as their meeting place, the big house also took on an official function. At Dinshawai, a big house served as the courthouse for the trials of 1906. It is still standing in the 1980s, and an empty weapons rack in a corner reminds us that defense was an important common concern to the kinsmen who ordinarily met there.

Other physical expressions of kin group solidarity included the family tombs, which were vaults built, maintained, and used by the group. Grain for all its members was ground in a cooperative mill. Collectively maintained waterwheels meant the group had to make decisions on their repair and use. Even religious structures expressed the solidarity of the kinspeople who had joined forces to build them.

Common activities also reaffirmed kin group solidarity. The men met to decide issues, such as the sharing of irrigation water. The kin group gathered at the big house for family occasions. Today one still sees parties of children in the fields pulling weevils off the cotton plants. Some religious observances had family significance, particularly if a family member was claimed as a saint. Finally, there was the common defense. Normally, only a few constables, under the control of the village headman, represented the forces of law and order in the village. Disputes over irrigation water, or over injuries to the persons or the honor of kinspeople, could give rise to feuds that went on for generations, marked by destruction of crops and other acts of violence, including murder. Every kin group included some men ready to sleep in the fields to protect the crops, or to defend the family against other families or against agents of the government. Some of these valiants became village heroes, like Zahran.

The Kinship Society and the World Outside

Because the kin group meant so much, village society de-emphasized not only the individual but also larger social groupings. The sole exception was the common religious bond among all Muslims.* Countless features of Islam emphasize the equality and solidarity of all believers. But a spiritual message, even one so often repeated, can be difficult to apply in everyday life. In the village, only a few occasions brought together members of different kin groups. The most important were the nativity festivals for the saints of the village and for the Prophet Muhammad.

Apart from economic links, the village was isolated from the outside world. Even the bright boys who went to study at the higher religious schools of the major towns, especially at the Al-Azhar Mosque University in Cairo, seldom returned, forming a human tribute that the village paid to the outside world, receiving little in return. Their social system was so self-contained that villagers had little sense of political integration into any entity larger than the kin group. The "politics" that meant most to them worked itself out in discussions of matters like marriage and irrigation, or in meetings of the village elders, or in feuds among kin groups.

Villagers knew about the khedive in Cairo and the sultan in Istanbul, and they had some notion of the British. But they also had the apathy of people whose opinion was never asked. Agents of the central government usually came to the village to collect taxes, conscript soldiers, or exact forced labor. In their dealings with officials, villagers were typi-

---

*A Muslim is a believer in Islam. Islam is a form of monotheism (faith in one God), and is based on scripture, the Qur'an (Koran) revealed to the Prophet Muhammad. Islam is related to Judaism and Christianity, and resembles them in many ways. Islam was founded in the seventh century.

Villagers tilling the soil with a wooden plow, al-Agami Village, Shar-qiyyah Province, 1983.
(C. V. Findley)

cally submissive but evasive. The officials generally responded by treating the peasants as little better than brutes.

Among Egypt's urban elites, nationalist movements had been working for political mobilization at least since the 1870s, but the villagers knew little of these. The Dinshawai incident of 1906 helped set the stage for political mobilization of the villagers by causing the urban elites to take a greater interest in them. The villagers themselves had little concern about national politics until the revolution of 1919, Egypt's response to the pressures of World War I.

Economic Life of the Village

In the economic life of the village, agriculture reigned supreme. Tilling one's own land was virtually the only occupation that had prestige among villagers, who were aptly known as *fellahin* ("cultivators"). Many things about Egyptian agriculture seemed changeless, but in fact the rustic drama had unfolded over the nineteenth century in ways that reflected the establishment of European domination.

Had the villagers been left to themselves, their economic life in 1906 would have resembled that of many other culturally conservative societies. Villagers would have spent their time cultivating and irrigating their fields, divided into many small plots by the provisions of Islamic inheritance law. Villagers would have consumed some of their produce, used some for hospitality, bartered some, sold some, and yielded up a good part for rents or taxes. They would have given little thought to saving or investment, except to buy more land. True wealth, in their view, would have consisted in having many kinsmen—and land to support them. The economic world of the Delta villager would have been radically different from that of the European capitalist. Instead of profit and growth for the individual, the village would have emphasized the communal interests of the kin group and the equitable distribution of resources within it.

But Delta villagers had not been left to themselves, and a new economic order had come into existence, much closer to European capitalist norms than to kin group communalism. Until the rapid population growth of this century, Egypt produced agricultural surpluses. Since the early nineteenth century, the family that governed Egypt had sought to take advantage of this productivity. The rulers introduced changes in land tenure that led to the formation of huge estates, owned by individuals associated with the government; they undertook large-scale public works to extend irrigation, with permanent irrigation in the Delta. Thus, Delta agriculture no longer depended on the annual Nile flood, and cultivators could work year-round, producing several crops.

Together with other factors, expensive public works projects led to tax increases that strained the resources of peasant families. Because the government wanted to maximize agricultural ex-

ports, new crops were introduced—in particular, long-staple cotton. But cotton cultivation required more investment than other crops, further straining villagers' resources. And increased emphasis on production for export compounded a problem common to all colonial economies: vulnerability to unforeseen price shifts in world commodity markets. During the U.S. Civil War, for example, when the South could not export its cotton, the price of Egyptian cotton more than tripled. But between 1865 and 1866, when U.S. cotton reappeared on the world market, Egyptian cotton prices fell by more than half. The collapse of cotton brought ruin to Egyptians and helped push the khedive's government toward bankruptcy—preparing the way for the British occupation in 1882.

More and more village families sank into debt as their taxes and operating costs grew; finally they lost their lands. By 1906, less than a quarter of the rural work force consisted of landowners who cultivated their own lands. The remainder were sharecroppers, tenants, or wage laborers, many of whom had formerly owned land. Some villages now consisted entirely of landless fellahin, often working for absentee landlords. Peasants who had once cultivated their own fields of wheat, vegetables, and clover spent most of their time growing cotton for the landowners and in the remaining hours worked small plots to produce the crops—especially beans and onions—that formed their meager diet.

Agricultural Egypt was being integrated into the world economy under conditions of colonial subordination. Also Egypt was becoming a market for goods that its colonial masters had to sell, although villagers were too poor to buy much. Shifting tastes in beverages illustrate this point. Historically, the villagers preferred coffee, consumed in the Middle East long before it became known in Europe. But in 1906, a visitor would probably have been offered tea. For Egypt was then ruled by the British, who dominated the world's tea trade. Today, a visitor to an Egyptian village is just as likely to be offered a soft drink, like Coca-Cola.

Although they made no headlines, the changes in village economic life were as drastic as the violence of 1906 at Dinshawai.

The Life of the Spirit

The aspect of village life that the appearance of monotony most misrepresented was the life of the spirit. Egyptian villagers' religious life was a rich mixture of elements ranging from formal Islam, through a variety of popular religious practices sanctioned only by custom, to superstition and magic. Although the people were Muslims, or sometimes Coptic Christians, their religious life included traces of beliefs that had prevailed in Egypt in pre-Islamic, or even pre-Christian, times.

Formal Islam was based directly on the Qur'an and the Islamic religious legal system (shari'ah). Formal Islam included the profession of faith, the five daily prayers, almsgiving, the fast during the month of Ramadan, and—for those who could afford to do so once in a lifetime—the pilgrimage to Mecca. Annual observance of the two major religious festivals and the birthday of the Prophet was another part of formal Islam, while Islamic law regulated countless features of daily life—from concepts of cleanliness to details of inheritance. In the village, as elsewhere, the Islamic world view also expressed itself in many

pious forms of speech. For example, one never expressed any intention about the future without saying In sha'a 'llah ("if God wills"). "If God wills, I'll help you pick cotton tomorrow."

Popular Islam included practices that did not grow directly out of the Qur'an and religious law, but had been established by immemorial custom. Eventually, religious reformers began to attack these practices precisely because they had no justification except custom, but this change was not felt in Delta villages until the 1930s. The two main expressions of popular Islam in the village were mystical societies and the nativity festivals of the local saints.

The mystical societies, branches of orders (tariqah) found in many parts of the Islamic world, met periodically to engage in specific religious exercises, ranging from repetitive prayer to music and dance, in an effort to deepen their religious experience. These societies combined religious fulfillment with social interaction in an environment that offered few leisure activities. They might also appeal to kin group loyalty, for society members often belonged to a single kin group. One of the village saints might be remembered as founder of both kin group and mystical society.

The tombs of the saints, which were thought to radiate grace, were places for prayer and visitation at all times. Once a year, a nativity festival (mawlid) was held at the tomb. A pole was erected on an open space near the tomb, and village families set up tents at the site. The pious and the mystical societies passed in procession. Litanies were recited in a circle around the pole. Supplicants circulated around the saint's tomb, seeking intercession. But the mawlid also included an earthier component. Merchants came from far and wide to set up booths. Musicians and snake charmers delighted the crowd. Boys circulated in hopes of catching a glimpse of pretty girls. The nativity festivals were thus fairs, communal celebrations, and religious events, all in one. The nativity of the Prophet produced a similar celebration on grander scale. Then and now, these festivities were the high points of the villagers' year.

Modern scholars believe that some local saints' shrines were shrines of Christian saints in pre-Islamic times and of ancient Egyptian gods in pre-Christian times. If so, the shrines are among many links with pre-Islamic types of religious consciousness. Such links are especially abundant in the realm of superstitious and magical practices.

Generally, these practices can be grouped under the heading of *animism*: the belief that the natural world is inhabited by spirits. Egyptian villagers believed in many spirits. A magic serpent haunted houses. A barren woman could conceive if she went inside an abandoned tomb. Certain practices could help ward off the evil eye. Physical and mental disturbances were also attributed to spirits. Against these afflictions, villagers relied on the folk remedies of the barber or wore amulets. A special cult called the *zar*, normally frequented by women, used rituals—music, dance, song, and sacrifice—as means of exorcism.

By identifying the spirit world with that of nature, animism fosters an intense spiritual involvement in the processes of nature. Many beliefs and practices of Delta villagers expressed this involvement. The fellahin loved the land, and their ideas of what was good for them were dominated by their concept of what was good for land, crops, and livestock. For example, muddy canal water was not only good for irrigating

A woman using canal water to wash, al-Agami Village, Sharqiyyah Province, 1983. (*C. V. Findley*)

fields, it was also better than clear water to drink. Canal water was best for washing clothes. To improve an inadequate milk flow, a nursing mother would wade into the canal up to her breasts and express a few drops of her milk into the water. And the same practice was used to increase a buffalo's milk. To Berliners of the age of Lister, such beliefs would have been unthinkable. Nothing better expresses the nondifferentiation of village life than the assumed fusion of human, natural, and spiritual realms.

Conclusion: Berlin and Dinshawai

It would be hard to imagine two environments more different than Berlin, the fast-moving urban machine, and Dinshawai, scene of the rustic drama. In terms of virtually all the twentieth-century themes defined in Chapter 1, these two communities were opposites. Berlin was the capital of a great power, while Dinshawai claimed European attention only momentarily as an example of how great power dominance made itself felt in remote corners of the colonial world. Berlin was a crucible of change, while Dinshawai was a refuge of cultural conservatism. In the Berlin of 1914, the age of national integration and mass politics had begun, though the kaiser's regime still retained many old-fashioned attributes. In Dinshawai, the incident of 1906 marked one of the first steps in the political mobilization of the villagers. Berlin was a product of the most advanced technologies of its day, while the villagers of Dinshawai were pitifully vulnerable to the forces of nature and relied on technologies two thousand years old. Berlin embodied many of the values that would shape the twentieth century, while Dinshawai still represented those that had molded the human experience through earlier ages.

In 1914, the Berlins and Dinshawais of the world were radically different, but linked by invisible chains. A discerning observer could sense these connections on a day-to-day basis, and a crisis like that of 1906 made it impossible to ignore them. Greater crises, like World War I, would subject the linkages existing in 1914 to strains that they could not bear. The result has been to transform and tighten, but never to break, the bonds of global integration.

Notes

1. Anwar El-Sadat, *In Search of Identity: An Autobiography* (New York: Harper & Row, 1978), pp. 16–17.
2. Jacques Berque, *Histoire sociale d'un village égyptien au XXe siècle* (Paris: Mouton, 1957), p. 9.

Suggestions for Further Reading

Berlin

Kollmann, Wolfgang, "The Process of Urbanization in Germany at the Height of the Industrialization Period." In *The Urbanization of European Society in the Nineteenth Century*, ed. Andrew Lees and Lynn Lees (1976).

Liang, Hsi-Huey, "Lower-Class Immigrants in Wilhelmine Berlin." In *The Urbanization of European Society in the Nineteenth Century*, ed. Andrew Lees and Lynn Lees (1976).

Masur, Gerhard, *Imperial Berlin* (1970).

Dinshawai

Ayrout, Henry Habib, *The Egyptian Peasant*, trans. John Alden Williams (1963).

Berque, Jacques, *Histoire sociale d'un village égyptien au XXe siècle* (1957).

Fakhouri, Hani, *Kafr el-Elow, An Egyptian Village in Transition* (1972).

Richards, Alan, *Egypt's Agricultural Development, 1800–1980: Technical and Social Change* (1982).

Vatikiotis, P. J., *History of Egypt, from Muhammad Ali to Sadat* (1980).

Part 2

CRISIS IN THE EUROPEAN-DOMINATED WORLD ORDER

Chapter *3*

WORLD WAR I: THE TURNING POINT OF EUROPEAN ASCENDANCY

The collapse of Europe's world dominance began with an assassination. It took place on June 28, 1914, in Sarajevo, the capital of Bosnia, then under Austro-Hungarian rule but now part of Yugoslavia. A nineteen-year-old terrorist, Gavrilo Princip, stepped up to the car in which the Archduke Franz Ferdinand, heir to the Austrian throne, was making an official visit to the city. With a shaking hand he pumped bullets into the archduke and his wife, fatally wounding them both.

Because the Austrian government correctly suspected that Princip's terrorist organization, the Black Hand, had the covert backing of the head of intelligence of the neighboring kingdom of Serbia, Austria-Hungary retaliated by threatening and then declaring war on Serbia. The hostilities soon expanded, however. One after another, honoring commitments made in secret treaties with their allies, the major powers of Europe entered the most costly war the world had yet witnessed.

In the end, some 10 million young men were

killed and another 20 million crippled. In France, more than 1.3 million died, representing a quarter of all the men of draft age (between twenty and thirty-eight) in 1914; in addition, half the draft-age population had been wounded by 1918. Death reaped a rich harvest among civilians as well. Millions died in Germany from malnutrition, as the British blockade cut off food supplies, and in Russia, where the still-developing economy could not cope with both total war and normal requirements.

Other consequences of World War I had even longer-lasting significance. To mobilize manpower and material, governments extended their control over the lives of citizens, creating a precedent for later government management of society to meet crises. To meet the gigantic costs of World War I, governments resorted to methods of financing that continued to strain the world's economy for generations. The stresses of the war gave communism its first opportunity when V. I. Lenin and the Bolsheviks seized control of the revolution of 1917 against Russia's tsarist government. Thus began the formation of the hostile blocs that divide the world in the 1980s. Above all, the impact of the war and its aftermath helped Adolf Hitler take power in Germany in 1933. The rise of a man dedicated to reversing the outcome of World War I by force probably made a second world war inevitable. From that conflict, Europe would emerge in ruins in 1945, too feeble ever to re-establish control over the dependent peoples of the rest of the world.

Causes of World War I

The shots fired by Gavrilo Princip at Sarajevo in 1914 killed not only the heir to the Hapsburg throne, but eventually the European-dominated world system. They marked one of the great turning points of history. When the slaughter stopped in 1918, people groped for an explanation of its origins. How could a political assassination, in a town unknown to most Europeans of 1914, have led to such a disaster?

Aggression or Accident?

In the peace treaty they wrote at Versailles, the "winners" of World War I (France, Britain, and the United States) naturally held the "losers," especially Germany, responsible—though it makes little sense to speak of winners and losers after a conflict that mortally weakened every country involved, except the United States. Article 231 of the Versailles treaty placed the blame on decisions made by German leaders between the shooting of the archduke on June 28 and the outbreak of general war in early August.

If we could believe, as the victors claimed at Versailles, that World War I was caused by the deliberate aggression of evil leaders, we would have the key to preventing future wars. Peace could be maintained by preventing people with such intentions from obtaining power, or by constantly resisting them if they already held power. In fact, however, most historians believe that well-meaning, unimaginative leaders in every capital stumbled into World War I. By doing what most people believed was normal for defense, they produced a result none had ever intended.

Ideas cause wars: ideas of how the world is divided and how to resolve conflicts within it. Ideas of nationalism and of alliances underlay World War I. The

The capture of the assassin of Archduke Franz Ferdinand and his wife in Sarajevo, June 28, 1914.
The Granger Collection

idea of South Slav nationalism inspired Gavrilo Princip to fire his fatal shot. The local conflict between South Slav nationalism, represented by Serbia, and the Austro-Hungarian Empire escalated into a world war because of European leaders' notion that their nations' safety depended on maintaining credible alliances. These two ideas were reflections of some more basic characteristics of the European-dominated world of 1914. We cannot explain why South Slav nationalists like Princip wanted to destroy the Austro-Hungarian Empire, and why Europe was tangled into alliances that pulled everyone into the conflict, without understanding the nature of international relations in 1914, the assump-

tions that Europeans made about their obligations to national community, and even the general mood. A full appreciation of these factors makes it much easier to understand the link between the shots at Sarajevo and a war of 30 million casualties. If that assassination had not triggered a world war, some similar event elsewhere might have done so.

The Multinational Empire

The shots at Sarajevo might never have been fired had multinational Austria-Hungary not survived into the twentieth century. A state that included people of a dozen ethnic groups seemed out of date to an age that believed every ethnic group should have a country of its own. Austria-Hungary was a mosaic of ethnically diverse provinces collected over a thousand years of wars and dynastic marriages. Some of these ethnic groups felt they were unfairly treated by the German-speaking Hapsburg rulers, and by the twentieth century their rebelliousness had been encouraged by developments on the empire's borders. Nations like Italy had emerged as independent homelands for some of the same ethnic groups that felt oppressed under Hapsburg rule.

In the capital, Vienna, it was feared that a rebellion by another ethnic minority would mean the end of the empire. The nightmare was that the independent kingdom of Serbia would do for the empire's South Slavs what Italy had done for its Italians. Since a palace revolt in Serbia had replaced rulers sympathetic to Austria-Hungary with fanatical nationalists, discontented South Slavs within the empire could look across the border for arms and encouragement. Through the assassination of the archduke, Princip and his fellow terrorists, Austrian subjects who sought a country of their own, aimed to provoke a war that would destroy the Austro-Hungarian Empire.

They succeeded. In Vienna, the Austro-Hungarian government took the assassination as a historic opportunity to eliminate the Serbian menace. On July 23, Austria-Hungary dispatched to the Serbs an insulting set of demands that no independent nation could have been expected to accept.

Alliances and Mobilization

The ultimatum to the Serbs set off a chain reaction that within ten days involved almost all the major powers in war. Government leaders believed that in a showdown the loser would be the first country that did not stand with its allies. A power that proved a weak or disloyal ally would soon have no allies left.

In 1914 Europe was divided into two great alliances: the Triple Alliance of Germany, Austria, and Italy, and the Triple Entente of France, Russia, and Britain. Ironically, these alliances had both been originally formed for defensive purposes. In a clash over European or colonial issues, diplomats had felt their countries would face less risk of attack or defeat if backed by a strong ally.

The events that led to the outbreak of World War I suggest that the leaders had miscalculated. The alliances made it easier, not more difficult, to go to war. The more aggressive partners in each alliance tended to recklessness because they were counting on allied help. The less aggressive partners were afraid to restrain their ally, lest they appear unreliable and thus find themselves alone in the next crisis. Had the rulers of Austria-Hungary not been sure of German support, they might not have risked war with the greatest Slavic nation, Russia, by attacking Serbia. But the German government essentially gave the Austro-Hungarian government a blank check to solve the Serbian problem as it chose. Due to their own blundering foreign policy of the past quarter-century, the Germans felt encircled by unfriendly nations. Ringed by France, Britain, and Russia, the Germans felt they could not let down their one reliable ally.

▶

Map 3.1 Ethnic Groups in Germany, Austro-Hungarian Empire, and the Balkans Before World War I

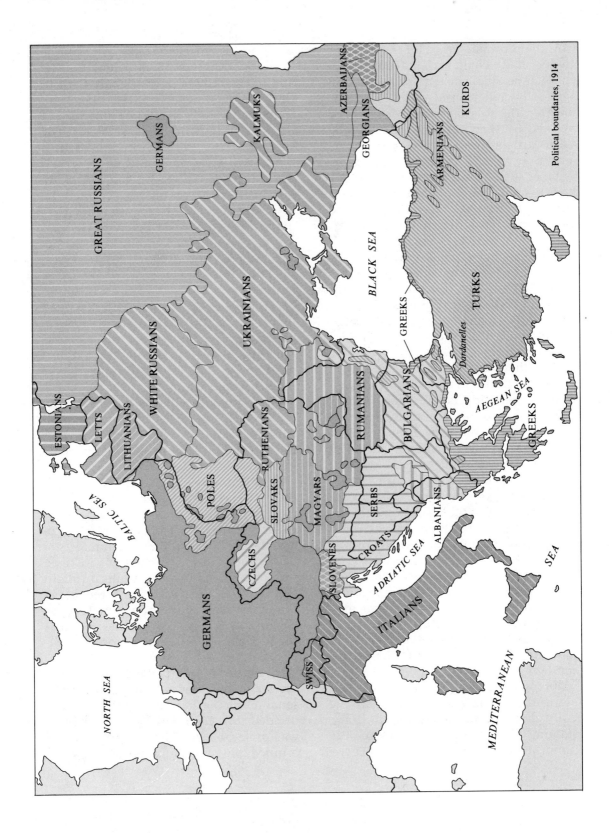

Political boundaries, 1914

In the Bosnian crisis of 1908–1909, Russia had challenged Austria-Hungary's annexation of that province, but eventually had backed down. In 1914, however, the Russians were determined to stand by their South Slavic kinfolk. When Austria-Hungary declared war on Serbia on July 28 (despite Serbian acceptance of all but one of the demands), the Russians began mobilization. Tsar Nicholas II, who had recently sponsored two international disarmament conferences, would have preferred war against Austria-Hungary alone. Russian military experts, however, explained that mobilization for modern war did not permit that kind of flexible response. The tsar had only two choices, they said. He could remain at peace or he could launch total war on all fronts.

When the tsar chose the latter course on July 30, the events that followed were almost automatic. Though some German leaders began to think of drawing back, it was too late. With the Russian army mobilizing on their borders, they felt forced to launch total war themselves. Germany expected to fight both France and Russia; its only hope of success would be to finish off France quickly before the slow-moving Russians posed too great a threat. Thus German mobilization meant a direct threat to France. The French, outnumbered almost two to one by Germany, believed that their national survival depended on the Russian alliance. Having done little to restrain Russian belligerence, the French now responded to the German threat by mobilizing.

Although they had been enemies for centuries, Britain and France had recently drifted into some joint military planning. Thus the British felt a moral commitment to help the French. (There were no formal treaty obligations.) The new friendship of Britain and France, and the cooling of once friendly British-German relations, resulted above all from the German decision at the turn of the century to build a high seas fleet. The ensuing arms race convinced the British that the new German battleships were a direct threat to the Royal Navy. Even so, the British public probably accepted the need for war in 1914 only when the Germans invaded neutral Belgium. German military planners, guided by strategic rather than diplomatic priorities, thought the quickest way to defeat France was to attack through Belgium. The British government could now lead its people to war for the moral cause of defending a violated neutral country. Thus, by August 4, all the major European powers but Italy had toppled over the brink into war.

The immediate blame for this catastrophe falls on the monarchs and ministers who made crucial decisions with the aim of either bluffing their opponents into backing down or entering a war with maximum allied help. All considered the preservation of their national interests more important than the vaguer general European interest in maintaining peace. The vital interests of Serbs, Austrians, and Russians justified waging a local war even if it might spread. The Germans and French believed they served their own interests by backing even aggressive allies, because the loss of an ally seemed more dangerous than the risk of war.

In one sense, then, World War I was the result of a series of apparently reasonable calculations, as national leaders decided that each new step toward war was preferable to a backward step that implied national humiliation or isolation. Thus the confrontation was played out to the point of collision.

Nationalism and Interdependence

To avoid the trap into which they fell, Europe's leaders would have had to go against people's perceptions of the nature of the world and against values derived from those perceptions. In a general sense, World War I was caused by the fact that people felt themselves to be not Europeans but Frenchmen, Germans, Russians, or South Slavs. Although new technological and economic realities were making this vision of an ethnically divided continent obsolete, most Europeans knew no higher goal than national self-preservation.

The decade before the war had seen a few steps toward internationalism. An International Office of Public Health and a World Missionary Congress had been created; these institutions recognized that neither disease nor the word of God was restrained by borders. Over half of Europe's trade union members belonged to internationally affiliated unions, united by the idea that workers of all countries had more in common with each other than with their employers. A growing peace movement placed its hopes in the permanent International Court of Arbitration recently established in The Hague.

Such expressions of internationalism counted for little against the prevailing nationalisms, which exalted individual countries. Many people interpreted international politics as they believed that Charles Darwin had interpreted the world of nature: in the struggle for survival, the weak perished, and the strong dominated.

To many people the major European powers seemed already locked in economic struggle for raw materials and markets. Germans resented the fact that their belated achievement of national unity had denied them a colonial "place in the sun" like the empires of Britain and France. By creating a navy to assert its aspirations to world power, Germany came into confrontation with Britain, even though each country was the other's best export customer. Substantial sectors of both economies would have collapsed without the markets provided by the "enemy."

This perception of the world as an arena of conflict rather than interdependence weighed heavily on the calculations of statesmen in 1914. Most people everywhere had been taught to accept this view. Even Russia was fumbling toward making elementary education compulsory by the time of the war. In parts of Germany all young children had been educated since the early nineteenth century. Britain and France had made their educational systems universal in the 1880s. After school came military service. All the major powers except Britain had universal conscription—the draft.

The patriotism young men learned from their schoolmaster and the drill sergeant was reinforced by what they read in the newspapers. Now that most of the population could read and write, mass journalism entered its golden age. The number of European newspapers—the first of the twentieth-century mass media—doubled in twenty years. And patriotism sold papers. The international conference held at Algeciras in 1906 to deal with a colonial confrontation between Germany and France was the first to be covered by a pack of reporters. Although nations continued to keep their treaties secret, diplomats would henceforth have to negotiate their way out of international showdowns with patriotic public opinion looking over their shoulders.

An Age of Militarism

Hemmed in by public opinion, statesmen struggling to resolve international issues also had to reckon with increasing military influence on decison making. Europe in 1914 was in the grip of *militarism*: the dominance of a military outlook and of the men who embodied it. Of the major heads of state, only the president of the French Republic never appeared in uniform. The German kaiser, the Austrian emperor, and the Russian tsar always wore uniforms. This custom suggests the supreme prestige of soldiers—especially the generals who commanded the vast armies the draft made possible.

Europe's generals and their allies in industry, finance, and journalism formed a kind of military-industrial complex. The creation of the German fleet, for example, was facilitated by a publicity campaign financed and managed by admirals and shipbuilders. Lucrative contracts were their reward.

Military spending did not mean that a country's leaders were planning aggression. Armaments were heaped up in the name of defense to provide a "deterrent" against attack. These build-ups did not prevent war in 1914, however. Indeed they had the opposite effect. Measuring their armaments against those of a potential enemy, some commanders became convinced that they had the upper hand and could risk war. Others feared they were about to lose their advantage and argued that if a war was to be fought, it should be soon. Estimations of this kind were particularly dangerous because military men were specialists trained to think almost entirely in military terms. Such were the advisers who persuaded Nicholas II that partial mobilization was impractical in 1914. And General Alfred von Schlieffen's strategic masterstroke of attacking France through Belgium brought Great Britain into the war, thus leading to the German defeat.

Against this background of intense national rivalry and expanding militarism, the decisions statesmen made in 1914 are understandable. None of them had any idea of how long and devastating a war between countries armed with twentieth-century technology would be. Neither did the public. Cheering crowds filled the streets of every European capital in the summer of 1914, greeting declarations of war with delirious enthusiasm.

Europeans had been taught that war was the real test of the nation's toughness. Only those past middle age could remember a war between major powers in Europe. For the young, war meant a short-lived colonial contest that occurred far away, involving someone else, and brought profit and prestige to the victor. For the last ten years, tension had been mounting domestically and internationally. Within each of the major powers, social conflicts had produced strikes and violence. Europe had gone from one diplomatic crisis to another, all ended unheroically through negotiation. Now a crisis had come along that diplomats could not solve, and many people felt relief. The whole society could unite against a common enemy.

As they rushed off to fight that enemy, the soldiers of 1914 could not know that they were embarking on the first of two European civil wars that would end Europe's domination of the world.

Battlefronts, 1914–1918

The war that began in 1914 led to fighting in almost every part of the globe. In Africa south of the Sahara, invasions from British and French colonies quickly captured most of Germany's holdings, though in East Africa a German force continued the battle against a British Indian army until 1918. In the South Pacific, British imperial troops from Australia and New Zealand seized German outposts. Britain's ally Japan snapped up other German possessions and appropriated the German slice of China.

Closer to Europe, the long-decaying Ottoman Empire entered the conflict on the side of the Central Powers (Germany and Austria-Hungary). This move threatened not only Russia's southern flank but also Britain's link to India through the Suez Canal. The British not only fought the Ottomans, but also encouraged revolt among the Ottomans' Arab vassals, while making a conflicting promise that Ottoman Palestine would become a national homeland for Jews. As a result, the war provoked by the frustrated aspirations of the Serbs, once Ottoman subjects, helped unleash the turmoil of conflicting national aspirations that still torments the Middle East.

All these conflicts were extensions of the European battle lines. Only in 1917 did the war become a world war in the sense that whole continents were pitted against one another. Then the weight of the United States, dominant in North and South America, had to be thrown into the scales to match a Germany that had overrun much of continental Europe, penetrated deeply into Russia, and fought Britain and France and their worldwide empires to a standstill.

The Entente versus the Central Powers

Though hardly anyone in 1914 foresaw a bloody stalemate of the European war, calculation might have predicted such an outcome. The Central Powers and the Entente Powers were rather an even match. Britain's naval might gave the Entente the advantage on the seas. Though the construction of the German fleet had made Britain an enemy, the two nations had only one significant naval encounter, at Jutland in 1916. There the Germans sank more British ships than they lost of their own, but they did not risk a second confrontation. Too precious a weapon to be hazarded, the German battleships rusted in port while the British blockade cut Germany off from the overseas world. Against blockade, Germany could muster only its submarines, the weapon that would eventually make the United States another German enemy.

On land the two alliances were more equally matched, despite the Entente powers' two-to-one advantage in population. Russia's millions of peasants in uniform were so inadequately equipped that some were sent into battle unarmed and expected to find the weapons of dead or wounded comrades. France and Britain could do little to help, for their prewar lines of communication to Russia were blocked by the Central Powers and their Turkish ally. Indeed, Germany's enemies never successfully coordinated their strategies. The war effort of the Central Powers, by contrast, was effectively directed from Berlin.

Since the citizens of each nation were convinced that they were defending their homeland against unprovoked attack, neither alliance had an edge in morale. Both were sufficiently determined to fight the land war to a draw. Thus victory could only be achieved by mobilizing overseas manpower and material, either by squeezing resources from the colonial empires or by drawing the world's most powerful neutral nation, the United States, into the conflict. Since British control of the sea lanes gave the Entente Powers better prospects of developing these advantages in a long war, the Germans felt they had to score a quick victory.

Stalemate in the West

The campaign of 1914 failed to produce the hoped-for victory. Germany's initial rush through Belgium carried its advance guard up to the Marne River, scarcely twenty miles from Paris. The French victory on the Marne was a very close brush with destruction, but it was a victory.

The Battle of the Marne may have decided the war. By Christmas 1914 the armies' rapid advances and retreats had given way to stationary front lines. Both sides dug into the soil of a corner of Belgium and northeastern France, creating a line three hundred miles long from the English Channel to the Swiss border. The French drive against Germany failed, and the Germans reversed the Russian advance on their eastern border. But these successes could not compensate for

the loss of German momentum in the west. Germany now found itself in the very situation its prewar strategy had tried to avoid: a protracted war on two fronts. Though few sensed it at the time, Germany had perhaps already lost the war.

Many million lives were to be sacrificed, however, before that loss was driven home. During 1915 and 1916 the war was dominated by both sides' futile efforts to punch a hole in the enemy front. Launched against elaborately fortified lines of trenches, these offensives became massacres. The German attack on the French fortress at Verdun in 1916 cost each side a third of a million men. In the same year the British attack on the Somme River won a few square miles of shell-torn ground at the cost of over a half-million lives. The defending Germans lost nearly as many.

Numbers like these do not convey what life in the trenches was like. Probably no earlier war, and perhaps no later one, imposed such strains on fighting men. Soldiers spent months in a filthy hole in the ground, their boredom interrupted only by the occasional crack of a sniper's rifle or a dogfight between airplanes. (Both sides had quickly learned to put this new technology to military use.) Sometimes the clang of the gas alarm warned the men to put on their masks as a poisonous cloud drifted toward them. When the rumble of artillery fire in the background had risen for a few days or weeks to a roar, they knew they would soon have to go "over the top," out of their trenches and across no man's land toward the enemy's barbed wire, under a hail of machine gun and heavy

▶

Map 3.2   World War I in Europe, 1914–1918

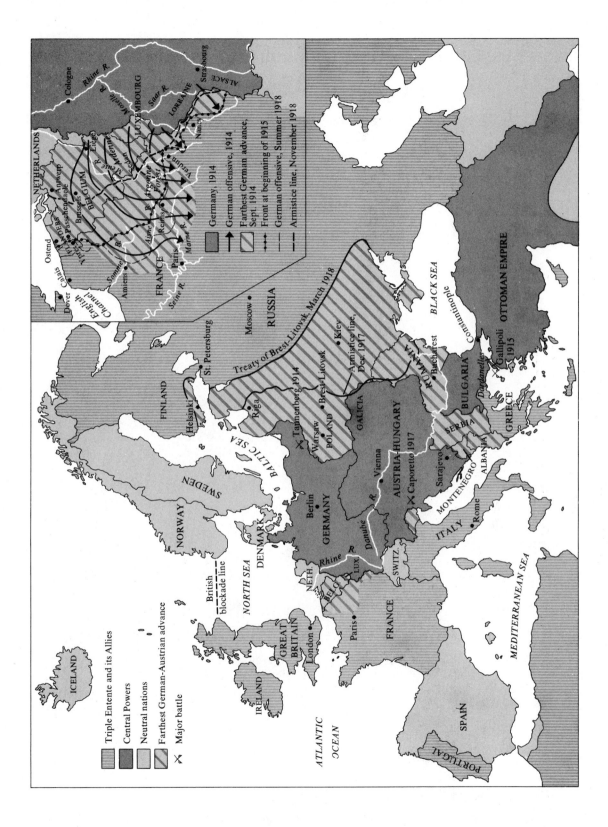

Triple Entente and its Allies

Central Powers

Neutral nations

Farthest German-Austrian advance

✕ Major battle

British
blockade line

Germany, 1914

German offensive, 1914

Farthest German advance,
Sept. 1914

Front at beginning of 1915

German offensive, Summer 1918

Armistice line, November 1918

ATLANTIC
OCEAN

ICELAND

IRELAND

GREAT
BRITAIN

London

Paris

FRANCE

SPAIN

PORTUGAL

MEDITERRANEAN SEA

NORTH SEA

DENMARK

NORWAY

SWEDEN

BALTIC SEA

FINLAND

Helsinki

St. Petersburg

Moscow

RUSSIA

Treaty of Brest-Litovsk, March 1918

Armistice line,
Dec. 1917

Riga

✕ Tannenberg 1914

Warsaw

POLAND

Brest-Litovsk

Kiev

GALICIA

VIN

RUMANIA

Bucharest

BLACK SEA

Constantinople

Dardanelles

Gallipoli
1915

OTTOMAN EMPIRE

BULGARIA

SERBIA

GREECE

ALBANIA

MONTENEGRO

Sarajevo

✕ Caporetto 1917

Vienna

AUSTRIA-HUNGARY

Danube R.

Berlin

GERMANY

Rhine R.

SWITZ.

NETH.

BELG.

LUX.

Rome

ITALY

NETHERLANDS

Cologne

Rhine R.

Moselle R.

Saar R.

ALSACE

Strasbourg

LORRAINE

LUXEMBOURG

BELGIUM

Antwerp

Liège

Ardennes

Meuse R.

Verdun

Namur

FLANDERS

Ostend

Passchendaele

Brussels

Ypres

Dover

Calais

Somme R.

Amiens

Aisne R.

Reims

Argonne
Forest

Marne R.

Paris

Seine R.

FRANCE

English
Channel

weapons fire. The result of these offensives was always the same—failure to break through.

Both sides tried, but failed, to break through on other fronts. The Entente Powers attracted neutral Italy into the war by promising it a share of the spoils. The Italian challenge to the Austrians soon bogged down, however, giving the Entente's leaders another stalemated front to worry about. They also tried, half-heartedly, to establish a closer link with the Russians by sending an expedition to seize the Ottoman-controlled straits that connect the Mediterranean to Russia's Black Sea ports. Ottoman forces, led by the future creator of modern Turkey, Mustafa Kemal, offered effective resistance. The expedition to Gallipoli proved another fiasco.

The Central Powers also tried to break the deadlock by expanding the conflict. Bulgaria was encouraged to join the German side and successfully invaded Serbia. By 1917 Germany and its satellites controlled most of southeastern Europe,

Lloyd George talking with Indian soldiers near Fricourt on the Somme River, in September 1916.
The Trustees of the Imperial War Museum, London

but this success was no more decisive than the continuing German victories against the Russians.

The German submarine effort to cut Britain's ocean lifelines had to be suspended after a U-boat torpedoed the giant liner *Lusitania* off the Irish coast in May 1915. Though it was rightly suspected that the ship carried a secret cargo of munitions, most Americans did not believe that excused the drowning of more than twelve hundred people, among them over one hundred Americans. American outrage compelled the Germans to abandon the practice of torpedoing without warning.

The two sides staggered into 1917 with no hope of victory in sight. By now the enthusiasm of 1914 had evaporated, and the mood everywhere was one, at best, of determination to survive. Some people, particularly socialists, urged that the war be stopped by declaring it a draw. But leaders everywhere shrank from such a solution. Without a victory, the previous butchery would seem pointless. And there would be rich prizes for winning. German industrialists and military men expected to annex Belgium and parts of northeastern France, as well as a huge swath of Russia. For France, defeat of the Central Powers would mean recovery of the northeastern provinces of Alsace and Lorraine. Victory would enable Italy to incorporate within its borders the remaining Italian-speaking regions of Austria. For Britain it would mean ending the German challenge to its commercial and naval pre-eminence. Hard-liners were now in control in almost every capital, and they used their wartime powers of censorship and arrest to silence the doubters. Because technology seemed to have made defensive positions impregnable and offensives unbearable, the weary armies of Europe faced a prospect of apparently endless struggle.

1917: The Turning Point

In fact, two events made 1917 the decisive year of the war. Russia withdrew from the conflict, and the United States declared war against the Central Powers. The net result was an advantage to the Entente side.

Why did the United States enter the war? Idealists point to a U.S. feeling of kinship with the Western democracies. Cynics note that an Entente defeat would have cost the U.S. industrial and financial communities a great deal in contracts and loans. In any case, a U.S. entry into the war probably became inevitable when the Germans decided, in January 1917, to resume unrestricted submarine warfare. This was a calculated risk. The German high command expected that renewed Atlantic sinkings would bring the United States into the war, but hoped to starve Britain into submission before American intervention could become decisive. The Germans also tried to incite Mexico to reclaim vast territories lost to the United States in the nineteenth century. The disclosure of this plan by British intelligence showed Americans just how far the Germans were prepared to go.

The entry of the United States marked the turning point of World War I. But it took time for the Entente's new advantages in manpower and materiel to become apparent. Meanwhile, the emergence in Russia of a revolutionary government determined to make peace at any price seemed a devastating blow to Entente hopes. The Bolsheviks believed the war had given them a historic opportunity to make a revolution by fulfilling the yearning of the Russian masses for peace. Even so, they hesitated for a time to pay the price the Germans demanded. The Treaty of Brest-Litovsk (March 1918) required them to hand over a quarter of Russia's prewar territory, a third of its population, and half of its industrial plant. When Lenin signed, he ratified a decision many Russian peasant soldiers had already made by starting home from the battlefield.

The final phase of the war, from the spring to the autumn of 1918, amounted to a race between trains carrying German troops west to France from the Russian front and ships transporting U.S. soldiers eastward to France. Reinforced from the east, the German spring offensive did break through. Once again the Germans were at the gates of Paris. This second Battle of the Marne, however, was Germany's last gasp. In August the German army's chief strategist, General Erich Ludendorff, admitted to the kaiser that he had no hope of victory. Germany's enemies were counterattacking its collapsing allies. As the Austro-Hungarian Empire disintegrated, its subject peoples declared their independence.

The Hapsburg crown was the oldest, but not the greatest, to fall in 1918. In Germany, sailors mutinied rather than sail on a final suicide mission. This spark of rebellion set the whole country alight. Deserted even by the generals who had once been his staunchest supporters, the kaiser fled. Democratic and socialist politicians proclaimed Germany a republic.

It was their representatives who met the supreme commander of the Entente and American armies, French General Ferdinand Foch, aboard his command train. The terms he demanded were stiff. Germany must withdraw its armies, which were still fighting deep in their enemies' territory, behind the Rhine River. It must renounce the Treaty of Brest-Litovsk and hand over much of its railway rolling stock and shipping to the victors. With the British blockade threatening their country with starvation, Germany's representatives had no real choice. Protesting bitterly, they signed an armistice.

Thus at eleven o'clock on the morning of November 11, 1918, the guns at last fell silent in ruined northeastern France. There have been other wars since 1918, and we now celebrate Veterans Day, not Armistice Day. We do not always recall that the occasion commemorates men who died fighting, they believed, a war to end war. The generation that first observed November 11, however, was vividly aware that it had survived an experience unparalleled in history, not only for the men in the trenches, but even for those who remained at home.

Home Fronts, 1914–1918

World War I was fought on the "home front" as well as on the battlefield. Everyone in each country, not just the men in uniform, was in the battle and must make his or her contribution to the national effort.

Though the air blitz and guided missile attacks of World War II were foreshadowed thirty years earlier by German bombing raids on London, the technology of 1914–1918 was inadequate to make every citizen a target of enemy attack. In a sense, however, Europe's shops, factories, and farms became another fighting front. As it became clear that neither side was going to win a quick victory, leaders realized that it was essential to harness the efforts of every individual. Unprecedented coordination and coercion would be required. No aspect of people's lives could be left unmanaged.

In this way, World War I had a revolutionary impact on the societies of all the major powers. The new controls imposed on citizens were justified as wartime expedients, and many were relaxed when the war was over. Even so, they established precedents that made the postwar world a very different place. Many of the basic trends in twentieth-century government, politics, economics, and thought can be traced back to the experience of total war in 1914–1918.

War and Government

The war gave a new dimension to the role of government. Before 1914, Western governments had gradually made themselves more and more responsible for the welfare of their citizens, insuring them against old age or disability, limiting their hours of work, forbidding unhealthy work places. Germany was the most protective; France and the United States were the least. Every new measure met vigorous opposition, however, for political thought was still dominated by the basic nineteenth-century liberal conviction that the best government is the one that governs least. Government today is the largest and most powerful organization in society. But in most major European powers in 1914 the "government" was a committee of legislators who exercised limited functions as long as they enjoyed the confidence of a parliamentary majority (or, in Germany and Russia, the confidence of the monarch).

The committee, or cabinet, of ministers oversaw bureaucracies whose numbers and powers varied from one nation to another. Nowhere, however, were bu-

reaucrats very numerous, nor did their responsibilities extend much beyond providing the basic services for which governments had long been responsible. They maintained law and order and raised the modest taxes needed to balance the budget every year, while providing defense and the few other essentials not left to private initiative.

All this changed radically after 1914. Prolonged war demanded a more effective mechanism for planning and decision making than could be provided by the prewar parliamentary system, in which government was essentially a debating tournament. Even in countries with long-established parliamentary tradition, prime ministers emerged who personally exercised wide emergency executive power, tolerating little parliamentary interference: David Lloyd George in Britain and Georges Clemenceau in France. World War I pushed aside even venerable traditions "for the duration." The British Defense of the Realm Act, for example, allowed the government to censor or even silence newspapers, violating one of the most cherished British freedoms.

The number of government employees increased enormously. Twenty clerks had handled the purchase of munitions for the prewar British army. But by 1918, when the draft had put 3 million in uniform, the procurement of arms was the work of a Ministry of Munitions employing 65,000 civil servants. The wartime concentration of power into a few hands and the extension of that power into every sphere of life was most marked in Germany, where the tradition of parliamentary government was weaker and political tradition had long subordinated the citizen to the state.

In Germany, as in the rest of the modern Western world, private economic power had become concentrated in trusts and *cartels** before 1914. Nevertheless, the belief remained strong that the best economy was one of free competition, with a minimum of government interference. Now, cut off by the British blockade from many essential supplies, the German government began to make all the economic decisions. Scarce commodities were rationed, and skilled workers were directed by government order to the jobs where they were needed. The government mobilized the scientific community in fields like industrial chemistry to develop synthetic substitutes for unavailable imports like rubber. A government bureaucracy headed by Walter Rathenau, the prewar head of the giant German General Electric Company, oversaw the distribution of available raw materials to the most efficient producers, usually the largest. In the process the prewar economy was altered beyond any hope of restoration.

By the war's end, the German government managed so much of the economy that the system was described as "war socialism." It was operated, ironically, by the conservative military men and industrialists who had been most hostile to socialism before the war. The individual German had become a cog in the military machine: every man between the ages of seventeen and sixty was mobilized under military discipline. And the German case is only the most extreme example. In each of the countries involved in the war, government authority was concentrated and expanded.

---

* Cartels are associations of private producers who agree to share markets and fix prices, thus limiting competition.

War, Economics, and Society

In addition to changing ideas about the proper functions of government, the war altered conventional notions of how governments should get and spend money. Traditional methods could not produce the vast sums needed. The British and French governments liquidated between a quarter and a third of their citizens' foreign investments to pay for essential goods purchased overseas, but still emerged from the war owing enormous debts. In every belligerent country, new taxes were introduced and old ones raised. Nowhere was the resulting income more than a fraction of what governments were spending. They made up the difference by borrowing from their citizens, harnessing the new art of advertising to exhort savers to invest in the war effort. The supply of money was further enlarged by the easiest and most dangerous means of all: printing more and more of it.

The result was staggering inflation, though its full impact was not felt until after wartime price and wage controls were abolished. Only then did people realize what a new and terrifying financial world they lived in. The budget of the French government, for example, was forty times larger in 1918 than at the beginning of the war. The sum the French treasury had to pay out in interest alone was more than its entire annual budget before the war. The financial legacy of the war made the years 1918–1939 a period of almost constant economic strain.

Such economic changes inevitably produced profound social changes. For some social groups the war meant new opportunities. For example, as U.S. factories tooled up to produce the munitions the Entente demanded, industrialists took labor wherever they could find it. Thus began the migration of blacks from the rural South to the industrial North, a trend that continued into the post–World War II years, profoundly transforming American life. In the increasingly interconnected world of the twentieth century, sharecroppers from Georgia found jobs in steel mills in Pittsburgh because farm boys from Bavaria were finding death in northeastern France.

European societies that had drafted a large proportion of their male populations, exempting only workers with critical skills, also recruited a "reserve army" of labor by hiring women for jobs monopolized before the war by men. Thereafter it was more difficult to argue that women's place was in the home. In fact, wartime necessity may have done as much as prewar agitation to break down the distinctions between the roles of men and women. In 1903, a bill giving British women the vote had been laughed down in the House of Commons. The next decade saw continuing lobbying and occasional violence by Emmeline Pankhurst's Women's Social and Protective Union, whose suffragettes threatened ministers with horsewhips and burned the slogan "Votes for Women" into golf course greens with acid. But not until after the war, in 1919, did British women get the vote. American and German women obtained the vote a year later. Only France, among the major democracies, restricted suffrage to men until after World War II.

World War I created new opportunities for some groups, but ruined others. Governments obsessed with maintaining production proved readier than prewar private employers to engage in collective bargaining. Trade unions thus won greater recognition. But workers felt

Women munitions workers during World War I.
The Trustees of the Imperial War Museum, London

they had not received just compensation for their contribution to the war effort, and a wave of strikes swept around the world with the coming of peace. In fact, workers' gains were vastly exceeded by the fortunes of profiteers who borrowed to build armaments factories, then paid their debts in a currency depreciated by inflation. Those hit hardest by the war, however, were the people who had lived comfortably before 1914 on a fixed income provided by a pension or on the interest from government bonds. In 1919 an income in British pounds (not by any means the most inflated currency) bought only a third of what it could purchase in 1914.

These economic distortions deepened prewar social divisions. When people had to accept a decline in their standard of living because of inflation, they naturally assumed that others must have gained at their expense. Wartime social upheaval laid the groundwork for the success of postwar political movements based on hatred and an appeal to vengeance, like those founded by Mussolini and Hitler.

War's Psychological Impact

The postwar years were marked by a mood of cynicism and disillusionment, an inevitable reaction against the war enthusiasm every government had tried to drum into the heads of its citizens. World War I prompted the first systematic efforts by governments to manage information and manipulate mass emotions. Such efforts were inevitable in twentieth-century society. All the major powers except Russia were approaching universal literacy and universal male suffrage by 1914. People who could read and felt they had a right to vote could not be commanded to blind obedience; they would have to be shown reasons for making the sacrifices the national cause demanded.

Thus each government in World War I mounted a vast propaganda campaign to persuade its public, and potential allies, of the justice of its motives and the wickedness of the enemy. British propagandists convinced a generation that Germany had ordered its soldiers to chop off the hands of Belgian children. But even more damage was done by the *positive* slogans of the propagandists: that soldiers were fighting for the de-

fense of civilization against barbarism, or for democracy against militarism, or for the abolition of war.

The postwar world quickly revealed that these slogans had been hollow half-truths. Postwar cynicism was a direct reaction to wartime campaigns that had played on pride, shame, and fear to mobilize opinion. When the Bolsheviks published the secret Entente treaties, showing that neither side's motives had been pure, when none of the lofty goals for which the war had supposedly been fought materialized even for the "winners," public opinion turned on the leaders whose official news turned out to be lies. The very values that had supposedly motivated the war were now discredited. Wartime idealism, deliberately overheated, turned very sour in the postwar world.

The postwar mood also reflected a more basic change in the human outlook. No generation since 1914–1918 has ever matched the nineteenth century's confidence in progress. The world had gone through an orgy of destructiveness that seemed to prove false everything the prewar world believed in. In the words of the soldier in Erich Maria Remarque's classic novel *All Quiet on the Western Front,* "It must be all lies and of no account when the culture of a thousand years could not prevent this stream of blood being poured out." No wonder the postwar Dadaist movement of artistic rebels mocked the pretensions of the past by exhibiting a copy of the Mona Lisa wearing a moustache, or suggested that poetry should henceforth be written by cutting a newspaper into scraps and shaking them at random out of a bag. Such painting and poems might make no sense, but, as the war had just proved, neither did anything else. This was a dangerous discovery, for, as the great

Russian novelist Feodor Dostoevski had warned, "If nothing is true, then everything is permitted." Today, when human beings have permitted themselves cruelties on a scale that earlier ages could not have imagined, we know what he meant.

World War I accelerated trends in every sphere of modern life already visible before 1914 and still powerful in the 1980s. Politically it stimulated the growth of executive authority and government power. Economically it spurred the concentration of economic power in large corporations increasingly interlocked with government, while destroying forever the comforting idea that money retains a constant value. The war leveled social distinctions between groups and destroyed some altogether. In every country, for example, the sons of Europe's landed aristocracies became the second lieutenants of the elite regiments and were killed out of all proportion to their numbers. At the same time the war gave greater status to working men and women. By lessening the distances between social classes, however, the war may well have heightened tensions, for now the class enemy was closer at hand.

Spiritually, too, World War I marked a real turning point. Before 1914, only a minority doubted the nineteenth century's faith in the future. The skeptical mood became general after 1919, as the world began to guess how unsatisfactory a peace had been made.

Peacemaking, 1919 and After

No international meeting ever aroused such anticipation as the conference that convened in Paris in January 1919 to write the peace treaties. Surely, people thought, so great a war would result in an equally great peace.

The Wilsonian Agenda

Many hopes focused on U.S. President Woodrow Wilson. He arrived in Europe to a welcome greater than any other American leader has ever received. Wilson seemed to embody a new kind of international politics based on moral principles, rather than on selfish interests.

Early in 1918, Wilson had outlined American objectives in the war. Some of his Fourteen Points simply called for a return to prewar conditions. Germany must evacuate Belgium and restore its freedom, for example. But other points seemed to promise change in the whole international order. Wilson called for an end to the secret alliances that had dragged all the major powers into World War I. He advocated the removal of tariff barriers between nations and a general reduction of armaments. In settling the European powers' disputes over colonies, he declared, the interest of the colonized must be taken into account. The implication was that all peoples had an eventual right to choose their own government. This indeed was what Wilson promised to the subject peoples of the Austro-Hungarian and Ottoman empires. To the Poles, too, Wilson promised a restoration of the country they had lost when Austria, Russia, and Prussia carved up Poland among themselves during the eighteenth century.

For many critics of prewar power politics, the most hopeful of Wilson's Fourteen Points was the last, which proposed to reconstruct the framework of international relations. The countries of the world should form an association—a

League of Nations—whose members would pledge to preserve one another's independence and territorial integrity. In this way, the system that keeps the peace in a smaller human community—willingness to obey the law and condemnation of those who defy it—would replace the international anarchy that had brought disaster in 1914.

Wilson had not consulted his allies about any of his proposals. The United States entered the war in 1917 with no obligation, Americans believed, to support the objectives of earlier entrants. The Fourteen Points seemed to promise Europe a just peace and to recognize the national aspirations of colonial peoples. Unfortunately the Paris Peace Conference produced no such results. To the rights of the non-Western peoples it gave little more than lip service. To Europeans it gave a postwar settlement—the Treaty of Versailles—so riddled with injustices that it soon had few defenders.

Colonial Issues in 1919

Four years of world war had undermined European rule over non-Western peoples. In their frantic search for essential war materials, European powers increasingly treated their colonies as extensions of their home fronts. The non-Western peoples were thus subjected to many of the same strains that eventually broke the morale of European populations. In fact, European governments used much greater coercion on their non-Western subjects than they dared try at home. The British, for example, used methods of drafting labor and requisitioning materials that would have been enough in themselves to explain the postwar explosion of Egyptian nationalism. Colonies were also a reservoir of

manpower. Almost 1.5 million Indians, for example, fought for Britain, and 62,000 of them were killed in the Middle East, Africa, and the trenches of France. The French recruited in their colonies in black Africa, as well as among the Arab population of Algeria.

To dress a man in your own country's uniform is implicitly to admit that he is not your inferior. The French recognized this by opening French citizenship to Algerians who had fought under the French flag. But many Algerians had greater ambitions than becoming honorary Europeans. Their pride demanded an Algerian nation of their own. The image of European superiority had been drastically undercut by World War I. Hearing the propaganda Europeans published against each other, non-Western people could conclude that the real savages were their colonial masters. As fighting spread around the world, some non-Western peoples actually saw their European conquerors beaten and driven out. A successful defense often depended on the help of the non-Western population. These developments—economic, military, and psychological—undermined the prewar colonial order and launched a wave of postwar restiveness from Africa to China.

Trusting Wilson's rhetoric of self-determination, some non-Western nationalists journeyed to Paris in 1919 to argue their case. But the peacemakers hardly acknowledged them. They handed over to Britain and France the territories in Africa and the Middle East that had belonged to Germany or the Ottoman Empire. The only concession to Wilsonian rhetoric was that these territories became "mandates" rather than colonies. This new term implied that Britain and France did not own these lands, but held them in trust for the

League of Nations. The European country was responsible for preparing the territory for eventual self-rule. In practice, however, there might be little difference from prewar colonial rule. The French, for example, responded to Syrian complaints with tanks and bombers.

Ultimately, the statesmen in Paris not only refused to redefine the power relationship between the world's whites and nonwhites, but rejected the principle of racial equality proposed by Japan—the nonwhite great power that could claim a place among the victors. The Latin Americans, the Italians, and the French supported the Japanese. The British, speaking for Australia—a thinly settled white outpost that greatly feared its neighbors on the Asian mainland—opposed the proposal. Without U.S. support, the Japanese initiative came to nothing. It was clear that the peacemakers intended, despite all the noble rhetoric, to recreate the European-dominated world of 1914.

This outcome had a tremendous impact on a whole generation of ambitious young Africans and Asians. Western ideas of democracy were now shown to be things reserved for Europeans. As the Wilsonian promise faded, some future Asian and African leaders turned instead to the country the Paris peacemakers had outlawed from the international community: revolutionary Russia. Only Lenin and his regime seemed inclined to offer sympathy and support to the wave of protest that swept the colonial world after World War I.

Whatever the intent of the Paris peacemakers, European colonial rule could never again be as secure as it had been in 1914. In Egypt, something close to full-scale revolution broke out against the British. In India, a local British commander in the Punjab demonstrated the firmness of British authority by ordering his soldiers to fire on an unarmed crowd. Brigadier Reginald Dyer's troops killed nearly four hundred people and wounded more than a thousand. A century earlier, this massacre at Amritsar would hardly have been news. Now, however, the world reacted with horror. General Dyer was reprimanded by his military superiors and censured by the House of Commons.

Times had changed. Colonialism had acquired a bad conscience, perhaps in part because of all the wartime talk about democracy. By the early 1920s, Britain had launched both Egypt and India on the road to self-government. Indeed the colonial powers had little choice. Bled white by four years of war, no European country could devote the same level of resources to colonial pacification as it had spent before 1914. But it took many years and another world war to persuade the British, and even longer to persuade the French, that their empires were too costly to maintain.

The Peace Treaties

The fate of the colonial peoples was a side issue for the peacemakers of Paris, whose real task was to draft the treaties ending the war with the Central Powers and their allies. They produced five such treaties. The Treaty of Sèvres imposed on the Ottoman Empire is discussed in Chapter 10. The three treaties that dealt with southeastern Europe essentially ratified what had happened in 1918. Out of the wreckage of the Austro-Hungarian Empire had emerged a country for each of its peoples: the Czechs and Slovaks, the Hungarians, and the South Slavs. Prewar Balkan nationalists like Gavrilo Princip had gotten what they wanted.

Whether their desires were wise remains a question. Most of these new countries remained economically little developed. Their ethnic animosities made cooperation among them unlikely. Miniature versions of the empire they had replaced, most of them contained dissatisfied minorities within their borders. Even so, most of these countries felt they had been cheated of the borders they deserved.

These states suffered a dismal fate. They were dominated after Hitler's rise by Germany, and after his fall by the Soviet Union, as they still are to varying degrees. (Yugoslavia today is an exception.) As separate victims of Hitler and Stalin, these countries suffered much more than when they all belonged to the Hapsburg emperor. But there was no hope of resurrecting his regime in 1919, even had the peacemakers wanted to.

Delegates to the Peace Conference of 1919. In the foreground is Prince Faysal, third son of King Husayn of the Hijaz and spokesman for Arabs at Versailles. T. E. Lawrence (Lawrence of Arabia) is the British officer second from right in the middle row.
The Trustees of the Imperial War Museum, London

The real task was to decide what to do about Germany. To justify the loss of millions of lives, the statesmen in Paris had to ensure that future generations would not have to fight another German war. One approach that appealed to much of European public opinion and to military minds, notably in France, was to destroy Germany's military capability and economic strength. Now that the nation had surrendered, it should be broken up, so that there would be several weak Germanies, as there had been through most of European history.

The emotions that prompted demands for such a drastic solution are easy to understand. Would it have worked? After Russia's collapse, the Entente Powers had not been able to defeat Germany without the help of the United States. Was it likely that this wartime alliance could be maintained indefinitely in the postwar period to hold down an embittered German population? Moreover, in a world of economic interdependence, a country's former enemies are its future trading partners. A bankrupt and broken Germany might drag the whole world's economy down.

Considering such dangers, some concluded that a harsh peace was not the answer. The kaiser and his regime, who bore responsibility for the war, had been driven from power. Germany was now in the hands of democratic leaders. Why not let it return on relatively moderate terms to membership in a world community ruled by law?

Not surprisingly, this point of view was far more widely held in Britain and the United States than in France, on whose soil the war had been fought and whose richest farming and industrial regions the Germans had totally devastated. It would be difficult to convince the French to give up their guns. In 1919

the prevention of aggression by the League of Nations was only the dream of idealists.

The peacemakers of Paris failed because of this conflict of views between the wartime allies. It is just possible that World War II might have been avoided if one of these approaches to the German problem had been fully applied. The Treaty of Versailles, however, was a compromise that combined the disadvantages of both approaches. Despite some Wilsonian language, it imposed on Germany a peace no patriotic German could accept. But it did not cripple Germany enough to prevent it from eventually challenging the verdict of 1919 by force.

This outcome may have been inevitable. Wartime alliances usually come apart as soon as the common objective has been attained. Though all twenty-seven countries that had declared war on the Central Powers sent delegations to Paris, most of them, notably the Latin Americans, had made insignificant contributions to the war. The major powers shunted them into the background. Though Italy was considered a major power, it fared little better. Believing that their country had been denied its fair share in the spoils of victory, the Italian delegates left the conference for a time. Neither their departure nor their return could win them a larger share of the remains of the Austro-Hungarian Empire or any of Germany's former colonies.

The important decisions of the Paris peace conferences were the work of the Big Three: President Wilson, French Prime Minister Clemenceau and British Prime Minister Lloyd George. Lloyd George was caught in the middle. He could foresee the dangers of a harsh peace, but he represented an exhausted country, some of whose newspapers had mounted a campaign to "hang the kaiser." The worst clashes were between Wilson and Clemenceau, who were temperamentally far apart.

Clemenceau's determination had made an unmeasurable but real contribution to France's victory. Cynical and sarcastic, he cared for nothing but his martyred country. France had suffered, he believed, as a result of incurable German aggressiveness; in time the Germans could be expected to attack again, and only force would stop them. All the talk about new principles in international affairs left him cold. "Fourteen Points!" he snorted. "Even the Good Lord only had ten points." Yet Clemenceau knew that France's safety depended on British and American support, especially since Russia had disappeared into a dark cloud of communist revolution.

Wilson, the sublimely self-confident former professor, believed that his country had no selfish motives—a position easier to maintain in relation to the United States' role in Europe than to its role in Latin America. He thus spoke from a position of moral superiority which people who did not believe that morality ruled international affairs, like Clemenceau, found hard to endure. Wilson spoke with the zeal of a missionary from the idealistic New World to the corrupt Old World. But he may not have spoken for U.S. public opinion. The congressional elections of 1918 had gone against his party, and a reversal of wartime enthusiasm would soon lead the United States back to its traditional isolation from European affairs.

Only the necessity of producing some conclusion enabled two such different men to hammer out a treaty both could sign. When its terms were published, both were bitterly attacked by their countrymen. French hard-liners condemned Clemenceau for not insisting on the territorial demands they thought essential to French security. Many of Wilson's advisers thought he had too often given in to European-style power politics, sacrificing the principle of a people's right to choose its own government.

Wilson's supreme goal was the creation of the new international organization, the League of Nations. Clemenceau could hardly take the idea seriously, for Wilson could not promise that membership would require any nation, least of all the United States, to help a future victim of aggression. (The U.S. Constitution clearly prohibited any such commitment.) The same difficulty arose when the United Nations was created in 1945. Sovereign nations proved unwilling to subject their freedom of action to international authority.

In return for French agreement to the establishment of the League, Wilson allowed Clemenceau to impose severe penalties on Germany. The German army was to be limited to 100,000 men. Germany could have neither submarines nor an air force. Characteristic of the compromise nature of the treaty, this virtual disarmament of Germany was described as the first step toward the general disarmament called for in the Fourteen Points. The Treaty of Versailles was full of provisions intended by Clemenceau to weaken Germany. The new Republic of Austria, the German-speaking remnant of the former Hapsburg state, was forbidden to merge with Germany, though a national vote made it clear this was the solution preferred by most Austrians.

With the Russian alliance gone, Clemenceau intended to surround Germany with strong French allies to the East. The new state of Czechoslovakia was given a defensible mountainous border that put millions of Germans under Czech rule.

The Poland the Paris peacemakers resurrected included a "Polish corridor" cutting through German territory to the Baltic Sea. Such terms made sense if the aim was to cripple Germany. But they flouted Wilsonian principles, and the Germans complained that the principle of self-determination had been honored only when it worked against them.

The Paris peacemakers also demanded that Germany should pay reparations. The word implies that Germany was to repair the damage its war had caused—not an unreasonable demand. But the bill drawn up by the victors was so astronomical—132 billion gold marks—that the Germans would still be making huge payments today if anybody were still trying to collect them.

The old idea of collecting large sums from a defeated enemy may well be outdated in the twentieth century, when national economies are so interdependent. If the Germans had to turn over everything they earned, they would be unable to buy the goods the victorious nations wanted to export. The economists who raised such questions were drowned out by the insistence that "the Germans will pay." Indeed when the Germans did not pay enough, soon enough, French and Belgian armies reoccupied German territory to collect what was due. Germans then concluded that reparations were not a bill for damages but an excuse for Germany's enslavement.

To prevent another German invasion like those of 1870 and 1914, many Frenchmen felt German territory should be amputated in the west as well as the east. In particular, they wanted to detach the Rhineland—the region between the French-German border and the Rhine—and place it under reliable French control. (Map 3.3 makes it clear why the French would have liked to control this territory.) Even as the conference was meeting in Paris, renegade Germans working for the French tried to establish a separate Rhineland Republic, though the effort soon collapsed. The Rhineland issue provoked the bitterest of the many quarrels of the Paris conference. Wilson, backed by Lloyd George, warned that taking the Rhineland from Germany would create a permanent German grievance, comparable to Germany's taking of Alsace-Lorraine from France in 1871. Speaking for a country that had suffered casualties at thirty-six times the rate the Americans had, Clemenceau insisted that French control of the Rhineland was essential for French security. But he finally agreed to a compromise. The Treaty of Versailles stipulated only that the Rhineland be demilitarized. The Germans would keep it but could not fortify it or station troops there. In return for this concession, Wilson and Lloyd George signed a separate treaty committing their countries to help France if it was again attacked by Germany.

After months of argument, the Treaty of Versailles was complete. The victors handed it to the Germans to sign—or else. Germany's representatives were horrified. Their contacts with Wilson before the armistice had led them to expect a compromise peace. Now they were told to confess that Germany alone had caused the war and to pay a criminal's penalty.

By accepting the Treaty of Versailles, Germany's new postwar democracy, the Weimar Republic, probably signed its own death warrant. But its critics, like Adolf Hitler, never explained how the republic's representatives could have avoided the "dictated peace" of Versailles. Germany had lost the war. Because the fighting ended before Germany had been invaded, many Germans did not recognize this harsh reality. They saw the Treaty of Versailles as a humiliation to be repudiated as soon as possible. Its reputation among the victors was hardly better. French hard-liners charged that Clemenceau had conceded too much and thrown France's victory away. "This is not a peace," said Marshal Foch, "but an armistice for twenty years."

The pessimism of these critics was confirmed within six months as the United States repudiated the agreements its president had negotiated. In November 1919 the Senate refused to ratify the Treaty of Versailles or the treaty promising American help to France. Americans were increasingly impatient with Europe's messy, faraway problems. The Old World, which had seemed so close in 1917–1918, again became remote: another world, a week away by the fastest ship. The 1920 presidential election was won by a likable, small-town newspaper publisher from the Midwest, Warren G. Harding. The choice reflected Americans' longing for a return to what Harding called "normalcy"—the way things had been before the United States became involved in a European war.

This American return to isolationism suggests the fatal weakness in Wilson's vision of a new world order. An international organization like the League of Nations could keep the peace only if its members committed themselves to use force against any country determined to be an aggressor. Yet Wilson himself could offer no such commitment on behalf of the United States. The Senate's rejection of the Treaty of Versailles showed that Americans, like other people, still insisted on judging international conflicts in terms of their national interests. With no power of its own, the

League of Nations proved pathetically inadequate to the task of keeping the peace when international tensions mounted again in the 1930s.

The limitations of the League were particularly serious because the balance of power in Europe had been destroyed. The collapse of Austria-Hungary had left a vacuum of power in central and southeastern Europe. Russia was in the hands of communists who openly encouraged the overthrow of all other governments; no one could form an alliance with such an outlaw regime. Britain, like the United States, now decided that the costs of getting involved in Europe outweighed the likely benefits. Using as their excuse the American failure to honor Wilson's commitment, the British also repudiated their pledge to defend France. This left an exhausted France alone (except for resentful Italy) on the Continent with Germany. And Germany, though disarmed and diminished, was still the same nation that had held off the British Empire and two other major powers for most of the war. Its fundamental strengths—its numbers and its highly developed economy—could be mobilized by some future regime less willing than the Weimar Republic to accept the Versailles verdict.

World War I had not ended until U.S., Australian, and Indian troops had become combatants. If peace were to be maintained by some renewed balance of power, that balance would have to be global. But many people in all countries were unable to draw this conclusion. Americans tended to see their intervention in international politics as a choice

▶

Map 3.3 Post–World War I Boundary Changes

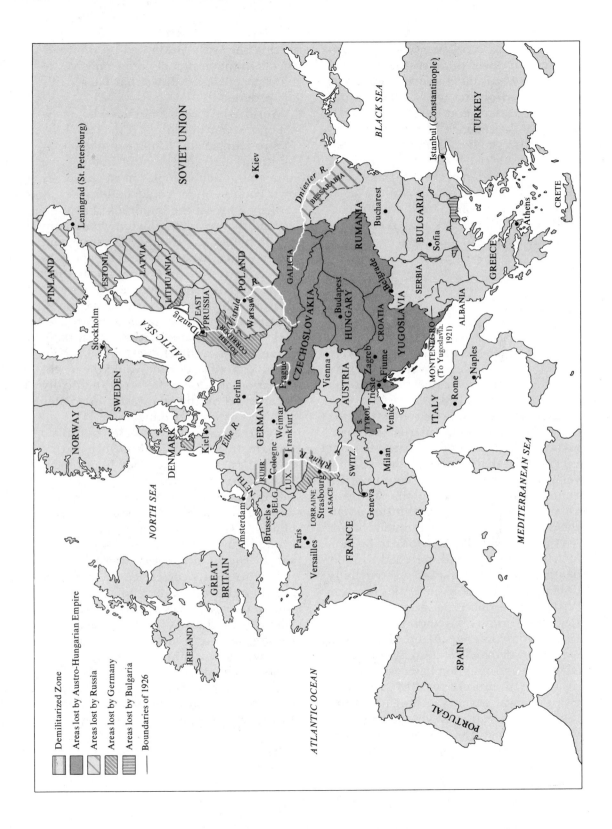

Demilitarized Zone

Areas lost by Austro-Hungarian Empire

Areas lost by Russia

Areas lost by Germany

Areas lost by Bulgaria

Boundaries of 1926

rather than as a necessity of the twentieth-century world. Over the next decades, they continued to come and go as they pleased on the world stage. Similarly, Australians and Indians claimed a greater independence of Britain in foreign affairs. The British Empire soon became the British "Commonwealth of Nations," whose members did not automatically follow where Britain led. It would take a second world war to persuade all these peoples that they had a permanent stake in the global contest for power.

Conclusion

Although it is sometimes said that wars do not settle anything, World War I resolved several prewar questions, though hardly ever in the way the people who started the war had hoped. It settled the fate of the ramshackle Austrian, Russian, and Ottoman empires. It showed that Europe, the smallest though the most developed of the continents, could not indefinitely dominate the globe. The war also settled prewar uncertainties about the possible limits of government power over individuals. The disciplined fashion in which millions had marched to their deaths showed that power was virtually unbounded. At the same time, the war settled some questions about inequalities of civil rights based on birth or sex. Distinctions among citizens had given way to the demands of total mobilization (though discrimination had certainly not disappeared entirely in 1918). And certainly the war gave a shocking answer to the prewar question of whether progress was inevitable. The art of surgery, for example, had advanced significantly

during the war—prompted by improvements in the design of high explosives to blow people apart. It was hard to see this as "progress."

World War I also created a whole new set of postwar questions. If the fall of the Austro-Hungarian Empire proved that multinational states could not survive and that each people must have its own country, how could nations be established for all the hundreds of peoples around the world? And what would happen in places like Ireland, Palestine, and South Africa, where more than one people claimed the same territory as their home? What would happen if government expansion continued? If the mobilization effort had created a greater social equality, would that eventually mean equal rights for everyone, or an equal loss of freedoms? Would the mechanization of human life, so dramatically accelerated by the war, result in greater comforts or greater dangers?

By the mid-1920s some optimists thought they could see hopeful answers to all these questions. They found them in a country that was seeking to replace the European-dominated world system with a new one based on worldwide revolution. There an experiment in unlimited government power was taking shape. The country's goal was said to be the creation of a society based on literal equality. Its officially anointed heroes were its steelworkers and tractor drivers, whose machines would modernize a peasant land and make it the model for the twentieth century. Like those optimists of the 1920s from the West, but with a more analytical eye, we shall look at the Union of Soviet Socialist Republics (USSR)—the country that emerged, after the Bolshevik Revolution of 1917, under Lenin and Stalin.

Suggestions for Further Reading

Albrecht-Carrié, R., *The Meaning of the First World War* (1965).

Birdsall, Paul, *Versailles Twenty Years After* (1941).

Bruun, Geoffrey, *Clemenceau* (1943).

Falls, Cyril, *The Great War* (1959).

Feldman, Gerald D., *Arms, Industry, and Labor in Germany* (1966).

Horne, Alistair, *The Price of Glory* (1962).

Lafore, Laurence, *The Long Fuse* (1965).

Mayer, Arno J. *The Politics and Diplomacy of Peacemaking* (1968).

Nicolson, Harold, *Peacemaking, 1919* (1933).

Remarque, Erich Maria, *All Quiet on the Western Front* (1928).

Roth, Jack J., ed., *World War I: A Turning Point in Modern History* (1967).

Tuchman, Barbara, *The Guns of August* (1963).

Chapter 4

RESTRUCTURING THE SOCIAL AND POLITICAL ORDER: THE BOLSHEVIK REVOLUTION IN WORLD PERSPECTIVE

World War I did not only begin the decline of European world dominance. This "European civil war" also opened the way for the triumph of a revolutionary movement in Russia: Bolshevism, committed in principle to destroying the social and economic bases of the European-dominated system worldwide. The Bolshevik Revolution of 1917 therefore influenced world history, as well as Russian history. This chapter explains why Russia's prewar tsarist regime was vulnerable to revolution, how Lenin and the Bolsheviks seized and held power after the tsarist collapse, and how Stalin in the 1930s began to transform the Soviet Union from a backward country into an industrial superpower rivaling those of Europe and North America.

Russia's was the most important revolution of the early twentieth century. It was not the only one. By 1917, revolutions had also occurred in Iran (1905–1911), the Ottoman Empire (1908), Mexico (1910), and China (1911), challenging the dominance of the European great powers or (in Mexico) of the United

States. Whereas the Bolsheviks were able to defeat their internal and external enemies and to establish their independence, none of these earlier revolutions succeeded in either achieving independence from great power dominance or restructuring the society of the country where the rebellion occurred. They failed partly because they lacked leadership comparable to Lenin's. But more importantly, these earlier revolutions had essentially nationalist goals. They aimed to free a particular country, but offered no model for the transformation of the world. An examination of the Mexican revolution will illustrate this problem. (See also Chapter 8.)

The Bolshevik Revolution, by contrast, claimed to liberate Russians by implementing a set of relatively simple ideas about history and politics—Marxism-Leninism—that were equally applicable everywhere. Economic forces determined the course of history, in Marx's view. Liberal capitalist industrial societies emerged when middle-class interests overthrew feudal societies dominated by monarchs and aristocrats. The liberal capitalists then created the means of their own eventual destruction by exploiting industrial workers. Eventually, workers would rebel and overthrow capitalism in a revolution inaugurating the communist millennium. As imperialistic capitalism spread its control over the world, the revolutionary potential would become an international, ultimately a global, one.

Lenin applied Marxism in a country where industrial workers made up only about 1 percent of the population. His innovation was to insist that the proletariat be guided in establishing its dictatorship by a tightly organized and disciplined party in which power flowed from the top down.

After 1917, people in the colonial world inevitably asked themselves whether Marxism-Leninism was an effective way to shake off European domination. While the situation of colonial peoples differed fundamentally from that of workers in industrial societies, the global dominance of capitalist societies had created a powerful connection between the two groups. In Russia, Marxism-Leninism had provided a way to topple despotism in one of its European homelands. Could it do the same in the colonial lands?

Non-Western leaders' answers to this question covered a broad spectrum. At one extreme, Mohandas K. Gandhi produced an ideology that challenged European dominance but was radically different from Bolshevism. His career illustrates what could be accomplished through a reformist, rather than a revolutionary, approach to national independence and regeneration. Despite his radical differences from Marxism-Leninism, it is important to remember, however, that Gandhi's movement succeeded partly because the global balance of power had changed since 1917. A new great power, the Soviet Union, had emerged that was dedicated to the overthrow of European dominance.

At the other end of the spectrum from Gandhi, Mao Zedong (Mao Tse-tung) was perhaps the most important non-Western political leader of the twentieth century. His early career shows how much Marxism-Leninism could do, compared with the less radical ideology of Sun Yat-sen and the Chinese Nationalists, to lay the basis for the resurgence of the world's most populous nation. But first Mao had to adapt Marxism-Leninism to the Chinese setting by formulating the ideas that later became known as Mao Zedong thought. Mao's ideas provide the best example of the influence of the Bolshevik Revolution on the wider world, and of the limits and ambiguities of that influence.

The End of Tsarist Russia

Russia had always loomed menacingly over Central and Western Europe. In the nineteenth century, however, Russia was dreaded by Europeans not as the homeland of revolutions, but as the crusher of revolutions. Russian troops repeatedly snuffed out the Poles' hopes for independence. Russia's tsar saw himself as Europe's policeman and played an equally autocratic role at home. Even as it had expanded 5,000 miles across a continent, subjecting a hundred nationalities to its rule, the Russian Empire never departed from its inherited political system. Its law was the will of the tsar, whose secret police still curbed freedoms taken for granted in Western Europe or North America—freedom of speech, press, association, and self-expression.

Society and Politics

At the beginning of the twentieth century, Russia was still socially and economically backward. Nine out of ten Russians were still peasants. Until 1861 their grandparents had been serfs, literally the property of the aristocrat or the state whose land they worked. Even now the peasants were Russia's "dark people," largely illiterate, often lacking sufficient land to feed themselves. Their tradition was one of endurance, interrupted periodically by violence, as in the 600 separate serf rebellions of the first half of the nineteenth century. Between the peasants, at the bottom of Russian society, and the wealthy, untaxed aristocracy at the top was a small middle class. The economic functions of a middle class—commerce and industry—had developed slowly in nineteenth-century Russia. Until 1830 there had not even been a paved road connecting Moscow and St. Petersburg, the empire's two principal cities.

In the early twentieth century, middle-class political liberals hoped to convert the tsarist autocracy into a Western-style constitutional monarchy. But by 1900, many intellectuals had despaired of any peaceful evolution of Russia's government. So grim was the tsarist record of repression and resistance to change that Social Democrats believed that Marxist revolution offered the only hope. Others—the Social Revolutionaries—favored the distinctively Russian politics of assassination that had killed one tsar and dozens of high officials since the mid-nineteenth century. Many members of both groups paid for their political beliefs with their lives, or with long terms in Siberian prisons. Others fled Russia to await the coming of revolution. The tsarist regime was happy to see them go. There was no room for people influenced by Western notions of freedom and tolerance in a society that used the state-dominated Orthodox Church to control popular opinion, that imposed rule by Russians on the many ethnic minorities, and that systematically persecuted Jews. To official Russia, Western ideas were alien and dangerous.

The Western Challenge

Russia could not do without Western ideas, however. If it was to remain a great power as its rivals modernized, Russia must modernize too. This lesson had been painfully driven home in the mid-nineteenth century when Britain and France defeated Russia in the Crimean War. One of its consequences was the tsar's decision to emancipate the serfs in 1861—a decision inspired less by humanitarian concern than by economic calculation. A modernized agricultural system no longer based on serfdom might produce more grain for export— and grain was what Russia had to exchange for the products of Western ingenuity. By the turn of the century, Russia had become a large exporter of grain, even in years, like 1891–1892, when famine killed millions of peasants.

Apart from the large loans it received from Western Europe and particularly from France, Russia could finance its industrialization only by exporting food even while its own people went hungry. Although it claimed to be a great power, preindustrial Russia stood in almost the same colonial economic relationship to Western and Central Europe as the dependent peoples of Africa and Asia. By the 1890s progressive ministers had persuaded the tsar that Russia must undertake a crash program of industrialization.

The program produced impressive economic results. Russian industry doubled its output from 1900 to 1913, raising the nation from near insignificance among industrial powers to fifth rank. Russia still had a long way to go, however. Its per capita income was one-sixth that of the United States, one-third that of Germany.

The social consequences of rapid industrialization were explosive. The capital needed for development was literally wrung out of the peasantry, already burdened by the debt they owed their former masters for emancipation. Their taxes increased 50 percent in a decade.

A more immediate danger to the government was the condition of Russia's rapidly growing cities. As in almost every other country, the first phase of industrialization was a grim era for workers. The Russian factory worker often returned home after an eleven-and-a-half hour day under relentless supervision to a hovel he shared with ten other people. He could not protest such conditions to anyone, for strikes, like unions, were illegal. Many Russian factories were huge places where the worker had no human contact with his employer, only with his fellow employees. In such settings, though propaganda could circulate only secretly, the Marxism of the Social Democratic party gained ground among the urban working class.

The massacre of hundreds of working people on Bloody Sunday (January 22) triggered the Revolution of 1905. Their peaceful attempt to petition the tsar— the "Little Father," Nicholas II (1894–1917)—by gathering outside his palace in St. Petersburg ended in a hail of bullets. The uprising that followed was inconclusive, a dress rehearsal for the Revolution of 1917. Nevertheless, it revealed the deep disaffection of almost all of Russian society.

Military defeat had already exposed the regime's weaknesses. The tsar's advisers had led him confidently to war with Japan in 1904, expecting to defeat the "little monkeys" easily and end their interference with Russian expansion in East Asia. The Russo-Japanese War turned out instead to be the first major defeat of a European great power by a non-Western people. Admiral Heihachiro Togo's battleships sank much of the Russian fleet in a single battle. It was just one in a seemingly endless series of revelations of the government's incompetence. By the time Russia sued for peace, the government had been wholly discredited.

After Bloody Sunday, Russia's cities became the scene of continuous strikes and demonstrations until the army could be moved back from the front to restore order. Reinforced by violence in the countryside, this wave of revolt compelled the tsar to yield concessions, including a constitution. He even promised that the new parliament, or Duma, would have real power. But the tsar's heart was never in such promises; he had come to the throne denouncing petitions for reform as "senseless dreams." He intended to rule Russia exactly as his forefathers had. As his government gradually regained control of cities and countryside, he took back most of the concessions he had made.

Thus Russia was still an autocracy as it entered World War I. The electoral system had been rigged to give the Duma, which was virtually powerless, a conservative majority. The parliament consequently provided no real outlet for the grievances of the middle class, workers, or peasants. Despite the failure of the 1905 revolution, the tsarist system seemed doomed to fall before long.

Lenin's Russia, 1917–1924

Revolutions seldom begin among people who have no hope. Like many others, the one that occurred in 1905 was a "revolution of rising expectations." Rapid modernization had showed Russians the possibility of change. It also increased their frustration with a government that seemed both incompetent and oppressive. People seem able to endure a harsh, efficient government, or an inept government that is not harsh. But they will rebel against a government that combines harshness and ineptitude if its defenders lose confidence. This is what happened to the tsarist government in March 1917.

World War I proved disastrous for Russia. As German armies drove deep into Russian territory, the government showed itself incapable of mobilizing society for total war. It was so frightened of losing control that it prohibited the patriotic efforts of citizens to organize to help the war effort. In 1915 the tsar took personal command of his armies, asserting his autocratic responsibility. But his bureaucracy could not organize Russia's industrial and transport system to supply those armies. The home front was no better managed. Shortages of food and fuel led to ceaseless protests. The prestige of the imperial family vanished as it became known that a sinister faith healer, Grigori Rasputin, had become the power behind the throne.

By the spring of 1917 the only support remaining to the autocracy was its forces of law and order, and they were wavering. When the troops disobeyed orders to fire on food rioters in Petrograd (formerly St. Petersburg), joining the rioters instead, Nicholas II could do nothing but give up his throne. It would be four years before it became clear to whom power had passed.

The Provisional Government

As often happens in revolutions, the people who first came into power could not hold on to it. The Provisional Government of Duma liberals that proclaimed itself the tsar's successor immediately enacted reforms. It prepared to convene a democratically chosen assembly to give Russia a real constitution. Nevertheless, the government quickly became almost as unpopular with the masses as the tsar had been. It could not bring order out of the chaos into which Russia had fallen. As honorable men, its leaders insisted on continuing the war at the side of Russia's allies, even as millions of peasant soldiers had declared *their* war over by simply starting to walk home from the front. Moreover, an explosion of grassroots democracy challenged the provisional government's authority. Workers and soldiers everywhere elected Soviets (councils) to govern each factory and regiment. These Soviets in turn elected a hierarchy of Councils of Workers' and Soldiers' Deputies that amounted to a rival government.

In this confused situation one of the most formidable figures of modern times saw his opportunity to change the course of history. Vladimir Ilyich Ulyanov, better known by his revolutionary name of Lenin, was forty-seven in 1917. Child of a middle-class family of academics, he had been a revolutionary already at seventeen, when his older brother was hanged for conspiring to assassinate the tsar. In exile since 1900, he had taken a leading role among Russian Social Democrats abroad.

Lenin combined tactical brilliance and ruthlessness. He was convinced that he knew how to make a revolution that would change the world, and was prepared to use any means and to destroy any opposition. Thus in April 1917 he accepted the offer of the kaiser's generals to send him from Switzerland through the German battle lines into Russia. Their intent was that Lenin should undermine the provisional government's continuation of the war, and he did not disappoint them. As soon as he arrived in Russia, he announced that the revolution should provide "peace, land, and bread." The Provisional Government, having failed to produce these, should be swept aside: "All power to the Soviets."

Lenin believed that his faction of the Social Democratic party, the Bolsheviks, could now seize power and make Russia's revolution real. The Menshevik faction believed that Russia must industrialize further before it could have the proletarian revolution Marx envisioned. But Lenin saw the possibility of capturing power now by giving Russia's masses, represented in the Soviets, what they demanded. End the war, even by accepting defeat. Give the peasants the land many were already beginning to seize. Feed the starving cities, imposing whatever controls were necessary.

Second Revolution, 1917

So exactly did this program correspond to the aspirations of war-weary Russians that Bolshevik representation in the Soviets continued to climb through 1917. In vain the Provisional Government tried to fight back. Ineffective, torn by dissension, threatened both by tsarist generals and by Bolsheviks, it could not endure. Hardly a shot was fired in its defense during the second (November) revolution of 1917. When Bolshevik soldiers occupied government headquarters, it was all over. Lenin had been right, and everyone else wrong. The Bolsheviks, a tiny minority of Russian society, could capture the power the tsar had let fall.

As often happens in revolutions, power had passed from the moderates to a small band of dedicated extremists with a vision of an entirely changed society. Only after four more years of civil war, however, did the Communist party (as the Bolsheviks renamed themselves early in 1918) secure its victory. Lenin

Lenin with Stalin in 1922. This was the year in which Lenin (left) suffered his first stroke—he died in 1924—and Stalin became Secretary-General of the Communist party of the Soviet Union.
The Mansell Collection

swiftly implemented changes that inevitably turned much of his country and the world against him. He made peace on Germany's terms in the treaty of Brest-Litovsk in March 1918, surrendering Russia's most fertile and industrialized regions and a third of its population. He abolished private ownership of land.

It was more difficult to meet the goal of providing bread from Russia's war-ravaged economy, though he sent the army to seize food from recalcitrant peasants. But Lenin did not hesitate to decree complete economic reorganization. In the name of "War Communism,"

he nationalized Russia's banks. He confiscated industries and merged them into giant government-controlled trusts. He repudiated Russia's foreign debts. Private property was not the Communists' only target, however. They attacked the patriarchal family by establishing legal equality of women with men, easing conditions for divorce and abortion, and providing for universal compulsory education.

Lenin did not seek popular consent to these changes. He knew that many of them would not have commanded majority support. Indeed, the Bolsheviks won only about 25 percent of the votes cast for the Constituent Assembly the Provisional Government had ordained. Lenin's solution to this problem was simply to dissolve the Assembly on the first day it met. So vanished the only democratic parliament Russia has ever known, unmourned by most Russians. Parliamentary democracy was not part of the Russian tradition. Since 1905 the Soviets *had* been part of the revolutionary tradition, and in theory the Council of People's Commissars, dominated by Lenin, now governed as the delegates of the All-Russian Congress of Soviets. In reality, now that the Soviets had served their purpose, Lenin had no intention of letting them continue their disorderly experiments in direct democracy. He quickly brought them under control of the Communist party.

Invasion, Civil War, and New Economic Policy

In concentrating power in the hands of a few, Lenin was following his deepest instincts. He had always believed that a revolution was made by a small elite, a party "like a clenched fist," which directed the masses. In 1918 to 1921, moreover, his regime was fighting for its life against enemies within and without. Russia's former allies sent in 100,000 troops (British, French, Japanese, and 7,000 Americans) to occupy strategic points in Russian territory. The goal was first to bring Russia back into the war and later, as Winston Churchill put it, "to strangle Bolshevism in its cradle." Most of the troops were withdrawn by 1919, but their presence symbolized the world's refusal to recognize the Communists as Russia's masters. This refusal encouraged some non-Russian national-

ities within the former tsarist empire to rebel, and raised the hopes of several high-ranking tsarist officers, who mobilized "White" armies to march against the new "Red" regime. Against these multiple enemies the Red Army was fighting at one time on two dozen fronts.

The White counterrevolution failed. The mutual suspicions of the White leaders made cooperation impossible. Moreover, fighting to turn the clock back, they could not win the support of the majority of Russians. However disillusioned they might become with Communist rule, the people had gained from the revolution.

There was soon much reason for disillusionment. In his fight for survival Lenin had not hesitated at any step. He re-established the secret police, for example, and ordered the shooting of hostages. If he did not order the murder of the captive tsar and his family, Lenin certainly did not regret it. In protest against the iron rule of his party dictatorship the sailors at the Kronstadt naval base rebelled in May 1921. Though they had once been ardent Bolsheviks, Lenin crushed their uprising without mercy. Within four years, "heroes" of the revolution had become "traitors."

Many of the world's revolutions have followed a similar path from enthusiasm to disillusionment. In the resulting atmosphere of cynicism, the extremist leadership has often been overthrown by leaders less bent on total change. Lenin's pragmatism, however, told him that he must temporarily slow the pace of revolution to consolidate Communist rule. The revolution's enemies had been beaten, but the economy was a shambles. Thus in 1921 his New Economic Policy (NEP) ended War Communism by re-establishing the free enterprise system in agriculture and retail trade, though not in heavy industry.

There was no corresponding relaxation of political control. After 1921, disagreement with the Communist party line meant expulsion from the party. To the distress of some old Bolsheviks, by the time Lenin died in 1924 the party was becoming the privileged, conformist bureaucratic machine that governs the Soviet Union today.

At the end of his life Lenin seemed clearly to regret that he had created a party dictatorship rather than a truly egalitarian society. For this reason his defenders try to dissociate him from the later totalitarian regime of Joseph Stalin. But it was Lenin who laid the foundations for the one-party police state that Stalin built. Lenin could hardly have done otherwise. His genius had been to see how his party could capitalize on war-weariness, land hunger, and economic chaos to take power. But only for that brief interlude did the Bolshevik vision of the future coincide with the ideas of most Russians. Once in power, the Bolsheviks had to use force to turn their vision into reality. To do that required recreating the kind of authoritarian bureaucratic class the revolution had just overthrown. The only means to the Communist end were means that mocked that end.

died, leaving no clear successor, the question of the USSR's future direction divided the Communist party leadership.

In this debate, also a power struggle, the advantage lay with the man who dominated the bureaucratic machine. This was General Secretary of the Communist party Joseph Stalin (1879–1953). Though a Bolshevik since his youth, Stalin came from a background very different from that of most of the men who surrounded Lenin. Son of a cobbler and grandson of serfs, Stalin had emerged from among the "dark people." Like them, he had little to say. When he did speak, it was often in the peasant's earthy proverbial language. He had never lived in the West and had none of the old Bolsheviks' fluency in Marxist theory. By 1927, however, Stalin's ruthless ambition allowed him to gain control of the Soviet party and state. The party congress of that year forbade any deviation from the party line as Stalin defined it. This final blow to party discussion drove many old Bolsheviks into retirement or exile. Some of them concluded that the Russian Revolution, like others, had convulsed an entire society only to end up in the dictatorship of a tyrant.

Stalin's Soviet Union, 1924–1939

The realities of the Union of Soviet Socialist Republics (USSR), as Russia was renamed in 1922, were never anticipated by Marxist theory. Communism had won its first great victory not by a worldwide workers' revolution, but by imposing a party dictatorship on a largely peasant country. There was no clear Marxist prescription for what to do next. After Lenin

Socialism in One Country

Because the world had not yet followed Russia into revolution, Stalin was convinced, the task of Marxists must be to strengthen "socialism in one country." This could only be done by making the Soviet Union a mighty industrial power. As he declared in 1931, "We are fifty or one hundred years behind the advanced countries. We must make good this lag in ten years. Either we will accomplish this or we will be crushed."[1]

The USSR's first Five-Year Plan, launched in 1928, made it clear that Stalin intended to squeeze capital for industrialization out of agriculture, just as the last tsars had done. To do this, Stalin believed, required smashing the agricultural society that had developed under the NEP. Wealthy peasants (kulaks) were to be "liquidated" and the millions of family farms abolished. Surviving rural Russians were to be massed on collective farms a thousand times bigger than the typical peasant holding and presumably more suitable for mechanized agriculture. The immediate results of this agricultural revolution were catastrophic. Peasant resistance reduced agricultural productivity to nothing, and Russia endured mass starvation during 1931–1933—only the first of the Stalinist horrors of the 1930s.

Meanwhile the industrial sector grew enormously—by a factor of three during the 1930s, according to one evaluation. Production rose at an annual rate of 14 percent. The Soviet Union rose from fifteenth to third rank worldwide in production of electricity, fulfilling Lenin's definition of communism as "socialism plus electricity."

The contrast between this frenzied Soviet development and the stagnation of the Western economies during the Depression was striking. Soviet propaganda attributed the nation's accomplishments not only to Stalin's genius but to the heroism of Soviet workers like the miner Stakhanov, who supposedly exceeded his production quota by 1,400 percent in 1935. Some Western visitors came away marveling at such achievements. But shrewder observers could guess at some of the human costs. Soviet workers, who had no right to strike, were not spurred to produce by any hope that their low earnings would purchase consumer goods. Hardly any were available. Soviet workers were goaded to productivity by all the managerial tricks of early industrial capitalism, including piecework rather than hourly pay. They could not change jobs. Any protest meant arrest and deportation to one of the large projects being built with slave labor. Under Stalin, some twelve million Russians were prisoners on such sites, or in Siberian camps, or in jails—far more than the tsars had ever incarcerated.

Assessing the Soviet Experience Under Lenin and Stalin

On the eve of World War II, the Soviet Union projected two sharply contrasting images to the world. The image of progress emphasized the great dams, factories, even whole new industrial cities sprouting across the land. But there was also the image of terror, particularly during the great purge of 1936–1938, when Stalin got rid of most of the surviving old Bolsheviks. Courtroom cameras filmed them confessing to improbable crimes against the state before disappearing forever.

Defenders of Stalin's historic role explain that these contrasting images are inseparable. The factories, they maintain, could not have been created so quickly without the threat of the prison camps. By forcing the discipline of modernity on Russian society, he transformed a largely peasant nation into an industrial superpower in just two decades. Because we cannot rerun history to see the results of alternative approaches, we cannot know whether the Soviet Union could have industrialized quickly without Stalin's inhumanity.

For world history, the important consideration is the import of what Lenin and Stalin did. They showed that it was possible to break away from the European-dominated world system. The Soviets had done so both politically, by rejecting Western liberal democracy, and economically, by undertaking their own industrial development. Western capitalist societies had industrialized over several generations, as their citizens slowly adjusted their lives to the rhythms of the machine age. The Soviet Union seemed to provide a model for accelerating this process and overcoming economic dependency rapidly. In the Bolshevik model, modernization was imposed from above by force. But for the vast majority of the world's people, who had never known Western-style liberal democracy, this criticism was not necessarily compelling. Comparing the results of the Russian Revolution with those of less radical revolutions and independence movements elsewhere, the aspiring revolutionary might well find the Bolshevik model more attractive.

Construction of the Volkhov River Power Station, 1926. The USSR's first hydroelectric generating station was located near Leningrad. Expanding generating capacity became a prime objective of the First Five-Year Plan (1928). *Sovfoto*

Contrasts in Revolution and Mass Mobilization

The Russian Revolution has been the most influential of twentieth-century revolutions. To understand its impact, it helps to consider the most nearly comparable experiences of some other countries. Many examples offer themselves for comparison. One type includes national, but not social, revolutions—that is, revolutions that aimed to achieve national independence, but not basic social change. The experience of Mexico illustrates what could happen to a revolution that had neither a clear-cut ideology of social change nor a leader as dominant as Lenin. Another phenomenon that merits consideration is the unique Indian case of an independence movement that advanced a powerful ideology—Mohandas Gandhi's philosophy of nonviolence—and achieved mass mobilization under this charismatic leader, but again stopped short of a thoroughgoing restructuring of society. Last, for an example that includes a commanding leader who called for both national and social revolutions, and that provided the first major test of Soviet ability to export Marxism-Leninism, we shall look at the rise of Chinese communism and especially at the early career of Mao Zedong.

The Mexican Revolution

The Mexican revolutionaries of 1910 hardly recognized the difficulty of their task. Mexico still shared many characteristics of the rest of Latin America. It was principally agricultural, with much of the land belonging to huge plantations or haciendas. Though three out of four Mexicans tilled the land, only 2 percent of them owned the land they worked—and the proportion of owners had steadily diminished for a half-century. Mexico was a federal republic in form, but political forms meant little in a country where 84 percent of the population was illiterate, and most pure-blooded Indians (a third of the population) spoke no Spanish. In reality, Mexico was a dictatorship, ruled for thirty-four years by one man, Porfirio Díaz (1830–1915), and a small clique of wealthy associates, many of them hacienda owners.

Díaz typifies the conservative ruler who undermines his own rule by encouraging change. His regime was spectacularly successful in encouraging Mexican economic development. Railroad mileage, for example, increased more than fortyfold during his dictatorship. The national income doubled in the decade before the economic panic of 1907, which plunged Mexico and the rest of the world into crisis. But the boom had side effects that worked against the dictatorship. Mexico's small but growing middle class resented the disparity between their economic importance and their political impotence. The urban working class complained of their low wages, long hours, and poor working conditions. Both groups condemned Díaz as the instrument of American economic domination. The dictator had once sighed, "Poor Mexico! So far from God, so near the United States!" But Mexico needed U.S. capital for its development. With Díaz's encouragement, U.S. investment poured into Mexico, more than doubling in the decade before the revolution. By 1910 Americans had invested twice as much in Mexico as Mexicans had. U.S. companies controlled three-fourths of Mexico's mines and almost three-fifths of its oil production. To protect these investments, the United States interfered in Mexican politics so often that the nationalist revolutionary slogan became, "Mexico for the Mexicans!"

Mexico was a powderkeg of political, social, and anti-foreign discontent. The revolutionary leaders who lit the match sought only to make real the democracy Mexico already had on paper. Most of the men who challenged Díaz in 1910 and forced him into exile in 1911 were members of the upper classes, like Díaz himself. They touched off a decade-long firestorm of violence. The original revolutionaries were quickly overwhelmed. As Mexican politics became militarized, rival politicians mobilized armies to seize the capital and the presidency. By 1920 two Mexican presidents had been murdered on the orders of, or with the connivance of, their successors. Before the revolution was over, about one of every eight Mexicans had died, either in the violence or as a result of the collapse of the economy.

From this political chaos, a pattern emerged. In their struggle for power, rival politicians made commitments to social change, in order to secure alliances with worker and peasant forces that joined in the conflict for their own reasons. Once in power, however, the politicians tended to play down their commitments and try to bring workers and peasants under government control as quickly as possible.

The fate of the social and economic provisions of the Mexican constitution of 1917 illustrates this pattern. It was a radical document for its time, compared to everything but the Bolshevik program of the same year. Going beyond the standard political language of liberal democracy and its guarantees of universal suffrage, it gave Mexican workers the right to organize and strike, authorized an eight-hour day and a six-day week, and specified a minimum wage. The constitution called for the redistribution of some land to landless peasants, though the former owners were to be compensated for the loss of their property. And it declared that Mexican resources, including mineral wealth, belonged to Mexico and could not be sold or given away to foreigners.

Those provisions reflected the state of the revolutionary power struggle in 1917. The "constitutionalist" politicians needed the help of the workers and peasants not only to restart the economy but also to suppress rival claimants to power. These included Pancho Villa, whose army ranged through much of northern Mexico and briefly occupied Mexico City. Known to the peasants who made up his army as the avenging angel, he seemed to pose the threat of rural social revolution, though his actions were more those of a bandit than of a revolutionary.

The only revolutionary leader with a genuine commitment to land redistribution seems to have been Emiliano Zapata, who led a peasant army in the south under the banner of the Virgin of Guadalupe. "We fight," he declared, "so the people will have lands, forests, and water."[2] He proposed to give one-third of the haciendas to landless peasants, with prior compensation to the owners. This was hardly a radical objective compared with the Bolsheviks' confiscation of all privately owned land in 1918, yet it made Zapata suspect to the constitutionalist politicians. They had him killed in 1919. (They pacified Villa by giving him a hacienda of his own.)

The land reform envisioned in the constitution of 1917 was intended to remedy the tremendous imbalance of the Mexican social pyramid. Similarly, the constitution's restrictions on the use of Mexican resources was a response to the cry of "Mexico for the Mexicans." But once the politicians in Mexico City had eliminated guerrilla leaders like Zapata and Villa and had begun to establish control over the country, the promises of the constitution were only partly fulfilled. Labor won the right to organize, but only in a single big union under firm government control. By 1919, less than one-half of 1 percent of Mexico's land had changed hands. Little more was accomplished in the 1920s. And in 1923, President Álvaro Obregón (1880–1928) promised the U.S. government that he would not enforce the constitution's claim to safeguard Mexico's resources for Mexicans. This bargain won his regime the official recognition Washington had previously refused. American companies continued to drill and sell most of Mexico's oil—a quarter of the world's supply at the time.

With so little real change after so much bloodshed, it can be argued that the Mexican Revolution had failed, or at least stalled, by 1920. Many factors worked against real change: the politicans' selfish ambitions; a political style that favored pistols rather than princi-

Villa and Zapata. Both Francisco "Pancho" Villa (left) and Emiliano Zapata led peasant movements. Despite their shared scorn for middle-class Constitutionalist politicians, their contact was limited, and their movements did not unite.
Special Collection, University of Texas, El Paso

ples; the limited, mainly verbal, objectives of most politicians; and the failure, despite Zapata, to mobilize the Indian peasants who had most to gain from change. Two obstacles were probably fatal: the absence of any ideology calling for a thorough redistribution of power in Mexico, and U.S. opposition.

None of those who sought power could unite most Mexicans behind his program, for none capitalized effectively on the needs of the majority, as Lenin had done in 1917. Moreover, none of the revolutionary programs could really challenge U.S. interests in Mexico, because U.S. recognition was essential to whoever ruled in Mexico City. Without U.S.

recognition, a Mexican head of state could not borrow money or buy arms. He might even have to contend with an American occupation of Mexican territory, like those President Wilson dispatched in 1914 and 1916.

Defenders of the Mexican Revolution argue that it laid the foundations for the more sweeping land reforms and nationalizations of foreign property that came in the 1930s. The earlier years of chaos, so this argument runs, were no time to further cripple the economy by undertaking social experiments. By opening the way to economic development and establishing a semidemocratic political system, according to these defenders, the revolution by 1920 had at least fulfilled the objectives of most of the rebels against Díaz. They sought no more than to move Mexico in the direction of democracy and free enterprise.

The debate between critics and defenders of the Mexican Revolution is likely to continue as long as the present single-party regime, which traces its origins to 1910. One key fact, however, reveals the limits of Mexico's revolutionary experience. Mexico in the 1920s had not broken out—still has not broken out—of its subordinate position in the global configuration, in which, by 1910, the United States played the dominant role in relation to Latin America.

Gandhi's Nonviolence—a Means to Revolution?

Before World War I, only a small minority of Westernized Indian intellectuals and politicians actively challenged British rule in their country. Then a charismatic personality, inspired by a unique mixture of Indian and Western ideas, made the drive for Indian independence a mass movement. The philosophy of Mohandas K. Gandhi (1869–1948) proved a powerful means for change, though its methods and effects differed greatly from Marxism.

Gandhi was the son of the prime minister—we might say secretary—to the Hindu ruler of one of the tiny native states the British permitted to survive within their Indian empire. Earlier the family had been grocers. In fact, the surname Gandhi was a term for the subcaste of grocers in the larger Banya subcaste of shopkeepers that belonged in turn to the *Vaisya* caste of traders and farmers. This was one of four hereditary castes into which tradition divided all Hindus, except the casteless untouchables, at birth. The other castes were those of priests and scholars (*Brahman*), warriors and nobles (*Kshatriya*), and manual laborers (*Sudra*).

Tradition weighed heavily on Hindu society. Only members of the top three castes were entitled to an education, for example, and the mere shadow of an untouchable was spiritually polluting to a caste Hindu. Gandhi's early life reflected the force of tradition in countless details, such as the extended family household into which he was born and his arranged marriage. His parents found a bride for him when he was about twelve.

To assure his future, however, Gandhi's family decided he must complete his education in England. He had to leave his wife and newborn son behind. His mother—an orthodox, vegetarian Hindu—made him take a vow not to touch meat, liquor, or women while he was away. Because he had crossed the "black waters," the elders of the Banya subcaste pronounced Gandhi an outcaste.

Gandhi arrived in England in 1888, aged nineteen. He had been an indifferent student so far. Over the next three years, he completed his legal studies, which were not exacting, and qualified as a barrister. More importantly, he discovered a new world of ideas. At first, Gandhi identified with his new environment in superficial ways, paying much attention to dress and taking dancing lessons. Then realizing that he could not fit in, he began to seek out people with whom his own way of life gave him something in common: first vegetarians, then enthusiasts of various religions and cults. These contacts led Gandhi to wide reading in religious texts, ranging from Christ's Sermon on the Mount to the great Hindu scripture, the Bhagavad Gita, or "Celestial Song," which he read first in English translation. In both, God summoned human beings to a life of selfless dedication to the welfare of others. This, not the law, became Gandhi's lasting lesson from his years in England.

Returning to India at twenty-one, Gandhi had trouble readjusting to life with his uneducated wife, Kasturbai, and lacked the self-confidence needed to succeed in legal practice. Within two years, he was so frustrated that he leapt at a chance to go to South Africa to represent an Indian merchant in a legal case there. Though he had gone through religious rites to be received back into his caste, Gandhi again set out across the "black waters." He was to remain in South Africa most of the time from 1893 to 1914. There he developed the methods he later applied in India.

Gandhi had not been in South Africa long before he discovered the racial discrimination to which Indians and all other non-Europeans were subject. One of his earliest experiences there was being forced off a train, although he had the proper ticket, because a European objected to his presence in a first-class compartment. Gandhi soon began meeting with other members of the Indian community and studying the discriminatory legislation. Although he had originally planned to stay only a year, he decided to remain in South Africa to work in behalf of his fellow Indians.

Over the next twenty years, Gandhi worked out a distinctive way of life and political action. He read widely, studying the scriptures of Hinduism and Islam, India's two most widespread religions; the works of Henry David Thoreau, the U.S. apostle of civil disobedience; and the later pacifist writings of the Russian novelist Leo Tolstoy. In his personal life, Gandhi became noted for his ascetic emphasis on diet, fasting, and nature cures. From 1906 on, he formulated his principles as *brahmacharya*, the ancient Hindu vow of celibacy (within marriage in Gandhi's case); *ahimsa*, or nonviolence; and *satyagraha*, the force of truth and love. Gandhi himself developed the last concept, which he equated with passive resistance. His ability to express partly new concepts in terms drawn from Hindu tradition enhanced Gandhi's appeal greatly, as did his selflessness in living according to those principles. Gandhi would clean latrines as a spiritual discipline, for example, and he led ambulance units in hazardous service during the Boer War.

Gandhi was no solitary ascetic. He organized his family and closest followers into communal settlements that became models for the *ashrams* (a Hindu term for a religious retreat) he later created in India. In these settlements, he propagated a life of egalitarian self-reliance. He also became a mass mobilizer, championing the interests of women and untouchables. In fact his emphasis on latrine cleaning and self-reliance was part of his attempt to persuade Indians to forget their differences of religion and caste, which condemned untouchables to do jobs that Hindu tradition classed as unclean. Finally, Gandhi became a political organizer and leader. He staged the first of his great passive resistance campaigns against laws that required Asians to carry special registration certificates, and that made only Christian marriages valid in South Africa. By the time Gandhi left South Africa, he and his followers had won at least some concessions from the government.

Returning to India in 1915, Gandhi soon took up the cause of Indian independence, as we shall discuss in more detail in Chapter 10. In the communal settlements he founded in India, Gandhi elaborated his ideas of self-reliance into a Constructive Program. His goal was to revitalize village India by getting villagers to breed cattle, learn elementary sanitation and hygiene, take up useful crafts like beekeeping or pottery, spin and weave their own cloth, form cooperatives and village assemblies, overturn hereditary bars to learning, learn Hindi so that India could have one national language, and eliminate religious hatred and discrimination against untouchables, whom Gandhi began to call *harijans*, or children of God. He also advocated equality for women, prompting the Indian National Congress party to adopt a bill of rights (1931) that called for equality without regard to religion, caste, or sex. Politically he worked through the Congress party and organized a number of passive resistance campaigns. Above all, Gandhi identified with the poor by traveling among them and living in the style of a Hindu holy man. India's poor responded with enthusiasm. Gandhi could command the attention of a crowd with a gesture. His fasts, which he used not just to discipline himself but also to pressure others, could halt widespread intercommunal violence. Indians hailed him as a *mahatma* ("great soul"), or even as a manifestation of divinity.

Compared to other revolutionaries and nationalist leaders, Gandhi had an unusual combination of strengths and limitations. The most important limitation is that he was ultimately not a revolutionary. True, Gandhi, like others, used nonviolence as a powerful instrument for change, but his goals for social change were limited. Although he wanted independence from the British, his aspirations for Hindu society did not go beyond ending discrimination against untouchables and women. Gandhi never took a consistent stand against the caste system, the heart of the Indian problem of inequality. Although he favored unity among members of India's religions, he never seemed to realize how much the overtly Hindu character of his ideas and style irritated some non-Hindus. Finally, his Constructive Program, though it anticipated later rural development concepts, represented a move more toward the past than the future. Gandhi rightly perceived that Indians could hurt Britain by refusing to use British textiles, and by spinning and weaving their cottons by hand instead. He was correct, too, in seeing the dehumanizing effects of industrial labor. But Gandhi was almost unique in the non-Western world of his day in not calling for economic independence *through* industrialization—the path India ultimately pursued.

Gandhi's great strength was his ability to bridge the gap between Hindu tradition and Western ideas, and to combine new elements with old in a form of political action that was probably the only realistic alternative for an India faced with overwhelming British power. Thirty years after his death, many of his disciples thought that the rulers of independent India had more in common with the British than with Gandhi. But his ideas have not been forgotten. They have influenced people all over the world, many of whom compare Gandhi to the greatest figures of all time.

Marxism as a Challenge to Imperialism: Mao Zedong

To find another twentieth-century revolutionary or nationalist leader comparable to Lenin or Gandhi in impact on his nation and the world, we must look to China and Mao Zedong (Mao Tse-tung, 1893–1976).* For most of Mao's life, however, his later importance was far from obvious. In 1911, a revolution toppled the entire combination of traditional institutions and Confucian ideology that had dominated China for two millennia. The underlying causes of the revolution were European imperialism, which had undermined the traditional Chinese imperial system without establishing direct foreign rule (except in some enclaves), and the nationalism that developed among Chinese as a result. But the revolution of 1911 merely started China down the road to mass mobilization and popular sovereignty. The change was not complete before 1949.

Meanwhile, the greatest question facing China's leaders was how to organize a new regime that could re-establish China's independence and survive the stresses of mass politics in a rapidly changing world. For years, the Chinese Communists were not the most successful contenders in the struggle (see Chapter 10). Their eventual triumph was in great measure the work of Mao Zedong. An examination of his early career will show how Marxism came to the non-Western world, and changed in the process.

Unlike many Chinese political leaders, even Communists like Zhou Enlai (Chou En-lai, 1898–1976), long-time premier of the People's Republic, Mao came from a peasant family. Mao's father, an authoritarian with whom he often clashed, eventually became a "rich" peasant, owning a bit over three acres, on which the family produced five or six tons of rice a year. In addition he traded in grain.

The family's relative affluence enabled Mao to go to school. His education began in the conventional way, with memorization of Confucian classics in the local primary school. But China's changing politics also was changing education; new types of schools were coming into existence. By his mid-twenties, Mao had been in and out of a number of schools and had studied for a time on his own. Along the way, he acquired enough Confucian culture to be able to write essays and poems in the traditional style. He also absorbed China's traditional popular literature; from some of its Robin Hood–like heroes, he learned military strategies that he later applied. He began to write for newspapers, and he read some of the most influential works of Western literature in translation. At a time when many Chinese took an unprecedented interest in the army as a way to throw off imperialism, he was briefly a soldier.

When other future leaders, including Zhou Enlai, went to France on a work-study program during World War I, Mao stayed behind, perhaps because he was not good at languages. Mao remained close to China's common people, read foreign books only in translation, never left the country in his early years, and could deal with foreign ideas only by ex-

---

* Following current usage, this book will use the Pinyin, rather than the Wade-Giles, system for the rendering of Chinese names and terms. At the first appearance of each name or term, the Wade-Giles version will, however, be shown in parentheses following the Pinyin. The only exceptions will be where the two forms are identical, or in the cases of individuals who are well known under the Wade-Giles forms of their names and whose identity would be obscured by the Pinyin form. Two such individuals mentioned in this book are Sun Yat-sen and Chiang Kai-shek; the Pinyin forms of their names are Sun Yixuan and Jiang Jieshi.

pressing them in Chinese. These factors may explain why it was he who naturalized Marxism into the Chinese setting.

Ultimately, of course, Marxism was the intellectual influence that affected Mao most. In 1918, when the Bolshevik Revolution was beginning to attract attention in China, Mao spent a half-year in Beijing (Peking) as assistant to the university librarian, Li Dazhao (Li Tachao), who organized a Marxist study group. Chinese like Li and Mao did not then really understand Marxist theory and had not committed themselves fully to it. What appealed to them, following the shootout of 1914–1918 among the Western—and also imperialist—nations, was the idea that the Bolshevik model offered an alternate way to reorganize China and improve its place in the world.

On May 4, 1919, a massive student demonstration broke out in Beijing to protest Japanese encroachment on China and the decision of the Paris Peace Conference to support Japanese territorial claims. The demonstration created a lasting excitement, the May Fourth Movement, that favored the spread of new ideas, including Marxism. In his native Hunan Province, Mao took an active role in political organization and helped found the Chinese Communist party (CCP) in 1921.

Mao and his colleagues, still not proficient in Marxist theory, were uncertain how to launch revolution in China. The country hardly had the urban working class that Marx assumed. Mao's work in the countryside convinced him of the revolutionary potential of the peasantry. But party leaders of the 1920s thought that the peasants wanted only land and would lose interest in revolution once they got it.

The CCP sought help from the Soviet Union through the Communist International, or Comintern, founded in 1919 to serve as a "general headquarters" for world revolution. But neither the Comintern advisers in China nor the Soviet leadership understood Chinese conditions. Under Stalin, whose real goal was socialism in one country, the Comintern became a mere tool of Soviet foreign policy. Soviet advice to the CCP generally ranged from bad to disastrous. Because standard Marxist theory held that the overthrow of feudalism (the imperial system in China) should lead to a period of bourgeois capitalism (like the liberal capitalist societies of Western Europe) before the proletarian revolution, the Soviets called on the CCP to ally with the larger Nationalist Party, the Guomindang (GMD, Kuomintang). The GMD was based in the port cities and among the landlord class. Its leader, Sun Yatsen (1866–1925), agreed that Communists could join the GMD and work within it as individuals. Mao was one of those who did so. But as the GMD began to consolidate its control throughout China, Sun's successor, Chiang Kai-shek, turned violently against the CCP in 1927, killing a great many of its supporters. Nevertheless, Stalin continued for months to advocate GMD-CCP cooperation, and the influence of Moscow-trained leaders in the CCP remained a problem into the early 1930s.

Among those who survived the GMD terror, Mao again went south to Hunan Province. After an unsuccessful uprising, he joined other Communists in the mountains on the border of neighboring Jiangxi (Kiangsi) Province, becoming chairman of their Jiangxi Soviet. Isolated from the CCP Central Committee and Comintern representatives in Shanghai, Mao developed his own ideas of organization and tactics, emphasizing

Mao Zedong with peasants of Shensi Province during the war against Japan. According to the official caption supplied for this picture, "Chairman Mao cherishes the masses most ardently."
Eastfoto

rural base areas, agrarian revolution, and development of the Red Army.

In 1930, Chiang Kai-shek began a series of campaigns against the Jiangxi Soviet that eventually forced the Communists to strike out on the Long March. During this six-thousand-mile trek, which led from Jiangxi to a new base in the northwest, Mao emerged as the leader of the CCP. Of the hundred thousand people who began the Long March, only a fraction lived to complete it. At Yan'an (Yenan), the CCP base during 1935–1947, Mao finally came to grips with Marxist theory and began evaluating the Chinese experience in its light.

With this effort began the modification of Marxism-Leninism that later became known as Mao Zedong thought.[3] The main themes of Mao's thought underscore its potential for conflict with Soviet Marxism-Leninism. One theme was Mao's emphasis on will. He had become a Marxist out of excitement over the 1917 revolution, without knowing Marx's ideas about the stages of history. For Mao, revolution emerged from will and activism, not from predetermined levels of economic development. From this idea followed the emphasis on thought reform as a way of bringing people into conformity with the party line. From this also followed a concept of class struggle that made class identification more a matter of how one thought than of how one earned a living. If Mao's ideas made a muddle of Marx's stages of revolution, so be it: China would have ongoing, permanent revolution. For a society where cultural conservatism had lately reigned supreme, change would become permanent.

A second Maoist theme was nationalism—anathema to Marx, but a powerful force in the political awareness of most Chinese. Mao's nationalism expressed itself in his closeness to China's traditional culture and his hostility to the Comintern and the Soviet Union. Some reasons for the Sino-Soviet split in the late 1950s went back more than thirty years. Mao's nationalism also appeared in his tendency to see the real enemy of the revolution as foreign imperialism, to identify class struggle with national struggle, and so to allow willing Chinese of any class background to join the revolution.

Perhaps the most important Maoist theme stemmed from his origins: populism, or emphasis on the common people. Mao's radicalism showed itself most clearly in his romantic faith in the revolutionary potential of the peasantry. Since this faith conflicted with strict Marxist theory, Mao became distrustful of theorists and experts in general. Differing not only from Marx, but also from Lenin, who thought that the vanguard party could impose revolutionary consciousness on the workers, Mao came to believe in a "mass line," a revolutionary consciousness among the peasant masses, which the party must understand before it could guide them. From this view followed a commitment to mass mobilization that enabled the CCP, unlike the GMD, to succeed in dealing with peasants, who might not have responded favorably to communism otherwise.

Like most Chinese of his time, Mao also thought an effective military was necessary for overcoming imperialism. He believed his cause required a military force that could survive among the people—as it did during the Long March—without alienating them. That meant treating peasants like human beings, paying for supplies, and a host of other things not done in the past.

Mao's ideas enabled the CCP to survive through World War II, during which it again cooperated with the GMD against the Japanese. His ideas enabled the CCP to win support, while the GMD's crumbled, setting the stage for the civil war (1946–1949) that gave the Communists control of the country at last. In Chapter 16, we shall see how Mao's thought left its mark on the history of the People's Republic of China.

Conclusion: Revolutions Compared

Revolutions vary widely in scope. Some affect only the domestic political order. Some reach beyond politics to restructure underlying social and economic relationships. Others transform the society's culture as well. Internationally, revolutions may, or may not, transform a society's place in the global configuration.

The examples in this chapter suggest that for a country with a domestic history of exploitative social and economic relationships, the only real revolution is a social revolution that not only changes political institutions, but also redistributes wealth and power. The Bolshevik leaders did this in Russia, and so did the Maoists when they gained control of China. The Mexican revolutionaries failed to effect such redistribution; so did the Chinese Nationalists (GMD). As these and similar failures show, revolutions need to have an ideology that provides a program for action, as Marxism-Leninism did in Russia and as Mao's adaptation of those ideas did in China. The contrast between successful and unsuccessful revolutions also underscores the importance of effective leadership and a well-organized movement or party.

In addition, for a country that has been in a subordinate position in the global pattern of power relationships, the revolution does not reach completion until it improves these external relationships. Mexico failed in this respect. The Bolsheviks succeeded by breaking links of debt and investment that made the tsarist regime, though supposedly a great power, dependent on Western Europe. Both the GMD and the CCP contributed to ridding China of imperialist encroachment.

The Soviet experience with revolution has been so influential in the twentieth century that it is difficult to discuss the requirements of successful revolution in terms that do not seem to refer to this example. Gandhi's significance lies in his showing the possibility of other ways. Although his movement did not produce revolutionary change, it included the aspiration to socioeconomic and cultural change, the ideology to chart a course for change, the charismatic leader, organized movement, and mass mobilization. Clearly, too, Gandhi aimed to transform India's place in global power relationships. The main limiting factors were that Gandhi sought to reform Indian society but not systematically to eliminate the bases of inequality in the caste system, and that Gandhi's method perhaps also assumed a certain type of adversary, one accessible to moral arguments. The method worked against the British, and in some other settings, especially in the U.S. civil rights movement. Could it have worked against a more ruthless adversary, like some of the other leaders discussed in these pages?

Notes

1. Theodore H. Von Laue, *Why Lenin? Why Stalin? A Reappraisal of the Russian Revolution, 1900–1930* (Philadelphia: J. B. Lippincott, 1964), p. 212.
2. Ramón E. Ruiz, *The Great Rebellion: Mexico 1905–1924* (New York: W. W. Norton, 1980), p. 203.
3. This summary of Mao's ideas follows Maurice Meisner, "Yenan Communism and the Rise of the Chinese People's Republic," in James B. Crowley, ed., *Modern East Asia: Essays in Interpretation* (New York: Harcourt, Brace, and World, 1970), pp. 283–296.

Suggestions for Further Reading

Carr, E. H., *The Meaning of the Russian Revolution* (1979).

Crowley, James B., ed., *Modern East Asia: Essays in Interpretation* (1970).

Mehta, Ved, *Mahatma Gandhi and His Apostles* (1976).

Moon, Penderel, *Gandhi and Modern India* (1969).

Ruiz, Ramón E., *The Great Rebellion: Mexico 1905–1924* (1980).

Schram, Stuart, *Mao Tse-Tung* (1966).

Snow, Edgar, *Red Star over China*, rev. ed. (1968).

Stavrianos, L. S., *Global Rift: The Third World Comes of Age* (1981).

Treadgold, Donald W., *Twentieth Century Russia*, 5th ed. (1981).

Von Laue, Theodore H., *Why Lenin? Why Stalin? A Reappraisal of the Russian Revolution, 1900–1930* (1964).

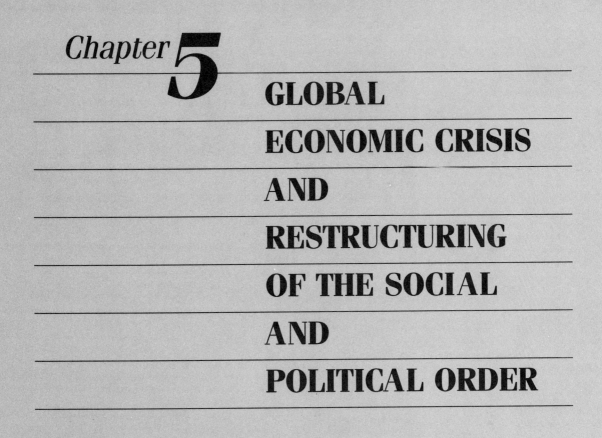

Chapter 5

GLOBAL ECONOMIC CRISIS AND RESTRUCTURING OF THE SOCIAL AND POLITICAL ORDER

The triumph of communism in Russia challenged the European-dominated global pattern of 1914 in three ways. It offered an alternative to the liberal capitalist model for the organization of an economy, society, and government. It severed the links that had subordinated Russia economically to Western Europe. And it encouraged revolutionaries everywhere who dreamed of restructuring their own societies and freeing them from foreign domination.

This challenge to the pre-1914 order produced panic that the communist "disease" might spread. Politicians blamed communists for the 1919 wave of strikes in which workers protested their loss of purchasing power under wartime wage controls. In the United States, the postwar "red scare" led to the so-called Palmer raids, in which Wilson's attorney general rounded up and deported foreigners without regard to their rights. In France, the right-wing parties won a landslide victory in the elections of 1919 partly by playing on voters' fear of "the man with a knife between his teeth"—a hairy and terrifying Communist depicted on conservative election posters.

By the mid-1920s, however, it seemed clear that the Russian Revolution was not going to spread. Conservative forces overturned the communist regime established in Hungary after the Hapsburg collapse. The new German republic crushed communist attempts to seize power in 1919 and 1923. Arguing that communist subversion was still a threat probably helped British Conservatives defeat the first Labour cabinet in 1924. But by then Europeans and Americans were beginning to see communism as a Russian abnormality.

People could more easily believe that the Russian Revolution had not changed the course of world history because some semblance of the prewar world seemed re-established by the late 1920s. In the great democracies, politicians whose very ordinariness reassured people that nothing had changed replaced dynamic wartime leaders like Wilson and Clemenceau. Humorist Will Rogers said of Calvin Coolidge, who became the U.S. president after Warren Harding's death in 1923, that "Silent Cal" did exactly what Americans wanted: nothing. His administration was reminiscent of the nineteenth century, when U.S. presidents had been relatively inconspicuous. In Britain and France, too, conservative prime ministers—Stanley Baldwin and Raymond Poincaré—held power for much of the 1920s. They also were committed to the pre-1914 view that the government's role in a free society should be minimal.

Prelude to Depression

After the mid-1920s, some nations' economies seemed to have regained or ex-ceeded their prewar levels. By 1929, for example, U.S. industrial production was 75 percent greater than in 1913. British factories in 1929 were producing only 10 percent more than they had before the war. The war had seriously weakened the British economy, around which the world economy had pivoted throughout the nineteenth century. Nevertheless, Britain took the controversial step of returning to the gold standard in 1925. That is, the British government again offered to sell gold for an established price in pounds. As a result, the pound became overvalued, making British exports too expensive for many countries to buy. But deeply felt psychological need, rather than economic calculation, motivated the return to the gold standard. By the mid-1920s, people wanted to see World War I as a short and accidental interruption of "normalcy"—in President Harding's phrase—rather than as the beginning of a grim new era of change. So Britain declared that the pound would once again be "as good as gold."

Because people wanted so much to believe that World War I had not fundamentally changed the world, they ignored the ominous structural faults that were the war's legacy to the global economy. Wartime demand had everywhere expanded both agricultural and industrial capacity beyond peacetime needs. By the late 1920s prices were beginning to fall and unsold goods to pile up. The prewar pattern of international finance was replaced by an absurd system of overextended international credits that reflected political pressures rather than economic good sense. A prime example was American loans to Europeans to enable them to pay the debts Americans insisted they owed—all very well as long as the lenders continued to lend, but calamitous when they stopped.

Thus the prosperity of the late 1920s rested on fragile foundations. Because the economies of the developed world were so interdependent, a catastrophe in any one of them would quickly spread to the rest.

When prices on the New York Stock Exchange collapsed in October 1929—the biggest loss stocks have ever experienced—the eventual result was a world-wide Great Depression far worse than any earlier downturn.

In economic terms, a *depression* is a time when the curves on all the graphs—prices, wages, employment, investment, international trade—head persistently downward. After 1929 all these variables dropped to, and stayed at, unprecedentedly low levels.

The Great Depression wrecked more than the global economy. By 1932, with one American in four and two Germans in five unable to find jobs, much of the world was living in psychological depression. Economists, business leaders, and politicians admitted they could not find a cure. No experience from the pre-1914 world was relevant to an economic disaster this big and this long-lasting.

Gravely eroded by World War I, the foundations of the European-dominated global pattern were further undermined by the Depression. The dependent peoples of the world had already seen their European masters locked in a death-struggle that left none unscathed. After 1929, Asians, Africans, and Latin Americans saw that the technological dynamism of Western civilization had not averted an economic calamity that engulfed them, too. The Depression of the 1930s cruelly drove home to the dependent peoples the extent of their economic subordination, and further discredited the Western claim to rule the globe by right of cultural superiority. Though most colonial peoples would win political independence only after the second "European civil war" (World War II), 1929 like 1914 was a fateful date on the way to the post-1945 "end of empire."

In the developed Western nations, despair and rage led people to reject many of the economic and political ideas taken for granted until the crash, and stimulated frantic demands for new ideas that could put people to work again. Now interest in the communist alternative really began to develop. When European and American coal mines were closed for lack of sales while unemployed people froze to death for lack of coal, the Soviet idea of a government-planned and -managed economy suddenly seemed to make more sense.

In Western Europe, political parties had emerged since 1917 that accepted the need for socialism but argued that it was not necessary to destroy parliamentary democracy in order to institute government ownership and management of the economy. In Britain and France, the Great Depression would provide a first test of this idea of democratic socialism.

Still powerful today in Europe and much of the rest of the world, democratic socialism was never a strong movement in the United States. Its most successful presidential candidate, Eugene Debs, won no more than 6 percent of the vote in 1912. Yet many critics of President Franklin D. Roosevelt, elected in 1932, attacked his New Deal programs as "socialistic." Though incorrect, the label reflected the deep controversy the New Deal provoked among Americans. All agreed that it profoundly changed the bases of American life—but was it for better or for worse?

What role the federal government should play in controlling the U.S. economy is still a matter of hot controversy. Americans tend to debate that issue without placing it in historical context or drawing comparisons with the experiences of other nations. But, as we shall see, in the light of world history the New Deal is best understood as the U.S. answer to a worldwide problem revealed after the Wall Street crash.

From Wall Street Crash to World Depression

In the summer of 1929, American ingenuity seemed to have produced an economy invulnerable to the ups and downs of economic history. The new president, Herbert Hoover, an engineer and self-made millionaire, proclaimed, "We in America today are nearer to the final triumph over poverty than ever before in the history of any land . . . we shall soon with the help of God be in sight of the day when poverty will be banished from this nation."[1] Such confidence seemed justified when all but 3 percent of the work force had jobs, and manufacturing output had risen by 50 percent in a decade.

At the New York Stock Exchange on Wall Street, the mood was euphoric—and why not? Stock prices were climbing with unprecedented speed, as much in June and July alone as in all of 1928. After Labor Day, the rise slowed, but few of the million or so Americans speculating in stocks were disturbed. They trusted authorities like the president of the National City Bank, who declared, "Nothing can arrest the upward movement of the United States."

In October, however, the bottom fell out. October 29 was the worst day in the history of the exchange, and probably of any stock market anywhere. As panic-stricken investors tried to sell, an unheard-of 16.5 million shares were dumped. Some found no buyer at any price. Within two months American stocks lost half their value. Paper millionaires in August were bankrupt by Christmas.

The impact of this disaster was not limited to investors, or even to Americans. As business leaders' confidence sagged, they reduced production, throwing employees out of work. As the unemployed stopped buying anything but necessities, reduced demand put more people out of work. As the unemployed failed to pay what they owed to banks, the bankers called in the loans they could collect. Because U.S. banks had made huge loans to Europe, panic spread there. After one of Vienna's leading banks, the Credit-Anstalt, failed in the spring of 1931, the cycle of fear and economic paralysis spread quickly into neighboring Germany and from there to the rest of the Continent.

By 1932, the Depression was everywhere. In the United States, its symptoms were padlocked factories, vacant stores, deserted transportation terminals, and empty freight yards. City streets were relatively empty, for many people now had no place to go. On the sidewalks were unemployed people attempting to sell apples for a nickel or simply seeking a handout. The fortunate were those who were still working, though at reduced wages, and those who still had their homes, though they might have lost their savings. Others, homeless, huddled in improvised shantytowns bitterly called Hoovervilles, or rode the rails in empty freight cars, crisscrossing the country in a hopeless search for work.

Such were the human realities behind

the grim statistics. In the United States, gross national product had fallen by nearly a half, and the number of suicides had increased by a third. Things were as bad in Düsseldorf as in Detroit. Worldwide industrial production in 1932 stood at only two-thirds of its 1929 level. World trade had fallen by more than half.

Nothing better illustrated the twentieth-century global pattern than the Depression's impact on parts of the world whose peoples knew nothing of stock markets and little of industrial development. Because natural rubber prices fell 75 percent from 1929 to 1932, for example, fewer jobs were available on the rubber plantations of Ceylon (now Sri Lanka). Because Western manufacturers were ordering less rubber for automobiles and appliances, half the Indian laborers who had worked on the Ceylonese rubber plantations had to return jobless to their homeland.

The Depression stretched to the ends

A West Virginia company town. Coalminers were part of the "third of a nation" President Roosevelt described as "ill-housed." *Library of Congress*

Depression charity. Even well-dressed New Yorkers endured the humiliation of lining up for a free meal. *Franklin D. Roosevelt Library*

of the earth. What was worse, it seemed to go on forever. The world's earlier economic crises had been short and sharp, followed quickly by recovery. But despite politicians' assurances that prosperity was "just around the corner," the current economic decline seemed beyond remedy. How had this disaster of unprecedented size and duration occurred?

Origins of the Crisis

Economics is not an exact science. Moreover, the history of an economic crisis cannot be discussed without evaluating opposing economic policies. For these reasons, explanation of the Depression is controversial. Although historians generally agree on why the stock market crashed, they differ as to what the crash implies about the structure of the U.S. economy. Still more controversy surrounds the relation of the crash to the worldwide slump. In attempting to explain the crisis, we shall move from the surest ground to the most contested: from Wall Street to the U.S. economy and finally to the world scene.

Stock Market Collapse

The Wall Street crash that triggered the Depression was the collapse of a house of cards. It ended a decade of speculation that involved dangerous though hidden risks for the speculators, the bankers who lent them money, and the brokers who sold them shares. During the 1920s all three groups began to assume that financial paper like shares of stock had a value of its own that could only increase. Buyers bought stock "on margin,"

paying only 10 percent of the price and borrowing the rest from the broker; they expected the stock's value to increase fast enough to allow them to pay off the loan. Often the initial 10 percent was lent by bankers who accepted the stock itself as collateral, while investing their depositors' money in similar shares. Shady financiers created glittering opportunities for these eager investors by launching holding companies whose only assets were paper ones: shares of other companies. They also bribed financial advisers and newspaper columnists to circulate tips that would stimulate a rush to buy shares in these paper creations.

The stock market's climb owed as much to psychology as to economics. For example, people borrowed money at high interest to purchase the stock of Radio Corporation of America (RCA) not because they expected to collect dividends—RCA had never paid any—but because they were sure its price would continue to soar. And while the optimism lasted, its price quintupled in a single year.

Once the mood changed, and people became convinced that the market could only go down rather than up, the plunge was as steep as the climb had been. As prices fell, brokers demanded a larger margin. When speculators could not pay, their shares were dumped onto the market, depressing prices still further. Meanwhile the holding companies simply melted away as their paper assets became worthless.

In one sense, the 1929 crash was simply the inevitable end of a financial boom generated within the small world of Wall Street. But it had a devastating impact on the entire U.S. economy. It wiped out much investment capital and made investors cautious about risking what they still had. The resulting damage to individual purchasing power, to international lending, and to trade would not be repaired in the next ten years.

Mass Production and Underconsumption: Basic U.S. Economic Flaws

Many economic historians believe the Wall Street crash was only a symptom of basic flaws in the U.S. economy that would inevitably have produced a depression at some point. These flaws were not apparent at the time. Throughout the 1920s, U.S. industry continued the rapid growth stimulated by the war. By 1929, there were 26.5 million automobiles on American roads, compared to 1.3 million in 1914. Once a curiosity, radio became an industry of mass entertainment. Americans in the the Far West and the Deep South listened to identical network programs. In 1929, expenditures on radios were forty times the level of 1920, when they were first mass-produced. The apparent affluence represented by American ownership of automobiles, radios, and other gadgets did not surprise visiting Europeans. They knew that World War I had transformed the United States from a debtor nation to the principal creditor of the rest of the world. With industry booming and the rest of the world owing them money, Americans thought nothing could be wrong with their economy.

But the distribution of wealth in U.S. society may have been too unequal in the 1920s to create demand for all the goods that industry was pouring forth. Some domestic markets were becoming glutted with unsold goods as early as 1926.

The productivity of American factory workers rose by almost 50 percent in the 1920s, as mergers created firms large enough to afford more efficient machinery. But firms' cost savings were channelled primarily into corporate profits, which tripled during the decade. Prices were not substantially reduced, and even in unionized plants, wages rose less than profits.

Thus the purchasing power of the U.S. labor force was not greatly increased. Nor was the boom creating jobs. The number of Americans employed remained fairly constant through the 1920s. In some industries mechanization actually reduced the number of jobs steeply while increasing output. The problem of *technological unemployment*—of human workers displaced by machines—dates back to the beginning of mass production.

In human terms, these trends meant that the average American might be able to maintain a car in the 1920s, but not to trade it in for a new one. Industrial expansion proceeded on the assumption that consumers could afford to keep buying indefinitely, though the 20 percent of Americans who worked in agriculture did not realize even the modest gains of industrial workers.

World War I had been a bonanza for American farmers, who vastly expanded their acreage to provide the food once grown on European battlefields. When European production revived after the war, the world's markets were soon glutted with agricultural produce. Long before the Wall Street crash, world farm prices had collapsed to about half their level of 1919. When the Depression began, the wages of American farm and factory workers were further apart than they had been in 1910.

While some of the poor were getting

poorer, the rich were getting richer. The proportion of total U.S. income earned by the wealthiest 5 percent of the population had grown since 1910 from a fourth to a third. In 1929, almost a fifth of American income was collected by the top 1 percent. Wealthy people's purchases of yachts and jewelry could not sustain a boom.

The United States had developed an economy of mass production without a corresponding society of mass consumption. The concentration of wealth had been less important during the nineteenth century, when Americans had been building and equipping a nation of continental dimensions. Now, however, the railroads the tycoons had built were all finished. Stringent postwar laws restricted immigration, which had increased the American population by as much as a million people a year before World War I. With nation building complete and population growth greatly reduced, the possibilities for constructive investment were less obvious. There was no guarantee that the wealth increasingly concentrated in fewer hands would be invested in ways that benefited the economy as a whole. The stock market boom, like an earlier craze for buying Florida land, showed that too much money was at the discretion of people who could afford to spend it foolishly. The purchasing power of most consumers was far more limited. The shrewdest investors recognized these warning signs. In 1928, when they noticed that company profits were not increasing nearly as rapidly as stock prices, they began the trickle of selling that became an avalanche in October 1929.

Maldistribution of income also helps explain why the Depression persisted so long. Although the economy would remain stagnant without investment, the wealthy few who could afford to invest were afraid to do so. The vast majority of Americans confined their expenses to necessities. Thus a vicious circle developed. With no hope of sales, there was no inclination to invest. With no investment, there were no jobs, no income, and consequently no sales.

The Spread of the Depression

If the Depression resulted from weaknesses in the U.S. economy and society, how did it spread to the rest of the world? Historians disagree on this question. But it is clear that the U.S. crash and U.S. government policies in reaction to it were the final blows to a world economic order already mortally weakened by World War I.

The European-dominated global pattern of 1914 was centered on Great Britain. Because the British were committed to free trade, many goods could enter their country tariff-free, even when British industry and agriculture were suffering from an economic downturn. British wealth had been so great that the bankers of the City of London continued to make long-term loans to the rest of the world regardless of the fluctuations of the British economy. When investment opportunities at home were limited by an industrial slump, British investment abroad actually increased. Whenever a banking crisis threatened anywhere in the world, bankers turned to the London banks for prompt help.

After the Wall Street crash it became clear that Britain could no longer play the central role in the global pattern, and that the United States, Britain's logical successor, would not do so.

Britain had been the first nation to industrialize. In 1914 its industrial plant was already outmoded in comparison with those of its later-starting competitors. During World War I, Britain sold many of its overseas assets to buy arms, but nevertheless amassed huge debts to the United States. The war enabled nations like Japan to invade British markets. Whereas over three-fifths of India's imports in 1914 came from Britain, by 1929 fewer than half did.

Britain's weakness became obvious when the Depression struck. After nearly a century of free trade, it adopted protective tariffs in 1932. A year earlier, the drain on British gold reserves had forced it to stop paying gold for pounds. Once again off the gold standard, and with a depreciating currency, Britain was in too much trouble itself to help reinflate the world economy with new investment. A large British loan might have saved Vienna's Credit-Anstalt after the recall of American loans and might have forestalled the economic collapse of Central Europe. But the Bank of England would offer only a comparatively small loan, to be repaid in weekly installments: hardly the terms of a long-term offer of salvation.

Britain could no longer be the world's financier, and the United States declined to take on any such responsibility. Throughout the 1920s the U.S. government rejected European arguments that war debts and reparations destabilized international payment balances and should be cancelled. "They hired the money, didn't they?" retorted President Coolidge. Not until 1932 were these economic reminders of wartime hatreds abandoned. The German economy increasingly relied on short-term American loans to make its reparations payments—which in turn were needed by Britain and France to pay their American debts. Germany was already in trouble before October 1929, as U.S. bankers reclaimed their money to invest it on Wall Street. After the crash, demands for immediate repayment completed the damage.

In 1930, Congress passed the Hawley-Smoot Tariff Act, imposing the highest import duties in history. Ignoring protests from thirty countries, President Hoover signed it into law. Now foreign countries could no longer sell their goods in the American marketplace to earn dollars to buy American products. Nor could they borrow dollars, for after the crash American banks became much more cautious lenders. Meanwhile, U.S. producers found they sold less abroad, for many countries retaliated by shutting their doors to U.S. products.

Because the United States produced nearly half the world's goods, it was the obvious candidate to assume Britain's former role of financial leadership. But instead of providing a market and loans in a crisis, the U.S. government signaled that in a world Depression, it was every nation for itself. In such an atmosphere, what were the weak to do?

The Depression in the Developing World

The peoples of the developing world, whether living in colonies or in technically independent countries like those of Latin America, were even less able to combat the Depression than Europeans and North Americans. The more a developing country's economy had been integrated into the European-dominated global pattern, the more it suffered after 1929.

Those who fared best were the few nations whose principal economic activity was still subsistence agriculture—growing food to feed themselves. By 1929, however, many countries of Latin America, Africa, and Asia were economically dependent on their sales of agricultural or mineral products to Europeans or Americans. In many cases a single crop or mineral constituted most of a country or colony's exports.

The world agricultural glut had cut into export earnings well before 1929. To many crop-exporting countries the Depression was the final blow. The price of rice, the principal export of Siam (today Thailand) fell by one-half within a year. As the factories of Europe and the United States shut down, the bottom fell out of the market for industrial raw materials like copper and tin. The value of Chile's exports fell by 80 percent, and that of other Latin American exports by at least half. Despite international efforts to restore prices by agreeing to limit production, the countries that had earned their living by selling goods like tea, rubber, and copper remained in deep trouble throughout the 1930s. Unable to sell, they could not buy what their trading

Indian boycott of British products, 1931. Preparing to burn an effigy of the British cotton cloth industry, these followers of Gandhi were protesting colonial dependency.
Popperfoto

partners might offer, nor were they credible risks for loans. Their wealth of natural resources was now worthless. In two years, for example, Brazil burned or shoveled into the ocean enough coffee to fill the cups of the whole world for a year. Although Brazil had been ostensibly independent since the 1820s, the Depression showed that its economic well-being was at the mercy of prices set in markets it did not control.

The experience of India, still a British colony, suggests that colonies beginning to develop economies less dependent upon a few commodities might actually benefit from the Depression's impact on their masters. After World War I, British industry never regained its prewar dominance of Indian markets. When Britain in response to postwar unrest granted its colony power to manage its own economic affairs, India promptly erected tariff barriers to protect its infant industry from foreign competition. In the twenty-five years after India opened its first large steel mill in 1913, Indian steel production grew more than eightfold. Though raw cotton remained India's principal export, its own cotton-spinning industry grew rapidly, encouraged both by protective tariffs and, after 1930, by Gandhi's campaign to boycott British goods. In 1939 modern textile mills—largely owned by Indians, not Englishmen—produced almost three times as much cotton cloth as the primitive hand looms Gandhi's campaign had encouraged.

India did not escape the Depression entirely. In 1939, total steel consumption, including imports, was still less than in 1929. Agricultural exports fell, partly because of a 15 percent growth in population in the 1930s. (The population explosion began in much of Asia during this period, as these countries' rates of population growth overtook those of Europe and North America.) The need to feed many more people encouraged the overcultivation and exhaustion of Indian soil. Already one could foresee the question that became critical for India during the 1980s: could industrialization raise the standard of living among so many hungry mouths? Even so, India came through the Depression far more easily than countries wholly dependent on raw material exports.

Britain, France, and the Dilemma of Democratic Socialism

An astute observer in the 1930s might have realized that if the rest of the dependent world followed the Indian example and made its own cloth and steel, the global pattern of European and North American dominance would eventually collapse. By the 1980s, in fact, the American steel industry was shrinking as steel imports increased—some from countries like Brazil and India. Few foresaw this development in the 1930s, however. Europe and North America still made the economic decisions. If a remedy for the Depression was to be found, it was up to them to find it.

The Failure of Economic Liberalism

As the Depression deepened it became clear that the old remedies were not working. According to the liberal school that dominated economic thinking throughout the nineteenth century, governments could do little about a depression. They could no more legislate their way out of a depression, President Hoover declared, than they could "exorcise

Map 5.1   Percentage of Unemployment in European Countries During the Depression

a Caribbean hurricane." What governments could do was *deflate*. If people were not buying, the remedy was to push prices down to a level low enough to stimulate demand. This also meant driving down the price of labor: wages. If people lacked confidence in the future of their money, the way to restore it was to balance the government's budget. Since a depressed economy produced fewer tax receipts, government would have to reduce its expenditures and raise taxes.

Most economic historians agree that these measures actually made the Depression worse. Higher taxes further reduced the public's purchasing power. With government spending also limited, there was no stimulus to boost confidence and revive the economy.

As the 1930s dragged on, the failure of traditional politics and economics drove more and more Europeans into a search for alternatives. The longest-established alternative was Marxism, which had always warned that capitalism was ultimately doomed by its failure to pay workers enough to buy the things they made. Now that the warning seemed to have come true, the Marxist alternative had much appeal. In a society where income was evenly distributed and the government planned and controlled production, Marxists argued, a disaster like the Depression could not have happened. Nor would government be indifferent to the sufferings of the jobless. But although many Europeans were attracted to a vision of a fairer social system, they shrank from the Soviet model of violent revolution and totalitarian government, preferring instead the nonrevolutionary socialist path.

The Socialist Alternative

To combine a socialist economy with political democracy was the central hope of the Social Democrats, or Socialists. In the 1930s, as today, they constituted the principal opposition to conservative or liberal parties in many countries with a democratic political tradition.

The Bolshevik Revolution had caused a split in all pre–World War I Marxist movements. To be allowed to affiliate with the Comintern, non-Russian Socialist parties had to accept the Soviet model of change. Many Socialists, however, were already sick of Bolshevik methods. At the 1920 annual convention of the French Socialist party, for example, a minority led by Léon Blum, a future prime minister, walked out rather than accept Moscow's control. The majority accepted Moscow's terms and became the French Communist party. Blum and his followers refounded the Socialist party. Germany's Social Democratic party broke apart during the war,

and in the chaotic first years of the postwar republic, the German Socialist party (SPD) and the German Communist party (KPD) fought each other in the streets.

Deep differences of principle divided socialists and communists. To communists, it was a dangerous illusion to believe that it would be possible to create a socialistic society by winning an election. Why, communists asked, would capitalism yield to anything but force? Socialists, on the other hand, believed that Lenin had made an unacceptable sacrifice of political freedom to achieve the socialist goal of a society based on economic equality.

Who was right? The Depression provided several tests of the idea that a socialistic society could be created through democratic politics. In Scandinavia the formula proved partially successful. After socialist electoral victories, Denmark, Norway, and Sweden developed a kind of "mixed" economy. Although most businesses were still privately owned, the mixed economy made government responsible for protecting all citizens' welfare "from the cradle to the grave." The high taxes needed to sustain the welfare state have prompted continuing protests. Nevertheless, Scandinavian Socialists and their political opponents still seem to agree on the necessity for this "middle way" between capitalism and socialism.

The record of democratic socialism during the Depression was much more disappointing in larger countries like Britain and France. The failures of the British Labour party and the French Popular Front were not entirely their own fault. But their experience shows some of the obstacles that can arise to restructuring society within a democratic system.

Britain

When leaders of the British Labour party had formed the first "socialist" cabinet in European history in 1924, middle- and upper-class Englishmen were filled with anxiety. Supported chiefly by working-class voters organized by Britain's increasingly powerful trade union movement, Labour had made an official commitment to socialism in 1918. The party's prime minister, Ramsay MacDonald, was the illegitimate son of a Scottish tenant farmer—a very different kind of person from the aristocrats and conservative businessmen who had previously occupied his office. But the fears of the well-to-do were soon allayed, as they saw that Labour was not going to make many changes. MacDonald's government, which lasted less than a year, made no attempt to convert Britain to a socialistic economy. Its most radical measure was to construct public housing with controlled rents, a measure continued by the Conservative government that replaced it.

To the second Labour government, formed after elections in 1929, fell the task of finding a remedy for the Depression. By 1931, one Englishman in four was unemployed. Unemployment benefits—"the dole"—were meager. Nevertheless, conventional economic wisdom demanded that this burden on the budget be reduced. A majority of the Labour cabinet resigned in 1931 rather than accept such a cut, which they saw as a betrayal of Labour's responsibility to the poor. MacDonald formed a new cabinet, composed largely of Conservatives but called a "National" government because all parties were represented in it. The Labour party expelled MacDonald as a traitor, but remained crippled by its internal divisions. Labour did not get another chance to govern until after World War II. Meanwhile, under the governments of MacDonald and his Conservative successor Stanley Baldwin, the country muddled through the Depression without imagination. There would be no experiment in democratic socialism until after 1945.

In 1929 as in 1924, most Labourites leaned toward preserving the political consensus that had enabled Englishmen of all classes to live together in democracy. Then as now, the party was an uneasy alliance of trade unionists (the majority) and radical middle-class intellectuals. However much they hated Britain's class society, the trade unionists were not sure it could be replaced with a socialist alternative within the existing institutional framework of crown and parliament, which most of them cherished. MacDonald's cautious policies corresponded to their views, not those of Marxist intellectuals. Even the Labour ministers who broke with MacDonald when he agreed to inflict deflation on the unemployed in 1931 did not urge the socialist alternative. If the British Labour party was an example of a democratic socialist movement, it clearly emphasized the democratic, even at the expense of the socialist.

France

In France the question of creating socialism within democracy presented itself somewhat differently. Here the ideas of Karl Marx had more influence than in Britain. While bitterly opposing each other until the mid-1930s, both French Socialists and French Communists proclaimed their allegiance to his ideas. Dividing the votes of France's Left,* they allowed the conservative Right repeated victories. Those French who wanted a different society, particularly members of the urban working class, became deeply frustrated.

In 1935, however, faced with the threat posed to the USSR by Germany after the arch anti-communist Adolf Hitler became German dictator, Stalin imposed a complete reversal of policy upon the Comintern and the Communist parties of Europe. Instead of reviling Socialists, Communists henceforth were to ally with them and other democratic parties in a Popular Front against the fascist threat. In France, after the formation of the Popular Front, Communists and Socialists united with the middle-of-the-road democratic Radical party to back a single candidate in each electoral district in the general election of 1936.

The victory of the Popular Front aroused tremendous hope in the French working class. At last, it seemed, a re-united Left could impose a socialist alternative to the capitalistic economy that had collapsed. But the Socialist party leader, Léon Blum, faced a terrifying dilemma when he became France's prime minister. Some of those who had voted for the Popular Front wanted it to make France a socialist country. But the majority, including supporters of the Radicals, did not want a socialist France.

---

* The use of the terms *Right* and *Left* to designate opposing political beliefs dates back to the parliament of the French Revolution of 1789. Supporters of the king and the existing society happened to sit on the right side of the hall, the supporters of the revolution and of change on the left. Ever since, opponents of change—conservatives—have been described as the Right, and proponents of change—from progressives to radicals—have been the Left.

If Blum did not implement a socialist program, he would be undercut by his Communist allies. But if he did, he would lose the support of Radicals, whose votes he also needed to maintain a majority in parliament. Both groups would turn on him unless he found a way to relieve the Depression.

Blum hoped to escape from this dilemma by improving the conditions of the French working class enough so that its rising productivity and purchasing power would stimulate recovery. Thus, when a wave of strikes followed the victory of the Popular Front, he pressured French employers into making such concessions as the forty-hour work week, annual paid vacations, and workers' rights to bargain collectively. Although he encouraged working-class demands, Blum moved very slowly toward actual socialism. He took over from private ownership only the railways, munitions factories, and the Bank of France.

Blum's efforts to conciliate all groups in French society ended by satisfying none. Productivity fell with the establishment of a shorter work week. Meanwhile, fearing a socialist tax collector, the wealthy sent their money abroad for safekeeping. Reluctant to aggravate their fears, Blum did not impose strict controls to keep money from crossing the border. Many poor voters concluded that he was not really committed to socialism.

With productivity declining and investors frightened, France remained mired in depression while Blum's coalition of Communists, Socialists, and Radicals quarreled over the direction he should take. One year after coming to power, Blum, no longer able to muster a parliamentary majority, resigned.

France's experiment with democratic socialism ended on an ambiguous note.

A "stay-in" strike at a French factory during the Popular Front period. The workers have occupied the plant and locked management out. Similar U.S. strikes were called sit-down strikes.
Popperfoto

Some Popular Front legislation had a lasting effect on French society. Annual paid vacations brought the first working-class families to France's beaches, for example, shocking the middle-class people who had always had these resorts to themselves. Yet Blum's inability, after winning a majority in democratic elections, even to begin to create a socialistic society, raises questions about the possibility of democratic socialism. It may seem that his failure resulted from the particular French circumstances of 1936, notably the need to satisfy a coalition of groups with very different aspirations. Yet this was a problem likely to confront all democratic socialists in power. To give a genuinely socialistic direction to the French economy, Blum would have had to defy the rules of the democratic game, which require a parliamentary

majority. Using undemocratic means, however, would have violated his convictions. Moreover, it would have confirmed the communist view that social change can be imposed only by revolution.

Conventional economic thinking had proved to be of little use in countering the Depression. For whatever reasons, Europe had not found democratic socialism an effective alternative. How much more successful was the United States?

The New Deal in Global Perspective

President Franklin D. Roosevelt promised Americans a New Deal after his election in 1932. Despite the charges of

Roosevelt's critics, the New Deal was not socialistic in any sense European socialists would have understood. Nevertheless, the measures Roosevelt adopted to combat the Depression fundamentally altered the role of government in American life, setting a pattern that persisted without real challenge until the inauguration of President Ronald Reagan in 1981. Today most Americans seem to resent and distrust the role of the federal government in their lives. Relatively few recall how that federal role developed in response to the worst economic collapse the country had known. Americans turned in desperation to government in 1933 because all other sources of leadership were helpless.

Roosevelt was inaugurated in March 1933, almost four years after the Wall Street crash. A quarter of the work force was unemployed. Farmers were threatening to hang bankers who tried to repossess their farms. Bankers had just closed the doors of all U.S. banks after a wave of failures created panic among depositors. Public opinion, the business community, and even Congress were ready to follow wherever Roosevelt led. He had already made it clear that he would seek "broad executive power to wage a war against the emergency, as great as the power that would be given to me if we were in fact invaded by a foreign foe."

During the first "Hundred Days" of the New Deal, Congress passed whatever legislation the administration proposed. The banks were reopened, with depositors' savings guaranteed by a Federal Deposit Insurance Corporation (FDIC). A Federal Emergency Relief Act replenished the funds used by states and cities to relieve the distress of one out of seven Americans.

The "Roosevelt Revolution"

Beyond such rescue measures, Roosevelt tried to attack the basic problems of the American economy. The descendant of generations of aristocratic Hudson River Valley landowners, he was not committed to any particular doctrine. Despite his Harvard education, he was as skeptical of the theories of economics professors as of the platitudes of businessmen. Launched helter-skelter, the New Deal's programs were usually vote-catching, often ineffective, and sometimes inconsistent. Nevertheless, the whirlwind of activity rekindled hope. Skillfully projecting his cheerful optimism in radio "fireside chats," FDR became a hero to a majority of Americans.

The New Deal's congressional supporters attacked the farm problem by legislating limits on production. The Agricultural Adjustment Act (AAA) paid farmers not to contribute to the glut. Thus began the federal administration of farm markets that continues in the 1980s.

To combat mass unemployment, the federal government became an employer of last resort. The Civilian Conservation Corps (CCC), for example, hired idle young men and set them to work on improving the American environment.

To promote industrial recovery, the New Deal allowed business to escape some of the stress of free market competition. In 1931, the president of General Electric had called for the establishment of government-enforced cartels to fix prices and regulate competition in every industry. The National Recovery Administration met this demand by establishing so-called "codes of fair competition" in some 800 industries. These rules were designed to limit competition so that all businesses might survive. When the Supreme Court struck the NRA down as unconstitutional, the New Dealers retorted by creating a series of "little NRAs" in separate industries.

Though such legislation, and loans from the Reconstruction Finance Corporation (RFC), helped to keep many businesses afloat, most business leaders came to hate Roosevelt and the New Deal. Perhaps this was because the Roosevelt administration also supported labor, especially in the so-called second New Deal after 1935. The Wagner Act endorsed trade unions and collective bargaining, prohibited employers from opposing unionization, and set up a National Labor Relations Board (NLRB). The Fair Labor Standards Act of 1938 established a forty-hour week and a forty-cent minimum hourly wage.

Even this summary list of New Deal legislation suggests how much the role of the federal government, and its impact on the individual, had grown. A host of new agencies was created—like the SEC (Securities and Exchange Commission), intended to prevent the kind of Wall Street malpractices that had led to the crash. How effective were these laws and agencies?

Evaluating the New Deal

The New Deal did not end the Depression. Unemployment still stood at 17 percent in 1939. Only the need to make weapons for a new world war provided jobs for virtually every American man who wanted one, and for some women too.

Today, as in the 1930s, the New Deal remains controversial. Conservatives think its basic mistake was to attempt, vainly, to alter the normal operations of a free market economy. Spending more money than the government had collected, Roosevelt began the system of federal budget deficits that have become so enormous in the 1980s. Deficit spending had been recommended as a depression remedy by the most innovative economist of the day, the Englishman John Maynard Keynes. But conservatives argue that deficit spending was a double mistake. It proved ineffective, and it taught Americans to rely on an overgrown federal government rather than their own efforts.

Such criticism is rejected by liberals, the New Deal's most ardent supporters. Their support has given a special American twist to the word *liberalism*. Unlike their nineteenth-century European predecessors, New Deal liberals favored an active role for government in social and economic life. Liberals see in the New Deal a sensible progressive adjustment of American institutions to the new reality of a world depression. In this view, by humanizing and democratizing the economy, and above all by restoring people's hope, the New Deal became one more chapter in the continuous success story of American history.

This interpretation was challenged, especially in the 1960s, by the historians of the New Left. Looking back from the decade of the Vietnam War and ghetto riots, they wondered whether American history really was a success story. In their view, far from undermining American capitalism, as conservatives charged, the New Deal had given it a new lease on life by alleviating its worst abuses. Liberals were equally mistaken, according to the New Left, when they applauded the New Deal for its concern for the common people. Ordinary people actually benefited little. It was the big farmers, the future founders of agribusiness, who were helped by government management of the marketplace.

Organized labor tripled its membership between 1933 and 1941, unionizing one of four American workers, but organized labor was almost entirely white and male. Unorganized labor—like blacks and women—did not fare so well. Moreover, the New Deal had not eliminated "unjust concentrations of wealth and economic power," the professed goal of one piece of legislation. In 1941, the poorest 20 percent of American families collected 4.1 percent of American personal income, compared with 3.5 percent in 1929. The richest 20 percent were still collecting 49 percent of national income in 1941, a small decline from the 54 percent they earned in 1929, and a very long way from the equal shares prescribed by socialism.

There is some truth in each of these conflicting assessments of the New Deal. The federal government did grow: it had 50 percent more employees in 1937 than in 1933. Federal spending rose from 3 percent of the gross national product in 1929 to 14 percent a decade later. The deficits required to pay these employees and fund this spending were unprecedented—though minuscule compared with those of the 1980s. The rich did pay more taxes: the rate in the highest income bracket went up from 20 to 79 percent. Nevertheless, the New Deal was far from a social revolution. At the end of the 1930s, Roosevelt admitted, one-third of Americans remained "ill housed, ill fed, ill clad."

Those same words can be cited as evidence that the New Deal had created a norm of government responsibility for the economic well-being of its citizens. Though he was probably more hated than any other twentieth-century American president, Franklin Roosevelt was also more loved. He was re-elected to an unprecedented four terms. Above all his popularity was inspired by his willingness to mobilize the forces of government against economic disaster (though the New Left historians are correct in asserting that New Deal benefits were unequally distributed).

After the New Deal, the federal government became a "guarantor state."[2] Before 1933 the American government had guaranteed its citizens practically nothing. Thereafter, at least until the 1970s, the federal government sought to guarantee more and more to all citizens: an education for the young; a safe and adequately paid job for adults, with compensation if the job was lost; an adequate standard of living; and medical care for the elderly.

Conclusion: The Global Trend Toward the Guarantor State

The New Deal was the American example of a worldwide trend toward enlarging governments' responsibility for their people. Perhaps the emergence of the guarantor state was inevitable in democratic societies, once World War I had shown that a government could coordinate an entire society and the Depression had reduced whole peoples to despair. Though democratic socialism failed in Britain and France during the 1930s, both countries eventually established more elaborate welfare states than the New Deal created. So did other developed industrial nations, and even some Third World countries.

Despite the current disenchantment with big government, the guarantor state may have become indispensable in the complex, mobile, urban societies of the late twentieth century. Who else today will take care of young and old as the extended family did before 1914 in villages of the non-Western world like Dinshawai?

The growth of governmental power can pose grave risks, however. Democratic socialism and New Deal democracy were not the only possible answers to the Depression. President Roosevelt once declared: "My desire is to obviate revolution. . . . I work in a contrary sense to Rome and Moscow." If he could not make the New Deal work, in other words, the American people might turn from democracy to another model of government and society. We already know the Moscow model. We must now examine the model that began in Mussolini's Rome: fascism, which seemed on its way to conquering the world in the 1930s.

Notes

1. Quoted in Robert L. Heilbroner, *The Making of Economic Society*, 6th ed. (Englewood Cliffs, N.J.: Prentice-Hall, 1980), p. 140.

2. The term *guarantor state* is taken from Carl N. Degler's essay "The Establishment of the Guarantor State," in Richard S. Kirkendall, ed., *The New Deal: The Historical Debate* (New York: Wiley, 1973).

Suggestions for Further Reading

Childs, Marquis, *Sweden, The Middle Way* (1936).

Colton, Joel, *Leon Blum: Humanist in Politics* (1966).

Galbraith, John Kenneth, *The Great Crash* (1955).

Heilbroner, Robert L., *The Making of Economic Society*, 6th ed. (1980).

Johnson, Paul, *Modern Times: The World from the Twenties to the Eighties* (1983).

Kindleberger, Charles P., *The World in Depression, 1929–1939* (1973).

Kirkendall, Richard S., ed., *The New Deal: The Historical Debate* (1973).

Latham, A. J. H., *The Depression and the Developing World 1914–1939* (1981).

Orwell, George, *The Road to Wigan Pier* (1937).

Taylor, A. J. P., *English History, 1914–1945* (1965).

Chapter 6

RESTRUCTURING THE SOCIAL AND POLITICAL ORDER: FASCISM

The word *fascism* derives from the Italian *fascio* (*di combattimento*) and originally referred to the street-fighting combat groups of an Italian political movement. But in the 1920s and 1930s, the fascist label was applied indiscriminately to virtually every government in the world that was clearly neither democratic nor socialist. As a term of abuse, the word is still carelessly used to refer to almost anybody politically to the right of center.

To deal precisely with such an ambiguous concept, this chapter begins by defining fascism. It then discusses the two most important fascist regimes, those of Mussolini in Italy and Hitler in Germany, and shows how Hitler's rise prepared the way for World War II. Like other models of social and political organization that developed in Europe, fascism influenced political movements in other parts of the world. As strictly defined, fascism may seem to have perished in World War II. But the stresses that produced European fascism could some day lead to a similar phenomenon anywhere.

The Varieties of Authoritarianism After 1918

The years between the world wars were not healthy ones for democratic government. Initially the new states of eastern and southeastern Europe created from the ruins of the German, Austrian, and Russian empires all had democratic constitutions. Within a few years, however, most of those governments had been forcibly replaced by some form of authoritarian or dictatorial rule. Poland became a military dictatorship in 1926. After years of chronic political chaos, the kings of Yugoslavia and Rumania abrogated their countries' constitutions and became dictators in 1929 and 1938, respectively. In the other least-developed corner of Europe, a 1926 military coup in Portugal paved the way for the dictatorship of Dr. Oliveira Salazar, an austere economics professor. His regime lasted from 1930 to 1968—long enough to become an accredited part of the free world through its membership in the North Atlantic Treaty Organization. In Spain, General Francisco Franco led the army in rebellion against the Popular Front government of the Republic in 1936. After a three-year civil war that cost a million Spanish lives, Franco established a dictatorship that endured almost as long as Salazar's—until Franco's death in 1975.

All these governments were sometimes called fascist. But their appearances were deceiving. Though most borrowed language from fascism and occasionally mimicked fascist rituals, fundamentally these regimes were simply dictatorships by conservatives. Challenged by real or imagined threats of democracy or socialism, the long-established elites of these little-developed countries—landowners, the Church hierarchy, the army officer corps—abolished politics and began to govern by force. Their goal was to restore or perpetuate their own rule by forestalling all change. Once they had consolidated their power, they usually domesticated and sometimes annihilated the fascist movements whose slogans and cooperation they had borrowed.

Borrowings from Left and Right

The elites feared fascism's revolutionary potential. Authentic fascism—the fascism preached by Mussolini and Hitler and their imitators around the world—did not fit into the usual political categories of Left and Right. It borrowed some of the ideas of both. Like the right-wing regimes established in places like Portugal, fascism was ferociously hostile to liberal democracy and Marxist socialism. Like most conservatives, fascists were intransigent nationalists. Moreover, fascists proclaimed their determination to restore law and order in society using whatever force was needed—another favorite conservative theme.

Yet much about fascism should have alarmed a genuine conservative. Like movements of the Left, fascism was avowedly revolutionary. Fascists said they intended to smash the existing order of things—including much that conservatives held dear. Fascists often declared that their mission was to replace capitalism with a "national" socialism, although this bore little resemblance to the Marxist variety, which stressed international worker solidarity.

Fascism's leaders were young men, drawn not from the old elites but from the lower strata of society. They sought power by mobilizing mass movements whose disciplined readiness for violence was symbolized by their uniforms. Italian Fascist Blackshirts and German Nazi Brownshirts had counterparts around the world, from the tan shirts of the Lebanese *Phalange* to the green shirts of the Brazilian *Integralistas*.

Once in power, many fascists aspired to a new kind of unified society, ruled by an all-powerful state that would mold every individual's life. None of these themes is conservative, and some were clearly borrowed from the Left, indeed from the far Left.

Faced with this basic ambiguity in fascism's nature, historians and political scientists have long argued about how to interpret it. Most would probably agree, however, that fascism is a revolutionary movement whose mass appeal is achieved by invoking largely conservative values. Fascism triumphant was a revolution from the Right.

Economic and Social Change and the Growth of Fascism

Why did people on the Right, who usually oppose change, flock to join fascist movements that promised to change everything? Some powerful trends that underlay fascism's success were already apparent in European society and culture on the eve of World War I. The war, its aftermath, and the Great Depression accentuated these trends, bringing Mussolini to power in 1922 and Hitler in 1933.

One trend was the impact of social and economic change upon those groups in every society least able to defend themselves. These groups included small businessmen, small farmers, and self-employed craftsmen. Before 1914 they saw themselves as being crushed between big business and big labor. Chain stores belonging to anonymous corporations reduced the sales of the corner shopkeeper. The exchanges of a worldwide economy meant that the small dairy farmer of northwest Germany now had to compete with New Zealand butter brought halfway round the world in refrigerated ships. Ingenious machines designed for high-speed mass production threatened the livelihood and status of handworkers everywhere.

Parliamentary politics, which often seemed a mysterious and corrupt game benefiting only the politicians, offered no protection against these looming dangers. Nor could these people turn to Marxist socialism, for they were proudly respectable citizens who looked down on proletarian factory workers, who voted Marxist. These middle-class groups and low-level office workers—the fastest-growing component of society in much of Europe in 1914—derived their sense of security from identification with such apparently solid institutions as the German monarchy. When World War I swept these institutions away and the following decade of uncertainty led into the Depression, these groups stampeded into fascist movements that promised to restore order and security.

Paradoxically, however, fascism also drew support from groups that found the complacency of pre-1914 European society unbearably confining. The quality of life had improved dramatically. In 1914, Europe had not had a major war for fifty years. For the first time in history, medicine was beginning to cure as many patients as it killed. The younger generation found itself in a world without prospect of the glorious conflict that patriotism taught it to value. As the older generation lived longer and longer, young people's wait for opportunity was indefinitely prolonged. Fascist ideas reflected the rebellion of this prewar younger generation.

This generation was inspired by an intellectual revolt against many of the dominant ideas of the nineteenth century, such as scientific materialism and parliamentary democracy. The prophets of this revolt saw in the civilization of Imperial Berlin a symbol of decay rather than progress. The routine of technological society had produced, they complained, a contemptible kind of human being: selfish, complacent, weak, irreligious. Parliamentary democracy had given political authority to the clever people who knew how to manipulate these gullible masses. They had tamed even the threat of revolutionary socialism. The time was coming to sweep all this away, to replace what one fascist derided as "the politics of ink, saliva, and ideology" with a real politics of "soil, flesh, and blood."

This contrast between the artificial and the real sums up fascism's revolt against modernity. While capitalists and socialists argued about what should become of "economic man," fascists held up the ideal of "heroic man," strong and cruel, joyful believer in the destiny of his nation or race. Fascists, Mussolini declared, were "against the easy life," because only a life of continuous hardship and struggle, like that of peasants of earlier centuries, could retrieve modern human beings from the decay of a world grown too comfortable. Only a movement dedicated to such a life of primitive virtues could reunite nations divided by the social strife of the twentieth century.

Without World War I, such ideas might have remained confined to the fringe of European society. It was the war and its aftermath that made them meaningful to millions and decisively encouraged the growth of fascism.

Their experiences in the trenches of World War I deeply affected the first fascists, those who joined up in the hard days before their movement had won power. The more thoughtful of them found in those horrors a condemnation of the whole prewar way of life. At the same time, the anguish of life on the front line produced a camaraderie among young men who in peacetime Europe would have been kept apart by sharp class distinctions. As veterans, many of these men tried to prolong this wartime sense of belonging by joining paramilitary street-fighting movements dedicated to smashing the prewar social order that had condemned them to the battlefronts. In its place they wanted to install the kind of government World War I had brought to the home front of every belligerent: one that would use centralized authority to impose a united society and a controlled economy.

Such movements emerged in all the countries that fought in World War I. Only in Italy and Germany, however, did they win control of the government. Why did these two societies prove especially vulnerable to the fascist temptation?

Both Italy and Germany were new nations, united only in the second half of the nineteenth century. Defeat—or, for Italy, a victory that seemed like defeat—in World War I revealed their internal fragility and external helplessness. Both

Italy and Germany were rocked by near civil war at the very moment they were humiliated by the Versailles settlement. Frustrated nationalism and widespread fear of a Bolshevik-style social revolution thus reinforced the appeal of fascism.

Neither Italy nor Germany had the kind of long-established liberal or democratic institutions that gave some confidence to Englishmen and Frenchmen. Faced with social chaos or economic disaster, the Italian and German middle classes preferred to abandon their feeble newborn democracies for the strong government the fascists promised. They acquiesced in a revolution that they hoped would end the disturbing changes brought by the war—a revolution from the Right.

We now turn to an examination of the fascist experience in particular cases, first Italy, then Germany. Six years after Adolf Hitler came to power, his Nationalist Socialist regime had drawn the nations into a new world war. By then, as we shall see, fascism's apparent success had spawned a host of imitations throughout Europe and beyond.

The Original Fascism: The Italian Model

Italy had gained little from its alliance with the winners of World War I. This disappointment was only the last in a series of frustrations since the unification of the nation in 1870. It had become clear that Italy's status as the sixth great power was a fiction barely tolerated by the others. The country remained desperately poor. The Italian South was notorious for the backwardness of its huge landed estates. Recent industrialization in the North had added urban social ten-

sions to the age-old clash between peasant and landowner.

Nor could Italians take much pride in their constitutional monarchy. The nation's parliamentary system, long based on corrupt bargains and rigged elections, faced paralysis after every Italian male became eligible to vote in 1912. This mass electorate did not provide support to the traditional liberals and conservatives, but divided it between two mass parties, Socialists and Catholics. Each was strong enough to prevent the other (or anyone else) from governing, but they were separated by differences too deep for compromise.

The Versailles settlement gave Italy far less of the disputed territories on its borders than Italians felt their country deserved. Only nine thousand square miles compensated for the loss of 600,000 young men. Moreover, this "mutilated" victory brought Italy the same economic dislocations and social unrest that other nations faced. Cabinets based on parliamentary coalitions that typically collapsed after a few months did little to combat the fourfold increase in the postwar cost of living, the sevenfold increase in the public debt, and the rising rate of unemployment. When discontented workers seized control of factories in the fall of 1920, it seemed that the contagion of revolution might have spread from Russia to northern Italy.

Benito Mussolini (1883–1945) skillfully mobilized his compatriots' anxiety and disgust. Since his adolescence he had been a rebel against Italian society, though originally, like almost all rebels, on the Left. His radical father, a blacksmith, had named him after Benito Juárez, the leader of a nineteenth-century Mexican revolt. At the outbreak of World War I, the younger Mussolini was a leading Socialist journalist. But he dis-

Mussolini marches with the Blackshirts, 1922. Photographed a week before the "March on Rome," the leader is shown surrounded by bemedalled veterans at a Fascist meeting in Naples.
The Mansell Collection

agreed with the Socialist party's position that Italy should stay out of the war, and broke with the Left permanently over that issue. For Mussolini the violence of war was a promise of revolution. In war, a proletarian nation like Italy might throw off its dependence on the more developed industrial nations. When Italy entered the war on the Anglo-French side in 1915, partly as a result of Mussolini's agitation, he promptly joined the army.

The war won as little for him as for his country. As a demobilized veteran, Mussolini became a spokesman for his comrades' rage for something better. On March 23, 1919, with about 145 friends, including former *arditi* (shock troops) whose black uniform he adopted, Mus-

solini founded the first *Fascio di Combattimento*.

The Rise of Fascism

During its first year, Mussolini's Fascism, championing such radical causes as votes for women and the eight-hour day, attracted little attention. Its real growth began when frightened conservatives recognized its potential to suppress social disorder. Industrialists, landowners, and the army rushed to bankroll the movement, whose brutal *squadristi* beat up strikers and other troublemakers, often forcing them to drink near-fatal doses of castor oil. By late 1922, growing as fast as the unemployment lines, Fascism had a membership of over 300,000. Its leaders loudly demanded at least a share in the government. With Fascist thugs controlling the streets of many major Italian cities, their threat of a march on Rome, the capital, seemed plausible.

Yet Mussolini did not take power by violence. Power was handed to him. Rather than challenge so formidable an enemy of their own enemies—Socialists and Communists—the king and his conservative advisers decided to name Mussolini prime minister. In October 1922, Mussolini "marched" comfortably on Rome in a railroad sleeping car, with a royal invitation to head a fourteen-member cabinet including only three Fascists.

For a time he appeared content with this role, although many of his followers called for a "second wave" of revolution to transform Italy's society and political system. Behind his bluster, Mussolini was a hesitant adventurer: a "roaring rabbit," as he was once called. It took a major threat to his new position to force him into the final steps to dictatorship. Fascists close to Mussolini kidnapped and murdered a Socialist member of parliament, Giacomo Matteotti, who had exposed Fascist misdeeds. In reaction to this scandal, Catholic and some liberal politicians began to boycott parliament, hoping to force Mussolini to resign. Instead this show of opposition apparently pushed him, after months of wavering, to establish a dictatorship.

By 1926, after dissolving opposition parties and independent unions, establishing strict press censorship, and reducing parliament to subjection, Mussolini appeared to be Italy's only master. Whenever he appeared on the balcony of his Roman palace, frenzied crowds saluted him as leader with cries of *"Duce! Duce!"* A similar, if more restrained enthusiasm was expressed by many foreign visitors. Fascism, it appeared, had taught the formerly "undisciplined" Italians to "make their trains run on time." Mussolini's propaganda machine proclaimed that his genius had created a successful alternative to both capitalist democracy and Soviet communism. A closer examination of the regime's record and its relationships with various groups in Italian society, however, suggests that this was a gross exaggeration.

Fascist Myth versus Fascist Reality

The Fascist remedy for social conflict was corporatism, a concept partly borrowed from Catholic social thought, which had always been troubled by the individualism of the free enterprise system. *Corporatism* sought to unite members of the same economic calling—both employers and employees—by abolishing political parties and geographical election districts. In place of these divisive institutions, "corporations" were to be established for each sector of the economy. In these institutions representatives of bosses and workers could resolve their differences in an atmosphere of mutual understanding.

Mussolini eventually created twenty-two such corporate bodies and in 1938 replaced his rubber-stamp parliament with a Chamber of Fasces and Corporations. Far from fulfilling Catholic hopes of social reconciliation, the system was a façade disguising the repression of Italian labor. The leaders of big business effectively controlled the corporate bodies. Italian workers, forbidden to strike, had little voice in them. By 1939, workers' real wages—the purchasing power of what they had earned—had fallen below the level of 1922.

Workers had never been Fascism's best supporters. Small businessmen were generally much more enthusiastic, but even they got little help from the regime when the Depression struck. Government planning consistently favored big businesses over small ones, which were allowed to fail while their larger competitors got loans from the Agency for Industrial Reconstruction. The effort to build an efficient industry took precedence over Fascist rhetoric about preserving the little man. Perhaps the best-rewarded of Fascism's early supporters were the students and white-collar workers who found jobs in the expanding party and government bureaucracies.

Fascist propaganda declared that these bureaucracies gave new unity and direction to Italian life. In reality Mussolini's movement never began to achieve his totalitarian dream of integrating every individual in society. Long accustomed to political cynicism, many Italians simply went through the Fascist motions. In Sicily, for example, members of the Mafia put on black shirts and continued business as usual.

Nor was the Mafia the only group beyond Mussolini's control. He tried to placate the Catholic church by signing a treaty in 1929 that ended the long quarrel over Italy's seizure of Rome, the pope's city, as its capital. But the Church objected to his efforts to enroll children and young people into Fascist youth movements that rivaled the Catholic ones. Though much overshadowed, king and court also remained a potential rival power center. And despite all the talk about a new social order, the leaders of industry continued to direct the economy much as before, in cozy consultation with the higher bureaucracy. The

Duce had not fully realized his boastful slogan: "Everything for the state, nothing against the state, no one outside the state."

The original Italian Fascist regime bore some striking resemblances to systems like Franco's and Salazar's because such conservative groups as the church, the court, and big business remained influential. By the mid-1930s, Fascism appeared to be a gigantic bluff even to some of its original supporters. It had not saved Italy from the Depression. After 1929 Italians who had emigrated to the United States sent less money home—a heavy blow to the Italian budget. Despite Mussolini's emphasis on public works projects, all his construction sites could not provide jobs for the many who fled the poverty-stricken countryside for the cities.

Mussolini's policies were crippled by contradictions. It made little sense, for example, to try to keep people on the overpopulated farms while encouraging Italians to have more children. But Fascist ideology insisted on both agricultural self-sufficiency and an ever-growing population to make Italy strong. Similarly, the goal of an "autarkic" economy, independent of foreign suppliers, had patriotic appeal. But in practice the Fascist regime restricted the purchasing power of the working-class majority without planning systematically for investment—hardly a recipe for economic growth.

No wonder Mussolini raged as he became entangled in the contradictions between Fascist myths and hard reality. Or that he turned again to violence in 1935,

▶

Map 6.1 German and Italian Aggressions, 1935–1939

ICELAND

Germany and Italy
Italian possessions in Africa before 1935
German aggressions, 1935-1939
Italian aggressions, 1935-1939

NORWAY

SWEDEN

FINLAND

DENMARK

BALTIC SEA

ESTONIA

LATVIA

Moscow •

NORTH SEA

Memel • LITHUANIA

SOVIET UNION

IRELAND

NETHERLANDS

GREAT
BRITAIN

London •

Brussels •
BELGIUM

Paris •

LUXEMBOURG

ATLANTIC
OCEAN

Danzig •

EAST
PRUSSIA

POLISH
CORRIDOR

• Warsaw

GERMANY

Berlin •

SUDETENLAND
1938

POLAND

RHINELAND
1936

Weimar •

Nuremberg •
Munich •

Prague •

CZECHOSLOVAKIA
1939

Vienna •
AUSTRIA
1938

HUNGARY

RUMANIA

FRANCE

SWITZERLAND

YUGOSLAVIA

BLACK
SEA

BULGARIA

PORTUGAL

• Madrid

SPAIN
(Civil War, 1936-1939)

• Barcelona

ITALY

• Rome

ALBANIA
1939

GREECE

TURKEY

MEDITERRANEAN SEA

LIBYA

ERITREA

AFRICA

ETHIOPIA
1935-1936

IT. SOMALILAND

A   F   R   I   C   A

launching an invasion of Ethiopia to avenge Italy's humiliating defeat there in 1896, a rare victory of Africans over Europeans. Instead of establishing an Italian empire, however, this adventure began the undoing of Fascism. For a country as underindustrialized and poor in raw materials as Italy, war would eventually mean dependence on a more powerful ally. Hating (and spurned by) the domineering democracies, England and France, Mussolini eventually turned to his fascist neighbor, Nazi Germany. Its leader had come to power much as Mussolini had. But Hitler had created a far more terrifying regime. In the end, he would drag Mussolini with him to destruction.

From Weimar Republic to Third Reich

In Germany as in Italy, fascism owed its success to a masterful demagogue who mobilized popular anger against a feeble democracy during a period of upheaval. In Germany too, the conservative establishment handed the fascist leader supreme power in the expectation of exploiting his movement. Hitler had a far greater impact on world history than did Mussolini, however. From the moment a leader determined to reverse the humiliation of Versailles took power in Germany, another European civil war became likely. That conflict brought the final collapse of European domination of the world.

Weakness of the Weimar Republic

Like Fascism's, the story of Nazism's triumph begins with the end of World War I. The conditions imposed on Germany by the Versailles settlement were an enormous liability for the new republic. Right-wing propaganda implanted in the minds of many the lie that the war would not have been lost had the German army not been "stabbed in the back" by the Republican "November criminals," who had allegedly preferred revolution to victory. The Weimar Republic's first five years were a constant struggle for survival against attacks from both Left and Right. In 1919, the Socialist-dominated government mastered Communist uprisings only by using both the old imperial army and private armies (*Freikorps*) of right-wing veterans. The old army remained unsympathetic to the republic, however. When several of the Freikorps backed the attempt of a right-wing bureaucrat, Wolfgang Kapp, to overthrow the government in 1920, the army refused to move against them. The republic defeated Kapp only by calling out its worker supporters in a general strike.

This sequence of events already revealed the Weimar Republic's fatal weakness. On paper it was a model of democracy. Its bill of rights guaranteed freedoms never before recognized in Germany—including the vote for women. But in reality the republic was aptly described as a "candle burning at both ends." It faced a continuous Communist threat on its Left and also had to contend with a hostile Right that included many of its own officials, as the Kapp putsch proved. In truth the German revolution of 1918 had hardly been a revolution at all. Far from stabbing the army in the back, the republicans had merely occupied the political vacuum temporarily created by its collapse. They did not shatter the old power structure, for they needed the empire's bureaucrats and officers. Many of these, though ostensibly serving the new government, remained as contemptuous of democracy as they had been before 1914.

The republic might have endured if it had won the support of the German middle classes. But this group lost its savings when a terrifying wave of hyperinflation—the worst ever recorded anywhere—destroyed the value of the German currency overnight in 1923. Soon a billion marks were worth only about twenty-five cents, and many people blamed the republic. Few recalled that the imperial government had begun the inflation by printing floods of money to fight the war. Meanwhile, to force the payment of reparations, France occupied the Ruhr, Germany's industrial heartland, thus compounding the financial crisis.

To many, the Weimar Republic appeared to be on the point of collapse in 1923. Communists attempted a rising in Saxony. In Bavaria, Adolf Hitler led his Nazi storm troopers from a Munich beer hall in an attempt to overthrow the Bavarian state as a prelude to destroying the central government. The Beer Hall putsch was a fiasco. The police fired on the advancing Nazis, killing several, and arrested Hitler, who was sentenced to a five-year prison term. This apparent failure marked a turning point in the career of one of the most sinister figures of modern history.

Born in Austria, the son of a minor customs official, Hitler left his provincial birthplace for Vienna at the age of eighteen. Failing to get into art school, he drifted, like many unsuccessful migrants to the great metropolis, into a lonely and marginal life. From his observations of Viennese society and politics, he developed two basic beliefs. The German nationalists there, who despised the multi-ethnic Hapsburg monarchy, taught him the necessity of uniting the Germans of Europe into one nation. Viennese anti-Semitism persuaded him that Jews were Germans' worst enemies in the worldwide struggle for survival. Though Hitler exploited these themes to move the masses, these were also his deeply held beliefs. World war and genocide would later prove how sincerely he meant them.

When World War I broke out, Hitler chose not to fight for the Hapsburgs, but for Germany. Though he did not advance beyond the rank of corporal, he thrived in the army as he never had done in civilian life, winning decorations and commendations. The worst day in his life was the one in November 1918 when, lying wounded in a hospital, he heard the news of Germany's defeat. Later, drifting in bewilderment like so many demobilized veterans, he came to Munich, where army intelligence hired him as a political agent. His job was to infiltrate an obscure group called the National Socialist German Workers Party—Nazi for short. Hitler soon took it over from its founder, a locksmith whose aim was to combine German nationalism with a socialism dedicated not to Marx's proletarian revolution but to the protection of respectable little men in the middle—like locksmiths.

German society included millions of people to whom such a mixture would appeal. Hitler had exceptional gifts for reaching such an audience. Films of his speeches show that he had an uncanny ability to rouse crowds to frenzy by expressing their rage and frustration. He articulated the grievances of the many Germans who believed their nation was destined by racial superiority to rule Europe, but was now disarmed and held captive by a conspiracy of alien forces:

Jews above all, but also Communists, Socialists, Catholics, and democratic politicians. It was wholly irrational to attribute Germany's misfortunes to the cooperation of such ill-assorted groups, or even to any one of them alone. But Hitler knew that emotion, not reason, wins political commitment.

For a time Hitler's message of hate went unheeded as a renewed currency and a reviving economy gave the Weimar Republic a respite after 1924. Hitler served only eight months of his prison sentence, an indication of the Weimar judges' leniency toward right-wing revolutionaries. He emerged from prison to find Nazism largely forgotten. In the 1928 elections, his party won only twelve seats in the Reichstag, with only 3 percent of the popular vote. It remained largely a refuge for a hard core of men unable to readjust to civilian life. They reveled in the brown-shirted uniforms of the Nazi storm trooper brigade, or SA (for *Sturm-Abteilung*).

From Hindenburg to Hitler

It was the Depression that finally doomed the Weimar Republic and gave German fascism its opportunity. As in Britain, parliamentary factions became deadlocked over the issue of reducing government spending by cutting unemployment benefits. A government based on a Reichstag majority became impossible. After 1930 the president of the republic, the aged Field Marshal Paul von Hindenburg, governed with the emergency powers unluckily included in Article 48 of the constitution. Thereafter the political battle was fought in two places: between the SA and the uniformed brawlers of the other parties in the streets, and among rival factions in

the circle of conservative intriguers who surrounded Hindenburg.

Desperate economic circumstances intensified political violence in the streets. By 1932, two of five trade union members were unemployed and another was working short hours. Meanwhile, trying to break the political deadlock, the government held one election after another. In this atmosphere of economic despair and political frenzy, the extremes gained at the expense of the middle-of-the-road parties. The Communist vote rose dramatically, but not nearly as fast as the Nazi totals. The Nazis had 12 seats in the 550-member Reichstag in 1929, 107 in 1930, and 230 in the summer of 1932.

Sensing that momentum was with them, some Nazis urged Hitler to overthrow the republic. But he had learned from Mussolini's experience and his own failure in 1923. As leader of the largest party, he could simply wait for the conservatives around Hindenburg to offer him a deal that would enable them to end emergency government under Article 48. On January 30, 1933, an agreement was reached: Adolf Hitler became chancellor of Germany as head of a coalition government whose 11 members included only 3 Nazis.

Many groups share the blame for this development. Conservative German politicians sneered at Hitler's "gutter" following but still tried to use his mass movement for their own purposes. Convinced that the Socialists were their real enemies, the Communists joined the Nazis in attacking the republic. Yet it should not be forgotten that Hitler could claim power because so many Germans backed him. Careful comparison of election results shows that the Nazis had little success among working-class Socialist voters or the Catholic voters of the Center party. Many Nazi votes came at the expense of the conservative middle-class parties, which were virtually wiped out. Others were cast by new voters, especially the young. A third of the Nazi party's membership was made up of young people between eighteen and thirty.

Disgusted with the floundering of the Weimar government, which could not restore sanity to an economy gone crazy for the second time in ten years, these voters saw a striking contrast in Nazi dynamism. They also expected Nazi force to restore law and order to a turbulent political scene. Eighty-two people had been killed and hundreds wounded in six weeks of street fighting in one German state alone. If the price of an end to chaos was the establishment of a dictatorship, many were prepared to pay it—indeed looked forward to it.

The Nazi State

Dictatorship was not slow in coming. When a fire devastated the Reichstag building less than a month after Hitler's inauguration, the Nazis proclaimed that Germany was faced with a Communist plot. As a "defensive measure against Communist acts of violence," they "suspended" constitutional guarantees of personal freedom—never to be restored. As the first concentration camps opened to hold Communists and other Nazi enemies, the Reichstag convened to consider an Enabling Act that empowered Hitler to make laws, even unconstitutional ones, on his own authority for the next four years. With Communist members of parliament under arrest, only the Socialists were there to vote against the proposal. Combining his Nazis' votes with those of the Catholic Center party

and what remained of the other parties of the Right, Hitler won an easy victory.

Now invested with unlimited authority, Hitler swiftly destroyed most of the institutions of a free society. He outlawed rival political parties or prodded them to dissolve themselves. He abolished the federal system, making Germany a country with an all-powerful central government for the first time in its history. When Hindenburg died early in 1934, Hitler simply absorbed his office into his own. Never was the Weimar constitution modified. The "constitution" of the new Third Reich was simply whatever the Nazi *Führer* (Leader) commanded.

He gave fearful demonstration of the extent of his power in the summer of 1934. By then, many Nazis, especially in the SA, were complaining that the political revolution had not gone far enough. Taking the socialism of National Socialism seriously, they were impatient to see Germany's old elites displaced. The SA's leaders dreamed of replacing the old officer corps, dominated by aristocrats, with their own street brawlers. Their demands forced Hitler to choose between some of his earliest supporters and the conservative and army leaders who had just given him power. He favored his most recent benefactors, ordering his black-uniformed SS bodyguards to massacre his most troublesome SA followers. When this Night of the Long Knives (June 30, 1934) was over, Hitler bluntly warned the Reichstag that if anyone "raises his hand to strike the State, then certain death is his lot."

Nazi Society and Economy

The Nazis overhauled German life and institutions through a process of "coordination" (*Gleichschaltung*) designed to compel obedience by peer pressure. To prevent individuals from combining to oppose the regime, Hitler ordered the Nazification of every organized activity in Germany, right down to clubs of stamp collectors and beekeepers. He dissolved the labor unions and made every German worker a member of the Nazi Labor Front—without, of course, any right to strike. He ordered the consolidation of the Protestant denominations into a single church under Nazi domination. In addition to bringing these older institutions under control, the Nazis also created new ones like the Hitler Youth, to enroll whole categories of the population.

All these groups were organized according to the *Führerprinzip*, the idea that authority comes from the top down and must be obeyed without question. Nazi society thus became an example of mass mobilization carried to its most extreme and authoritarian form. Until 1938 the army high command seemed exempt from "coordination." But in that year Hitler took advantage of scandals involving the most senior officers to retire them and take the supreme command into his own hands. Unlike Mussolini's Italy, Nazi Germany seemed to have fulfilled the fascist revolution; the prefascist power structure was forced into obedience.

Joseph Goebbels, Hitler's propaganda minister, described the Third Reich as "one great movement of obeying, belonging, and believing." Historians have shown that this image was only partially accurate. Behind the facade of totalitarian efficiency was a bureaucratic nightmare of confusion and rivalry. Hitler was bored by the routine of government and ignored it, while deliberately encouraging organizational enmities that only he

could resolve. Nevertheless the accomplishments of his regime, particularly its economic achievements, were enough to make it genuinely popular with a majority, at least until war came in 1939.

Six million Germans were out of work in 1932. By 1938, the figure had dropped to 164,000 and was still declining. Three factors contributed to this success. First, the Nazis—unwitting Keynesians—used government spending, even at a deficit, to restart the economy. These appropriations went originally for public works—the Nazis built the world's first network of superhighways—and later almost exclusively for rearmament. By 1938, the Nazis were committing at least half the budget—far more than any other country—to an arms build-up. Second, they brought the economy under tight government control. The government fixed prices, established production quotas, and allocated raw materials according to a Four-Year Plan, practically abolishing the forces of the marketplace. The third anti-Depression tactic was an effort—called for by the Plan—to make Germany's economy self-sufficient. The chemical industry, for example, was stimulated to develop synthetic substitutes to replace imported oil and rubber.

Together these policies produced a full-employment economy that contrasted sharply with the stagnation of the democracies. Not that all Germans fared equally well. Industrial workers, who had never been enthusiastic Nazis, were the least rewarded. The fate of farmers and small businessmen was only marginally better, though they had provided much of Nazism's voting strength. Their earnings increased faster than those of factory workers—but not nearly as fast as industrial corporate profits, which grew fourfold in the 1930s. Nazi promises to safeguard the little man proved hollow. The flight from the farm continued, and the number of small businesses actually declined faster than in the 1920s.

Like Fascism, Nazism in practice proved a disappointment to those who had supported it as a conservative revolution, against change. Under the Third Reich, change actually accelerated, further eroding German small-town and rural society. The reason is quite simple. Hitler's goal was a powerful Germany. That meant a modern Germany equipped for war by the latest technology, which only large corporations could supply. The little people who had flocked to Hitler in fear of change could contribute little to that goal. He sacrificed them ruthlessly to the needs of war.

The Road to War

Compared to the causes of World War I, the causes of the European part of World War II, at least, have provoked little debate. The story of European international relations between 1933 and 1939 is the story of how Hitler dismantled the Versailles treaty piece by piece, unresisted by the democracies—until they finally went reluctantly to war in defense of Poland. Although one might conclude that Hitler was the cause of World War II, the leaders of the democracies are often also blamed for giving in to him. Even in the 1980s, this interpretation remains an important historical model in the minds of foreign policy planners. The lesson American leaders felt they had learned from the sorry outcome of the 1930s was surely one reason for the prolonged U.S. involvement in Southeast Asia in the 1960s and 1970s. The lesson appeared to be that any failure to resist an aggressor nation, even in the remotest and most unimportant-seeming place, simply emboldened it to further aggression. Today, too, the world situation is often analyzed by analogy to the 1930s. We need to know precisely what happened then if we are to judge the aptness of the analogy.

Design for Aggression

Sometimes the suggestion is made that the democracies' failure to resist Hitler in the 1930s was the more inexcusable because his book, *Mein Kampf*, made no secret of his objectives. This rambling, unreadable work, written during his short stay in prison, clearly reveals his basic beliefs. Hitler was a "social Darwinist," who applied to human life the evolutionary vision of nature as a struggle among species for the survival of the fittest. For Hitler, history was a struggle for survival among biologically distinct races. The German race would not be able to compete effectively unless all Germans were brought within one country—a program that implied the destruction of independent Austria, Czechoslovakia, and Poland, where many "racial Germans" lived. Because France had consistently blocked German unity, another French war was probably essential. Yet Hitler's ambitions for the Germans did not stop with their unification, for he believed all the lands they inhabited to be overcrowded. They must conquer additional *Lebensraum*—living space—in the east, taking land from the racially inferior Slavs, particularly of the Soviet Union.

Mein Kampf thus does contain a kind of "design for aggression." Moreover, we know that Hitler vaguely contemplated still further struggles—ultimately, perhaps in the late 1940s, a war with the United States for mastery of the world. Yet we cannot really blame democratic statesmen for not taking the message of the book seriously. Many politicians out of power have made promises that they later failed to keep. *Mein Kampf* was dismissed as this kind of election propaganda.

Hitler's Destruction of the Versailles System

As chancellor, Hitler at first proceeded very cautiously in foreign policy. He had no predetermined timetable for destroying the Europe of the Versailles treaty, though this remained his goal. Instead he took advantage of opportunities as they arose, avoiding risks and accepting whatever successes circumstances gave him. His speeches stressed his own experiences of the horrors of war and his determination to prevent a new one. Moreover he was always careful to stress that whatever changes Germany sought in the Versailles settlement were only what was "fair." Hitler's rhetoric appealed to the guilty consciences of many people in the democracies. They had forgotten that the Versailles treaty had not been intended to be fair to Germany, but to weaken and control it.

Arguing that the Versailles treaty had called for all countries to disarm, but that only Germany had been forced to do so, Hitler withdrew Germany from international disarmament talks and the League of Nations in the fall of 1933. He used a similar justification in 1935 when he announced the creation of a German air force, or *Luftwaffe*, forbidden by the Versailles treaty, and the expansion of the German army to five times its permitted size.

Perhaps encouraged by the failure of Britain and France to counter these challenges, Hitler began moving troops in the spring of 1936. In violation of the Versailles treaty and later agreements, he "remilitarized" the German Rhineland. This strengthening of Germany's western defenses would make it much harder for the French to move into Germany—the only way they could really help Germany's eastern neighbors if Hitler threatened them. But the French confined themselves to an ineffectual protest. On the eve of their Popular Front experiment, they were divided domestically and dreaded a new war after the fearful toll the last one had taken of their youth. They surrendered European leadership to Britain. The British could see nothing wrong with Hitler moving German troops into German territory. So Hitler got away with it.

It is sometimes suggested that the Rhineland crisis of 1936 was the one time when Hitler could have been stopped without much bloodshed. Armed resistance to remilitarization might have forced him to retreat, destroyed his prestige, and perhaps prompted the German generals to overthrow him. But it is not clear that the German generals would have had the courage to mount a coup. Moreover, Hitler's ambitions were not his alone. Most Germans wanted to reverse the Versailles treaty. Their country had territorial ambitions long before Hitler came to power, as illustrated by the peace it imposed on the Russians in 1917. A rebuff in the Rhineland might not have toppled Hitler. Even if it had, he might have been followed by a German government no more peacefully inclined.

In 1937, Hitler directed his generals to be ready for war in connection with his next move. This precaution proved unnecessary, for the democracies did not oppose his annexation (*Anschluss*) of Austria in the spring in 1938. Hitler arranged a plebiscite after he marched in, in which a majority of Austrians approved the annexation. This result eased the consciences of people in the democracies, who thought in terms of national self-determination rather than strategic realities.

The annexation of Austria left Czechoslovakia in the position of a man with his head in the lion's mouth. By September 1938, Hitler was preparing to devour the Czechs. The complaints of the more than 3 million Sudeten Germans who lived under Czech rule served as his justification this time.

The Czech situation brought the most severe of the prewar crises, for France and the Soviet Union were committed by treaty to protect the Czechs. At every Czech concession Hitler escalated his demands and threatened a solution by force. He was not bluffing. In May, he had issued secret orders stating his "unalterable intention to smash Czechoslovakia by military action in the near

Hitler and Chamberlain at Munich, September 29, 1938. The German leader (left) and the British Prime Minister (third from left) review a Nazi honor guard before Chamberlain's return flight to London. *Popperfoto*

The Nazi occupation of Warsaw, September 1939. Air raids and shelling during a three-week siege reduced much of the Polish capital to ruins. *Popperfoto*

future."[1] But he was also willing, grudgingly, to let the democracies deliver Czechoslovakia to him without war.

It was the British prime minister, Neville Chamberlain, who obliged him. Chamberlain made three frantic trips to Germany to negotiate a settlement. In Munich, with Mussolini's encouragement and France's acquiescence, Chamberlain and Hitler made terms. The Czechs, who were not represented, lost their defensible mountain frontier regions, where the Sudeten Germans (and nearly a million Czechs) lived.

The Munich agreement made *appeasement* a dirty word and Chamberlain's umbrella a symbol of surrender. But in 1938, most Europeans were relieved by this settlement. They were not anxious to go to war again. It is in hindsight that Chamberlain's sacrifice of the only remaining democracy in Eastern Europe has been condemned.

Often such condemnation has been made without any understanding of Chamberlain's position. He was no admirer of Hitler, whom he regarded as half-crazed. Nor was he simply yielding to threats. He was pursuing a deliberate policy of peacefully eliminating sources of conflict. He foresaw correctly that another bloodbath like World War I would mean the end of the European-dominated world order. He had little faith in help from the Soviet Union, as frightful a regime as Hitler's, or from the United States, whose citizens clearly wanted to avoid further involvement in Europe. In this perspective, the sacrifice of a small remote country seemed a lesser evil than a new war.

Chamberlain's error was to believe that Hitler, like most people, would prefer peace to war, especially if his grievances were satisfied. In fact, Hitler was glad to get what he demanded without war. But if Chamberlain had not appeased him, the war that began in September 1939 would probably have begun in September 1938, and the British would have been even less well prepared than they were a year later.

When Chamberlain returned to Britain, he announced that the Munich agreement heralded "peace in our time." But in the spring of 1939, Hitler seized what was left of Czechoslovakia. In retaliation, the British government promised support to Poland, clearly destined to be his next victim. Even so, Hitler probably did not expect his invasion of Poland to produce full-scale war, which German planning anticipated would come only in 1943 or 1945.

In August 1939, preparing to attack Poland, Hitler cynically signed an agreement with the Soviet Union that ensured Germany would not have to fight on two fronts. In return, the Nazi-Soviet pact guaranteed Stalin a share of the Polish spoils and at least temporary immunity from German attack. Hitler probably calculated that such odds would prove daunting to Britain and France, and indeed those countries hesitated to respond for almost two days after German troops crossed the Polish border on September 1. But the Poles refused to have a surrender negotiated over their heads, as had happened to the Czechs. And so,

with the British and French declarations of war on September 3, Europe's second world war began.

The Record of the 1930s and the Lessons of History

What "lessons of history" are to be learned from the story of the 1930s? Winston Churchill, soon to become Britain's prime minister, had systematically condemned each successive failure to curb Hitler. The prestige of his wartime leadership has lent much weight to the lesson he preached: the need for timely resistance to dictators. Yet it cannot be proved that following his policy would have allowed Europe to avoid war, or even to fight on terms more advantageous to the democracies. We cannot know what would have happened if Hitler had been forced to back down in 1936. And by 1938 he was eager to fight. In historical perspective, Churchill's lessons no longer seem so certain.

Ironically, Neville Chamberlain in 1938 was convinced that he had learned the lessons of history. How incredible it was, he said during the Munich crisis, that the British government should be issuing gas masks to its civilians and digging trenches in London "because of a quarrel in a faraway country between people of whom we know nothing." Clearly he was remembering the origins of World War I. The lesson Chamberlain had learned from 1914 was that great wars began when great powers were dragged into them by alliances with quarrelsome small powers like Serbia. Hence his determination to defuse a similar crisis, as he saw it, by opening a dialogue.

Perhaps there was no way to stop German expansion except by war. Hitler was in a hurry, believing that destiny called him to realize Germany's ambitions and that his own days were numbered. It may be that the fascist revitalization of Germany, always potentially the strongest power on the European continent, forced the democracies to choose between war and submission. As we shall see, Germany's power was finally destroyed only by invading and dismembering the country, as the French hardliners had wanted to do in 1919. Chamberlain at Munich may have been wrong to believe that negotiation allowed the democracies to avoid both war and surrender. But no one can be certain that earlier resistance to Hitler would have offered a way out of the dilemma.

War or submission? Our views of what should have been done to stop Hitler in the 1930s are influenced by hindsight— by knowledge of World War II and the ghastly sufferings the Nazis inflicted on six million Jews and many other victims. We find it difficult to imagine how Chamberlain could have believed it wise to accommodate Germany in hope of avoiding a conflict that seemed to him the greater evil. Perhaps the greatest wisdom is to realize that the lessons of history do not repeat themselves exactly. Chamberlain correctly recognized that World War I resulted from the great powers' failure to manage a peripheral crisis effectively. But the origins of World War II lay rather in the limitless ambitions of a revived Germany. Before applying the lessons of history to the present and future, we need to examine carefully the validity of the analogy linking our own situation with the past.

Despite the rapidity of twentieth century change, 1914, 1939, and the 1980s do have one thing in common. Now as then the world is divided among sovereign nations that acknowledge no law

except that of self-preservation, by force if necessary. In such a world fascism, with its glorification of patriotism and violence, found imitators almost everywhere.

Fascism Around the World

As Hitler systematically overturned the obstacles to German power set up by the Versailles system, the momentum of fascism seemed irresistible. In imitation of this success, fascist or fascist-inspired movements appeared all over the world—testimony to the power of the European-dominated global configuration in shaping the ideologies of other countries as well as their economies.

Other European Fascist Movements

Few of these fascist movements succeeded in capturing power and some did not even command much attention. In developed northwestern Europe, British, Dutch, and Scandinavian fascists were insignificant political forces. In linguistically divided Belgium, ethnic tension produced two fascisms, one speaking Flemish and the other French, that together captured 20 percent of the vote in 1936. Militant right-wing leagues rioted in Paris in 1934, arousing fears of a fascist coup in France. But they were conservative rather than revolutionary, tamely submitting to dissolution by Léon Blum's government.

In southeastern Europe, by contrast, substantial fascist movements included the Hungarian Arrow Cross and the Rumanian Iron Guard. In both Hungary and Rumania, however, the conservative dictatorships were at least as ruthless as the fascists. Corneliu Codreanu, leader of the Iron Guard, was "shot while attempting to escape" after King Carol II suspended the Rumanian constitution and threw him into jail. When the Iron Guard attempted to regain control, the army crushed it.

The Brazilian Integralistas

A similar fate befell the most interesting of the Latin American fascisms of the 1930s, the Brazilian *Integralistas*. After borrowing many of their slogans, the dictator Getúlio Vargas prudently outlawed his fascist allies.

The Depression caused a collapse of Brazilian coffee prices. The ensuing crisis dealt the final blow to Brazil's republican government, which had been run by a tiny minority of the wealthy. In 1930 it was overthrown by Vargas, an ambitious provincial governor. This coup marked the beginning, not the end, of political uncertainty. The new constitution of 1934 extended the right to vote, launching Brazil on the perilous new course of democratic politics in a time of growing social unrest. An abortive Communist coup in 1935 expressed the discontent of industrial and plantation workers.

Amid similar anxieties, the middle classes of Italy and Germany had turned to fascism. In Brazil the urban lower middle class and small landowners made up three-quarters of the Integralista movement founded by Plinio Salgado in 1932. The movement copied European fascism in many respects, from its emphasis on centralized and authoritarian government and a corporatist economy to the stiff-armed salutes exchanged by its green-shirted militia. But it also reflected Brazil's particular circumstances. In a fervently Catholic country, the fascist motto was "God, Country, and Family." Moreover, Salgado explicitly condemned the racism of some European fascisms as inappropriate for a country with Brazil's mixed racial heritage.

As Brazil's first truly national political party, the Integralistas initially expected to take power by legal means, the only ones Salgado admitted. They were also encouraged by the tacit support they received from President Vargas, whose speeches stressed themes similar to theirs. But Vargas refused Salgado's offer of Green Shirt help against the Communists. He would tolerate no armed power to rival his own. The Integralistas would not, he explained, "Hindenburg" him. In 1937 he carried out a new coup d'état and established a more authoritarian political system, the Estado Novo (New State). To their horror, the Integralistas discovered that the new system's press censorship and prohibition of political parties applied to them, too. When some of them attempted a coup against Vargas in 1938, the ensuing shoot-out marked the end of the movement.

The Integralistas failed partly because of their own political naiveté. Trusting in Vargas and nonviolence, Salgado had none of Hitler's cunning. But the parallel failures of fascist movements in Mexico and Chile suggest that Latin American societies lacked some of the essential ingredients for successful fascism. None of these countries had experienced the mass mobilization and disruptive horror of World War I. Indeed, Latin American armies rarely fought wars. They devoted their time to politics instead, often providing their own brand of authoritarian rule. Moreover, despite some industrialization, most of Latin America in the

1930s had not yet developed mass movements of the proletarian Left, such as those that had made fascism attractive to the European middle classes. For all these reasons, fascism failed in Latin America in the 1930s.

The Lebanese Phalange

The 1930s also produced short-lived protofascist movements in the Middle East—Blue Shirts and Green Shirts in Egypt, Gray Shirts and White Shirts in Syria, Khaki Shirts in Iraq. Arabs under British and French rule had reason to copy the political style of Germany and Italy, the enemies of their enemies. But in the Middle East, the social groups that constituted the core of European fascism were too small or too strictly controlled to permit Arab fascism to develop fully. Nonetheless, at least one such movement founded in the 1930s survives in the 1980s, a reminder of the permanent temptation of fascism for people who feel that history has wronged or is threatening them.

Five young Western-educated Christian Arabs founded *Al Kata'ib*, otherwise known as the Lebanese *Phalange*, on November 21, 1936. Their leader was pharmacist Pierre Gemayel. Captain of the Lebanese soccer team at the 1936 Berlin Olympic games, Gemayel had been struck by German discipline, which contrasted sharply with the bitter division of his homeland.

Historically, the name Lebanon referred not to a state, but to a smaller region within a larger one, Syria. Mountainous Lebanon had long been a refuge for religious minorities. When the League of Nations gave France control of the region after World War I, it created the Republic of Lebanon, which contained some seventeen religious sects.

Maronite Christians, like Gemayel, who had important historic links to the Papacy and France, were the largest sect, even though they represented less than a third of the population. Most of the rest were Muslims. Most Muslims resented Maronite dominance, which they believed rested on foreign support. Then and now, many Muslims even resented the French-imposed idea that Lebanon should be a country separate from Syria and the rest of the Arab world.

In such a situation, the task of Gemayel's Phalange was obvious. It recruited Maronite students, apprentices, shopkeepers, and minor bureaucrats into a militia that could defend their community and the Maronite-dominated Lebanese order. Their slogan was "God, Country, Family"—the same as the Brazilian Integralistas'. Members between the ages of eighteen and thirty-five were organized into 600-man "phalanxes," which carried out military drills in their tan shirts. The motto, the military trappings, and the early insistence of the Phalangists that they were not a political party, all link this movement with fascistic movements elsewhere. After Lebanon became independent from France in 1943, however, the Phalange gradually evolved into a political party. Yet it never lost its military dimension and still had 70,000 men under arms a generation after Pierre Gemayel's visit to Berlin. In the Lebanese civil war that began in 1975, it played a leading role in defending the Maronite position.

Conclusion: The Permanent Temptation of Fascism

To what extent has fascism survived into the 1980s? Appearances may be deceptive. Genuine fascism appears to have disappeared. The fascism of Hitler and Mussolini arose in response to a specific set of conditions in the aftermath of World War I and ended with the destruction of their regimes in 1945. Their defeat has discredited most of the ideas and symbols we associate with them. Though the Lebanese Phalange still exists, it may never have fully met our definition of fascism. Its founders were primarily reacting to Lebanese problems and had little real knowledge of the European fascism that vaguely influenced them.

On the other hand, fascism was a response to central themes of twentieth-century life. Its nationalism appealed to the resentment of peoples who felt oppressed. Its revolutionary conservatism was a violent protest against the erosion of traditional societies by the acceleration of change. Fascists boasted that they had succeeded, where democracy failed, in combining mass politics with effective government. Ideologically, fascism curiously mingled the twentieth century's mania for technology with its uneasy feeling that human beings were losing touch with their roots in nature. Above all fascism gave its adherents a set of values—belief in the nation and its leader—that were comforting in an age when most values were questioned.

These themes remain central to today's world. Thus, we should not be surprised to see something like the fascism of the interwar period reappear, though under a different guise and bearing a different name.

Notes

1. Alan Bullock, *Hitler: A Study in Tyranny*, rev. ed. (New York: Harper & Row, 1964), p. 408.

Suggestions for Further Reading

Adamthwaite, Anthony, *The Making of the Second World War* (1979).

Aycoberry, Pierre, *The Nazi Question: An Essay on the Interpretations of National Socialism* (1981).

Bullock, Alan, *Hitler: A Study in Tyranny* (rev. ed. 1964).

Cassells, Alan, *Fascism* (1975).

Hilton, S., "*Ação Integralista Brasileira:* Fascism in Brazil, 1932–1938," *Luso-Brazilian Review*, 9 (December 1972).

Laqueur, Walter, ed., *Fascism: A Reader's Guide* (1976).

Smith, Denis Mack, *Mussolini: A Biography* (1982).

Taylor, Alan, *The Origins of the Second World War* (1962).

Weber, Eugen, *Varieties of Fascism* (1964).

Chapter 7

WESTERN INTELLECTUAL AND ARTISTIC LIFE BETWEEN THE WORLD WARS

At the beginning of the twentieth century, Western societies still took a largely optimistic view of the world and human nature. This confident perspective had almost been destroyed by the end of the 1930s. The slaughters of World War I, the degeneration of the Bolshevik Revolution into Stalinist dictatorship, and the success of fascist movements that glorified violence and scorned liberal values made nonsense of the idea that the future would be a story of progress. The twentieth century had become, in the words of poet W. H. Auden, the "age of anxiety."

Much earlier in the twentieth century, new discoveries had undercut confident nineteenth-century assumptions about the nature of the universe and human beings. These new ideas, reinforced by postwar disillusionment, eventually colored social scientists' assumptions, artists' forms of expression, and political philosophers' analysis of that characteristic form of twentieth-century life, the mass society.

The Optimistic Vision Shattered

The Nineteenth-Century World of Certainty and Uniformity

Through history, social studies, the arts, and political analysis have evolved to reflect each era's understanding of the universe and of human personality. The liberalism that dominated the Western world at the end of the nineteenth century, for example, took for granted a model of the universe that any informed person could comprehend. Two hundred years earlier Isaac Newton had worked out physical laws describing the motions of the planets and of the particles that made up matter. This "majestic clockwork" universe ticked along as the result of invariable interactions between forces and masses. Energy was assumed to impart motion to matter in a uniform manner, for example, regardless of the place in space and time of the person observing their interaction. On this Newtonian model of a uniform nature, all the scientific and technical triumphs of modern Western civilization had been based. At the end of the nineteenth century, though new instruments and experiments were revealing some unaccountable deviations from Newton's laws, they had not yet been fundamentally challenged.

Human beings held a privileged place in this regular universe. By the end of the nineteenth century most educated people probably accepted the Darwinian view that human beings were a species of animal that had evolved from "lower" species over millions of years. Many scientists and philosophers argued that human actions and thoughts were determined by the same chemical and physical reactions that governed the rest of nature. They hoped eventually to work out laws of behavior that would make

human beings as predictable as the physical phenomena of the Newtonian universe.

Still, people's ability to comprehend their own nature and that of the world around them set them apart from the rest of the animal world, at the top of the evolutionary ladder. And Westerners felt that their particular capacity to understand the working of the universe and the mind set them above people of other cultures. Europeans and Americans tended to regard the customs and ideas of the African or Asian societies they had subjected to Western dominance as primitive or savage, characteristics of people less "evolved" than Westerners.

Until late in the nineteenth century, the mainstream of Western literature and art also embodied these basic assumptions about the nature of the world and of humanity. Graphic artists since the Renaissance had seen their task in much the same way. They devoted their skill to recreating the beauties of a natural world everyone could see and understand. Or they illustrated traditional themes—from the Greek and Roman classics, for example—taken from the long story of the human struggle with nature, including human nature.

Nineteenth-century Western artists differed in their choice of means to their goal—academic painters emphasized careful formal draftsmanship, whereas the impressionists valued vivid colors more. But all believed that their paintings instructed their audience in the nature of visible reality. Some artists insisted that art existed for itself alone and required no social or intellectual justification; but even they regarded themselves as educators.

Education was the cherished priority of late nineteenth-century Western liberalism. Its belief in the possibility of educating humanity is what links the nineteenth century's understanding of physical and human nature with its faith in liberalism and even democracy. If human intelligence had already understood the physical universe and might one day discover laws of human behavior, then governments must eliminate all obstacles to the development and use of the mind. Democracy was mobilizing great masses of people for participation in the political process. Universal education could raise even these masses to the level of rational decision making the nineteenth century's small middle-class elites believed they had achieved.

The Discovery of Relativity and the Unconscious

Even before 1914, this optimistic vision of the world and humanity had been undermined—ironically, by thinkers who themselves believed in an unvarying universe and in the rational powers of the human mind. Albert Einstein's equations depicted a universe of unknowable size whose operations flouted conventional notions of cause and effect. (Later scientists, better able to look out into space and within the atom, confirmed Einstein's theories experimentally.) At almost the same time, Sigmund Freud asserted that conscious reasoning was only one facet of the human mind, and not the basic one. Much human behavior sprang from feelings of which the individual remains unconscious. This revelation proved as devastating to nineteenth-century certainties as Einstein's equations. Among their other effects, Freud's discoveries undermined the assumption of Western cultural superiority by showing that "primitive" drives were common to all human beings.

Though both Einstein and Freud had completed their most important work before the end of World War I, they became famous only after 1918. In the disillusionment that followed the war, people were more receptive to their conclusions, which helped discredit the sometimes smug certainties of 1914. Similarly, authors and painters after 1918 used experimental techniques developed before the war as weapons against prewar society's basic assumptions.

The events of the 1920s and 1930s did little to restore prewar certainties. It was discouraging to find that large numbers of democracy's new mass electorate freely voted for fascist dictators. Insensible to liberal politics, mass humanity sometimes also seemed indifferent or hostile to modern literature, art, and architecture. People's readiness to consume mass-produced entertainment led some intellectuals to despair of the future of both democracy and traditional high culture.

On the eve of World War II, not much was left of the optimistic synthesis of Newtonian physics, rationalist psychology, objective literature and painting, and political and economic liberalism. The foundations of nineteenth-century certainty had been so undermined that there could be no going back. Everywhere one looked, uncertainty reigned. To discuss the Einsteinian natural world of astromechanics and atomic physics, for example, one had to use terms that only "relatively" approximated what they attempted to describe, rather than corresponding to the bedrock reality earlier centuries had taken for granted.

Einstein's Universe: Curved Space and Subatomic Particles

In the history of scientific understanding, occasional revolutions have interrupted long periods in which investigators accumulated experimental detail to confirm pre-existing assumptions. A scientific revolution occurs when new data cannot be fitted into the old framework of understanding. Scientists are then forced to abandon their old assumptions and propose new explanations. This new framework of basic explanations in turn stimulates experiments to develop new data to confirm it.

Such a revolution transformed physics, the science of matter and motion, between 1900 and 1950. Today we have grown accustomed to the practical consequences of its discoveries, from nuclear weapons to space vehicles. Early in the century, however, the men and women who provided the vision and the data for this physics revolution were so few that they met in quite a small room at the annual Solvay conferences.

Well before 1900, some of these scientists had noted experimental results that were hard to reconcile with the Newtonian model. In the Newtonian world of matter bounded by an absolute space and an absolute time, the same causes invariably produced the same results. In 1900 the German physicist Max Planck demonstrated that energy on the atomic scale proceeded not in a continuous flow but by periodic emissions he called *quanta*. Attempts to reconcile such internal phenomena of atoms with the Newtonian model of matter and motion proved unsatisfying.

At that moment in its history, physics needed not more observations, but a revolution. It was Albert Einstein (1879–1955) who provided a new insight into the nature of the universe as all-encompassing as Newton's had been.

Although it is impossible to explain genius, certain of Einstein's youthful traits help to explain how, at the age of twenty-six, he was able to "rebuild the universe in his head."[1] He grew up in the Jewish community of Munich, a mediocre student who dropped out of school at fifteen. By then, however, he had educated himself by wide reading, especially in the works of critical philosophers. This reading made him skeptical of most widely accepted ideas, including the tenets of formal religions. But Einstein had a special faith: though God might be unknowable, he would not have created a world unintelligible to humankind. The idea of such a world offended the young Einstein's sense of beauty as well as his faith.

Einstein's aesthetic sense of the necessary unity and order of the world, reinforced by a remarkable self-confidence, enabled him to set aside the accepted formulas of physics and to conceive new ones that better explained recent experimental findings.

The Theory of Special Relativity and $E = mc^2$

When Einstein finally completed his education in Switzerland, the only job he could find was as a patent examiner, evaluating the work of Swiss inventors. On the backs of discarded patent applications, he scribbled the equations that would make the twentieth century the age of atomic energy, the laser, and space flight. In 1905, within a few months, he published three papers that began a basic redefinition of space and time, matter and energy. The first paper, for which Einstein was awarded the Nobel Prize in 1921, demonstrated mathematically that light is composed of particles whose energy can be characterized by the quanta Planck had described.

A greater leap of the imagination was involved in Einstein's famous paper "On the Electrodynamics of Moving Bodies." As a boy he had wondered, "What would the world look like if I rode on a beam of light?" Sitting up in bed one morning, he suddenly found the answer to this question. To someone traveling at the constant speed of light, time on the earth would appear not to pass. What we observe of the passage of distance and time is "relative" to our own motion within the universe. Absolute distances and times do not exist.

This theory of special relativity had no practical consequences in 1905. (Today it explains why an astronaut in orbit sees the earth tumbling rapidly through space, while we on the earth's surface are unconscious of any such motion.) But in space and in the invisible world of subatomic particles, the theory had revolutionary implications. Einstein used it to arrive at a conclusion developed in his third 1905 paper and later expressed in the momentous equation "$E = mc^2$." This meant essentially that energy and mass were equivalent (so that, for example, the sun must lose mass as it dispenses the energy of sunlight). This equation proved fundamental to the future of both astronomy and atomic physics.

These papers established Einstein's reputation, and in 1914 he won a prestigious appointment at the Kaiser Wilhelm Institute in Berlin. There, a year later, he published his theory of general relativity, which argued that because light had mass, it was subject to the force of gravity. He suggested that the theory be tested by measuring how the light

from a distant star was deflected as it passed through the sun's gravitational field. In 1919, two British expeditions traveled to the coasts of Africa and of South America to take the prescribed measurements. When their results confirmed his prediction almost exactly, Einstein, to his amazement, suddenly found himself world-famous. The *London Times* proclaimed "Revolution in Science: Newtonian Ideas Overthrown."[2]

The rest of Einstein's life became a long anticlimax. For almost four decades he continued to elaborate his mathematical idea of a curved universe with both space and time as dimensions. Forced to flee Germany in 1933, he found refuge in the United States, becoming a professor at Princeton's Institute for Advanced Study. He worked there until his death in 1955.

From Atomic Physics to Atomic Weapons

By the time he died, Einstein had become a figure out of the past to younger physicists. He found it difficult to accept some of their new theories about the atom. A significant example was Werner Heisenberg's "principle of uncertainty" (1927), which held that the motion of subatomic particles (which we cannot directly observe) cannot be predicted except within a range of statistical probabilities. "God does not throw dice," declared Einstein. Though his discoveries had overthrown the predictable regularities of Newtonian physics, Einstein always hoped to construct a new framework for the universe that would not have to allow for such uncertainty.

Einstein was also unsympathetic to those who charged that in the relativistic world he had revealed, there could no longer be any absolute rules, even of moral conduct. He did not hesitate to condemn on ethical grounds the development of nuclear weapons, a stand that cost him some of his popularity in the cold war years.

Nuclear weapons were the most spectacular consequence of the revolutions in astronomy and nuclear physics that followed upon Einstein's demonstration that energy has mass, and mass has energy. In the 1920s, American astronomers, measuring the distances of stars by spectrographic analysis of their light emissions, confirmed the vision of an infinite universe of countless billions of stars. Another German refugee physicist, Hans Bethe, working at Cornell University in 1939, dramatically illustrated that Einsteinian principles could be simultaneously applied to both astrophysics and nuclear physics. Bethe showed precisely how the sun's loss of mass produces the energy of sunlight by transforming hydrogen into helium. In this way, he traced the origins of the matter that composes us and our world to the energy of stars that disintegrated several billion years before the sun and earth existed.

In 1905, Einstein had proposed testing his theory of special relativity by experimenting with the newly revealed phenomenon of radioactivity. By 1939 much more was known of the subatomic components of matter. Experiments at Cambridge University in England in 1932 confirmed Einstein's formulation of the relationship of energy to mass and revealed that the nucleus of the atom was not the basic unit of matter. Nuclei were composed of protons and neutrons. Within two years, at the University of Rome, Enrico Fermi applied this discovery by bombarding the nuclei of various atoms, including that of the heaviest element, uranium, with neutrons.

Fortunately for Nazism's future opponents in World War II, Fascist racism now diverted the unfolding of scientific inquiry. Fermi, whose wife was Jewish, had to flee Rome in 1938, when Mussolini imposed anti-Semitic laws similar to Hitler's. By then, nuclear scientists everywhere had learned of the tremendous energy that could be released in a chain-reaction splitting of uranium atoms. Politicians reacted slowly to this revelation. Hitler gave the potential weapon a low priority. Not until late in 1941 did the U.S. government decide to go all out to make a bomb. By then most of the physicists with the knowledge to undertake the task were refugees, like Einstein, in North America. Fermi led the team that achieved the first self-sustaining chain reaction releasing nuclear energy, at the University of Chicago on December 2, 1942. This date marked the dawning of the atomic age and the first step toward the atomic bombs that would be exploded over Japanese cities in 1945.

When Einstein learned of the first test of an atomic weapon, he groaned aloud. The equations he had developed in the Swiss patent office had led indirectly to the most destructive weapon yet devised. The advent of nuclear weapons heightened the uncertainty of the twentieth century. Nor in the long run were the implications of relativity theory and probabilistic quantum mechanics reassuring. Scientific popularizers interpreted those implications in the best light for the societies they addressed. The British astrophysicist Sir Arthur Eddington, a Quaker, firmly denied that the Einsteinian view of the world in any way invalidated the Christian view. At the same time, Soviet physicists contended that Einsteinian physics affirmed the material reality underlying Marxist dialectical materialism.

Historically, people have reassured themselves of their grasp on reality by citing scientific discoveries to bolster their basic beliefs. Still the world view of Albert Einstein revealed that human perceptions of the realities of both space and matter are imperfect: subjective, not objective. The psychological doctrines of Freud re-enforced this humbling evaluation of human capacities.

Freud: The Path into the Unconscious

Sigmund Freud (1856–1939) launched another intellectual revolution. Freud was guided by a nineteenth-century faith that reason can ascertain regular causes for all behavior. Like Einstein, he was tough-minded enough to persevere in his explanations even when they led him to conclusions that contradicted his initial assumptions. But Freud's investigations of the human personality had a far more direct influence on intellectuals and the public than Einstein's theories of the cosmos. Freud's conclusions were far more controversial. Although he emphasized dimensions of human nature that many people would prefer not to discuss, his ideas have been assimilated into the foundations of twentieth-century Western culture.

The Founding of Psychoanalysis

Though he had won some earlier international recognition among psychologists, Freud's work became popularly

Sigmund Freud with his fiancée Martha Bernays, 1885. Much of this year the young doctor spent studying with a famous neurologist in Paris.
The Granger Collection

known only in the disillusioned aftermath of World War I. His emphasis on the irrational elements of human motivation appealed to a generation outraged by a pointless war. Ironically, however, it was Freud's nineteenth-century faith in the ability of the reasoning mind to discover the causes of phenomena that led him into the realm of the unconscious. He based his model of the mind's workings on analogy with the nineteenth-century concept of energy. To the end of his life, he regarded himself as an experimental scientist. Although some people felt his discoveries had revealed the hypocrisy of conventional Western standards of behavior, Freud remained a moralist.

All these traits can be traced to his youth in Vienna, where he spent almost all his life. The son of a Jewish merchant, he was a voracious reader, like Einstein. Freud felt strong artistic inclinations, but decided he must discipline this side of his personality by pursuing a scientific career. He wrote a postgraduate thesis on the reproductive system of the eel. Ultimately he became a doctor of medicine, specializing in neurology.

By the late nineteenth century, physicians had begun to try to treat the victims of mental disorder, rather than simply locking them up as earlier ages had done. Their working assumption was that mental illness arose from organic causes—for example, damaged brain cells. This was a natural assumption in an age that was discovering the bacterial causes of most infectious diseases. But there was evidence that an organic explanation did not always apply.

An older friend and colleague, Josef Breuer, described to Freud his treatment of a patient, "Anna O.," whose hysterical symptoms included occasional paralysis, inability to drink water, and trances. Breuer had experimented with the novel technique of hypnosis. When hypnotized, Anna O. recalled memories of which she had been unconscious, but which were related to her symptoms. Recalling them relieved the symptoms. Such evidence made Freud doubt that the workings of the mind were determined wholly by physical causes. Mistrustful of hypnotism, he began asking his patients to relax and concentrate on their symptoms while he questioned them to evoke related memories. Bringing such memo-

ries up to the surface often relieved the symptoms. Clearly, then, some symptoms of mental illness had a "functional" cause: the mind itself, under the pressure of unconscious memories, generated painful symptoms.

Freud's next advance along the path into the unconscious came when a patient told him not to interrupt the stream of her recollections with questioning. Freud started to encourage his patients to "free-associate": to tell him whatever came into their consciousness, however shameful or absurd it might seem. He found that patients who talked in this way repeatedly brought up suppressed memories of a childhood sexual seduction by a parent. Freud soon decided that not all these parental sexual assaults could really have occurred. The origins of such "recollections" were as mysterious as the strange events of his patients' dreams. Yet Freud had been schooled in the nineteenth-century conviction that all phenomena have definite causes.

To find the cause of his patients' fantasies and dreams, Freud began to look within his own personality, following his own free associations wherever they led, regardless of pain. This self-analysis took him over the threshold of the unconscious mind. He did not "discover" that world, which had long haunted artists. Freud's achievement was to demonstrate the influence of the unconscious on human behavior and to develop a therapeutic method for dealing with that influence.

The model Freud developed for explaining the workings of the human mind is already visible in his book *The Interpretation of Dreams* (1899). His fundamental metaphor derived from pre-Einsteinian physics. Like physical energy, Freud believed, psychic energy—thoughts and emotions—might be transformed but not eliminated altogether. Dreams, for example, offered a harmless way to express feelings forbidden to daytime consciousness. Neurotic behavior and hysterical symptoms like paralysis were other forms of transformation. The unconscious found a variety of outlets for the pressure of unthinkable thoughts.

Freud gave the name *id* to the dynamo within the human personality that produces all this emotional energy. The id's power comes from primitive drives toward physical, essentially sexual, pleasure. But human societies could not function if the only outlet for emotional energy were the satisfaction of animal instincts. Therefore, Freud held, another element of the mind, the *ego*, redirects psychic energy into socially acceptable channels. These are defined by the *super-ego*, which enforces parental and social standards of behavior. Freud thus saw the human personality as a system of emotional energies in constant tension. The ego faces a continuous challenge to transform the animal impulses of the id, which are always present in the unconscious, into behavior acceptable to the strict superego. Sometimes this transformation is successful, as when the sexual impulse Freud called *libido* is "sublimated" into the creative artistic impulse. Sometimes it is not: unconscious drives then become neurotic behavior or even disabling mental illness. The treatment Freud developed for such conditions is called psychoanalysis.

In his later years, Freud increasingly turned from the specifics of psychoanalysis to wider concerns. Like Einstein, he aspired to a comprehensive explanation of the phenomena he studied—all human behavior. Comparing the myths and taboos of "primitive" peoples with those of the West, he concluded that the tension between instinct and repression affects human societies as well as individual personalities. The price human beings paid for social organization was an immense burden of guilt over repressed instincts (incestual ones, Freud believed). Because guilt found its outlet in violence, civilization was a fragile creation, in which people's instinct to love was perpetually counterbalanced by their impulses to destroy one another.

The destructiveness of World War I thus came as no surprise to Freud. Nor was the postwar emergence of political movements like Nazism unpredictable. When Hitler annexed Austria in 1938, Freud had to flee the city that had been his home for over eighty years. While the Nazis gleefully burned his books, he died a refugee in London in 1939.

Freud's Influence

An attempt to assess Freud's impact on the twentieth-century world yields a complicated verdict. Even psychologists who acknowledge their debt to his inspiration have modified his ideas by stressing nonsexual motivations and the effects of social as well as instinctual drives, and adult as well as childhood experiences, on personality development.

Since 1973, a new organic interpretation of behavior has arisen from the dramatic development of "molecular psychology." Scientists have identified chemical reactions in the brain corresponding to such mental states as depression or aggressiveness. As one leader of this school explained, "People who act crazy are acting that way because they have too much or too little of some chemicals . . . in their brains. It's just physical illness! The brain is a physical thing!"[3] If this molecular approach eventually revolutionizes psychology's basic framework of assumptions, we may conclude that science has come full circle since Freud abandoned purely organic explanations for mental illness before 1900. Indeed, critics are now arguing that many of the human characteristics Freud believed universal were merely the peculiarities of his middle-class, turn-of-the-century Viennese patients. For example, Freud asserted that women think of themselves as incomplete men. But feminists have rightly pointed out that Freud's view reflects the male dominance in Viennese society of his day, not a universal truth.

None of these developments means that Freud has lost his importance for the twentieth-century world. On a nontechnical level, his model of human psychology has been so widely diffused through Western culture that we are almost unaware of its influence. Terms like the "Freudian slip"—the slip of the tongue that betrays our unconscious feelings—or "wish fulfillment"—the process by which we fantasize what we cannot have—have become part of the everyday vocabulary of educated people. Everyone from advertising copywriters to political campaign managers assumes that our decision making reflects subconscious as well as conscious motivations.

In the 1920s, popular oversimplification led many people, especially in the United States, to conclude that the chief lesson of Freud's teachings was that human beings should not feel guilty about their sexual impulses. Freud himself was no advocate of unbridled permissiveness, but he recognized the intensity of the conflict between the dictates of instinct and the rules of society. In the long run, his work has probably led to greater tolerance of those who fail to resolve that conflict—not only the officially mentally ill and the socially deviant, but the many "normal" people who suffer breakdowns or violate the moral standards set up by some authority. Such tolerance has proved to have narrow limits, however, and twentieth-century societies are periodically confronted by demands for a return to punitive standards. Freud's demonstration that every society develops its own repressive codes to control the universal impulses of the unconscious was another example of the twentieth-century collapse of certainty. It implied that far from being absolute, ethical standards, like the physical observations of the Einsteinian universe, are not absolute but "relative" to whoever pronounces them.

Cultural Relativism: Non-Western Societies and European Global Dominance

The years after World War I also produced a relativist revolution in the study of human societies and cultures. A new kind of anthropology significantly altered Western intellectuals' perspective on the many other peoples of the twentieth-century world.

The methods and assumptions of Western study of non-Western peoples remained ethnocentric well into the twentieth century. Information about non-Western customs and beliefs was typically collected as quaint behavior of peoples who had not yet reached the "higher" levels of civilization prevailing in the West.

If any single individual was responsible for rejecting this approach and founding modern cultural anthropology, it was Bronislaw Malinowski (1884–1942), professor of anthropology at the

University of London and later at Yale. Born a Polish subject of the Austro-Hungarian Empire, he studied in Germany, did research in the Southwest Pacific, and taught in Britain and the United States. His career is an illustration of the shrinking of the twentieth-century world. Its turning point came when he accompanied a team of British anthropologists to study Australian aborigines. When the outbreak of World War I made him an enemy alien, the Australian authorities consented to intern him in the Trobriand Islands of eastern New Guinea. His first book about the islanders, *Argonauts of the Western Pacific* (1922), marked an anthropological revolution. In the next thirteen years he wrote six more books about every aspect of Trobriand life, from sexual behavior to methods of cultivation.

Like Einstein and Freud, Malinowski began with a conviction that careful observation would yield universal laws—in this case, of societal organization. A man of cosmopolitan background, he was shocked by the ignorance of white people who had lived in places like the Trobriands for years, learning nothing of a "native" culture they scorned. A Westerner could not understand such a culture by looking at it from outside. Intensive fieldwork, such as Malinowski had used to study the Trobrianders, was necessary. That meant living among the people, speaking their language fluently, learning "to grasp the native's point of view, his relation to life . . . *his* vision of *his* world."[4]

To Malinowski, a culture was a totality. Every part of a people's system of customs and beliefs, however odd it might appear, served an essential social function, sometimes better than the corresponding Western ones did. Although a Westerner might dismiss the Trobrian-ders' magic as superstition, for example, it served the essential function of relieving human anxiety about the unknown. Every culture was a complex structure functioning to meet basic human needs. Descriptions like "savage" or "primitive" were all relative, and every culture had its own value.

This "functionalist" revolution in anthropology challenged the easy assumption of Western cultural superiority. The principle of cultural relativism, though now taken for granted by social scientists, was not immediately accepted by everyone. European colonial administrators joked scornfully about the mythical anthropologist who would tolerate head-hunting if it was an authentic tribal custom. For many other people in the West, Hollywood's stereotype of the prancing, grunting, simple-minded "native" probably remained intact.

Ironically, as revolutionary movements aimed at throwing off Western dominance developed in the non-Western world, especially after World War II, some of their leaders denounced anthropological interest in traditional ways of life. They saw it as a neocolonial attempt to keep Africans and Asians dependent by isolating them from Western progress. Nevertheless, in the years after World War I, Western cultural superiority was seriously questioned—in part because of the advent of cultural relativism, but also because of the war's revelation that Western peoples, too, lived by myths. It was myth, for example, that mobilized men in the trenches of 1914. Malinowski wrote:

We cannot possibly reach the final . . . wisdom of knowing ourselves if we never leave the normal confinement of the customs, beliefs, and prejudices into which every man is born. Nothing can teach us a better lesson . . . than the habit of mind which allows us to treat the beliefs and values of another man from his point of view. Nor has civilized humanity ever needed such tolerance more than now, when prejudice, ill will, and vindictiveness are dividing each . . . nation from another. . . .[5]

For many Western intellectuals who thought as Malinowski did, twentieth-century standards of culture and social organization, like observations of physical phenomena and moral norms, revealed not an absolute but only a relative truth.

Modern Art and Architecture: Mind versus Eye

Twentieth-century art underwent a transformation as dramatic as the revolutions in physics and psychology. Artists came to believe that their quest for absolute truth demanded more than faithfulness to the appearances of nature and to traditional themes. Even before 1914, an "advance guard" of painters and architects were experimenting with radically new forms. World War I reinforced these artistic revolutionaries by discrediting the prewar order of things. As modern physics penetrated behind appearances to a subatomic reality it could describe only by abstractions, and as modern psychology probed the human unconscious, avant-garde modern art tried to express these new aspects of experience through continued experimentation with new forms. Some of these artists portrayed a world whose reality was so relative to their own perceptions that it appeared absurd. Most, however, still believed that the function of art was to explain experience, though they now used new idioms to express the new realities. Within the first generation of the twentieth century, a cultured minority of Western art lovers had accepted these radical new forms of modern art as standard. But their abstract quality opened a gap between artistic standards and popular tastes wider than Western civilization had yet known.

Probably the most popular school of painting in the history of art, and one that still delights gallery-goers today, was the French impressionists. They were the advance guard of the 1870s, who attempted to achieve a genuine "impression" of nature by using color to depict the play of light over objects. By 1900, however, their appeal to the eye had become routine. Some of the greatest impressionists by then were experimenting with new forms, which were avidly taken up by a younger generation. Monet practically dissolved nature into an indistinct shimmer of light. Cézanne tried to get beneath the impressions of the eye to an underlying reality that was almost geometric. Landscape painting, he declared, "is not copying the object, it is realizing one's sensations."[6]

Around 1905, the same goal inspired the painting of the Fauve (Wild Beast) group. This short-lived school was given its name by a critic startled by the contrast between the painters' distorted lines and violent colors and the cool moderation of the classical tradition.

It was the cubist movement that most dramatically signaled twentieth-century artists' new idiom. In one painting (*Les Demoiselles d'Avignon*, 1907) the young Pablo Picasso (1881–1973) summed up the revolutionary currents that combined to launch the modern art of the twentieth century. Like many artists before him, Picasso represented a group of standing female nudes—but in a manner than has been called "the first radically new proposition about the way we see

Pablo Picasso's *Demoiselles d'Avignon* (1907). In this work, Picasso painted faces like tribal masks; he admired what he saw as the imaginative distortion of African art. For Africans, however, the design of masks was traditional (see example on page 208).
Museum of Modern Art, New York, Lillie P. Bliss Bequest

that painting had made in almost five hundred years."[7] The faces are those of African tribal masks. (Picasso, a Spaniard then living in Paris, had seen such masks at a colonial exhibition.) The jutting, distorted angles and planes seek to capture the underlying geometric essence of being, not its superficial appearances. "I paint forms," Picasso explained, "as I think them, not as I see them." Addressed to the mind rather than the eye, *Les Demoiselles* still shocks us by its bold-

ness. So does another classic of modern art, Marcel Duchamp's *Nude Descending a Staircase*. Derided as "an explosion in a shingle factory" when it was exhibited in New York in 1913, *Nude* had to be carefully guarded against vandals. Its effort to portray muscular motion seemed as outlandish as Einstein's vision of a universe in which space-time was a dimension.

Twentieth-century physicists' discovery of an ultimate reality that we cannot actually see—the subatomic particle—helped to inspire another revolutionary prewar artistic school, abstract expressionism. *Expressionism* simply meant that artists' task was to tell the truth as they perceived it. For the Russian Vasili Kandinski (1866–1944) the truth of this invisible subatomic world was God's presence everywhere. The artist who sought to convey spiritual reality must therefore teach his audience to disregard what they saw in favor of symbols of what they could only sense. In this way, Kandinski's expression of truth became an art of pure abstraction, representing no recognizable object at all. Although Kandinski's abstractions expressed a joyful, personal truth, many expressionists' truth was a lonely, fear-ridden existence in the twentieth-century metropolis. A forerunner of expressionism, Norwegian Edvard Munch (1863–1944) anticipated the world of Freudian psychology, in which human reason was torn between instinctual needs and society's constraints. The terrified face in *The Scream* (1893) is modeled on that of an Incan mummy Munch had seen in a Paris anthropological museum. The picture itself became one of the twentieth century's most frightening images of the human experience: a cry of personal, subjective horror to a merciless sky and indifferent passers-by. Munch wrote on the canvas, "Can only have been painted by a madman." Before 1914 his vision was an isolated one. World War I, however, made the madman's nightmare real.

The Night by Max Beckmann (1918–1919) is the work of a German stretcher-bearer who became so depressed at what he saw in the front lines that he was given a medical discharge. The obscene and senseless violence of this grisly canvas shows a truth of war very different from the heroic images projected by the parades and monuments of prewar Berlin.

Not all artists shared Beckmann's dark vision of the human future. Most of the brilliant Russian painters who had made Moscow a center of the avant-garde before 1914 enlisted their art in the service of the Bolshevik Revolution. They were encouraged by Lenin's commissar of education, Anatoli Lunacharski, who believed as they did that art could reach the masses and inspire political commitment. Thus modern art became part of the "agitprop" effort to mobilize Russia's peasant masses for the revolution through agitation and propaganda. Artists decorated railroad cars to become rolling billboards for the Bolshevik cause: a modernization of the long Russian tradition of painting icons—religious images—to inspire the faith of the illiterate.

The association of modern art with Soviet communism ended with Lenin's death. Stalin rejected the forms of modern art as pretentiously middle-class, demanding instead "socialist realism": portraits of smiling, heroic, muscle-bulging tractor drivers, for example. By the 1930s, as modern-minded artists like Marc Chagall fled Stalinist censorship, official Soviet art sank into mediocrity. For the Russian school of modern art, revolutionary hope ended in cruel disappointment.

In most of the rest of Europe, where there was no revolution to inspire the postwar artistic generation, the most important school during the 1920s was the surrealists. They took their inspiration not from politics but from their radical break with the Western tradition of perceiving reality. They saw the destructiveness of World War I as disastrous proof of the Western error of detaching human

Max Beckmann, *The Night* **(1918–1919).** The painting reflects the artist's horror at the cruelty and chaos of both World War I and the postwar German revolution. The sinister figure in the cloth cap at far right is clearly modelled on Lenin.
Kunstsammlung Nordrhein-Westfalen, Dusseldorf

beings, as supposedly independent observers, from their own natural surroundings. Westerners' tendency to attribute reality to only certain objects of their imperfect sense perceptions was leading them to eventual annihilation. The French poet André Breton, spiritual leader of surrealism, remarked after 1945, "The atomic bomb had its origin in Descartes' brain." He meant that Western civilization had been on the wrong track ever since the seventeenth-century philosopher had declared that human existence was defined by the capacity for rational thought: a capacity that enabled people by the twentieth

century to design a weapon of total destruction.

Challenging the stubborn Western insistence that things must be what perception says they are, the surrealists sought artistic truth as far from reason as possible. They found it in the unconscious, as it emerged from the perceptions of children and madmen, from the "primitive" art of non-Western peoples, and from dreams. The young, the mad, the savage, and the dreamer were more in touch with the real world, surrealists believed, because their thought remained unfocused, unlike the specialist thinking of Westerners. The goal of art was to free the mind from reason's constraints, enabling it to break though to the surreal—the "more than real"—these nonreasoners could perceive. Surrealist painting extended the forms of World War I Dadaism, which had tried to shock people into rethinking their assumptions by offering the familiar in a jarringly unfamiliar way. Salvador Dali's limp watches outrage our sense of reality, but remind us that in the Einsteinian universe time is relative to the observer and can be told as well by a melting watch as by a normal one. The message of modern art, like the message of twentieth-century physics and psychology, was that things were not as they appeared to the eye, but as they appeared to the mind.

The principal idea of the dominant twentieth-century school of architecture was that if decoration were stripped away, buildings could reveal their underlying essence, appearing to the eye what they were to the mind. Form should reflect function: a railroad terminal should look like just that, not like a Roman bath. Improvements in build-

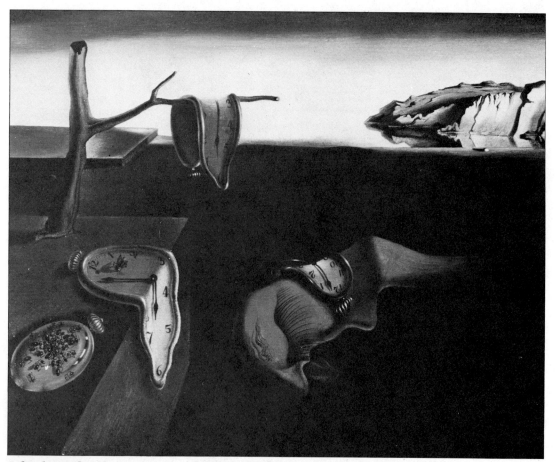

Salvador Dali, *The Persistence of Memory* (1931). Another surrealist lesson in the unreliability of the senses. The objects are real; the whole landscape madly unreal.
Collection, The Museum of Modern Art, New York

ing materials and methods in the late nineteenth century prepared the way for this architectural revolution. A steel framework, rather than the walls, now could carry the load of a structure. The structure itself could be built of lighter materials like reinforced concrete and glass. The Bauhaus architects (who took their name from the famous school of design that flourished briefly in Weimar Germany) used these materials to build the severely unornamented buildings they felt realism required. The most famous example is New York's Seagram Building, built in the 1950s to the design of Ludwig Mies Van Der Rohe. By then, Bauhaus architecture had become the so-called international style, spreading its undecorated glass boxes around the world.

By the 1950s, this avant-garde style had become standard. What had once been revolutionary became ordinary. The same fate befell modern art. Its institutionalization began as early as 1929, with the establishment in New York of the Museum of Modern Art. Collection in a museum was a sign of acceptance for modern styles like cubism and abstract expressionsim. A late cubist painting like Picasso's *Guernica* (1937), his protest against the Nazi bombing of a Spanish republican town and by extension against all inhumanity, quickly became an antifascist symbol recognized far beyond the circle of artistic connoisseurs.

Acceptance did not come without a struggle. For many people, modern art expressed everything that was new and disturbing about the twentieth century: the crumbling of a comprehensible universe, the exposure of once unmentionable human drives, the suggestion that "primitive" cultures had something to teach the West, the growth of uncertainty about everything. Stalin was not

the only dictator to reject it. In 1937 Hitler ordered the staging of two contrasting exhibitions, one of "degenerate" modern art, the other of "German" art, depicting the blond and muscular Master Race at work and play. His goal was to demonstrate how politically motivated art could restore the certainty undermined by modernism and its questions.

The Emergence of Mass Culture

Hitler had at least one thing in common with many modern artists: a belief that art's function was to instruct and inspire as many people as possible. In the 1920s and 1930s, however, it became clear that a great many people—"the masses"—were not much interested in art-gallery art of any kind. To the dismay of many intellectuals, a new kind of popular culture was emerging. It was very different from either the high culture of the nineteenth-century middle-class elite or traditional folk cultures.

Sociological and technological change both fostered a new mass culture in the twentieth century. As improved transportation and universal schooling broke down rural isolation and people migrated from the countryside to the cities, the old peasant folk cultures—the regional costumes, dances, dialects, and legends—began to disappear well before the end of the nineteenth century. Increasingly they were replaced by a commercial, standardized culture. By the late 1930s, most households in Western Europe and in the United States had radios, for example. The movies had become an international industry. The products of these mass media—radio soap operas and quiz shows, movie serials and Westerns—helped to fill the urban masses' new leisure time, made possible by shortened work weeks. To intellectual critics, such entertainment amounted to little more than escapism—empty diversions from reality. Moreover, they were increasingly the same the world over. Jazz, for example, once the special music of New Orleans, spread in the 1920s over the airwaves of the world.

Many critics were profoundly disappointed by people's uncritical enthusiasm for the trite and trivial. A basic assumption behind the nineteenth-century drive for a democratic political system was that a majority would decide intelligently when offered a choice. After World War I, the revelation of the level of mass taste reinforced many intellectuals' doubts about the practicability of the democratic ideal.

Even before 1914, the conservative Italian political philosophers Vilfredo Pareto and Robert Michels had argued that every government or political movement, even a democracy, really expresses the power of an elite, which legitimizes its rule with slogans calculated to win mass support. Max Weber, the leading German figure in the new twentieth-century science of sociology, suggested that in modern Western societies the growth of democratic participation was a less significant trend than the expansion of bureaucracies' power to control whole populations by subjecting them to standardized rules. He also warned that as other forms of government broke down, the masses would follow with religious zeal leaders who had the magical attribute of charisma—a prediction soon borne out when Mussolini and Hitler came to power.

It was a Spanish philosopher, José Ortega y Gasset, who offered the most sweeping indictment of mass society. His *Revolt of the Masses* (1930) predicted that Western societies would be overwhelmed by masses too numerous to educate in the art of critical thinking essential to freedom. Swamping the cultured minority, they would impose their low standards on everything from art to politics, ultimately destroying the fragile foundations of a civilization whose material benefits they took for granted. "The world is a civilized one," he wrote; "its inhabitant is not":

. . . he does not see the civilization of the world around him, but he uses it as if it were a natural force. The new man wants his motor-car, and enjoys it, but he believes it is the spontaneous fruit of an Edenic tree. In the depths of his soul he is unaware of the artificial, almost incredible character of civilization, and does not extend his enthusiasm for the instruments to the principles which make them possible.[8]

We may dismiss such criticisms as the complaints of an educated elite that had lost its political dominance. Nevertheless they reflected still another twentieth-century uncertainty. Just as Newtonian physics, rationalist psychology, and the assumption of Western cultural superiority had been undermined, late nineteenth-century faith in the future of liberal democracy was profoundly shaken.

Conclusion: An Age of Uncertainty

Developments in physics, psychology, social science, and art together amounted to a cultural revolution. In fact, the twentieth century produced or reinforced breaks with the past in almost every field. The twelve-toned compositions of Arnold Schönberg, for example, designed to appeal to the mind more

René Magritte's *Treason of Images* (1928–1929). The painting stresses the surrealist theme that images are treacherous clues to reality. "This," says the inscription in French, "is not a pipe." Instead, it is an image of something people agree to *call* a pipe.

Los Angeles County Museum of Art. Purchased with funds provided by the Mr. and Mrs. William Harrison Collection

than the ear, marked a radical departure from classical music's traditions of harmony and melody. In philosophy, the publication in 1921 of Ludwig Wittgenstein's *Tractatus Logico-Politicus* was a fundamental turning point. Wittgenstein contemptuously dismissed centuries of philosophical speculation about ethics and the causes of things as mere superstition. Henceforth, he declared, philosophy should consider only propositions that could be expressed mathematically.

From these multiple breaks with the past emerged the Western intellectual and cultural world we know today. One of its most noteworthy features is its unintelligibility as whole. In the nineteenth century, it had still been possible for an individual to grasp the basic principles of most categories of human knowledge. In the twentieth century, knowledge became increasingly fragmented. No one thinker any longer claimed to provide an interpretation of the whole of experience. Scientists, psychologists, authors, artists, and philosophers all specialized in providing particular sorts of difficult abstractions from reality, ranging from the language of astrophysics to that of molecular biology. Less and less were the discoveries of each set of specialists understandable to others, let alone to the vast majority of nonspecialists.

To the extent that ordinary people associated scientific discoveries with the advent of bountiful new technologies, they welcomed them. Mass media made Einstein and Freud popular celebrities. But like the masters of modern literature and art, they also encountered a great deal of hostility, for the uncertainties they revealed tended to undermine some valued human convictions. Though Einstein was deeply religious in his own way, it was difficult to see his infinite, only "relatively" comprehensible universe as the work of a Creator. Freud's model of unconscious motivations threatened the foundations of traditional morality, which assumed that people could readily distinguish right from wrong. Anthropologists' comparisons of non-Western and Western societies, not always to Western advantage, implied to many people an insulting disregard of Western civilization's achievements. The incomprehensible quality of much modern literature and art offended people accustomed to more conventional images, reminding them again that everything once apparently solid and unassailable had become fluid and problematical. Instead of providing reassurance, novels and paintings strained the understanding in an effort to prove that all human judgments were subjective, and all human statements about reality merely relative.

The twentieth century's vision at its bleakest was embodied in Franz Kafka's famous novel *The Trial* (1925). Its hero is matter-of-factly tried and executed, amid the bustle of a great city, for some crime of which he knows nothing and which is never explained to him by his bland judges. The novel is a powerful metaphorical statement of the human predicament as it appeared to many twentieth-century thinkers. The individual seemed a lonely, uncomprehending speck in a universe where nothing was as it appeared and nothing meaningful could be said. Faced with such a vision, people have continued to search desperately for something to replace the lost certainties of 1900: an ideology, a faith, something to hang on to. For many thoughtful Europeans in the 1930s, this anguish of uncertainty was heightened by their consciousness that European global dominance was waning and that another war was approaching.

Notes

1. Nigel Calder, *Einstein's Universe* (New York: Penguin Books, 1979), p. 12.
2. Raymond V. Sontag, *A Broken World* (New York: Harper and Row, 1971), p. 181.
3. Dr. Candace Pert of the National Institutes of Health, quoted in the *Baltimore Evening Sun*, July 23, 1984.
4. Bronislaw Malinowski, *Argonauts of the Western Pacific*, (New York: E. P. Dutton, 1922) p. 25.
5. Malinowski, *Argonauts*, p. 518.
6. Quoted in Robert Hughes, *The Shock of the New* (New York: Alfred A. Knopf, 1981), on which this section is largely drawn, p. 125.
7. Hughes, *Shock of the New*, p. 15.
8. José Ortega y Gasset, *The Revolt of the Masses* (New York: W. W. Norton & Co., 1957), p. 82.

Suggestions for Further Reading

Bronowski, Jacob, *The Ascent of Man* (1974).

Calder, Nigel, *Einstein's Universe* (1980).

Ellenberger, Henri F., *The Discovery of the Unconscious* (1970).

Graham, Loren R., *Between Science and Values* (1981).

Hall, Calvin S., *A Primer of Freudian Psychology*, new ed. (1983).

Hoffman, Banesh, *Albert Einstein, Creator and Rebel*, (1972).

Hughes, H. Stuart, *Consciousness and Society: The Reorientation of European Social Thought, 1890–1930* (1958).

———, *Contemporary Europe: A History*, 5th ed. (1981).

Hughes, Robert, *The Shock of the New: Art and the Century of Change* (1981).

Jones, Ernest, *The Life and Work of Sigmund Freud*, 3 vols. (1953–1957).

Kafka, Franz, *The Trial* (1925).

Kuhn, Thomas S., *Structure of Scientific Revolutions*, 2nd ed. (1970).

Kuper, Adam, *Anthropology and Anthropologists: The Modern British School*, rev. ed. (1983).

Malinowski, Bronislaw, *Argonauts of the Western Pacific* (1922).

Ortega y Gasset, José, *The Revolt of the Masses* (1932).

Paxton, Robert O., *Europe in the Twentieth Century* (1975).

Sontag, Raymond V., *A Broken World* (1971).

Watson, Robert I., *The Great Psychologists*, 4th ed. (1978).

Part 3

LATIN AMERICA, AFRICA, AND ASIA THROUGH WORLD WAR II

Chapter **8**

LATIN AMERICA'S STRUGGLE FOR DEVELOPMENT

Some readers may wonder why a chapter on Latin America appears in the same part of this book as chapters on Africa and Asia. Whereas settler colonies were the exception in Asia and Africa, the Latin American countries began as European settler colonies—in this way, Portuguese became the national language of Brazil, while Spanish prevailed almost everywhere else. Most Latin American nations have been politically independent since the early nineteenth century, while in Asia and Africa, only a handful of countries were independent in 1914. Yet in the Latin America of 1914, as in the few Asian and African countries that were formally independent then, the impact of imperialism was so great as to make independence virtually a sham. The struggle to change this situation had already begun in many places. But the progress made before World War II was limited.

This chapter begins with an overview of how Latin America in general was integrated into the global configuration of 1914. In this context we shall speak of a *Western*-dominated, not *European*-dominated, global pattern, for the United States had become the dominant outside power in this region. The chapter then illustrates the themes of the continental overview more concretely by examining the development of three of the most important Latin American nations—Argentina, Brazil, and Mexico—through World War II.

Continental Overview: The Illusion of Independence

Whatever their differences, the Latin American countries have much in common. They share many social, economic, and political traits, and show common patterns in their relations with the outside world.

Latin American Societies

To a large extent, the similarities and problems of the Latin American nations stem from the way their populations developed. In comparison with English-speaking North America, what is most striking historically is the much greater number of native Americans and blacks in relation to the number of people of European origin. When the Spanish arrived on the mainland following Columbus's voyages of 1492–1504, some 60 million Indians, perhaps more, inhabited the region. Mexico, Guatemala, and Peru had the greatest numbers. By the nineteenth century, probably over 10 million blacks had been imported as slaves. In contrast, fewer than one million Europeans immigrated to Latin America during the colonial era.

Disease, spread by the sudden mixing of peoples, became a major factor in shaping Latin America's population. Perhaps 90 percent of the Indians were killed by the newly introduced diseases of smallpox and measles in the sixteenth century. Malaria and yellow fever afflicted non-Indians, too. By the early nineteenth century, the population of the continent had fallen to perhaps 20 million.

Another important influence on the Latin American peoples was the mixing of races. In some countries, most people—in Brazil virtually all—are of mixed ancestry. Since independence, the human blend has changed. The importation of blacks stopped with the abolition of slavery, and European immigration increased in the later nineteenth century. Still, the mixed pattern of the colonial era remained.

Latin American societies were not really integrated, however. Spanish and Portuguese settlers had a capitalist outlook, but one wedded to ideas of class and privilege developed in their homelands in earlier centuries. They did not come to work the land with their own hands. Instead, they saw themselves as conquerors who would exploit the resources of the New World by commanding the labor of others, starting with the Indians. Rather than pushing aside the original inhabitants, as North American settlers did, the Spanish and Portuguese settled where they could exploit Indians in greatest numbers. Where this was not possible, they brought in black slaves. The Spanish and Portuguese crowns supported settlers' aspirations by issuing land grants, so laying the foundation for the huge estates that continue to exist, often inefficiently run. The melding of races began with sexual exploitation of the conquered.

Meanwhile, the conquerors elaborated their ideas about social relations into a virtual caste system. At the top stood the Europeans, followed by mixed-bloods of all types. Last came black slaves and native Americans. At independence, Latin American countries declared a policy of legal equality, and some nonwhites rose into the elites. But unofficial discrimination persisted. Social and economic institutions still permitted those who were, or could pass for, white to dominate the rest.

Latin American Economies

Because Latin American economies remained predominantly agricultural, the most important expression of white dominance was the great estates—known as *fazendas* in Brazil, *estancias* in Argentina, and *haciendas* in other Spanish-speaking countries. Some estates were almost unimaginably vast. The Diaz d'Avila fazenda in colonial Brazil was bigger than some European kingdoms. Around 1900, the Terrazas-Creel clan of the state of Chihuahua, Mexico, owned fifty estates having 7 million acres. Few estates were so large, but land-ownership was extremely concentrated. By 1914, urban middle and working classes were forming and assuming important roles. But Latin American society still consisted mostly of small landowning elites and huge peasant masses.

The gulf between the elite and the masses was wide in every respect. Members of the elite were well dressed, well fed, relatively well educated, European in culture as well as origin, and keen to preserve a way of life that assured them power, wealth, and leisure. The poor were ill fed, ill clad, largely illiterate, and attuned to folk cultures in which Indian and African elements and older communal ways played a major role. Among elite and mass alike, women were repressed by factors ranging from the elaborate etiquette of the elites to the crude cult of male dominance, or *machismo*, found throughout society.

In general, the poor were subordinated to the elites, either as slaves (through the late nineteenth century) or as peons working on the haciendas. The difference between the two conditions was often slight, thanks to the debt servitude promoted through the hacienda store. Many hacienda owners paid their peons with scrip or tokens usable only at the store, which charged artificially high prices that forced the peasants into permanent indebtedness. Under the law, the peasants could not leave the hacienda as long as they owed money. They responded with passivity and occasional rebellion, a combination that led the elites to regard them with a mixture of paternalism and fear. No wonder hacienda agriculture was inefficient. Recent critics have described the world of the hacienda in terms of "internal colonization."

If internal colonization was the key domestic reality in Latin America's economic history, its key external reality was dependency. Europeans first came to South and Central America in search of new ways to reach Asia. They stayed in the "Indies" of the New World to exploit their mineral, agricultural, and human resources. In keeping with the then widespread economic philosophy of mercantilism, Spain and Portugal each set out to organize its colonial trade as a monopoly producing a positive balance of trade for the mother country. Mercantilist trade restrictions were never entirely successful, but they implanted on Latin American economies a pattern they have never completely shaken off: that of sup-

Carnival time in Rio de Janeiro, Brazil. This scene at an open-air cafe, taken in the 1920s, shows that Brazil's culture, like its population, blends European, African, and local elements.
Popperfoto

plying raw materials to more powerful economies abroad and importing finished goods.

Latin American elites profited from this arrangement and have done much to maintain it. Their imitation of highly developed economies has tended to focus on patterns of consumption, rather than patterns of production. European fashions were easier to adopt than advanced techniques of agricultural and industrial production, although the result was increased demand for imports and deepened dependency.

In the long run, Spain and Portugal were too weak to remain the dominant outside powers in the region. When Latin American countries won independence in the first quarter of the nineteenth century, they opened their ports to world trade—that is, to a flood of British industrial goods. The British had aided the Latin American independence movements with this end in view. Great Britain was then the greatest naval and commercial power and the only industrial power.

Free trade set in motion a sequence of events that became familiar around the colonial world in the nineteenth century: the ruin of local merchants and manufactures (in the old sense of production by hand), a drain of precious metals toward the countries from which industrial imports came, accumulation of foreign debts by the local governments, and eventual bankruptcy or near-bankruptcy, with the risk of intervention by foreign governments to protect the investments of their citizens. Some major steps toward economic development and industrialization occurred in Latin American countries in the later nineteenth century. But these advances were usually the work of foreign capital and tied the local economies more tightly into the world economy. The railroad networks, for example, developed in a characteristically colonial pattern. They were designed to drain the products of the interior toward the ports, rather than to link the various parts of each country in a way that would serve the needs of the inhabitants.

By the end of the nineteenth century, the focus of Latin American dependency was shifting to the United States. In 1823, President James Monroe announced the policy that became famous as the Monroe Doctrine: the United States would regard any European attempt at colonization of the independent Americas as a threat to its own peace and safety. At that time, the United States had neither the strength nor the interest to protect Latin America. For decades, the dominant outside influence remained that of Great Britain, which was interested in economic domination rather than outright colonization. By the post–Civil War years, however, U.S. interests had grown to the point that the United States began to insist on the Monroe Doctrine. By the end of the century, the British had to concede U.S. primacy in Latin America. U.S. investments in the region had increased substantially. The Panama Canal (completed in 1914) is perhaps the best-known example. And the United States was prepared to use military force to protect these investments, as it did in Cuba during the Spanish-American War (1898).

By 1914 it was clear that the independence of the Latin states was limited and that their economies were still colonial. The powerful industrial nations had indeed established colonial economic relations all over the globe. The fact that a country could achieve political independence but remain economically dependent was simply one variation, now often called neocolonialism, on the theme.

Economic colonialism has many disadvantages for the dependent countries. In Brazil, for example, a long series of export products—dyewood, sugar, gold, diamonds, tobacco, cotton, cacao, coffee, rubber—have succeeded one another as the major determinants of prosperity. There were several reasons for these changes. Mineral resources do not last indefinitely, nor does demand for a given country's production of a given crop. Cheaper sources of the crop may be found elsewhere. New processes or products, such as synthetics, may wipe out demand entirely. Even when such changes are not occurring, the colonial economy remains at risk because it has little or no influence over the price of its exports, which is determined far away in international trade centers. During the Great Depression, for example, the value of Latin American exports fell about two-thirds between 1929 and 1932.

That experience fueled Latin American desires to diversify economically through industrialization—under local, not foreign, auspices. Industrialization efforts had, in fact, begun earlier and been stimulated by import shortages during World War I. After 1929, however, the virtual stoppage of international trade and investment created an opening for a major push to escape economic colonialism. Now the larger Latin American countries intensified their efforts to industrialize, first through import substitution (local production of previously imported goods) and then through development of heavy industry. High tariffs and other measures were used to protect the budding industries from competition. These policies produced unexpected consequences, and the relation between agricultural and industrial development was not always well thought out, as we shall see. But a new era in Latin America's economic history had begun.

Politics and International Relations

Nineteenth-century revolutions freed most of Latin America from European rule, but the new states did not fit local reality. By 1914, the independent Latin American countries were officially all republics, though Brazil had been ruled by an emperor until 1889, and Mexico also had had a couple of imperial episodes. But Latin American republicanism was a façade, behind which the governments displayed the authoritarianism and instability familiar in the Third World today.

Political power in Latin American republics belonged to elite factions and military strong men (*caudillos*), who either emerged from the factions or cooperated with them to seize power. The conservatives among these powerful groups favored political centralization and maintenance of colonial social patterns. The liberals favored federalism, guaranteed individual rights (for propertied males), and limitation of the privileges of the clergy and military. Intellectual members of the elites adopted imported ideologies, such as positivism, which stressed science and elitist politics, or social Darwinism, which believed progress grew out of the struggle for survival of the fittest (that is, the elites). In practice, none of these outlooks had much to offer women or the poor.

While the intellectuals argued about ideology, the caudillos manipulated republican institutions. They rigged elections or voided their results. They told legislators what laws to pass, and judges what decisions to render. They kept administration inefficient and corrupt. The military forces they commanded did little but interfere in politics. To preserve the wealth of the elites, the caudillos kept direct taxes very low. Until World War II, import and export duties alone provided half the revenues of many governments. With such narrow resource bases, caudillos could usually do little for the masses—though the few who tried could win an enthusiastic popular response. By World War II, the demand for democratization was spreading. Effective mass politicians, such as Lázaro Cárdenas in Mexico, Getúlio Vargas in Brazil, and Juan Perón in Argentina, had appeared, and broad-based political parties had emerged in Argentina, Uruguay, Peru, and Mexico. Some of the cruder features of the caudillo pattern were fading. But the result was more likely to be a modernization of military dictatorship than a real democracy.

International politics also reflected the weaknesses of the Latin American states. Their most important economic relations were always with countries outside the region. Partly to compensate for their poorly developed relations with one an-

Map 8.1 Latin America, 1910

▶

UNITED STATES

ATLANTIC OCEAN

MEXICO

Mexico City • • Veracruz

Havana •

CUBA

BR. HONDURAS

JAMAICA   HAITI

Guatemala •

GUATEMALA   HONDURAS

NICARAGUA

COSTA RICA

PANAMA

DOMINICAN REP.

PUERTO RICO

CARIBBEAN SEA

Caracas •

VENEZUELA

BR. GUIANA

DUTCH GUIANA

FR. GUIANA

Bogota •

COLOMBIA

Quito •

ECUADOR

Amazon

PERU

Lima •

B R A Z I L

• Bahia

La Paz •

BOLIVIA

MINAS GERAIS

SÃO PAULO

São Paulo •

RIO DE JANEIRO

Rio de Janeiro •

PARAGUAY

Paraná

RIO GRANDE
DO SUL

PACIFIC

OCEAN

Valparíso •

Santiago •

CHILE

URUGUAY

Buenos Aires •

• Montevideo

ARGENTINA

Bahía Blanca •

PATAGONIA

Falkland/Malvinas Islands

Independent nations

0   1000 Km.

0   1000 Mi.

other, Latin American states joined in international agreements and organizations, such as the Pan American Union (1889)—although U.S. sponsorship made it an object of suspicion—and later the League of Nations.

The Latins' biggest international problem was U.S. power and aggressiveness. While Woodrow Wilson was arguing for national self-determination at the Paris Peace Conference, five Caribbean nations—Cuba, the Dominican Republic, Haiti, Nicaragua, and Panama—lay under U.S. rule, a situation that Washington saw as necessary to preserve order and protect U.S. interests. Later, under Franklin Roosevelt's Good Neighbor Policy (1933), the United States backed away from interventionism. But the corollary of this policy was increased reliance on pro–U.S. regimes. These were often brutal dictatorships—like the Somoza regime in Nicaragua (1936–1979).

The Latin American states eventually entered World War II on the U.S. side, though they provided primarily bases, supplies, or intelligence, rather than combat troops. The war illustrated that U.S. interests were global in scope, rather than hemispheric, like those of most Latin American states. Tensions have continued to arise from this disparity, as well as from new episodes of U.S. interventionism, especially in the Caribbean area in such countries as the Dominican Republic, Guatemala, Nicaragua, and El Salvador.

Context of the Struggle for Independence and Development

Lack of social integration, the inequities of the hacienda system, neocolonial economic relations, caudillo politics behind a republican façade, and domination of external relations by economic dependency—these common traits provide the background against which individual Latin American states evolved through the interwar period. As we look more closely at Argentina, Brazil, and Mexico, we shall see that they shared not only these problems but also developmental patterns reflecting major themes of twentieth-century history around the world. All three countries experienced a major growth of demand for political participation. Eventually, each country produced a charismatic leader who catered to that demand by adopting a populist stance, usually combined with a strong dose of authoritarianism. Economically, the main theme of this period was the attempt to break out of neocolonial dependency through a strategy of industrialization aimed at import substitution followed by development of heavy industry. This development strategy proved as problematic as Latin American political life. Still, the progress made and the limits encountered, both politically and economically, essentially defined the basis for Latin American development in the post–World War II era.

The Amazing Argentine

Argentine history may be thought of in terms of the development, in corresponding stages, of the nation's economy and political system. In the colonial period, economic interest centered on the Andean region, which supplied agricultural and manufactured products to the nearby silver-mining centers of what is now Bolivia. By the late eighteenth century, with the decline of the silver mines, the economic center began to shift to the grassy plains of the coast, the pampas,

Argentine gauchos of the 1930s. These cowboys' costumes and customs helped give Argentine culture a distinctive stamp. The gauchos' work with livestock was important for the country's economy.
The Bettmann Archive/BBC Hulton

which lie inland and southward from Buenos Aires, and contain some of the richest soil in the world. The agricultural system that developed on the pampas spread to the windy plateaus of Patagonia in the south and to the northern lowlands, tying the country into a unit dominated by the port-capital, Buenos Aires.

The foundations for agricultural prosperity had been created by accident in the sixteenth century, when Europeans introduced horses and cattle to the New World. Some of those animals escaped and flourished on the pampas. By the eighteenth century, people had begun to hunt these animals for their hides. The hunters began to form herds and stake claims to vast landholdings, which remained sparsely settled and inefficiently managed. Gradually, people learned to exploit Argentina's natural resources more intensively, always with political results. In the 1780s the introduction of meat-salting plants made it possible to export meat, as well as hides. This development increased the commerce of Buenos Aires, heightened resentments of Spanish commercial restrictions, and led to the proclamation of independence—at Buenos Aires in 1810 and in the interior in 1816. Politically, independence brought disunity and caudillo politics.

In the mid-nineteenth century, a new chapter opened in Argentine history with the rise of sheep-raising and wool exports. Since a given amount of grazing land could support four or five times as many sheep as cattle, sheep-raising led to more intensive use of established grazing lands near Buenos Aires, and cattle-raising shifted to new lands to the south and west. The growth of the sheep economy attracted European immigrants, and the extension of the frontier climaxed with a military campaign against the Araucanian Indians of Patagonia in 1879–1880.

This campaign, which added 100 million acres to the supply of grazing land, coincided with the development of techniques for transoceanic shipment of frozen meat. Together these two events touched off a major boom in the 1880s. This transformed Buenos Aires into one of the first supermetropolises of the New World. Henceforth the city dominated the rest of the country politically and economically. By 1914, Buenos Aires had a population of one million, and the province of Buenos Aires contained 46 percent of the national population. The rail network converged on the city, by far the most important port.

Radiating out from the metropolis, patterns of land use had assumed a distinctive form. This emphasized production of livestock and grains on huge estates by small numbers of laborers or tenants, then often immigrants who lacked the rights of citizens. This pattern of development distinguished Argentina from other Latin American countries in an important way: Argentina never acquired a large peasant class, and land reform never became a key issue, as it often did elsewhere.

Politically, the period after 1880 was one of oligarchical domination by the National Autonomist party (later known as the Conservatives), whose corrupt politicians ruled in the interest of large landowners and foreign capitalists. In 1889–1890 as the boom collapsed, a protest movement emerged from the growing middle class, itself a by-product of urbanization. With this movement, the twentieth-century political history of Argentina began.

The Radical Period

By 1892, the protest movement had taken form as the Radical Civic Union and found a charismatic leader in Hipólito Yrigoyen. The party was not really radical—for example, it did not attack economic neocolonialism, although it did talk about "revolution" to overthrow the oligarchy. Like other Latin American movements of the period, the Radicals represented nineteenth-century political liberalism, with little thought given to social and economic issues. Their demands for honest elections and broader power-sharing were important, for they pointed toward further political mobilization. Fearing the Radicals and seeing that genuinely leftist forces were starting to form, the Conservatives finally granted the reforms the Radicals demanded—universal male suffrage and the secret ballot—in 1912.

These reforms enabled the Radicals to win the election of 1916. Yrigoyen became president for six years, but found himself in a difficult situation. He could not antagonize the oligarchy, which was still powerful and might depose him. At the same time, he needed to gratify his middle-class supporters, who wanted power and patronage. To make matters worse, the Radicals did not control the legislature or most of the provincial governments. And they had no real program for dealing with the needs of most Argentines. When pressures related to World War I began to distort the economy and produce strikes, Yrigoyen initially supported the strikers but soon yielded to Conservative and British pressure and used force against them. A later economic upswing enabled the Radicals to retain the presidency through the 1920s. But they were toppled by a military coup in 1930, after the Great Depression again drew attention to their lack of social and economic policies. The Radicals had tried to broaden political life. But their vision was not yet broad enough to meet the needs of most Argentines in a crisis.

The Depression and the "Infamous Decade"

Just as economic changes had been associated with earlier political milestones in Argentina, the same correlation occurred in the 1930s. Until the Depression, its agriculture-based export economy had made "the amazing Argentine" Latin America's most developed economy. Thereafter, the emphasis was increasingly on industrialization. World War I had already stimulated industry by creating needs for import substitution and even some opportunities to supply wartime needs of the Allies. The Depression made it still more important to expand domestic production because the price of Argentina's exports fell faster than those of the goods it had been importing. The Conservative politicians who succeeded the Radicals in 1930 restricted imports to protect Argentine industry, and fought to defend their share of the British market for agricultural commodities. One economic develop-

ment with future implications was that U.S. manufacturers, suffering from discriminatory import restrictions, began in the 1930s to establish plants inside Argentina.

Such changes essentially ended the Depression for Argentina by 1936. World War II provided another stimulus to the economy. An inflationary export boom ensued, and the war left Argentina with $1.7 billion in accumulated foreign exchange reserves. Argentina was now an industrial, as well as an agricultural, country. Because industry was concentrated around Buenos Aires, industrialization further heightened the dominance of the country's one great city.

The period known as the Infamous Decade (1930–1943), which began with the coup against Yrigoyen, marked a move away from democracy, but ended with a further step toward mass mobilization under authoritarian auspices. Politically chaotic, this period featured a coalition between a splinter group of Radicals and the Conservatives, with the military in the background. After a military coup in 1943, generals dominated the government directly for the next three years.

Behind this familiar phenomenon of Third World politics, significant developments were occurring. The army officers of this period were mostly middle-class, keenly nationalistic, and eager for industrialization and technology, which they saw as a means to end neocolonialism. (As so often in the colonial world, their pro-German feeling was largely an expression of anti–British and anti–U.S. sentiment.) Despite their desire for industrialization, the generals feared a politically awakened working class. At first, they tried to dominate labor by force. When this approach threatened to wreck industrialization, the military had the good fortune to produce from its ranks one of the most effective political mobilizers of Latin American history: Colonel Juan Perón, a man with ideas about the social and economic needs of the increasingly numerous workers.

The Rise of Perón

Perón took charge of the Department of Labor in 1943 and had it upgraded to become the Ministry of Labor and Welfare. He encouraged workers to organize and used the influence of his ministry to support them in negotiations. Wages and labor's share of national income grew, thus increasing purchasing power and stimulating the drive for industrialization. Perón also created a system of state pensions and health benefits. At the same time, he deprived the unions of independence, bringing them under his own control. All the while, his power (and conservative resentments of it) grew.

Perón was an impressive figure, and his readiness during speeches to pull off the jacket that Argentine politicians had always worn and identify with the shirtless workers (*descamisados*) won him their loyalty. His opponents overthrew and jailed him in 1945, but, bewildered by the massive labor demonstrations that followed, released him. He then retired from his governmental and military posts, organized his followers as the Labor party, and campaigned for the presidency in 1946. In one of Argentina's most honest elections, Perón won with 56 percent of the popular vote.

The story of what followed belongs to the postwar era (see Chapter 14). Yet Perón's rise to power, and the charisma that surrounded both him and his politically active wife, Eva Duarte Perón, decisively advanced the trend, observable ever since the Radicals' heyday, toward broadened political participation. Events would show that this was mass politics in the authoritarian mode. Politically as well as economically, Argentina had many problems yet to face.

Brazil from Empire to New State

Brazil has such great natural promise that it has been known for centuries as the "land of the future." Unfortunately, the struggle to fulfill this promise has encountered most of the difficulties found elsewhere in the continent, together with some distinctive problems.

In the colonial period, Brazil presented the spectacle of a huge colony—now the fifth-largest nation in the world—dependent on a tiny mother country, Portugal, which itself slipped into dependency on the most powerful economy of the day, Britain. During the Napoleonic wars, which provided the European background for independence in Latin America, the Portuguese government responded to its danger in a unique way: fleeing to its most important colony. Rio de Janeiro became the imperial capital from 1807 to 1821. This episode led to a political consolidation that enabled Brazil to weather the transition to independence and later political crises without loss of unity or much political violence. Another consequence was that the Portuguese court, which fled to Brazil in British ships, immediately opened Brazil to free trade, and so to British economic domination.

When the king returned to Portugal in 1821, he left his son, Pedro, as regent in Brazil. Frictions soon developed between colony and mother country, and Pedro declared independence in 1822. In what amounted to a bloodless coup, he assumed the title emperor of Brazil.

For most of the nineteenth century, Brazil was dominated by the emperor in alliance with slave-owning coffee planters concentrated in the three adjoining states of Rio de Janeiro, Minas Gerais, and São Paulo. The alliance was so close that when Brazil abolished slavery in 1888 (the latest emancipation date in the Western Hemisphere), the emperor also fell in a bloodless coup a year later. Emancipation had alienated the slave-owners, who got no compensation for the loss of their "property." Other groups were already estranged from the regime of crown and coffee. Especially alienated were the urban populace, from which a commercial-professional middle class and an industrial proletariat would soon emerge.

The Old Republic

The period from 1889 to 1930 became known as the Old Republic. At first it resembled the Radical period in Argentina, in that the urban elites replaced the coffee interests as the politically dominant group. By 1893, however, the clumsy efforts of the new government to stimulate the economy and promote industrialization, coupled with fluctuations in coffee prices, had produced economic crisis and revolts against the regime. The government could cope with these only by striking a deal with the coffee planters of São Paulo, who controlled a well-trained militia: support against the rebels in return for the presidency at the next elections. Thus in 1894, the political emergence of the urban middle class—something that came only later in other Latin American countries—ended for the time being, and the coffee interests regained political ascendancy.

After 1894, the Old Republic became politically and economically regressive. With no political parties in existence, the two richest coffee states, São Paulo and Minas Gerais, made a deal to monopolize the presidency. Such an arrangement was possible in part because the electorate was small and geographically concentrated. Illiterates could not vote, so the electorate never exceeded 5 percent of the adult population before World War I. And since education and wealth went together, over half the electorate lived in just four of Brazil's twenty states: São Paulo, Minas Gerais, Rio de Janeiro, and Rio Grande do Sul.

With the coffee interests securely in power, the industrialization efforts of 1889–1894 were abandoned. Economic policy concentrated on the agricultural interests of the leading export-producing states. For example, one of the government's chief concerns was coping with the oversupply that resulted from the spread of coffee production. In 1906, the government set up a system of *valorization*: large government coffee purchases to drive prices up. This helped Brazilian growers, although no measure taken by a single producing country could entirely overcome the problems of the global commodities markets. Another problem of the agricultural export economy was lack of diversification. The second most important export of this period—rubber, which rose from 10 percent of Brazilian exports in 1890 to 39 percent in 1910—was not cultivated, but collected from trees growing wild in Amazonian jungles. When the British began to cultivate rubber in Asia, they destroyed Brazil's position in the world market in a few years. This time, valorization could not save the day.

Between 1910 and 1930, the political alignment that dominated the Old Republic fell apart. When the president died unexpectedly in office in 1909, Brazil's first hotly contested presidential race developed. Neither candidate was from one of the big states, and new demands for democratization were heard. After the election, the country faced revolts, fed by resentment of oligarchical rule. World War I relieved the tension by touching off an agricultural export boom and boosting industrial production. But the boom collapsed soon after the war.

Politicians from São Paulo and Minas Gerais continued to occupy the presidency by turns, but scattered events in the 1920s showed that discontent was spreading. In February 1922 a Modern Art Week was organized in São Paulo to celebrate the centennial of independence. Young artists used the occasion to express rebellion against European forms and determination to develop a Brazilian culture. Here, as later in Mexico, cultural nationalism had political significance, for it meant a growth of interest in the common people. The year 1922 also saw the formation of the Brazilian Communist party. Perhaps more important, army officers began to join the opposition. A handful of junior officers decided to revolt at a fort on Copacabana Beach at Rio de Janeiro, where they fought to the death for their ill-defined cause. Their seemingly foolish heroics started a series of revolts that lasted until 1930, culminating in the overthrow of the regime. The ideas of the "lieutenants' movement" gradually became widely held demands for revolution, modernization, national integration, and expansion of political participation. Soon even the Catholic church was displaying an active concern for the plight of workers.

The Depression Destroys the Old Republic

When the price of coffee was high, the government could contain pressures like these, but a drop in coffee prices threatened the status quo. When the Depression drove coffee prices down from 22.5 cents a pound in 1929 to 8 cents in 1931, making valorization unworkable, everything fell apart. The presidential election of 1930 destroyed the Old Republic.

The trouble began when the outgoing president selected another man from his state, São Paulo, to run for the office instead of allowing Minas Gerais its turn at the presidency. The Minas Gerais politicians then joined opposition groups from all over the country in a Liberal Alliance, which selected Getúlio Vargas, from the southernmost state of Rio Grande do Sul, as its presidential candidate. As always, the candidate favored by the incumbent president won. But when the congress refused to seat some Liberal Alliance deputies, and when Vargas's vice presidential candidate was assassinated, the Liberal Alliance overthrew the government and brought Vargas to power. He was to dominate Brazil continuously from 1930 to 1945, and again from 1951 to 1954.

Vargas and the New State

Vargas's rise was a new victory for the urban elites and set the stage for important social and economic changes. Since he came to power with the backing of a broad coalition, and since there was an urgent need to deal with the problems of the Depression, Vargas proceeded cautiously at first. Economically, he did what he could to help the coffee interests raise prices by limiting production. He promoted agricultural diversification—for example, into cotton. More importantly, he encouraged industrialization to supply the goods Brazil could no longer afford to import. His policies included increased import duties, tax exemptions for industry, low-interest loans, and government operation or ownership of certain enterprises. These efforts paid off in a doubling of industrial production between 1931 and 1936. National income began to increase again in 1933, much earlier than in the United States.

Gradually, too, Vargas laid the bases for a new political order. Maneuvering among the interests he had to consider, he won the support of important elements of the population—business, labor, the military, some landowners, nationalists—and gave his regime a character of authoritarian populism. Political reforms began with an electoral code of 1932 that granted the secret ballot, lowered the voting age to eighteen, and enfranchised working women, though still not illiterates. The new constitution of 1934 preserved federalism, but strengthened the president, who was to serve for a single four-year term. Under this document, the Chamber of Deputies dutifully elected Vargas president. The constitution also proclaimed government responsibility for economic development, provided for gradual nationalization of minerals and energy resources, and granted benefits to workers under control of the Ministry of Labor. There were still no national political parties, except the small Communist party and a new fascist movement, the Integralistas. Repressing the Commu-

Brazil's President Getúlio Vargas (center) during an interview. For Brazil, Vargas's rule meant authoritarianism, but also populism and political mobilization. *Pictorial Parade*

nists, Vargas moved to the right. Because he could not legally be a candidate in the scheduled 1938 presidential election, he prepared a coup.

Vargas announced over the radio on November 10, 1937, that he had cancelled the elections, dissolved the legislature, and assumed dictatorial powers under a new constitution. So began the New State (*Estado Novo*), which resembled the fascist regimes of Europe in its organization and repressiveness (see Chapter 6). Vargas abolished political parties and violated many rights. He used fascistic language to expound his mass-mobilizing authoritarianism. Attacking democracy as decadent, he said, "The New State does not recognize the rights of the individual against the collective. Individuals do not have rights; they have duties. Rights belong to the collective."[1] But in 1938, Vargas used his troops to put down a challenge from Brazil's real fascists, the Integralistas. In fact, his regime had few opponents, for it represented the regimented approach to modernization that the lieutenants' movement had called for.

Vargas's real priority was not fascism, but Brazil's development. His economic policy made this clear. An economic nationalist, Vargas expanded trade with Germany and Italy primarily as an alternative to trading with the United States. The New State reaffirmed restrictions on foreign exploitation of natural resources and adopted policies of centralized economic planning and government initiative to develop major industries in energy, metallurgy, and chemicals. Brazil began its first five-year plan in 1940. By then, industry employed 944,000 workers, more than three times as many as in 1920, and could satisfy domestic demand in many fields. At last, the economy no longer depended solely on agricultural and mineral exports.

Brazil's active support for the Allied side in World War II—another indication that Vargas was not really a fascist—further accelerated industrial development. Wartime shortages made it possible to begin exporting manufactures, especially textiles. Because the Allies had little to sell back at the time, this export boom enabled Brazil to accumulate over $600 million in foreign exchange during the war. Brazil's industrial development also moved beyond import substitution into heavy industry, a fact symbolized by the accomplishment of one of Vargas's most cherished goals—the opening of the Volta Redonda steel mill—in 1946.

Brazil's 40 million citizens did not share equally in the benefits of development. Industrialization would surely have proceeded more rapidly if Vargas had reformed the agricultural sector, so as to increase the purchasing power of the impoverished rural masses. Yet, Vargas, born into the landowning class, could not afford politically to antagonize it. It was an innovation even to visit the interior of the country—he was the first Brazilian head of state ever to do so. Those who benefited most from Vargas's development policies were in the cities, to which he shifted the center of power. Under his regime, the growing urban population became divided into a middle class of business and professional people and an industrial working class. That Vargas was concerned for workers' welfare is clear from the labor code of 1942, then one of the most advanced in the world, though not systematically enforced.

Toward the end of World War II, Brazilians who had fought against fascism in Europe while living under authoritarian government at home began to demand change. Calls for an end to the New State prompted Vargas to readjust his policies and announce presidential and congressional elections. When it appeared that he might manipulate the elections and mount another coup, the military staged their own coup first and forced him to resign. In the election, one of the generals who had led the coup emerged as president, and a new constitution was drawn up. Vargas was elected senator from two states and congressmen from a half dozen others. There would be more to hear from him politically, up to his death in 1954. But the part of his career most significant for the economic development of Brazil and the political mobilization of its people was over.

Mexico and the Legacy of the Great Rebellion

What is commonly called the revolution of 1910 overshadowed Mexican history throughout the first half of the twentieth century. Chapter 4 has already raised the question of whether this really was an "epic revolution" or merely a "great rebellion."[2] Some historians interpret each of Mexico's later phases as a continuation of the revolution—an approach suggesting that Mexico's experience did lack the finality and decisiveness normally associated with revolution. We must therefore return to the outbreak of the crisis to understand its significance for Mexico through World War II.

The End of the Díaz Regime

After dominating Mexico for three decades, the regime of Porfirio Díaz faced increasing stress as the twentieth century opened. A worldwide increase in supply had reduced the value of Mexican silver so much that the peso lost half its value between 1871, when it was worth a U.S. gold dollar, and 1905, when Mexico switched painfully to the gold standard. Hacienda agriculture was so inefficient that Mexico had to import wheat and corn for the last twenty years of Díaz's rule. Liberal critics did not fail to attack. The most noted were the three Flores Magón brothers, whose Liberal Plan of 1906 demanded guarantees of basic freedoms, protection for industrial workers, redistribution of uncultivated lands, and return of communal lands to the Indian communities. These were demands of which more would be heard. Strikes, such as those at the American-owned Cananea copper mines in 1906,

became increasingly serious and produced international repercussions due to foreign ownership of many enterprises. The most important factor in precipitating Díaz's fall, however, was the international financial crisis of 1907, which began in the United States and hit Mexico during a long period of drought (1905–1910).

Díaz also contributed to his own undoing in a strange way. In 1908, he announced that he would retire when his term ended. Candidates to succeed him immediately stepped forward. The most influential was Francisco Madero, who published a book entitled *The Presidential Succession in 1910*. Somewhat like Yrigoyen in Argentina, Madero took a narrowly political view of Mexico's ills, arguing that the greatest danger was military dictatorship and that the best remedies were effective suffrage and prohibition of presidential re-election. These concepts gained salience when Díaz accepted nomination for re-election despite his earlier announcement. In the race that followed, Díaz had Madero and many of his followers arrested, thus assuring his own victory.

The Great Rebellion

When released from prison, Madero fled to the United States. He issued a statement that declared the last election "illegal" and called for the republic to "rise in arms" on Sunday, November 20, 1910, at 6 P.M.[3] Widespread fighting broke out, and the rebellion spread. Díaz found it increasingly difficult to control an uprising that had popular support. He resigned in the spring of 1911. That was the end of Díaz. It was barely the beginning of the rebellion.

The main problem of the rebellion

(and the reason why it is more accurate not to call it a revolution) was that it expressed in politics the lack of integration of Latin American societies. Madero and most other revolutionary caudillos came from the elite class. Their ideas seldom went beyond basic political principles of the sort enunciated in Madero's book. Any thought of social and economic change that would upset their interests was enough to turn most of them into defenders of law and order. From the Flores Magón brothers on, some leaders did identify with the masses, and their appeals roused passions that could not be ignored. Yet the only prominent rebel leader with a consistent social program was the southern caudillo Emiliano Zapata, who was radical only by comparison with his northern colleagues. He called for a partial redistribution of hacienda lands, with compensation to the owners. Such limited demands were popular. They are not the stuff of which social revolution is made.

While radical hopes were destined for disappointment, the rising against Díaz plunged Mexico into a decade of violence that brutalized the nation. More than anything else, it is this impact on the populace, and the vast military and political mobilization that occurred at the same time, that justified Mexicans in remembering what they went through as an epic struggle. Within a few years, the army numbered a quarter million, or twelve times its size at the fall of Díaz. Vast forces were also mobilized to fight against government troops. Those drawn into the struggle found their lives transformed, and not necessarily for the worse. Hacienda peons now escaped into a life of adventure as revolutionary soldiers, or—in the case of the women—as camp-following *soldaderas*, many of whom also fought. By their own testimony, these men and women found their experiences a great improvement over their former lives.

At the top, meanwhile, the rebellion pursued a zigzag course as different leaders occupied the presidency. First came Madero, elected in 1911. A member of one of Mexico's wealthiest northern families, he showed a continuing faith in political democracy as president. But he never developed a program for social and economic reform, and he appointed many conservative relatives to high office. The forces that had united to overthrow Díaz soon disintegrated. Madero was murdered in 1913 by one of his generals, Victoriano Huerta, who then assumed the presidency. U.S. Ambassador H. L. Wilson, attempting to defend U.S. business interests, played a key role in the coup. As president, Huerta faced revolts by all the "revolutionary" caudillos. His most serious problem, however, was U.S. President Woodrow Wilson, who did not share his ambassador's enthusiasm for the Huerta regime and did everything possible to undermine it. In 1914, U.S. Marines occupied Veracruz, forcing Huerta to pull troops toward that city and to abandon the rest of the country to his opponents. When he saw he could not regain control, he resigned. A chaotic period followed, from which Venustiano Carranza emerged as president, partly because Woodrow Wilson gave U.S. recognition to him as the most conservative contender. Angry that he was not the one recognized, Pancho Villa led a raid into U.S. territory, provoking the punitive expedition sent into Mexico under General John Pershing in 1916–1917.

In 1917, Carranza called a constitutional convention. It expressed the lack of focus in the Mexican revolution in that when it met, radicals proved, despite Carranza, to be in the majority. The constitution of 1917 consequently embodied many of their demands. It limited the power of the Catholic clergy, whom many Mexicans regarded, with reason, as antirevolutionary. It made primary education free, obligatory, and secular. It provided for restoration of lands seized illegally from the peasantry and expropriation of land not in use. It restricted foreign ownership of land and natural resources. Provisions for labor were advanced for the period. Workers were guaranteed the eight-hour day, the six-day week, a minimum wage, equal pay for equal work, and the rights to organize, bargain collectively, and strike. The problem was to get these principles enforced.

As president, Carranza showed that he had no intention of implementing such provisions of the constitution. Zapata was bitterly critical of Carranza, who retaliated by having Zapata killed in 1919. At last, however, the decade-long violence began to subside. By 1920, reconstruction was beginning.

Reconstruction and Depression

The period of reconstruction, which lasted until 1934, was dominated by two presidents, Álvaro Obregón and Plutarco Calles. Both went further than Carranza in fulfilling the constitution, but not far enough to revolutionize Mexican society. Obregón distributed about 3 million acres of land during his term (1920–1924), and Calles distributed 8 million acres by 1928, mostly as communal lands (*ejidos*) for the Indian villages. This was enough to worry hacienda owners, but not to satisfy radicals. In education, there were significant efforts to develop rural primary schools to teach the Indi-

ans Spanish and draw them into national life. The new interest in the Indians also had a profound effect on the arts. Young artists like Diego Rivera and David Alfaro Siqueiros were commissioned to paint murals in public buildings. Their Indian-inspired works were meant for the people, but also won international acclaim.

Calles in particular enacted important measures for business and industry. Road-building, electrification, and the founding of the Bank of Mexico all assisted economic development. Government subsidies and high tariff duties on imports also stimulated the growth of Mexico's consumer goods industries. But U.S. interests could still find ways to flourish inside Mexico's tariff walls, as illustrated by the opening in 1925 of a Ford assembly plant, organized on terms highly favorable to the parent company. And there were continuing frictions with U.S. oil companies, which feared that the constitutional restrictions on foreign control of natural resources would be applied to them after all.

In the later 1920s, just as the Argentine Radicals and Brazilian coffee oligarchs seemed to run out of ideas, the momentum of Mexico's reconstruction gradually faltered. Latent church-state conflict gave rise to a unique church "strike"— all religious services were suspended throughout Mexico for three years—and a guerrilla war between militant Catholic *Cristeros* and government forces. Other problems emerged when the presidential election of 1928 degenerated into violence. Two candidates were executed for starting rebellions before the election, and the winner, Obregón, was assassinated by a Cristero before he could take office.

Though a recent constitutional amendment prevented any president from suc-

Mural by Diego Rivera: *The Distribution of Land to the Peasants.* This Indian-inspired work illustrates one of the most important issues raised by Mexico's "great rebellion."
Instituto Nacional de Bellas Artes de Mexico/Art Resource

ceeding himself, only Calles was then influential enough to run the government. He arranged for puppets to serve out Obregón's term, while he pulled the strings. Calles also organized the National Revolutionary Party (PNR in Spanish), which, with changes of name, has dominated Mexican politics ever since. The creation of a single mass party in support of the regime suggests the influence of European fascism. The virtual suspension of land reform and other social programs in the later Calles years also indicates a shift to the right, which the Depression confirmed. Fortunately for those who still believed in the revolution, a progressive wing was forming in the PNR.

Cárdenas and the Revolutionary Legacy

The PNR nominated Lázaro Cárdenas, former party chairman and leader of the progressive wing, as its presidential candidate for 1934, and he was duly elected. Calles proved unable to control the new president. Democratic in style, Cárdenas made himself accessible to peasants and workers. When Calles made threats, Cárdenas excluded Calles supporters from his cabinet and then deported Calles.

Cárdenas proved himself the most committed reformer so far. He distributed 49 million acres of land, roughly twice as much as all his predecessors. By 1940, about a third of the population had received land, much of it through the communal ejidos. The historical patterns of the hacienda system and peasant servitude had been broken. The government also provided other facilities—roads, credit, electrification, medical care. A six-year plan for economic development had gone into effect shortly before Cárdenas came to power. He added new credit facilities and further tariff protection to foster industrialization. Under his regime, industry grew even more than agriculture. Cárdenas also supported creation of a new Confederation of Mexican Laborers, thus strengthening the labor movement while maintaining government control over it.

In 1938, Cárdenas reorganized the official party along corporatist lines, with agrarian, labor, military, and "popular" (essentially middle-class) sectors. One reason for the continued dominance of Mexico's single party, known since 1945 as the Institutional Revolutionary Party (PRI in Spanish), may well be the fact that Cárdenas mobilized both workers and peasants, but kept them separate in competing sectors.[4]

Cárdenas also scored his most dramatic foreign policy success in 1938. When the controversy with U.S. oil companies flared up again after a strike by Mexican workers, Cárdenas went on the air to announce nationalization of the companies' holdings. This assertion of economic independence created a sensation all over Latin America. The companies were outraged, but because the Roosevelt administration had decided on a policy of nonintervention in Latin America, they had to settle for monetary compensation.

The events of 1938 marked a high point for Cárdenas and for the effort to fulfill the revolutionary ideal. Conserva-tive fears over Cárdenas's policies prompted a flight of Mexican capital abroad and a scaling back of reform during his last two years in office. World War II opened a long period of rapid economic growth, but confirmed the rightward political shift. Since Cárdenas, the "revolution," supposedly institutionalized in the PRI, has been increasingly a conservative force.

Conclusion: Charismatic Leaders Compared

By World War II, three of Latin America's most important countries had produced memorable charismatic leaders: Perón, Vargas, and Cárdenas. We can sum up the significance of the first half of this century for their countries by comparing these men and their policies.

Each came to power only after demands for wider political participation had already produced some changes in his country. To varying degrees, the electoral victory of the Argentine Radicals in 1910, the brief ascendancy of the urban elites in the early years (1889–1894) of Brazil's Old Republic, and Mexico's great rebellion of 1910 all signified such a broadening. Then and later, however, most politicians had only a limited concern for the common people. Neither Madero in Mexico nor Yrigoyen in Argentina had clear policies for attacking socioeconomic, rather than political, problems. Even Zapata made only limited demands.

More than anything else, the Depression exposed the inadequacies of such leadership and prompted the emergence of a new approach. The collapse of the markets for Latin American exports toppled both the Argentine Radicals and the coffee oligarchs of Brazil's Old Republic. Coming after the church-state crisis of the 1920s and the violence of the 1928 election, the Depression also heightened the confusion of the later Calles years in Mexico.

Out of this disruption, Perón, Vargas, and Cárdenas emerged as leaders who would carry political mobilization into a new phase. In doing so, they displayed important characteristics and policies in common. To varying degrees, they all took an authoritarian approach to mass mobilization. Especially in Perón and Vargas, one can see traits of the caudillo tradition. All three also displayed fascist influence, if only in the monolithic character of the movements they headed. In Argentina, Perón's followers, drawn largely from organized labor, became the largest party, though not the only one. Vargas used fascist-style language and methods, and his New State completely monopolized political life, allowing no parties. Even Cárdenas contributed to the development of the corporatist single party in Mexico.

Nationalist goals of political and economic development meant more to most Latin Americans of the 1930s, however, than did imported ideologies. In addition to broadening political participation, Perón, Vargas, and Cárdenas therefore also pushed for industrialization as a way to overcome the effects of the Depression and the structural limitations of the colonial economy. Assuming power when Argentina's drive for industrialization was already well launched, Perón championed the working class, thus creating for himself a wider base of support than earlier politicians had enjoyed. Vargas ended the political dominance of the coffee interests, introduced centralized planning for economic devel-

opment, carried Brazil into the age of heavy industry, and shifted power to the cities, where both the middle class and the workers benefited from his authoritarian paternalism. Emphasizing service to the common people, Cárdenas not only took seriously the constitutional promise of land reform, but also presided over significant industrial development.

In order to break out of economic dependency, Latin American leaders of the Perón-Vargas-Cárdenas era typically pursued a strategy of industrialization that aimed first at import substitution behind high tariff barriers, and then at heavy industry, without necessarily reforming the agricultural sector. How sound was this strategy?

Adopted in the Depression era, when high tariffs became almost universal, the protectionist import-substitution strategy did produce some positive results. Yet neglect of the agricultural sector was unwise. An agricultural policy aimed at reducing inequality in the countryside would have enlarged the market for industrial products by increasing the income of the majority. A development policy that reduced the inefficiency of hacienda agriculture could also have helped make it possible both to accumulate capital for industrial investment and to feed a population of which a growing proportion worked in factories rather than in fields. Finally, mass education in the countryside would have produced a more skilled and productive labor force.

A sound approach to industrialization would have required starting with agriculture and fundamentally changing Latin America's historic pattern of internal colonization. Argentina was a partial exception because it lacked the large peasant class found in other Latin American nations. Mexico was also exceptional because its reforms, especially under Cárdenas, met some of this approach's requirements. But Argentina and Mexico were only local variations in an agrarian problem of continental scope, still unsolved in the 1980s.

The high import duties characteristic of the Depression posed another danger to the import-substitution strategy: the protected industries might not develop the ability to compete in an international market. As long as domestic need for basic consumer goods remained unmet, only Mexicans, or Brazilians, or Argentines had to put up with the inferior goods. But a time would come—in the 1960s for these countries—when domestic demand for light industrial goods was substantially satisfied, and industrialization could continue only by mastering more advanced technologies or by facing the competition of international markets. By then, too, the response of U.S. manufacturers to the creation of protective barriers (the establishment of subsidiary firms in countries like Argentina and Mexico) would show that protectionism offered no sure way to overcome subordination to foreign economic interests. Like the political problems of authoritarian mass mobilization, the economic issues raised by the protectionist import-substitution strategy of development were to remain major Latin American issues of the post–World War II era.

Notes

1. Bradford Burns, *A History of Brazil*, 2d ed. (New York: Columbia University Press, 1980), p. 410.
2. Ramon Ruíz, *The Great Rebellion: Mexico, 1905–1924* (New York: W. W. Norton, 1980); Charles C. Cumberland, *Mexico: The Struggle for Modernity* (New York: Oxford University Press, 1968), p. 241 ("epic revolution").
3. Michael C. Meyer and William L. Sherman, *The Course of Mexican History*, 2d ed. (New York: Oxford University Press, 1983), p. 499.
4. Thomas E. Skidmore and Peter H. Smith, *Modern Latin America* (New York: Oxford University Press, 1984), p. 240.

Suggestions for Further Reading

Burns, E. Bradford, *A History of Brazil*, 2d ed. (1980).

Keen, Benjamin, and Mark Wasserman, *A Short History of Latin America*, 2d ed. (1984).

Loveman, Brian, *Chile: The Legacy of Hispanic Capitalism* (1979).

Meyer, Michael C., and William L. Sherman, *The Course of Mexican History*, 2d ed. (1983).

Ruíz, Ramon, *The Great Rebellion, Mexico, 1905–1924* (1980).

Scobie, James R., *Argentina: A City and a Nation*, 2d ed. (1971).

Shafer, Robert J., *A History of Latin America* (1978).

Skidmore, Thomas E., and Peter H. Smith, *Modern Latin America* (1984).

Chapter 9

SUB-SAHARAN AFRICA UNDER EUROPEAN SWAY

Most of Africa became integrated into the European-dominated global pattern later than either the Americas or Asia. Yet the European voyages of exploration began decades before Columbus, as Portuguese navigators inched their way down the Atlantic coast of Africa. Although Asia was the principal source of the silks and spices that the early European explorers sought, Africa also produced precious commodities, such as gold and ivory. Why then did Africa remain so long outside the sphere of European domination?

Disease and topography hindered Europeans in Africa, as did the presence of strong African kingdoms controlling trade to the interior. Europeans introduced diseases, such as smallpox, that had extremely serious consequences for Africans. Until the advent of modern tropical medicine, however, the impact of endemic African diseases on Europeans was greater. Yellow fever and malaria caused very high death rates among newly arrived Europeans. Diseases spread by the tsetse fly made animal transport impracticable in many places. Topography slowed European penetration of the continent; the rivers all had high cataracts near the coast, and existing paths were not suitable for wheeled vehicles. For a long time, much of direct European trade with Africa entered into established networks controlled by Africans and Arabs. For these reasons, Europeans knew so little of Africa's interior that they had to leave it blank on maps.

European conquest came to most of Africa only in the late nineteenth century after the gradual penetration of African kingdoms, the discovery of effective malaria preventives, and an agreement among European powers not to sell firearms to Africans. The last factor created a technological gap that made it relatively cheap and easy to establish and maintain European rule.

To study this epoch-making change, this chapter begins with an overview of Africa and its recent history up to World War II. Later sections will look more closely at the two largest African colonies: Nigeria, where few Europeans went, and South Africa, where many settled. The comparison of these two countries sheds light on the conditions in which the processes of social and political mobilization characteristic of the twentieth century proceeded where Africans did, or did not, have to contend with large numbers of Europeans.

Continental Overview: African Diversity, European Domination

Africa comprises a vast array of environments and societies. We need to consider some key dimensions of the continent's diversity—topography, modes of adapting to the environment, language, forms of social organization—and some common traits, before examining the European impact and African responses to it.

African Diversity

Of the many indicators of African diversity, the most basic are the ecological differences that divide the continent into zones running mostly east and west across the continent. Northernmost, in Algeria and Morocco, lies a small coastal zone with a Mediterranean climate, like that of Spain and Italy. Below this zone, the Sahara Desert extends from the Atlantic coast to the Red Sea. Below the Sahara, the desert grades into the savanna, a zone of grassland and scattered trees, running from Senegal in the west to the southern Sudan, from which the same environment also extends to the southeast. Next comes the tropical forest, found in a coastal strip running from Senegal through Nigeria, then widening to the east and south to cover the Zaire (Congo) River valley. Pockets of rain forest recur farther south and east. South of the Zaire River valley, much the same zones as in the north appear in reverse order: a zone of woodland and shrub; a savanna zone; an arid zone—the Kalahari Desert in the west, grassy steppes in eastern South Africa; finally, a small zone with a Mediterranean climate at the Cape of Good Hope. These regions produce many products not found in Europe—rubber, cacao, palm oil, and ivory, not to mention gold and diamonds.

One way to classify African peoples is according to how they have adapted to the different environments, that is, how they survived and obtained food. Historically, in Africa, the two more prevalent adaptations are agriculture and pastoralism, while the two less common are fishing, and hunting and gathering.

In the most ancient way of life, hunting and gathering, people subsist on plants and animals that grow wild, without either agriculture or animal husbandry. This way of life survives for a few Africans: the Mbuti of the rain forest and the San of South Africa's open grassland. Hunting and gathering communities have to remain small and migratory in order to find subsistence year-round. In such communities, which never exceed a few hundred, the need for chiefship has never been felt. Decision making and control of conflict are communal responsibilities. Communal egalitarianism and highly developed skills for taking advantage of difficult landscapes are attractive features of this way of life.

The first communities to settle permanently in one place were probably fisherfolk, located along the shores of rivers, lakes, or the ocean, which provided an adequate food supply year-round. A permanent food supply permitted the formation of larger communities, specialization of roles, and the emergence of chiefs. Few fisher communities survive, but they probably provided the setting for development of a sedentary (as opposed to migratory) lifestyle, such as later became known in agricultural communities.

Agriculture spread to Africa from the Middle East by 5500 B.C. By cultivating plants and domesticating animals, agriculturists could use the environment more intensively than hunter-gatherers, and could spread over a much larger part of the landscape than fisherfolk. Agriculture has long been the most widespread of the environmental adaptations. Its productivity made possible the formation of larger societies, in which people's roles and statuses became more differentiated, trade began, and the institution of chiefship evolved into kingship as the societies grew larger.

Where conditions were, or became, too dry for agriculture, as in the Sahara, pastoralism appeared. This way of life depends on herding livestock, such as sheep or camels, in arid zones where there is too little water to support grazing year round. Pastoralism is necessarily a migratory or nomadic way of life, requiring intimate knowledge of the environment, because the survival of the community depends on knowing how to find grazing and water throughout the year. Chiefship is sometimes an important social institution in the pastoralist community, normally an extended kin group. Alternatively, some pastoralist groups have stateless societies, in which elders keep order with no centralized government.

Whatever their mode of environmental adaptation, another factor differentiating African societies is language. The continent has over 800 languages and many more dialects. Yet virtually all of them belong to only five language families, with common structural traits that indicate a common origin. For example, the Afro-Asiatic family includes the Arabic and Berber languages of North Africa and various languages of Somalia and Ethiopia. In western South Africa and adjacent territories are the speakers of the Khoisan languages. The Nilo-Saharan family is found in a zone running from Chad, through the southern Sudan, to the eastern side of Lake Victoria. The fourth language family, the Austronesian, is of Southeast Asian origin. This family is found on the island of Madagascar, whose people migrated from Indonesia long ago, bringing a language closely related to Malayo-Polynesian. The most widely dispersed language family of sub-Saharan Africa is the Congo-Kordofanian. These languages are spoken across much of the savanna belt of West Africa, through the forest zone, and across most of the southern part of the continent. Finally, some European languages, such as English, French, or the Dutch-derived Afrikaans, remain in use by either European settlers or Africans for whom these languages provide a common medium of communication in regions that might otherwise not have one.

Variations in concepts of kinship provide yet another way to classify African societies. Historically, some African societies were patrilineal, organizing themselves in terms of descent relationships among males; some were matrilineal; and some recognized bilateral kinship. Some societies were endogamous, preferring marriage among kin, and some were exogamous, preferring marriage among non-kin. African societies differed vastly in scale, from bands of a few hunter-gatherers to huge kingdoms ruling over many kin groups. In some societies, exotic variations on the kinship theme appeared. For example, the Lunda people of central Africa practiced "perpetual succession" (each successor to an office took the name, as well as the title, of the original incumbent) and "positional kinship" (later occupants of the offices assumed the same kin relationships to one another as the original incumbents had had). If originally several chiefs were brothers, generations later the chiefs bore the same names and were still considered brothers. In some societies, too, non-kin relationships could function as extensions to the range of kinship ties. Slavery especially served as a way to expand the master's household. The contrast with the plantation slavery of the New World could be very great.

The Ijo people of the Niger Delta, for example, developed an organizational form known as the canoe house, which began as an extended family plus the slaves of the family head. The slaves were regarded as full members of the household and might succeed to its headship.

Kinship and its extensions, such as slavery or blood brotherhood, were certainly not the only meaningful social relationships. Shared religious orientation could be extremely important. The Sokoto caliphate of northern Nigeria was one of many African states to grow out of an Islamic reform movement. Groups defined in terms of age and sex were also sometimes important. The Zulu regiments of nineteenth-century South Africa consisted of contemporaries who went through initiation rites together as youths. A Zulu ruler bent on military expansion could use these age-grade societies to separate young fighters from their kin and form them into units dependent on himself alone. At Aba, in Nigeria, the local women used their age-grade societies and trading contacts to organize a revolt in 1929.

Yet the preceding examples remain exceptions to the general rule that African societies were basically kinship societies. The societies' structural variations were largely variations on the kinship theme. Because differences among kinship groups often coincided with differences in language and culture, and because kinship groups often acknowledged no political allegiance to any larger body, the kinship groups were the key entities of African society.

One approach to the study of Africa is to classify its societies along the dimensions just discussed—the different types of environments, environmental adaptations, languages, and kinship structures. Such an approach can lead to very extended discussion, especially since additional criteria should be considered. For example, in religion, some African societies are historically Christian, some are Islamic, and many are animist, venerating spirits thought to inhabit the natural world. Cultural borrowings can also complicate the picture by creating close relationships in certain respects—religion, artistic styles, ideas of kingship—among societies that are otherwise different.

Common Traits

Let us shift emphasis from the diversity of African societies to shared traits that have important implications for twentieth-century African history. Two themes are noteworthy: the implications of kinship society for efforts at political integration on larger scale, and the problems resulting from the fact that the centers of the world's most influential civilizations lay outside Africa.

Especially because they so often coincided with linguistic, cultural, and political differences, the distinctions among kinship groups and the rivalries among African states of the precolonial period made it easier for Europeans to take power in Africa. As they consolidated their domination in the late nineteenth century, most African societies proved too small, and too underdeveloped technologically, to resist effectively. Africa then had some states that were large and powerful by African—but not European—standards, many microstates of village size, and stateless societies. Ironically, the larger monarchies were often easiest for Europeans to master, since if they could defeat the ruler, his subjects then became theirs. Stateless societies

were hardest to subdue, because practically the only way to gain control was to make each member of the society submit. This fact supports anthropologists' view that the ability to live in a stateless society is a great African achievement. Only Ethiopia approached the size of a major European nation, and it was one of just two African states to remain independent throughout the nineteenth century.

When Europeans established control, they consolidated African societies into larger entities. But Africans could not easily shift their primary loyalty from accustomed social and political entities to the new-formed colonies, or the "nations" that emerged from them. The result has been splits within independence movements and a continuing tendency of post-independence national politics to degenerate into regional or ethnic conflict. If no European state fully lived up to the ideal of the nation-state, the nations that colonialism created in Africa were far less coherent.

Faced with European expansionism, Africa also suffered from the fact that the four zones where the most influential civilizations of the Old World had developed lay outside it, one in Europe and three in Asia (centered in the Middle East, in India, and in east Asia). Influences from two zones in particular—the European and Middle Eastern—strongly affected much of Africa for millennia. The importance of Islam in Africa provides evidence of this influence. Throughout their history, African cultures also displayed great sophistication and creativity in their own right. Indeed, African societies have produced achievements with a unique place in the human heritage. African sculptures, for example, have become highly prized in other parts of the world and have exerted a

Sixteenth-century ivory mask from the Bini people of Nigeria. Such masterpieces of African artistic achievement exerted a major international influence in the twentieth century.
The Metropolitan Museum of Art, The Michael C. Rockefeller Memorial Collection, Gift of Nelson A. Rockefeller, 1972

major influence on Western art. Yet Africa's remoteness from the centers of the most influential civilizations had its cost, especially when the rapid growth of Western power altered relations among those centers and began to bring

the entire non-Western world—great centers and hinterlands alike—under European domination. Once science learned how to cope with the tropical diseases that had shielded most of Africa up to that point, and once Europeans agreed not to sell weapons to Africans, the technological gap between industrial Europe and African societies grew tragically wide. Then Europeans were able to establish control over the continent with a suddenness unparalleled elsewhere.

Integration into the Europe-centered Global Pattern

Africa's integration into the European-dominated world progressed in several stages. The first stage centered on the transatlantic slave trade. Africans were already trading in slaves when the Europeans appeared off their coasts. The European export of African slaves quickly began and grew as European explorers and settlers spread the plantation system of agriculture in the Americas. In the end, some 12 million slaves were exported, most of them from West and Central Africa. Not all of them survived the crossing. An older pattern of slave exportation across the Sahara and the Red Sea also continued, accounting for perhaps 3 million people during the period of the transatlantic trade. Blacks thus became the second most widely distributed of the world's races.

Though Europeans were long unable to penetrate the African interior, the slave trade produced profound changes there too. In the Niger Delta, the rise of the Ijo canoe houses, which used their manpower to staff large canoes for slave trading and war, was one example of how African societies adjusted to their new economic opportunities. Accustomed to trading in prisoners of war and criminals and knowing little of the nature of slavery across the Atlantic, many Africans were little more shocked by the trade than Europeans. The Ijo, for example, did not realize how the experience of slaves sold to Europeans differed from that of slaves who became members of their canoe households.

In the nineteenth century, "legitimate" trade in industrial, agricultural, and mineral products replaced slaving as the principal link between Africa and the world economy. This transformation owed more to economic factors than to the efforts of idealistic abolitionists. Britain's abolition of the slave trade (1807) coincided not only with growth of interest in human rights, but also with the early phases of the Industrial Revolution. British ships had new products to take to Africa, and British demand for raw materials began to exert a more powerful influence on African exports than did American demand for slaves.

African societies had to reorient themselves, as trade shifted in character and grew in volume. In the Niger Delta, which had been the most prolific source of slaves for export, the volume of legitimate trade increased 87 percent between 1830 and 1850. At the same time, Europeans began to extend the influence of their coastal representatives: consuls, explorers, missionaries, and merchants. There were also efforts to resettle freed blacks in Africa—the British settlement at Sierra Leone (1787) and the U.S. settlement in Liberia (1822). The pace of European involvement was quickening.

The 1880s were the critical phase in the consolidation of European control. Several factors combined to touch off the "scramble for Africa." In Europe, the unification of Italy and Germany (1870–1871) had intensified international rivalries and increased the number of would-be colonial powers. Medical breakthroughs—starting with the use of quinine against malaria—reduced the mortality rates that had plagued Europeans in the tropics. The advances of European industry increased demand for goods like vegetable oils and rubber. Military applications of new technologies widened the gap between European and African military capabilities. The significance of these advances grew when European nations made treaties with one another forbidding sale of guns to Africans. That left Africans with breechloaders to face Europeans with maxim guns, an early form of machine gun. In South Africa, fabulous mineral discoveries—the Kimberley diamond finds of 1867 and the Witwatersrand gold finds of 1886—whetted European greed. In the north, the French, who had controlled Algeria since 1830, established a protectorate over Tunisia in 1881, and the British occupied Egypt in 1882. But the scramble was most intense in the tropical forest of the Niger and Congo basins, once medical advances made that region accessible to Europeans. To deal with competition for that region between a number of powers, the European nations convened a congress at Berlin in 1884–1885. The conference defined a procedure for Europeans to follow to gain international recognition of their African claims, a procedure summed up in the phrase "notify and occupy." The European powers had only to notify one another of their claims and then stake them.

Over the next three decades, the scramble continued, until only Liberia and Ethiopia remained independent. In a continent where precise linear boundaries were scarcely heard of, Europeans carved out their possessions as they pleased. The result was a system of territorial divisions that reflected the perspective of someone entering from the coast. Togo was just a thin strip running in from the sea. The Belgian Congo, in contrast, was mostly a vast interior expanse, but it too had an outlet to the sea. Capital cities grew up on the coast, as beachheads of imperialism. Everywhere, boundaries cut across the patterns of settlement and economic life that mattered to Africans. European imperialists did not worry about that. Their concern was to plant the flag and claim their place in the sun.

By World War I, virtually all of Africa was divided into dependencies of seven European states. France and Britain had emerged as the winners, though they had almost come to blows in the process. In addition to Morocco, Algeria, and Tunisia, France held vast tracts of sub-Saharan Africa grouped into two federations: French West Africa and French Equatorial Africa. The British held Gambia, Sierra Leone, the Gold Coast (now Ghana), and Nigeria in West Africa. They also held a strip that ran from north to south, from Egypt to South Africa, broken only by German East Africa (the Tanganyika of the interwar period, now the mainland part of Tanzania). In 1898 a major war almost broke out between England and France when both countries tried to claim the Sudan. If the French had been successful, they would have emerged with a strip of territories running across the continent from east to west. Instead, they backed down, allowing the British almost to fulfill their dream of controlling territory from "Cape to Cairo."

After Britain and France, Belgium and Germany probably won most in the scramble. Belgium acquired the Belgian Congo (now Zaire). King Leopold, acting on his own account, had begun to establish claims there in the 1870s. His personal regime exploited the country scandalously, and the Belgian government took it over in 1908. Germany acquired Togo, Cameroon, South-West Africa, and German East Africa. The government tried—with little success—to get Germans to settle in those territories, rather than emigrate to America.

Although World War I weakened the European powers, and Wilson's principle of self-determination attracted attention around the world, European dominance of Africa appeared to become even stronger during the interwar years. Defeated Germany lost its colonies, but they were entrusted to Belgium, France, South Africa, and Britain under mandates from the League of Nations. The mandates theoretically differed from old-fashioned imperialism, as the mandatory powers were supposedly accountable to the League of Nations. Since the League was not a strong organization, the mandatory powers did not all live up to their obligations. South Africa, in particular, continues to administer the adjoining territory of South-West Africa (Namibia) virtually as if it were another province. One consequence of the transformation of German East Africa into the British-mandated Tanganyika was that Britain briefly acquired its band of territory running the full length of the continent. European empire-building in Africa did not stop, even with the mandates. In 1935, Mussolini's Italy invaded Ethiopia—the last campaign in the conquest of Africa, and the first for Africa in World War II. The Italians held

Map 9.1   Africa, 1914

▶

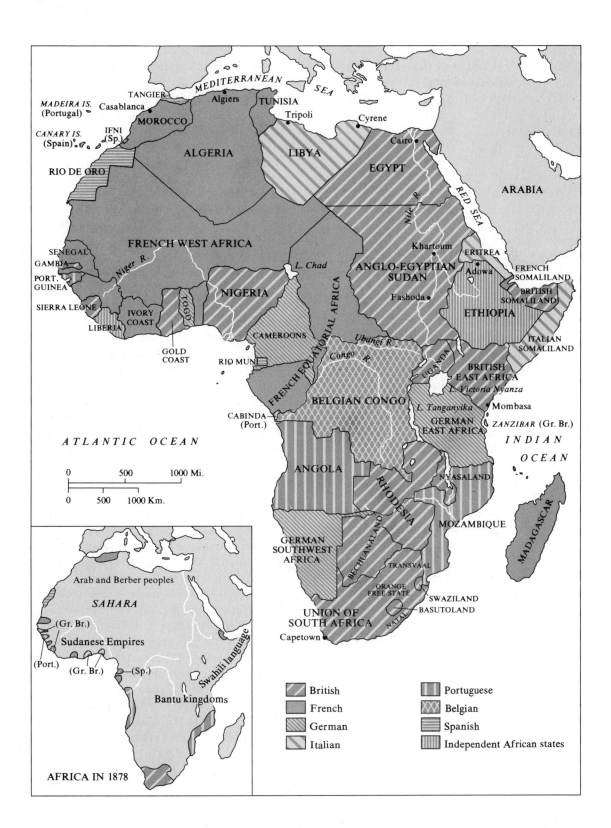

MEDITERRANEAN SEA

TANGIER
MADEIRA IS. (Portugal)   Casablanca   Algiers   TUNISIA
                                                      Tripoli
CANARY IS. (Spain)   IFNI (Sp.)   MOROCCO   Cyrene
                        RIO DE ORO   ALGERIA   LIBYA   EGYPT   Cairo

                                                                        ARABIA

ARABIA

FRENCH WEST AFRICA

SENEGAL
GAMBIA
PORT. GUINEA   *L. Chad*
SIERRA LEONE   Khartoum   ERITREA
LIBERIA   IVORY   NIGERIA   Adowa   FRENCH SOMALILAND
           COAST   ANGLO-EGYPTIAN   BRITISH SOMALILAND
           GOLD   SUDAN
           COAST
RIO MUNI   CAMEROONS   Fashoda   ETHIOPIA
                                                                    ITALIAN SOMALILAND
Niger R.   TOGO
Ubangi R.
Congo R.
FRENCH EQUATORIAL AFRICA   UGANDA   BRITISH EAST AFRICA
                                                              L. Victoria Nyanza

BELGIAN CONGO   *L. Tanganyika*   Mombasa
CABINDA (Port.)   GERMAN EAST AFRICA   *ZANZIBAR* (Gr. Br.)

ATLANTIC OCEAN   *INDIAN OCEAN*

ANGOLA   NYASALAND

0   500   1000 Mi.
0   500   1000 Km.
                        RHODESIA   MOZAMBIQUE   MADAGASCAR

GERMAN SOUTHWEST AFRICA
                        BECHUANALAND   TRANSVAAL
                                        ORANGE FREE STATE   SWAZILAND
                        UNION OF SOUTH AFRICA   NATAL   BASUTOLAND
                        Capetown

Nile R.   RED SEA

Arab and Berber peoples
SAHARA
(Gr. Br.)
Sudanese Empires
(Port.)
(Gr. Br.)   (Sp.)   Swahili language
Bantu kingdoms

AFRICA IN 1878

British	Portuguese
French	Belgian
German	Spanish
Italian	Independent African states

Ethiopia only until 1941. During those few years, Liberia was the only independent African nation, and even it was virtually a colony of the Firestone Rubber Company due to its millions of acres of plantations.

Impact of Colonial Rule

Inside the colonies and mandates, political and economic conditions varied. The biggest difference was whether or not a colony attracted white settlers. The settler colonies developed regimes that allowed for political participation by whites, while the political rights of blacks were limited, at best. In other colonies, Europeans regarded government as a matter of administration, not politics, and scarcely allowed questions of political participation to come up. There were also differences of national style in colonial administration. Yet conditions everywhere had enough in common to permit generalizations.

The foremost common trait was Europeans' limited understanding of Africans. Even in the best-administered colonies, the African populations were apt to be dismissed as savages. Those who acquired a Western-style education were still viewed as "trousered natives." They also risked becoming alienated from their own peoples. The French and Portuguese encouraged just this by offering full rights of citizenship to members of their colonial populations who met certain cultural standards. The Portuguese called such people *assimilados* (assimilated). The French used the patronizing term *évolués* (ones who have evolved or developed).

All forms of colonial rule were disrup-tive. Where white settlers were not present to contend for power, the organization of colonial rule ranged from military despotism to the British ideal of "indirect rule." This meant taking local chiefs and kings under "protectorate" and giving them places in a colonial hierarchy with only a few Europeans at the top. Some African rulers were removed. Others found their powers and their relations with their people changed as Europeans tried to turn them into cogs in the colonial machine. In stateless societies, Europeans sometimes arbitrarily appointed "warrant chiefs," on the ground that chiefship was the African way to rule. One African response to colonial rule was dual chiefship. An African people would put forward one "chief" to deal with Europeans, while quietly keeping another to perform the many functions the people needed from their leader. Under this unhappy compromise, the Europeans dealt with—and perhaps knew about—only the first chief, while the people respected only the second.

Colonial administrators showed little concern for political participation or for social needs, such as education and public health. The administrators at first relied on missionaries to meet such needs, and only slowly broadened the range of government functions. Some imperialists acknowledged a responsibility to prepare the people of their colonies for self-government in the remote future, but they felt no responsibility to develop the colonies' resources for the benefit of the populace. Instead, they exploited those resources for the world market.

In Africa, the colonial economic pattern assumed even starker contours than in Latin America, and no country except South Africa came close to throwing off economic dependency prior to World

War II. African prosperity, too, rested on exports of raw materials produced by mining or single-crop agriculture. Working conditions were scandalous, and highly unequal for blacks and whites. In 1939, South African blacks in mining or industry received one-eighth the wages of whites in the same jobs. Export agriculture centered on such crops as palm kernels and palm oil, peanuts, cotton, rubber, and cocoa. Plantations did not totally dominate the agricultural scene, especially in West Africa. Yet even independent peasant households suffered exploitation indirectly by the complex of interests—colonial trading companies, local middlemen, banks, shippers, insurance companies—that intervened between African producers and the faraway markets for colonial goods. The colonial governments were intimately linked to these interests and aided them by such means as requiring forced labor or imposing taxes that could only be paid in money, thus forcing Africans to produce new crops for export or to hire out as wage laborers.

One principle of colonial administration was that each colony should be financially self-sufficient. In places like the Belgian Congo, this policy degenerated into an "economy of pillage." Everywhere, colonial economies were at the mercy of fluctuating commodity prices. The Depression of 1929 underscored this fact so strongly that Britain and France began to consider economic diversification and improvements in public welfare for their colonies. But few practical improvements emerged before World War II. Economically, then, colonial rule did not prepare Africa for independence, but led in general to what radical critics call "the development of underdevelopment."

African Responses to Imperialism

African responses to Europeans have a long history. Even before the late nineteenth-century European scramble for Africa, many African social and economic systems had developed as responses to European-created changes, such as the transatlantic slave trade. Examples include the Ijo canoe houses and distinctively African Christian sects, which broke away from the missionary churches' organization, and sometimes also their doctrine.

To respond to European inroads, African rulers had a range of choices running from armed resistance to accommodation. Armed resistance was seldom totally successful. By defeating the Italian attempt of 1896, Ethiopia became the only African country to defend itself successfully against imperialism, until it fell to Mussolini in 1935. But resistance was seldom entirely futile, for it forced the thinly staffed European administrations to realize that their power had limits. Accommodation, too, had advantages, as it sometimes enabled Africans to influence the terms of colonial rule.

After colonization, Africans developed new institutions to advance their interests. In French-controlled Senegal, public letter writers helped develop a communications network linking the French-educated urban leaders to the rural populace. In South Africa, efforts to form broadly based African political organizations began during the 1880s.

Although World War I began when the colonization of Africa was not fully complete, the continent felt the war's effects in important ways. Thousands of Africans from the French colonies served on the Western front, as noted in Chapter 3. Because African territories under German and Allied control shared borders, there was some fighting in Africa. The Allied seizure of Togo, Cameroon, and South-West Africa presented little difficulty, but the campaign for German East Africa lasted for most of the war and involved many African troops. For Africans as for other colonial peoples, the spectacle of a brutal war among their colonial masters raised new questions about European supremacy.

Consequently, Africans became more assertive after World War I. In West Africa, wartime pressures produced widespread rioting in Sierra Leone, and a political association, the National Congress of British West Africa, was formed in 1920. In the towns, recent migrants from the countryside began to form voluntary associations—alumni groups, dance societies, sports clubs, religious or ethnic associations. Such groups provided important supports to people who were not yet at home in the towns. In addition, the societies served as channels of communications between towns and hinterland. In time, overtly political organizations grew out of organizations formed for other purposes. One sign of the limited extent to which Africans had yet adjusted to the boundaries created by the scramble was that nationalist ideas focused at first on large-scale entities: unity for all of English-speaking, or French-speaking, West Africa, even pan-African unity.

World War II precipitated the end of colonial rule. In 1935, the Italian attack on Ethiopia—the ancient Christian kingdom, which symbolized for blacks everywhere all that the scramble denied them—started a process of radicalization. From 1941 to 1943, North Africa provided the stage for some major campaigns of the war. Africans everywhere felt the impact of wartime shortages and

restrictions. Far more than in World War I, Africans were drawn into fighting forces in far parts of the world, where they saw that Europeans were not all governors and generals: many were peasants and privates who fought and died as they did. Broadened awareness and increased confidence gave new impetus to the pressures for social and political mobilization already at work. For nonsettler colonies like Nigeria, the age of independence was coming, although it did not open for most until the 1960s. For settler colonies like South Africa, the struggle would be longer and more difficult.

Nigeria Under the British

Nigeria today is Africa's most populous state and one of its most important. Like most African nations, it is a colonial creation and shares the diversity of the continent as a whole. The many peoples of Nigeria speak several hundred languages or dialects, from various language families. Four peoples have been especially prominent in Nigeria's modern history, however. The Hausa and Fulani live in the semiarid northern savanna, where Muslims form a majority. In the forest near the coast, where animist religions historically prevailed, are the Yoruba in the west and the Ibo (or Igbo) in the east.

Unification Under British Rule

Nigerian history had its unifying factors, even before the arrival of Europeans. Yet their coming redirected the economy from an orientation toward the trans-Saharan trade routes to a seaward orientation, really tying the various regions together. Through the early nineteenth century, the main theme in this reorientation was the slave trade, which drew many of its victims from the historically overpopulated Ibo lands of the southeast and Yoruba lands of the southwest.

For a long time, Europeans had little effect on the northern parts of Nigeria, which continued to evolve in response to stimuli coming from other Islamic lands across the Sahara. The most important event of the century preceding British rule was one of the Islamic reform movements then sweeping the savanna region of Africa and other parts of the Islamic world. The movement began among Fulani townsmen who criticized the religious laxity of the Hausa rulers under whom they lived. Led by the religious activist Usman dan Fodio, the movement erupted in 1804, toppled the Hausa kings, and established a *caliphate*—the term implies a state organized strictly according to the practice of the early Islamic community—centered at Sokoto. When the British eventually took control in northern Nigeria, they did so by defeating the Sokoto caliphate.

First, the British had to take the coastal zone. This occurred as slaving gave way to legitimate trade. Not all parts of Africa had commodities, other than slaves, that Europeans valued. But

Village near Zaria, Nigeria, early twentieth century. The village is in the grasslands of northern Nigeria.
The Mansell Collection

the Niger Delta had several. The most important was palm oil, used for soap making (hence the name Palmolive) and as an industrial lubricant in the prepetroleum era. By midcentury, British naval and consular personnel were increasingly intervening to regulate trade. In 1861, the British annexed Lagos on the western coast, and appointed a governor soon afterward. Lagos later became the capital of all Nigeria, a fact that gave the Yoruba people of the vicinity disproportionate prominence in Nigerian politics.

European interest also began to extend into the interior. In 1854, an exploration mission, using quinine against malaria, penetrated 900 miles into the interior without the horrible loss of life that had accompanied earlier attempts. Missionaries and merchants then enlarged their efforts. Some practices of the forest peoples, such as human sacrifice and the murder of newborn twins (thought to be the work of evil spirits), confirmed the missionaries' view that religious conversion required total cultural change. This outlook brought the clash of cultures into the starkest form.

It was the traders who put Nigeria together as an economic and political entity. In the 1870s, Sir George Goldie, one of the two most influential figures in the establishment of British rule, combined the companies trading on the Niger into the United African Company. The British government then gave the company the right to make treaties with local chiefs. Goldie's work enabled the British to claim the territory around the Niger after the Berlin Africa Congress of 1884–1885. By 1900, the British had established several protectorates inside what is now Nigeria, and created a military force, the West African Frontier Force, to operate in the interior under command of Frederick Lugard. He did more than anyone else to consolidate British rule in Nigeria.

In 1900, rivalry with the French to the west and a desire for greater coordination inside Nigeria led the British government to take over the functions of Goldie's company, then known as the Royal Niger Company. The country was then reorganized into the Lagos Colony and separate Northern and Southern Protectorates, with Lugard as governor in the north. In the south, British control was a reality. In the north, it was Lugard's mission to make it so.

Lugard had at his disposal only a small force to conquer the Sokoto caliphate, which, though in decline, presented a huge target. This situation suggested to Lugard what became known as indirect rule, a policy that he is often thought to have created, though the British had long used it in India. The strategy was to defeat the rulers of the caliphate, then take over their governmental apparatus and dominate their former subjects through it. By skillful use of superior technology, Lugard achieved military success by 1903, and then went on to consolidate indirect rule in the north. In 1912, he was appointed governor general of Nigeria with the task of amalgamating the entire country under a single administration, a task formally completed on January 1, 1914.

Nigeria's Development Under the British

Between 1900 and 1914, the consolidation of British rule quickly broke down accustomed ways of life. Economic development was extensive, although starting from levels so low that the results were impressive only on a colonial scale.

Chief Auyama, a British-appointed warrant chief in Enugu, eastern Nigeria, shown with some of his subchiefs.
Popperfoto

Political amalgamation created a huge free trade area, for example. Many local rulers were deprived of trade tolls they had collected, but trade grew and the distribution of wealth and power changed substantially. A major integrating factor was the extension of the railway into the interior. When it reached Kano, a key city of the Sokoto caliphate, in 1911, peanut shipments from that town rose to 19,288 tons, up from 1,179 tons in the preceding year. Amalgamation also gave Nigeria its first uniform monetary system.

Cultural and administrative change accompanied economic development. Missionaries challenged traditional beliefs and offered the country its first common system of literacy. Initial suspicion of missionary education waned as people realized that it offered opportunities in economic life and in the central administration. Western-educated Nigerian men who moved into lower central administrative jobs became the first Africans oriented to thinking of Nigeria as a whole. In the north, where the Sokoto caliphate survived under British protection, indirect rule made government less flexible and more autocratic. More serious consequences followed Lugard's attempt to introduce his pet policy to the south. For example, among the stateless Ibo, who historically had no chiefs, Lugard appointed "warrant chiefs," who proved highly unpopular.

The pace of change slowed during the interwar years. The administrative system, which had been introduced abruptly on the eve of World War I, evolved only gradually after the war. Economic change slowed as well, especially during the Depression. Nigeria still had only 1,903 miles of railroad track in 1945. Foreign trade grew in value from 0.2 British pounds for each Nigerian in 1900 to 1.3 pounds in 1945. This was a substantial rate of increase, yet at low levels that clearly indicated limited purchasing power. By World War II, industrialization had barely begun outside the mining sector of the economy. Low per capita incomes limited the internal market for industrial products and made it difficult for the governor to raise revenue to support development projects. As in all colonial economies, severe fluctuations in export prices were a major obstacle to development. During the Depression, the value of Nigerian exports fell by about half, and did not recover before World War II. After the vigorous beginning of 1900–1914, colonialism had done little for Nigeria's development.

Rise of Nigerian Nationalism

Nigerian political activism first emerged as a demand for political participation, not independence. The National Congress of British West Africa, a political association founded in 1920, included representatives of the four British colonies of Gambia, Sierra Leone, Gold Coast, and Nigeria. Its demands included an end to racial discrimination in civil service appointments, the right to control specific administrative positions and functions, and the founding of a university in West Africa.

In 1920, Europeans still felt they could just reject such demands. Yet, small concessions occurred. The Lagos town council became elective in 1920. More important, under the constitution of 1922, elected African representatives joined the colony's legislative council, though they were outnumbered there by the governor and his staff. Comparable provisions appeared in the constitutions enacted for Sierra Leone in 1924 and the Gold Coast (now Ghana) in 1927. Several political parties quickly formed at Lagos to contest the seats, and newspapers sprang up to support the parties.

This kind of political activity initially remained largely localized at Lagos, among the Yoruba people. In other regions nationalist political activity emerged only later, or took different forms. In the north, as in the princely states of the Indian maharajas, indirect rule fossilized the political forms of a bygone era. In the southeast, the main problem was resentment of warrant chiefs. Here a crisis developed, following a census that counted women as well as men, over a rumor that women were to be taxed. In 1929, the women of Aba and Owerri responded to this threat, and to the economic effects of the Depression, in an uprising that became known as the Aba Women's War. Organizing through their age-grade societies and market associations, the women attacked unpopular chiefs and institutions, causing enough damage to provoke armed police retaliation. The British then recognized the failure of indirect rule in this region and began efforts to devise a policy better suited to it.

In the 1930s, the Depression, the growing integration of the country, and the spread of education stimulated the emergence and diffusion of new forms of political activity. One of the first new organizations, the West African Students' Union formed in London, exerted a major influence on nationalist leaders of later decades. The next important organization, the Nigerian Youth Movement, was formed at Lagos in 1936. It became an organization of national importance under leadership of Dr. Nnamdi ("Zik") Azikiwe, an American-educated Ibo, the first prominent non-Yoruba politician. The Nigerian Youth Movement suffered because of quarrels among its leaders, and the fact that different leaders came from different peoples injected ethnic rivalries into the national movement.

As the 1930s wore on, Nigerian nationalists pressed for economic and social concessions, as well as political participation. World War II, which stimulated the growth of the economy and the labor movement, heightened these demands. In 1944, after the virtual disintegration of the Nigerian Youth Movement, Azikiwe founded the National Council of Nigeria and the Cameroons (NCNC), a confederation of trade unions, small parties, ethnic associations and other groups, to pursue these demands. When the British introduced a new constitution in 1947 without consulting Nigerians on its terms, virtually all the nationalists attacked it, and Nigerian politics began to move toward—not participation—but independence.

As far as British-Nigerian relations were concerned, the transition to independence would prove relatively easy. The greater challenge would be to divide power among Nigeria's peoples and regions so as to create the basis for peace and unity.

South Africa: A History of Two Struggles

Today's South Africa is the product of two struggles. One was between two white communities—the English and the Boers, who are largely of Dutch origin—for political control. The other was between whites—of either community—and blacks for control of the land.

White settlement in South Africa began almost accidentally. In the seventeenth century, the Dutch East India Company set up a station at the Cape of Good Hope on the way to its possessions in what is now Indonesia. In 1657, the company allowed colonization of the countryside. Gradually, a Dutch-speaking, slave-owning agricultural community developed, favored by the moderate climate near the Cape. The *Boers* (Dutch for peasant or farmer) believed that every settler was entitled to 6,000 acres. Over generations, this policy forced the Boers to spread out, coming into conflict with the black populations. As the Europeans expanded from the sparsely settled territories of the west into the more thickly settled territories of the Bantu speakers in the east, these conflicts became serious. Adapting their Calvinist faith to justify their intentions, the Boers identified white dominance with the will of God. Enough racial mixing occurred to form a "colored" population—in South Africa meaning people of mixed ancestry—but racial mixing remained less extensive than in Latin America.

Boer expansion to the east worsened competition for land among Africans there. By the early nineteenth century, a Bantu-speaking people that needed more land for its cattle could expand only at the expense of its neighbors. One people, the Zulus, did this with dramatic results, referred to in Zulu as the *mfecane* (crushing) of the peoples.

The Zulus' rise to military power was the work of a chief named Shaka (1787–1828). Becoming chief in 1816, he began to reform and adapt an existing system of military organization based on age-regiments. He tightened discipline over his regiments and improved their tactics and weapons. In addition, he enlarged the customary scope of war into a total effort to wipe out his enemies' resistance and incorporate the survivors into his own kingdom. In 1818, Shaka embarked on a career of conquest. The effects were felt far and wide. Some peoples fled his regiments, clashing with one another. Some fled toward Cape Colony, worsening conflict with the Boers. Some started their own campaigns of conquest, extending as far as Lake Victoria. The mfecane became one of the most widely felt upheavals of nineteenth-century Africa. The Zulus remained a small independent nation on the Indian Ocean coast of Natal into the late 1870s, and a Zulu rising occurred as late as 1906.

Meanwhile, conflict had developed within the white population of South Africa. The democratic ideas that swept Europe and America in the late eighteenth century also influenced the Boers at the Cape of Good Hope, awakening a concern for individual rights (their own, at least) and republicanism. Then as a consequence of the Napoleonic wars in Europe, Cape Colony came under British control, permanently so in 1806. After that, the ideas of Boer rights and republicanism became ways to express anti-British feeling.

British settlers, who began to arrive in 1820, disapproved of many things the Boers said and did. British missionaries were shocked at the way Boers treated Africans. The British soon abolished slavery and enacted other reforms. In 1853, they granted the Cape Colony a constitution that allowed for parliamentary government and a nonracial franchise, in which males of all races who met a property qualification were registered in common as voters. Ultimately, differences between the British and the Boers gave rise to Afrikaner nationalism and spurred the development of Afrikaans, derived from Dutch, into a language in its own right.

Many Boers had had too much of British policy long before 1853. By the 1830s, many had decided on migration (*trek* in Dutch) beyond the frontiers of Cape Colony. They would create a republic, their ideal political form, where they could assure "proper relations" between blacks and whites. At this point, their frustrations and the mfecane interacted, for the Boers learned that lands to the east of Cape Colony had been depopulated and turned into grazing land by the Zulus. By 1839, Boer migrants had defeated the Zulus and set up a republic in Natal. Unwilling to accept this arrangement, the British annexed Natal in 1845. But most Boers, still determined, migrated again and created the republics of the Transvaal and the Orange Free State to the north. The British recognized these states in 1852 and 1854. At that point, the area now covered by South Africa consisted of two British colonies (Cape Colony and Natal), the two Boer republics, and numerous African chiefdoms and kingdoms.

In the late nineteenth century, both the black-white struggle for land and the Afrikaner-British struggle for political dominance grew more intense. The land struggle proved tragically unequal, as it did in many other cases where capitalistic and communalistic economic outlooks confronted each other during the age of Western expansion. Whites took much land by conquest and much by other means. They entered the struggle for land armed with tools and ideas unfamiliar to Africans: surveying instruments, title deeds, and the very ideas of individual ownership and a market for land sales. Conquest gave the whites power to create a legal environment that enforced their ideas. In one part of the country after another, unwary blacks traded land rights for guns or liquor, or, where formerly communal lands had been divided into individual holdings, lost them through inability to adjust their way of life quickly to the new conditions. In a few cases, African rulers avoided annexation by getting their kingdoms made protectorates of the British crown. By this means, Swaziland, Bechuanaland (now Botswana), and Basutoland (Lesotho) remained separate as High Commission Territories when the Union of South Africa was formed in 1910. They acquired formal independence in the 1960s.

Competition for the land and its resources was also a major factor in the struggle between British and Afrikaners. In 1867, diamonds were discovered near the junction of the Orange and Vaal rivers, just outside the western edge of the Orange Free State. That began a race between the British—who won—and the Orange Free State to annex the diamond territory. Then, in 1886, gold was discovered in the Transvaal at Witwatersrand, near Johannesburg. An influx of gold-hungry outlanders (*uitlanders*) ensued, and the building of railway lines toward the mining centers accelerated. South Africa had 4,000 miles of track by 1899. The Boers felt threatened, for most of the great entrepreneurs were British. The outstanding example was Cecil Rhodes (1853–1902), who acquired immense wealth from gold and diamonds, served as prime minister of the Cape Colony in the early 1890s, and personally directed British expansion into the regions that became Northern and Southern Rhodesia (now Zambia and Zimbabwe), so blocking Boer dreams of expansion to the north.

In the 1890s, Anglo-Boer tensions built toward a climax. Rhodes tried to destabilize the Transvaal government by encouraging the outlander gold-seekers to revolt. In 1895, a raid led by a Rhodes agent, Leander Starr Jameson, tried to raise a revolt, but failed. Reactions to this episode finished Rhodes's political career. But because the monetary systems of most major nations were based on gold, the British government was willing to take over the struggle for control of South Africa and provoke a showdown. War broke out in 1899 and lasted until 1902.

Compared to other colonial wars, the Anglo-Boer War proved trying indeed. Boer commandos used their accustomed guerrilla tactics deep in British territory. Not prepared for that kind of war, the British responded brutally, burning farms, and moving civilians into concentration camps, where over 25,000 died of disease. Finally, the war turned into one of attrition, which the Boers could not win. The British got peace on their terms in 1902, after a bitter foretaste of coming twentieth-century conflicts.

The Union of South Africa: Politics and Economy

The Anglo-Boer War set the stage for the unification of South Africa. Having bullied the Boers, the British now yielded to many of their demands. For their part, the Boers found that they could get more through conciliatory tactics, for example, by soft-pedaling their wish for a republic. In 1910, after several years of negotiation between the two white communities, but with no consultation of nonwhites, the four colonies became the Union of South Africa under a constitution that recognized the union as a *dominion* (a term used for former colonies that acquired autonomy within the British Empire). The government was headed by a governor general representing the British monarch, and there was a two-chamber parliament. Dutch and English were both official languages. Because the British feared that extending the color-blind franchise of the Cape Colony to the entire union would wreck the unity movement, voting rights were left as they had been in each of the colonies before union. As a result, nonwhites remained permanently disenfranchised in Transvaal and the Orange Free State. Peace with fellow whites mattered more to the British than votes for blacks, whose cheap labor mattered perhaps most of all.

So began the Union of South Africa, as the country was known until it formally became a republic and broke with the British Commonwealth in 1961. Three trends dominated the country's development through World War II. The Afrikaners, who formed the majority among whites (about 60 percent in the 1970s), gained political control. The rights of nonwhites—the real majority—were steadily reduced. Finally, thanks to its mineral wealth and the exploitation of black labor, the country completed the transition from an economy based on mining to one that combined mineral exports with industrial self-sufficiency. South Africa's success in industrialization was a rare achievement in the co-

lonial world, but one produced at terrible social and political costs.

The political life of the Union began auspiciously. The first two prime ministers, Louis Botha (1910–1919) and Jan Smuts (1919–1924), belonged to the South African party. Both Boer generals who had fought the British, they now tried to unite the two white communities. They also participated in the Paris Peace Conference and influenced the emerging concept of the British Commonwealth. Smuts suggested the mandate concept that was adopted by the League of Nations, and South Africa acquired South-West Africa (Namibia) as a mandate. Smuts gained a reputation as a world-class statesman.

The untroubled mood of 1910 did not last long. In 1913, the National party formed under the leadership of J. B. M. Hertzog, with an Afrikaner nationalist platform. Because the government participated in World War I, it was unable to make peace with the Hertzog movement, for many Afrikaners sympathized with the Germans, to the point of open rebellion. In race relations, though Botha and Smuts were moderate compared to later prime ministers, the passage of restrictive laws soon began. The Native Land Act of 1913, for example, confined African land ownership to Native Reserves, based on former chiefdoms. The reserves then contained only 7 percent of the land for 78 percent of the population. Africans were supposed to be in other parts of the country only as temporarily resident workers. A system of passes controlled their movements, and the Native Urban Areas Act of 1923 imposed residential segregation.

South Africa's economic growth nonetheless caused thousands of African laborers to migrate to urban centers.

Development thus produced racial interdependence, not separation. Conflict was bound to result. When gold prices fell after World War I, for example, mine owners attempted to cut costs by admitting blacks to jobs previously held by whites. White workers responded with the Rand Rebellion of 1922. When Smuts used troops to put down the protest, his popularity waned, and Hertzog's Nationalists came to power in alliance with the Labour party in 1924.

The policies of the Hertzog government of 1924–1933 were those of Afrikaner nationalists, opposed to the British Empire and unabashedly insistent on white dominance. Hertzog played a key role in hardening racial segregation and in launching South Africa's drive for industrial self-sufficiency. Politically, he pushed for recruitment of Afrikaners into government service, formerly dominated by English speakers. He made Afrikaans (as well as Dutch) an official language, required it to be taught in public schools, and campaigned for all civil officials to be bilingual in Afrikaans and English. Hertzog also moved toward greater independence from Britain, a process favored by the British Statute of Westminster (1931), which transformed the empire into a Commonwealth of Nations and gave the dominions complete independence to make laws and conduct foreign relations.

Hertzog's economic policies reflected a desire to further the interests of the Afrikaners. Since British capitalists dominated the economy, he pursued this goal largely through state intervention in it. In 1927, the government set up the South African Iron and Steel Corporation as a public enterprise, intended to create jobs for Afrikaners and use the country's abundant coal and iron ore to achieve economic independence. Other state enterprises followed, for electric power, radio, and air transport. South Africa was becoming an industrial economy and a regional economic power. From 1933 on, the country entered a sustained boom that lasted into the late 1970s. Yet the majority could not enjoy this boom, for it depended on a black underclass working for minimal wages to pay taxes enacted to force them into wage labor. At the same time, the government passed laws to reduce white unemployment by barring nonwhites from many of the better jobs (the "color bar").

Because of gold exports, the impact of the Depression on South Africa was relatively slight and brief. Hertzog's popularity suffered nevertheless, and he merged his Nationalist party with Smuts's South African party in 1934 in an effort to stave off electoral defeat. Extremist Afrikaners naturally resented this compromise, and Daniel Malan formed a Purified National party. Meanwhile, the Smuts-Hertzog fusion government (1933–1939) pushed through further segregationist legislation. The Native Representation Act of 1936 effectively eliminated Africans in the Cape Province from the common voter rolls. Thereafter, Africans of the various provinces were to vote separately to select whites who would represent them in parliament. Another law of the same year enlarged the native reserves, but only to 13 percent of the country's land surface, while extending territorial segregation elsewhere.

Segregation was hardening. The influence of European fascism compounded South African racism in these years, a fact illustrated by Malan's Purified Nationalist party and many hard-line Afrikaner organizations. With Afrikaner opinion moving in this direction, the Smuts-Hertzog United party had difficulty holding together.

On September 2, 1939, the government split over the question of war with Germany. The British governor general asked Smuts to form a new government without Hertzog. The Smuts government (1939–1948) devoted itself primarily to the war, but showed some signs of moderation in racial policy. War made it necessary to set aside some of Hertzog's segregation policies, for labor needs could only be met by hiring blacks without regard to the color bar (though at lower wages than whites). Smuts, whose ideas on racial policy were more moderate than Hertzog's, also created a "Native Laws" Commission, whose report of 1948 urged concessions. Observing that blacks were already incorporated in the economy, the report recommended that they be included in the country's political life too.

Most whites reacted to the report as if it were a bombshell. Hertzog's Nationalists and Malan's Purified Nationalists had by then reunited, and the more extreme Malan had captured party leadership. In the 1948 election, Malan's Nationalists won by capitalizing on white anxiety. It was then that the Nationalists unveiled their doctrine of *apartheid*, which elaborated Hertzog's policies into a program of strict racial separation.

Nonwhite Responses to Consolidation of White Supremacy

For nonwhites, the political developments of 1910–1948 meant a steady erosion of rights, against which protest proved less and less effective. Part of the problem was lack of unity, for the non-white category included three types of people: racially mixed coloreds, Asian (mostly Indian) migrants to South Africa, and Africans belonging to many peoples. White governments reinforced this fragmentation by legally defining the status of different groups in different ways, and by setting up the native reserves on tribal lines. In the preunion period, rights of nonwhites also differed from one colony to another.

Political activity among nonwhites developed first in the relatively free atmosphere of Cape Colony. There, in 1884, John Jabavu founded the first African political newspaper. An Aborigines Association was founded in 1882 to encourage cooperation among religious denominations, an effort motivated in part by the proliferation of separatist churches. In 1902, the colored population of the Cape established the African Political Organization, which had branches outside Cape Colony and was reportedly the first political organization for nonwhites from all parts of South Africa.

Natal was the original center for the Indian population, and laws discriminating against them were passed there in the 1890s. Chapter 4 noted the importance of Gandhi's South African years (1893–1914) for his development, and his contributions to the South African Indian community. He formed the Natal Indian Congress in 1894, patterned after the Indian nationalist movement. His passive resistance campaigns also won concessions from the Union government in the Indian Relief Bill of 1914.

The fact that the Union of South Africa was created without consulting nonwhites gave new impetus to political mobilization and to cooperation among nonwhite communities. In 1909, a South African Native Convention met to protest the terms of union. In 1912, the

South African Native National Congress was formed. Its name was shortened in 1923 to African National Congress (ANC), and it is still the most influential political organization among South African blacks, although illegal. Influenced by Gandhi, the ANC long remained a small organization dominated by moderates. Its goal was not revolution, but political participation and equal rights. It remained committed to nonviolence for almost half a century. Gradually, however, the deteriorating political situation of South African blacks led to radicalization and broader efforts at political mobilization. The Native Representation Act of 1936 was a special shock that helped to bring forth new leadership. Alfred Xuma, a U.S.–educated physician, became president of the ANC in 1940 and broadened it into a mass movement of national scope. During World War II, a still more radical generation formed the Congress Youth League and toppled Xuma from ANC leadership in 1949.

The ANC and the many other political organizations that emerged during the interwar years all faced certain common problems. One was reaching agreement on how to respond to government policy changes. Even a measure as drastic as the Native Representation Act of 1936 divided nonwhites. Some thought it was to their interest to cooperate in the procedures of indirect representation provided by the law. Others opposed cooperation. The question of political methods was also difficult. Some have asserted that Gandhi's nonviolence and passive resistance are ideal methods for a people confronting oppressors who use superior force to impose morally indefensible policies. Yet, when South African blacks tried the same methods, whites responded with violence, not

concessions. Smuts, the scholar-statesman, was personally impressed by Gandhi. Hertzog candidly admitted that white settlers' fears of being deluged by the African majority lay behind his segregationist policies. One of the greatest dangers to nonwhite unity lay in the possibility of exclusive black nationalism, opposed to other nonwhites as well as to whites. In fact, a movement of this type, the Pan-Africanist Congress, eventually broke off from the ANC.

In the years immediately following World War II, a new era was clearly beginning. The racial gulf was widening inside South Africa, and its racial policy was also beginning to attract criticism abroad. A sign of the change was the leadership of newly independent India (1947) in attacking South African racism at the United Nations.

By then, the Afrikaners had won political control from the British, and the whites together had wrested control of the land from the blacks. In the process, South Africa had diversified economically and had embarked on a sustained period of economic growth. But these accomplishments rested on a radical denial of majority rights, an injustice that had begun to isolate South Africa in world opinion.

Conclusion: South Africa in the Perspective of World History

The development of the South African racial system represents a radical attempt to deny the processes of mass mobilization that have elsewhere typified the twentieth century. That being the case, the final question that this chapter raises is why South Africa has evolved as it has.

No doubt there are many reasons. Racial exclusivism is one possible response to an environment where majority rule, or even a more equal income distribution, would destroy the ruling minority's privileged way of life. This is not the only possible response, as is clear from the case of Latin America, where Europeans also first appeared as dominant and racially distinct settler minorities. The fact remains that Afrikaner opposition to identification with the majority hardened very early, and even the relative liberalism of the British had eroded by 1910, although there continue to be some who oppose apartheid. The presence in South Africa of two white communities, one of which, the Afrikaners, felt threatened by the British and the nonwhites, no doubt worsened the exclusivist trend. Once committed to exclusivism, the white minority no longer had the choice of mobilizing the masses. Instead, it could only rally behind the leaders who were most uncompromising in defense of its interests—not Smuts, but Hertzog and later Malan.

Meanwhile, once the majority's demand for political participation had been denied, its political mobilization could only occur in opposition to the established order. Economic discrimination limited the majority's means for the struggle, but heightened their incentives. Ultimately the struggle would become very difficult. For South Africa's majority would face not a few colonial troops and administrators as in Nigeria, but a long-established European population with all the political and military institutions of a sovereign state.

Since World War II, all the rest of Africa has gained independence under majority rule. Everywhere but South Africa, white settler regimes have proved transient, unable to survive for long after the collapse of European global dominance. Can the history of South Africa ultimately be any different? It is difficult to believe that the themes noted in Nigeria will not appear in South Africa too: the advent of the mass society, problems of unity and cohesion, and the dual struggle to achieve political power for the majority and socioeconomic change in its interest.

Suggestions for Further Reading

Abrahams, Peter, *Mine Boy* (1976).

Achebe, Chinua, *Things Fall Apart* (1959).

——, *Arrow of God* (1969).

Crowder, Michael, *The Story of Nigeria* (1978).

——, ed., *West African Resistance: The Military Response to Colonial Occupation* (1971).

Curtin, Philip, Steven Feierman, Leonard Thompson, and Jan Vansina, *African History* (1978).

Davenport, T. R. H., *South Africa: A Modern History*, 2d ed. (1978).

Ekundare, R. Olufemi, *An Economic History of Nigeria, 1860–1960* (1973).

Hafkin, Nancy, and Edna Bay, eds., *Women in Africa* (1976).

Hull, Richard W., *Southern Africa: Civilizations in Turmoil* (1981).

Oliver, Roland, and Anthony Atmore, *Africa Since 1800*, 3d ed. (1981).

Shostak, Marjorie, *Nisa: The Life and Words of a !Kung Woman* (1983).

Wilson, Henry S., *The Imperial Experience in Sub-Saharan Africa since 1870* (1977).

Wilson, Monica, and Leonard Thompson, eds. *The Oxford History of South Africa*, 2 vols. (1969–1971).

Chapter 10

ASIAN STRUGGLES FOR INDEPENDENCE AND DEVELOPMENT

Culturally, Asia is more diverse than either Latin America or Africa. Extending from the Eastern Mediterranean and the Ural Mountains of the Soviet Union to the Pacific, it represents slightly more than half the Afro-Eurasian land mass. It includes three of the four zones that gave rise to the world's most influential civilizations: the Middle East, India, and East Asia, the fourth being the European zone. Asia also includes Central Asia and Siberia in the north, as well as mainland and island Southeast Asia, from Burma to Indonesia and the Philippines.

During much of their long history, Asian civilizations were the world's most brilliant. At a time when these civilizations excelled that of Europe, the attraction of their richness launched Europeans on the voyages that helped establish Western dominance and make Western civilization the most advanced of all. In the twentieth century, Asians have struggled to escape this dominance and to recover something like their earlier standing in the world.

In tribute to Asia's diversity, this chapter will depart from the pattern, used in the last two, of a continental overview followed by closeups of several countries. We shall discuss Asia's three major centers of civilization along with specific countries from each. We shall emphasize the Western impact on the Asians and their efforts, rooted to an important degree in their own traditions, to reassert their independence. In the period discussed here, the West's impact on Asia was tremendous. Although parts of Asia remained free of formal European domination in 1914—the Ottoman Empire, Iran, Afghanistan, Siam, China, and Japan—European influence was so great that real self-determination was almost nonexistent.

The pattern of 1914 was destined for change. Japan, uniquely successful in escaping the common Asian fate, had already accomplished the most important part of its modern transformation, gaining formal recognition as a great power before World War I. Between the wars, Turkey became the Asian country next most successful in reasserting its independence. Neither of Asia's two most populous countries, India or China, regained meaningful independence in this period, but both would do so shortly after World War II.

We shall examine the three major Asian zones in the order in which they came under European sway and highlight the experiences of India, Turkey, China, and Japan. Comparison of their experiences in the conclusion will suggest four factors that governed the success of each country's adaptation to twentieth-century conditions: responsiveness to foreign ideas, consensus about the definition of national identity and about the way to organize political life, basic social change to support the drive for independence, and the ability to devise an economic development strategy that could overcome the effects of colonialism.

India Under the British

Colonialism hit India first and hardest, although the results were ultimately benign by colonial standards. After the arrival of the Portuguese in 1498, a succession of European peoples vied for control of India's trade. By the eighteenth century, the leading contenders were the officially chartered trading companies representing Britain and France. The British East India Company won against its French competitor and began consolidating its control, a formidable task. The country was large—about half the size of the continental United States today. India's peoples spoke hundreds of languages and dialects, including almost twenty major languages. Among the half dozen religions, the Hindus were far the most numerous, although the Muslims had long been dominant politically. And the political situation was chaotic. The Mughal Empire, the last independent state to rule most of India, had fallen apart in the eighteenth century. In the 1790s, the British directly controlled only a little territory, mostly in the northeast, but the East India Company repeatedly extended its zones of direct control. Elsewhere, it sought alliances with local rulers, cultivating cooperative ones as supporters of British rule.

From Company Rule to Crown Rule

Company rule lasted until 1858. By then, essentially all of India lay under direct or indirect British rule. With this unification, company rule brought many changes. The British abolished *sati*, the ritual suicide of Hindu widows on the cremation pyres of their husbands, and promoted English-style education. They introduced the ideas of nineteenth-century liberalism—for example, through the Charter Act of 1833. Politically, this act promised equal rights for all Indians, including the right to employment under the East India Company. Economically, the act abolished the company's monopoly over most branches of trade and opened India to unrestricted British immigration and enterprise. Although the political provisions of the act were not fully enforced, the economic ones were. Free trade had come to India.

These measures had mixed effects. Intervention in matters of Hindu or Muslim religious belief provoked the Sepoy Mutiny of 1857–1858. This Anglo-Indian war, the bloodiest conflict ever fought in India, created lasting distrust of the "natives" and prompted the British government to take control away from the company. In the long run, because Britain was the only industrialized state of the first half of the nineteenth century, free trade was more devastating than the mutiny. For an unindustrialized country like India, free trade meant the collapse of production by hand, huge unemployment, and economic subordination.

When crown rule replaced company rule in 1858, India assumed the status in the British Empire that it retained until independence in 1947. With its huge markets and large production of spices, tea, and other exotic goods, India was the "jewel of empire." Queen Victoria became sovereign over the country and assumed the title empress of India in 1877. A viceroy represented her there. In London, where the Colonial Office managed most of Britain's overseas dependencies, a special ministry, the India Office, managed India. Its head, the secretary of state for India, was a member of the prime minister's cabinet.

In India, crown rule had a conservative impact in some ways. British control over the Indian army was tightened. Many local princes were left in place (indirect rule). But technological modernization continued, as steamships, telegraphs, and railroads tied India more tightly into the imperial system. As usual, colonial administration siphoned off much of the country's wealth. By 1892, about a fourth of the annual expenditures of the government of India went for overseas expenses. Indians had little to say about this. The governance of India remained mostly in the hands of British bureaucrats.

Gradual Progress Toward Self-rule

From 1858 to 1947, Indian participation in public affairs enlarged slowly. Indians were recognized as eligible for certain appointments in the civil service in 1854. But until 1921, the examinations required for appointment occurred only in England, not in India. The first steps toward giving Indians control of municipal and other local affairs, and representation on the councils that assisted the viceroy and the governors of Bombay and Madras, also took place during the first half-century of crown rule. But not until 1907 were the first Indian members appointed to the council of the secretary of state for India in London.

Far-reaching change began only after World War I. In 1917, Secretary of State for India Edwin Samuel Montagu promised "increasing association of Indians in every branch of the administration," "gradual development of self-governing institutions," and "progressive realization of responsible government." Delivery on these promises came with two acts of the British Parliament, the Government of India acts of 1921 and 1935. These created a governmental system that, more than any other in the colonial world, represented genuine progress toward self-rule.

The 1935 act provided for India to have a federal form or organization, in which the local princes would retain their territories. The princes failed to agree about implementation of this principle, thus dooming themselves to political extinction after independence. But other provisions of the two acts took effect. Most importantly, these acts transferred virtually all government responsibilities at the provincial level, and selected ones at the central-government level, from colonial administrators to ministers responsible to the provincial and central legislative assemblies. In other words, these responsibilities passed into Indian hands. Both Government of India acts also extended the franchise. In 1935, some 35 million men and women, one-sixth of the adult population, were eligible to vote. Although the act of 1935 initially dissatisfied Indian nationalists, large sections of it were incorporated into the constitution of independent India in 1950. Other important reforms of the interwar period included the beginning of modern-style social legislation and efforts to recruit large numbers of Indians into the Indian civil service and the officer ranks of the Indian army.

What had brought about this transition from the colonial pattern of bureaucratic government to internal self-rule? A major factor was the duration and depth of the British influence. In India there had been time for reality to catch up part-way with rhetoric about preparing colonial peoples for self-rule. The Indians had also learned a lot. By the early nineteenth century, some Indians had acquired a good Western, as well as Indian, education. In time, such leaders learned not only the principles that governed political life in Britain, but also the methods that citizens used to exert pressure on their rulers. The results included the founding of India's major nationalist party, the Indian National Congress, in 1885—exceptionally early by colonial standards.

The Congress was Hindu dominated from the start, and tensions with Muslims and other communities soon arose. The Hindu majority had certain qualities, however, that enabled it to react to the British more positively than many colonial peoples could. The Hindus had not been sorry to see the advent of the British end the earlier Muslim domination. In addition, Hinduism lacked the doctrinal definition or closedness of some other religions. Hindus could absorb Western ideas into their outlook with less sense of conflict than Muslims. Finally, there was charismatic leadership, furnished by Muhammad Ali Jinnah (1876–1949) to the Muslims and, even more, by Mahatma Gandhi (1869–1948) to the Hindus. In the long run, the British were forced to make concessions. Among the many who contributed to this outcome, Gandhi holds a unique place.

Gandhi and Nonviolence

We have already examined Gandhi's background and ideas in Chapter 4. When he returned to India in 1915, he was already known for his work in South Africa and his writings. He soon began

Mahatma Gandhi and his wife, Kasturbai, on their return to India, 1915.
D. G. Tendulkar

don cooperation with the British and brought Gandhi to leadership of the movement.

In 1920 Gandhi opened a major campaign of noncooperation—refusal to work for the British, to pay taxes, to use British products, to associate with the British in any way. He predicted that this strategy would produce self-rule by the end of 1921. When that date passed without self-rule, disillusionment spread, and outbreaks of violence occurred. The British imprisoned Gandhi in 1922. By the time of his release in 1924, enthusiasm for noncooperation had waned, and Hindu-Muslim tensions had increased dangerously.

It was time for a different approach. Later Gandhi mounted two more large civil disobedience campaigns: one in 1930–1932 against the British salt monopoly and salt tax (salt was a major dietary requirement for poor workers in this hot country), another in 1940–1942 in protest against the fact that Indians were forced to fight in World War II as subjects of the British. But for most of the 1920s and 1930s, he devoted himself to his Constructive Program, symbolized by his spinning wheel and the homespun cloth he wore and tried to popularize. With this program went continued reformist efforts to improve the lot of women, whom Gandhi regarded as having a greater capacity for nonviolence than men, and untouchables. Meanwhile, India's industrialists—including some extremely wealthy ones who became Gandhi disciples and bankrolled his ashram experiments in communal poverty—pursued goals of import substitution and heavy industrial development, much as in other non-Western countries. In a sense, Gandhi and the industrialists pursued the same goal: self-sufficiency. The industrialists were on the path of the fu-

applying his nonviolent techniques on behalf of the poor and dispossessed. When the British prolonged the wartime suspension of civil liberties into the postwar years, after having promised reforms that eventually became policy in the Government of India Act of 1921, Gandhi called for a nationwide campaign of civil disobedience. The ensuing tensions climaxed in 1919 at Amritsar, where the British commander, who had forbidden gatherings, led the massacre of a crowd that had peaceably assembled to celebrate a Hindu festival. National outrage then led the Congress to aban-

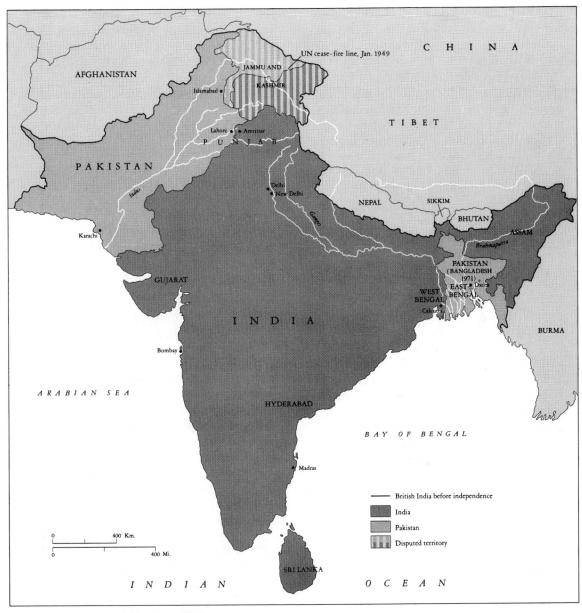

Map 10.1   The Partition of British India, 1947

ture, but Gandhi knew better how to capture the popular imagination of the day.

Gandhi was politically astute. For example, sensing the danger of a split in the Congress party in 1928, he worked to elect Jawaharlal Nehru as its president, even though the younger man's reformist socialism placed him well to the left of Gandhi's own views. Later, although he disliked certain features of the Government of India Act of 1935, Gandhi decided that members of the Congress should participate in elections and take office. Congress leaders had waited so long for power that many used it badly. Muslims protested, but they had fared poorly at the polls, while the Congress won a smashing victory. Soon Jinnah and many other Muslims became committed to the goal of a separate state. Nevertheless, officeholding unquestionably helped prepare the Congress leadership for independence.

With time, especially under the stresses of World War II, Gandhi's hold over the masses seemed to weaken, although it never vanished. As British rule approached its end and preparations were made to divide the country into separate Hindu and Muslim states. Gandhi devoted himself to restraining violence and trying to maintain good will among religious communities. He had always opposed the "vivisection" of India. But on August 15, 1947, India and Pakistan became independent as separate states. The Muslim state, Pakistan, combined two widely separated territories under a single national government. The mood of India had shifted away from Gandhi's vision. In January 1948 he was assassinated by a member of an extremist Hindu movement.

Even in his own country, Gandhi's methods have not been the ones most used to solve the political and economic problems of peoples trying to escape from colonialism. Yet his memory lives on. His nonviolent principles have exerted a far-reaching influence, from the African National Congress in South Africa, to Martin Luther King and the U.S. civil rights movement, to the European antinuclear movement of the 1980s.

The Middle East and North Africa in the Era of European Expansionism

Unlike India, most of the Middle East survived to World War I without formal colonization. But this region had a special significance for European colonialism from the beginning. For a long time, as noted in Chapter 1, Europe's prime source of exotic goods was the Islamic ports of the eastern Mediterranean.* Knowing that many of those goods were produced farther to the east, Europeans began to seek direct access to their sources, so opening the age of oceanic

---

* A note on terms: *Islam* is the dominant religion of the Middle East and North Africa, a culturally cohesive region that is historically centered in Southwest Asia, although it straddles two continents. *Islamic* is an adjective referring to this religion, the civilization that grew up around it, or the people who adhere to it. *Muslim* is the Arabic term for a person who accepts this faith. The term *Arab* refers not to religion, but to language and ethnic identity. Most Arabs are Muslims, but some are Christians, and some Jews also used to live—a few still do—in Arabic-speaking countries. Among Middle Eastern Muslims, the most important non-Arab linguistic groups are the *Turks* and the *Iranians.* Elsewhere, Muslims are numerous—often in the majority—in places as far apart as West Africa and the Philippines.

exploration that brought Columbus to the Americas and the Portuguese to India.

Dimensions of European Dominance

Europeans first undermined the economy of the Middle East. The sea route they established around Africa diverted the trade that had enriched the Middle East, slowly choking off its economic vitality. And although they did not take control, Europeans intervened in the internal affairs of Middle Eastern countries. By continuing to allow foreign trade to be organized along traditional lines, Islamic rulers opened the way for this intervention.

Originally, when Europe had few goods to entice Muslim merchants, Islamic rulers granted Europeans the right to trade in their countries in return for payment of certain duties. Traditional Islamic states were officially committed to maintaining Islamic religious law, but they typically allowed European traders in the Middle East to be governed by their own law in dealings among themselves. Islamic rulers applied the same legal policy to the non-Muslim communities among their subjects. The term *extraterritoriality* is often used to refer to the foreigners' legal and commercial privileges. The name does not mean that Europeans acquired control of territory inside the Islamic lands. It means the opposite: they were allowed to operate under the law of their homelands, even though they were in an independent country that gave them this privilege only as a matter of convenience.

As long as Islamic civilization excelled that of Europe, extraterritoriality did not harm Islamic interests. When the balance shifted, Islamic rulers were slow to recognize the change. Gradually, Europeans acquired a technological lead and began to import into the Middle East goods they had once exported from it: staples like sugar and coffee, as well as manufactures. Because of the Europeans' commercial privileges Islamic rulers could not raise import duties to protect local producers and merchants. Europeans also kept up constant pressure for enlargement of their privileges.

The process reached the point in 1838 where the Ottoman Empire—which then included all of the Middle East except Iran, as well as much of southeastern Europe and part of North Africa—had to accept a treaty with Britain that introduced the principle of free trade. In the Middle East, the British thus obtained by treaty what they had obtained in India by the Charter Act of 1833. The economic effects were predictable. Trade balances shifted strongly in Europe's favor. Local manufactures and monetary systems fell into disarray. By the 1870s, Middle Eastern governments were going bankrupt and Europeans were seizing control of their revenues to repay European creditors. The Ottoman Empire and Iran might have fared better had they become additional jewels of the British Empire. In that case, the British government might have taken the same interest in railway building and other improvements in these countries that it took in India. As it was, Middle Eastern governments had to strike their own deals with hard-nosed European capitalists.

European governments also pressed for enlargement of their noncommercial privileges. In the Ottoman Empire, these included the right to enroll a few locals, serving on consular staffs, as subjects of European governments. This privilege gradually extended into a virtual sale of passports. Merchants who were subjects of the Ottoman sultan were eager buyers, since acquiring foreign nationality was the only way for them to enjoy as many advantages in their own country as their foreign competitors did. The ability of local merchants to acquire foreign nationality further weakened the Ottoman economy and the government's ability to raise revenue. Because many merchants who acquired foreign nationality were non-Muslims, the passport trade also worsened relations among religious communities. In time, European states extended their protection beyond individuals to entire religious communities. The French claimed protection of churches that acknowledged papal authority. The Russians claimed to protect Orthodox Christians. So it went, until almost all the religious communities had foreign protectors—except the Muslims.

By the nineteenth century, both the Ottoman Empire and Iran had been so undermined politically and economically that they probably had less real independence than the Latin American republics. The Ottoman Empire made determined efforts at reform, and the results were sometimes impressive, creating the basis for more successful twentieth-century reforms. But the great powers still regarded this partially European empire on their eastern borders as the "sick man of Europe." When they wished, they took outlying provinces. France helped itself to Algeria (1830) and Tunisia (1881). England took Cyprus (1878) and occupied Egypt (1882). When not grabbing territory, the European powers acted together to preserve the Ottoman Empire, whose condition was so favorable to their interests. Nineteenth-century Iran was in a sorrier state, chiefly because the government was weaker, even after the revolution of 1905–1911 turned it into a

supposedly constitutional monarchy. In Iran, the dominant outside powers were Russia and Britain.

Political Fragmentation and the Drive for National Independence

After World War I, European dominance seemed to become even stronger, as Europeans divided the territories of the Ottoman Empire and extended various forms of political control over much of the Middle East. In a part of the world that had until recently had only two states of consequence, the Ottoman Empire and Iran, this change created a new degree of political fragmentation, which a map of the region still reflects. Uncomfortable with this innovation, many Middle Easterners have since sought to re-create unities of larger scale, such as have historically prevailed in the Middle East and in other great Asian centers of civilization. For the short run, however, a more immediate problem was to recover independence at what appeared on the redrawn map of the region as the "national" level. As this struggle began, European control proved less solid in some places than at first appeared. For illustrations, we shall look first at Iran, then at the succession to the Ottoman Empire.

Iran

Although Iran declared neutrality during World War I, it still suffered. Afterward, while the Bolsheviks took the Soviet Union temporarily out of the imperialist game, the British tried to fill the gap. In

▶

Map 10.2 The Middle East, Post–World War I

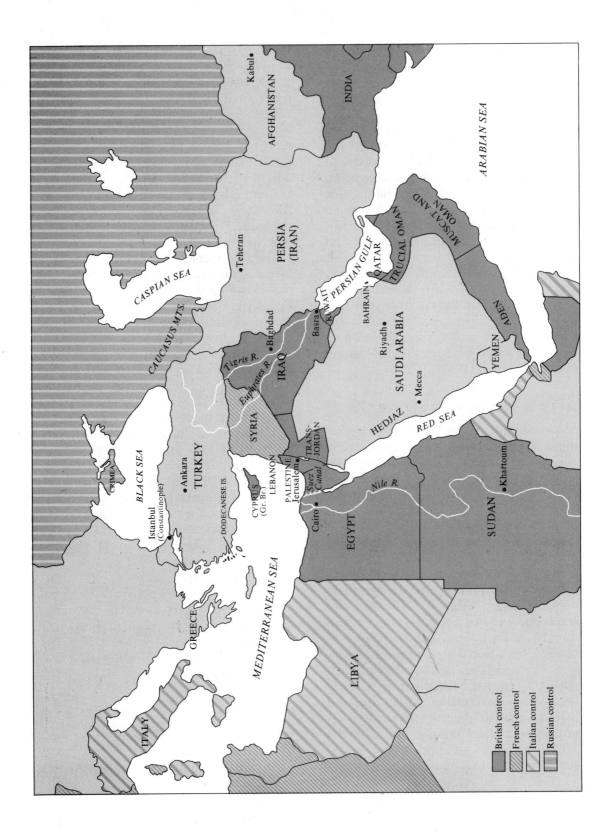

1919, they prepared a treaty that would turn Iran into a virtual British protectorate. When Iranian and foreign opposition forced abandonment of this idea, the British withdrew.

Shortly afterward, a military officer, Reza Khan, emerged as shah (1925–1941), founding the Pahlevi dynasty. At the time, many Iranians suspected him of being a British pawn. Yet he became Iran's first effective modernizing ruler. He created the nation's first real army, founded its first modern university, and began to build its national railway network—sadly overdue reforms—before abdicating in 1941, when the British and Russians occupied Iran in order to use it as a conduit for Allied war aid to the Soviet Union. On that inauspicious note began the reign of Reza's son, Muhammad Reza Shah (1941–1979).

The Succession to the Ottoman Empire

The consequences of World War I were more serious for the Ottoman Empire, which had entered the war on the German side. During the war, Britain and its allies began planning to liquidate the empire. Ultimately, they made too many plans. To start an anti-Ottoman revolt in the Arabian peninsula, the British encouraged Arab aspirations to independence in certain territories. To smooth relations with France, Britain agreed to divide some of those territories into zones that the two powers would control directly or indirectly. There was also to be an international zone around Jerusalem. Then, in 1917, Britain aligned itself with the Zionist movement by issuing the Balfour Declaration, which declared that the British government favored establishment of a "national home for the Jewish people" in Palestine and would support efforts to realize this goal on cer-

tain conditions. Many Zionists, and many of their opponents, interpreted the declaration to mean British support for creation of a Jewish state, or even a British promise of such a state.

At the peace conference, it proved impossible to reconcile all these commitments. British and French interests won out in the Treaty of Sèvres, intended as the epitaph for the Ottoman Empire. The Zionists were able to get their goals recognized. The Arabs were not so lucky. Nor were the Turks at first.

The treaty disposed of every part of the former empire. Istanbul and the straits that flowed past it, connecting the Black Sea with the Aegean, were to form an international zone. Other regions around the edge of what is now the Republic of Turkey were to go to various foreign powers or local non-Turkish peoples (the Kurds and the Armenians). The Turks were to have only what remained. Mandates from the League of Nations assigned Syria, including what is now Lebanon, to France, and Iraq to Britain. A special mandate, including many Zionist goals, gave Britain control of the territory that is now Israel and Jordan. Other provisions of the treaty recognized the British position in Egypt and Cyprus. Thus direct European domination came to parts of the world that had not previously known it.

The struggle for political independence consequently became the main theme of the interwar years in the former Ottoman territories. As examples, we shall consider the cases of Egypt, Palestine, and the Turkish Republic.

Egypt

In Egypt, a nationalist movement predated the British occupation of 1882. Nationalism re-emerged in anti-British form in the 1890s and erupted in what Egyptians remember as the revolution of 1919. Unable to suppress this, and unwilling to negotiate with the nationalists, the British unilaterally declared the country independent under a constitutional monarchy (1922–1923). But they attached conditions that required negotiations. Not until 1936 could the British and the Egyptian nationalists agree on these conditions. Abolition of extraterritoriality followed in 1937. Although Egypt was supposedly fully independent after 1936, the British retained a "preferential alliance," giving them special rights in wartime. During World War II they exercised these rights with such force as to nullify Egypt's independence and discredit the Egyptians who had negotiated the 1936 treaty.

This experience showed just how elusive independence could be for a colonial country. A new push for independence required the emergence of a new leader, Gamal Abdel Nasser, in 1952.

Palestine

The three League of Nations mandates, meanwhile, worked out in ways that depended on local conditions and the policies of the European power in charge. One familiar problem was that boundaries drawn—in some cases—by Europeans had little relation to local social and economic realities. And although the British tried to adhere to the mandate ideal, the French in Syria and Lebanon did not. In Palestine, even the British failed.

The mandate concept required preparation for self-government. But Palestine included two communities with incompatible goals: the Zionists, most of them immigrants from Europe, and the local Arabs. The goals of the Arabs were initially less clear-cut: Palestinian nationalism developed only gradually. But an international Zionist movement had been active, even before World War I. Its goal was to redevelop Palestine as a Jewish homeland, with a Jewish culture and all the social and economic institutions needed for self-sufficiency. The idea of a Jewish state had been current in the movement at least since one of its founders, Theodor Herzl, published a book called *The Jewish State* in 1896. For a long time, however, an independent Jewish state seemed a far-off goal. Not until May 1942 did the Zionist movement in general become formally committed to the demand to establish a sovereign "Jewish commonwealth" after the war.

After World War I, Palestinian Arabs began to realize what extensive Jewish immigration could mean for them. Outbreaks of violence began in 1920 and culminated in the Arab Revolt of 1936–1939. The British struggled to define a policy that would satisfy both sides. The mandate permitted them to specify that the terms of the Balfour Declaration would apply only to part of the mandated territory. In 1922 they exercised this option, setting aside the territory east of the Jordan River to be an Arab state, now known as the Kingdom of Jordan. West of the river, British difficulties in bridging the Arab-Zionist gap continued. They grew worse after the rise of Nazism in Europe increased the demand for unlimited Jewish immigration. Ultimately, the British could not devise immigration and land policies that satisfied both the Zionists and the Palestinian Arabs, who feared that they would become a minority in their homeland.

By the time World War II broke out, the Zionists bitterly resented the British. They hated the Nazis still more, however, and backed Britain in the war. But resentment of British policy played a major role in prompting the Zionist demand of May 1942 for a sovereign state. Later, as the horrors inflicted on European Jewry became known more fully, Zionist feeling grew even stronger. By the time the war ended, the British could no longer manage Palestine. They decided to turn it over to the United Nations (UN), as successor to the League of Nations, and withdraw.

In the melee that followed, superior Zionist organization and will proved decisive, even after five Arab countries sent in forces to support the Palestinian Arabs against the new state of Israel, which declared its independence on May 14, 1948. The story of this remarkble state, which has more in common with the Western than the non-Western world, will merit fuller attention in Chapter 16.

Turkey

Among Middle Eastern countries, the Turkish Republic came closest to defying the apparent postwar strengthening of European power. Sure that the multinational Ottoman Empire was finished, the Paris peacemakers did their work as if the Turkish people, among whom the empire had arisen, were also finished. Yet a mass-based Turkish nationalist movement, led by a charismatic leader named Mustafa Kemal, emerged from the collapse of the empire and took up arms in 1919. Its goal was to create a nation-state and prevent the carving up of what is now Turkish territory.

By 1922, the military effort had been so successful that attempts to divide the territory were abandoned. The nationalists then destroyed what was left of imperial government and declared a republic, with Ankara as its capital. The Western powers convened an international conference to negotiate a new peace, in which they renounced their extraterritorial privileges (1923). Turkey's nationalist revolution had enabled it to become the only defeated power of World War I to force revision of the peace terms.

But the "national struggle" of 1919–1922 was only the beginning of revolutionary change in Turkey. With Mustafa Kemal as president, the new republic went on from political revolution to social and cultural changes that were revolutionary in important respects. After a century of Ottoman agonizing over the confrontation of Western and Islamic civilizations, the new state sought to overcome this conflict by turning its back on the heritage of Islamic empire. Instead, retaining many of the late Ottoman reforms, it became a pro-Western, secular, nationalist republic.

In the twentieth century, at least one other Asian country, Japan, has been more successful than Turkey in learning from the West, but none has remade its own culture so completely in the process. Geography gave Turkey a unique potential for this kind of reorientation, for it lies immediately next to Europe. In fact, part of its territory is on the European continent. This fact gave a distinct stamp to the Turkish effort at state formation, the most successful such effort in the Islamic world of the interwar period.

Turkey's westernizing reforms began in 1924 with abolition of the institutions that had made Islam an official part of the imperial political system. Henceforth, as in the West, religion was to be a matter of private conscience. The old religious bureaucracy, religious courts, and religious schools were abolished or drastically modified. The legal system was almost completely secularized through adoption of Western-style codes.

Then came social and cultural reforms of other types. Western dress was prescribed for men. For women, veiling was discouraged. Polygamy was abolished, and civil marriage became mandatory. Major efforts were made to improve education for women and bring them into professional and public life. Mustafa Kemal, as political mobilizer, played an important role in the advancement of Turkish women, who became eligible to vote in local elections in 1930 and in national ones in 1934—exceptionally early dates by Asian standards. Another important social reform was the adoption of Western-style family names, which became compulsory in 1935. It was then that Mustafa Kemal acquired the surname Atatürk, "father Turk." Among other things, the family names made it easier for the government to implement modern systems of census registration, taxation, and military recruitment.

To strengthen the national character of its culture, Turkey adopted a modified Latin alphabet and launched a language revolution to purify Turkish by eliminating many borrowings from other Islamic languages. Simultaneously, the spread of education doubled the literacy rate, from a tragically low 11 percent of the population in 1927 to 22 percent in 1940. The cultural inheritance of the Ottoman Empire would soon be inaccessible to generations schooled only in the new language and ideas.

By Atatürk's death (1938), Turkey had gone through a cultural revolution and a great deal of social reform, but not a social revolution. The people had experienced considerable political mobilization, but no radical redistribution of

Heroes of Turkish Independence, 1922.
Mustafa Kemal (left), first president of Turkey (1923–1938), with his deputy Ismet (president, 1938–1950). In 1935, under Turkey's surname law, they become Mustafa Kemal Atatürk and Ismet İnönü.
The Mansell Collection

wealth and power. In some sense, the replacement of the multinational empire by a Turkish nationalist state had substituted for structural change in Turkish society. Yet this substitution left some important problems unsolved. The collapse of the empire had turned once-internal nationalist antagonisms largely into international problems. Despite the peace of the Atatürk years, lingering tensions between Turks and Greeks or Armenians illustrated this fact. The economic record under Atatürk suggests that the lack of structural social change limited Turkey's revolutionary achievement internally, as well.

Economic change under Atatürk was not radical, although the government assumed responsibility for development of major sectors of the economy. In 1933, Turkey became one of the first non-Western states to adopt the new Soviet practice of centralized planning for economic development. As in Latin America, the industrial drive aimed first at import substitution and then at heavy industry. The first five-year plan accomplished its goals in a number of fields, and the second produced an iron and steel mill, though an inefficient one. In the 1930s, industry's share of gross national product almost doubled, reaching 18 percent. A Turkish managerial and technocratic class had also begun to develop. It would play a major role in economic and political life after World War II.

Yet Turkey had made no fundamental effort to reform or develop the agricultural economy. Land-ownership was probably less concentrated in Turkey than in most of Latin America. But as late as the 1970s, 22 percent of Turkey's farm households owned no land and another 20 percent supplemented what they owned by renting or sharecropping other fields. A stronger push for agricultural development would no doubt have aided industrialization by increasing the domestic market for industrial products.

Not all of Atatürk's reforms were equally successful. But together they created a new concept of a Turkish nation and helped mobilize the populace into citizenship. This intent is clear from the organization of Atatürk's followers into the Republican People's party (1923), and from the nationwide creation of "people's houses" (*halkevi*) and "people's rooms" (*halkodasi*) as political and cultural centers.

Democratic values played a key role in the mobilization process. Like other major Asian cultures, Turkey had no heritage of political pluralism. Under Atatürk it was a one-party state. But he and many others believed Turkey should be democratic, though they were also willing to borrow from the Soviet Union the practice of economic planning. Atatürk encouraged two experiments with opposition parties. After World War II, his successor, Ismet Inönü, authorized the formation of a second party. When this Democrat party won national elections in 1950, the Republican People's party stepped aside, opening an era of two-party—soon multiparty—politics. Turkey's democratization has since faced many obstacles, but it remains an outstanding chapter in the political history of the non-Western world.

Comparison with Japan shows a wide developmental gap between the two countries. The causes of this gap must include Turkey's low starting levels in development of its economy and human resources (witness the low literacy levels) and the limits of its social transformation. Nevertheless, the Turkish success in creating a new order was impressive. It is little wonder that Atatürk became an inspiration to Middle Eastern leaders of his own and later generations, from Reza Shah in Iran to Presidents Nasser and Sadat in Egypt.

China and Japan: Contrasts in Development

The easternmost of the great Asian centers of civilization did not feel substantial effects of European expansion until much later than either India or the Middle East. Although the Portuguese reached China and Japan in the sixteenth century, those countries were long able to limit their contacts with the faraway West. Japan isolated itself almost entirely from 1639 on, confining contact with both Europeans and Chinese to the single port of Nagasaki. In the eighteenth century, China almost entirely limited its Western contacts to trading posts at Guangzhou (Canton).

Both traditional values and geography insulated Japan and China from European expansionism. Much as Muslims long rejected the idea that a non-Muslim culture could be on a par with their own, the Chinese traditionally saw other peoples as inferior. China was the "middle kingdom," and other peoples had to acknowledge its cultural and political superiority. Though China's relations with the outside world were more complex, the Chinese view of them was that representatives of other peoples could present themselves at the court of the Son of Heaven only as payers of tribute. The Chinese entered the nineteenth century thinking of Europeans—when they thought of them at all—in such terms and saw nothing to learn from the West. Having borrowed from the Chinese and others in the past, the Japanese were more ready to learn. Their decision to exclude foreigners reflected a desire to avoid foreign domination and to escape acknowledging Chinese superiority in the way the Chinese world view required.

In the mid-nineteenth century, isolation ended, as Westerners forcibly "opened" first China, then Japan. British merchants first went to China from India. For a time, the trade was profitable to the Chinese. The only way the British could achieve a positive trade balance with China was to import Indian opium, fostering drug addiction in China in the process. When the Qing (Ch'ing) ruling house tried to stop the drug traffic, the British responded with high-sounding rhetoric about free trade, and with force. The First Opium War (1839–1842) was a sordid affair. But something like it would have happened sooner or later. Europeans had means to exert force and goods to sell, but no intention of accepting the status of "barbarians" owing tribute to the Chinese emperor.

The British used their victory to create the *unequal treaty system*, which completely turned the tables on the Chinese. This system, which remained in force until 1943, reduced a formally independent country essentially to colonial status. The unequal treaties were patterned after the extraterritoriality of the Ottoman Empire, but eventually went further. By the end of the nineteenth century, China had made many treaties, and the number of ports open to foreign trade had increased from one to about fifty. In China, extraterritoriality meant that foreign law covered foreigners anywhere in the country, and everyone—including Chinese—who resided in the treaty ports. Opium was legalized. Restrictions on missionary activities were eliminated. Tariff rates were set low by treaty, so that the Qing government lost part of its power to raise revenues. As the government slipped into debt to foreign interests, its revenues were placed under foreign control as security for the loans.

At the end of the century, as doubts about the Qing monarchy's survival increased, emphasis shifted from extraterritoriality to the carving out of *spheres of influence*—zones where the interests of a particular power would take precedence.

In the mid-nineteenth century, Japan seemed headed for a fate no better than China's. The United States took the lead in "opening" Japan. Naval missions commanded by Commodore Matthew Perry visited the country in 1853 and 1854 to press U.S. demands. Over the next several years, the unequal treaty system was established in Japan, too.

The process of "opening" was similar in both countries, but later events differed greatly. For a long time, China remained one of the least successful of modernizing non-Western societies. Japan quickly became the most successful.

China's Crisis of Authority

China was slow in responding to outside challenge for many reasons. One was the vast size and population of the country, which had 300 to 400 million people by the early nineteenth century. Even after many ports had been opened to foreign trade, most Chinese lived far in the interior, isolated from foreigners. Culturally, China was more homogeneous than other large empires. A monolith with tremendous inertia, it was extremely difficult to change. The rich intellectual tradition and self-centered world view of the Chinese gave them many ways to explain external challenges in traditional terms. They had done this many times before. More than other Asian cultural centers, China first reacted to the West with a reinterpretation of its own traditionally dominant value tradition, Con-

fucianism. Only at the very end of the nineteenth century did it begin borrowing from Western cultures on significant scale.

The Qing Dynasty and the Western Challenge

The decline of the Qing ruling house (1644–1912) complicated China's reaction to the Western challenge. The Qing were not Chinese, but Manchu, a tiny minority trying to rule the most populous country in the world. Partly in reaction against European encroachment, a series of provincial rebellions broke out in the second half of the nineteenth century, complicating the dynasty's problems. The Taiping Rebellion (1850–1864), the most serious of all, probably caused 20 million deaths, more than World War I. Unable to quell such disturbances with its own forces, the Qing government had to rely on forces led by the local gentry. Thereafter the central government became increasingly unable to control the provinces, and local affairs became militarized. At the turn of the twentieth century, the empress mother, who hated Europeans, backed the antiforeign Boxer Uprising. Her policy backfired when foreigners intervened. They put down the Boxers and imposed disastrous terms that inflamed nationalist resentments, thus undermining the dynasty more than ever.

Under the circumstances, serious reform efforts were slow in beginning. Once underway, they further weakened the Qing regime. In the 1860s, as part of a larger effort to reassert the Confucian ideal of government, the Chinese made their first experiments in defensive westernization. They tried to obtain modern military technology and organized something like a foreign ministry and a system to train interpreters. Japan's victory in the Sino-Japanese War of 1894 revealed how much more rapidly that nation had modernized; this triggered a new seriousness in Chinese reform efforts. A brief burst of reform ensued in 1898, soon frustrated by the opposition of the empress mother. But the catastrophic end of the Boxer Uprising left the old empress and her supporters no choice but to carry through many of the reforms thwarted only a few years earlier.

The last decade of Qing rule thus became one of major reforms. The examination system that had capped the traditional educational system was replaced by new schools with a mixed Chinese-Western curriculum. Efforts were made to create new military schools and military forces. Changes in administration included the creation of ministries and attempts at legal and budgetary reform. Under a plan to create a constitutional system, elective provincial and national assemblies came into being. Meanwhile, widespread demand to nationalize China's developing railways, and disagreements about how to do so, helped politicize the populace.

Revolution was on the way. Sun Yatsen, China's first professional revolutionary, and others were already at work in the 1890s. In 1905, he helped to found a United League, intended to bring together all opposition elements. When revolution broke out in 1911, however, it was not entirely the work of this organization. The elective provincial and national assemblies played a critical role, becoming rallying points for opponents of the dynasty. Another essential factor was a government plan for nationalizing the railways on terms favorable to foreigners. When the assemblies' protests against the plan went unheeded, fifteen provincial assemblies proclaimed their independence in the fall of 1911. The provincial military forces that had grown up since the mid-nineteenth century then assumed a leading role in overthrowing the Qing regime. At that point, Sun, who was outside the country, returned to assume the provisional presidency of the Chinese Republic. The three-year-old emperor, bowing to the "mandate of Heaven . . . manifested through the wish of the people," abdicated in February 1912.

Nationalists versus Communists

Recent emperors had been weak, but their office remained the focus of familiar ideas of authority. Now the dynasty had fallen, and the entire Confucian system of ideas that supported it had come into question. What could hold China together? The revolutionary leadership set about expanding the United League into a National People's Party (Guomindang, GMD) and made an attempt at parliamentary government. But the GMD had great difficulty gaining control of the country. Sun relinquished the provisional presidency of the republic to General Yuan Shikai (Yüan Shih-k'ai) after the latter forced the emperor to abdicate. But Yuan turned into a dictator and would have made himself emperor, had he not died in 1916. After 1912, real control of much of the country passed to local "warlords," military men with their own armies. The GMD did not gain control over all China until 1928. Even then, GMD control proved only an episode in China's authority crisis, which continued through the civil war of 1946–1949.

Japanese expansionism worsened China's problems. During World War I, Japan tried to exploit China's weakness by ignoring its neutrality, by occupying

Sun Yat-sen (right) and Chiang Kai-shek, 1923.
Camera Press

educational institutions had done much to promote political mobilization. New political ideas were also spreading, including Marxism. The GMD tried to keep abreast of the changes and absorb the newly politicized elements of the population. Still, in 1921, the Chinese Communist party (CCP) was founded. The GMD and the CCP became leading forces in the struggle to create a new order.

Initially, in keeping with Soviet thinking on Asian national revolutions, the CCP worked with the larger and stronger GMD in hopes of achieving power from within it. Sun Yat-sen himself became interested in the Soviet model, tried to reorganize the GMD along Soviet party lines, and was eager for Comintern aid. Believing he could control the Communists, he accepted them as members of the GMD. One example of this collaboration occurred at the Huangpu (Whampoa) Military Academy. There, Chiang Kai-shek, who later succeeded Sun as head of the GMD, was superintendent, while Zhou Enlai (Chou En-lai), later premier of the People's Republic of China (1949–1976), had charge of political education.

In the 1920s during the struggle to eliminate the warlords, the relationship between the GMD and the CCP degenerated. A year after Chiang's succession to GMD leadership in 1925, he launched his Northern Expedition, intended to reunify China. By 1928, this campaign had been so successful that foreign powers recognized the Nationalist regime and began to give up some of the privileges of the unequal treaty system. Meanwhile, GMD-CCP relations worsened to the point of civil war in 1927, and the Communists were defeated—for the time being. Many Communists were killed, and many were forced underground or into exile.

the German positions on the Shandong (Shantung) peninsula, and by presenting twenty-one demands that would have given Japan far-reaching control over China's government. China resisted some of the demands, but had to accept a treaty recognizing Japan's claims in Shandong, Southern Manchuria, and Eastern Inner Mongolia. After the war, the Paris Peace Conference failed to restore Chinese interests; this provoked the May Fourth movement, a patriotic outburst that marked a new phase in the growth of Chinese nationalism (see Chapter 4).

Students, both male and female, were prominent in the movement, for the new

For the next several years, the Communists struggled for survival. In time, they would emerge as the most effective mass mobilizers in China. The key to their success was the idea, discussed in Chapter 4, that the revolution could be based on the peasantry, rather than on the proletariat, which scarcely existed in China. Mao did not invent this idea, but it came to dominate CCP policy as he became leader of the party during the Long March (1934–1935), which led the Communists to their new northwestern base at Yan'an in Shaanxi Province (Yenan, Shensi). Mao expressed his understanding of the relationship between mass mobilization and the military struggle in memorable terms: "such a gigantic national revolutionary war as ours cannot succeed without universal . . . mobilization. . . . The popular masses are like water, and the army is like a fish. How . . . can it be said that when there is water, a fish will have difficulty preserving its existence?"[1]

Meanwhile, the GMD faced huge problems in governing China. Chiang spent much of his time manipulating factions within the GMD. In a country that had no tradition of political pluralism, he tried to turn his party into a political machine that would include everyone of political importance. "Generalissimo" Chiang also had only limited control over the GMD military and the countryside. Limited administrative control meant a weak fiscal system. In the 1930s, the government still got about half its revenue from customs duties—a familiar indicator of fiscal underdevelopment—compared with about 1 percent in the United States at the time. Based on Sun's Three People's Principles—nationalism, democracy, and "people's livelihood" (a classical concept sometimes later equated with socialism)—the GMD

ideology also lacked the clarity and attractiveness of communist thought. Largely oriented to urban areas, the GMD regime failed to work effectively among the peasantry. The GMD's economic development efforts, too, almost exclusively benefited the modern sector of the economy, centered in the coastal cities. The agricultural sector, in which some 80 percent of the populace worked amid serious problems of landlessness and exploitation, remained nearly untouched—except where the Communists gained control.

Japanese Aggression

The GMD also had to contend with Japanese aggression in Manchuria. The population of that region was almost entirely Chinese, but the Japanese felt they had acquired interests there through the Russo-Japanese War of 1904–1905. Most of the foreign investment in Manchuria was Japanese, too. In the days of the warlords, Japan wielded considerable power in Manchuria behind a front of Chinese sovereignty. But the spread of Chinese nationalism challenged all that. In 1931, Japanese officers in Manchuria therefore attacked the Chinese at Mukden. This led to creation of a Japanese-dominated puppet state of Manchukuo. Interfering further south, the Japanese combined five Chinese provinces into a Japanese-influenced North China-land in 1935.

As in 1918, Japanese aggression raised Chinese nationalism to a new intensity. Chiang knew he was not strong enough to take on Japan. The Communists posed a more direct threat to his government. But his strategy of mounting military campaigns against the Communists, rather than the foreign invader, inflamed Chinese resentment all the more, until Chiang found himself forced to form a second common front between GMD and CCP in 1937. By then, a full-scale war between China and Japan had begun. For China, it was the beginning of World War II.

As in the Russia of 1917, war became the midwife of revolution. Japanese attacks forced the Nationalists to retire into the interior, where they were cut off from the major cities, their main bases of support. The landlord class, which had supported them in the countryside, either had to flee with them or remained helpless behind. The Japanese, in turn, had enough manpower to occupy the cities, but not to control the rural areas. There the Communists were left to extend their bases, undermine the two-thousand-year-old domination of the landlord gentry, and apply their skills in guerrilla warfare. With the Nationalists

Japanese invasion of Manchuria. The rail line built by the Japanese replaces one that the Chinese blew up in 1939. Control of the railroads was a key strategic issue during both the Japanese invasion of China and the later conflict between the Chinese Nationalists and the Communists.
Popperfoto

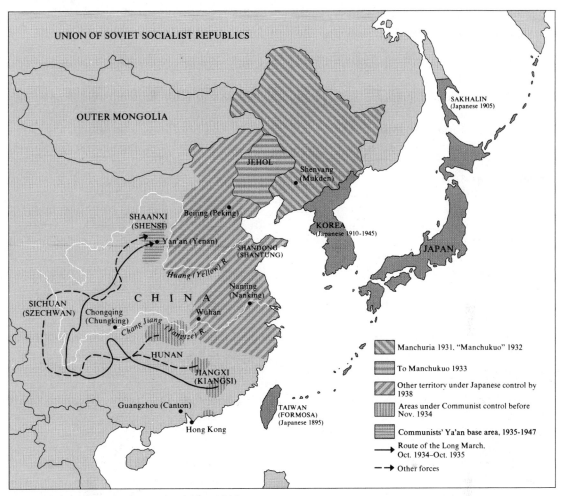

Map 10.3 China and Japan in the 1930s.

unable to defend the nation, the Communists seemed increasingly like the real nationalists. Anti-Japanese feeling led thousands to slip away from the cities and join the Communists, and also helped rally the peasantry to their side. By the end of the war, the authority of the Nationalist government had declined seriously, and the economy was edging toward collapse. The stage was set for Communist triumph in the civil war of 1946–1949.

Japan's First Rise to Great Power Status

U.S. Commodore Matthew Perry's visits to Japan in 1853 and 1854 touched off a major crisis that illustrates important differences between Japan and China. Those differences help explain why Japan's response to the West was so different from China's.

Whereas China's emperor remained the central figure of political life despite the decline of the dynasty, real power in Japan had for centuries been in the hands of a leading member of the warrior class, the *shogun*, though the emperor retained legitimacy and prestige. In China, the leading social class was that of scholar-officials, in service of the emperor; in Japan, it was the warrior class of the *samurai*. All samurai felt themselves superior to commoners and jealously guarded their monopoly over the skills and privileges of the warrior class. But they differed significantly in wealth and power. After the shogun the most important samurai were the lords (*daimyo*) of large and supposedly autonomous domains. There were 260 such domains in the nineteenth century. Each daimyo had many samurai retainers. It took a strong shogun to maintain authority over this complex system, and by the 1850s the shogunate was in decline. The question of how to respond to U.S. demands touched off its final crisis.

Japan needed consensus about such a controversial question. Although most Japanese wanted the foreigners repelled, the nation lacked the strength to do so. The shogun thus found himself forced to make treaties with the United States, and later other powers, granting extraterritorial privileges of the sort foreigners enjoyed in China. The shogun's inability to implement the policy most Japanese preferred, and the disruption of the economy following the sudden opening of the country, brought the shogunate into question. Samurai discipline began to collapse. The prestige of the emperor remained intact, however, and in 1868, a rebellion broke out under the slogan of "restoring" the rule of the emperor. The shogunate fell.

Revolution by Way of Restoration

This event is known as the Meiji Restoration, after the current emperor. Of course, the Meiji emperor (1867–1912) did not wield real power, which remained in the hands of the men who made the rebellion. The changes they introduced mark the beginning of modern Japan and deserve the name of revolution.

Major changes began with organization of the central governmental system. In 1868, a Council of State was created, with a series of ministries under it. The leaders of the revolution soon assumed control of these ministries. In the same year, the imperial capital was moved from Kyoto to Tokyo, which—under its old name of Edo—had been the center of the shogunate. The next priority was to reassert the authority of the central government over the autonomous domains. Otherwise there could be no coordinated Japanese response to the Western challenge. The new leaders persuaded the daimyo to return their holdings voluntarily to the emperor. At first the daimyo were allowed to stay on as governors. But soon the domains disappeared entirely as the country was redivided into prefectures, the basis of the centrally controlled system of local government that still exists. The next step was to create a modern army and navy. The leaders of the revolution came from daimyo domains in which experiments in military modernization had begun before the revolution. The new leaders now made such experimentation a national policy. They also undermined the status of the lower samurai by requiring universal military service for men (1873). Thus the new government eliminated Japan's old social class distinctions almost entirely.

A key problem for the new regime was

finance. Existing revenue sources had been inadequate for the shogunate. Because the new regime did not have good enough credit to borrow abroad, and did not want to, Japan escaped the slide into bankruptcy and foreign financial control that other non-Western countries experienced in this period. The new government was forced to limit its borrowing to the internal market, and to concentrate on improving its finances by reforming its monetary, banking, and taxation systems. The land tax reform gave land-ownership in the countryside to the peasant cultivators who actually paid the tax. Its effect was to stimulate growth in agricultural output and provide much of the capital for the first phase of Japan's modern economic development.

At first, economic growth was most rapid in traditional sectors—agriculture, commerce, and handicrafts. The main stimulants to growth included domestic security, expansion of foreign trade, unification of the national economy, and improvements such as modern shipping, telegraphs, and railways. A distinctive combination of government leadership and private enterprise also developed in this period. The government took the initiative in certain fields of industrial development, later selling many of the enterprises it founded to private investors. Even in the Meiji period, however, the individual initiative of Japan's businessmen probably contributed more to industrialization than did the government.

In fact, the readiness of the Japanese to respond to opportunities for economic growth was extraordinary by Asian— and many other—standards. Even before the Meiji Restoration, Japan may have had an adult literacy rate of 40 percent, the highest in Asia. Because of the country's isolation and ethnic homogeneity, its commerce remained essentially in the hands of Japanese, as opposed to foreigners or unassimilated minorities. Japan was also unusual among Asian cultures in not associating low prestige with commerce. Outside the samurai class, the Japanese had a long history as eager businessmen. With the eclipse of the warrior class following the Meiji Restoration, even former samurai assumed important roles in business. In time, Japanese business and industry developed a dual characer, with both huge conglomerates (zaibatsu, "financial cliques") and many small enterprises. By the early twentieth century, Japan's industry was diversified and strong, and the economy had enjoyed a quarter-century of significant growth.

By 1900, then, Japan had responded to the Western challenge more successfully than any other non-Western country, including ones that had faced serious challenge centuries earlier. The contrast with China reflected major differences between the two countries. Japan lacked China's size and inertia, but was at least as uniform in culture and much more so in population. Japan had no vast interior, isolated from contact with foreigners. And Japan had much more of a history of cultural borrowing. Once Japan was "opened," revolution quickly followed, and change proceeded rapidly in many fields. For example, Japanese writers produced popular books about the West, introduced journalism, and translated Western literary successes. The Japanese were popularizing Western ideas on a large scale by the 1860s and 1870s, much earlier than the Chinese, and almost as early as the Ottomans, whose contacts with Europe went back centuries earlier. The Japanese government fostered these cultural developments by becoming the first in Asia to develop something like a Western-style, national, secular school system, from compulsory elementary schools through universities.

Japan as a Great Power

Japan's leaders wanted to gain acceptance from the major powers as an equal. This concern had important implications for internal politics. Japanese leaders like other non-Western leaders of the time, assumed that representative government had something to do with the success of the great powers. They also had to contend with demands from former samurai for political participation. As a result, the Meiji regime introduced representative bodies at the prefectural level in 1878. Political parties began to emerge in the 1880s. In 1889, the country received a constitution, drafted along German lines.

The constitution of 1889 vested supreme authority in the emperor, who held vast executive, legislative, and military powers. Ministers were responsible to the emperor, rather than the parliament. As in Germany, the chief of staff remained independent in matters of command from the army minister. In other words, the military was not under civilian control. There was to be a parliament, known in English as the Diet, with two houses. The budget and all permanent laws required approval of both houses, although the government could continue to operate under the budget of the preceding year, if the Diet failed to pass the new one. For the people, the constitution guaranteed a number of rights, usually with restrictions.

If one considers what Japan had been like a quarter-century before, the constitution was a remarkable change. But it contained problems. It did not specify who would actually exercise the many powers formally vested in the emperor. As a practical matter, the top civil and military officials would have to do so. The Constitution also did not clearly regulate relations among the various power centers. What would happen if the Diet tried to assert control over the cabinet, as is normal in parliamentary systems? What would happen if military commanders used their independence of command to launch operations the cabinet opposed? Both these things eventually happened, and the latter produced tragic results.

Their wish for recognition as a great power required Japan's leaders to pay particular attention to foreign policy. Their method, typical of the time, was imperialist expansion. By 1895, Japan had seized the Ryukyu Islands and gone to war against China, winning Taiwan and other concessions. These gains were economically significant, for Japan was ceasing to be self-sufficient in rice. From then on, it could supply its needs with cheaper rice from its new dependencies.

But Japan's diplomatic gains were more important. The Western powers were now so impressed with Japan's rise that they began to conclude new treaties surrendering the unequal treaty privileges. In 1902, Britain entered into an alliance with Japan—the first military alliance on a basis of formal equality between a Western and a non-Western nation. Most astonishing of all was Japan's victory in the Russo-Japanese War of 1904–1905, which Russian expansion in Manchuria had triggered. This was the most dramatic case in which a non-Western people defeated a great power before World War I. The victory was also memorable as a step in the development of Japan's interests in Manchuria.

By 1914, then, Japan had risen from semicolonialism to nominal equality with the great powers, and had acquired overseas dependencies of its own. Entering World War I on the British side, it did little militarily, but used the occasion to pick up German possessions in China and the Pacific. Japan was the only non-Western power to sit with the victors at the peace conference. There the great powers showed that they still did not accept Japan fully as an equal. For when it tried to get a clause on racial equality inserted into the Versailles Peace Treaty, U.S. and British opposition thwarted the effort. But the conference did leave Japan the territories it had acquired in China, so aggravating Chinese nationalist grievances.

Democratization or Militarism?

Between the wars, Japan's development into a great power continued. From 1914 on, the economy enjoyed a spectacular growth that lasted into World War II. The record was marred by unimpressive performance from 1920 to 1932. But Japan was already recovering from the depression by 1932—earlier than any other major power. By 1940, less than half of all Japanese workers were employed in agriculture, and some of the zaibatsu firms had grown into the largest financial empires in the world. In the economy, as in other spheres, Japan no longer developed by simply imitating the West. By the 1930s, for example, the Japanese were able to design and build their own battleships, including the most formidable ever built.

Political parties became increasingly influential during this period. At first, this development seemed likely to answer the question of how much influence the parliament would exert over the cabinet. Although it never became a principle that the majority leader in the Diet would become prime minister, from 1924 to 1932 the prime minister was always the head of one of the two major parties. Suffrage was broadened in 1925 to include all men of twenty-five and older (women did not get the vote until 1947). Through 1937, the popular vote showed public support for this trend of political development.

Japan did not manage to consolidate its democracy during the interwar period, however. The main reason was the lack of civilian control of the military. A series of developments—the Depression, conflict with China over Manchuria, the rise of fascism—prompted the military to assert its independence in ways that upset the liberal trend.

The Depression contributed by raising questions about the extent to which the parties and the great firms were to blame. Rightists and militarists asked whether Japan could afford to depend on world markets, or whether it should expand its empire. By 1931, the army was also concerned that the progress of the Chinese Nationalists threatened its position in Manchuria. Two Japanese colonels organized a plot, not without complicity at higher levels. A Japanese-staged railway bombing at Mukden became the pretext to attack Chinese troops in Manchuria, and the conflict spread. The Manchurian episode had serious effects on the credibility of the Japanese government. Repeatedly, the government announced that it had limited the scope of conflict, only to have further military initiatives follow. By 1932, Japan had been condemned by the League of Nations, had withdrawn from it, and had moved beyond Manchuria to occupy parts of Inner Mongolia. Inside Japan, extreme rightist groups went into action, using violence against first the Left, then the liberals. By 1937, when the war with China began, militarists had essentially captured control of the cabinet. For all their electoral support, the parties were reduced to an oppositional role. Japan's naval commanders, meanwhile, resented international treaty limitations on the seapower of Japan and other states. By 1937, Japan had withdrawn from the disarmament system and begun a naval build-up.

Japan never acquired the charismatic dictator, mass movement, or clear-cut ideology of a fascist regime. But it was moving toward authoritarianism and militarism. Japan's aggression in China and its naval expansion upset relations with the United States and Britain, while many of the Japanese responsible for these developments found Fascist Italy and Nazi Germany more attractive. In September 1940, impressed by German victories, the Japanese signed an alliance with Germany and Italy. The alliance bound each country to go to war against any nation attacking any one of them. Japan had committed itself to the Axis, a decision that would bring it to virtual destruction in World War II.

Conclusion: China, India, Turkey, and Japan Compared

With the integration of Asia into the European-dominated world order, no Asian country escaped the effects of European expansion entirely. In reaction, independence movements emerged almost everywhere. A comparison of the two most populous Asian countries, China and India, and of the two most successful independent Asian nations of the interwar period, Turkey and Japan, suggests several prerequisites for the success of these efforts at independence. These are: openness to new ideas, consensus about the definition of constitutional principles and national identity, effective social change to support the drive for independence, and the formulation of an economic development strategy that could overcome economic colonialism. A comparison of the four countries will illustrate the significance of these points.

During the interwar period, China was less successful than any of the other countries. It had to survive not just a change of dynasty, but the collapse of the imperial regime and the Confucian value system that had formed its core for two thousand years. China's traditional resistance to foreign ideas greatly compounded its problems. Despite the ideological efforts of the GMD, only the Communists would finally overcome this resistance. Meanwhile, consensus about the definition of national identity was not a major issue for the hundreds of millions who were ethnically and culturally Chinese, despite their differences of dialect. Achieving consensus on how to organize a new political order proved extremely hard, however. The effort produced two rival nationalist movements and, after 1949, two regimes—the People's Republic on the mainland and the Republic of China on Taiwan—each professing to be the real China. The prolonged political struggle reflected the difficulty of mobilizing China's huge population. In this, the GMD failed, and the CCP under Mao succeeded. CCP membership rose from 40,000 in 1937 to over 1.2 million in 1945. For the GMD, failure in social and economic change went together in this period. After 1949, revitalization of the economy would remain one of the greatest challenges for the Communists.

India, in contrast, found it impossible to forge a broad enough consensus about national identity to prevent partition into separate Hindu and Muslim states in 1947. In other respects, however, India's record through 1947 was at least partly positive. Gandhi epitomized the Hindus' openness to foreign ideas. The exceptionally long period of British rule helped to forge a consensus about constitutional principles that has made contemporary India the world's largest democracy. Like Turkey, India has experienced no radical revolution in social structure, and some of India's major problems today reflect this lack. But some of the social reforms undertaken before 1947—the Gandhian mobilization of women and untouchables, or the extension of the vote to both sexes—were major social gains. India's record was perhaps most unusual in the economic sphere. Fortunately for India's later development, the less publicized efforts of others to achieve self-sufficiency through industrialization balanced Gandhi's call to regain self-sufficiency through hand production. Gandhi's methods remain a moral inspiration, however, and they proved highly successful in a situation where an outside power, responsive to moral arguments, dominated a huge population that it knew it could not master forever.

In Turkey, the resistance of the dominant Islamic tradition to borrowing foreign ideas was such that, as in China, a real reorientation of the country required the drastic means of cultural revolution. Its geography made Turkey unique among all non-Western countries in its potential for the reorientation toward the West that Atatürk carried out. Because of the Ottoman Empire's collapse and the success of the Turkish independence movement (1919–1922),

Atatürk's Turkey came through this readjustment with relatively high levels of consensus about national identity and the structure of its political system. Change stopped short of a revolution in the structure of Turkish society, however. For most Turks who remembered the past, the shift from polyglot empire to Turkish republic and the many social and cultural reforms of the Atatürk years probably seemed revolutionary enough. But the absence of structural social change made itself felt in Turkey's economic record. Like Latin America, Turkey bypassed agrarian reform to attempt industrialization. Partly for this reason, Turkey has achieved far less economically than Japan.

Japan, indeed, performed superlatively along all four dimensions considered here. Its openness to foreign ideas was exceptional. By the interwar period, Japan's use of modern ideas and techniques—as in industrial production—had gone beyond cultural borrowing to a synthesis between Japanese tradition and Western—or now international—ways. This uniquely homogeneous Asian country had no need to redefine national identity concepts. A redefinition of constitutional principles did occur with the Meiji Restoration, a change of revolutionary significance. But the fact that the Japanese could conceptualize the shogunate's elimination as a re-emphasis on another institution of ancient and unimpaired legitimacy, the imperial throne, greatly eased their transition. The Japanese emperor, though powerless, thus illustrates the importance of long-established symbols for legitimating the political order in a rapidly changing society. Socially, Meiji Japan experienced significant structural change with the destruction of the samurai, the elimination of the old class distinctions, and the land tax reform, which gave land-ownership to the peasant cultivators. Thereafter, the ethnic and cultural homogeneity, high literacy, and business spirit of the Japanese contributed to an extraordinary transformation of the economy. By the interwar period, Japan could supply many agricultural needs from its colonies and had become internationally competitive in industry.

A nation-state with a powerful industrial economy and a colonial empire, Japan had truly become a great power. Some problems remained unresolved—especially the lack of civilian control over the military. These flaws would bring Japan defeat in World War II—the final crisis of the European great powers it had come to resemble—before its extraordinary rise resumed.

Notes

1. Michael Gasster, *China's Struggle to Modernize*, 2d ed. (New York: Alfred A. Knopf, 1981), p. 78.

Suggestions for Further Reading

India

Fischer, Louis, *The Life of Mahatma Gandhi*, (1950).
Moon, Penderel, *Gandhi and Modern India*, (1969).
Spear, Percival, *A History of India*, vol. 2 (1965).
Wolpert, Stanley *A New History of India*, 2d ed. (1982).

The Middle East

Aroian, Lois, and Richard P. Mitchell, *The Modern Middle East and North Africa* (1984).
Goldschmidt, Arthur, Jr., *A Concise History of the Middle East*, 2d ed. (1983).
Lewis, Bernard, *The Emergence of Modern Turkey*, 2d ed. (1968).
Shaw, Stanford J., and Ezel K. Shaw, *History of the Ottoman Empire and Modern Turkey*, vol. 2. (1977).

China and Japan

Fairbank, John K., *The United States and China*, 4th ed. (1979).
Fairbank, John K., Edwin O. Reischauer, and Albert M. Craig, *East Asia: Tradition and Transformation* (1978).
Gasster, Michael, *China's Struggle to Modernize*, 2d ed. (1983).
Reischauer, Edwin O., *Japan: The Story of a Nation*, 3d ed. (1981).

Part 4

WORLD WAR II AND THE PERIOD OF SUPERPOWER RIVALRY

Chapter *11*

WORLD WAR II: THE FINAL CRISIS OF EUROPEAN GLOBAL DOMINANCE

The habit of looking at the twentieth-century world from the perspective of European dominance is hard to shake. Even now, four decades after that dominance collapsed at the end of World War II, historians often date the war from Hitler's invasion of Poland in 1939. Americans often date the war from the Japanese attack on the U.S. fleet at Pearl Harbor on December 7, 1941. By then Britain had been fighting Germany for a year alone, while German armies overran most of Europe. Britain found an ally against Hitler only when he invaded the Soviet Union on June 22, 1941, the day the war begins in Russian history books.

For many non-Europeans, however, World War II dates from well before 1939. For the Chinese, it began in 1931 against the Japanese in Manchuria. For the Ethiopians, virtually the only Africans not under European rule, it began with the Italian invasion in 1935.

The significance of these conflicting dates is that World War II merged originally separate drives for empire into one conflict. One drive began with Hitler's war with Britain and France over Poland, the last surviving creation of the Versailles system. This last of Europe's "civil wars" became a German campaign for "living space," which culminated in a Hitlerian empire stretching across Europe.

The second drive for empire began with Japan's penetration of China. Profiting from Hitler's attack on the European colonial powers, the Japanese extended their control over a large part of the East Asian mainland and the islands of the southwest Pacific, including the Dutch East Indies and the Philippines. By the end of 1941, the German and Japanese drives for empire had converged to make World War II a conflict of continents. It pitted Europe, under Hitler's rule, against the worldwide British Empire, which also had to face much of Asia, under the dominance of Japan. Had Germany not attacked the Soviet Union, and had Japan not attacked the United States, those other two continent-sized powers might not have been drawn into the struggle. Until Hitler attacked, Stalin had adhered to the Nazi-Soviet pact of August 1939. A clear majority of U.S. citizens favored neutrality in the war until the Japanese attacked them.

Russian and American participation brought World War II to a turning point by mid-to-late 1942. Until then, the so-called Axis powers (Germany, Japan, and Italy) had achieved an unbroken series of victories. German armies surged to the northern tip of Norway, to the shores of the Greek peninsula and the Black Sea, and over much of the North African desert. The Japanese swept to the eastern frontiers of India and to the arctic fringes of North America in the Aleutian Islands.

Even in this early period, however, the Axis leaders made fateful mistakes. Hitler failed to defeat Britain. He neither invaded it nor cut its lifelines across the Atlantic and through the Mediterranean. Meanwhile, he repeated Napoleon's fatal blunder of invading Russia while Britain remained unconquered. The Japanese leaders did not join in this attack on their hereditary enemy, but tried to avert U.S. interference with their empire-building by destroying the U.S. Pacific fleet. Following the attack on Pearl Harbor, it was Hitler who declared war on the United States, not the United States on Hitler.

It was these uncoordinated Axis attacks that forced together what Churchill called the Grand Alliance of Britain, the Soviet Union, and the United States. Together, these dissimilar Allies were too strong for the Axis. Consistently victorious through most of 1942, the Axis encountered nothing but defeat thereafter. Germany and subjugated Europe had been a match for Britain, despite the troops sent by the Dominions, like Canada, Australia, and New Zealand. But the Russian war destroyed Hitler's armies, and the U.S. agreement to give priority to Germany's defeat made it certain. After mid-1942, the Americans, the British, and their allies also steadily pushed the Japanese back. When the Soviet Union, after Hitler's defeat, joined Japan's enemies in 1945, Japanese prospects became hopeless, even without the awful warning of two American nuclear attacks—the first in history and the last, so far.

Throughout the war, the Axis powers failed to cooperate effectively. They also did not mobilize their home fronts as effectively as the Allies. Despite German rhetoric about uniting the peoples of Europe and Japanese claims to be leading an Asian crusade against imperialism, neither Germany nor Japan was able to mobilize the enthusiasm of a majority in the lands they overran. Instead their treatment of conquered peoples was marked by cruelty and greed, which inspired even civilians to abandon passivity for active resistance.

After World War I, people quickly concluded that most of the slogans for which they had fought were hollow. After World War II, the revelations of Japanese and Nazi brutality kept alive the sense that this second global conflict had been fought for a just cause. But if the war defeated evil regimes, this struggle of continents also destroyed the power of Europe as a whole and the European-dominated global system. Within a generation after 1945, even Britain, bankrupt and exhausted in victory, would grant independence to most of its Asian and African colonies. From this "end of empire" would soon emerge the Third World of countries reluctant to subordinate themselves to either the United States or the Soviet Union, the only great powers left after 1945.

Not only in the already threatening conflict of these two superpowers does the world of 1945 foreshadow the world of the 1980s. Even more intensively than in 1914–1918, the pressures of total war had expanded the powers of governments, transformed societies, and revolutionized the economies of the world. Moreover, with official encouragement, scientists had produced a weapon so incomparably deadly that thoughtful people wondered whether human beings still had a future. We still live with that unprecedented uncertainty of 1945. In this respect as in most, World War II marks the turning point of the twentieth-century world, though few people foresaw this transformation when Hitler's armies crossed the Polish border on September 1, 1939.

From Phony War to Operation Barbarossa, 1939–1941

The German attack on Poland revealed the revolutionary impact of the internal combustion engine on warfare. *Blitzkrieg* (lightning war) used fast-moving masses of tanks, closely supported by aircraft, to shatter opposition. The gallant charges of Polish cavalry could not stop them. Within a month Poland ceased to exist. Russian troops moved in to occupy the eastern half of the country, where a majority of the population were not Poles, but Ukrainians. They deported over a million Poles eastward, most to their deaths. Stalin now had a common border with his German ally, some 200 miles west of the former Soviet-Polish frontier.

The Phony War and the Fall of France

Meanwhile the British and French did nothing, though they had declared war on Poland's behalf. The French army and a small British contingent moved into defensive positions and bombarded the Germans with propaganda leaflets. For the moment, they were unwilling to attack, and Hitler was unready. The resulting "phony war" profoundly damaged the morale of Germany's enemies, especially the French. Governments that had gone reluctantly to war now debated where to fight it. Defeatists who had argued it was crazy to go to war for Poland now declared it was even crazier to fight after Poland had been destroyed. Communist propaganda explained the war as a conflict between equally greedy imperialist powers. Meanwhile Hitler occupied Norway, whose location was strategically essential in an Anglo-German naval and air struggle. The Norwegian king and his ministers fled to London, the first of many governments-in-exile to find sanctuary there. Hitler established a puppet government headed by Vidkun Quisling, a Norwegian fascist. His name has become a generic term for traitors who do a conqueror's dirty work.

The lull ended when Hitler launched the Blitzkrieg westward on May 10, 1940. Horrified by the destruction of Rotterdam—the first European use of aerial bombardment to terrorize civilians—the Dutch soon surrendered. Belgium held out little longer. No one had expected these small countries to withstand Hitler. The great shock of 1940 was the fall of France.

The country that had held off Germany for almost five years in 1914–1918 now collapsed within six weeks, suffering over a quarter-million casualties. Such losses are proof that despite the prewar quarrels that had continued through the phony war, many of the French still believed in their country's cause. What they lacked was not courage, but the weapons and especially the leadership needed for mechanized war. France's elderly generals had ignored the warnings of the soldier-scholar Charles De Gaulle that the machine had revolutionized warfare. Unable to hold a line as they had in 1914–1918, they could only surrender.

Hitler savored his revenge for Versailles, forcing the French to capitulate in the very railroad car where Foch had accepted the German surrender in 1918. Hoping to make the French reliable satellites, he allowed them to keep their fleet and colonies. There would still be a French government in the southern two-fifths of the country, where German columns had not penetrated. Thus the little resort of Vichy replaced Paris as the capital, and Marshal Philippe Pétain, a hero

of World War I, set up an authoritarian regime to replace the fallen democratic republic. Stunned by defeat, most Frenchmen at first accepted this dictatorship. Few heeded the radio appeal of General De Gaulle, who had fled to London, for Frenchmen to join him in continuing the battle overseas.

"Their Finest Hour"

Within a few weeks of Hitler's attack, the British found themselves all alone against him. Hitler publicly proposed peace. He had never really wanted a war with the British Empire. His onslaught, coming after the British failure to keep the Germans out of Norway, had discredited Neville Chamberlain's government. The new prime minister, Winston Churchill, replied that Britain would make peace if Hitler gave up all his conquests.

Churchill combined apparently contradictory traits into a remarkable personality—the last great figure of the age of European global dominance. Child of an old aristocratic family, he had been a political maverick throughout his forty years in the House of Commons. As First Lord of the Admiralty at the beginning of both world wars, he had been at the center of the British military establishment, yet remained a consistent champion of military innovations. Excluded from government through the 1930s because he opposed appeasing Hitler, he became Britain's leader chiefly because the policies he had criticized had failed. But the vision, energy, and determination that had made him a loner were now the qualities Britain needed.

Steeped in history, Churchill did not always see the future clearly. He had opposed concessions to Gandhi as resolutely as he opposed them to Hitler. Churchill's understanding of the past, however, gifted him with words to unite Britain's class-ridden society in old-fashioned patriotism. The battle of France was over, he declared on June 18.

I expect that the Battle of Britain is about to begin . . . Hitler knows that he will have to break us in this island or lose the war. . . . [If] we fail, then the whole world . . . will sink into the abyss of a new Dark Age. . . . Let us therefore brace ourselves to our duties, and so bear ourselves that if the British Empire and its Commonwealth last for a thousand years, men will say "This was their finest hour."[1]

Since Churchill ignored Hitler's prophetic warning that the British Empire would not long survive another world war, the Nazi leader reluctantly ordered his staff to plan an invasion. As his generals and admirals wrangled over how to carry the Blitzkrieg across twenty miles of the English Channel, the *Luftwaffe* (air force) offered the alternative of bombing Britain into submission.

Through the summer of 1940 the Battle of Britain raged in the English skies. Just as it was devastating British air bases, the Luftwaffe made the mistake of switching its target to London. Thus Londoners became the first to prove, as the citizens of Tokyo and Berlin later confirmed, that people can continue to live and work under the stresses of nightly air raids. Meanwhile the Royal Air Force, aided by a radar early-warning system in operation only since 1939, shot down two Germans for every plane it lost. Unable to establish air superiority, Hitler "postponed" his invasion of Britain—a delay that proved to be permanent.

The Battle of Britain may have determined the entire future course of the war. Hitler now faced the prospect of a long war, requiring a level of preparedness he had told his planners to expect only in 1944 or 1945. Moreover, though Britain was as incapable of attacking Germany as Germany was of attacking Britain, Britain might find an ally. Striving, while half-prepared, to eliminate such potential allies, Hitler was drawn into an ever-widening, eventually global, war he could not win.

Mediterranean Campaigns

The failures of Mussolini provoked the first dispersions of German strength. Having remained neutral, except for a belated attack on defeated France, the Duce decided that Italy would risk less by joining the general war than it would by failing to profit from Germany's victories. In September 1940, he struck from Libya, Italy's North African colony, at the British in Egypt. A month later, he invaded Greece. Both attacks were fiascos. The British pushed the Italians out of Egypt; the Greeks pushed them out of Greece. Hitler had had little notice of the Italian plans—only one example of the general Axis failure to coordinate strategies. But he had to retrieve Mussolini's failures. If he did not, the British might overrun North Africa and return to the Continent by way of the Balkans. In the spring of 1941, German troops arrived in North Africa to stiffen the Italians. Hitler thus involved himself in a seesaw desert battle that would end in an Axis defeat two years later. Almost simultaneously, he invaded Greece and Yugoslavia, quickly defeating them.

Neither of these campaigns proved decisive. Hitler never really accepted the idea that the way to defeat Britain was to cut its Mediterranean link to the Empire at both ends—at Gibraltar and at the Suez Canal. Though the Spanish dictator Franco coveted Gibraltar, he was too wily to let Hitler draw him into the war. Hitler never gave the *Afrika Korps* sufficient means to dislodge the British from Egypt. Most of the Balkan countries had already become economically dependent on Germany before the war began. The campaign to reinforce this dependency militarily delayed for five critical weeks the blow Hitler thought really would decide the war: invasion of the Soviet Union.

Operation Barbarossa

In December 1940, Hitler decided to "crush Soviet Russia in a quick campaign even before the end of the war against England."[2] The failure to defeat Britain had reinforced his long-standing purpose of expanding German "living space" at Russian expense. Though Stalin had lived up to the Nazi-Soviet pact, to "crush" him was the only sure way to prevent him from changing sides.

Because the Soviet Union and the West have been antagonists since World War II, few Westerners realize the stupendous dimensions of the conflict Russians call "the Great Patriotic War." On June 22, 1941, four million Germans began crossing the Soviet frontier in Operation Barbarossa. They constituted the biggest invading army in history. Within three weeks they had advanced two-thirds of the way to Moscow, taking a million prisoners. Surprised by the attack, despite ample warnings, Stalin could only trade space for time, retreating deeper and deeper into the vastness of Russia. Hitler's optimism—he had neglected to equip his armies with warm clothing or antifreeze—seemed justified. But in December 1941, "General Winter" took

command, halting the German advance only twenty miles from Moscow. The Blitzkrieg had stalled, and Barbarossa proved to be no quick campaign.

Stalin counterattacked, in thirty degrees below zero, with troops transferred from Siberia, where they had been guarding against a Japanese attack. His spies in Tokyo had reassured him that the Japanese would honor their non-aggression pact with the Soviet Union. A coordinated Axis strategy would have forced Stalin to fight on both fronts. But to the extent they listened to Hitler at all, the Japanese agreed with him that their interest lay in attacking the United States.

Meanwhile, on the other side, Churchill, a lifelong anticommunist, pledged all-out British help to the Soviets when they were invaded. "If Hitler invaded Hell," he explained, "I would at least make a favorable reference to the Devil in the House of Commons."[3] He understood that mutual interests dictated Allied cooperation. No such commitment bound the Axis powers together. The attack on Pearl Harbor on December 7, 1941, surprised Japan's allies as much as its victims.

The Japanese Bid for Empire and the U.S. Reaction, 1941–1942

By the 1930s Japan had produced the most successful non-Western response to European global dominance. Both the ancient and the modern elements of that response inclined the Japanese toward empire-building. Aloof from democratic politics, the Japanese officer corps still lived by the code of *Bushido*, the way of the warrior, whose fate was to die for the Emperor. Many leaders of big business saw more practical reasons for war. Japan was an overcrowded set of islands practically devoid of essential raw materials and dependent on exports for survival. The impact of the Great Depression had confirmed these harsh realities. Economic motives inspired the Japanese thrust into China in 1931. When the League of Nations condemned this act, the feeling grew within military-industrial circles that Japan was besieged.

This feeling was heightened by the constant rebukes of the United States, whose traditional insistence on an "open door" for American trade in East Asia clashed directly with Japanese ambitions. In 1940 President Roosevelt reinforced his moral condemnations with an embargo on scrap iron and weapons for Japan. In July 1941, after the Japanese took advantage of the fall of France to seize French Indochina, he extended the ban to include oil and steel. In the ensuing negotiations, the United States made it clear that its condition for lifting the ban was Japanese withdrawal from China.

Pearl Harbor

As these negotiations failed to resolve the embargo issue to Japan's satisfaction, power within the Japanese government shifted to the military-industrial advocates of war against the United States and the European colonial powers. Japan's decision to enter the war was not prompted by any sense of solidarity with the fascist powers. Hitler had not warned the Japanese he would invade Russia, despite the German-Japanese pact signed in 1940, nor did the Japanese consult him before Pearl Harbor. Rather, the war they planned had three objectives: to break the stranglehold of embargo, to end interference with their conquest of China, and to build an overseas empire that would give Japan the supplies and markets it lacked.

Early on a Sunday morning, December 7, 1941, Honolulu awoke to the roar of explosions. The surprise Japanese air attack sank or damaged much of the U.S. Pacific fleet at its moorings in Pearl Harbor. Having disabled their most-feared enemy, the Japanese quickly overran Hong Kong, the Dutch East Indies, Burma, and Malaya. The surrender of the great base at Singapore dealt a lasting blow to the prestige of the British Empire in East Asia. By May 1942, American and Filipino resistance in the Philippines had also ended in surrender.

At the time of Pearl Harbor, U.S. intelligence had cracked the Japanese codes and was expecting an attack someplace. Why then was the Pacific fleet so unprepared? No credible evidence supports the terrible allegation that Roosevelt deliberately allowed the attack so that outraged public opinion would accept war. Several factors contributed to the disaster: the secrecy that shrouded the Japanese strike force, the racist overconfidence of commanders who believed the "little yellow men" would not dare attack Hawaii, and the habits of peacetime routine.

The End of U.S. Isolation

Pearl Harbor undoubtedly simplified Roosevelt's foreign policy problem, which arose from the clash between two enduring characteristics of American thinking about foreign relations. Protected by oceans and bordered by far weaker neighbors, Americans had little experience of adjusting foreign policy to the necessities of the balance of power, as Europeans did. The threat to Britain of a Europe dominated by Germany, for example, spurred Churchill's opposition to Hitler far more than his distaste for Nazi politics. Americans, with their strong Puritan heritage, were more likely to judge others in moral terms. This view implied that the United States should help "good" countries and oppose "bad" ones. By the late 1930s most Americans probably judged Nazism and Japanese imperialism to be bad. But an equally powerful American tradition urged against any "entangling alliance" abroad. The widespread feeling that the United States had been led into World War I under false pretenses had reinforced this tradition. To prevent its happening again, Congress had passed a series of neutrality acts aimed at preventing any peripheral involvement in foreign wars that could be used to justify U.S. intervention.

In keeping with this isolationist sentiment, Roosevelt had proclaimed U.S. neutrality in 1939. Despite his growing conviction that the United States' vital interests required opposition to both Japan and Germany, he could not do more than public opinion would permit. Thus

A Japanese war artist's painting of Kamikaze pilots. In the last year of World War II, one in five of these suicide pilots succeeded in crashing his bomb-laden plane into a U.S. ship.
U.S. Army Signal Corps

in the fall of 1940, when Britain desperately needed escort ships for its Atlantic convoys, Roosevelt could only trade Churchill fifty obsolescent U.S. destroyers for ninety-nine-year U.S. leases on six British bases in the Western Hemisphere.

In the spring of 1941, polls showed that no more than one American in five favored entering the war. By then Britain had sold all its dollar holdings at a loss in order to pay for munitions. U.S. legislation stipulated that foreigners could buy arms in the United States only on a "cash-and-carry" basis. Roosevelt now persuaded Congress to pass the Lend-Lease Act, empowering him to lend or lease the British whatever they needed. However, the Act stipulated that U.S. ships must not enter combat zones. In August, Roosevelt and Churchill met at sea and promulgated the Atlantic Charter. This document set forth the kind of general principles Americans liked to affirm, including the right of self-determination. Churchill could only accept it, perhaps not fully conscious that it outlawed Britain's empire as well as Hitler's.

Thus step by step Roosevelt edged Americans toward war. As U.S. warships escorted convoys across the Atlantic, there were clashes, despite Hitler's orders, with German submarines. These encounters enabled Roosevelt to declare that the country was already virtually at war. Even after Pearl Harbor, however, he did not ask Congress to declare war on Germany. Hitler solved Roosevelt's dilemma by aligning himself with the Japanese, against whom Americans had been roused to fury. Vastly ignorant of the United States and contemptuous of its racially mixed society, Hitler saw no reason not to declare formally a war that had already begun in the Atlantic.

The Turning Points, 1942

Churchill immediately recognized the significance of the Pearl Harbor attack. From that moment he knew Britain would not lose the war. With the formation of the "Grand Alliance," the tide of war began to turn in mid- to late 1942. By the spring of 1943, the Axis had lost battles in Pacific jungles and North African deserts, in the snows of Russia and the storms of the North Atlantic.

The momentum of the Japanese seemed irresistible in early 1942. Their planes bombed northern Australia, their fleet raided Ceylon. But in May 1942, in the Battle of the Coral Sea, the U.S. Navy parried the threat to Australia. A month later, a smaller U.S. force repelled the huge Japanese fleet sent to take Midway Island, only 1,100 miles from Hawaii. In August, U.S. Marines landed on Guadalcanal in the Solomon Islands, a British possession occupied by the Japanese. Six months of fighting in the steamy, malarial jungle ended in an American victory. It was the first in the long running battle that would lead from island to island to Japan itself.

In November, at El Alamein, less than one hundred miles from the Suez Canal, the British counterattacked and drove the Germans out of Egypt. Retreating westward, the Germans encountered the British and American troops that had landed in Operation Torch, in French North Africa. Caught between these two fires, the Germans surrendered in Tunisia in May 1943. Meanwhile, enraged by the French failure to resist the landings, Hitler ordered the total occupation of France. This invasion shattered the illusion of the Vichy regime's independence. Frenchmen began to realize that the only independent French regime was the one De Gaulle soon installed in North Africa.

The war in the Soviet Union also reached a turning point in November 1942 with the savage house-to-house battle of Stalingrad. Hitler refused to allow any retreat. In three months he lost a half-million men. Thereafter the Soviet advance did not halt until it reached Berlin.

Despite these Allied successes, Churchill was still haunted through the spring of 1943 by the one German threat he really feared: the submarine campaign against ocean convoys. In the first years of the war the North Atlantic crossing demanded a quiet heroism of every merchant seaman. For fifteen days they battled through mountainous seas, dreading what they called the hammer: a torpedo slamming into their ship to send it to the bottom in minutes. In the eighteen months after the fall of France, Britain lost a third of its prewar merchant tonnage. The British convoys dispatched through the Arctic to supply north Russian ports confirmed the Grand Alliance at a terrible cost in ships and lives. By late 1942, however, the Americans were building ships faster than the Germans could sink them. By deploying more escorts and wider-ranging aircraft, and by perfecting submarine detection by underwater radar, the British destroyed an unprecedented forty-one submarines in March 1943. A turning point had been reached on the Atlantic sea-lanes too, allowing the Allies to bring the full weight of their home-front production against the Axis.

The Home Fronts

Even more than in World War I, the home front was a real fighting front in World War II. Not only were civilians much more subject to attack by enemy bombers, but victory or defeat depended largely on the governments' success in mobilizing their productive skills for the war effort. This was a war between economies as well as between armies. Churchill actually created a Ministry of Economic Warfare. Its responsibilities included organizing sabotage of the German-dominated European economies and denying Hitler vital raw materials by offering neutrals a better price for goods they would otherwise have sold to Germany.

Allied Mobilization

The battle of home fronts was above all decided at home. The Churchill all-party government, depending on a parliamentary majority, felt it could ask at least as much of its citizens as more authoritarian regimes imposed on theirs. The British National Service Act of 1941 put every adult from eighteen to fifty at the government's disposal, to be sent to work wherever he or she was needed. The government controlled prices and rationed essentials like food and fuel. It paid part of the soaring costs of war by deducting compulsory savings from every paycheck. By 1945 it had allocated one-third of the British work force to war industry.

The Soviet government took equally drastic steps. Though the Five-Year Plans of the 1930s had begun locating industry farther from Russia's European border, German armies had seized one-third of the Soviet industrial plant by

▶

Map 11.1 World War II: The European Theater

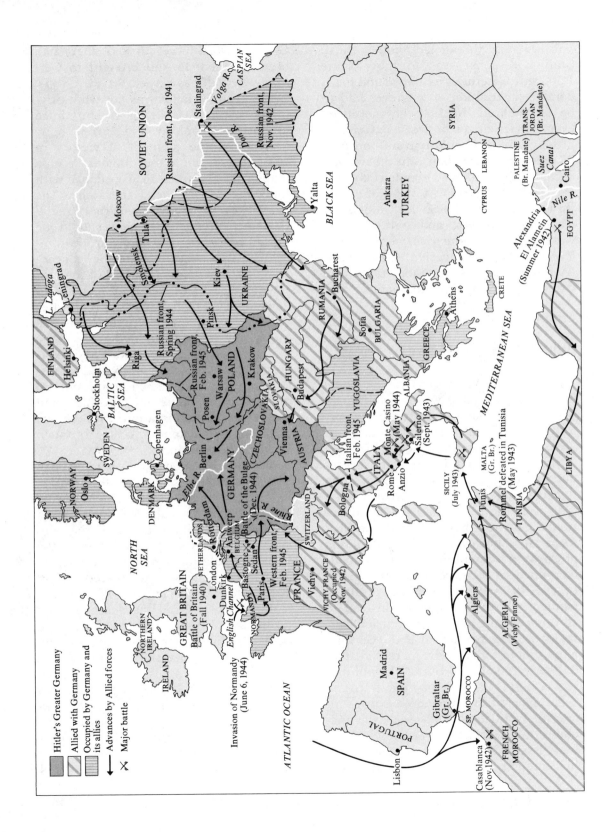

Hitler's Greater Germany

Allied with Germany

Occupied by Germany and
its allies

→ Advances by Allied forces

✕ Major battle

ATLANTIC OCEAN

NORTH SEA

IRELAND

NORTHERN IRELAND

GREAT BRITAIN

Battle of Britain (Fall 1940)

London

English Channel

Dunkirk

NETHERLANDS

Rotterdam

Antwerp

BELGIUM

Bastogne

Battle of the Bulge (Dec. 1944)

Sedan

NORMANDY

Paris

Invasion of Normandy (June 6, 1944)

Western front, 1945

FRANCE

Vichy

VICHY FRANCE (Occupied Nov. 1942)

SWITZERLAND

Rhine R.

Elbe R.

Berlin

GERMANY

DENMARK

Copenhagen

Oslo

NORWAY

SWEDEN

Stockholm

BALTIC SEA

Helsinki

FINLAND

L. Ladoga

Leningrad

Riga

Russian front, Spring 1944

Moscow

Smolensk

Tula

SOVIET UNION

Russian front, Dec. 1941

Stalingrad

Volga R.

Don R.

Russian front, Nov. 1942

CASPIAN SEA

Russian front, Feb. 1945

Posen

Warsaw

POLAND

Krakow

Pinsk

Kiev

UKRAINE

CZECHOSLOVAKIA

SLOVAKIA

Vienna

AUSTRIA

HUNGARY

Budapest

Bologna

Monte Casino (May 1944)

Rome

Anzio

Salerno (Sept. 1943)

ITALY

Italian front, Feb. 1945

RUMANIA

Bucharest

Sofia

BULGARIA

YUGOSLAVIA

ALBANIA

GREECE

Athens

BLACK SEA

Yalta

TURKEY

Ankara

SYRIA

LEBANON

CYPRUS

PALESTINE (Br. Mandate)

TRANS-JORDAN (Br. Mandate)

Suez Canal

Nile R.

Cairo

Alexandria

El Alamein (Summer 1942)

EGYPT

MEDITERRANEAN SEA

CRETE

MALTA (Gr. Br.)

SICILY (July 1943)

Tunis

TUNISIA

Rommel defeated in Tunisia (May 1943)

LIBYA

Algiers

ALGERIA (Vichy France)

SP. MOROCCO

Gibraltar (Gt. Br.)

FRENCH MOROCCO

Casablanca (Nov. 1942)

Lisbon

PORTUGAL

Madrid

SPAIN

late 1941 and threatened another third. Stalin's response was to move some 1,500 entire factories eastward and to order the destruction of whatever had to be left behind. In 1942 he mobilized every Soviet citizen between sixteen and fifty-five. With twenty-two million men in uniform, more than any other combatant, the slogan "women to the tractors" came true. At the war's end, three-quarters of the Soviet Union's agricultural workers, and half of those working in war industries, were women. By 1943, despite invasion, these industries were turning out more tanks and planes than German factories did.

Hitler's European Empire

The mobilization of the German home front began late and was less thorough. Although Germany began the war woefully short of such essential weapons as ocean-going submarines, easy victories prompted Hitler actually to cut war production. Only at the end of 1941, when it became clear Germany was in for a long war, did he order total mobilization. Such were the rivalries of the Nazi hierarchy, however, that production of some nonessential consumer goods continued to increase into 1944. Moreover, Hitler's views precluded drafting women, who were supposed instead to stay home and breed children for Germany. During World War II the German female labor force hardly increased at all (while in the United States the number of working women rose by one-third).

Foreigners from conquered Europe increasingly filled the places at the machines that German women might have been assigned. By 1944, more than 7 million foreigners represented a fifth of the German work force. Most of them had been rounded up and brought to Germany virtually as slaves.

The need for labor was not what originally inspired the Nazis to shift huge numbers of people around Europe, however. From the moment of victory in 1940, they began to rearrange the ethnic map of the continent in accordance with their notions of racial hierarchy. The Nazi "New Order" decreed that "racial Germans" living elsewhere should be moved to Germany, where European industry was henceforth to be concentrated. The peoples of the rest of the continent were to be reduced to colonial dependency. The harshness of their fates would depend on how much "Nordic blood" the Nazis thought they had. The fortunate peoples of northern and western Europe, who supposedly had a measure of it, were subjected at first only to puppet governments like Quisling's and to systematic confiscation, through the payment of "occupation costs," of much of what they produced.

In Nazi eyes, non-Nordic peoples like the Poles and Russians were sub-human, fit only for enslavement. After erasing Poland from the map, the Nazis closed Polish schools and massacred the educated elite. They subjected the rest of the Polish population between the ages of eighteen and sixty to forced labor. Forced to wear a purple "P" on their clothing, Poles faced the death penalty for having sex with a German. As for the Soviet Union, Hitler declared his intention to "Germanize the country by the settlement of Germans and treat the natives as redskins," to be killed or herded onto reservations like American Indians.[4] Eighty percent of the Soviet prisoners taken by Germany died of overwork and starvation.

Historically, most empire builders

have justified their conquests as the means of spreading some idea of general benefit to mankind. Nazi ideology is remarkably barren in this respect. The Nazi vision of the future depicted a Nazified, static world stretching from the Atlantic far into the Eurasian land mass. Thousand-mile expressways and oversized trains would connect the monumental fortresses from which the German racial masters would rule their enslaved inferiors. By implementing this vision as his armies advanced, Hitler made enemies even of ethnic minorities within the Soviet Union who had initially welcomed the Germans as liberators from Stalin. As the war began to go against the Nazis, Europe eventually became one large prison. Its restive populations made as small a contribution to the Nazi war effort as they dared.

Those carried off to the labor camps established by the SS or German industry could not choose how hard they worked. Nazi-occupied Europe did not only contain camps intended to work people to death, however. The Nazis designed some camps for the immediate extermination of minority groups they deemed unfit to live on any terms. Among these were Gypsies, Jehovah's Witnesses, and especially Europe's Jews.

The Holocaust

Long before the war, the Nazi Nuremberg Laws (1935) had deprived German Jews of their civil rights, and storm troopers had wrecked their businesses and places of worship (1938). But the war provided the opportunity for the "final solution" of what the Nazis called "the Jewish problem." After Poland's defeat, its three million Jews were sealed into walled urban ghettoes. Special extermination units accompanied the German army into the Soviet Union. But their primitive massacres, in which thousands were shot and hastily buried dead or alive in mass graves, struck Heinrich Himmler, the head of the SS, as unnecessarily harrowing as well as inefficient.

Himmler called on modern technology to equip the extermination camps opened in 1941–1942 with a kind of production line of death, including specially designed gas chambers and crematoria. Into these camps the Nazis slowly emptied the Polish ghettoes. They also deported Jews from the rest of Europe "to the east," never to return. So essential did the Nazis consider this task of extermination that they continued it even when Germany was on the brink of defeat. Sometimes they gave trainloads of deportees destined for the death camps the right of way over ammunition trains for their retreating armies.

Six million Jews perished in this Holocaust. The camp at Auschwitz probably established the killing record: a million people, not all Jews, in less than three years, 12,000 in a single day. The rest of the world did little to hinder the slaughter. Poles did not come to the aid of the rebellion in the Warsaw Ghetto. The Allies failed to bomb the death camps. Such indifference reinforced the Zionist argument that Jews could only be safe in a country of their own that they could defend themselves.

When the extent of these crimes became known after the war, some explained them as the result of a uniquely German sadism. Unfortunately, however, the underlying causes of these attempts to wipe out whole peoples arose from characteristics of human thinking not at all peculiar to the Germans of the

Liberation of a Nazi concentration camp, 1945. The U.S. army compelled German civilians to view atrocities at Buchenwald, including thousands of starved bodies.
UPI/Bettmann Newsphotos

1940s. Human beings have always been too ready to deny the humanity of other people by stereotyping them; to believe that the problems of their own group could be solved by eliminating such a dehumanized enemy; and to excuse from moral responsibility those who are "just following orders." Sheer inability to imagine the agony of other people also played its part in the Holocaust.

To acknowledge that these common human traits helped make the Holocaust possible is not to deny its unique horror, but to recognize the kinds of thinking humanity has to unlearn if it is to escape future holocausts.

The Defeat of the Axis, 1943–1945

Italy was the first of the Axis powers to fall. British forces had ousted the Italians from Ethiopia in 1941. The alliance with Germany that had sent 200,000 Italians to the Soviet front had never been popular. When British and U.S. forces crossed from North Africa to invade Sicily in July 1943, even many leading Fascists concluded it was time for Italy to change sides. Within two weeks of the landing, the king ejected Mussolini from office and had him arrested.

When Italy surrendered to the Allies in September, Hitler's armies turned northern Italy into another German front line. German paratroopers rescued Mussolini from imprisonment and made him the head of a puppet state. Stubborn German resistance slowed the Allied advance up the Italian peninsula to a crawl. When the Germans finally surrendered in the spring of 1945, Italian anti-Fascist guerrillas executed Mussolini and hung his bullet-riddled body up by the heels in a gas station as an object of public contempt.

Despite the doubts of U.S. military planners, Churchill had imposed his preference for attacking Italy, rather than launching a cross-channel invasion in 1943. Italy, he said, was the "soft underbelly" of Hitler's Europe. In actuality, the Italian campaign proved anything but easy. It did not satisfy Stalin's demand for the opening of a second front. This fact helps explain the compromises Churchill and Roosevelt made when they met Stalin in Tehran, the Iranian capital, late in 1943. The location was symbolic of the Grand Alliance, for some American Lend-Lease supplies reached the Soviets through the Persian Gulf and the Trans-Iranian Railway.

At Tehran the "Big Three" recognized their need for each other's help. They therefore tended to put aside any issue that might divide them. Churchill and Roosevelt were keenly aware that Stalin commanded most of the soldiers actually fighting Germans. Having put him off in 1942, and again in 1943, they now gave him a firm date in 1944 for the cross-channel invasion of France. Roosevelt and Stalin rejected as a dangerous diversion Churchill's suggestion that the United States and Britain also attack another "underbelly" in the Balkans, so as to "join hands with" the Soviets. In re-

turn for the second front, Stalin pledged Soviet support for a postwar world organization to replace the League of Nations, and a Soviet declaration of war against Japan soon after Hitler was defeated.

Stalin made it clear that he intended to keep the territories annexed by the Soviet Union in 1939. Though the Soviets had severed relations with the Polish government in exile in London, Churchill concurred with moving the Polish-Russian border westward and compensating Poland at German expense. Roosevelt, characteristically mindful of the large Polish-American vote in the coming presidential election, preferred to avoid discussing territorial adjustments until the war was won. Like Woodrow Wilson, he envisioned a totally new postwar world order, in which the new United Nations would decide such questions. At Tehran, in fact, the president began to feel he had at least as much rapport with Stalin, who agreed with him that World War II should end European global dominance, as he did with Churchill, champion of the British Empire.

Thus, the outlines of the postwar world remained largely undefined as Hitler found himself between the closing jaws of a gigantic vise in the summer of 1944. While the Soviets drove his armies out of their homeland, the Americans, British, and Canadians hit the beaches of western France on D-day, June 6. Operation Overlord was a technological and managerial feat as well as a military one. The Allies towed entire artificial harbors across the Channel to provide ports for the landing of a million men in a month. Four pipelines laid on the seabed pumped fuel for the Allied advance across northern France.

In August, French and U.S. tanks

reached Paris, where fighting had already begun between the forces of the underground Resistance movement and the retreating German garrison. General De Gaulle, the lonely exile of 1940, returned to be acclaimed as his country's liberator.

While Parisians rejoiced, the people of German cities had few illusions about the war's outcome by late 1944. When the Royal Air Force discovered early in the war that it could not hit precise targets like particular factories, it adopted a policy of simply loosing its bombs indiscriminately on the populations below. In the summer of 1943, a week of incendiary raids on Hamburg had generated fire storms that killed 50,000 and left a million homeless. The strategic effectiveness of this tactic is doubtful. Postwar studies have shown that air raids did not even begin to slow German war production until the summer of 1944, when American "precision bombing" started. Even then, postwar polling revealed, only a bare majority of Germans would have favored surrender.

The last months of Hitler's Germany provide an eerie demonstration of the capacities of human determination—or madness. Hitler withdrew to an underground bunker in Berlin, from which he issued orders forbidding retreat to units that had already ceased to exist. To the end he hoped that his new secret weapons would save him. In addition to the world's first jet aircraft and robot flying bombs, these weapons included the V-2s, missiles carrying one-ton warheads. Five hundred V-2s, crude prototypes of today's weapons, fell on London alone. Too few of them had been produced too late, however, to reverse the outcome of World War II.

Eventually Russian tanks overrode the elderly men and teen-age boys Hitler had mobilized as a last line of defense and began shelling the ruins above his bunker. Only then did Hitler admit that the war was lost. On April 30, 1945, after marrying his mistress and writing a will blaming the Jews for his failure, he shot himself. She took poison. SS men burned their bodies in the courtyard above while the Russian shells continued to fall. Only then was the spell of this man, who had risen from obscurity to command the largest European empire ever known, finally broken. A week later, Germany surrendered.

Like Hitler, the Japanese warlords failed to mobilize their home front as effectively as the Allies had done. Just as the Nazis claimed that their conquests were building a united Europe, the Japanese asserted that they were establishing a "Great East Asian Co-Prosperity Sphere" and reserving Asia for the Asians. These claims were belied by the cruelty of their occupying armies, however. Like the Germans, the Japanese people displayed great tenacity as defeat closed in on them.

In China the Japanese faced little danger from the Nationalist armies of Chiang Kai-shek, despite heroic American efforts to arm him by airlifts over the Himalayan Mountains. But by the time of Germany's surrender, a British army including African and Indian troops was driving the Japanese from the Southeast Asian mainland. The Americans had begun the reconquest of the Philippines, and their bloody island-to-island campaign had won them air bases within easy striking distance of Japan itself. A single air raid by General Curtis Le May's B-29s on March 10, 1945,

▶

Map 11.2 World War II: The Pacific Theater

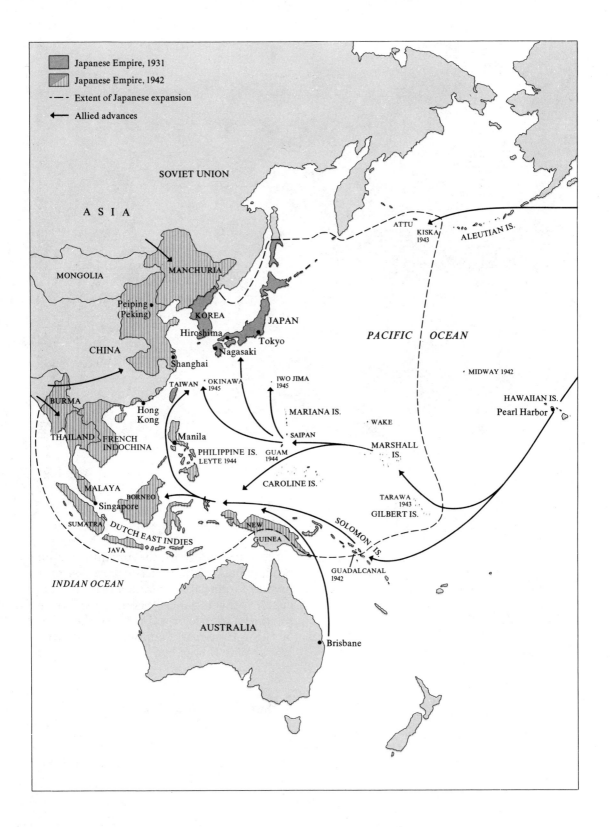

Japanese Empire, 1931
Japanese Empire, 1942
Extent of Japanese expansion
Allied advances

SOVIET UNION

ASIA

MONGOLIA

MANCHURIA

Peiping
(Peking)

KOREA

CHINA

Hiroshima

Nagasaki

JAPAN

Tokyo

Shanghai

TAIWAN

OKINAWA
1945

IWO JIMA
1945

BURMA

Hong
Kong

THAILAND   FRENCH
INDOCHINA

Manila

MARIANA IS.

WAKE

MIDWAY 1942

HAWAIIAN IS.
Pearl Harbor

PACIFIC   OCEAN

ATTU

KISKA
1943

ALEUTIAN IS.

SAIPAN

PHILIPPINE IS.
LEYTE 1944

GUAM
1944

MARSHALL
IS.

MALAYA

Singapore

BORNEO

CAROLINE IS.

TARAWA
1943

GILBERT IS.

SUMATRA   DUTCH EAST INDIES

JAVA

NEW
GUINEA

SOLOMON IS

INDIAN OCEAN

GUADALCANAL
1942

AUSTRALIA

Brisbane

Hiroshima, August 6, 1945. Controversy continues over whether it was necessary to level whole cities with the world's first atomic weapons.
National Archives

burned nearly half of Tokyo to the ground, killing or maiming 125,000 people.

Nevertheless the Allies dreaded the invasion of Japan. They expected suicidal resistance of the sort displayed by the kamikaze pilots, who deliberately crashed their planes into American warships. Considering the gloomy estimates of American casualties, Harry S Truman, who had become president at Roosevelt's death, unhesitatingly ordered the dropping of the first atomic bomb upon Hiroshima on August 6, 1945. This single bomb, tiny in comparison with today's nuclear weapons, destroyed at least 100,000 people. The only other atomic bomb then in existence fell on Nagasaki three days later. In the meantime, the Soviets had hastened to declare war and invade Japanese-held Manchuria. On August 15, the Japanese people heard over the radio, for the first time ever, the voice of the Emperor, announcing defeat. World War II was over.

A World Divided into Three

The distribution of global power we know in the 1980s was already taking shape in 1945. Hitler's defeat left Europe divided down the middle into blocs dominated by his two strongest enemies, the United States and the Soviet Union. In the next decade, Western Europeans would begin to recognize that recovery depended on European economic cooperation and political unity, not a vain attempt to reestablish global dominance. As their former colonies won independence, a host of new nations would emerge in Asia and Africa to form a Third World seeking to stay out of the superpower conflict that divided Europe.

The Yalta Conference

Despite the Nazis' hopes, the Grand Alliance against them held together until they were defeated. Allies usually tend to diverge as soon as their common goal is in sight. Knowing this, and fearing a Soviet advance into the vacuum left by Germany's collapse, Churchill approached Stalin to propose a southeast European deal. The Soviets would be dominant in Bulgaria and Rumania, Nazi allies already invaded by Soviet armies. Britain would dominate in Greece. Each would have a half-interest in Hungary and Yugoslavia. Stalin seems to have been agreeable. He did not object when British troops crushed a communist attempt to seize power in Greece and imposed the monarchist government that had spent the war in London.

But after June 1944 there were more American than British soldiers fighting Hitler. Churchill became the junior partner of the Western Allies. Henceforth it would be the Americans who set the tone in relations with the Soviets, and they contemplated no deals. Likewise American military planners rejected as "political" Churchill's insistence that Western strategy should aim "to shake hands with the Russians as far east as possible," and notably in Berlin.

The Big Three met for a second time at Yalta in the southern Soviet Union in February 1945. Once again the emerging differences among the Allies were papered over with ambiguous formulas. Roosevelt had reacted to Churchill's deal with Stalin as Woodrow Wilson had reacted to European power politics a generation earlier. He insisted that the Allies guarantee free postwar elections everywhere in Europe. In Poland elections were to be held by a new government that would somehow merge the Poles of the London government-in-exile into the pro-Soviet regime the Soviets recognized.

Stalin accepted these proposals, but told a confidant, "Any freely elected government in eastern Europe would be anti-Soviet and that we cannot permit." He could not believe the Americans would not understand this, or that they intended the pledge of free elections everywhere as more than propaganda. In fact, U.S. foreign policy is often made by such a statement of principle, and Americans were outraged at Stalin's violations of it. From these differing perspectives eventually arose the East-West confrontation Churchill had tried to avoid.

Critics have sometimes accused the dying Roosevelt, who survived Yalta by only two months, of conceding too much to Stalin. Such criticism forgets the actual situation at the time of the Yalta conference. The war was not over. The Western Allies had yet to cross the Rhine, while the Soviets were already a hundred miles from Berlin. Disillusioned at last with the inactivity of Chiang Kai-shek, Roosevelt accepted Stalin's demands for Chinese territory in order to

The Big Three at the Yalta Conference, February 1945. Winston Churchill (left) and Stalin (right) flank President Franklin D. Roosevelt. Already, Churchill feared that Roosevelt had a "slender contact with life."
National Archives

ensure Soviet help in the final campaign against Japan. Expecting to withdraw U.S. troops from Europe as rapidly as they had left after World War I, Roosevelt secured whatever postwar commitments he could. Though he clearly overestimated his personal influence on Stalin, in early 1945 Roosevelt had no reason to doubt his cooperation. Nor would American public opinion then have favored opposition to Stalin, for since 1941 Americans had been encouraged to see the Soviets as allies fighting the good fight.

In the end, as Churchill had expected,

the realities of power, not declarations of principle, determined the division of the postwar world. For Stalin, the war before the German invasion of the Soviet Union had been a contest between equally dangerous capitalist powers. His country had narrowly escaped being defeated by one of them. Afterward, as a victor, he attempted to win control of as much territory as possible between the

▶

Map 11.3 USSR Western Border Changes, 1914 to the Present

▨	Areas lost by Russia after 1917
▥	German territory to Poland, 1945
▦	Acquired by Soviet Union, 1939-1945
▧	Soviet satellites
▨	Communist, nonsatellite nation
▬	"Iron Curtain" after 1950

NORWAY

SWEDEN

FINLAND

Helsinki

Leningrad

Stockholm

ESTONIA

Moscow

BALTIC SEA

LATVIA

SOVIET UNION

DENMARK

Copenhagen

LITHUANIA

Gdansk (Danzig)

Hamburg

Elbe R.

Berlin

EAST GERMANY

Vistula R.

Warsaw

POLAND

WHITE RUSSIA

NETHERLANDS

WEST GERMANY

Kiev

Bonn

Prague

CZECHOSLOVAKIA

UKRAINE

Dnieper R.

Rhine R.

Munich

Vienna

Dniester R.

BESSARABIA

SWITZERLAND

AUSTRIA

HUNGARY

Budapest

RUMANIA

CRIMEA

Po R.

Belgrade

YUGOSLAVIA

Bucharest

BLACK SEA

ITALY

ADRIATIC SEA

Danube R.

BULGARIA

Sofia

Istanbul

CORSICA

Rome

Tirane

ALBANIA

GREECE

AEGEAN SEA

TURKEY

Ankara

SARDINIA

Athens

SICILY

CYPRUS

MEDITERRANEAN SEA

Soviet Union and the other capitalist powers. He expected the Americans to do the same. As Stalin said, "Everyone imposes his own system as far as his army can reach." And in fact today—except in Germany, where the Americans withdrew westward some 100 miles to their predetermined occupation zone, and in Austria, from which the Soviets withdrew in 1955—the European frontier between the "free world" and the Soviet bloc runs where the respective armies stood at Hitler's defeat.

The End of the European Empires

Even more than this division into two blocs, the rapid dissolution of Europe's colonial empires after 1945 revealed the end of European global dominance. In 1939, a quarter of the world's population, most of them nonwhite, lived under the British flag. They produced three-quarters of the world's gold; half of its rice, wool, and tin; and a third of its sugar, copper, and coal. France's overseas empire was twenty-six times larger than France itself, with three times the population. The Dutch ruled an empire with a population nine times larger than that of the Netherlands. Few of the colonial peoples enjoyed in 1939 even the limited self-government the British had conceded to India. Almost everywhere, however, an elite had emerged who had absorbed from their European masters the modern political ideal of a self-governing national state. World War II, and especially the Japanese campaigns, showed that the Europeans could be beaten. Moreover, it left Europeans too exhausted for vigorous efforts to restore colonial rule. Wherever they attempted such a restoration, they encountered the opposition of both the Soviet Union and the United States.

Americans took seriously Article 3 of the Atlantic Charter, which proclaimed "the right of every people to choose the form of government under which it desires to live." As promised, they granted independence to their Philippine dependents in 1946, and they expected others to do likewise. Whether this attitude reflected the United States' own experience as a colony, as Americans often asserted, or its eagerness to penetrate more non-Western markets, as embittered Europeans complained, the effect was the same. In 1945 and 1946 U.S. agents encouraged Ho Chi Minh and other Indochinese nationalists to resist the reimposition of French rule after the Japanese departure. When the Dutch refused to recognize the independent Republic of Indonesia established in their former East Asian empire as the Japanese left, U.S. pressure through the United Nations forced them to abandon their military intervention. Over three hundred years of Dutch colonialism came to an end in 1949. The United States began to reverse its anticolonial pressure only in the 1950s, when it began to perceive colonial nationalists as communist agents or dupes.

The Soviet Union also supported the non-Western drive for independence. Under this double pressure, Europeans gave up their empires more or less gracefully. The British habit of indirect rule simplified their surrender of power to native elites in Burma (1948), Malaya (1957), and much of sub-Saharan Africa (after 1957). The Commonwealth provided a kind of club within which former colonies could preserve a loose affiliation with Britain, though not all chose to join it. Thus the rich and gigantic empire of

1939 had dwindled to a few bits and pieces by the 1970s.

After the debacle of 1940, the French found it harder to relinquish the overseas symbols of great power status. France was almost the last European country to remain involved in colonial warfare. It fought for eight years (1946–1954) to hold Indochina, and another eight (1954–1962) to hold Algeria—all in vain.

The Revolutionary Impact of World War II

In several respects, the end of World War II marked the beginning of the world we know today. As we have seen, the globe was soon divided into American, Soviet, and Third World blocs. Unlike the temporary controls of World War I, lasting changes in the relationship between government and the individual emerged from the experience of wartime government or, in German-occupied Europe, from social conflict between those who collaborated with the Nazis and those who resisted them. The war also did much to stimulate the technologies that now pervade our lives.

The War and Postwar Society

In much of Europe World War II laid the foundations of the postwar welfare state. In Britain the wartime government had made great demands on citizens, but it had also assumed unprecedented responsibility for them. The population became accustomed to the provision of extensive social services—and to the high taxes needed to pay for them. When the Labour party defeated Churchill's Conservatives in the elections of July 1945, the new government moved rapidly to nationalize much of private industry and to implement such wartime proposals as a compulsory social security program and free secondary education.

On the continent, the ideas of the underground Resistance movements provided much of the impetus for postwar social change. Resistance originated with the lonely decisions of individuals that Nazism was intolerable and that they must oppose it somehow. Gradually they found others who felt the same way and began publishing clandestine newspapers, or smuggling downed Allied airmen to safety, or transmitting intelligence to London. As Resistance movements grew with Germany's defeats, they inevitably became politicized. Because the regimes that collaborated with Hitler—like Pétain's Vichy government—were drawn from the prewar Right, the Resistance inclined to the ideas of the Left. This was true even of Catholic Resisters, who later founded Christian Democratic parties committed to programs of social reform.

In France, for example, General De Gaulle, like the leftist thinkers of the Resistance, was convinced that the defeat of 1940 reflected basic weaknesses of France's society and economy. The provisional government he headed until 1946 set out to transform both. It imposed government ownership of the big insurance companies and the coal, steel, and energy industries. It laid the foundations of the system that still sets goals for the French economy today: cooperative development of five-year plans by industry, labor, and government. And it greatly expanded the prewar welfare state. Thus one legacy of World War II was the idea that government has a comprehensive responsibility for the quality of its citizens' lives.

The War and Postwar Technology

The war was even more revolutionary in its acceleration of the pace of technological innovation. The Battle of Britain was an early clash in what Churchill called "the wizard war" (because it seemed magical to laymen)—German electronics experts devised a guiding beam for bombers, and British engineers found ways to deflect it. In this war of scientists the most formidable feat was the transformation of a 1939 concept of nuclear physics into the bomb dropped on Hiroshima in 1945. To turn its design into an actual weapon, the Manhattan Project constructed whole new factories employing 120,000 workers, including the first entirely automated plant in history. The total cost came to some 2 billion dollars. Ever since, government-sponsored research has continued to demonstrate the possibilities of invention on demand—at vast cost.

Nuclear weaponry was only the most dramatic example of the technological breakthroughs stimulated by the needs of war. In 1940 the British invented *operations research*, the statistical study of war, a discipline that would profoundly influence postwar ideas of industrial management. In 1943 U.S. factories began to mass-produce the pesticide DDT and the antibiotic penicillin. Before long these two substances had fundamentally altered the conditions of human life. The application of DDT in Ceylon after the war, for example, reduced the death rate by half in one year by wiping out disease-bearing insects. Penicillin and the sulfonamides were the first of the wonder drugs that since 1945 have virtually eliminated infectious diseases in areas where the drugs are available.

Conclusion: The High Point of U.S. Power

Even in the United States, where no battles had been fought, World War II had a revolutionary impact. After Pearl Harbor, formerly isolationist Americans threw themselves into the war effort with an enthusiasm no war since 1945 has generated. U.S. industrial production quadrupled as assembly lines turned out over a quarter of a million aircraft and vast quantities of other goods. Such feats demanded substantial relocations of population, as new factories opened in underindustrialized regions like the South and the Pacific Coast. Everywhere new opportunities drew rural people from the countryside to the cities. The demand for labor led to Roosevelt's creation of the Fair Employment Practices Commission, the first federal agency charged with protecting minorities from discrimination.

By 1945, war-induced patterns of migration and economic growth had produced a society very different from the one Americans had known in 1941. The war effort carried over into peacetime, too, for the development of military technology had acquired a dynamic of its own. In 1945 the U.S. and Soviet military establishments raced to capture Hitler's missile designers. Those efforts marked the beginning of what has been called the warfare state, dedicated to developing new technologies of destruction. World War II had already hinted what a future war fought by such means might be like. Almost half of its fifty million dead were civilians (compared with only 5 percent during World War I). Many of these were victims of indiscriminate aerial bombing—a weapon that had seemed so terrible in the abstract that many people in the 1930s believed that it never would be used, or even that it had made war itself unthinkable. World War II proved otherwise, and after 1945 the use of aerial bombing was taken for granted in all nations' defense planning.

The outcome of World War II suggested that future combatants in such a full-scale war would have to be as populous and industrially powerful as the United States, which then had more than 140 million people. Former great powers with populations of 40 to 50 million, like Britain and France, were already dwarfed. On this superpower scale, the only possible rival to the United States was the Soviet Union. A Soviet challenge seemed unlikely, however, for that country was exhausted and devastated. It had lost 20 million people, sixty times more than the United States.

In the face of such Soviet weakness, the United States had probably reached in 1945 the high point of its twentieth-century power. So strong was the U.S. position that Americans redesigned the world's political and economic systems to their own specifications. The new United Nations, created to replace the League of Nations, set up its headquarters not in Europe, like the League, but in New York. Among the five permanent members of its Security Council, charged with keeping the peace, the United States could usually count on the votes of Britain, France, and China as well as its own. Similarly the new International Monetary Fund, designed to balance international payments, and the World Bank, established to make loans

to needy nations, conformed to the specifications of the U.S. delegation to the international financial conference held at Bretton Woods, New Hampshire, in 1944. Though ostensibly international, both institutions were actually subject to U.S. influence.

In many ways, then, the destiny of the world after 1945 seemed to be in American hands. World War II marked the climax of an incredibly swift U.S. ascent to world power. Until the 1890s, the United States had been seen as a second-rate power, not even accorded full ambassadorial representation by the great powers. Over the next half-century, it began to play a world political role corresponding to the fantastic growth of its economy. But the U.S. advance to world power had been interrupted by apparent retreats, like the return to isolationism after 1918. Today, when U.S. armed forces are stationed in more than a hundred countries around the world, it is hard to imagine the situation of 1940, when the Pentagon had not been built and the U.S. army was smaller than that of Belgium. It was World War II that marked the turning point to the global involvement we have learned to live with in the 1980s. For U.S. power did not long remain unchallenged. Only a few years after the war's end, the United States and the Soviet Union found themselves locked in cold war confrontation.

Notes

1. Winston S. Churchill, *Their Finest Hour* (Boston: Houghton Mifflin, 1949), pp. 225–26.
2. Alan Bullock, *Hitler: A Study in Tyranny*, rev. ed. (New York: Harper & Row, 1964), p. 574.

3. Winston S. Churchill, *The Grand Alliance* (Boston: Houghton Mifflin, 1950), p. 370.
4. Peter Calvocoressi and Guy Wint, *Total War: Causes and Courses of the Second World War* (New York: Penguin Books, 1972), p. 212.

Suggestions for Further Reading

Calvocoressi, Peter, and Guy Wint, *Total War: Causes and Courses of the Second World War* (1972).

Churchill, Winston S., *The Second World War*, 6 vols. (1949–1954).

De Gaulle, Charles, *War Memoirs*, 3 vols. (1955).

Feis, Herbert, *Churchill, Roosevelt, Stalin* (1967).

Fourcade, Marie-Madeleine, *Noah's Ark: A Memoir of Struggle and Resistance* (1974).

Hersey, John, *Hiroshima* (1946).

Horne, Alistair, *To Lose a Battle: France 1940* (1969).

Hughes, Terry, and John Costello, *The Battle of the Atlantic* (1977).

Liddell Hart, Basil H., *History of the Second World War* (1970).

Prange, Gordon W., et al., *At Dawn We Slept: The Untold Story of Pearl Harbor* (1982).

Rupp, Leila J., *Mobilizing Women for War: German and American Propaganda, 1939–1945* (1978).

Wright, Gordon, *The Ordeal of Total War* (1968).

Chapter *12*

EMERGENCE
AND DECLINE
OF SUPERPOWER
BIPOLARITY

After their tremendous efforts to defeat the Germans and the Japanese, the winners of World War II hoped they had established peace for good. In one sense, they were soon undeceived. Within five years most nations were compelled to choose sides between the two superpowers World War II had left confronting one another in a "cold war," the United States and the Soviet Union. Nevertheless, the world has managed to avoid a World War III. It has been forty years since World War II—twice as long as the interlude that separated that conflict from World War I. As we trace the postwar history of international relations in this chapter, the fundamental question to keep in mind is why the hostile peace of the last forty years has not, so far, ended in war.

To understand how global conflict has been avoided, one must recognize what is at stake. Publicly, the leaders of both superpowers have asserted that their confrontation is between ways of life. The U.S. government has declared, and most Americans believed, that confrontation with the Soviet Union is essential to the defense of political democracy and what is called the free enterprise system. The Soviet government has proclaimed, and most Soviet citizens believed, that confrontation with the United States is essential to the defense of revolutionary socialism.

Clearly the political and economic systems of the two superpowers are very different. And there is little doubt that one of them is more attractive to most people than the other. Since 1961, the Soviets have maintained a barrier—the Berlin Wall—separating their part of the world from the rest. Its purpose, despite Soviet denials, is to keep people *in*. The United States, by contrast, has recently been considering legislation to strengthen its border with Mexico to keep people *out*.

Interpreting Post-1945 International Relations

Despite the genuine differences between the two systems, some aspects of the U.S.-Soviet confrontation suggest that it is not fundamentally driven by ideology. To counter Soviet influence, for example, the United States has supported regimes around the world that have had little more regard for freedom than a communist regime would. Nor has the Soviet Union consistently supported communist regimes and movements. In the 1960s the two largest communist powers, the Soviet Union and China, became open enemies. In the same decade, the democracies of Western Europe were becoming increasingly impatient of U.S. direction.

What has really been at stake since 1945 is the world distribution of *power*. If this interpretation is correct, then statesmen of the last forty years have been pursuing much the same objective as those who maintained the European-dominated world order until it broke down in 1914. Their task has been to reduce conflicts by maintaining spheres of influence in a rough balance of power.

The conflicting ideologies of the superpowers have obscured this fundamental task, encouraging both sides to understand the aftermath of World War II by drawing analogies with the 1930s. As the wartime Grand Alliance dissolved in suspicion, American policymakers came to assume that the Soviet Union's aims, like Hitler's, were unlimited: the creation of a universal empire by conquest and communist revolutions. Soviet policymakers expected U.S. capitalism to envelop and try to destroy the homeland of communism.

Each side feared an ideological crusade by the other. But in practice neither superpower has been willing to let ideological goals override its interests, defined by its power. The nonaligned nations of the world soon came to see the U.S.-Soviet confrontation as a power struggle, regardless of ideology. In 1955, at a conference in Bandung, Indonesia, many of these nations declared their unwillingness to line up with either superpower.

This perspective of the nonaligned Third World sometimes surprises Americans. Although isolationism was no longer a practical option after World War II, Americans were still significantly influenced by the idea that had lain at the heart of their earlier aloofness from international affairs: the sense that the United States was a uniquely superior society that might be defiled by contact with a more sordid world. This notion reinforced a strong impulse to improve the world and make it conform to the

U.S. model. If the United States could no longer remain aloof from the world, then the world had to be made a safer place for U.S. ideals. Americans did not understand that other nations perceived these ideals as a smokescreen covering the use of U.S. power to promote U.S. interests.

The Soviets approached the postwar world in much the same spirit. They too have tried to impose their ideals on their neighbors, and as much of the rest of the world as possible. Because both U.S. and Soviet policies have been embodied in alliances, the world since 1945 has come to resemble less that of the 1930s than the pre-1914 European world of armed alliances, confronting one another in successive crises. Whether their standoff will continue indefinitely, or whether, as in 1914, some crisis will eventually lead to war is not yet clear.

In the postwar history of international relations, the period from 1945 to 1962 was dominated by the bipolar contest. This *cold war* was an unequal contest, though the Americans, who dominated it, did not always see it that way. It pitted the United States, dominant in Latin America and Western Europe, against the Soviet Union, which controlled (beyond its own vast territories) only the band of adjacent lands overrun in World War II. The crises of the cold war all occurred along this periphery of Soviet control, in Korea, in southeastern Europe, in Iran, in Berlin. In every case the Soviets' attempt to expand their perimeter was rebuffed, as was their probe of the U.S. perimeter in support of Cuba in 1962. The Soviets' strength was still so inferior that when President Kennedy gave them an ultimatum, they could only retreat. The Cuban missile crisis seemed to confirm American primacy in the world.

U.S. self-confidence was shattered in the 1960s—a decade that really ended in 1973 with withdrawal of U.S. combat troops from Vietnam. The debacle seemed to prove that the United States could not defeat Third World revolutionaries determined to pull their country out of the U.S. orbit. Meanwhile, a prosperous Western Europe, spurred by a France once more led by General De Gaulle, increasingly challenged American dominance. Soviet power also seemed to be eroding in the 1960s. It was then that relations between the Soviet Union and China flamed into open hostility.

The thrust of the 1970s toward superpower *détente*—the word means relaxation of tensions—reflected a multipolar world that included other significant powers besides the United States and the Soviet Union. With a weakening economy, the United States was eager to come to an understanding with its perpetual antagonist. The Soviet Union, in even worse economic shape, was ready to reciprocate. A mood of mutual uncertainty made possible some limited accommodations between the superpowers.

It is not yet possible to tell how sharply the 1980s mark a break with détente, or whether the emergence of multipolarity, to the extent that it is real, has reinforced the forty-year stalemate in international relations. The world of the 1980s still pits a U.S. economy and culture of incredible worldwide power and attractiveness—witness the universal preference for English as a second language—against the Soviet Union. The Soviets are still encircled on the Eurasian landmass by a hostile China and an unsympathetic Europe. Despite large infusions of aid and arms, neither superpower has won the advantage among the hungry peoples of the nonaligned Third World.

It does not seem likely that, for all his denunciations of the Soviet "evil empire," President Reagan will be any more able than Secretary of State John Foster Dulles in the 1950s to roll it back. Nor will revolutions in the Third World necessarily profit the Soviet Union, though they may challenge American hegemony. The outlook for Americans and Soviets alike is rather for uneasy coexistence in the shadow of nuclear missiles, requiring painful adjustments between unfriendly neighbors. Clearly the Soviet Union is now "contained," as the first postwar American strategists planned. But forty years have revealed far more constraints on U.S. power than were foreseen in 1945.

The Cold War to 1953

Allies in World War II, the United States and the Soviet Union did not become opponents overnight. The cold war developed gradually between 1945 and 1950. There has been much controversy over who was to blame. Most historians now agree that the cold war began as the Soviet Union, seeking to expand in accordance with historic Russian ambitions, aroused American fear that it would contest the U.S.-dominated world system created by European and Japanese collapse. Each side reacted to successive challenges by taking new steps that it regarded as defensive but that appeared to the other as new threats. A dynamic of confrontation developed.

There were three stages in this process. During the first stage, which ran from Hitler's defeat to the spring of 1947, cooperation was curiously mixed with growing antagonism. Communists held seats in coalition governments in Western Europe, noncommunists in Eastern Europe. Expecting a permanent peace, the United States reduced the number of Americans in uniform from twelve million to only a million and a half. The Soviets also demobilized, but less completely. American soldiers handed over Soviet refugees in their jurisdiction to the Soviet authorities. As Truman and Stalin had agreed, the Soviets collected reparations from the other three occupation zones—American, British, and French—into which Germany had been divided.

In the meantime, however, the Soviets sought to expand into areas that Russia had long coveted. They encouraged separatist movements in northwestern Iran and demanded a revision of the historic agreement by which Turkey controlled the passage to Russia's warm-water ports on the Black Sea. In the past, Britain had often pushed the Russians back when they attempted to encroach on these regions. Bankrupt postwar Britain, however, could no longer play this role.

In February 1947, the British indicated they could no longer afford to give aid to Turkey, or to the royalist government Churchill and British troops had installed in Greece, under attack from Communist guerrillas. Unwilling to allow what they interpreted as Soviet pressure in southeastern Europe to succeed, American policymakers took a step that marked a second stage in the development of the cold war. On March 12, 1947, President Truman announced that the United States would aid the Greeks and Turks. It would be American policy, he declared, "to support free peoples who are resisting subjugation by armed minorities or by outside pressures."[1] He thus linked resistance to historic Russian ambition to ideological principles. In fact, however, the governments to which the United States extended protection were not necessarily very "free." This Truman Doctrine marked a major turning point in the history of American foreign policy. The U.S. president had offered an open-ended commitment to forestall revolution or aggression anywhere.

Prostrate Western Europe, where cooperation between Communists and the other parties in coalition governments broke down in the spring of 1947, seemed especially vulnerable. In June, Secretary of State George Marshall committed the United States to rebuilding the European economy. His offer of aid was extended to all the war-torn countries, including the Soviet Union. Americans, who saw the Marshall Plan as an act of spontaneous generosity, could not understand why the Soviets walked out of the Paris conference convened to implement it.

In fact, unsurprisingly, the Marshall Plan was designed as much in U.S. self-interest as for Europe's benefit. It required its recipients to accept U.S.-made goods—shielding the U.S. economy from a postwar slump—and to account to the U.S.-managed European Recovery Administration for aid expenditures. In effect the Marshall Plan tied the European market securely to the U.S. economy. It is not surprising that the Soviets rejected such subordination in a U.S.-dominated world economic system.

Integration into the U.S. economic orbit brought Western Europeans a rapid postwar recovery. By 1952, when Marshall Plan aid ended, European industrial production was a third higher than it had been before World War II.

Two separate European economies began to emerge: one oriented to the Atlantic, the other to the Soviet Union. Now Europe was truly divided by the Iron Curtain that Winston Churchill had described in 1946. In February 1948, a coup d'état in Czechoslovakia overthrew the last Eastern European coalition government and imposed a communist dictatorship. President Truman responded by reinstituting the American draft and encouraging the formation of the Brussels Pact, including Britain, France, and the "Benelux" countries (Belgium, the Netherlands, and Luxembourg). As the two blocs solidified, a key uncertainty was the fate of divided Germany.

At the beginning of 1947, the Americans and British merged the economies of their two occupation zones. Clearly, it was only a matter of time before a western German state dependent on the United States emerged as a barrier to any further Soviet ambitions in Central Europe.

Even if they had no such ambitions, the growth of a resurgent Germany aligned with a hostile United States was a terrifying prospect for the Soviets. Stalin's countermove, in June 1948, was to cut off access to Berlin, which lay deep within the Soviet occupation zone of Germany. The ruined former capital, itself partitioned into zones, was to be used as a Soviet chip in the international poker game. But Truman raised the ante by airlifting all the needed supplies—including coal—into Berlin, and by stationing bombers capable of carrying nuclear weapons at British airfields. Once again the Soviets backed down, abandoning their Berlin blockade after a year. When the Federal Republic of West Germany was created in May 1949, the Soviets could only counter by establishing a communist-led German Democratic Republic in East Germany.

▶

Map 12.1   NATO, the Soviet Bloc, and the Third World

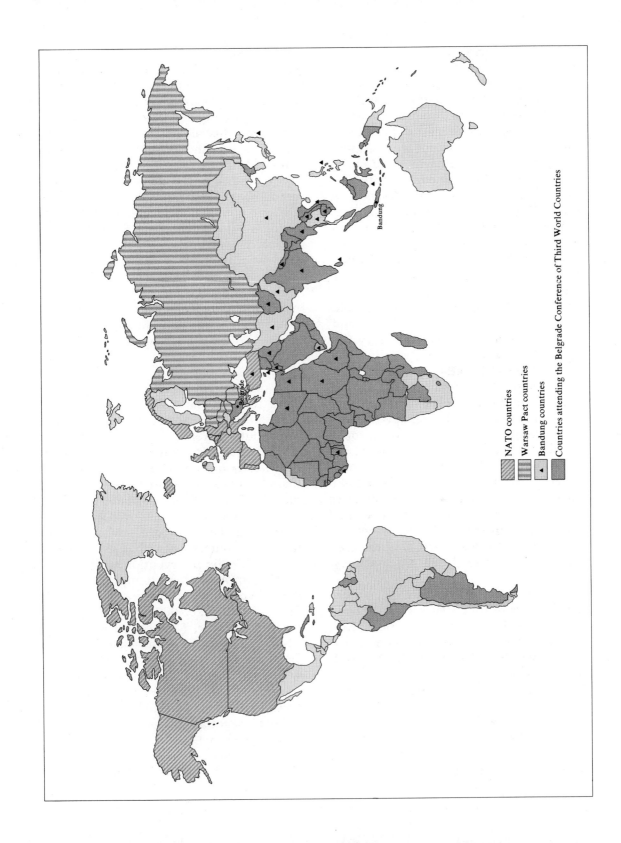

NATO countries

Warsaw Pact countries

Bandung countries

Countries attending the Belgrade Conference of Third World Countries

Belgrade

Bandung

The U.S. strategy of containing the Soviet Union had not yet led to major American rearmament. The United States remained confident in its monopoly of the ultimate, nuclear weapon. When the Soviets exploded an atomic bomb in July 1949, a major reassessment was required. According to "NSC-68," a secret planning document prepared by the U.S. National Security Council in April 1950, the Soviet Union was a rampant aggressor bent on overrunning all of Europe and Asia. To counter the threat, "NSC-68" declared, the United States must develop a thermonuclear bomb and European air bases from which the Strategic Air Command could deliver it. In Europe, U.S. troops should reinforce the North Atlantic Treaty Organization (NATO) formed to link the United States, Canada, Denmark, Norway, Iceland, Italy, and Portugal to the countries of the Brussels Pact. Moreover, it would be necessary to rearm West Germany, despite the reluctance of Europeans whose countries had been ravaged by German armies. The implementation of "NSC-68" marks the third and final stage in the development of the cold war. For the first time in its history, the United States began massive peacetime preparations for war, including the creation of the Central Intelligence Agency (CIA).

The sudden attack of North Korea on South Korea in June 1950 seemed to confirm the need for such preparations. Korea had been the object of imperial rivalries between Russia and Japan until the Japanese victory in the war of 1904–1905 placed it firmly under Japanese control. The defeat of the Japanese in 1945 left Korea divided between Soviet and American occupying armies. Each superpower established a client regime, north and south of the thirty-eighth parallel of latitude. The U.S. secretary of state, however, had excluded South Korea from the list of countries the United States was prepared to defend.

Thus emboldened, the North Koreans attacked. This seemed to be a clear case of aggression, and an opportunity for the United Nations to demonstrate its ability to restore peace. Any one of the five permanent members of the UN Security Council could paralyze action by exercising a veto. At the time of the Korean attack, however, the Soviet representative was boycotting Security Council meetings to protest the UN's refusal to recognize the Chinese Communists in place of Chiang Kai-shek's regime. In the Soviets' absence, the United Nations prescribed collective action against aggression in Korea. Such a step has rarely been taken since.

In fact, the so-called UN forces mustered to meet the North Korean attack were 50 percent American (and 40 percent South Korean). They were successful in containing the North Koreans' initial headlong advances and pushing them back. Then the American UN commander, General Douglas MacArthur, became overconfident. He moved his forces close to the Chinese border while ostentatiously conferring with Chiang Kai-shek about his intervention in the war. Fearing an American attempt to reverse their revolution and restore Chiang, the Chinese rushed 200,000 "volunteers" into the Korean War. They soon pushed the UN forces back to the line where the conflict had begun. Forced to choose between this Korean stand-off and the unknown risks of full-scale war with China, President Truman agreed in June 1951 to begin negotiations for a cease-fire, finally signed in June 1953.

This outcome of the Korean "police action"—after the loss of 54,000 American lives—illustrated how frustratingly inconclusive peripheral bipolar conflicts could be. But the experience stimulated the American government to extend its guarantees wider still: to the Philippines, Australia, and New Zealand. During the 1950s, it gave a quarter of a billion dollars annually to Chiang Kaishek's Taiwan, no small factor in that country's "economic miracle." The key to securing the Pacific was Japan, which now, like Germany, changed rapidly from an American enemy into an American friend. In 1951–52, the United States signed a peace treaty and withdrew its occupation troops. Many American servicemen remained in Japan, however. Japanese bases were a key link in the chain the United States had drawn around the Soviet Union from Norway through Greece and Turkey (added to NATO in 1952) to South Korea and Taiwan. Americans saw this strategy as containment or the defense of freedom—though strong-man regimes like that of South Korea were hardly free. But to the Soviets it undoubtedly looked like encirclement. It would be up to Stalin's successors after his death to find ways to break out.

The Containment of Khrushchev, 1953–1962

The Soviet Union of the early 1950s was a country transformed. When Stalin had first asserted his supreme authority, it was still a backward nation. Now it was beginning to rival the United States in heavy industry. Stalin's industrial revolution had been imposed on Soviet society at a ghastly cost. The last nightmare years of his rule, when he sank into paranoia and ordered the arrest or execution of everyone he distrusted, climaxed an era in which literally millions of Russians were confined in slave labor camps. Ordinary citizens who escaped that fate had to struggle with the daily shortages and hardships of an economy in which the consumer had the lowest priority.

After Stalin's death in 1953, Soviet citizens of all sorts, hoping for change, welcomed his successors. Even in a totalitarian system, public opinion can make its weight felt when there is a struggle for succession to supreme power.

If the new Soviet leaders hoped to reduce discontent by easing international tensions, it was not clear how their conciliatory gestures would be received in Washington. President Eisenhower's secretary of state, John Foster Dulles, had come to office in 1953 arguing that the mere containment of the Soviets was not enough. Dulles professed to see international relations as a contest between good and evil, in which the Soviet rule over Eastern Europe should not go unchallenged. He did not, however, explain how the United States could drive the Soviets out of that region without going to war. Because Eisenhower was reluctant to unbalance the U.S. budget for a build-up of conventional forces, Dulles could only back up his aggressive language by threats of "massive [nuclear] retaliation" for any Soviet transgression. That threat became far less credible, however, when the Soviets exploded their hydrogen bomb in 1953, only nine months after the Americans detonated their first such weapon. For many years the United States retained an advantage in capabilities for delivering the fearsome new weapon. Nevertheless, the Soviet hydrogen bomb, rapidly evening up the arms race, was a vivid reminder that the two superpowers could not wish away each other's power.

Khrushchev at the United Nations. Nikita S. Khrushchev, Stalin's successor, once became annoyed by the UN president's gavel during an assembly, took off his shoe, and used it as a gavel of his own.
UPI/Bettmann Newsphotos

als at Geneva to de-escalate the nuclear arms race failed, as they almost invariably have since, to overcome each side's suspicions that the other would cheat in any process of negotiated disarmament. Still, the discussions marked a departure from cold war unconditional hostility. So did such Soviet concessions as withdrawal from Austria, on condition that it remain nonaligned.

The neutralization of Austria reflected the conviction of Nikita S. Khrushchev, the Communist party secretary-general, that Stalin's system had been as overextended abroad as it was overrepressive at home. He gave the signal for a new course in a sensational secret speech to the Twentieth Congress of the Communist party of the Soviet Union in 1956. Khrushchev stunned his colleagues by denouncing not only the errors, but the crimes of Stalin. Coming from a former henchman who had inherited Stalin's powerful position, such a denunciation shook Eastern Europe to its foundation—far more than Khrushchev had intended.

The new Soviet leadership had to try to reach accommodation with the United States without alienating factions within the communist bloc that insisted the Americans were not to be trusted (the Chinese, for example). For this reason, Soviet policy alternated between concessions and intransigence through the 1950s. In 1955, for instance, the Soviets countered the entry of West Germany into NATO by forming the Warsaw Pact, an alliance of their Eastern European client states—but they also met with Western leaders in Geneva, in the first "summit conference" since 1945. Propos-

The Soviet Union in Eastern Europe

The countries that vanished behind the Iron Curtain in 1945—East Germany, Poland, Czechoslovakia, Hungary, Rumania, and Bulgaria—all received virtually the same treatment under Stalin. Drab police states imposed Soviet-style modernization, including the collectivization of agriculture and the build-up of heavy industry at the expense of consumer production. After his 1948 break with Tito of Yugoslavia, Stalin feared that other nationalistic communist leaders might also rebel, so he kept rigid control over the governments of the Eastern European states. Leaders accused of "na-

tionalist deviationism" from unconditional obedience to the Soviets were
purged or even executed.

Now, in yet another repudiation of
Stalinism, Khrushchev publicly recon-
ciled Soviet differences with Tito. The
populations of Eastern Europe interpreted such concessions as a weakening
of Soviet control and rebelled against the
conditions of economic exploitation and
political suppression under which they
lived. In Poland, where hatred of Russian
rule dated back long before the Bolshevik Revolution, workers' rioting forced
the Polish Communist party to install
Wladyslaw Gomulka as leader. Formerly
imprisoned by Stalin as a Polish nationalist, Gomulka confronted Khrushchev
and won consent to a liberalized communist regime in Poland. The new order
recognized the continuing influence of
the Catholic church among Poles. Thus
began a curious combination of ostensi-
ble hostility and quiet cooperation between communists and Catholics, a combination that continues in the 1980s in
Poland.

Gomulka never forgot the immense
power of the Soviets as he tried to whee-
dle concessions from them; though his
policies have often been criticized, they
were more effective than overt resistance. Hungarian communists tried to
break more dramatically with Moscow.
After students and workers clashed with
Soviet tanks in the streets of Budapest
in October 1956, another formerly dis-
graced, nationalistically inclined communist, Imre Nagy, was installed in
power. At first it appeared that he could
satisfy both Hungarian demands for
greater freedom and Soviet anxieties
about losing control. Including noncommunists in his cabinet and promising
free elections, Nagy nevertheless talked
the Soviets into withdrawing the tanks

from Budapest. But not for long. As some
Hungarians continued to demonstrate
their hostility to communism and the
Soviet Union, Soviet leaders decided
they had made enough concessions. The
tanks rolled back into Budapest, crushing the revolt. Nagy was arrested and
later executed. János Kádár became premier of Hungary and still governs there
in the mid-1980s.

The lesson of Budapest was that
even the post-Stalinist Soviet leadership
would not tolerate Eastern European
liberalization that threatened Soviet
control. Meanwhile, despite all the encouragement of the Hungarian rebels by
CIA-financed radio stations like Radio
Free Europe, the United States could do
nothing for them but take in some of the
nearly 200,000 Hungarians who fled
their land. Despite Dulles's bombast, the
United States was not going to intervene
directly in a region tacitly conceded to
be in the Soviet sphere of influence.

The U.S. government in October 1956
brought pressure not against the Soviets
but against its own allies—the British,
French, and Israelis—when they provoked the other international crisis of
that month (a godsend to the Soviets) by
invading Egypt in retaliation for President Nasser's seizure of the Suez Canal.
Khrushchev threatened a nuclear war,
but Eisenhower's warnings to the U.S.
allies were far more effective in ending
the invasion. The future of the Arab
world lay with Nasser-style Third World
nationalism, U.S. policymakers decided,
and not with a resurgence of European
influence in the region. Thus, nations on
both sides of the world's bipolar divide
received sharp reminders in 1956 of their
dependency—the Hungarians, of course,
far more tragically than the British and
French.

Meanwhile, relations between the two

superpowers continued to oscillate between cordiality and confrontation. Khrushchev, who by 1958 led both the Soviet Communist party and the government, alternated blandishments and threats in his efforts to force the United States to recognize Soviet equality.

The Soviet Union and Berlin

A perennial bone of contention was the status of Germany and its capital. By surviving the siege of 1948, Berlin had become a symbol of freedom, a democratic and affluent island in a totalitarian and destitute sea. The official position of the West German government was that Germany should be reunified by free elections, with Berlin again becoming the capital. Official U.S. policy supported this scenario, though privately American policymakers, like those in Western Europe and the Soviet Union, were doubtless content to see Germany remain divided. Fearful of the power that West Germany alone contributed to the U.S.-led NATO alliance, the Soviets repeatedly tried to force the United States to recognize the permanent division of the country, including the Soviet domination of East Germany. Their lever once again was the vulnerability of isolated Berlin. Late in 1958 Khrushchev threatened unilaterally to end Berlin's privileged status as a free city within communist East Germany, a status which had provided an escape route for some 2 million fugitives. Encountering united Western resistance where perhaps he had hoped to expose disunity, he cancelled this Berlin ultimatum in March 1959.

Confrontations of this sort alternated with attempts at communication. On a visit to the United States later that year, Khrushchev met with President Eisenhower at Camp David, Maryland. Those talks produced little except agreement for another summit meeting in Paris. The president and the premier made no progress on disarmament, though by now the Soviets had created a strategic bomber force (still far smaller than the U.S. Strategic Air command) to deliver their nuclear weapons, and both nations were hard at work developing ballistic missiles. Khrushchev aborted the Paris summit meeting as soon as it convened, by revealing that the Soviets had shot down an American high-altitude U-2 spy plane over Soviet territory and by demanding an apology for the flight.

In June 1961, this turn toward renewed confrontation was followed by an ultimatum to U.S. President John F. Kennedy. Within a year, Khrushchev declared, he would sign a peace treaty with East Germany and relinquish to the East Germans control over access to Berlin. A few months later he ordered the erection of a wall separating East and West Berlin to end the hemorrhage of Eastern European labor and talent from the Soviet empire. Kennedy's only response was to draft more young Americans into the army and send some of them to West Berlin. Forced to choose between acquiescence and war, the United States preferred to acquiesce.

The Cuban Missile Crisis

Though it solved a Soviet problem, the Berlin Wall was hardly a Soviet success. Presumably challenged by Soviet and Chinese hard-liners to show more results in the continuing duel with the United States, Khrushchev took a step in 1962 that brought the world as close as it has yet come to nuclear war. He ordered the installation of Soviet missiles in Cuba.

The ultimate cause of the Cuban missile crisis was the Cuban revolution of January 1959, in which Fidel Castro overthrew the right-wing, U.S.-backed dictatorship of Fulgencio Batista. Castro soon attacked Cuba's dependency on the United States by seizing control of economic assets—sugar mills, oil refineries, banks—that were largely American owned. The United States retaliated by virtually excluding sugar, Cuba's principal source of export income, from the American market, and by denying Cuba most American goods. In such a situation, Cuba and the Soviet Union inevitably drew together. Khrushchev saw opportunities to extend Soviet influence by helping developing countries. He had already promised aid to those seeking to escape dependency by fighting "wars of liberation." Castro had no alternative ally. By the end of 1960, the Soviet Union had agreed to buy half of Cuba's sugar crop and to provide Castro with the essentials the U.S. embargo denied him.

Unwilling to tolerate a Soviet client state ninety miles off U.S. shores, the Eisenhower administration ordered the CIA to develop a secret plan for overthrowing it. But the plan, executed in April 1961, proved a deeply humiliating fiasco for President Kennedy. Castro's forces easily killed or rounded up the 1,500 Cuban refugees the CIA landed at the Bay of Pigs. Contrary to Washington's expectations, the Cuban population did not rise up to welcome the invaders.

Castro's demands for Soviet protection against a renewed American attack undoubtedly prompted Khrushchev's decision to send missiles to Cuba. But he must also have had other motives for taking such a tremendous gamble. Soviet missiles in Cuba would put much of the United States at the same nuclear risk the Soviet Union already faced from American missiles in Turkey and Western Europe. They could be used as bargaining chips against a German settlement. Their emplacement would prove to Khrushchev's critics that he could get tough with the Americans.

In October 1962, when U.S. aerial reconnaissance revealed that launching sites were under construction in Cuba, a terrifying thirteen-day crisis began. Few voices in the U.S. administration called for negotiation—most favored some show of force. Rather than attacking the launching sites without warning, as some recommended, Kennedy chose to impose a "quarantine" on Cuba. That term was used because a naval blockade amounted to a declaration of war. In fact, however, the U.S. navy blockaded Cuba; it was prepared to stop and search approaching Soviet ships that might be carrying the missiles. As television news plotted the course of those ships, the world waited and wondered whether a clash on the high seas might lead to nuclear war. Kennedy himself is reported to have thought that the odds of war were at least one in three, and at worst even. The suspense ended only with the news that the Soviet ships were turning back.

Once again, and this time very publicly, Khrushchev had to back down. He paid for this humiliation in 1964 when his colleagues in the Politburo, the Soviet cabinet, fired him from office. Whatever credit he might have earned for ending the crisis was negated by the fact that he had provoked it. In exchange for his retreat he had received U.S. commitments not to invade Cuba and to remove

American missiles (already obsolete) poised on the Soviet border in Turkey. But the Soviet Union had visibly failed in an attempt to project its power as close to American borders as U.S. power hemmed in its own frontiers.

The lessons of this hair-raising episode remain obscure. The Soviets concluded that they must never again be caught in such a position of inferiority and began constructing a navy and nuclear delivery systems that could challenge the Americans. In the United States, critics on the left accused Kennedy of a strident, macho posturing that made the crisis worse, while those on the right complained that the Castro regime survived unscathed. One thing was clear, however. The crisis proved that twentieth-century leaders were ready to go to the brink of nuclear war to defend what they saw as their nations' vital interests.

Challenges to Bipolarity, 1962–1973

During the Cuban missile crisis, most of the world stood on the sidelines, at risk of destruction if the two superpowers clashed. This episode vividly illustrated the continuing danger for other nations of "annihilation without representation." That danger helps to explain the theme of the next decade of postwar international relations: the apparent breakdown of the bipolar world into a multipolar world. A resurgent Western Europe increasingly challenged U.S. leadership. At the same time, the U.S. assumption that Moscow orchestrated every move of world communism proved stunningly false as the Soviet Union and the People's Republic of China moved from mistrustful friendship to the verge of war.

The growing importance of Europe and China in the international power game seemed to mark the eclipse of the bipolar system that had emerged in 1945.

The Integration of Europe

The first steps toward Western European resurgence were taken while the Continent was still rebuilding after the war. As the cold war undercut the parties of the Left, power passed to Christian Democratic leaders. Their Catholic faith, transcending national loyalties, helped them to see that the European nations had become dwarfed and obsolete in a world of superpowers. Only by merging into a "United States of Europe" could Europeans regain even part of their former power. The first institutional embodiment of European integration was the European Coal and Steel Authority, established in April 1951. It merged the mines and steel mills of France, West Germany, Italy, and the Benelux countries. This proved to be only the first of many such supranational European organizations. In 1957 the same countries signed the Treaties of Rome, establishing the European Economic Community (EEC). Its members committed themselves to creating a "Common Market," eventually eliminating tariffs on one another's goods.

Nearly three decades after its foundation, the EEC has not yet fulfilled all the hopes of its founders. Mobilizing some 10 percent of the world's population to produce about a third of its goods, the EEC has become a formidable competitor, outproducing the United States in such basic commodities as steel. With the addition of Britain, Ireland, and Denmark in 1972, Greece in 1981, and Spain and Portugal in 1985, it has become a community of twelve members. It has even paved the way for a degree of political integration. The first all-European parliament—with very limited powers—convened in 1979.

In the mid-1980s, European unification is yet to be accomplished. Polls show that almost half of the citizens of the EEC countries never think of themselves as citizens of Europe. The budget of the Common Market itself has been the cause of bitter wrangling among the members.

The Gaullist Challenge to U.S. Leadership

Though he was prophetically skeptical of European integration, General De Gaulle, as president of France from 1958 to 1969, tried to make multipolarity a reality by compelling Western Europeans to abandon their dependency on the United States. He aimed to make a revived Europe, led by France, a power to reckon with in the world again. The Europe he had in mind extended from the Atlantic to the Urals (the western mountains of the Soviet Union), combining the two blocs created by the cold war.

Western Europe's subordination to an American NATO commander, De Gaulle maintained, was frightening and unconvincing. Frightening, because as the Cuban missile crisis showed, in a confrontation with the Soviet Union the United States would not consult its allies before acting. Unconvincing, because as the Soviet Union developed its nuclear capability, it was no longer credible that the United States would risk destruction to save Europe from a Soviet attack. Therefore De Gaulle did all he could to foster an independent European defense sys-

tem. He gave the highest priority to developing delivery systems for France's nuclear weapons, developed without U.S. assistance and over U.S. objections. Meanwhile he refused to allow the installation of NATO nuclear weapons on French soil, withdrew French forces from NATO command, and in 1966 ousted NATO from France. Similarly, when the British agreed in 1962 to replace their obsolete nuclear bombers with U.S. missiles, De Gaulle retaliated by vetoing Britain's application for membership in the EEC.

For a time, De Gaulle hoped the West Germans, unlike the British, would back his efforts for an independent Western Europe. He tried to persuade them to abandon their unrealistic, U.S.-backed insistence on a formula for German reunification that was unacceptable to the Soviet Union because it threatened the existence of East Germany. De Gaulle believed that a reduction of the German threat might persuade the Soviet Union, faced with a growing Chinese menace, to relax its grip on Eastern Europe. Then Europe's bipolar division might end and the Continent, from the Atlantic to the Urals, could return to world power.

In hopes of restoring European economic independence, De Gaulle attacked the international monetary system created under American auspices at Bretton Woods in 1944. Under this system, the dollar had become the world's principal "reserve currency." De Gaulle argued that the dollar's privileged status enabled the United States to escape the discipline the world economy enforced on other currencies. The United States could ignore growing inflation and an ever-growing imbalance in the payments it exchanged with other countries. Its reserve-currency role protected the dollar from depreciating even when Americans spent more abroad than they earned. The endless outflow of dollars enabled U.S.-based multinational companies to buy heavily into the economies of other countries. Until the world monetary system could be revised, De Gaulle's remedy for France was to demand payments in gold, largely depleting the U.S. supply.

Many Americans denounced De Gaulle as an enemy of their country. In fact, however, Gaullist foreign policy was only the most outspoken expression of a widespread European aspiration to break free of the post-1945 bipolar system. When the Soviets in 1968 crushed the attempt to create a "communism with a human face" in Czechoslovakia, it appeared that De Gaulle's ambitious strategy of reuniting the Continent had failed. But the Gaullist drive for European solutions to European problems, taken up by less abrasive leaders like Chancellor Willy Brandt of West Germany, would become a significant factor in the détente of the early 1970s.

Playing the China Card

In January 1964, De Gaulle's France extended diplomatic recognition to the People's Republic of China. To many Americans, this seemed another example of Gaullist unfriendliness. American policy was that "China" meant Chiang Kai-shek's refugee regime on Taiwan. De Gaulle, however, was bent on enlarging the number of players in the global power game, and recognizing China was one step in this process. Only in this way, he believed, could the world escape endless bipolar confrontations, or the equally grim prospect of an agreement between the superpowers to rule the world, such as had occurred at Yalta in 1945.

By 1964, Communist China was turning out not to be the obedient creature of Moscow once imagined. The Chinese had both ideological and practical reasons to complain of the Soviet Union. Mao Zedong was convinced that the Soviet Union was becoming a nonrevolutionary society closer in outlook to the capitalist nations than to China. At the same time, the Soviets, whose economic aid had always been niggardly, reneged on their promise to equip China with nuclear weapons. In 1960, as Sino-Soviet relations worsened, Khrushchev withdrew the Soviet technicians sent to facilitate Chinese development. By the mid-1960s, border clashes revealed the depth of hostility between the two communist giants. As De Gaulle saw, the West now had an opportunity to draw closer to a potentially powerful enemy of the Soviet Union, thus complicating Soviet calculations. Unfortunately, it would be nearly a decade before the United States could play this "China card" in the international game. For American leaders had become obsessed with victory on another Asian front—in Vietnam, where they mistakenly believed they were resisting Chinese expansion.

The American Misadventure in Vietnam

The total costs of the Vietnamese conflict, the United States' longest and most costly war, are not easily reckoned. Over 57,000 Americans—and hundreds of thousands of Vietnamese—died. Total American expenses have been calculated at over a trillion dollars. Less tangibly, the lost war dealt a blow to Americans' self-confidence from which they began to rally only in the 1980s. The United States' obsession with Vietnam, and then its apparent renunciation of power when it withdrew, hastened the transformation of international relations to a multipolar system. Thus the Vietnam War must be regarded as a pivotal event. Certainly its impact has been far out of proportion to the size of this small Southeast Asian country. The tragedy unfolded in four acts.

The first act—the end of French rule in Vietnam—involved the United States only tangentially. Vietnam had been part of the French empire at the beginning of World War II. The Japanese defeat of the colonial powers created a power vacuum at the war's end when Japan itself was defeated. Vietnamese nationalists seized the moment to reclaim independence. Their leader was Ho Chi Minh, who as a young emigrant to France in 1919 had vainly petitioned the Versailles Peace Conference for self-determination for his country. Disappointed by the indifference of Western leaders, he became a founding member of the French Communist party. The French had no inten-

Vietnam, New Year's Day, 1966. A U.S. paratrooper is pinned down by sniper fire while assaulting a "Viet Cong" stronghold. Caught in the middle, Vietnamese civilians wait for the shooting to end.
AP/Wide World Photos

tion of surrendering Vietnam to the Vietminh, the name given the movement Ho founded when he returned to his country in 1941. Negotiations between them ended in bloody clashes in 1946, the prelude to eight years of war.

American sympathies in this conflict shifted with events. U.S. undercover agents had cooperated with Ho's resistance to the Japanese. During the cold war, however, Americans began to perceive Ho as a creature of Moscow, rather than as a nationalist fighting for liberation. The French took advantage of this shift to enlist U.S. aid against Ho. By 1954, the United States was paying three-quarters of France's war costs, and 300 advisers were in Vietnam. Though Vietnam's mineral wealth was sometimes cited as the reason for U.S. involvement, the real explanation seems to have been the *domino theory*. In this view the countries of Southeast Asia were like a row of dominoes standing on end: push one over and all the rest would immediately fall to communism.

This theory became critical when the Vietminh defeated the French at the battle of Dien Bien Phu early in 1954. A new French cabinet indicated its intention to get out of Vietnam as swiftly as possible. An international conference in Geneva agreed to partition Vietnam temporarily, though it was to be reunited after free elections within two years.

These Geneva accords mark the beginning of the second act of the American drama in Vietnam. Having refused to sign them, Washington felt free to disregard them. The promised elections, which all agreed would have given a majority to the Vietminh, were never held. Instead, as had happened elsewhere around the periphery dividing the spheres of the superpowers, two countries emerged. As it protected South Korea, the United States took under its protection the Republic of South Vietnam. Its President was Ngo Dinh Diem, a fervent anticommunist from the country's Catholic minority.

Diem's regime was corrupt, and its contempt for the country's Buddhist and peasant majorities soon provoked revolt. In 1960, a National Liberation Front (FLN) began guerrilla operations in South Vietnam's jungles and villages. From the start, though the FLN claimed to be a multiparty, strictly southern movement, it received supplies and direction from Ho Chi Minh's North Vietnam.

This situation gave the Kennedy administration an opportunity to test its theory that guerrillas could be beaten by tactics of counterinsurgency, including programs to "win the hearts and minds" of a peasant populace by land reform and social change. By 1963 12,000 American advisers were in South Vietnam, helping Diem's army regroup peasants to prevent the FLN from living among them. However, the Diem regime's continued repression of Buddhists and other "enemies" made it impossible to claim that the United States was defending democracy in South Vietnam. Early in November, with U.S. encouragement, elements of the South Vietnamese army overthrew Diem.

The third act of the Vietnam tragedy began a few weeks later when Vice President Lyndon Johnson succeeded Kennedy. To understand why Johnson turned American involvement into a tragedy by vastly increasing the U.S. commitment to Vietnam, it is necessary to examine the perceptions of the policymakers who advised him.

In the context of twentieth-century history Ho Chi Minh is a familiar type. He is only one of many leaders who have mobilized mass movements against the European-dominated global configuration. Ho had warned the French that even if they killed ten of his men for every French soldier killed by the Vietminh, he still would win. He had.

U.S. policymakers, however, looked at the Vietnamese situation through a veil of American preconceptions. Americans knew, and cared to know, practically nothing of Vietnamese history, culture, or society. Vietnam was a peasant country still struggling with the heritage of colonialism, but Americans saw it as a "cornerstone of the free world," a place to "stand up to" the Soviet Union and China. Before it became an American nightmare, Vietnam was an American fantasy—and the mightiest nation on earth was prepared to invest powerful energies in making the fantasy a reality. The policymakers who directed those energies wanted to make sure that events conformed to their preconceptions, because their careers and reputations were at stake. For such reasons many young men sometimes die.

Within a year of Johnson's 1964 pre-election promise not to expand the U.S. commitment, there were 200,000 American troops in Vietnam. When North Vietnamese patrol boats clashed in the Tonkin Gulf with U.S. warships, Johnson seized the occasion to force a resolution through Congress giving him virtually unlimited powers to expand a war against the North Vietnamese without declaring it. Out of more than 500 members of Congress, only 2 voted against the resolution. While American infantrymen sweated through search-and-destroy missions in the South Vietnamese countryside, the U.S. Air Force dropped on Vietnam, North as well as South, nine times the tonnage of bombs dropped throughout the Pacific during World War II. This was massive support indeed for the dozen-odd mostly military governments that succeeded one another by plot and coup in the South Vietnamese capital, Saigon, between 1963 and 1965.

But it did not work. The North Vietnamese matched the Americans escalation for escalation, infiltrating regular troops into the South to back up the FLN. One of the many ironies of this terrible story is that both sides were obsessed with the "Munich analogy"—belief that surrender to aggression would mean never-ending subjection to it, as in 1938. American failure in Vietnam, Johnson and his advisers deeply believed, would expose the United States to a never-ending series of Communist aggressions. The prime minister of North Vietnam, Pham Van Dong, declared in 1966, "Never Munich again, in whatever form." He meant that Vietnam had been cheated of total independence twice, in 1946 and 1954, and had no intention of negotiating anything away again.

In this contest of wills the turning point for Americans came with the FLN offensive during the Vietnamese month of Tet, in January 1968. The Tet offensive ended in military defeat for the FLN, but it was a psychological success. The nightly television news depicted an apparent American debacle. Coordinated FLN operations showed that not even the American Embassy in Saigon was safe from guerrilla attack. After Tet, influential figures in the administration joined campus protesters in doubting that victory could ever be achieved. Faced with these doubts, Lyndon Johnson abandoned the presidency.

The election of 1968 opened the final act of the drama—the slow facing up to the reality of defeat. The successful Republican candidate, Richard M. Nixon, knew the war could not be won. His "secret plan" for Vietnam turned out to consist of trying to cut U.S. losses by beginning withdrawal while trying to bomb the North Vietnamese into a settlement that would save American face. For four years negotiations dragged on in Paris. At last the United States agreed to essentially the same terms the North Vietnamese had held out for from the beginning: prompt U.S. withdrawal, with few effective guarantees for South Vietnam.

South Vietnam did not long survive the departure of the U.S. combat troops in 1973. Nixon's plan for "Vietnamization" of the war—preparing the South Vietnamese to defend themselves—proved illusory. In April 1975 the North Vietnamese army entered Saigon. U.S. helicopters lifted the last Americans out of the embassy compound, while Marines pried loose the clutching hands of desperate South Vietnamese supporters who wanted to flee too. It was a scene remarkably like that of the French departure from Vietnam twenty years earlier.

In 1975, most Americans probably considered the nation well out of Vietnam, even at such a price. With the passage of time, however, myths have begun to grow up, as often happens when a nation has suffered a defeat. One is almost reminiscent of the "stab-in-the-back" legend of post-1918 Germany in blaming defeat on civilian irresolution. It alleges that the Vietnam War was lost not by the army but by Washington's unwillingness to fight with sufficient determination. In crude terms, this view holds that, "next time, we should go in with everything we've got!"

As we have already seen, however, the lessons of history are not always clear. Certainly, hostility toward Washington by some Vietnam veterans is understandable. They neither caused the war nor failed in their duty—but after anguishing experiences, they returned to an indifferent or hostile home front. Moreover, the extension of North Vietnamese rule to the whole country since 1975 has belied the assurances of anti-war protesters that an FLN victory would bring freedom to South Vietnam. The unlucky South Vietnamese have exchanged a regime of stark social inequality and fast-changing dictatorship under Diem and his successors for Soviet-style scarcities under the enduring dictatorship of Ho Chi Minh and his successors.

Had the U.S. gone all out for victory, some argue, none of this would have happened. But the implications of such a statement demand careful analysis. In pursuit of victory the United States extended the Vietnam War to the rest of Indochina, devastating once neutral Laos and Cambodia (Kampuchea). What further steps would have been involved in "going all out"? The United States could have gone to war with China, which was supplying the North Vietnamese (as was the Soviet Union). But none of the presidents who had to face the Vietnamese nightmare was willing to risk the American public's reaction to such steps. Far from favoring war with China, most Americans later welcomed improvement of Chinese-American relations. Meanwhile, once the Americans were gone, relations between Vietnam and China, traditional enemies, deteriorated into actual war in 1979.

If the risks of enlarging the war outweighed the possibilities of thereby winning it, could the United States have made a greater effort in Vietnam itself? This question cannot be answered without doing something American policymakers rarely did: understanding the mentality of their opponents and particularly their different understanding of *time*. To Americans of the television era, a year is a very long time, and three years of inconclusive fighting by large American forces in Vietnam proved insupportable by 1968. In the Vietnamese perspective, nearly a century of French colonialism had been a mere interlude—their history is one of a thousand years of resistance to outsiders, principally the Chinese. Even if the American forces had concentrated on defeating the North Vietnamese regular army instead of the FLN guerrillas, the resulting "victory" would probably not have been definitive. Vietnamese resistance would doubtless have continued, requiring an American occupying army. And Americans have shown little enthusiasm for commitments that would keep draftees indefinitely at risk. In the light of these considerations, the idea of victory in a place like Vietnam becomes elusive and problematical. Perhaps the best way of achieving victory would have been to follow the wise counsel of a senator who advised Johnson simply to announce that the United States had won—and then withdraw as quickly as possible.

Multipolar Détente versus Renewed Confrontation, 1973–1984

Since the end of the Vietnam War, international relations have been marked by an exploration of the possibilities and limits of diminished tension—*détente*—in a multipolar world. Through the mid-1970s, détente made it possible to set aside many of the festering issues of the cold war. More recently, Soviet-American relations have taken another turn for the worse. The inability of the rest of the world to prevent this development suggests that bipolar conflict remains the inescapable fact of international relations.

The Making of Détente

American diplomacy during the period of relative détente until 1976 was orchestrated by Secretary of State Henry Kissinger. Unlike many of his predecessors and successors in his office, Kissinger had a coherent world view shaped by the European tradition of diplomatic *Realpolitik*—policy based on cold-blooded realism. Now that the revolutionary ardor of the Soviet Union and China had diminished, Kissinger believed, the United States could maneuver between them to secure its own interests and the balance of power. Though he too ritually denounced the Soviet Union on occasion, Kissinger did not see the world's future as the triumph of American right over communist wrong. Rather he envisioned an everlasting process of adjustment of interests among five centers of power: the United States, the Soviet Union, China, Western Europe, and Japan.

The most spectacular result of this idea was the reversal in Chinese-American relations. The process wound its way from secret negotiations, to the American table tennis team's visit to China, to a climax in a solemn state visit by President Nixon to China early in 1972. His televised toasts to Chinese leaders marked a dramatic contrast to the decades during which the United States had ignored the existence of the People's Republic. The new friendship of the two countries raised deep concern in the Soviet Union, which by the early 1970s was maintaining up to a quarter of its armed

U.S. President Nixon and Chinese Premier Zhou Enlai toast U.S.-Chinese friendship in Beijing, February 1972. The world power balance had changed since U.S. Secretary of State Dulles refused to shake hands with Zhou at the Geneva Conference in Switzerland, in 1954.
UPI/Bettmann Newsphotos

forces in the east against possible Chinese attack.

The Soviet Dilemma

Partly because of Soviet concern about China, President Nixon was warmly received when he visited Moscow in May 1972, three months after his trip to Beijing. But many motives, both international and domestic, impelled the Soviets toward détente.

On the international plane, the Soviet Union had overcome the inferiority in nuclear weaponry so evident during the Cuban missile crisis. In the second half of the 1960s, it had more than tripled its land-based intercontinental ballistic missles (ICBMs), its principal deterrent force. Each superpower now had enough nuclear warheads to destroy the other many times over. When President Nixon admitted there was no possibility that the United States could win a nuclear war, the Soviet Union could feel it had finally been accepted as an equal.

Domestically, however, Soviet society by the 1970s had weaknesses that could be addressed, if at all, only by achieving détente with the United States. The Soviet economy was in trouble. Although the weakness of the world economy was partly responsible, to a much greater extent the problems were peculiar to the Soviet Union.

The pattern of Soviet growth since 1945 had been much like that of the Western democracies. Annual growth of the Soviet gross national product (GNP) began slowing down in the 1970s. Though Western growth slowed in similar fashion, the poor Soviet figures reflected the worsening of perennial Soviet problems, above all comparatively unproductive agriculture. Fully one Soviet citizen in four is still engaged in agriculture (compared with under 3 percent of the population in the United States). Although they seeded almost twice as much land as the Americans, the Soviets reaped only three-quarters of the American harvest. Sometimes they did not produce enough to feed the country, as in 1972 when détente enabled them to make essential purchases of grain from the United States and other countries.

It is a measure of the frozenness of Soviet ideology that Soviet politicians insist that the solution to agricultural insufficiency is further heroic clearing and irrigation of land. The heirs of the Bolsheviks cannot admit what Soviet economists have been insisting since the 1960s: the Stalinist model of a rigidly controlled economy does not work very well. For twenty years, the Soviet government has tinkered with what everyone agrees is the problem, in industry as well as agriculture: centralized, bureaucratic management, and poor morale and discipline on the farm and the shop floor. Attempt after attempt has been made, on a limited basis, to galvanize production by offering management and workers the incentive of the profit mo-

tive. All have proved unavailing against the passive resistance of the bureaucracy and of workers in an economy where officially there can be no unemployment.

By the time of Nixon's visit it was becoming urgent to close the efficiency gap with the West. Soviet society was changing, becoming gradually more like that of the United States. Twenty-five years ago, visitors who penetrated into the villages where half of the Soviet population of nearly 275 million lived found conditions not very different from those found in Third World villages. Since the 1960s the same currents of change that transformed Western societies have swept into the Soviet Union as well. Today only a third of Soviet citizens are villagers. This wave of urbanization has created masses of more sophisticated city dwellers eager for the products of an advanced society. Significantly, the ninth Five-Year Plan (1971–1975) was the first to give priority to production for mass consumption. Its goals were far from fulfilled. Indeed, there is disturbing evidence that Soviet society is becoming too inefficient to provide the cradle-to-grave care that has been one of its boasts. Soviet life expectancy seems to be falling, and infant mortality rising.

To remedy all this was perhaps beyond the abilities of the aging Communist hierarchy that continued to rule by relentless repetition of Marxist-Leninist slogans. It was inconceivable that they should repudiate them. Leonid Brezhnev, an orthodox party functionary, had captured an uncontested place at the top of the hierarchy by 1969, and occupied it until his death in 1982. Under him, vast numbers of dissenters no longer disappeared into concentration camps (though they might be sent to mental hospitals instead—a strategem devised by the chief of secret police, Yuri Andropov, who briefly succeeded Brezhnev in 1982–1983).

Nevertheless, the increasingly educated, urbanized Soviet public expected Brezhnev to deliver on the party promises of greater Soviet modernity. Here was another good reason—in addition to the Chinese threat—for the Soviets to broaden their contacts with the Western democracies, whose trade would provide them with the technology and hard cash they needed. Détente would also enable Brezhnev to divert scarce Soviet resources from defense to consumer-oriented demands. Small wonder he welcomed President Nixon to Moscow in 1972.

The United States in the World Economy

The cold war has also imposed severe strains on the U.S. economy. On August 15, 1971, Nixon had reacted dramatically to the new combination of inflation and recession called *stagflation* and to the decline of the dollar. He ended the dollar's convertibility at fixed rates to gold or foreign currencies. Henceforth, currencies would "float," exchanged at whatever rate the markets thought best. By this unilateral action, the United States destroyed the Bretton Woods system on which it had insisted in 1944. By refusing to pay in gold, the United States was repudiating part of its debts by depreciating the dollar. Its ability to do so without provoking protest was a testimony to continuing American power. But its need to do so suggested that American power was no longer what it had been in 1944.

Thus, the leaders who met in Moscow in 1972 both recognized their nations' limitations. Their meeting produced an agreement based on the Strategic Arms Limitation Talks (now known as SALT I) held over the previous three years. Both sides would retain the monstrous stockpiles of nuclear weapons they had already built, but future production of certain kinds of weapons would be limited. Modest though it was, this agreement was a sign of the "spirit of détente," which soon stimulated a sixfold increase in trade between the Western and Soviet blocs.

Détente for Europeans

This increased flow of goods reflected the détente that had developed between the subordinate states in each of the superpowers' spheres of influence. While the United States was preoccupied in Vietnam, Europeans east and west had seized the initiative to begin melting down the Iron Curtain that divided their continent. The credit belongs primarily to West German Chancellor Willy Brandt. His Socialist party wanted an *Ostpolitik*, an eastern policy that might lead to the reconciliation—perhaps even the eventual reunification—of the two Germanies. Brandt's first step was to calm Soviet fears of renewed German danger by signing a nonaggression treaty with the USSR in 1970. He also accepted Poland's western border with Germany. In 1972, the two Germanies acknowledged each other's legitimacy. Both were admitted to the United Nations the following year. Finally, in 1973 West Germany formally renounced the Munich Agreement of 1938 that had dismembered Czechoslovakia. Meanwhile, in 1971 the United States, the Soviet Union, Britain, and France had mutually recognized each other's rights, and those of East Germany, in Berlin. This period of détente climaxed in 1975 at the European Security Conference in Helsinki, Finland, where all the European countries, Eastern and Western, and the United States promised to honor each other's existing borders.

Critics of the Helsinki treaty contended that the East got considerably more out of it than the West. In return for Soviet promises to guarantee basic human rights, which soon proved valueless, the West acknowledged Stalin's expansion of the Soviet perimeter in Eastern Europe.

Yet, as De Gaulle had foreseen, the Soviet Union's rule in Eastern Europe had become so difficult that it found détente essential. Behind a facade of communist solidarity, the Soviets were trying to maintain Eastern Europe in a situation of dependency not unlike colonialism. Such a situation was wholly incongruous. Still developing itself, the USSR could not provide its satellites with capital. Meanwhile, some of the satellite states had reached a higher level of economic development than the Soviet Union. Thus, both the poor and the more affluent economies of Eastern Europe had economic reasons to complain of Soviet rule by the 1970s.

To the extent that détente offered an economic alternative to Soviet dependency, it was seized eagerly by the communist leadership of the various Eastern bloc countries. Moscow's tolerance of their growing indebtedness to western banks suggested it had no better solution. As economic exchanges multiplied, the life of Eastern Europe was unavoidably altered. By the 1980s, it was clear that its peoples, like those of Western Europe, desperately wanted to perpetuate détente. In Czechoslovakia, for example, where the government controlled all publication, newspapers published letters critical of the installation of Soviet missiles on Czech territory. The Bulgarian government, long considered the most subservient in the Eastern bloc, called for making Eastern Europe a nuclear-free zone.

Such gestures were trivial compared to the mass protests in Poland in 1980 and 1981, organized by the free trade union, Solidarity. Its suppression by the government of General Wojciech Jaruzelski has been much criticized in the West. But the leaders of Eastern Europe, including Jaruzelski, walk a narrow line between the demands of their peoples' nationalism and the danger that such demands would provoke Soviet punishment. Though there is still no doubt who is master in Eastern Europe, the voices of its peoples are now sometimes heard. They are a reminder to the Soviets that the world is moving from bipolarity to multipolarity.

The Carter Years: Détente Dissolved

The United States also found itself confronted with the realities of a multipolar world in the 1970s. Challenges arose from such unexpected sources as Iran, once a dependable U.S. client state. Meanwhile the American attitude toward the Soviet Union veered from ideological contempt to longing for accommodation, and back again.

President Jimmy Carter came into office in 1976 anxious to maintain détente. He left office with détente in shambles. Perhaps the rapid chill was inevitable, given the continuing rivalry of the superpowers. In October 1973, only a little more than a year after President Nixon's visit to Moscow, the Soviet Union had threatened to send troops into the Middle East to intervene in the fourth Arab-Israeli war. Nixon responded by ordering U.S. forces on nuclear alert. Fortunately for the world, this incident did not prove to be the present-day equivalent to 1914's mobilization crisis. A countdown to nuclear war was not begun.

The Carter administration continued the negotiations that culminated in 1979 in a second Strategic Arms Limitation Treaty (SALT II). Though this agreement was never ratified by Congress, both parties have continued to abide by its provisions, so far as is known.

Despite these continuing contacts, Carter's foreign policy advisers convinced him that the Soviet Union was taking advantage of détente. They were alarmed by growing Soviet involvement in the rivalries among African independence movements. Except for their sponsorship of Cuba, the Soviets had not previously committed themselves in countries so far from their borders. American policymakers found it unacceptable that the Soviets should feel free to intervene on a global scale. In response, the Soviets asked why it was only the United States that had a right to support its friends in faraway places.

The Carter administration's greatest indignation, however, was reserved for the Soviet invasion of Afghanistan in December 1979. The situation in this undeveloped mountain nation bore certain ironic resemblances to that of Vietnam, with the very important difference that Afghanistan lies on the Soviet Union's southern border. A series of pro-Soviet governments had displaced the former nonaligned regime. Many Afghans held them in contempt. When fighting broke out, the Soviet puppet government could control the capital, the cities, and the main roads, but it could not control Muslim fundamentalist tribesmen in the

hills, who had a proud tradition of warfare against all of Afghanistan's invaders. By the mid-1980s, the Soviets had still not mastered their resistance, despite extensive use of the kind of tactics—saturation bombing, helicopter gunships, napalm—employed unavailingly by the United States in Vietnam. There was little the United States could do for the Afghan rebels except secretly send them arms. But Carter took the initiative in several expressions of outrage, including stopping the sale of grain to the Soviets and boycotting the 1980 Moscow Olympics.

None of these measures had any effect on Soviet policy, but they did contribute to the end of détente and the renewal of bipolar confrontation. At the same time, however, the United States was discovering the power of the previously powerless—small countries rich in raw materials.

The OPEC Challenge and the Iranian Revolution

In 1973, when the Organization of Petroleum Exporting Countries (OPEC) embargoed the sale of oil to the West to protest its support for Israel, stocks on the New York Stock Exchange lost $100 billion in value in just six weeks. Even supposedly reliable U.S. allies among the oil producers, like the shah of Iran, were quite unapologetic about their new attitude. Oil prices quadrupled between 1973 and 1975.

Worse events followed in the oil-rich Persian Gulf. As we shall see in greater detail in Chapter 16, the shah's regime was overthrown in 1979 by a massive opposition front whose religious leadership regarded the United States as the "great Satan" of the world. After the shah sought sanctuary in the United States, Iranian militants seized the American Embassy in Tehran in November, taking sixty Americans hostage. All of the United States' might could not help the hostages. For many months, television brought before Americans the humiliating spectacle of their fellow countrymen paraded before the cameras by enemies filled with the Third World's rage against superpower dominance. President Carter was quite unfairly blamed for the hideous dilemma of a hostage situation—whether to sacrifice the hostages or give in. He succeeded in negotiating their release only minutes before Ronald Reagan was sworn in as president in January 1981.

The Return to Confrontation

Reagan represented the right wing of the Republican party, which had been deeply suspicious of Kissinger's design for détente. During his first term, Soviet-American relations continued the deterioration begun during the Carter administration. By the end of his first term, experienced observers in Moscow declared that Soviet suspicions of the United States had become deeper than ever before, even under Stalin. Reagan ordered a record military build-up, which included preparation for the militarization of space (matched by the Soviets). And he denounced the Soviet Union in language reminiscent of that of John Foster Dulles.

At the same time, the Reagan administration seemed keenly aware that while Americans liked a president who would "stand up to the Russians," they would be unsympathetic to belligerence that imposed sacrifices—such as the draft. Reagan preferred confrontational rheto-

ric to actual confrontation. U.S. Marines were sent to Lebanon on an ill-defined mission to show the flag. After Islamic terrorists blew up their barracks, killing over 200 Marines, the administration quickly withdrew the survivors. Critics claimed that the United States was signaling its unwillingness to maintain a presence in a region where its vital interests were at stake. In Latin America too, the Reagan administration has held back from full commitment. The United States has sent covert aid to rebels seeking to overthrow the revolutionary Sandinista government in Nicaragua, but no American troops.

When Reagan did send troops it was to a situation without strategic importance—but also without risk. To many Americans, their country's invasion of the tiny Caribbean island of Grenada in October 1983 seemed to be a turning point, after years of humiliation and frustration in Vietnam and Iran. To much of the world it seemed a grotesquely disproportionate, as well as illegal, assertion of American power. In fact, the Grenadan revolution and the American invasion that crushed it offer a summary illustration of the major themes of international relations since 1945.

At no time before, during, or after the Grenadan invasion did the American news media explain much to the U.S. public about Grenada. As always, a foreign situation was summed up from a narrowly American perspective, which saw the invasion as "restoring democracy" and ending a Marxist-Leninist threat. Grenada had been a very minor British possession. The independence it won could not emancipate its almost entirely black population from the typical poverty and dependence of a Third World country of the Hungry South. Its principal products, cocoa, nutmeg, and bananas, remained at the mercy of depressed world markets. A birth rate twice as high as that of the United States had produced a fast-growing population, two-thirds of them under the age of twenty-five and all in search of opportunity. But there was none: unemployment verged on 50 percent in 1979, the year that Maurice Bishop's New Jewel movement seized power.

Having appealed in vain to an unsympathetic Reagan administration for aid in developing his minuscule island (principally by building a jet-sized airport for it), Bishop accepted the help of the Cubans instead. This commitment strengthened the hand of the hard-line Marxists around him. In this way, as had happened over and over again since 1945 in all parts of the world, what was really the tragic and perhaps insoluble problem of Third World poverty became translated into an episode of bipolar confrontation.

When the hard-line faction deposed and murdered Bishop, the United States invaded the island, alleging that the new regime might harm American students there. There were few casualties. The U.S. troops were greeted as liberators by a majority of Grenadans.

When the invasion was over, Grenada disappeared from the television screens as suddenly as it had appeared. By the end of 1984, elections produced a government sympathetic to U.S. intervention. Unemployment mounted, however, again, reaching a level unofficially estimated at three out of five Grenadans. Despite pressing appeals from the Reagan administration, and the promise of an English-speaking work force content with $4.50 a day, only one American firm has located a facility in Grenada. On the other hand, the United States finished the jetport the Cubans had begun. Grenada thus will be ready to resume the classic dependent role—selling nutmegs, entertaining tourists—that Bishop's revolution briefly interrupted.

The story of Grenada illustrates the interplay of economic development and global power politics. A great many of the world's conflicts—transformed by American anticommunism and Soviet opportunism into conflicts of capitalist West and communist East—are really consequences of the economic differences between Affluent North and Hungry South.

Conclusion

If we recognize that the conflicts of the 1980s are not only between East and West, but also between North and South, we will be better able to analyze the system of international relations that has replaced the European dominance that broke down in 1945. In the 1940s, the publisher of *Time* predicted that the next hundred years would be the "American century." In fact, the era of unquestioned American primacy lasted barely a quarter-century. The defeat in Vietnam showed that U.S. power could not be infinitely extended. Other developments— European diplomatic initiatives, Japan's emergence as the world's third economic power, the strengthening position of China—also suggested that the world had begun to move from an unequal bipolar configuration toward multipolarity.

Close scrutiny of the power actually possessed by the supposed challengers of the United States and the Soviet Union suggests, however, that the evolution from bipolarity to multipolarity remains far from complete in the mid-1980s. Despite the hopes raised by the Bandung Conference in 1955, the efforts of the nonaligned Third World countries to act together have largely proved to be combinations of weakness. The grievances of the Hungry South have been given attention chiefly because of Western guilt at being rich in a world that is overwhelmingly poor. Since many in the West feel no such guilt, Third World nations will continue to have meager prospects. Their only opportunity to exert power themselves seems to be to combine to withhold their products. Third World countries could organize producers' cartels in emulation of OPEC. So far, however, no such cartels have emerged, and OPEC itself is now experiencing the classic difficulty of cartels in sticking together when demand drops.

If the Third World has little effective power, is it correct to speak of a five-sided configuration of international power: the United States, the Soviet Union, China, Western Europe, and Japan? In economic terms these five are indeed dominant—but not in international power. Despite their economic muscle, Western Europe and Japan have not chosen to make the sacrifices necessary to provide their own defense. To the extent that they remain dependent on U.S. arms, they remain U.S. subordinates. As for China, Napoleon once remarked, "Let China sleep, for when it wakes, the world will tremble." The revolution of 1949 has awakened China, but it will take many years of intense effort to modernize the life of a billion people.

Thus we are left with the two protagonists that had dominated the world of 1945: the United States and the Soviet Union. How have they avoided war so far? Part of the answer is certainly that *MAD* (mutually assured destruction by

atomic weapons) has been a powerful deterrent. War has historically been a means of getting what one wants. Now war seems unable to serve that function, for it would involve the destruction of both sides.

Moreover, despite much rhetoric, neither superpower has been willing to overextend itself for goals determined by ideology rather than interests. The United States was not willing to make war in aid of Eastern European revolts. The Soviet Union backed down from defense of Cuba. Conflicts in regions where both superpowers might assert that their vital interests are at stake—the Middle East, for example—have so far been contained. Since the end of World War II, which left Eastern Europe and North Korea under Soviet occupation and Communists poised to seize power in China, the bipolar balance has changed very little. Apart from Cuba and Afghanistan, the only territory to pass into the communist camp has been the three nations of former French Indochina. Though the United States lost the war in Vietnam, the East Asian "dominoes" have not fallen, as proponents of the war warned they surely would.

In this perspective, international relations since 1945 is a history of crises along the borders of two huge empires in basic equilibrium, not one of ideological crusades. The emergence of China, the restiveness of Europe, and the dynamism of Japan have markedly affected, but not determined, the interaction of these two empires. They are like two wrestlers who have pinned each other. Neither has won, neither has lost, neither has any prospect of winning or losing the struggle. The struggle weakens and immobilizes them both. Yet neither knows how to break the hammerlock each has upon the other. Neither remembers just how he got into this situation. Yet both hold on grimly and hope to prevail, for that is human nature.

Notes

1. Quoted in William R. Keylor, *The Twentieth-Century World: An International History* (New York: Oxford University Press, 1984), p. 272.

Suggestions for Further Reading

Calleo, David P., *The Imperious Economy* (1982).

Grosser, Alfred, *French Foreign Policy Under De Gaulle* (1967).

Hoffman, Stanley, *Gulliver's Troubles: The Setting of American Foreign Policy* (1968).

Kahler, Miles, "Rumors of War: The 1914 Analogy." *Foreign Affairs* (Winter 1980), 374–396.

Kennedy, Robert F., *Thirteen Days: A Memoir of the Cuban Missile Crisis* (1968).

Keylor, William R., *The Twentieth-Century World: An International History* (1984).

Treadgold, Donald W., *Twentieth Century Russia*, 5th ed. (1981).

Chapter *13*

POSTINDUSTRIAL SOCIETY IN THE POSTWAR DECADES

W hether they accepted U.S. dominance or, like General De Gaulle, contested it, Europeans seldom doubted that the history of their own countries since 1945 was "made in U.S.A." As the United States set the pace of technological, economic, and cultural change in the postwar world, and as English replaced French as the prime international language, European critics often denounced the "Americanization" of their own societies and politics. Americans, on the other hand, have tended to see their postwar history as being unique, like the rest of their history.

Both of these viewpoints are shortsighted. From a worldwide perspective, it is clear that developments since 1945 both in the United States and in Europe have reflected the basic twentieth-century trends emphasized throughout this book.

Many of these developments can be seen as the results of growing interdependency. The final breakdown of the European-dominated world system in 1945 has led, after a brief interlude of U.S. hegemony before Europe recovered, to a pattern of worldwide integration that can be summarized as "interdependence amid scarcity." The multinational corporation with headquarters in the United States, Western Europe, or Japan, but operating in dozens of countries, is the most visible manifestation of this integration. As these corporations pursued profits around the world, they made national borders meaningless. While the Ford Motor Company made automobiles in Bordeaux, France, the French-owned Michelin Tire Company made tires in South Carolina, helping to put Akron, Ohio—once "the Rubber City"—out of business. As a consequence of this growing integration, American workers and soon Europeans and Japanese too found themselves competing for jobs in a worldwide labor pool, which included the developing countries of Latin America and Asia.

Multinational corporations like IBM (International Business Machines Corporation), reflecting a second basic trend of the twentieth-century world, spread new technologies around the world within a few years of their invention. Since 1945, the process of self-compounding technological discovery that has characterized the Western world since the seventeenth century has dramatically accelerated. Humankind's "triumph over nature" now extends even to an ability to "splice" genes, rearranging the chemistry of the very substance of life. By the 1980s, in fact, most Americans, Europeans, and Japanese were more at home in the electronic environment created by computers and television sets than in the natural world that their grandparents had inhabited.

As a result, a new kind of society has emerged, first in the United States but soon after in Western Europe and Japan, that promises to be as different from the era when most people worked at the machines of heavy industry as that industrial world was from the ages when most people were farmers. In this new postindustrial society, most people earn their living neither on the farm nor in the factory, but by providing services. Already in the 1960s, the change to this kind of high-tech society had become so rapid that an influential book warned of "future shock"—an inability of humankind to adjust to the pace at which the future was overwhelming the present.

Such sweeping change naturally affected the political behavior of North Americans, Europeans, and Japanese. Many perceived the new patterns of relations between the races, the generations, and the sexes as threatening the last vestiges of admirable culturally conservative values. The efforts of the guarantor state in both the United States and Europe to manage change by meeting the new demands of minority groups, young people, and women made it the target of a growing conservative backlash by the 1970s. Conservatives also grew increasingly impatient at the state's redistribution of income to the disadvantaged.

Conservative protest was expressed in votes. When France, the last of the major democracies, gave women the vote in 1946, the process of evolution toward the mass society—a basic trend of the twentieth century—was complete. With the collapse of the Spanish and Portuguese dictatorships in the 1970s, politics everywhere in the West became democratic. The principal difference between the parties that alternated in office under these pluralistic political systems was over how much the guarantor state should manage the economy, and in whose interest. In no major country did any party any longer advocate violent revolution. The German Social Democrats, for example, representatives of "red Berlin" in 1914, in 1959 officially repudiated the ideas of Karl Marx.

Yet the prevalence of protest—sometimes violent protest—especially in the 1960s suggested that many Americans, Europeans, and Japanese doubted whether their votes really counted for anything. In a fast-changing world dominated by such gigantic organizations as multinational corporations, did the will of the individual really matter? If political decision making was really beyond the individual's reach and the only purpose of life was to assure one's own share of the products of the new technologies, who would take responsibility for the goals of society as a whole—for example, safeguarding the natural environment from spoliation? Though less often voiced in the 1980s, this kind of question continues to pose a crisis of values for all of the Western world.

The central themes of U.S. and Western European history since 1945 are the growth of global interdependency, the acceleration of technological change, and the resulting crisis of democratic values in postindustrial society. Dividing the history of the postwar world into four periods will aid us in examining the impact of these developments.

During the first period (1945 into the early 1960s), conservative political dominance followed the short era of social reform that immediately followed World War II. Behind the appearance of immobility of the 1950s, however, accelerating technological and social change was fundamentally altering U.S. and Western European society.

The stresses of change burst out in protests that made the second period, the 1960s, a decade of upheaval. Some who protested—such as blacks in the United States—were demanding their share in newly affluent societies; others were challenging the notion that society's only goal should be affluence, the apparent prevailing belief of Americans during the 1950s.

In the early 1970s, these combined revolts produced a third period—backlash against the apparent collapse of authority. Reassertion of conservative values, however, could not cope with the economic slump of the 1970s that followed the rise in OPEC oil prices. The slowdown of the world economy brought global interdependency to the attention of the West in the most painful way. Europeans and even the Japanese discovered, as Americans already had, that their heavy industries could not compete with products turned out in still-developing counties with lower labor costs. As the withering of their traditional industries brought them, ready or not, into the postindustrial age, the peoples of the world restlessly voted governments, whether of the Left or the Right, out of power in rapid succession.

With the fundamental disarray of the world's economy masked in the 1980s by a partial recovery that benefited principally the United States, the theme of the new decade seemed to be an American-style revulsion, echoing the slogans of President Reagan, against the whole idea of the guarantor state. Even French President Mitterrand—a Socialist elected in 1981 on a platform of expanding, rather than shrinking, the guarantor state—by mid-decade had reversed his position. Only time would tell whether the 1980s' reassertion of the slogans of classic nineteenth-century economic liberalism was an adequate response to the problems of economies still plunging into the postindustrial future.

The United States and Western Europe in the Cold War Era

To a considerable extent, bipolar confrontation with the Soviet Union shaped U.S. and Western European politics in the two decades following World War II. The momentum for postwar social reform died as the perceived necessity of resisting communism at home and abroad discredited the Left and brought moderate centrist and even right-wing governments to power by 1949 on the European continent and by 1952 in Britain and the United States. These governments did not, however, reverse the postwar expansion of the guarantor state.

In the United States, the principal beneficiaries of this expansion were veterans. The GI Bill of Rights gave them educational grants, loans, and jobs. Although this was really a governmental reapportionment of income in their favor, an entire generation of Americans perceived it as a right.

Generosity to veterans did not mean that conservatives intended to leave the New Deal intact. The Taft-Hartley Law of 1947 prohibited some of the unions' most effective tactics. By upholding the anti-union right-to-work laws of the South, the law spurred the flight of industry from the unionized Northeast and Middle West to what would later be called the Sunbelt. Thus, the end of World War II, when a third of nonfarm labor was unionized, marked the high point of the union movement in U.S. history.

This law proved to be as far as U.S. conservatives could go in reversing the New Deal. Congressional actions in the second term of President Harry Truman, re-elected in 1948, suggested that most Americans did not want to see the New Deal extended, however. Truman's Fair Deal program called for the establishment of an American national health insurance system comparable to those that most other developed countries established after World War II. But a coalition of conservative Republicans and southern Democrats blocked enactment of Truman's proposals. Thus, though established programs of the guarantor state continued, Congress resisted their extension to other groups, such as the ailing poor.

The last years of the Truman administration were overshadowed by the crusade of conservatives to root supposed communists out of the U.S. government. Republican nominee Dwight D. Eisenhower swept to victory in the election of 1952.

Under Eisenhower, as under Truman, the U.S. guarantor state grew slightly, rather than shrinking as Republicans hoped. Haunted by fear of runaway inflation, Eisenhower held it to a level of about 1 percent a year, maintaining the federal budget largely in balance. In his farewell address he warned, as only a former commander of Allied forces in Europe in World War II could, against the dangerous growth of the "military-industrial complex." The alliance of big business with the Pentagon, he declared, threatened not only war but economic ruin through uncontrollable inflation.

This prophetic warning was uncharacteristic of a president whose bland political style made the Fifties synonymous with political conformity. In Western Europe, similarly reassuring leaders from the past provided a sense of postwar continuity. In Britain, the 77-year-old Churchill led the Conservatives back to power in 1951. They held it under his successors until 1964. The political life of the new Federal Republic of Germany was dominated until 1963 by "the old man," Chancellor Konrad Adenauer, leader of the centrist Christian Democratic party. In France, no such dominant figure emerged after De Gaulle withdrew in disgust from postwar politics in 1946. The postwar Fourth Republic was governed after 1947 by the kind of unstable and short-lived coalition cabinets of the Center and the Right that had dominated prewar political life. Their inability to deal with rebellion in Algeria brought De Gaulle back to power with a Fifth Republic in 1958.

Like President Eisenhower's administration, these European governments maintained, but did not greatly expand, the activities of the guarantor state. However, behind the appearance of political continuity, technological change in the 1950s was fundamentally altering Western societies.

The Acceleration of Change

A tremendous economic expansion followed World War II throughout the Western world, which increasingly included Japan. The U.S. gross national product (GNP) doubled between the end of the war and the early 1960s. Despite recessions, real wages (taking inflation into account) rose 20 percent during the eight years of Eisenhower's administration alone. Fully a third of American families had been living in poverty (by the official definition) in 1940, and over a quarter of them were still officially poor in 1950. By 1960, however, only

about one American family in five was to be found below the poverty line.

Western Europe shared in the 1950s boom. By the end of the decade, the Continent produced a quarter of the world's industrial goods, though even West Germany's "economic miracle"—a growth in industrial production of over 100 percent—was outstripped by Japanese expansion. Although their standards of living were still only half of U.S. levels, Europeans' pay envelopes reflected the boom. Real wages doubled in Europe between 1950 and 1966.

In the midst of growing affluence, the ways in which Americans and Europeans earned their living were changing. In the mid-1950s, for example, the number of U.S. nonfarm workers employed in blue-collar jobs dropped below the number of white-collar office workers for the first time. This was a momentous turning point. Once office workers began to outnumber workers in factories, commentators began to talk of the United States as a postindustrial society. U.S. industrial employment was not yet contracting. But jobs in the service sector—government, retailing, finance, insurance, health care—increased by over 200 percent between 1945 and 1970. The number of local government employees tripled.

Western European societies soon followed the United States into the postindustrial age. In the mid-1950s, the farming, industrial, and service sectors of the French economy employed almost equal numbers of workers. By 1970, the postindustrial service sector, expanding much more rapidly than industrial jobs, employed almost half the French population.

Changing technology explains why industrial employment everywhere had peaked by the 1970s. Until then, cheap energy made it advantageous for industry to replace workers with machines.

The Computer Revolution and the Knowledge Explosion

Machines replaced workers in complex tasks as well as in simple ones. In 1955, an American automobile plant opened in which the most highly skilled jobs were performed by automated machine tools without human intervention. This breakthrough reflected the increasing speed with which new knowledge found practical application. The very idea of the computer dated back only twenty years.

Of all the technological innovations of our century, the computer is probably the most revolutionary. In 1936, Alan Turing, a British mathematician, first sketched the concept of a machine that could almost instantly solve calculations that would take human beings a lifetime. Electronic technology and wartime need transformed this idea into actuality. During World War II, Turing was one of the British code-breakers who designed machines to uncover by high-speed computation the random settings of German ciphering machines.

The first programmable digital computers ultimately derived from these wartime machines. The invention of the transistor soon made possible the development of ever-greater calculating capacity in ever-smaller machines. In the 1950s, magnetic tapes began to replace the clumsy punched cards on which computer data were first stored. Computers proliferated at incredible speed, for advanced technology and the increasing number of human interrelationships vastly expanded the demand for calculations and detailed record-keeping. By the 1980s, worldwide computer capacity was doubling every two years, with over 5 million machines in use in the United States alone. International Business Machines (IBM), the U.S.-based multinational corporation, continued to dominate production; as early as 1960, it was selling French-built equipment in over sixty countries.[1] By the 1980s, however, Japanese firms were planning to capture a third of the world market before the end of the decade. They already made most of the advanced computer memory chips.

People who have grown up with computers may find it difficult to imagine what life was like in the very recent past without them. In a sense the computer is simply one more machine with which human beings have harnessed nature to their purposes. This machine uses electrons moving in billionths of a second to manipulate numerical symbols. It is a kind of assembly-line of information, producing conclusions in the way that the assembly lines of the 1920s produced automobiles.

In fact, however, the computer is a wholly new kind of machine. It produces not goods or energy like earlier machines, but information, the chief commodity in a postindustrial society. By the 1980s, half of the American workforce was engaged in processing information of one sort or another. The more data computers produce, the more raw material they provide for processing to produce still more data. Thus, the "knowledge explosion" continues in a self-perpetuating cycle.

The computer may have potential for harm as well as for good. Since the 1950s, critics have warned that its capacity to store information about every individual could reinforce bureaucratic control of human life. Not everyone believes that the computerized automation of whole factories (already accomplished in Japan and soon to be imitated in the United States) will create more jobs than are lost as workers are displaced by robots. In the mid-1980s, the ultimate impact of the computer remains to be seen. Some believe the personal computer will restore to the individual some of the creative autonomy of craftsmen. Others feel computers directly threaten jobs. In this gloomier scenario, the service sector of postindustrial society will provide a dwindling number of jobs to low-paid operators, performing repetitive tasks before a video terminal under conditions of discipline reminiscent of the industrial assembly line.

The computer has proved to be an essential tool in the postwar knowledge explosion. By 1960, the U.S. government was spending 10 percent of its budget on research, compared to less than 1 percent before World War II. Many scientists complained that far too large a share of research expenditures—three-quarters or more—went to military technology. Nevertheless, such governmental expenditures powerfully influenced the shape of society. The knowledge explosion helps to explain why so many people by 1960—and not only in the United States—were doing different jobs and living in different places than in 1945.

The Flight to the Suburbs

As more and more of the population moved into service-sector occupations like computer-programming, people moved inexorably from farm and city to the suburbs. Machine technology in agriculture made it possible to produce far greater yields with ever-fewer farmers. As "agribusiness" produced huge stocks of food, what had remained in 1945 of the distinctive rural life of the small farmer faded away. Only 9 percent of Americans still lived on farms in 1960, compared to 17.5 percent in 1945. By the 1980s, French and West German farmers made up equally small minorities of their populations.

The distribution of population within the metropolitan areas to which these formerly rural people were migrating reflected the dispersion postindustrial employment made possible. The policies of the U.S. federal government accelerated flight to the suburbs in the 1950s. The Federal Highway Act of 1956, the most ambitious public works project ever attempted anywhere, revolutionized transportation. Fueled by an apparently limitless supply of cheap petroleum, automobile ownership tripled in the United States. By the early 1970s, there was almost one car for every two Americans. Unlike public transportation, the automobile conformed to Americans' longing for a private life. Since the suburban house fulfilled a similar aspiration, jobs and stores followed the new freeways to the new suburbs.

The landscape of the suburbia of the 1950s was semistandardized. An architecture of mass production produced neighborhoods that looked the same from one region of the country to another. Such sameness was reassuring to Americans who averaged a change of address every five years between 1945 and 1960. Postindustrial professional people engaged in research and development moved twice as often.

This apparent rootlessness of Americans and their willingness to conform to a single suburban lifestyle shocked Europeans. They were accustomed to a society where the ways of life of regions and social classes remained distinct. But by the 1960s, as global interdependency grew, the institutions of American suburbia were beginning to appear in Europe, too. The spread of fast-food chains and supermarkets provoked patriotic Europeans to decry the "coca-colonization" of their societies by powerful U.S. corporations. Though U.S. multinationals did market their products aggressively in Europe, it was really the transformation of European societies that made such marketing possible. European firms were producing ten times as many automobiles for newly affluent consumers in the mid-1960s as they did in the late 1940s, for example. The resulting congestion of its ancient cities encouraged Europe's suburban sprawl. By 1980, half of France's nonrural population lived in suburbs developed after World War II. Like suburban Americans, suburban Europeans turned increasingly to the electronic entertainment provided by television.

Television: The Electronic World View

Television has proved to be as momentous a postwar innovation as the computer. It has basically altered the way American viewers form their *cognitive maps*, their way of understanding reality. As the world increasingly becomes a single audience for the same programs, television may prove to have the same impact elsewhere.

In 1949 there were still only a million sets in operation in the United States, though broadcasting had begun in 1941. By 1960 there were 46 million sets, watched for an average of five hours a day in 90 percent of American homes. As the mass audience grew, so did the U.S. networks' advertising sales—by a phenomenal 50 percent a year in the 1950s. To keep such a lucrative audience in

Fast food in Paris. In the 1980s, there are nearly 1,000 American-franchised fast-food outlets in Paris. The appearance of such multinational corporations in the capital of *haute cuisine* reveals how U.S. patterns of mass consumption are spreading throughout the developed world.
David Moore/Black Star

front of their sets, television executives limited most programming to a predictable staple of quiz shows, comedies, and crime thrillers.

Such programming, endless commercials, and perhaps the very nature of the electronic medium itself have unquestionably affected the American consciousness. The average child has spent twice as much time in front of a television set as in the classroom. While growing up, most children watched some

30,000 repetitive and frequently violent "electronic stories." The experience of television appeared far more direct to them than that of school. It gave the impression of mirroring reality, allowing people to "see for themselves."

In fact, television offers only a peculiar and partial view of the world. Studies have shown that people who watch television more than four hours a day—a third of all Americans—have a distorted view of the society in which they live. Heavy viewers, it has been found, made their judgments about social groups and issues on the basis of what they had seen on the screen, where until recently the elderly, blacks, and career women seldom appeared.

Television has broken down the barriers between politics and entertainment. It appeals to feelings not thought, to the eye rather than the mind. In 1960, people who heard Richard M. Nixon and John F. Kennedy's presidential debate on the radio thought that Nixon had clearly worsted Kennedy on the issues. But the glamorous Kennedy, more skillfully made-up, projected a better image to those who watched television, and he won the election.

By the late 1960s, Americans were increasingly taking their political cues from television, rather than from the party leaders and influential opinion makers who had earlier guided them. Molding the politician's image—what he *appeared* to be—became crucial. In 1984, the same advertising agency that had created the "Pepsi generation" designed television "spot" commercials for the re-election of President Reagan. It used the same technique: endless repetition of simple and emotionally appealing themes.

Television has also shaped the political thinking of Americans through its treatment of news. With only twenty-two minutes per night to convey what happened throughout the world, television news cannot devote much time to any happening, however complicated. It trumpets events—preferably visually striking confrontations like battles or riots—as parts of an oversimplified saga. In political campaigns, this technique means a breathless day-by-day emphasis on who is ahead in the polls, rather than on any discussion of the issues. Jimmy Carter, an unknown in 1974, became president in 1976 largely because his media specialists managed his primary campaign with skill. Television declared him the "front-runner" when he had won only a third of the votes in a third of the primaries. The interpretation of video events that television commentators supplied often concentrated on exposing politicians as self-seeking bunglers. Television thus has confirmed many Americans' view of politics as a dirty business rather than as the mechanism for managing a complex society. In this way, television contributed to the steady decline between 1960 and 1980 in the number of Americans who voted for president.

Whether television will have the same overwhelming impact upon other postindustrial societies as it has had in the United States remains to be seen. In 1980, there were 63 television sets for every 100 Americans, but only 33 for every 100 West Germans and 29 for every 100 persons in France.[2] But in 1984 even the Chinese had as many sets as Americans had owned in 1960, and the Chinese government was purchasing its first package of programs from CBS.

Such worldwide proliferation of TV sets appeared to be at best a mixed blessing. By the 1980s the television medium had clearly not realized the hopes of its early years. Culturally, television faithfully reflected growing global integration. It shrank the world, in the words of one critic, to the dimensions of a "global village." But traffic within the "village" was virtually a one-way street. Twenty percent of British TV and 50 percent of French TV programming was imported, mainly from the United States. The number of people outside the United States who watched U.S.-made serials like "Dallas" far exceeded the number of Americans who could find on their TV screen a window into the lives of their fellow "global villagers" in Europe and the Third World. In fact, except in moments of international crisis like the seizure of hostages, American television largely ignored other countries. In an interdependent world where human survival depends on greater public understanding of complex issues, television offered instead an escape into a world of illusory images.

The Collapse of Authority in the 1960s

Though television entertainment re-enforced the escapism of the postindustrial suburban middle class, television news thrived on the dramatic images of protest of the 1960s. The first of the successive revolts that dominated the news of the 1960s came in the southern United States, as blacks protested its segregated society. Within a few years, television had shown young people throughout the world how to challenge authority by, for example, occupying a place and refusing to leave—the sit-in.

Protests against the Vietnam War reflected the growing integration of the Western world: a march on the Pentagon in Washington, D.C., in October 1967 occurred simultaneously with demonstrations in Amsterdam, Berlin, Oslo, Paris, Rome, and Tokyo.[3] Some of those who demonstrated were attacking not just the war but the technological, inhuman society that they blamed for the war's continuation. Thus challenged by Americans and faced with a no-win situation in Vietnam, President Lyndon B. Johnson had to abandon his ambitions to expand the guarantor state, and did not run for re-election. In France, the student and worker revolt of May 1968 so discredited General De Gaulle's government that he too had to retire within a year.

The Black Rebellion

Television images of policemen assaulting unresisting civil rights demonstrators brought home the conflict between American ideals and the realities of black life. Below the Mason-Dixon Line, the law segregated blacks from whites in their daily acivities. Even getting a drink of water was segregated, with separate fountains for "White" and "Colored." Intimidation prevented any challenge to this system through the political process.

Blacks also faced discrimination outside the South. The postwar mechanization of agriculture in the southern states reduced employment there and accelerated northward migration. As whites moved out of the inner cities of the Northeast and the Middle West, blacks moved in. The nonwhite population of the Northeast rose by one-third in the 1940s and by a quarter again in the 1950s. Though northern laws did not often sanction segregation, blacks there faced effective exclusion from opportunities in housing and employment.

Dr. Martin Luther King, Jr., at a press conference in Birmingham, Alabama, 1963. Before a camera and reporters, Dr. King discussed biracial negotiations to end demonstrations against segregation.
AP/Wide World Photos

In the South, the black revolt could be dated from December 1, 1955, when Mrs. Rosa Parks refused to give up her seat on a city bus in Montgomery, Alabama. (Mrs. Parks was already sitting in the "colored" rear section of the bus. The law required her to yield her seat to any white person who had none.)

Martin Luther King, Jr., a Baptist minister, began his rise to leadership of the civil rights movement by organizing a boycott of the bus system to bring economic pressure on segregation. King had been deeply impressed by Gandhi's success in compelling change in India by nonviolent resistance. The Southern Christian Leadership Conference, which

King founded in 1958, helped spread this tactic throughout the South. The first southern sit-in occurred in 1960 when blacks refused to be ousted from a segregated lunch counter in Greensboro, North Carolina. Within two months, the movement had spread over nine southern states.

Media attention to these nonviolent demonstrators soon brought the weight of worldwide disapproval against southern segregationists. The Nobel committee in Sweden, for example, awarded its 1964 Peace Prize to Dr. King. By then, federal legislation was overruling the state statutes that provided the basis for southern segregation. King now turned his attention to the plight of blacks in the northern urban ghettoes. Here it would not be enough to reassert political rights; the problem was to provide economic advantages for a minority. Such advantages, many white Americans believed, could only come at their own expense. As a result, King had made little progress by 1968, the year he was assassinated.

Some blacks had always doubted that white America would yield to moral persuasion. As King's drive for economic equality stalled, more and more began to see their struggle as part of a worldwide conflict. They identified with the African nationalists then winning their independence from the white dominance of the European world-system. It was symbolic of this change that in 1966 the Student Nonviolent Coordinating Committee, founded in 1960 by whites and blacks to bring Gandhian pressure on southern segregation, expelled its white members and adopted the slogan of "Black Power." Henceforth, "The Movement," as young people of the 1960s sometimes called their revolt, was divided.

The Rebellion of the Young

The movement that ended in racial separatism in 1966 had begun with a wave of youthful enthusiasm for interracial harmony. The three young men killed outside Philadelphia, Mississippi, on June 21, 1964, by a mob that included sheriff's deputies illustrate this idealism. Two were white New Yorkers, aged twenty and twenty-four, who had come south to help register blacks to vote. The third was a local black man of twenty-one. Their killers were never tried for murder. Some men were convicted on federal charges of violating the dead men's civil rights. The worldwide youth rebellion of which the three were a part has many explanations. Among these, however, the young men's own reason— a dedication to equal rights that cost them their lives—should not be forgotten.

The principal theaters of the youth revolt were college campuses. At the University of California at Berkeley in the autumn of 1964, students protested the arrest of distributors of political literature. The student organizers of the Free Speech Movement argued that the academic environment could not be insulated from the emotional issues of race and war then dividing the country. Students challenged the administration by organizing campus sit-ins. For the next eight years, Berkeley students intermittently disrupted the usual academic routines. There and on other campuses, calm returned only with the end of the Vietnam War and subsequent suspension of the draft.

This pattern of disruption was matched on many U.S. campuses. It reached a climax of horror in 1970 when nervous National Guardsmen opened fire on students demonstrating against the presence of the Reserve Officers' Training Corps (ROTC) at Kent State University in Ohio. Four young people were killed.

Campus unrest and even violence was not limited just to the United States. Throughout the world, students copied the methods of their American counterparts to protest what they saw as U.S. racism at home and imperialism in Vietnam. Japanese students marched on U.S. naval bases and boycotted their classes to protest Japan's tacit support of the U.S. war effort. The German movement, Students for a Democatic Society (SDS), like the U.S. organization of the same name, insisted that in the age of the mass society, democracy had become a sham. Since no political party anywhere, not even socialists, questioned the quality of life under the capitalist guarantor state, the young could challenge the managerial elite who really controlled postindustrial society only by demonstrating in the streets.

This revolt among European and Japanese students who did not risk, as American students did, being drafted for an overseas war baffled many observers. Conflict between generations, like conflict between the sexes and between social classes, has been a constant in history. But this young generation lived in the most prosperous societies that the world had ever seen. Why should they rebel?

A partial explanation for the rebellion is that the large size of the younger generation of the 1960s and its relative affluence made the usual generational conflict worse. When student protests began, American, Western European, and Japanese youth—in their late teens and on the verge of adulthood, but not yet accepted by their societies as adults— were the most numerous age group in the population. This generation had grown up with higher expectations than its predecessors. Before World War II, for example, only 15 percent of Americans between the ages of 18 and 21 had gone to college. As it became evident that postindustrial society would require more complex skills to find a job, by 1960 one-third of the same U.S. age group was attending college. Many Western European societies too were approaching this proportion. This extension of adolescence into college years brought young people both benefits and liabilities.

The benefits often included continuing parental support. The price for that support was continued subordination to the older generation. Yet such dependency seemed unreasonable to young people raised in postindustrial suburban households in which both parents worked. In their absence, young people found role models within their own generation; they developed their own uniform—T-shirt and blue jeans—and their own music. Rock and roll began as a celebration of adolescent defiance of adult authority. The grandest rock concert of all brought nearly half a million to Woodstock, New York, in August, 1969. It was the celebration of a generation apart, aptly called "the Woodstock Nation." Whatever the justice of their protests, it is not surprising that many of this generation, reared in affluence and enforced conformity and identifying with each other and with generous ideals, should have risen in revolt.

Moreover, the Woodstock Nation extended throughout the world, and its members watched one another on television. Attacking a worldwide society they believed to be economically integrated by multinational corporations, some leaders of the youth rebellion hoped to generate a protest movement that was equally integrated globally.

Television helped to link the protest movements. The original nucleus of protest in France was provided by students at a suburban branch campus of the University of Paris, who had been horrified by the daily spectacle of the carnage in Vietnam. But what fired the revolt of the French young was the changing nature of France's university system. In their ambition to move France into the postindustrial age, the technocrats of De Gaulle's government decreed a vast expansion of higher education. Like many American students, however, French students found the new campuses to be impersonal, bureaucratic, oppressive environments. Campus activists played on the general undergraduate feeling of powerlessness to provoke confrontations with university authorities.

Student occupation of the main campus of the University of Paris, the Sorbonne, in May 1968 provoked a crisis that paralyzed the whole economy. Following the students' lead, half of France's workforce went on strike. The Gaullist government finally resolved the crisis only by decreeing an inflationary 10 percent wage hike. Thus pacified, the workers went back to work, leaving the students alone to face police repression. Nevertheless, the "events of May" had destroyed De Gaulle's credibility as the defender of law and order.

The French explained the youth revolt of 1968 much as Americans did campus unrest in the United States. Conservatives dismissed it as the misbehavior of a spoiled younger generation, which got out of hand only because the authorities had not been firm enough at the outset. More tolerant commentators blamed the revolt on the stresses of adjusting the once-exclusive university system to a democratic mass society. New Left sympathizers discovered more basic causes.

The "Days of May" in France, 1968. Students attack advancing police in the Latin Quarter, the student neighborhood of Paris.
Bruno Barbey/Magnum

Scornful alike of Western technocratic capitalism and of Eastern bloc communism, these critics saw the French students as a vanguard of revolt against postindustrial society worldwide. The younger generation everywhere, in the New Left view, were resisting integration into a worldwide economy, refusing to become a new white-collar proletariat.

Understanding the youth revolts of the 1960s requires weighing the merits of all these explanations. Throughout the twentieth century, younger generations have oscillated between idealism and cynicism, as in the pre– and post–World War I eras.The generation that was coming to adulthood during the 1960s, buoyed by growing affluence and low unemployment, tended to take these blessings for granted. These young people questioned whether a comfortable lifestyle and a dull job were life's only goals. Assuming the economy would continue to prosper as it had in the last decade, they idealistically sought to assure that everyone would benefit from this growth, and set their expectations higher than any government could meet. Their increasingly shrill protests inevitably produced a backlash, but their rebellion forced the political retirement not only of Charles De Gaulle but also of Lyndon Baines Johnson.

The Postwar Welfare State in Europe and the United States

President Johnson aspired to make the United States a Great Society for all of its citizens. To many Americans, such a program seemed long overdue, since the country lagged far behind the powerful guarantor states of Western Europe in providing social services to its citizens. The so-called free market economy that enabled West Germany to increase its share of world trade from 7 to 20 percent in the 1950s and 1960s, for example, was in reality based on capitalistic concentration and extensive government services. The three biggest German banks voted almost three-fourths of the shares in industrial corporations, providing economic planning in all but name. The government collected 10 percent of German GNP in social security taxes to provide a range of benefits far greater than those afforded by Bismarck's original welfare state.

Johnson's plans for his Great Society were more modest. The programs he pushed through Congress in 1965–1966 involved the federal government in improving the environment. Federal grants would support the cleansing of the nation's water supply, for example, and help rebuild its decaying mass transit systems. Medicare and Medicaid finally realized Truman's Fair Deal aspirations, giving elderly Americans some measure of security against dying untreated and penniless.

Johnson could see that even when guaranteed legal equality by the Civil Rights Act of 1964, blacks had no hope of becoming equal members of U.S. society so long as most of them were poor. He did not, however, propose a socialistic redistribution of income to remedy black poverty. In fact, the portion of U.S. income earned by the poorest 20 percent of the population remained constant at about 5 percent from the 1940s through the 1970s. Instead, the Great Society launched programs designed to rescue blacks from a "culture of poverty" similar, in the eyes of social planners, to that of the shantytowns of the Third World. The Equal Opportunity Act of 1964, for example, fostered such ventures as a Job Corps and community action programs to stimulate economic development in the ghettos.

In the disillusioned 1980s, it is fashionable to decry these programs as failures. Certainly they were inadequate to fulfill Johnson's grand goal of eliminating poverty. Critics pointed out that they provided opportunities for waste and corruption, and filled ghetto-dwellers with unrealistic hopes. Revolutions coincide with rising expectations. The wave of rioting and destruction that swept black areas of inner cities in the mid-1960s can partly be explained as the result of the misleading impression given by the Great Society that things were going to change.

By 1968 the ghettos seemed out of control, and Johnson, who was facing antagonism from several directions, declared he would not run for re-election. The young carried their protest against the Vietnam War to the streets outside the Democratic convention in Chicago. The majority of Americans who regarded these protestors as spoiled and unpatriotic had no love for Johnson either. To suburban Americans, he was responsible for handouts to rioting blacks. Nixon's victory in 1968 brought a Republican to the presidency, and the Great Society programs became the scapegoat for these ill-assorted discontents.

History in the long run may prove kinder to Johnson than public opinion was in 1968. He thought that the U.S. economy was strong enough to support both a huge military commitment abroad and a Great Society at home. Professional economists had assured him that there was no risk in running a federal budget deficit to reduce unemployment. As Johnson left office, however, it was already clear that this had not been good advice. As inflation increased, so did unemployment. This *stagflation*—rising prices in a stagnant economy—became the central economic problem of all the developed economies in the 1970s.

The Struggle in the 1970s to Re-establish Authority

The anger of many Americans and Western Europeans at governments' inability to revive the economy or to master the protest movements of the 1960s made the 1970s a decade of conservative backlash. The early 1970s also saw the climax of yet another revolt: women increasingly demanded that in the postindustrial era they should no longer be confined to the stereotyped roles of earlier times but should enjoy the same rights as men.

The Women's Liberation Movement

In the United States, the most recent chapter of women's struggle for equality dates from the end of World War II. Veterans were demobilized and sought jobs that women had filled during wartime. Women were encouraged to be homemakers in order to reduce competition for work. An influential book derided feminism, women's demand for economic and social equality, as a "neurosis."

As so often happened in the 1950s however, accelerating social change was quietly undermining such apparent certainties as the exclusively domestic role of women. To help support the suburban lifestyle, more and more women returned to work. In 1940, only 15 percent of American married women had been employed. By 1960, almost a third of them had jobs. As female employment grew, more women sought educational qualifications. The number of U.S. female college graduates doubled in the 1960s. It was largely among such women that the liberation movement found its members.

The federal government had not been energetic in prosecuting cases of alleged sex discrimination under the Civil Rights Act of 1964. This lethargy pushed the women's movement toward what critics called "radical" feminism. "Radical" feminists asserted that relations between the sexes had evolved as a struggle for power in the same way that Marx had depicted relations between social classes. To liberate women from male domination, women's groups revived the demand for an Equal Rights Amendment (ERA) to the U.S. Constitution. To free women from economic dependence, they called for a national system of day-care and the elimination of laws forbidding abortion. To enforce such demands, groups like the National Organization for Women (NOW) mounted a campaign to raise the consciousness of women and to turn their sexual solidarity into political power.

This political mobilization paid off. In the United States, federally imposed quotas required affirmative action by employers to ensure that women were sufficiently represented among their employees. (In Western Europe, the European Economic Community monitored individual governments to see that women received the same pay as men for doing the same work.)

Under such governmental pressure, women penetrated in considerably greater numbers into professions once reserved to men. The percentage of U.S. lawyers who were women more than tripled during the 1970s, from 4 percent to

14 percent. The proportion of women doctors doubled, from 9 percent to 20 percent—a far cry from the 1930s, when most U.S. hospitals would not admit a female intern.

In France, the proportion of women among the younger generation of doctors rose even higher—to over a third. This represented a remarkable change in a country where, until the mid-1960s, a woman had to obtain her husband's legal permission to open her own bank account or run her own business. In 1974, the French parliament legalized abortion, one year after a historic U.S. Supreme Court decision upheld this most controversial of women's rights. In the same year, President Giscard d'Estaing appointed Françoise Giroud as the first French cabinet minister for Women's Affairs.

As opportunities for women grew, their tolerance for a subordinate role in marriage declined. By the 1980s, one French marriage in six ended in divorce. The U.S. divorce rate was far higher: half of all marriages. Fully half of American women were single, compared to only a quarter of them in 1960. The kind of household that Americans had taken for granted only a generation earlier—father, dependent mother, two or more children—by the 1980s represented only 12 percent of U.S. households, and this proportion was still declining.

The acceleration of change in such a fundamental institution as the family naturally produced a backlash. In 1982, the ERA failed by a margin of three states to secure ratification. In the 1984 U.S. presidential campaign, the Republican party platform demanded that future federal judges be pledged to oppose abortion. European conservatives similarly attacked women's liberation as destructive of the social order. Faced with such adverse reactions, the women's movement seemed in retreat in the 1980s. A younger generation of women appeared to be taking the hard-won victories of women's liberation for granted.

Nevertheless, it seems unlikely that women in postindustrial societies will ever return to the state of domesticity that the 1950s took for granted. Economic necessity and educational inclination—half of France's university students today are women, for example—continue to attract women to careers. Trends like these are viewed as intolerable by many people who grew up in a society with very different role models. In both the United States and Europe in the 1970s and 1980s, such people expressed their protest by voting for politicians who promised to restore traditional values.

Stagflation and the Search for Political Direction

Economic dissatisfaction, as well as nostalgic protest, dominated the politics of the 1970s. Political power changed hands with increasing rapidity in the United States and Europe as one government after another failed to grapple effectively with stagflation. The re-election of President Nixon in 1972 symbolized continuing backlash against the 1960s; he defeated Democratic Senator George S. McGovern, whose candidacy seemed to personify the revolt of blacks, youth, and women. Within two years Nixon resigned under threat of impeachment. Investigation of a burglary at the Democratic party's headquarters in Washington D.C.'s Watergate complex and of the subsequent cover-up revealed a trail of complicity leading back to the president. In 1976, Democratic nominee Jimmy Carter profited from this scandal to defeat President Gerald R. Ford, who had succeeded Nixon. Carter promised to restore Americans' faith in their government. But by 1980, with inflation at an annual rate of 13 percent and American hostages being held in Iran, the voters rejected Carter's presidency and elected former California Governor Ronald Reagan.

In the 1980 presidential election, half the eligible voters chose not to cast their ballots. Such a turnout, despite the new political technology of computer-generated mailing lists and television commercials, was evidence of widespread skepticism that in a mass society, voting had any meaning. Polls revealed that as many as two-thirds of the U.S. electorate saw themselves as helpless victims of monied interests. In fact, campaign contributions to political action committees (PACs), formed to promote a single issue or special interest, increased tenfold in the 1970s. The temptations of these funds increased the voters' suspicion that politicians cast their ballots for the highest bidder.

In Western Europe, a far higher percentage of citizens continued to vote. Often, however, they voted to punish governments they judged to have failed to restore economic health, much as Americans had judged Ford and Carter. The British electorate voted the Conservatives into power again in 1970, out in 1974, and back in again, under Margaret Thatcher, in 1979. In and out of power, the British Labour party remained as divided as it had been during the Depression. In fact, its more moderate members finally seceded in protest, as they doubted that the program of radical social change, with which the party proposed to combat stagflation, was compatible with democratic politics.

Similar quarrels disrupted the German Social Democratic party, and the voters ousted it from power in 1982. Chancellor Willy Brandt's efforts to placate the young rebels of the 1960s by taking steps toward social change had angered middle-of-the-road voters. His successor in 1974, Helmut Schmidt, angered the Left by his indifference to the social costs of his deflationary economic policies. A significant number of young Germans turned away from the Social Democrats to the "Green" party, which championed many of the 1960s causes, including protecting the environment. In Sweden, Socialists had been in power for generations, but in 1976 the voters defeated them.

The reason for the voters' growing impatience in the 1970s lies in the worldwide economic crisis. Its differing impact upon diverse social groups polarized politics. No longer did people believe, as they had in the 1950s and 1960s, that their economies would continue to grow indefinitely. Each social group within each nation had become preoccupied with casting its votes to defend its own threatened share in a stagnant, or even shrinking, global economy.

The crisis of stagflation spared no nation. Through most of the 1960s, Europeans had worried about "the American challenge." They feared that U.S.-based multinational corporations would buy up their basic industries while using superior technology to drive European companies out of world markets. This proved a groundless fear, for the economic troubles that appeared at the end of the Johnson presidency were symptomatic of a deeply troubled U.S. economy.

In some ways the developing crisis of U.S. industry had been foreshadowed by the fate of Britain after World War II. Despite their burden of debt, for a long while the British attempted to maintain the appearance of a great power, such as having a nuclear deterrent. At the same time, they provided the generous benefits of the guarantor state. Meanwhile, they failed to modernize industrial plants that were already becoming obsolete in 1945. The British share in production of the world's manufactured goods fell by a half between 1960 and the mid-1970s. The growth of aggressive global competition, as well as British inefficiency, explains this outcome.

Overseas competition began to challenge U.S. industry in the 1950s. Japanese clothing sales in the U.S. retail market cost American textile workers 300,000 jobs. In the 1970s, the United States increased its manufacturing output by a third, but employment in manufacturing grew by only 5 percent—testimony to the growing industrial applications of automation. But the products of many U.S. industries no longer dominated world markets. By 1970, the United States manufactured only one-fifth of the world's steel, for example, compared to nearly half of world production in 1950.

U.S. manufactured goods were at a disadvantage in world markets for interrelated reasons. From the mid-1960s onward, the rate of growth of U.S. productivity fell behind that of every other developed country except Britain. U.S. conservatives blamed wage inflation: paying people too much, while expecting them to do too little. In fact, wages rose rapidly in the 1970s, though they lagged behind prices. Others blamed declining productivity on industrialists' reluctance to modernize existing U.S. plants. All too often, it was more profitable for multinational corporations to build new plants abroad where labor was cheaper. So prevalent did this trend become that by the 1980s, had the industrial output abroad of U.S.-based multinationals all been produced by a single country, that mythical country would have ranked third in the world, after the United States and the Soviet Union.

Some economists concluded that the U.S. economy had entered a period of crisis comparable to the Great Depression. Certainly the economy had some impressive achievements to its credit. It had found jobs—often service-sector jobs—for a labor force swollen by half by the baby-boom generation. The "entitlement" programs of the guarantor state—many, like Medicare and Social Security, distributed regardless of need—had improved the lives of the elderly, the disabled, and some of the poor. The costs of these programs, however, increased in the 1960s and 1970s from 5 percent to 11 percent of the U.S. GNP. Taxpayers, uncertain of their own prospects as the economy swung from recession to recovery and back again, blamed such costs for the decline of their own standard of living. Increasingly, they made the guarantor state and the recipients of its benefits the scapegoats for their fears and frustrations. Less and less was heard of the generous notion of the 1960s that society had a collective responsibility for its most vulnerable and least fortunate members.

By the 1980s, there were really two American societies: one was poor, urban, and mainly black; the other was relatively affluent, suburban, and mainly white. Increasingly their ways of life diverged. For those left behind in the shrinking central cities, the ups and downs of the economy hit much harder. At the depths of the recession of 1981–1982, for example, the unemployment rate among laborers hit 19 percent and among factory workers 17 percent, compared to only 3 percent for mainly suburban technical workers and professionals.

A growing number of those left behind in the cities had no job and no prospect of finding one. In 1960, almost three-quarters of black males had been either employed or seeking a job. By the early 1980s that proportion had declined to a little over one-half. The "black revolt" of the 1960s produced few economic gains. Largely because of federally enforced employment guidelines, some blacks joined the middle class. Overall, however, the gap between the family incomes of blacks and whites was as wide in the 1980s as it had been in 1960.

Conservatives blamed this continuing gap on the mistaken generosity of the Great Society, which supposedly made it easier to collect government benefits than to work. Others thought the origins of black poverty were more complex. The kind of job that minimally skilled immigrants to U.S. cities had historically taken was rapidly vanishing, especially in the inner cities. The growing number of women in the work force took many of the low-paying jobs in the expanding service sector. The root cause of the desperate plight of most U.S. blacks was that postindustrial opportunity began deserting cities just as they moved in.

Visiting Europeans were often horrified by their glimpses of U.S. inner-city society. A stricken neighborhood like New York's South Bronx, for example, with its mile upon mile of abandoned buildings burned out by desperate landlords or tenants, reminded such visitors of the ruins of their Continent in 1945.

Europe in the 1960s had had no such army of the unemployed as occupied such U.S. neighborhoods. In fact, industrial northern Europe during the boom had to import labor from less-developed southern Europe and from such countries as Turkey and Algeria to do the jobs its own citizens did not want. Eighty percent of the workers on the Renault auto-assembly line in Paris, for example, were immigrants. But by the mid-1970s, European governments were attempting to induce or coerce such "guest-workers" to go home. For Europe did not long celebrate its resistance to the American challenge—its own economies soon became mired in the same stagflation as the U.S. economy, and for many of the same reasons.

The rise in OPEC oil prices in 1973 hit Europe and Japan at least as hard as the United States. The postwar boom for all had been fueled by a raw material whose price had been nearly stationary. Its sudden rise was a heavy blow to the economies of countries like France and West Germany. After 1945, they had shifted from coal to oil as their prime energy source although they had little oil of their own. After 1973, Europe responded more effectively than the United States to the need to conserve oil. The European Economic Community actually reduced its petroleum imports by 4 percent, while the United States, whose own domestic supplies had equalled demand into the late 1960s, increased its imports by a third.

Nevertheless the inflated cost of energy contributed to the spread of stagflation in Europe, as did other factors already familiar in the U.S. economy. The rate of growth of European productivity slowed. Average European hourly wages in manufacturing, which in 1960 had everywhere been less than half the U.S. rate, matched or even surpassed U.S. wages by 1980. Though most European governments centrally planned the growth of their economies, plans consistently emphasized the benefits of the guarantor state, rather than reinvest-

ment in plant modernization. European-based and even Japanese-based multinational companies began to locate new plants in places where taxes and wages were lower. Thus, steel made in Europe, for example, which had undercut U.S.-produced steel, itself was now undercut by steel produced in Brazil or India.

The effect of these developments on a country like West Germany, where one in five jobs depended on exports, was devastating. As high energy costs slowed the whole economy and as German industry became increasingly uncompetitive, unemployment grew, particularly among the young. With high unemployment, Germans could neither themselves buy the products unsold on world markets, nor provide the investment to retool German plants. Meanwhile, tax revenues fell while government expenditures tended to inflate to relieve the hardships of a stagnant economy.

To a greater or lesser extent, this combination of problems beset all the economies of the developed world by the end of the 1970s. As individuals experienced the crisis in the form of high taxes and a living standard reduced by inflation, they tended to vote for politicians who promised to cut taxes and halt inflation by reducing the costs of the guarantor state. Moreover, as the growth of a post-industrial society changed the social composition of the electorate, a majority of voters everywhere had less and less sympathy with the unlucky poor who would be hardest hit by government cutbacks.

Americans and Europeans who managed to escape into the service sector as the number of industrial jobs dwindled lived in a milieu much more hostile to collective social action than that in which factory workers had lived. The latter had often identified themselves as "us" (the union, often affiliated with the Left) against "them" (the management). Even so, one-half of the German and a third of the British working classes had usually voted for conservatives. Such a vote came even more naturally to postindustrial workers in the service sector, who tended to see themselves as individual middle-class competitors, not members of a group with shared goals. (Denounced as special interests, U.S. unions by the 1980s were weaker than ever, enrolling only 15 percent of the U.S. work force.) Though European unions were more successful than U.S. unions at organizing service-sector workers, nowhere did unions in the 1980s represent a force for change. Dwindling in numbers and political influence, all but a few concentrated on preserving the benefits of their aging membership.

Nor were the young any longer a force for change in the 1970s. Facing uncertain job prospects, they had little of the enthusiasm for collective action that had characterized the 1960s generation. Their college studies did little to encourage young people in the 1970s to think about the problems of society as a whole. The number of U.S. students majoring in the humanities—subjects that taught critical thinking about general human problems—fell by 50 percent. The number of graduates in subjects like business that supposedly could ensure success in a constricted job market rose correspondingly. In Europe, where the unemployment rate among the young ranged over 20 percent by 1982, there was a similar preoccupation with acquiring marketable skills.

The faltering world economy of the 1970s thus produced an ethic of every person for himself or herself, and each nation for itself. Politicians everywhere tinkered with economic solutions and, as they failed to work, were ousted by the voters. Such traditional sources of alternative vision as the Left and the young seemed unable to provide a fresh dream, while the world slid haplessly into the postindustrial future.

Continuing Problems and Old Slogans in the 1980s

Nations cannot, however, indefinitely muddle along in an atmosphere of political doubt. Eventually the voters will turn to leadership that promises a real change of direction. In the fall of 1980 and the spring of 1981, the United States and France chose new presidents, Ronald Reagan and François Mitterrand. Each promised, by diametrically opposed programs, to resolve his country's economic crisis. The extent of their success by the mid-1980s suggests that the problems of postindustrial society remain resistant to these most recent experiments in economic liberalism (which Americans call conservatism) and democratic socialism.

France Under Mitterrand

The OPEC oil shock of 1973 marked the end of three decades of rapid French economic growth, during which the standard of living virtually doubled. Still remembered as a land of picturesque backwardness by those who had not seen it since 1945, France by the 1970s had become the third producer of aerospace technology in the world, after the United States and the Soviet Union. Taking for granted that such dramatic modernization would continue, the government of President Giscard d'Estaing (1974–1981) failed to anticipate how quickly the industrial foundations of an economy could become outmoded in the postindustrial era. As in the U.S. and the rest of Western Europe, Giscard's government permitted wages and social services to increase at inflationary rates and at the same time failed to invest sufficiently in new technologies.

Thus when François Mitterrand, who revived the French Socialist party after it had disbanded in 1969, succeeded Giscard as President in 1981, he inherited an economy already in decline. During his first year in office, he and his Socialist majority in Parliament tried to combat stagflation by renewing economic growth. Like Léon Blum in 1936, they hoped to do this by ensuring a more equal distribution of wealth. Like Blum, Mitterrand decreed wage hikes, reduced the work week and expanded paid vacations. He went further than Blum by nationalizing eleven large private companies and many of the banks that had escaped nationalization at the end of World War II. The Socialist hope was to stimulate the economy by expanding worker purchasing power and by confiscating for public investment the profits of large corporations. To finance compensation to these companies' former owners and to pay for enhanced guarantor-state benefits, the Mitterrand government borrowed heavily abroad.

Within a year, the discouraging results of this program proved, as in 1936–1937, that in a globally interdependent economy, not even a major industrial power like France could single-handedly pursue the goals of democratic socialism. Inflation rose to an annual rate of 14 percent, yet unemployment remained unacceptably high due to the worldwide slump. Meanwhile, U.S. bankers, noting its growing debt, foreclosed further borrowing by France. By the spring of 1982, the policy of trying to stimulate growth by restoring full employment and redistributing economic rewards had clearly failed.

Mitterrand then completely reversed direction. His new program stressed cutting taxes and social expenditures. His government shut down unneeded capacity in loss-making nationalized industries like steel and shipbuilding, though this cost many Socialist voters their jobs. By the fall of 1984, this new policy had brought France's inflation rate down to 6.5 percent. But over 9 percent of the French workforce were unemployed, and among the young the rate was much higher. The political prospects of the Socialists in the legislative elections schedule for 1986 grew dim. Conservatives denounced the original inflationary program. Mitterrand's own supporters were hurt and bewildered by his new program of harsh austerity, which made a Socialist government appear as uncaring as any other.

Some factors behind Mitterrand's failure were beyond his control, such as the continued stagnation of world trade and the obsolescent state of French industry. Moreover, he faced the usual dilemma of governments in the age of the guarantor state. Though they denounced "big government," the French, like others in the developed world, insisted on receiving the governmental benefits the various constituent groups expected, regardless of the inflationary effect.

In practice, the French did not want what Mitterrand called "savage" liberalism: an economy of unrestrained competition in which producers found markets, workers found jobs, and the unfortunate survived by their own efforts. In practice, Americans did not want such a system either, though Ronald Reagan won the U.S. presidency in 1980 promising one.

The United States Under Reagan

Reagan's policies once he was in office, however, were more reminiscent of the Keynesian idea of deficit financing than Republicans who had denounced the New Deal cared to admit. Reagan cut taxes, especially for corporations and the very wealthy. Despite this reduction in revenue, he also called for an enormous military build-up. This combination of policies vastly increased the federal budget deficit. The Reagan administration's first years seemed to confirm the inability of governments in the postindustrial era to restrain inflation (through raised interest rates) without substantial unemployment. The recession of 1981–1982 was the worst the United States had experienced since the Depression of the 1930s: up to 10 percent of Americans were unemployed.

The recovery that began at the end of 1982 carried Reagan to re-election in 1984. Many voted for him because they perceived his economic policies as being more successful than his predecessor's. Such a judgment depended on which of the twin evils of the 1970s, inflation or unemployment, the individual voter dreaded more. Consumer prices did rise less rapidly between 1980 and 1984 than they had between 1976 and 1980. But unemployment averaged 8.6 percent through the spring of 1984 under Reagan, compared to 6.4 percent in 1980 under Carter. By the election in the fall of 1984, about as many Americans were unemployed as there were when Reagan took office.

These figures suggest that rather than solving the basic economic dilemmas of the 1970s, "Reaganomics" made some people "winners" and others "losers." Foreign, especially European, investors benefited, lending money at high rates to finance the U.S. deficit. Foreign workers suffered, for the European investment that might have expanded their own economies and relieved unemployment instead was flowing to the United States. The high interest rates that attracted such investment made the dollar so expensive that foreigners could not afford to buy U.S. products. These factors made those Americans who had to sell abroad—certain industries and most farmers—losers from Reaganomics. By 1984, Americans were buying more goods from overseas and selling less abroad than at any time in their history.

On the other hand, the chief executive officers of large U.S. corporations were clearly winners: they voted themselves salary increases averaging 40 percent in 1983. But many employees of these companies were losers. Over a million manufacturing jobs were lost between 1979 and 1984. For the first time, white males composed less than half of the U.S. work force, outnumbered by lower-paid women. Of the new jobs created by the recovery, most were in the postindustrial service sector, which paid, on average, one-third less than industry.

Being comparatively well insulated against unemployment and benefiting from reduced inflation, members of the suburban middle class were marginal winners. Blacks and the poor in general were losers. More people lived in poverty in the 1980s than at any time since the inauguration of the Great Society programs, many of which the Reagan administration cut or discontinued.

This enumeration of winners and losers helps explain why so many Americans "voted their pocketbooks" in 1984.

In the postindustrial United States, as in France, whether one was a winner or loser depended largely on how government, through taxation and domestic expenditure, redistributed economic rewards. In the election campaign of 1984, both candidates reassured the U.S. voters by reaffirming their commitment to Social Security and Medicare, which consumed about one-third of federal expenditures.

In 1980, the Republican party had moved adroitly to exploit Americans' unhappiness with the 1970s stagflation and the social changes of postindustrial society. Already the party of the nation's corporate leadership, it forged an alliance with groups opposed to such innovations as "abortion on demand." Outspending the Democrats five to one, the Republicans were able to set the tone of economic and social debate.

The legacy of the 1960s revolts had left the Democrats divided. Walter F. Mondale, their 1984 candidate, represented what was left of the New Deal coalition. But he had to fight off challenges from Gary Hart, who spoke for the party's affluent suburban wing, and from Jesse Jackson, who continued to represent the cause of Martin Luther King, Jr. Mondale chose a woman, U.S. Representative Geraldine M. Ferraro, as his vice presidential running mate—a historic milestone. Whether his choice helped or hurt his candidacy is disputed.

The Reagan Republican ticket easily defeated such a divided opposition. But it remained to be seen in the mid-1980s whether there would really be a "Reagan Revolution" to return the nation to the more traditional values and liberal economics for which nostalgic Americans longed. Like Mitterrand, Reagan inherited an economy where a few multinational corporations could set prices in many markets regardless of demand—very far from the unlimited competition envisioned in Reagan's speeches. His government, like Mitterrand's, continued to spend without regard to income, piling up huge deficits. Despite the president's anti-bureaucratic rhetoric, the number of U.S. federal employees fell by less than 1 percent between 1980 and 1984.

Ever-rising prices and the astronomical borrowing of governments had been two causes of the 1970s stagflation. With inflation lessened but with deficits mounting, Reagan's administration attacked a third cause by forcing the price of labor down. His summary firing in 1981 of over 10,000 air traffic controllers—postindustrial workers who were illegally striking—was an ominous warning to unions trying to compensate for lost industrial jobs by organizing the service sector. But it is uncertain how long such a policy can work. In a time of high unemployment, people are reluctant to jeopardize their jobs by striking and organizing. At the same time, however, it is hard to believe that as new technologies spread, workers will forever accept low wages, such as those paid to the minority women who assemble the electronic components in California's "Silicon Valley" companies. Such considerations raise some doubt whether Reaganomics will prove in the long run more successful than Mitterrand's socialism in resolving the economic problems that emerged in the 1970s.

Conclusion

In 1985, Ronald Reagan's political position appeared much more secure than François Mitterrand's. His experience as a film actor helped him project his jovial personality over television, dominating the medium by which the mass society received most of its information. But his popularity rested on more than appearances. The widespread belief in his effectiveness had reinvigorated a presidency tarnished by repeated disappointments.

Although Reagan described himself as a conservative, his greatest appeal was to those Americans for whom the transition to a postindustrial society represented a challenge rather than a disaster. To the relatively affluent suburban majority, many programs of the guarantor state now seemed increasingly irrelevant. They applauded his determination to dismantle a system of little personal benefit to them. They welcomed his message that unhampered by governmental restraints, they could make the postindustrial age their personal success story, as earlier generations of Americans had made successes of the transition from rural to industrial America. This hope for the future was a welcome change from the political and economic pessimism of the 1970s. Moreover, Reagan's opposition to such innovations as legalized abortion seemed to suggest that the future could be won without abandoning the certainties of the past.

Though Reagan's combination of hope and nostalgia was especially well suited to American audiences, his government represented only the most prominent example of conservative resurgence in the 1980s. In much of the developed world, the dogma of the decade was the need to return to free enterprise, whatever the cost. In Britain, for example, the Conservative government of Prime Minister Margaret Thatcher was trying to force the country into the postindustrial age by selling off the profitable parts of government-owned industries and shutting

down the rest, such as coal mines. Though this program produced British unemployment of at least 14 percent and social strife reminiscent of the Great Depression, it encountered little effective resistance. In power in all of the major developed countries but France, conservatives proclaimed that they had finally reversed the trend to governmental intervention in the world's economies begun during World War I and much heightened after World War II.

These governments sought a national advantage in the world marketplace by reducing their own inflation, even at the cost of unemployment. Their hope was, by reducing the costs of labor and government, to produce less expensive goods that would be attractive in world markets. Such success in international competition would reduce unemployment as well as inflation, making these some other nation's problems.

To assume, however, that this kind of government has solved the basic dilemma of stagflation and provided a definitive answer to the developed world's restless search for authority would be premature. Conservatives' nineteenth-century liberal model of national economies is of questionable relevance to today's world where human ingenuity is producing new technologies overnight, which are exploited immediately by multinational corporations wherever in the world they find labor cheapest.

Mitterrand's failure seemed to prove that a revived democratic socialism was not a practical solution to what was really the French case of global economic problems. On the other hand, Margaret Thatcher by mid-1985 was becoming almost as unpopular as Mitterrand. Even a significant number of Conservatives believed that her ruthlessly deflationary measures—such as cutting the medical care provided by the National Health Service—went too far.

Mitterrand and Thatcher provide the most sharply defined alternatives to the politics of the capitalistic guarantor state. If neither they nor Ronald Reagan prove successful in the long run, it is difficult to see what other alternatives the existing spectrum of democratic political parties could provide. For the moment this does not seem to matter. In the mid-1980s, prosperous voters everywhere are absorbed in the benefits of prosperity, while the less fortunate are politically apathetic. Yet neither mood could long survive the return of rampant inflation or a severe worsening of unemployment. Both remain real possibilities, however.

The mood of the 1980s reminded some observers of the complacent 1920s. Now, as then, people believe that the public problems of an interdependent world can best be solved if each individual and each nation pursues a policy of self-interest. Should the world economy prove that conviction wrong, it would compound the crisis of political values already created by the decline of socialism and the inequities of Thatcher's and Reagan's neoliberalism. Then it would be the responsibility of a new generation to invent new political values for a world still rushing headlong into the postindustrial era.

Notes

1. Richard J. Barnet, *The Alliance: America-Europe-Japan, Makers of the Postwar World* (New York: Simon and Schuster, 1983), p. 206.
2. Robert Wegs, *Europe Since 1945: A Concise History*, 2d ed. (New York: St. Martin's Press, 1984), p. 168.
3. Barnet, *The Alliance*, p. 274.

Suggestions for Further Reading

Ardagh, John, *France in the 1980s* (1982).

Barnet, Richard J., *The Alliance: America-Europe-Japan, Makers of the Postwar World* (1983).

Bolter, J. David, *Turing's Man: Western Culture in the Computer Age* (1984).

Edsall, Thomas B., *The New Politics of Inequality* (1984).

Garreau, Joel, *The Nine Nations of North America* (1981).

Gilbert, James, *Another Chance: Postwar America 1945–1968* (1981).

Lasch, Christopher, *The Culture of Narcissism: American Life in an Age of Diminishing Expectations* (1970).

Lukacs, John, *Outgrowing Democracy: A History of the United States in the History of the Twentieth Century* (1984).

Priaulx, Allan, and Stanford J. Ungar, *The Almost Revolution: France 1968* (1969).

Ranney, Austin, *Channels of Power: The Impact of Television on American Politics* (1983).

Toffler, Alvin, *Future Shock* (1968).

Wegs, J. Robert, *Europe Since 1945: A Concise History*, 2d ed. (1984).

Woloch, Nancy, *Women and the American Experience* (1984).

Part 5

INDEPENDENCE FOR THE THIRD WORLD?

Chapter **14**

LATIN AMERICA: MOBILIZATION AND DEVELOPMENT, OR NEOCOLONIAL MILITARISM?

The history of Latin America since World War II divides, economically and politically, into two phases. The trends toward industrialization and mass mobilization begun by the 1930s continued through the 1960s. Thereafter the region relapsed into economic neocolonialism and military authoritarianism. By the mid-1980s, another period seemed to be opening as several countries returned to elected civilian governments, but it was not yet clear how great the differences would actually be.

Living through these shifting phases, Latin Americans have had difficulty escaping political and economic subordination at either the national or—for most—the individual level. At the national level, subordination exists even in countries whose experience, through revolution, has seemed to differ most from that of their neighbors. An overview of the entire region, followed by closer looks at Argentina, Brazil, Mexico, Cuba, and Nicaragua, will illustrate these points. Although we shall focus on the period since 1945, we shall at times look back to earlier periods to introduce subjects not discussed in Chapter 8.

Continental Overview: The Shark and the Sardines

Since 1945, many of Latin America's old problems have persisted, while new ones have appeared. To make matters worse, the changing global distribution of power and wealth has widened the gap between wealthy and poor countries around the world. A survey of the most common social, economic, and political problems of the region suggests that the regressive trend, in evidence from the 1960s on, stems in general from these facts.

Mounting Social Pressures

Latin America today retains some of the worst of its old social problems: the hacienda system and debt peonage in some places, the abuse of native Americans (including elimination of whole tribes in Brazil and Guatemala), and discrimination against women. Only five Latin American countries—Ecuador, Brazil, Uruguay, Cuba, and El Salvador—gave women the vote before World War II. Argentina followed in 1947, Mexico in 1953, others even later.

Atop the old lack of social integration, new problems also appeared. Mass mobilizers discovered that the class structure of most Latin American societies had become more complex. The old pattern was made up of landlords and peasants, with rudimentary urban middle and working classes. But now many Latin American countries had a social structure more like that of industrial societies, in part because of rapid population growth.

Throughout the Third World, death rates began to decline in the 1930s, thanks mainly to improvements in public health, while birth rates began to fall only later. A similar demographic transition occurred in Europe in the nineteenth century, eventually leading to a new equilibrium between birth and death rates at lower levels. The Third World has yet to achieve any such equilibrium. Many poor Latin Americans— and Africans and Asians—still believe they have incentives to have large families. Traditionally, more hands meant more income, and numerous offspring were the only security for parents in old age, especially because infant mortality rates were so high. Now the death rates have declined, but the birth rates have not yet adjusted. The result has been a population explosion.

In the 1970s, Latin America as a whole had a population growth rate of almost 3 percent a year, about four times the rate for Europe. There were wide variations, from Cuba's 1.3 percent to Mexico's 3.4 percent. But population growth was a problem almost everywhere, with dramatic effects on the quality of life. For example, although Latin America had been the world's largest grain exporter in the 1930s, it now became an importer. In the 1970s, the region's food supply grew by less than 1 percent a year, while population growth was close to 3 percent—a damning commentary on agricultural policies that substituted purely technological modernization for structural reform of the agrarian sector. Thus, the distribution of incomes remained highly unequal in most Latin American countries. Though they had fallen, infant mortality rates also told a shocking story: 23 deaths per 1,000 live births in Cuba in 1976, 62 in Mexico, and 125 in Haiti, compared to 15 in the United States or 8 in Sweden. Illiteracy too was a problem. In both Brazil and Mexico, although the percentage of the illiterate population declined, the absolute number of illiterates increased throughout much of the post-1945 period because of rapid population growth.

Problems of population and living standards challenged Latin American societies on every level. They also challenged the United States, as the political controversy of the 1980s over illegal immigration made clear. The determination of Hispanics to escape the problems of their homelands had given the United States the fourth-largest Spanish-speaking population—about 20 million—of any country in the Western Hemisphere.

Economic change has channelled burgeoning Third World populations into the cities. Since about 1960, a wave of superurbanization has produced urban complexes in the Third World bigger than any in the affluent countries. Often focused on the single largest city of each country, superurbanization overloads every facility of these cities and leaves the center ringed with shantytowns, known as *villas miserias* in Argentina and by other expressive names elsewhere. In the leading example, Mexico City, the population grew from 8 to 16 million between 1970 and 1984. At that rate, it will become the world's largest city, with over 30 million people, in 2025.

The Uncertain Course of Economic Development

The economic and social problems of the Latin American countries are clearly inseparable. Economic conditions vary widely among nations. Brazil and Mexico have large, substantially industrialized economies. Some observers now class them in an intermediate status between the dominant economies and the less developed. In contrast, coffee still accounted for over half the exports of the Central American countries (Panama, Costa Rica, Nicaragua, Honduras, El Salvador, and Guatemala) in 1960. Bananas made up another 14 percent, and industrialization was just starting. Despite such differences, the Latin American economies have important traits in common, reflected in a regionwide debate over alternative development strategies.

The debate focused on two fundamental questions: where the resources for industrialization would come from, and how to use them. The historical answer was often to extract these resources from agriculture. Other sources were external: profits from foreign trade, or investment by foreigners. As industrialization progressed, the working class offered another possibility, for capital could be extracted by depressing workers' wages. The success of any of these strategies depends in part on the strength of those who accumulate capital—the state, industrialists, possibly landlords—in relation to those with whom they must deal, at home and abroad. Another question has been the goal of industrialization: what kinds of industries to create and for what market.

The larger Latin American countries, as noted in Chapter 8, began to answer these questions by the 1930s with a strategy aimed first at local production of formerly imported goods, then at heavy industry. The market for import substitution was by definition the internal one, and various devices, such as high import duties, were used to protect it. The governments played a role in industrialization by founding state enterprises or providing facilities, such as credit. Capital came from agriculture to some extent, perhaps most notably in Argentina. But only Mexico attempted any basic restructuring of agriculture, whose workings historically emphasized the landlords' dominance over the peasantry more than economic productivity. The usual failure to couple import substitution with agrarian reform undercut industrialization by restricting the productivity of agriculture, the size of the internal market, and the development of a skilled labor force.

The import-substitution approach to industrialization remained predominant through the 1960s. But by then, it was evident that the policy had limits. After a first "easy" phase that satisfied domestic demand for simple consumer goods, import substitution meant moving into industries that required greater capital and more advanced technology, that produced proportionally fewer jobs, and

Shantytown outside Rio de Janeiro, Brazil.
Paul Conklin

Modern São Paulo, Brazil.
Bruno Barbey/Magnum

Scenes from these two Brazilian metropolises show the contrasts that superurbanization produces in this developing country, which has one of the most unequal distributions of income in the world.

that could function efficiently only with large markets.

The rapid advance of technology compounded these problems; it was one thing to conquer heavy industry symbolically by building a steel mill, quite another to become self-sufficient in such fields as machine tools and chemicals, not to mention advanced technologies like microelectronics. Without such self-sufficiency—something small economies could not aspire to—import substitution merely shifted the frontier of import dependency from the finished product to the machines or parts used to make it. Protectionist policies could not overcome these problems, but merely led multinational firms to penetrate the protected economies by creating local subsidiaries.

The realization that import substitution was reaching its limits became a major factor in opening a new period in the 1960s. The decades since have displayed two distinct approaches to economic development. The less common, socialist policy seeks development through radical structural change in society and economy, including agrarian reform and attempts to sever relations of external dependency. Countries that have attempted this approach so far include Cuba under Castro (1959 to the present), Chile under Allende (1970–1973), and perhaps Nicaragua since the Sandinista revolution (1979). Only in Cuba has this approach become established in a lasting way, and even Castro's regime has only changed the form of dependency, not eliminated it. Like most of the 170 or so countries in today's world, Cuba may simply lack the potential to rise above a subordinate place in any global pattern of economic relations.

The more common economic policy since 1960 has been neocolonial. In crude form, this is a revival of the old "liberal" view of Latin America as an agrarian region whose role is to export agricultural and mineral products and to import industrial ones. In the sophisticated view of finance ministers, the policy seeks development largely through foreign investment, accepting the restrictions, including drastic squeezing of wages, that foreign investors and lenders like the International Monetary Fund (IMF) demand to secure their investment.*

The Brazilian experience shows that the neocolonial approach can produce certain gains. Brazil even became an exporter of industrial products. On the other hand, Brazil's growth proved badly unbalanced, worsening existing inequalities. In Brazil, as in other relatively industrialized countries, neocolonialism passed through two stages. Direct investment by multinational corporations characterized the first. Direct governmental borrowing from large international banks typified the second. The combined result of both phases was that foreign investment in Latin America, after declining during the Depression, rose again sharply after about 1960.

Both phases had important costs. Industrialization through direct foreign investment worsened balance-of-payments problems because money left the country to cover profits and royalties. The capital that multinational firms took out of Latin America probably exceeded their investments greatly. For example, Brazilian statistics record a total capital inflow for the period 1947–1960 of $1.8 billion, but a total outflow of $3.5 billion.

---

* The International Monetary Fund (IMF) is a UN agency created to aid member states in temporary balance-of-payment difficulties. The IMF extends aid to a country only if it has a plan for eliminating its deficit.

Other examples of fantastic profits are not hard to find. Latin American governments attempted to limit these outflows, but the multinational firms found it relatively easy to defeat these efforts by working with the region's historically foreign-oriented elites. In the military-dominated Argentina of the 1960s, for example, 143 retired military commanders held 177 positions in the largest and mostly foreign-controlled firms.

The foreign-debt approach to capital accumulation seemed to solve some of these problems, but ultimately made them worse. Government borrowing brought capital into Latin American countries under a guise of national control and enabled the governments to enlarge their role as investors or lenders. Yet while direct investment by foreign firms required remittances abroad to cover profits and fees, government borrowing required even larger foreign remittances to cover both principal and interest.

Before the foreign-debt approach had gone far, a critical tightening of global economic interdependency compounded these problems. This tightening was due to revolutionary oil price increases imposed by the Organization of Petroleum Exporting Countries (OPEC), which includes Venezuela and Nigeria, though most members are in the Middle East. The first increases almost quadrupled the price of oil on the world market, from $2.70 per barrel in 1973 to $9.76 in 1976. A second round of increases in 1979 led to a price of $33.47 per barrel in 1982.

These price increases had worldwide effects, especially in developing countries that had to import part or all of their oil. By 1979 various factors—such as conservation, shifts to alternative energy sources, and recession—had reduced world oil consumption. Price drops followed in the early 1980s. Then even oil-producing countries began to suffer—a fact suggesting that, despite their sudden wealth, they were not completely different from other economies dependent on the export of a single commodity.

By then, Latin American foreign debt had shot out of control. Argentina, Brazil, Chile, Peru, Ecuador, and even the oil exporters Venezuela and Mexico had to spend 30 to 65 percent of their export earnings just to cover interest on their foreign debts. By late 1983, Brazil and Mexico had the largest foreign debts of any developing countries ($95 and $91 billion respectively), while Argentina ($42 billion) came fourth. Much of this debt resulted from the recycling of Middle Eastern "petrodollars" to Western banks, which then made unwise loans.

The build-up of this enormous debt suggests that Latin America's neocolonial development strategy may have played itself out, just as the import-substitution strategy had a quarter-century earlier. The stabilization programs that the IMF imposed on the debtor nations required sacrifices whose political costs verged on the intolerable. The debt crisis even threatened the international banking system. But by 1984, Latin America's economic situation appeared to be improving. The prices of Latin American exports had risen while that of oil had fallen, thus improving foreign trade balances. Nevertheless, the outcome of the debt crisis and the economic future of Latin America remained unclear.

Political Reflections of Socioeconomic Stress

The major developments of Latin America's post-1945 political history followed from the region's social, and especially its economic, history. Each of the three major economic policies—import-substitution, socialism, and neocolonialism—has been associated with a particular type of politics and particular social groups. Since its origins in the 1930s, for example, the import-substitution strategy was associated with mass mobilizers, of whom Perón and Vargas still played leading roles after 1945.

Radical leftist policies, in contrast, have appealed to frustrated nationalists and the disadvantaged. Many radicals are communists of some type, and a larger number hold some ideas inspired by Marx, Mao, or Che Guevara, who figures in the discussion on Cuba later in this chapter. Yet the communists are not united, and not all radicals are communists. Castro's unsuccessful efforts to export revolution in the 1960s, when Moscow and other Latin American communist parties opposed such efforts, illustrated the first point. The political activation of the historically conservative Roman Catholic Church illustrated the second, though some Catholics, too, adopted Marxist ideas.

Radicals dominated the course of change in only a few places. But they produced a wide impact, especially in the 1960s when Latin America felt its share of the radicalism agitating the young and disadvantaged around the world. The heyday of such radical heroes of the 1960s as Che Guevara, Mao Zedong, and Ho Chi Minh came just as Latin Americans found themselves facing the problems of runaway population growth, superurbanization, and neocolonial militarism. The eclipse of the secular radicals followed with the tightening of military authoritarianism and the worsened economic conditions after 1973. Catholic radicals continued work into the 1980s from El Salvador to Brazil, although Pope John Paul II demanded an end to political officeholding by priests and the elimination of Marxist ideas from religious thought.

Neocolonial authoritarianism, finally, has clearly been associated with conservatives, especially military leaders. Not all Latin American military officers are conservative. But the shift to neocolonial policies coincided with the military installation of repressive regimes in Brazil, Chile, Bolivia, Uruguay, Paraguay, and Argentina. Of the large Latin American countries, the only one to escape military domination—for reasons that will merit further comment—was Mexico. By the mid-1980s, the trend appeared to be reversing. Elected civilian governments had assumed power in many countries, or were expected to do so soon. It was too early to be sure whether a real shift of policy would occur in all cases.

Why had narrowly based authoritarian regimes emerged in the first place? Throughout most of the twentieth century, the trend was toward mass-oriented political systems. To explain the Latin American experience, some observers focused on the neocolonial economic policies. According to this view, only a repressive military government could restrain the demands of the working class, which populist leaders had mobilized, and impose the huge sacrifices required for the economic stabilization needed to attract foreign investment. Another explanation, not unrelated to the first, emphasized relations between the Latin American governments and the United States.

U.S.–Latin American Relations, with a Chilean Example

At the end of World War II, U.S. influence in Latin America was at its highest point. Having long claimed a paramount interest there, the United States capitalized on its influence by persuading most Latin American governments to sever relations with the Soviet Union, ban their local Communist parties, accept a collective security agreement (the Rio Pact of 1947), and join the new Organization of American States (1948). After the Communist victory in China and the Korean War (1950–1953), the United States saw its struggle with communism as a global one. As a result, the United States concluded defense assistance agreements with ten Latin American nations, from Chile to Honduras, during 1952–1954. These agreements had important consequences. Latin American military elites acquired U.S. equipment, far beyond what their governments could have bought them, and participated in joint training programs with U.S. forces, such as the counterinsurgency courses at several U.S. army bases. Thus these elites became identified with the U.S. military and also acquired greater prominence in their own countries than they would otherwise have possessed.

Under different U.S. presidents, policy toward Latin America shifted, but the military emphasis never disappeared. Truman attempted to balance the military policy with the Point Four Program, which offered technical assistance to developing countries. Eisenhower (1953–1961) abandoned economic assistance in favor of free enterprise. Faced with the Cuban revolution and Soviet penetration of the Western Hemisphere, Kennedy (1961–1963) shifted again, producing the Alliance for Progress. One part of this program aimed at social and economic development. Latin American nations were to submit development plans covering specified topics, including agrarian and tax reforms, and the United States was to provide much of the financing for the plans. The Alliance for Progress also included a military component: a counterinsurgency program, to help Latin American governments protect themselves against guerrillas.

The Alliance for Progress touched off a great deal of optimism that was headed for disappointment. Hindsight shows that it was unrealistic to expect freely elected Latin American governments to achieve economic growth and social reform at the same time. The central economic assumption of the Alliance—that industrial development in Latin America could "take off" as it had earlier in Britain or the United States—proved wrong, largely because it ignored Latin America's continuing economic dependence. Indeed, the Alliance aid programs reinforced dependence. Much of the aid took the form of loans, with requirements to spend the funds on U.S. goods. Although more than $12 billion went into Latin America between 1960 and 1968, those years witnessed a net outflow of capital and a growth of foreign debt. By the mid-1960s, the democratic governments that corresponded to the Alliance concept began to founder and fall to the military in country after country.

In Washington, Kennedy's successor, Lyndon Johnson (1963–1969), abandoned the Alliance for Progress side of the Kennedy strategy, though not the military side, as his military intervention in the Dominican Republic in 1965 showed. Reacting to its experience in Vietnam, the Nixon administration (1969–1974) declared that the United States could not keep peace all over the world; it shifted attention to regimes that seemed able to play that role in their own regions—in Latin America, the military regimes. Despite the somewhat inconsistent Carter focus (1977–1981) on human rights, there has been no fundamental revision of the military emphasis through the mid-1980s.

The Chilean experience of the 1970s provides perhaps the most memorable example of the military-oriented U.S. policy. Chile's economy has long been dominated by U.S. interests, especially in copper mining, and by a small local elite with interests in land, industry, and finance. As rapid population growth and urbanization put Chilean society under increasing stress, it became clear that these interests could no longer control political mobilization. By the late 1950s, the country had a range of political parties including the Popular Action Front (FRAP in Spanish) that combined socialists and communists, a Christian Democratic Party appealing to Catholic workers, a centrist "Radical" party, and "Liberal" and "Conservative" parties on the right. In the 1964 presidential election, the Right temporarily checked the radicalizing trend by combining with the Christian Democrats to elect their candidate, Eduardo Frei, and defeat the FRAP candidate, Salvador Allende.

As president, Frei was not successful. He accepted aid under the Alliance for Progress and opened Chile increasingly to foreign investment, so deepening dependency. On controversial questions like land reform and nationalization, he attempted to define middle-of-the-road policies. Meanwhile, the Social Democrats undertook large-scale political mobilization, by creating unions, cooperatives, and the like, so competing with similar efforts of communists and socialists. The result was sharp political polarization. In the 1970 election, in which Frei was ineligible for renomination, this polarization led to the nomination of a conservative on the Right and two leftist candidates, one from the Christian Democrats, and one from the Left coalition then known as Popular Unity (UP in Spanish). UP candidate Salvador Allende won a plurality—36 percent of the vote. Because he had not received a majority, the election went to the Congress, which approved him. A second Marxist government had come to power in Latin America, this one freely elected, by a narrow margin.

The UP program called for a peaceful transition to socialism, a tall order for a government that lacked a majority and had to operate in the Western Hemisphere under U.S. scrutiny. Allende began by freezing prices and raising wages to redistribute income. He next sought complete nationalization of the copper companies. Nationalization then extended into other sectors, affecting both Chilean and foreign-owned firms. Allende also pushed ahead with land reform, and by the end of 1972 had liquidated the large estates. In the nationalization of firms and the takeover of the estates, Allende tried to proceed by legal means, but left-wing radicals often forced his hand. Nationalizations had soon gone so far that the government could not have compensated the foreign firms, even if it had wanted to.

Gradually, it became clear that the opposition to Allende precluded any peaceful transition to socialism. By the fall of 1972, agricultural production and copper prices had fallen, and inflation was getting out of control. Radicals to Allende's left demanded faster change, while the conservatives—who still controlled much of the media, the Congress, the bureaucracy, the military officer corps, and the church—organized actions such as a massive strike in the fall of 1972. The U.S. government and U.S. corporations with interests in Chile did everything possible to thwart Allende. The Nixon administration took steps to halt loans and private investment, while the CIA spent $8 million in three years—as later revealed in Senate testimony—to undermine the economy. Only to the Chilean military did U.S. aid continue—a fact that proved significant. As the crisis mounted, Allende made concessions to his opponents, but could not save the situation. In September 1973, military officers mounted a coup that left Allende dead and the Left crushed.

At the head of the new regime stood General Augusto Pinochet, an alumnus of the School of the Americas, founded by the U.S. army to train Latin American officers. Still in power more than a decade later, he presided over one of Latin America's most repressive military regimes. Pinochet wiped out modern political life in Chile, abolishing political parties and suspending the constitution, with its guarantees of civil liberties. He also undid Allende's economic reforms and turned over economic policy to technocrats who fulfilled the neocolonial program to the fullest. Their policies reduced import duties from 100 percent to 10 percent, attracted $18 billion in foreign investment, and placed under private control not only many businesses nationalized under Allende, but also social services such as schools and hospitals. Especially after the global recession of 1981 halved the price of copper, these policies ruined Chilean industry, left a third of the workers unemployed or marginally employed, and gave Chile a foreign debt that is one of the highest in the world on a per capita basis.

What Allende would have accom-plished in the long run had his regime been left undisturbed by outside power is not clear. Scholars debate the extent to which U.S. opposition, rather than internal opposition and his own mistakes, caused Allende's fall. But in the mid-1980s, as thousands of Chileans risked their lives to demonstrate against Pinochet, it was also unclear what good could come for Chile from his attempts to turn back the clock on the development of his country. Since U.S. policy supported leaders like Pinochet, the need for a new foreign policy seemed as clear as the need for a shift away from military authoritarianism in Latin America's domestic political life.

The Chilean experience illustrates not only problems of relations with the United States, but also the other Latin American themes discussed in this overview. These problems began with runaway population growth and superurbanization being added to the old social inequalities. Such problems overtaxed the capabilities of governments that aimed at both political mobilization and economic development. By the 1960s, the characteristic economic strategy of these governments, based on import substitution, was exhausted. This fact, and the fears touched off by radical alternatives, especially the Cuban revolution, then launched a trend toward military-authoritarian regimes. They pursued neocolonial economic policies more favorable to the foreign interests that supported them than to the local populace. Chile's experience was unusual only in that the radical alternative briefly triumphed with the election of Allende, between the Christian Democrat Frei and the military dictator Pinochet.

Pursuing the perceived interests of their nation, U.S. policymakers continued to favor stability and a secure climate for investment, and so normally disregarded the political environment that Latin American rulers created for their citizens. In this way, U.S. policy contributed to the resurgence of militarism more than most U.S. citizens realize. Indeed, the average U.S. citizen has little grasp of why former Guatemalan President Juan Arévalo (in office 1945–1950) described U.S.–Latin American relations in terms of "the shark and the sardines." Some Latin American countries are bigger than sardines, but U.S. leaders know what Arévalo meant.[1]

After the oil price increases of 1973 and 1979, economic pressures exposed the military regimes of Latin America to new difficulties. In the early 1980s, it appeared that the military regimes had not permanently thwarted the characteristic twentieth-century demands for mass political participation and economic development to benefit the people. To replace these regimes with more democratic ones would not be easy, considering how many parties and other institutions the military had destroyed. Moreover, partly because of the economic regressiveness of the military regimes, the continent still had no country that had risen to more than an intermediate position in the global pattern of economic relations.

Argentina: The Perils of Authoritarianism, with Charisma and Without

Since 1945, the lasting influence of Perón has given a distinctive stamp to Argentine history. Even so, the country passed through the same phases noted elsewhere, starting with the relatively democratic, development-oriented regimes of Perón (1946–1955) and his Radical successors (1958–1966), and followed by a period of military authoritarianism. Throughout, several factors proved specially important. Perón proved more effective at mobilizing the populace than at charting political and economic policy. The military not only had means to exert force, but were politically assertive. Their control of large government enterprises that manufactured military supplies made them economically influential as well. Argentina suffered acutely from lack of political consensus. Peronists, middle-class Radicals, the military, the Left—all had splits and disagreements that made orderly political life difficult. But the most important problem was the economy. Despite progress in industry, almost all of Argentina's foreign exchange still came from agricultural exports, which suffered from both domestic policy decisions and external factors that drove down Argentina's share of world trade. By the early 1980s, the once "amazing Argentine" had fallen to a new low of political and economic disarray.

Toward Democracy and Development

Chapter 8 describes Perón's career through his election to the presidency in 1946. As president, he embarked on a program of reforms intended to overcome dependency, redistribute income and benefits to his supporters, and broaden his constituency into an alliance of labor, management, and the military. He introduced a Five-Year Plan and created a foreign trade organization (IAPI, *Instituto Argentino de Promoción del Intercambio*). By monopolizing the marketing of agricultural exports, IAPI was to generate profits to finance industrializa-

Juan and Eva Perón at his presidential inauguration in 1952. To many Argentines, this charismatic pair symbolized the opening of an era of mass politics.
UPI/Bettmann Newsphotos

tion. To reduce the foreign role in the economy, Perón nationalized many foreign-dominated enterprises, including the central bank and the rail lines, using the accumulated export earnings of the war years to compensate the owners. In July 1947, he paid off Argentina's entire foreign debt. Meanwhile, industrial development made Argentina almost entirely self-sufficient in consumer goods by 1955, although there was still little heavy industry.

Perón's drive for development was clear, but his policies were questionable. For example, they were highly inflationary: living costs at Buenos Aires increased almost 700 percent from 1943 to 1955. Perón's government, which provided many services, was one of the costliest in the world. Despite his populism, the high taxes required to support the government were still mostly indirect, hitting the poor hardest. By substituting bureaucratic inefficiencies for the spur of competition, nationalization also made firms less productive. To make a profit, IAPI had to buy Argentina's grain and livestock at below-market prices, a practice that deprived producers of incentives and led to cutbacks in production and investment. Since Argentina still relied on agricultural exports to earn foreign currency, Perón was killing the goose that laid the golden eggs.

For some time, most Argentines probably believed conditions were getting better. Industrialists and the urban middle class were pleased by patronage in the growing bureaucracy and by the enlargement of the market for their goods and services made possible by improvements in working-class living standards. The military liked Perón's commitment to industrialization, and the salary increases and equipment they received. Given the vote in 1947 largely through the efforts of Eva Duarte Perón, women voted heavily for her husband. Thanks to the strong export market of the early postwar years, Perón was able to gratify labor with steady increases in purchasing power through 1949—another factor that helped diminish agricultural exports, because consumption grew at home. The flow of new benefits, such as improved health care, continued. Until her death from cancer in 1952, Eva Perón dispensed many of the benefits through her Eva Perón Foundation. Receiving endless streams of petitioners there, she became a cult figure.

Nationalism and populism on this scale are enough to explain the Peróns' lasting hold on Argentine affections. In 1949, Perón was able to secure a new constitution that embodied his principles and authorized presidential re-election to consecutive terms. Although military objections to the possibility of a female commander-in-chief blocked Eva's vice-presidential candidacy, Perón easily won the badly manipulated election of 1952. Yet economic conditions were turning against him.

The policies that made Perón popular depended on income redistribution and expanded government spending, both supported by postwar boom conditions. After 1948, recession and bad harvests, and increased competition in export markets, led to balance-of-payments deficits. Industrial production and real wages were declining by the early 1950s. Perón never coped successfully with this change.

Perón's political alliance began to fall apart, and he turned to erratic measures that led to his fall. In 1949, the government had introduced a program of economic stabilization, limiting wage and price rises, cutting spending, and restricting credit. After his re-election, Perón introduced a second Five-Year Plan that departed from the first by courting foreign investment, providing incentives for agriculture, and calling for a two-year wage freeze. As if to mask these changes, he tightened political discipline among his followers, became increasingly dictatorial (though never to the point of eliminating all opposition), and emphasized the "Justicialist" ideology that he—not a profound or consistent thinker—had made up to explain his policies. Still, the complaints grew. In 1954, for reasons still unclear, Perón attacked the Catholic church. Violent demonstrations resulted, the pope retaliated with excommunication, and the military abandoned Perón. Facing a military conspiracy in September 1955, he fled without a fight. For the next eighteen years, Perón overshadowed Argentine politics from afar. Meanwhile, his followers, though divided, remained a major force inside the country.

After Perón's fall, the military took control directly. But they had no effective policy beyond the wish to root out Peronism, and in 1955 they decided to return power to the civilians. The largest legal party was the Radicals, who had last ruled Argentina before the Depression. They were now divided into Popular Radicals and Intransigents. By striking a deal with the outlawed Peronists, the Intransigents won the election of 1958, and their candidate, Arturo Frondizi, assumed the presidency, with the military in the background.

Civilian presidents from the Radical party, which was middle-class in orientation, governed Argentina for most of the next eight years. Their rule represented a second phase in the postwar trend toward mass political participation and economic development. Frondizi had an economic plan that seemed well suited to Argentina's needs: speed up industrialization, stimulate agricultural exports, and reduce state intervention in the economy. But there was also the risky point of attracting foreign capital; moreover, Frondizi was asking consumers, whom Perón had favored, to sacrifice for the sake of investment. Economic nationalists also did not like Frondizi's agreements with foreign oil companies, though the goal of petroleum self-sufficiency was four-fifths realized within a few years—an accomplishment significant for the 1970s. When trade deficits and inflation continued, Frondizi ran into international pressure for a strict stabilization program: cuts in public spending and wages, and devaluation. Economic growth would resume for a time in the early 1960s. But industrial workers' incomes fell by one-fourth in 1959 alone.

These economic problems made it impossible for Frondizi to maintain his political support, and the Peronists began to sweep the elections. If the two Radical factions had reunited, they would have been stronger. But the Popular Radicals also disliked Frondizi's economic policies and refused their cooperation. The middle-class Radicals had again failed to rule Latin America's most middle-class country. In March 1962, the army intervened, and Frondizi fell. He was the Argentine president who came closest to fulfilling the expectations of the Alliance for Progress. The Popular Radicals got their chance in 1963, when their candidate, Arturo Illia, won the presidency. But he too proved unable to make peace with the Peronists and, after another economic slump, fell to a military coup in 1966.

Neocolonial Militarism in Argentina

The new government dismantled the fragile institutions of Argentina's modern political life by closing the Congress, suppressing political parties and the labor movement, purging the universities, and ruling through an alliance of military commanders, technocrats, and foreign investors. Its economic program featured a two-year wage freeze, the elimination of all restrictions on profit remittances by foreign firms and a devaluation of the peso. Devaluation produced dramatic effects, making it harder for Argentine firms to import machinery or pay royalties on imported technologies and easier for foreign firms to buy them out. Foreign dominance over Argentine industry now increased markedly.

Military rule could not make Argentines take such medicine quietly. In 1969, when troops fired on a labor demonstration in Córdoba, center of the automobile industry, the violence spread to other cities, opening a period of urban guerrilla activism. Numerous guerrilla groups emerged, such as the People's Revolutionary Army (ERP in Spanish) and the left-Peronist Montoneros. Many movements had their roots, not in Marxism, but in the populist side of the Peronist legacy, which the military had repudiated.

As political violence grew—with attacks on government installations, kidnappings of foreign businessmen, even the killing of a former president, and brutal retaliation by the government—Argentina drifted toward civil war. Military leaders finally struck a deal with the exiled Perón, hoping that his magic could still restore order. He returned to become president again, at the age of seventy-seven. This time, his wife, Isabel, was his vice president. They were elected in September 1973 with 62 percent of the vote.

From exile, Perón had made statements to encourage both Left and Right, for his one goal was to regain power. In office, he cracked down on the Left—the military commanders who allowed his return to power had not misjudged him. When Perón died in 1974 and his wife succeeded him, she showed her lack of qualification for office. The crackdown on the Left intensified, as right-wing death squads, thought to be linked to one of her advisers, mounted a counterterror. When the economy went out of control, the army removed her from office in 1976, and the era of military control resumed.

Determined to change Argentine politics permanently, the generals who seized power set out to stop terrorism, to cut back the public sector, and to reorder relations among the state, business, and labor. Their two biggest problems were the Left and the economy.

The military rulers expanded the attack on the Left into a "dirty war" in which some 10,000 people—perhaps several times that many—simply "disappeared." The memory of these *desaparecidos*—first publicized by a movement that emerged among their mothers—will continue to haunt Argentine consciences. Many of the rebels were university students or former students, middle-class in background, who aimed to create a revolutionary order in place of the neocolonial military regime that offered them so little. The guerrilla movements may have included ten thousand Argentines and, by robbery and ransom, may have accumulated $150 million for their cause. The military treated the struggle against the guerrillas as a war with no quarter. The military won, but only by terrorizing the country and killing many innocent people.

On the economic side, the military rulers introduced the predictable neoliberal policy. They sold off many state enterprises and tightened credit, as real interest rates rocketed to 20 to 40 percent. The living standards of workers plummeted. These policies slowed inflation and produced a positive payments balance, until the 1981 recession sent the economy into a tailspin.

In the spring of 1982, the troubled regime executed the classic maneuver of trying to rouse patriotic loyalty through a popular war, fought over the Falkland Islands. These islands, located about 300 miles off Argentina's coast, had long been ruled by Britain but claimed by Argentina. Argentina's defeat destroyed the prestige of the military, which then had no choice but to step aside and call presidential elections for October 1983.

Again Toward Democracy and Development?

The winner, in an upset of the Peronist candidate, was Raúl Alfonsín, a Radical with a record as a human rights activist. His victory, with 52 percent of the vote, roused excitement in Argentina and abroad. For Latin America, it seemed an encouraging sign of a new turn toward democratic government and—ideally—economic development in the national interest.

But Alfonsín faced huge tasks. He was committed to try those responsible for both the leftist and the rightist excesses of previous years, including three former presidents. If the humiliation of the military boded well for Alfonsín's effort to shrink its power, he still faced powerful vested interests, notably the Peronist-dominated General Confederation of Labor. But the greatest hurdle was the economy. Argentina had the fourth-highest foreign debt in the world and an inflation rate of 580 percent a year. The Alfonsín government unveiled a plan to slow inflation, raise wages, and restart the economy. Whether he would be able to reach all three goals at once was not clear. Alfonsín found himself caught between labor leaders, who understood democracy in terms of its effects on workers' wages, and international lenders, who insisted on austerity as a condition for rescheduling Argentina's debts.

Combining economic growth with social justice has proved very difficult in Argentina. Perón's first presidency showed how difficult a populist mass mobilizer found this problem. The record of his military successors showed the greater inadequacies of neocolonial authoritarianism. If Alfonsín could cope with this problem, he would—as many Argentines hoped—launch a "third wave," after those of Yrigoyen and Perón, in Argentine history. It would not be easy.

Brazil: Political and Economic Vacillations

Events in Brazil after 1945 paralleled those in Argentina, but with significant differences. Here too the closing years of the import-substitution phase were dominated first by a prewar populist leader, Getúlio Vargas (1951–1954), and then by two presidents who aimed, not very successfully, at nationalist economic development and political mobilization: Juscelino Kubitschek (1956–1961) and João Goulart (1961–1964). As in Argentina, the military was an important influence on the government and seized power completely in the mid-1960s. The Brazilian military also introduced neocolonial policies, although civilian rule resumed in 1985. Differences between the two countries included the existence of a sizable peasantry in Brazil. This fact prompted an attempt at political mobilization in the Brazilian countryside in the early 1960s. Another difference was Brazil's greater success in economic development, at least through the early 1970s. Finally, probably because of stronger links between the military and the middle class, repression never became as severe in Brazil as in Argentina.

The Second Republic

The postwar part of Brazil's import substitution phase coincided with the life of its Second Republic (1946–1964). In reaction against Vargas's New State, the new constitution adopted in 1946 reduced the powers of the presidency, separated the three branches of government more effectively, and extended the vote to all but military enlisted men and illiterates, who still made up 60 percent of the population. Several political parties formed in 1945 and helped to democratize the country over the next twenty years. Until 1950, the presidency remained in the hands of one of the generals who had overthrown Vargas in

1945. His frankly neocolonial regime wasted the foreign exchange accumulated during World War II on imported luxuries. In the elections of 1950, Vargas ran for president with a program emphasizing industrialization. A coalition of labor, industry, and the middle class supported him.

Resuming the presidency at age sixty-eight, Vargas gave prime attention to the economy. Faced with deficits and inflation, his administration formulated a middle-of-the-road policy that aimed to stimulate foreign investment, but also included nationalist components. Vargas proposed to limit profit remittances by foreign companies and to form a mixed public-private corporation, Petrobrás, to monopolize the petroleum industry. Like other middle-of-the-road programs, this one attracted opposition from both Left and Right, and from the United States.

As inflation and the foreign trade deficit continued to worsen, Vargas faced a cabinet crisis and other troubles in 1954. His finance minister tried to introduce a stabilization program, while his labor minister—the future president, João Goulart—demanded wage increases. Evidence of financial scandal also came to light. Then an attempt to assassinate an opposition journalist was traced to Vargas's security chief, though he had acted without Vargas's knowledge. The military demanded Vargas's resignation. His response was sensational: suicide.

Brazil's next elected president, Kubitschek, came to power in 1955, despite much maneuvering by military and political leaders. He committed the country to an inflationary development strategy summed up in his slogan, "fifty years' progress in five." From 1957 to 1961, the economy grew at the remarkable average annual rate of 7 percent. By the time Kubitschek left office in 1960,

Brazil's heavy industry supplied half of the country's needs, from machine tools to mining equipment. By 1962, Brazil was the world's seventh-biggest auto manufacturer. There were also vast public works projects. New dams supplied electrical power to support growth. The most spectacular innovation was the new capital city in the interior, Brasília, built in three years at huge cost. The new capital, with the network of highways leading to it, was meant to create a new sense of national unity.

Yet a reckoning had to come. Kubitschek's policies favored profits over wages, and he courted foreign capital by offering incentives not available to Brazilian enterprises. Foreign interests soon controlled half of all large Brazilian corporations. The foreign debt rose rapidly, reaching $2.7 billion in 1961—a level that already required more than half of export earnings for debt service. Refusing demands to stabilize the economy, Kubitschek let inflation continue. As a result, the value of the cruzeiro, and Brazil's export earnings, fell drastically. Unrest spread throughout the country. In the northeast, Peasant Leagues had formed, denounced by landowners as communist. Kubitschek's nationalist development strategy was proving inconsistent, no sounder than Perón's.

Kubitschek's successors faced crisis conditions. His immediate successor resigned after seven months. The next, Goulart, faced a congressional attempt to check his populism by amending the constitution to reduce his powers. Goulart regained full powers in 1963, but was not always so successful in his populist-nationalist policies. In economics, one ambiguous success was a law regulating foreign investment and restricting annual profit remittances to no more than 10 percent of the capital invested.

The law slowed foreign investment almost to nothing, creating a shortage of capital that forced a return to Kubitschek's inflationary method of expanding the money supply. The cruzeiro collapsed again. The number of cruzeiros required to equal one U.S. dollar rose from 390 in 1961 to 1,820 in 1964. Arguing that inflation and development went together, Goulart did nothing about this, and his moderate support began to disappear.

Goulart responded to his difficulties by moving to the left. Unable to get Congress to pass a program for tax reform and expropriation of large estates, he presented more radical proposals: immediate expropriation of certain types of landholdings, periodic wage adjustments, votes for illiterates and enlisted men, legalization of the Communist party. And he began to enact some of these measures by decree. His support of political activism in unaccustomed places—among the peasantry and in the enlisted ranks of the army—brought moderates and conservatives to the point of panic. Civilian opponents of the regime began to call for military intervention. Finally, faced with rebellion in enlisted ranks, the military commanders swung into action, and forced Goulart to leave the country in April 1964. The United States approved the coup in advance and sent a naval force to stand by off the Brazilian coast.

Goulart's policies were mistakes in many ways. He failed to tackle inflation and further politicized the military. Yet his was the only Brazilian government that has yet tried to complete political mobilization by carrying it into the countryside.

Brazil's Military Phase

Goulart's fall opened a twenty-year period of military rule. Compared to the Argentine situation, the Brazilian military was proportionately smaller and less well financed, had closer links with the middle class, and often acted politically in its behalf. Nevertheless, the 1964 coup ended the Second Republic, and a series of "institutional acts," followed by new constitutions in 1967 and 1969, set up a dictatorship. Any Brazilian could be deprived of his or her rights, as three former presidents were, and the generals replaced the old political parties with two new ones they created. Thereafter, the problems facing the military resembled those in Argentina: the Left, the economy, the demand for return to civilian rule.

Dissatisfaction with the new regime found expression throughout Brazilian culture, from popular songs to guerrilla attacks. By the late 1960s, moderates demanded a return to civilian government, while the Left demanded social revolution. Student groups began to riot, and a Mothers' Union formed to protest the violent treatment the students received. Urban guerrillas began action on the far Left, and government-linked death squads on the Right. By 1973, the radical Left had suffered enough that it gradually ceased to be a threat to the regime. Yet denunciations of rights violations continued. Among the most vocal critics were activist churchmen, like Archbishop Helder Câmara, in the arid northeast, one of the most impoverished and hunger-stricken places in the world.

Economically, the most important feature of the military period was the so-called Brazilian miracle. Seeking to slow inflation and boost investment, the military governments pursued a blatantly foreign-oriented strategy. Foreign investment increased so much that foreigners completely controlled the tire and auto industries, and were nearly as dominant in other industries. Though unbalanced, economic growth in Brazil averaged around 10 percent a year between 1969 and 1974. During this "miraculous" period, industrial products first surpassed coffee among Brazil's exports.

Unfortunately this change signified neither an end to dependence for Brazil, nor anything miraculous for most Brazilians. Inequalities among social classes and regions of the country widened during these years. Brazil's income distribution became exceptionally unequal by Latin American, indeed by global, standards. As multinational corporations tightened their grip on the economy, their profit remittances often exceeded their investments in Brazil eight or ten times over. Agriculture, still dominated by the inefficiently run estates, "modernized" by producing more for export, and less for Brazil's soaring population—soybeans rather than black beans.

The OPEC oil price increases finally destroyed Brazil's "miracle." The military government immediately raised gasoline prices to reflect the 1973–74 quadrupling of oil prices, but allowed later price increases to fall behind the rate of inflation. In effect they gambled that the increases were temporary and decided not to jeopardize Brazil's future growth by further raising domestic oil prices. Economic growth continued in Brazil through 1978, but the next major oil price increase, in 1979, exposed the error in the government's strategy. Oil imports began to consume the bulk of export earnings. Petrobrás stepped up exploration, and Brazil's oil production reached a half million barrels a day by 1984. The shift to other forms of energy also progressed rapidly, and Brazil acquired a world technological lead in the use of alcohol derived from sugar cane as a fuel. Still, inflation slipped out of control, and the foreign debt soared, especially after interest rates in the United States rose to unprecedented heights in the early 1980s.

The economic results were extremely threatening for Brazil, and for the international banking system as well. Political consequences also followed, as cooperation between the military and the middle class began to break down. By the early 1980s, military neocolonialism seemed to have reached the end of its road, just as the import-substitution drive had done twenty years earlier. Lopsided economic growth continued. The Brazilian armaments industry became an exporter to places like Libya, Iran, and Iraq. The microcomputer industry became the third largest in the world after those of the United States and Japan. The state-controlled steel industry also exported its products, even to the United States. By 1984, Brazil again showed a foreign trade surplus projected at $12 billion. Yet Brazilians shared the profits more unequally than ever. Living standards had declined since 1980 for about half of Brazil's 130 million people, and an estimated 35 million went hungry.

The Return to Civilian Rule

Pressures for a return to civilian rule mounted steadily. In 1982, when Brazil held the first direct elections since 1965 for state governors, many opponents of the regime were victorious. Opposition to the military took strength from this victory, and the military began preparing for election of a civilian president.

By 1984, up to a million people at a time turned out to demonstrate in favor of direct election of the president, rather than indirect election by an electoral college as in the past. In the still-indirect election of January 1985, the winner was not the choice of the outgoing military leaders, but rather the head of the opposition, Tancredo Neves, former governor of the state of Minas Gerais and holder of many cabinet-level posts. He promised direct elections and a new constitution, but fell sick and died barely three months after his election. As Vice President José Sarney succeeded to the presidency, it was not certain whether he could fulfill the hopes that the Neves victory had raised.

Mexico Drifts Away from Its "Revolutionary" Legacy

Mexico, too, moved through a sequence of phases—mass mobilization, then neocolonial authoritarianism—with modifications that reflect its exceptional history before World War II. After achieving a high point of reform under Cárdenas, Mexico moved to the right, rather than the left, though there was a populist reprise in the late 1950s and early 1960s. Thereafter, the single dominant party remained more strongly institutionalized and broadly based than any other in Latin America. Because it had a degree of control over the military that other Latin American countries could only envy, the renewed move to the right toward authoritarianism and neocolonialism occurred under party auspices, without military rule. By the early 1980s, Mexico's distinctive party-state combination remained more firmly established

than the military regimes then approaching their ends in Argentina and Brazil, and Mexico had also become a major oil exporter. Yet the rapid growth of oil revenue had distorted other sectors of the economy, creating social and political strain. Mexico's attempts to transform its economic place in the world appeared no more successful than its "revolutionary" experience of the early twentieth century.

The Single-Party Regime

The key to the relative stability of Mexican political history since Cárdenas is the system of one-party rule. As noted in Chapter 8, Cárdenas reorganized the official party along corporatist lines, with separate agrarian, labor, military, and "popular" (essentially middle-class) sectors. In this way he mobilized both workers and peasants, but kept them separate. In 1945, the party was again reorganized as the Institutional Revolutionary Party (PRI in Spanish), the name it still retains, with peasant, labor, and "popular" (middle-class) sectors. The PRI and related interest groups had 4 million members in the early 1960s and were still growing.

Good organization enabled the one-party regime to endure. The party had firm control of both organized labor and the countryside. Party governance remained highly centralized in Mexico City. As usual in one-party systems, political interest focused more on nominations, an in-party matter, than on elections. Government and party interpenetrated each other so deeply that they became virtually indistinguishable. Because the state controlled many enterprises, the state-party symbiosis extended into the economy as well. The president had vast powers over this combine. For example, he originated the budget and most legislation, which the Congress merely rubber-stamped.

Opponents accused the PRI of corruption and vote manipulation, and there was truth in such charges. The PRI was a huge patronage machine, and it seldom lost elections. To a degree, these very qualities, familiar from the caudillo tradition, helped it maintain support, especially among peasants used to authoritarian leadership. The PRI also proved effective in coopting a broad range of opinion that might otherwise have fed opposition movements. And it had inherited the revolutionary rhetoric of the great rebellion. Mexico had its opposition parties. Yet in a sense, even they came under PRI patronage, as the government, responding to criticisms of one-party rule, began to guarantee them representation in the Chamber of Deputies. The Institutional Revolutionary Party was not revolutionary, but it *was* institutionalized.

Emerging from party leadership ranks to head such a strong party-state apparatus, Mexico's recent presidents have mostly not had profound impact as individuals. But there have been differences among them. For example, Miguel Alemán (1946–1952), the PRI's first civilian candidate, reduced military expenditure to 7 percent of the budget, down from 30 percent in 1930 and 70 percent in 1917. Thus, Mexico escaped the military-dominated politics that still bedevils most of Latin America. Adolfo López Mateos (1958–1964) came closest to the Alliance for Progress ideal. He revived land distribution by giving out 30 million acres, more than any president had since Cárdenas. He also expanded

social services, introduced profit-sharing for workers, and began the system of assuring congressional representation for minority parties.

The regime of President Gustavo Díaz Ordaz (1964–1970) marked the beginning of the shift back to the right then occurring in other Latin American countries. The blackest mark on his record occurred in 1968, as the government prepared to host the Olympic Games—the first time a developing country had the chance to show off its achievements in that way. Amid preparations for the Olympics, antigovernment demonstrations began. As in other countries in that decade, students played a leading role—although up to 400,000 sympathizers would turn out to demonstrate with them. The government's response showed how much it had moved away from revolutionary populism. The climactic episode occurred on October 2, when troops killed perhaps several hundred demonstrators and imprisoned two thousand. The Olympic Games went off without trouble, and the guerrilla violence that followed was suppressed in the early 1970s. But Díaz Ordaz, whatever else he did, was remembered for the violence. Subsequent presidents have never regained the populist stance of a López Mateos, and economic problems have preoccupied them increasingly.

Economic Shifts

Stimulated by wartime opportunities to export labor and raw materials to the United States, the Mexican economy continued to grow rapidly through the 1960s. By then, Mexico was nearly self-sufficient in consumer goods and was developing heavy industry. Perhaps the major problem, through the mid-1950s, was inflation, especially for agricultural and industrial workers, whose incomes did not keep pace.

The government dealt with this problem in 1954 by shifting to a "hard-money" strategy. It devalued the peso, from 8.65 to the dollar to 12.5. Mexico's ability to maintain a fixed exchange rate, while allowing unrestricted exchange of the peso against the U.S. dollar or other currencies, became a treasured symbol of development—one that few Third World countries could match. The reform also made Mexican exports cheaper, and Mexico itself cheaper for foreign tourists. Most important, the change stimulated foreign investment. In dollars of constant value, such investment in Mexico in 1940 was still only one-third what it had been in 1911. While economic nationalism remained an official priority, the hard-money policy began a reversal of trend that vastly increased foreign—mostly U.S.—investment over the next twenty years, creating the usual problems about profit remittances. Eventually, Mexico tried to limit these dangers. The government borrowed in order to expand its role as investor and lender. It also limited foreign ownership to a 49 percent share of any company. These measures did not solve Mexico's economic problems, however. Government borrowing started Mexico's fantastic debt accumulation, and the limit on foreign ownership left many opportunities for elite Mexicans to cooperate with foreign interests as they always had.

The 1954 hard-money strategy reduced inflation, but led to new problems in the early 1960s. Mexico's population growth began to cause alarm in the late 1950s. Urbanization accelerated partly because a mechanized "new hacienda" was emerging in the countryside. As in other Third World countries, many urban migrants could not find factory jobs and had to scratch out a living as bootblacks, street vendors, or the like. The government had long had programs to restrict the costs of goods and services to the poor. In the 1960s and 1970s, those programs had to be expanded. When shortfalls in domestic food production necessitated imports, the costs of the programs became prohibitive. This problem compounded the effects of the oil price rise. Inflation resumed, the 1954 exchange rate became untenable, and the government finally had to devalue the peso twice in one month in 1976.

Soon after, the world learned that Mexico was a major oil power. Discoveries raised its proven oil reserves to 70 billion barrels by the early 1980s, and its potential reserves to more than 200 billion—impressive figures even by Middle Eastern standards. Mexico became more confident. Iran's experience had shown that rapid growth of oil income could produce undesirable effects in a populous country with a complex economy. Mexico, which was not a member of OPEC, therefore set out to increase production only gradually. Even so, Mexico's petroleum earnings increased more than twenty-five-fold from 1976 to 1981, when they reached $13 billion. Despite its intentions, Mexico had become dependent on oil exports. The slump in oil prices after 1981 forced an increase in foreign borrowing that gave Mexico the second-largest foreign debt in the world by the end of 1983. To get the loans and try to reduce inflation, the government had to devalue again and curtail consumer subsidies. As of mid-1984, the most optimistic economic signs on the horizon were that interest rates had fallen, and that Mexico, like Brazil, was again beginning to show a positive trade balance.

Unfortunately less optimistic signs also appeared. Because the petroleum industry creates comparatively few jobs, the Mexicans who had to sacrifice for stabilization were mostly ones who had not profited from the oil boom. Mexico's income distribution was more unequal than that of Argentina or Chile, though less so than Brazil's. The share of household income going to the wealthiest 20 percent of households in the 1970s was almost 50 percent greater in Mexico than in the United States. To make matters worse, the growth of oil revenue compounded the corruption that had always greased the PRI machine. Soon, reports of vast abuses, including drug trafficking, circulated about prominent government officials. Resistance was also rising against the election-rigging techniques that had always assured PRI victory.

Compared with other populous oil states like Nigeria or Iran, Mexico was not yet in critical trouble. But observers who remembered the violence of 1968 questioned whether the established system would be able to absorb the demands for change that socioeconomic stress created. Mexico had escaped military dominance, but its problems were not very different from those of Brazil and Argentina.

Cuba: Social Revolution Without an End to Dependence

The small countries of Central America and the Caribbean have experienced many of the common Latin American problems—single-crop export economies, caudillo politics, inability to resist outside powers—with special sharpness, without matching the developmental successes of their larger neighbors. Yet Cuba achieved Latin America's most successful social revolution to date, and gave the first clear sign that superpower dominance could be altered, if not escaped. How did this happen?

Whence the Cuban Revolution?

By the nineteenth century, Cuba had discovered its vocation as a producer of cane sugar and, secondarily, tobacco. A slave-based plantation economy suddenly blossomed, and by 1860 Cuba was producing almost one-third of the world's sugar.

Preoccupied with economic growth, Cuba's landowners did not rebel against Spanish rule in the 1810s and 1820s, when most of Latin America did. A half century later, however, Cubans were resentful of Spanish domination and economically tied to the United States more than to Spain. A first rebellion (1868–1878) ended without independence from Spain. U.S. nationals had acquired control of the sugar industry by the time another rebellion broke out, and U.S. intervention forced Spain to concede Cuba's independence in 1898. Cuban revolutionaries opposed the U.S. role. What followed after "independence" showed why.

Cuba became independent under U.S. occupation. Americans intended to see that Cuban independence took a form compatible with U.S. interests. They did not seem to realize that their wishes might infringe on the "independence."

The first U.S. act was to disband the rebel forces. Improvements in public works and sanitation followed—most notably, the elimination of yellow fever, made possible by a Cuban doctor's discovery that mosquitoes carried the disease. The United States encouraged Cubans to draft a new constitution (1901), then forced them to add the Platt amendment, which gave Washington extensive rights, whence the U.S. naval base at Guantánamo Bay. "Independent" Cuba was really a U.S. protectorate.

Economically, the protectorate meant an increase in U.S. investment, from $50 million in 1896 to $1.5 billion in 1929. Cuba was more than ever a colonial economy, painfully vulnerable to variations in the size of the sugar harvest and its price. Export earnings in 1932, for example, were less than one-fifth 1924's earnings. During the Depression, U.S. investment, at least in the sugar industry, began to decline, and by the late 1950s, Cubans owned more than 60 percent of the industry, up from 22 percent in 1939. Cuba remained tied to the United States through special trade arrangements, however. From 1934 to 1960, a quota system gave Cuba a set share of the U.S. sugar market at prices above world market prices. In exchange, Cuba had to accept U.S. manufactures.

Cuba's dependence on the sugar industry had significant political and social effects. Just as the technology and capital requirements of sugar milling led to a concentration of ownership and management, the requirements of cane cultivation affected the Cuban populace. Sugar cane needs replanting only after five to twenty-five years. That fact means laborers get work during the three-month harvest season, and little or no work the rest of the year. Unable to buy or rent land because of the concentration of ownership, the rural populace faced a bleak future, especially as they were often kept in place by debt servitude.

Most rural Cubans were not typical peasants whose main goal was to acquire land, but rather were workers whose main concern was wages. Moreover, they were in touch with their urban counterparts. By the early 1930s, there was considerable migration between the countryside and urban slums. Partly because of improvements in public health, the population also grew rapidly, more than doubling between 1899 and 1931, to almost 4 million. By 1950, almost 40 percent of Cubans lived in cities, mostly in extreme privation. Cuba's workers, rural and urban, were ready for political mobilization. Who would lead them?

As elsewhere in Latin America, the Depression produced important political changes in Cuba, but only briefly did these seem to answer the question just posed. The Depression led to the overthrow of the brutal Machado regime (1925–1933). What emerged at his fall was an alliance of army sergeants, radical students, and Ramón Grau San Martín, who took charge of the civilian side of government.

At first, significant change appeared to be under way. Grau proclaimed a socialist revolution and abrogated the Platt amendment. His government produced much social legislation—the eight-hour day, creation of a labor department, votes for women. But it antagonized Washington when it suspended loan payments and seized sugar mills. Then the United States encouraged Fulgencio Batista, one of the army sergeants in the governing coalition, to overthrow Grau. Washington was ready to give up the

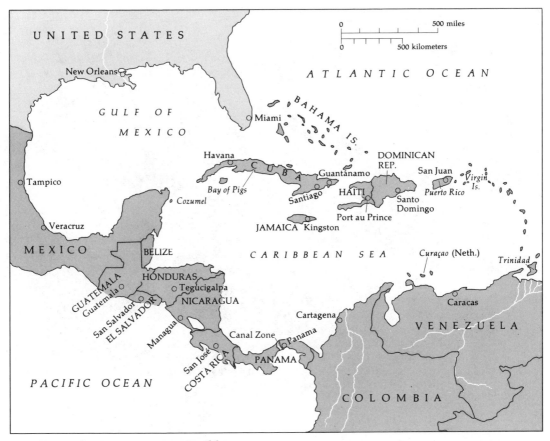

Map 14.1 The Contemporary Caribbean

Platt amendment, as it did by treaty in 1934, and was backing away from interventionism. But it had no hesitation in preferring a dictatorial regime that would collaborate with U.S. interests, to a democratic or populist regime that was economically nationalistic—especially if it talked of socialism. If anything, the abandonment of interventionism heightened the U.S. "need" for cooperative strong men, such as Batista.

Batista dominated Cuban politics through 1958. Sometimes he was the president. Sometimes others were his puppet presidents. Throughout the pe-

riod, corruption, violence, and popular disaffection marked political life.

Castro and the Revolution

Born in 1927, Fidel Castro grew up in the Batista era. While studying law, he became active in student politics. He mounted his first attack on the Batista regime on July 26, 1953, with an unsuccessful assault on a provincial army barracks. Fidel and his more radical brother, Raúl, survived but were sentenced to prison. Amnestied in 1955, Fi-

Cuba's Fidel Castro at the inauguration of President Ortega (right) and Vice President Ramírez (left) of Nicaragua, 1985.
Paolo Bosio/Gamma-Liaison

del fled to Mexico to plan a comeback. With him were Raúl and a young Argentine who would become one of the great martyrs of the revolutionary Left, Ernesto "Che" Guevara. In December 1956, Fidel set sail with eighty-one others to land in Cuba. Barely a dozen—including Fidel, Raúl, and Che—survived the landing, fleeing into the Sierra Maestra mountains to regroup their forces.

In the ensuing struggle, Batista proved to be his own worst enemy. His brutality alienated more and more Cubans, while Castro's guerrillas, like the Chinese Communists of the 1930s, had to learn how to operate among the people without alienating them. When Batista mounted a "liquidation campaign" into the Sierra Maestra, his army performed disas-

trously, and he fled. Castro's rebels, about three thousand strong, entered Havana at the beginning of 1959.

It took two more years to consolidate the revolution and define its character. In 1959, an initial episode of collegial rule ended with Castro in sole charge. An agrarian reform law expropriated farmland holdings over 1,000 acres and forbade foreigners to own agricultural land. Castro made two visits to the United States. He had not yet identified his regime with communism, but presented himself as a reformer. Yet the land reform law, and the accusations of Cuban refugees, made it hard to win good will. U.S.-backed operations by Cuban refugees began almost immediately.

In 1960, four major changes helped to

define Cuba's course. First, after a disagreement over U.S. oil refineries, Castro nationalized almost all of Cuban business and industry. The United States retaliated with an economic embargo and suspension of the sugar quota. Second, Cuba concluded a large trade agreement with the Soviet Union. Third, Castro laid the foundations for an authoritarian regime based on the army, the militia, local citizen groups known as Committees for the Defense of the Revolution, and controls over the press and almost all types of organizations. Mobilization became the watchword. Finally, the regime introduced an egalitarian social and economic policy, freezing prices, increasing wages, and launching a literacy campaign that halved the already low illiteracy rate (25 percent) in one year. In response, the United States severed diplomatic relations and, through the CIA, supported an abortive invasion by Cuban exiles at the Bay of Pigs (April 1961). The Soviet attempt to exploit this failure by placing missiles in Cuba led to the Cuban missile crisis of 1962, which ended with the withdrawal of Soviet missiles and a secret U.S. promise not to invade Cuba.

Meanwhile, in December 1961, Castro announced for the first time that he was a Marxist-Leninist. The statement proved epoch-making for several reasons. It signaled a shift in Cuba's dependency, from the United States to the Soviet Union. The choice of the Soviet model also facilitated what Castro perhaps most wanted: consolidation of his personal dominance. For other Third World countries, finally, here was something new on the Left. Instead of the complex developmental processes and struggles of either Marxism-Leninism or Maoism, Castro had shown that one could overthrow a government, simply announce that one was a communist, and so transform the position of one's country in the world. The pattern was hard to repeat in Latin America. Farther from the United States, in Africa, it found a number of imitators.

With its Marxist character set, Cuba experimented through the rest of the 1960s to define its policies. A second agrarian reform law (1963) made state farms the dominant form of cultivation. By 1965, Castro had also formed his revolutionary elite into a new Cuban Communist party. Meanwhile, debate raged over what to do about dependence on sugar. Che Guevara dominated the first phase of the debate with his Four-Year Plan for diversification and light industrialization, but the results soon proved disappointing. The emphasis shifted back to sugar then, with Castro prophesying that the harvest would reach a record 10 million tons in 1970.

Guevara now came out with an "idealist" strategy for reaching the new goal. His ideas recalled some of those of Mao Zedong in China. Guevara argued for a clean break with capitalism, total elimination of the market, and creation of a "new man," whose higher level of political consciousness would satisfy him with moral rather than material incentives. In this idealist view, consolidating the revolution in Cuba also required promoting it elsewhere—whence the international guerrilla strategy that led Che to his death in Bolivia in 1967. Not everyone agreed with Guevara. Some Cuban leaders advocated a more pragmatic approach, and the Soviet Union had little use for Guevara's pretensions to international revolutionary leadership. Castro began to back away from Che's view in international affairs in 1968, but held to it in domestic policy until 1970, when the cane harvest reached 8.5 million tons. That was an all-time record, but short of the goal that the idealist strategy was supposed to reach.

Recognizing the need for a change, Castro made a dramatic speech, taking blame for the failure to meet the goal and offering to resign. The crowd shouted *no*. Castro remained in power, but changed policy. With the adoption of more up-to-date techniques of economic planning and the reintroduction of material incentives, economic growth accelerated to over 10 percent a year from 1971 to 1975.

Other measures of the 1970s showed a new concern to expand political participation in ways compatible with the regime's character. For instance, Castro made changes in the labor movement and the Communist party to broaden their social bases. In December 1975, the party held its first congress. The next year, a new constitution instituted a system of Assemblies of Popular Power, with the directly elected members of the municipal assemblies electing members of the provincial assemblies and the national assembly. Cubans still could not form political organizations at will, and many elections were not conducted by secret ballot. But there were more opportunities for discussion of issues and greater mobilization into mass organizations. An official Cuban Women's Federation came into being, and a Family Code (1976) mandated equal division of household tasks—a departure from *machismo* but more on paper than in practice. The policy shift of the 1970s affected international relations, as other Latin American nations resumed diplomatic relations with Cuba, and demands to do so grew in the United States. The main obstacle, from the U.S. viewpoint, was Cuban intervention in Africa in the 1970s, and in the Caribbean basin in the 1980s.

Twenty-five years after he assumed power, Castro still presided over Latin America's most successful social revolution, although its accomplishments had limits. Cuba had altered its place in the world, but was still dependent on one of the superpowers. On the positive side, the Soviet Union was geographically remote and never acquired the stake in the Cuban economy that the United States once had. Cuba had still not diversified its economy. Sugar remained the mainstay, and the hazards of foreign markets had still to be faced: in some years, the Soviet price for sugar has been less than the world market price. With reason, not everyone was happy. Many Cubans continued to flee the island. Over the years, the virtual disappearance of the opposition helped consolidate the revolution. Even so, the government was thought in the late 1970s to be holding 20,000 political prisoners.

Yet this summary cannot capture the significance of the revolution. For most Cubans, the urban and rural workers who fared so poorly before 1959, the revolution meant improvement. Living standards rose. Illiteracy almost vanished. The establishment of a comprehensive school system gave many Cubans new power to shape their lives. The regime's record in economic growth was not impressive, but progress in equalizing distribution of available resources was significant. Over twenty years, improvements in public health increased life expectancy from sixty-three to seventy-three years, while the infant mortality rate fell by over two-thirds. The regime did more for women, on a formal level, than any other in Latin America. The government tolerated no dissent. For many of Cuba's 11 million people and for many elsewhere who learned about their experience, however, the important things about the Cuban revolution were its accomplishments.

Nicaragua and the Sandinista Revolution

For years, outsiders saw the small countries of Central America as places where issues of any significance, such as the Panama Canal or banana and coffee exports, lay in U.S. control. In fact, the Central American republics have many differences, but they also share many problems that follow from their weakness and their domination by the United States. Today the outside world can no longer ignore them, as the recent history of Nicaragua illustrates.

At the dawn of the twentieth century, Nicaragua was under the rule of dictator José Santos Zelaya (1893–1909). He patterned his regime after that of Díaz in Mexico and ruled in close alliance with local landowners and foreign interests. For the United States, one problem about Zelaya was his aim to unify Central America under his control. In 1909, a revolution broke out with U.S. backing, and Zelaya was replaced by a new president who had formerly worked for a U.S. mining company. When revolution threatened his regime in 1912, he called in U.S. troops, who occupied the country until 1932.

In reaction against a disputed presidential election, in which the United States interfered, a young Nicaraguan military officer, Augusto Sandino, rebelled in 1927 and took to the hills. For the next five years, he waged guerrilla war against both U.S. forces and the National Guard. A cultivated man from a wealthy family, Sandino had acquired his anti-Americanism while working for U.S. companies. He became a folk hero. The U.S. Marines could not find him or his followers among the peasants, and the Marines' bombing of peasant villages simply increased their support for him. Partly because of the Depression, partly to be in a better position to denounce the Japanese aggression of 1931 in Manchuria, the United States finally withdrew from Nicaragua, arranging for a presidential election to be held. Having promised to negotiate after the Marines left, Sandino emerged to meet the new president. After one such meeting, the National Guard commander, General Anastasio Somoza, had Sandino shot.

Somoza, his family, and the National Guard dominated Nicaragua for the next forty years. Educated in the United States, enthusiastic for all things American, and married into a Nicaraguan family of elite status, Somoza would stop at nothing to reach the presidency. In 1937, he seized the office, holding it until his death in 1956. Thereafter, his two sons took over.

In Managua stood the presidential palace, with the much-used torture chamber in its basement and the U.S. embassy next door. Eventually the Somozas and their cronies owned a fourth of the country's farmland. The government was blatantly a system to enrich the oligarchy, not to develop the country. U.S. officials were well aware of the corruption and occasionally lectured Somoza about it. But on balance, the Somozas' willingness to cooperate with the United States and their loud anticommunism made them too useful to give up. During the Alliance for Progress, Nicaragua received large amounts of aid, even though it was known that the required plans for reform were not implemented, and the money was going into private pockets. After the devastating earthquake of 1972, the Nicaraguan treasury could account for only half the U.S. aid funds, but National Guard officers were seen profiteering in emergency medical supplies, while the Somozas and their intimates made huge profits out of reconstruction.

In opposition to this corrupt dictatorship, the National Sandinista Liberation Front (FSLN in Spanish) began a terrorism campaign in 1966. Like Sandino, from whom it took its name, the group gained great support among the peasants. Soon, other sectors of society—business and the church—also turned against the regime and its abuses. For a while, the National Guard was successful against the FSLN, which lost several leaders and split into three groups. But the Guard had no hold on the loyalties of the people.

Eventually, as in Iran at the same time, President Carter's human rights policy also played a part in undermining the regime. To challenge an unpopular regime to ease repression of its opponents while doing nothing to promote reform of the problems that make the regime unpopular is to court revolution. Fearing the FSLN, the United States then made things worse by resuming arms shipments to the Somoza regime as soon as it eased repression at all. Meanwhile, the guerrillas grew more daring, their support increased, and the last Somoza president, Anastasio, Jr., responded more brutally than ever. By 1979, risings against the government were occurring spontaneously, and Venezuela, Mexico, Costa Rica, and Panama joined Cuba in supporting the FSLN. In late June, even the United States had to admit that it was all over.

Subsequent events were reminiscent of postrevolutionary Cuba. The Sandinistas quickly attacked basic social problems like illiteracy and disease. Nationalizing the holdings of the Somozas and their associates gave them a start on land reform. In 1980, they enacted an agrarian reform law that redistributed much land in cooperatives, but left large estates that were in productive use intact. The Nicaraguans also created organizations through which to mobilize the populace. The largest was the Sandinista Defense Committee, which by the mid-1980s claimed a membership of 500,000, or about one-sixth of the population. The Sandinistas, too, established an extremely close party-state identification. As Castro had done in 1959, they tried to avoid a break with the United States in foreign policy. It is true that they accepted 2,500 Cuban specialists in health care, education, and engineering, as well as Cuban military personnel to help defend the country against the expected counterrevolutionary attacks. But they also accepted aid from the United States in 1980, and larger sums from Western Europe. Initially, they welcomed U.S. business interests back into the country and—something revolutionaries seldom do—accepted responsibility for the debts of the Somoza regime. Castro had warned the Sandinistas not to follow Cuba's footsteps, but to retain a large private business sector and as many financial ties as possible to the United States.

Signs of moderation in Managua could not overcome U.S. antipathy toward revolutionary regimes, especially in Latin America. As happened earlier in Cuba, this problem generated conflict between the two countries and pushed Nicaragua to the left. When the United States cut off aid in 1981, the country moved toward a controlled economy along Eastern European lines, even though Nicaraguan leaders acknowledged that U.S. opposition would prevent them from accomplishing their developmental goals. Economic difficulties contributed to a split in the revolutionary leadership. One of its responses was to postpone elections—another step displeasing to Washington. As Nicaraguans feared, the CIA tried to destabilize the regime and supported its armed opponents, the *contras*, much as it had used anti-Castro Cubans.

By the time that Nicaragua's presidential election occurred in November 1984, the Sandinista regime had become increasingly authoritarian, though to a lesser degree than Castro's Cuba. The fact that a half dozen parties, representing a wide political spectrum, participated in the election, showed some openness. Still, given the Sandinistas' extensive mobilization apparatus, no one was surprised when their candidate, Daniel Ortega, won the presidency with 63 percent of the vote.

As U.S. opposition to the Sandinistas continued despite the questions of many U.S. citizens, the final outcome in Nicaragua remains difficult to predict. This tiny country may prove, as Iran has, that the possibilities of great-power dominance are no longer what they once were. Or, despite Castro's warning, Nicaragua may alter its place in the global configuration as Cuba has. Or the Sandinista revolution may end as another story of the shark and the sardines.

Conclusion

In forty years following World War II, Latin America moved through two historical phases and appeared about to begin a third. Import-substitution indus-trialization and democratizing mass mobilization set the trend through the early 1960s. The weakness of Latin America's democratic institutions, the exhaustion of import substitution, the political stresses of the 1960s, and the military emphasis of U.S. policy then led to a turn toward military authoritarianism and economic neocolonialism. With the 1980s came a trend back toward civilian rule. Whether this will mean mass mobilization and economic development in the interest of the people is uncertain. Alternatively, the demands of the debt crisis may simply bring into the limelight the civilian technocrats who shaped the neocolonial economic programs of the military governments, in place of the generals.

The experiences of specific countries showed significant variations in the regional pattern. Some countries were too small to experience each developmental phase fully or, for that matter, to function effectively as nation-states. Cuba and Nicaragua overturned old-fashioned caudillo rule only when they took a revolutionary turn to the left. Even then, they could not escape dependency. Some larger states also introduced variations into the pattern of phases, while following it more fully. Mexico and Brazil became highly enough industrialized that they could be regarded as middle-sized industrial powers. Mexico also became a major petroleum producer, although events of the 1980s showed that the ability to export large amounts of oil—one more mineral resource—was not in itself a cure for dependency.

No state escapes dependence on others in some sense. The crux of the Latin American nations' problems has seemed to lie in coping with the needs of their growing populations while trying to profit from participation in a world economy in which none of these nations holds a leading position. A long history of internal and external colonialism has helped shape this problem, but the rapid social and economic changes of the late twentieth century have made solving it more difficult than ever before. If Latin America's record has been this disappointing, have other parts of the Third World fared better?

Notes

1. Juan-José Arévalo, *The Shark and the Sardines*, trans. June Cobb and Raúl Osegueda (New York: Stuart L. Stuart, 1961).

Suggestions for Further Reading

Burns, E. Bradford, *A History of Brazil*, 2d ed. (1980).

Domínguez, Jorge I., *Cuba: Order and Revolution* (1978).

Keen, Benjamin, and Mark Wasserman, *A Short History of Latin America* (1984).

LaFeber, Walter, *Inevitable Revolutions: The United States in Central America* (1983).

Loveman, Brian, *Chile: The Legacy of Hispanic Capitalism* (1979).

Meyer, Michael C., and William L. Sherman, *The Course of Mexican History*, 2d ed. (1983).

Page, Joseph A., *Perón: A Biography* (1983).

Paz, Octavio, *The Other Mexico: Critique of the Pyramid*, trans. Lysander Kemp (1972).

Scobie, James R., *Argentina: A City and a Nation*, 2d ed. (1971).

Shafer, Robert Jones, *A History of Latin America* (1978).

Skidmore, Thomas E., and Peter H. Smith, *Modern Latin America* (1984).

Newspapers and Periodicals

Christian Science Monitor.
Latin American Newsletters.
Latin American Regional Reports.
New York Times.
Wall Street Journal.

Chapter 15

SUB-SAHARAN AFRICA: DEVELOPMENT OR COLLAPSE?

Since World War II, sub-Saharan Africa has passed through two historical phases. The years from 1945 to 1960 were the twilight of colonialism. The years since 1960—the period emphasized in this chapter—have been ones of formal independence, and neocolonialism. The record of the first quarter-century of African independence has proved disappointing, for many reasons. The African societies' lack of preparation for independence created some frustrations. Others stemmed from a combination of human and environmental problems for which neither Africans nor outsiders were prepared. At the end of this chapter, we shall attempt to sum up the contributing factors more fully. But first we shall consider the African experience as a whole and then look more closely at the continent's two largest countries, Nigeria and South Africa.

Continental Overview: The Hungry South par Excellence

Europeans established their dominance over sub-Saharan Africa very abruptly, at a time when enthusiasm for imperialism ran high among the great powers, and when European economies were the strongest in the world. The costs of taking control during this "scramble for Africa" were relatively low. By 1945, conditions had changed so much, and African nationalism had been so stimulated by experiences of the war years, that colonial rule ended even more suddenly than it had begun. The largest colonial powers, Britain and France, made some preparations for the transition. For example, Britain passed colonial development and welfare acts in 1940 and 1945, and France provided larger amounts of aid after the war. Some smaller colonial powers, like Belgium, failed to anticipate the end. Others, like Portugal, tried to hold on. Still, decolonization worked its way across the continent, leaving fifty-one independent countries, most of which gained independence in the early 1960s. Experience quickly showed how unprepared most of them were to face their demographic, economic, and political problems.

The Spread of Independence

The decolonization of sub-Saharan Africa began in 1956, when the Sudan, theoretically under joint Anglo-Egyptian rule, won its independence as a by-product of the Egyptian revolution of 1952. The next countries to become independent were in British West Africa—Gambia, Sierra Leone, Gold Coast, and Nigeria. They had few European settlers to contend with, and their black populations had benefited from greater opportunities to acquire education and political experience than were available in many other colonies. There were also some outstanding political leaders, no-

tably Kwame Nkrumah, under whom Ghana (formerly the Gold Coast) became the first West African country to achieve independence (1957).

Soon, French Africa also won independence. France was preoccupied with colonial struggles in Indochina (1946–1954) and Algeria (1954–1962). The latter conflict tied up as many as half a million French troops. Their resentments and those of French settlers in Algeria set the stage for the overthrow of France's Fourth Republic in 1958 and the advent of the Fifth. President De Gaulle then provided the leadership for decolonization, eventually in Algeria (1962), and immediately in France's other colonies, to which he offered a range of options. Guinea, under Sékou Touré, chose immediate independence in 1958. By the early 1960s, fourteen former French colonies had become independent, mostly as republics within a new French community.

Past this point, independence came less smoothly. In the Belgian Congo (now Zaire), Belgium failed to foresee that it could not hold on indefinitely. When faced with nationalist opposition, it realized that it lacked power to resist. The result was an abrupt grant of independence on June 30, 1960, and the immediate outbreak of civil war, as Katanga (now Shaba) province, with its rich copper mines, attempted to secede. By the time order was restored, the country had passed under the dictatorship of General Joseph Mobutu (1965)—one of many postindependence military takeovers.

In eastern and southern Africa, the presence of white settler communities complicated the transition to independence in some countries. In Kenya, where much of the best land was in large settler farms, the lands of the Kikuyu people were inadequate to support them and were becoming exhausted as a result. These pressures produced the Mau Mau rebellion of 1952–1956, which the British repressed with thousands of casualities. Still, Kenya, Tanganyika, and Uganda became independent under black rule in the early 1960s. The island nation of Zanzibar, becoming independent in 1963, joined with Tanganyika on the mainland to form Tanzania in 1964. A key factor in the smooth transition to black rule in East Africa was the care that leaders like Kenya's Jomo Kenyatta and Tanzania's Julius Nyerere took to reassure whites that the change would not hurt them.

Farther south, the British attempted to form a federation of Northern and Southern Rhodesia and Nyasaland, whose economies were interdependent. By the early 1960s, the British had decided on independence on a basis of one person, one vote. This decision broke the federation, for the white minorities in the two Rhodesias feared black domination. Nyasaland became independent as Malawi in 1964. Northern Rhodesia, despite white opposition, became independent under black rule as Zambia in 1964. Southern Rhodesia—where whites then formed 7 percent of the population, against 3 percent in Northern Rhodesia—followed a different course at first. The whites attempted to preserve their dominance with a unilateral declaration of independence in 1965. International opinion opposed the move, as did nationalist movements based largely among the Shona (Zimbabwe African Nationalist Union, ZANU) and the Ndebele peoples (Zimbabwe African People's Union, ZAPU). The white regime held out until 1980, when it too had to yield. Southern Rhodesia then turned into Zimbabwe under a government headed by Robert Mugabe, the ZANU leader. Although a professed Marxist, he took steps to reassure whites, whose economic roles remained crucial, even as he began to turn the state into a one-party regime. After 1980, South Africa, with its exceptionally large white minority, remained the last holdout of the settler regimes.

Portugal's resistance delayed independence for its colonies. In Angola, where violent outbreaks began in 1961, the independence movement soon divided into several parties. Nationalist violence broke out in 1962 in Portuguese Guinea (now Guinea-Bissau), and in 1964 in Mozambique, where there was a single nationalist party (FRELIMO, Portuguese acronym for Mozambican Liberation Front). Fighting dragged on into the 1970s, draining the Portuguese economy. Independence finally came in 1975 with an army mutiny that overthrew Portugal's government. In Mozambique, FRELIMO took over, setting up a Marxist government still in place in the mid-1980s.

Meanwhile, several parties contended for power in Angola, with foreign governments supporting their favorites. The United States, South Africa, China, the Soviet Union, and Cuba all intervened. The Angolan civil war became the largest-scale foreign intervention in Africa since decolonization began. By 1976, the Cuban-backed MPLA (Popular Movement for the Liberation of Angola) had come out on top, establishing a Marxist government that remains in power in the

▶

Map 15.1 Political Independence in Africa and Asia
The countries marked with an asterisk (*) on the map became independent in stages: Egypt in 1922, 1936, 1954; Iraq in 1932, 1947; and Lebanon and Syria in 1941–1945.

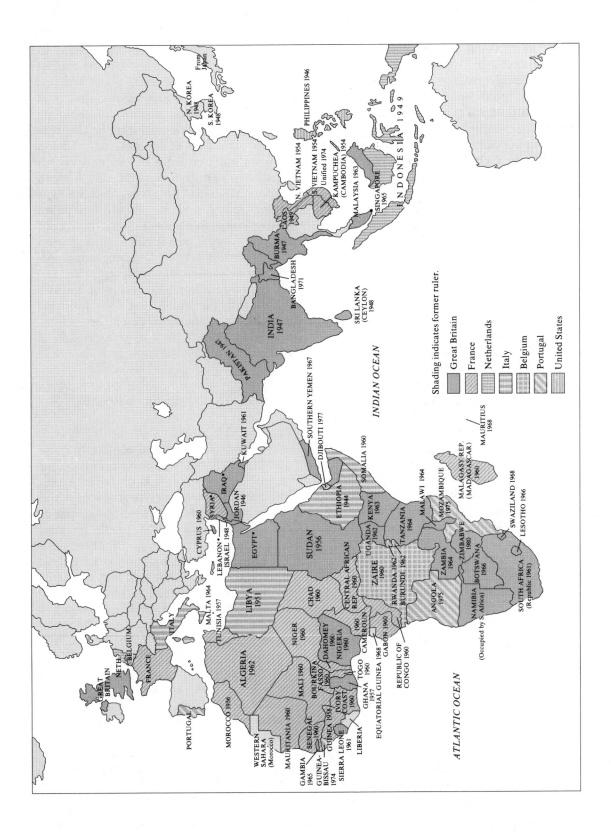

mid-1980s. About 25,000–30,000 Cuban troops stayed in Angola, protecting the government from domestic opposition as much as from South Africa. Tensions with South Africa continued over its military intervention in Angola, and over Angolan support for the Southwest African People's Organization (SWAPO) in Namibia, which remained under South African control.

As all of Africa but its southernmost tip achieved independence under majority rule, a number of common problems stood out. Given the artificiality of the colonial boundaries, it was striking how often they survived as national borders. Yet national integration proved difficult to achieve. Because virtually no African country had a cohesive population, political conflict among a nation's ethnic groups has been extremely common. All across West Africa are countries that have mostly Muslim peoples in the north and, in the south, linguistically distinct peoples who are either Christian or believe in indigenous religions. These countries, like many others in Africa, have experienced the kind of regional tensions that we shall see in Nigeria.

Although African nationalism had for many years expressed goals of regional or pan-African integration, those objectives remained less influential than nationalist goals. The Organization of African States (OAU) was established in 1963, and some succesful regional organizations have emerged. For example, most of the former French colonies belong to the West African Monetary Union (Union Monétaire Quest-Africaine, UMOA). With a common central bank and currency, which is linked to and convertible with the French franc, the UMOA spares its member states many of the monetary problems that most poor countries suffer. At the continental level, the OAU has been fairly successful in economic or social affairs. But its consistent inability to end armed conflicts has highlighted the limits of international African solidarity. Some of Kwame Nkrumah's experiences clarify the reasons for this lack of success. After Ghana won its independence, he turned his attention to pan-Africanism. Other African leaders thought, however, that he was trying to expand his small Ghanaian power base. Such suspicions have kept regional and pan-African integration from gaining greater momentum. Although most African countries lacked potential to function effectively as nation-states, they became Africa's key political entities once the leaders of the nationalist movements took over as heads of independent governments.

Africa's Population Explosion

Population growth was probably the most important problem confronting the new states. Africa's population problems resembled those of Asia or Latin America, but produced more severe social and economic effects. Population statistics are unreliable for Africa, partly because census taking can raise political tensions if it shows that the balance among rival ethnic groups has changed. But available estimates indicate that Africa had about 224 million people in 1954 and about 531 million in 1984. Africa then had the highest population growth rate of any continent.

Africa's population growth raised many problems. One was large-scale migration, both from rural to urban areas and across national borders. By 1960 estimates, one-fourth of all wage laborers in sub-Saharan Africa had been born in a colony or country different from their current residence. As for urban growth, in the mid-1980s no sub-Saharan African city was as large as the largest in Latin America, although Cairo, Egypt, had an estimated 14 million people. But urban growth rates were extremely high. By the late 1970s, Algiers (Algeria), Casablanca (Morocco), Abidjan (Ivory Coast), Lagos (Nigeria), Addis Ababa (Ethiopia), Soweto, and Johannesburg (both in South Africa) each had populations over a million. Kinshasa (Zaire) stood at 2.1 million. In 1984, Africa was the only inhabited continent, except Australia, with just one city larger than 5 million (Cairo). But if current rates of growth continue, it will have twenty-five cities that large by 2025, whereas Latin America will have only fifteen.

In fact, Africa's present rates of population growth and urbanization cannot go on unchecked. Many African cities are products of European imperialism, with sanitation and transportation facilities little expanded beyond the limited needs of the colonial era.

Throughout the continent, meanwhile, unemployment and poverty have created social and medical problems that challenge family structure and social discipline. For example, in the early 1980s, Ethiopia had a literacy rate as low as 15 percent, although figures as high as 50 percent were common elsewhere. In 1981, Africa combined the highest birth rate of any continent with the lowest life expectancy: fifty years, compared with seventy-five years for the most developed industrialized countries. Africa's infant mortality rate was 123 per thousand, compared with 11 per thousand for the most advanced industrial countries in 1981.

As in any case of rapid population growth, a large part of Africa's population was very young. In the West African countries, 40 to 50 percent of the population was under age fifteen in the 1970s. As a result, some of the most serious social problems clustered around youth-related issues: inadequate educational facilities, too few jobs for graduates, distinctive forms of political activism, crime, or violence. Even an Afro-Marxist regime, like that of Congo-Brazzaville (the former French Congo), might be denounced by the student left as neocolonial. In Soweto—officially not a city, but a government-planned shantytown for the black work force not permitted to live in Johannesburg—youth gangs were so violent by 1984 that the police were afraid to go out in the streets at night.

Economic Development in Reverse?

The gravest consequences of population growth were economic and ecological. As late as 1970, Africa essentially fed itself. By 1984, over a quarter of all Africans— 140 million—were vitally dependent on imported grains. Africa had become the Hungry South par excellence. Most African economies performed poorly, not just in agriculture, but in all respects. Between 1979 and 1981, World Bank statistics indicate that eighteen of the fifty-one African countries were increasing their gross domestic product no faster than 3 percent per year.* At that rate,

---

* A country's *gross domestic product* (GDP) is the total market value of all final goods and services produced in the country during a year, without allowance for earnings paid abroad or received from abroad, but including income earned by foreigners in the country. *Gross national product* (GNP) is the same measure, with the addition of income earned abroad by citizens of the country, and the exclusion of income earned inside the country by for-

their economic growth no more than kept even with population growth. Moreover, six of those eighteen countries had negative growth rates, a problem found in only two other countries, both Caribbean, during those years.

Many factors combined to depress Africa's economic performance, some of them dating back to the colonial past. The national boundaries had been drawn by outside powers whose interest in development did not go past the extraction of raw materials—a function that multinational corporations have continued since independence. Economically, as well as ethnically, most African countries lacked the makings of viable nation-states. Transportation and communication networks still reflected colonial purposes, so that even years after independence, telephone calls and airmail letters for a neighboring African country often had to go through Paris or London. Forms of corruption rooted in the impact of kinship ties on political life—a subject discussed further below—drained vast amounts of wealth from productive uses. Unequal income distributions were a problem everywhere. Why else would the Paris magazine *Jeune Afrique* (*Young Africa*), aimed at a French-speaking audience in this poor continent, carry advertisements for Mercedes-Benz automobiles, Cartier jewelry, and bullet-proof vests? In East Africa, Swahili speakers sarcastically referred to owners of Mercedes cars as an ethnic group, the "Wabenzi." Mining and industry suffered from a lack of highly trained personnel,

despite the expansion of education. As a result, outside South Africa, industrialization has hardly gone beyond limited import substitution, and most industries remain under foreign control. Political instability and civil war have also upset many countries. Finally, since only a handful of sub-Saharan countries—Angola, Gabon, Nigeria, Cameroon—were oil exporters, the oil price rises of the 1970s took a terrible toll. In Nigeria, so did the end of the oil boom of the 1980s.

Africa's worst problems, however, were agricultural. Some of these were inevitable—the aridity of the savanna, the infertility of rain-forest soils. But many were created by human beings— through unsound land-use practices, collectivization policies that reduced incentives to produce, or the government marketing boards. Supposedly set up to aid in marketing export crops, the boards forced farmers to sell at below-market prices. The boards thus became a means of indirect taxation, depressing production, as in Perón's Argentina. The worst agricultural problems, however, arose from the pressure of growing human populations on fragile environments.

By 1985, almost half of Africa's countries faced the prospect, and sometimes the fact, of mass starvation. Drought was the major immediate cause, but drought resulted largely from the mounting human pressure. Increased cutting of trees for firewood and overextension of cultivation had reduced the ability of the soil to retain moisture, accelerating rainwater runoff and soil erosion. These changes led in turn to possibly permanent disruption of the climatic patterns that had previously assured local rainfall—in short, to desertification. Although serious drought and famine had occurred in the early 1970s, African governments—and experts and policy mak-

---

eigners. Both concepts are ways of measuring a country's economic productivity. Only "final goods and services" are considered, because inclusion of intermediate products (for example, hides used to make shoes) would lead to double counting.

ers elsewhere—did not or could not check these consequences of unprecedented population growth in time to prevent their assuming catastrophic proportions. By then, relief efforts were too little and too late, offering no solution to the underlying problems.

Later in this chapter, we shall consider Africa's two largest economies. Both Nigeria and South Africa had GNPs of about $70 billion in 1981, and the two countries together accounted for about 60 percent of the combined GNP of all sub-Saharan countries. Here, to suggest the dimensions of Africa's problems more fully, we shall briefly consider a case from the less-favored end of the economic spectrum.

Among the many countries we could choose, Ethiopia is one of the most interesting and tragic. Until 1974, it retained its ancient monarchy, in which an ethnically Shoan Amhara aristocracy dominated a variety of other peoples, some of them hostile to Ethiopian rule. Economically, Ethiopia was unique in Africa in having a hierarchical feudal society with private landownership. Peasants were obliged to give service and anywhere from 25 to 80 percent of their crops to landlords, including the Coptic church. The drought and famine that ravaged much of Africa in the early 1970s caused 100,000 to 200,000 deaths in Ethiopia. Because the government of the aged emperor, Haile Selassie, did little more than try to suppress news of the disaster, protests arose that finally toppled his regime. In 1974, a body known as the *Derg* (committee) took power and overthrew the imperial regime.

Echoing the Cuban pattern, the Derg, once in power, gradually identified with Marxism-Leninism. In 1975, it began to nationalize the business sector and abolish private landownership, directing peasants to organize associations to carry out the land reform, and sending students into the countryside to assist in the process. What followed may well be Africa's closest approach so far to genuine social revolution.

What these efforts might have produced under favorable circumstances remained unclear, for famine conditions returned to Ethiopia in the early 1980s. By then, population growth had increased the demand for firewood until the forested area fell to 3 percent of the country, as opposed to 40 percent at the beginning of the century. For want of wood, peasants had to dry the droppings of their animals to use for fuel, so losing their only source of fertilizer. The growing food needs of the population, together with this loss of fertilizer, led to overcultivation, which, with deforestation, increased erosion. U.S. aid officials calculated as early as 1978 that Ethiopia lost a billion tons of top-soil a year through erosion and was headed for agricultural disaster unless something was done. Responding more to ideological than to practical considerations, the Derg government committed itself in 1979 to collectivization of agriculture, even though Soviet and Chinese experience should have made clear that collectivization offered no key to increased productivity. Separatist conflicts in both north and south also distracted the government from agricultural needs, as did prestige projects like the lavish celebration of its tenth anniversary in 1984.

Famine had become widespread by 1984, aggravated by virtual collapse of an overexploited agricultural environment. Not unlike its imperial predecessor, the government minimized the extent of suffering and prevented relief to famine sufferers in regions of separatist conflict. By the end of 1984, observers estimated that as many people had already starved as in 1973–1974, and that 6 million Ethiopians were in dire need of food. The end was hardly in sight, for the airlifting of sacks of grain from North America and Europe could never produce a real solution. That would require some restoration of a sustainable equilibrium between population and environment.

Comparison with many other African countries, from Mauritania to Mozambique, would show that Ethiopia's problems are unusual only in degree. It seems clear, then, that no sub-Saharan economy—unless the white-dominated exploitative one in South Africa—has excelled those of Latin America in development. By a 1982 estimate, about a third of the African economies had actually declined since independence. For most of them, food was the central problem. In global perspective, the African food problem may be only a warning of

Famine in Ethiopia. Refugees huddled in the morning cold at Korem Camp, 1985. A permanent solution for their problems would require far more than relief efforts.
Sebastiao Salgado, Jr./Magnum

what will happen elsewhere if human beings do not find ways to limit the stress that their growing numbers impose on the natural environment. We shall return to this question in Chapter 18.

Political Evolution: Common Phases and Themes

The political evolution of the independent African regimes was almost as problematic as their economic development. Partly because they were not well prepared for independence, partly because they had to adapt borrowed forms to the African environment, these new governments tended to pass through a common set of developmental phases marked by recurrent themes: overcentralized and ineffective governmental institutions, shared ideological preferences, ethnic tensions, and similar problems in relations with the outside world.

The political phases commonly began, in countries that had been under British rule, with an independent government headed by a prime minister responsible to the legislature. As in Great Britain, if the prime minister could not muster a parliamentary majority on a key vote, that government fell from office. These countries generally became independent as members of the British Commonwealth.

Most countries that began with a prime minister quickly changed, however, to a government headed by a president. The former French colonies began their independent life with this phase. The advantages of this system were that the president's tenure in office did not depend on the ability to command a parliamentary majority, and that the constitution could define presidential powers as extremely broad, even greater than those of the U.S. president. Ghana blazed the trail into this second phase. Nkrumah obtained a new constitution in 1960, under which he assumed the presidency, with vast powers over the budget and other legislation. He created a virtual presidential dictatorship, of a sort that has become widespread in the Third World.

The next phase was to move toward one-party government by abolishing all parties other than the one in power. Nkrumah did this in 1964 by making his Convention People's party the sole legal one. Most other African countries followed suit. We shall offer an explanation of this phenomenon in discussing the impact of regional and ethnic tensions on political life.

In the fourth phase in postindependence political life, a military dictatorship replaced the civilian presidency. In some countries, as in Ghana after the military overthrew Nkrumah in 1966, power shifted back and forth between military and civilians several times. Overall, however, the militarization of African politics has been unmistakable. The number of military governments has risen from two in 1963 to ten in 1968, eighteen in 1973, and twenty-four in 1984. Several factors contributed to this militarization. Colonial rule was imposed by force and often carried out by military officers. After independence, many African coup-makers were European-trained officers. Such officers had little difficulty seizing control of a weakly institutionalized government that lacked a strong tradition of military subordination to civilian authority.

As the military came to power, it became politicized. The most recent coups have tended to be the work of younger men of lower rank overturning generals or colonels. The younger men have been less likely than earlier military interventionists to shed their uniforms after taking over, or to promise a return to civilian rule. Lieutenant Jerry Rawlings, then in his early thirties, led two successful coups in Ghana in 1979 and 1981. Sergeant Samuel K. Doe led the 1980 coup that overthrew Africa's oldest republican government, that of Liberia, before he reached the age of thirty. The younger coup makers have argued that the corruption of the civilian presidents has discredited democracy—although the military are hardly immune to the same failing.

In each phase—parliamentary government, presidential republic, single-party dictatorship, and military rule—most governments showed only limited political or administrative capacity. A common attribute of underdevelopment, this problem had many manifestations. Governments were unable or unwilling to conduct an impartial election or an accurate census, to implement effective family planning or agricultural development programs, or to adopt more than rudimentary forms of revenue collection, such as the compulsory marketing boards that served essentially to tax exports. In most African countries, the excessive size of the public sector, and the lavish perquisites it inherited from colonial days, both reflected and compounded governmental inefficiency. On the positive side, it is worth noting that few African regimes have been as repressive as some found on other continents. Only a couple of other African regimes— like that of Jean Bedel Bokassa in the Central African Republic—have rivaled the violence of Uganda under Idi Amin, who killed over a hundred thousand Ugandans before his fall in 1979.

As the various states emerged, African rulers, civilian or military, justified their rule by official ideologies. Many of these were socialist in one of two senses.

The first was a fuzzy populist socialism that had little to do with Marx. Instead it reflected the desire for a program of mass mobilization and development, a program expressly suited for Africa. Formative influences on populist socialism have included Pan-Africanism and the idealization of African identity (négritude) by writers such as Aimé Césaire, a French-speaking West Indian of African ancestry, and Léopold Senghor, president of Senegal from 1960 to 1980 and a French-language poet of international distinction. Their notion of négritude had counterparts in Nkrumah's idea of "African personality," and in a widespread concern for authenticity that led, for example, to many name changes. The Congo became Zaire, Leopoldville became Kinshasa, and Joseph-Désiré Mobutu became Mobutu Sese Seko. Sometimes dismissed as "tinsel" modernization, this concern for authenticity was no doubt a needed adjustment to a new order, much as the re-evaluation of blackness in the United States was an adaptation to the conditions that the civil rights movement created. Julius Nyerere of Tanzania developed one of the most widely admired populist socialisms with his concept of ujamaa, or kinship communalism. There and elsewhere, one reason for the appeal of populist socialism was that it was easy to identify it with the communalistic heritage of African societies, even if historical fact sometimes got bent in the process.

The other type of African socialism was closer to Marxism-Leninism and has been called Afro-Marxism. The phenomenon was largely a by-product of the peculiar sequence of events in Cuba. Contrary to Marxist-Leninist assumptions, the revolution came first, then Castro announced that he was a Marxist-Leninist, then the regime created a new Communist party. Starting in Congo-Brazzaville in 1968–1969, a similar phenomenon appeared in Africa, as ruling military groups simply announced the advent of Marxism in a number of countries—Somalia (1970), Benin (1974), Madagascar and Ethiopia (1975–1976), Mozambique and Angola (1977).

The Afro-Marxist regimes were Leninist primarily in their concept of the party. It was not to be a mass movement, as in the populist-socialist regimes, but an ideologically pure elite vanguard that embodied the will of the masses. The most consistently Marxist-Leninist behavior of these regimes appeared in foreign affairs. Otherwise, they did not pursue pure Marxist-Leninist policies. Most of them—except Ethiopia—steered clear of agricultural collectivization, having observed the problems it created for the populist socialists. In other fields of economic policy, the Afro-Marxist regimes typically sought to create a state-controlled sector and nationalized foreign interests regarded as vestiges of colonialism. At the same time, however, almost all of them tried to attract new Western investment. In 1980, for example, Angola depended on Gulf Oil, a dominant firm in the international oil industry, for almost all its government revenue and foreign exchange, and used Cuban troops to guard Gulf's operations. In Zimbabwe, the Marxism of the Mugabe regime did not keep it from trying to reassure an economically indispensable white minority, or even from collaborating in some respects with the South African archenemy. The record of Afro-Marxism strikingly illustrates the variability of Marxism in the Hungry South. The lim-

ited economic rewards of collaborating with the Soviets heightened this variability, as we shall see.

Pre-existing sociopolitical patterns governed the political behavior of African regimes as much as did official ideologies. The political parties and movements that grew up in the various countries before independence were mostly regional, rather than national, in scope, and represented one or a few, but not all, of the peoples living in the country. The hasty organization of postindependence political life according to imported models meant giving power to one of these parties, or perhaps a coalition, and casting the others in the role of opposition. We shall see how this worked out in Nigeria, but there are many other examples.

Liberal democracies assume that all citizens are equal as voters—one person, one vote—and that the political parties succeed each other in office. The parties differ on matters of policy and political philosophy, but are all equally loyal to the political system, so that those out of office assume the role of "loyal opposition." But what happens if the primary loyalty of voters and parties is not to the nation and its constitutionally defined political system, but to their own ethnic groups or regions? Then there can be no loyal opposition, and the political victory of any party is likely to mean that a single sectional interest has captured the entire government. The importance of ethnic identifications helps to explain why Robert Mugabe's ZANU government in Zimbabwe, based among the Shona people, has been more lenient to the whites than to Joshua Nkomo's ZAPU movement. For ZAPU represents the Ndebele minority, who are potential rivals, as the whites no longer are, for control of the country. More generally, the political impact of ethnic conflict helps explain the shift to authoritarian presidential systems, which reduce the meaning of all forms of voting, as well as the preference for single-party rule, which gets rid of opposition parties.

But there is more to the intolerance of opposition than this. Many African leaders have pointed out that in kinship-based societies, decision making was conducted by discussion among the group's elders. The object was to achieve a consensus, after which no member would be allowed to oppose the group decision. The decision-making process progressively eliminated disageement, so that the decision could be regarded as unanimous. In the past, this kind of decision making was not unique to Africa, but characterized kinship societies in many places, including rural prerevolutionary Russia and the Middle East. Modern analysts cite this tradition of decision making as a reason for intolerance of political opposition today. In Africa, this intolerance goes so far that even the secret ballot, viewed in Europe or the United States as an indispensable safeguard of democracy, may be seen as "un-African," a suspect innovation.

Africa's problems with political corruption also stem from the tradition of the kinship society. Indeed, behavior that appears corrupt to us may not seem so to Africans who perpetrate it. Kinship societies traditionally tended to hold much property in common, and a major function of leadership was to distribute the group's wealth among its members. In such an environment, a ruler would head a great household, supporting many dependents, dispensing much hospitality, and seldom distinguishing between personal property and public goods.

Given this outlook, postindependence politics turned into a contest among parties based in specific regions or ethnic groups to control the entire country and parcel out its benefits as if they were those of the group's ancestral lands. Politicians saw no distinction between public funds and their personal compensation. At best, it would take time for their behavior to adjust to a situation that called for new standards. In the meantime, politics degenerated into runaway patronage, rampant misuse of public funds, and manipulation of political power to acquire private wealth. For example, after Nigeria's military coup of December 31, 1983, it was reported that an official of the fallen government had a house in England with a gold bathtub appraised at $5 million. The fact that the story was widely believed, whether true or not, gives some sense of the stakes of the political game in one of Africa's largest and wealthiest countries. The worst of the problem, to cite a point that Nigerian novelist Chinua Achebe made in his novel, *A Man of the People*, was that anyone who attacked the corruption of the leadership would be suspected of wanting to take power and follow their example.

How Africa's states could move beyond local loyalties to national integration remained unclear in the mid-1980s. For the time being, ethnic and regional interests prevailed, so much that British visitors were startled to hear people say they would like "the Queen to come back." Such wishes expressed the frustrations accumulated over a quarter-century of independence. They also expressed the need for an authority that could stand above petty interests, impartially embodying national unity.

Africa and Outside Powers

No single outside power has as much influence in independent Africa as the United States has in Latin America. However, a survey of African affairs would be incomplete without a consideration of international relations.

Both Britain and France tried to maintain ongoing connections with former colonies—for example, through the Commonwealth of Nations and the West African Monetary Union (UMOA). Both countries also had large investments in former colonies. In 1980 British interests held about half of the $25 billion invested by foreigners in South Africa. Although the South African government was strong enough to defend itself against the problem of foreign dominance, the age of African independence was typically also one of neocolonialism. The Ivory Coast, long an African "miracle" economy, had 150,000 foreign business people at work among a population of eight million in the early 1980s. Libyan and French intervention in the long-running civil war in Chad illustrated neocolonialism militarily.

Superpower rivalries also had their impact. Seeing the African independence movements of the 1950s and 1960s as a chance to advance its influence, the Soviet Union provided some of them with arms and military assistance. Eventually, however, African populist-socialist leaders either dissatisfied the Soviets ideologically or became disillusioned with Soviet aid. A more intense phase of Soviet involvement followed, with the rise of Afro-Marxist regimes in places like Ethiopia, Angola, and Mozambique. But in the long run, Africa commanded a low priority in Soviet policy. In the mid-1980s, the Soviet Union maintained a scholarship program that took many African students to the USSR. It also served as Africa's chief source of weapons—for which it demanded payment in hard currency. But African leaders found the Soviet system less and less credible as a model of economic development. Ugly incidents of racial discrimination against Africans in the USSR also created resentments. African leaders concluded that while the Soviets were eager for strategic and economic advantages in Africa, they were slow to provide development aid. Increasingly, the Soviet Union emphasized commercial exchanges with Africa, while seeking to keep the trade balance in its own favor and directing its development aid to a handful of states like Vietnam, Cuba, and Afghanistan.

From facts like these, Africans developed a critical view of "socialist imperalists." For example, Mozambique sought alternative diplomatic and economic relationships in the 1980s wherever it could find them—with Portugal, the United States, even South Africa.

If Soviet interest in Africa developed tardily and thinly, U.S. policy at first went little beyond general advocacy of an end to colonialism. Even after independence, the United States still assumed that the former colonial powers would be those most active in African affairs. Gradually, however, the United States became more active in pursuing certain interests of its own: ensuring access to its major sources of many minerals and a stable environment for U.S. investment, preventing the Soviets from acquiring strategic advantages in the continent, and protecting the shipping lanes around the Cape of Good Hope so as to assure U.S. and European oil imports. Gradually, too, the United States took greater interest in some of Africa's trouble spots—for example, joining in British efforts of the late 1970s to achieve a settlement in Rhodesia, or propping up the economically stricken Mobutu regime in Zaire in order to assure access to the country's minerals. Throughout the post-1945 period, however, the United States gave far less aid to all Africa than to the Middle East or the rest of Asia, and usually less than to Latin America. In the long run, the thorniest policy problem was that of defining a policy toward South Africa that could both satisfy U.S. interests and show black Africans that the United States opposed that country's racial policy with more than words.

Even without extensive outside interference, the period since independence has been difficult for most African countries. It was inevitable that an awkward period of transition would follow decolonization. The economic and environmental problems of the 1970s and 1980s have made things far worse. In Africa, even more than elsewhere in the Hungry South, the future seems uncertain and fraught with difficulties.

Nigeria: Independence plus Oil Dependency

Nigeria is Africa's largest black-ruled country and one of its wealthiest. Nevertheless it suffers many of the problems of its smaller, poorer neighbors. It provides a vivid illustration of factionalism and the slide into military rule. Above all, it illustrates the limits that even a populous, oil-rich nation faces in trying to overcome neocolonialism.

Rise and Fall of the First Republic

By the end of World War II, several rival nationalist movements had emerged in Nigeria, and experiences of the war years had raised political expectations. The British had not yet taken additional steps to broaden political participation, however. And despite Nigeria's wartime export boom, they had only begun to emphasize social and economic development. After the war, change accelerated on all fronts.

The quickening of the economy was dramatic. Government revenues rose between 1947 and 1958 from 14 million British pounds to 58 million, while the amount of money in circulation rose from 23 million to 55 million pounds. Over the same period, exports tripled, from 44 to 136 million British pounds in value, while imports quintupled, from 33 to 167 million. The shift from a positive to a negative foreign trade balance worried economists, but was associated with rapid growth of investment inside the country. The basis of the economy remained colonial exports, 85 percent agricultural and the rest mineral. The agricultural goods were now bought and marketed by government marketing boards, and industrialization was still only beginning. But the government made efforts at diversification, including oil exploration. The country began to export small amounts of oil by 1960.

These economic changes affected the Nigerian people profoundly. In particular, the growth of the economy, and the approach of independence, vastly increased the need for educated Nigerians. The colonial government expanded education greatly, especially at the secondary level. Many Nigerians received scholarships to study abroad, and in 1948 the University College of Ibadan was founded. Still the numbers of graduates remained far short of the need. Education became a political issue, too, for many nationalists preferred to emphasize universal lower-level education, even if that meant initially limiting expansion at higher levels. And the spread of education had economic effects. Rural youngsters with a primary education, especially boys, no longer wanted to work on farms as their parents did. Instead they flocked to the cities seeking jobs as clerks, so launching the superurbanization that has transformed Lagos.

As these economic and social changes unfolded, preparations for independence advanced. Nigeria received three successive constitutions in 1947, 1951, and 1954. The end result was a federal system of government, headed by a prime minister, with a directly elected federal legislature and three self-governing regions: Northern, Eastern, and Western. With some modifications, the 1954 constitution remained in force until 1966. Meanwhile, many political issues of continuing importance emerged.

The most troublesome point by far was ethnic and regional tension. The three regions were dominated by the Hausa-Fulani (Northern), Yoruba (Western), and Ibo peoples (Eastern). The Northern Region was larger and more populous than the other two combined. It was not long before the strongest national movement, the National Council of Nigeria and the Cameroons (NCNC), broke apart into ethnically based parties. Founded in 1944 by the Ibo nationalist leader Nnamdi Azikiwe, the NCNC initially had

▶

Map 15.2 Nigeria's Three Regions (1960), Twelve States (1967), and Nineteen States (1976)

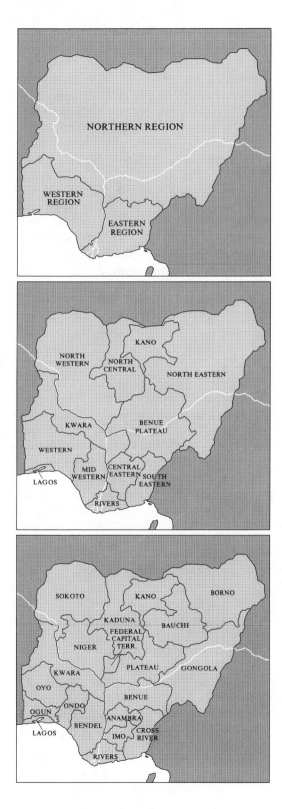

Yoruba as well as Ibo support, but relations between the two groups soon became strained. The northern Muslims also formed a political organization of their own. They feared that the southerners, who had been quicker to seek Western education, would gain political dominance after independence. Soon there were three regional parties based on specific ethnic groups: the Northern Peoples Congress (NPC, Hausa-Fulani), the Action Group (AG) in the Yoruba West, and the NCNC. This was basically an Ibo party centered in the East, although the fact that there were many Ibo migrants in other parts of the country gave it some following elsewhere and made its outlook less regional than that of the other parties. Many small ethnic groups demanded increases in the number of regions, so that more of them could acquire local dominance.

Despite these problems, Nigeria moved toward independence essentially by negotiation, rather than violence. The first federal general election (1954) produced a coalition government combining the Northern Peoples Congress and the National Council of Nigeria and the Cameroons. The NPC leader in the House, Abubakar Tafawa Balewa, a Muslim northerner from a small ethnic group, became the first federal prime minister. The three regions became self-governing between 1957 and 1959, and the country became independent in 1960, under a government still headed by Balewa as prime minister. Azikiwe assumed the mostly ceremonial role of governor general, or president, after the formal change to a republic in 1963.

With only a few years of preparation behind it, Nigeria's parliamentary government lasted only until January 1966 before falling to a military coup. Until then, Nigeria never abandoned multi-party for single-party rule. In that, Nigeria differed from the common African pattern. Yet by 1966, several factors, most of them quite typical, had discredited the republic. One factor was the corruption of most politicians and their lack of concern for their constituents in a time of rising prices and widening income inequalities. The government also failed to respect constitutionally prescribed procedures, especially in high-handed acts directed at the Western region and the Western-centered Action Group, then in the unfortunate role of opposition party. A third problem was regional imbalance. This became a chronic issue, affecting even census taking. After the last preindependence census in 1952–1953, Nigeria's next three produced results that were contested or officially disavowed. Some of the figures were surely wrong because of official ineptitude or manipulation. Others were unpopular because they indicated that the numerical dominance of the North had grown. As a result of problems like these, Nigeria was drifting toward chaos by the mid-1960s.

From the Biafran Civil War Through the Second Republic

After the overthrow of Nigeria's First Republic in January 1966, civilian rule was not restored for thirteen years. The mostly Eastern army majors who staged the coup killed the federal prime minister and finance minister, the premiers of the Northern and Western regions, and many of their military superiors, before a second group of officers, headed by Major-General J. T. Aguyi-Ironsi, another Ibo, took power. Ironsi began making plans for an early return to civilian rule and rushed through a constitution that

The Biafran Civil War, 1967–1970. An officer of the Nigerian army issues instructions through an interpreter to the chief of a captured Ibo village.
Bruno Barbey/Magnum

abolished the regions, creating a unitary rather than a federal state. By now, Nigerians had noticed the prominence of Ibo among the coup makers and their absence among the victims. Further, Nigerians saw the abolition of federalism as an attempt to gain power for the Ibo, who had a larger educated elite and were more widely dispersed around the country than other ethnic groups.

In July 1966, Northern officers staged a coup that killed Ironsi and installed a government under a Northern officer from a small ethnic group, Lieutenant-Colonel Yakubu Gowon. Discussion of re-

turn to civilian rule continued. Massacres of the Ibo also occurred, leading the Eastern Region to refuse to recognize the Gowon government. Thousands of Ibo residing in other parts of the country began returning to the Eastern Region, and secession seemed likely. In May 1967, Gowon attempted to defuse the issue by dividing Nigeria into twelve states, in place of the former regions, so breaking up the old blocs and appealing to the interests of small ethnic groups, in the East as elsewhere. Three days later the Eastern Region declared itself independent as the Republic of Biafra. This was a major challenge, because the majority of Nigeria's oil was in the East, though not in Ibo territory proper.

In the civil war that followed, Biafrans were initially successful. Nigerian forces soon turned the tide, however, reducing Biafran resistance village by village. The war roused much outside interest and support, partly because the Biafran government claimed, and overseas sympathizers believed, that the Nigerian forces intended genocide. When the Biafrans finally capitulated in January 1970, the Gowon regime responded with a magnanimous call for national reconciliation, and the former rebels were reintegrated into the nation in much that spirit.

With the civil war past, Nigeria entered a new period of opportunity, although military rule proved difficult to end. Even the war years brought some gains. The new states became established relatively smoothly, and the wartime foreign exchange shortage stimulated import substitution. By the early 1970s, Nigeria was becoming self-sufficient in some consumer goods, such as textiles, footwear, beverages, and soap. Foreign automobile firms had also opened assembly plants in the country, and the government was pressuring them to use Nigerian-made parts. As in other African countries, "indigenization" decrees were used, in 1972 and 1976, to force the sale of many foreign-owned firms, wholly or partly, to Nigerians.

What really propelled economic change, however, was Nigeria's emergence as a major oil exporter. Its annual petroleum production grew from 197 million barrels in 1970 to roughly 840 million in 1979. Overall, the current value of Nigeria's exports increased forty fold between 1960 and 1980. At the beginning of that period, agricultural prod-

ucts and tin represented 84 percent of the nation's exports. At the end, their share had fallen to 3 percent. Petroleum shot up from 3 to 96 percent of exports over the same interval.

Such changes necessarily produced economic and social distortions. Agricultural exports declined not only proportionally, but also in absolute amounts, largely because the agricultural marketing boards deprived producers of incentives to produce. This was one reason for the occupational shift out of agriculture. Unfortunately, petroleum, the most dynamic economic sector, could not absorb all the available labor, because the industry produced relatively few jobs—perhaps only 20,000 as of 1980. Meanwhile, rapid urbanization suggested a need to reorient agriculture from export crops to foodstuffs for domestic consumption. But neither the declining rural population nor the government responded to this need effectively.

Nigeria's emergence as a major oil producer coincided almost exactly with the price rises engineered by OPEC, which it joined in 1971. But waste and corruption kept Nigeria from making effective use of the gains. The growth of oil revenues seriously overstrained the country's supply of highly qualified technical and managerial talent. Since oil revenues went to the central government, increasing its power in relation to the states, the real problem was its inability to manage and redistribute these benefits advantageously. The fact that only one Nigerian in six had access to piped water in 1980, and that no Nigerian town had a central sewerage system illustrates the government's failure. After oil prices began to fall in the 1980s, Nigeria felt acutely the problems of dependence on a single export. The inflation rate soon passed 20 percent, the foreign debt reached $20 billion, and debt service appeared likely to require 50 percent of export earnings in a few years.

Part of Nigeria's problem was its leadership. The Gowon military government (1967–1975) became increasingly ineffective. After the Biafran war, Nigerians expected a return to civilian rule. Instead, Gowon announced that the change would take six more years during which the military would implement a nine-point program, including a national development plan, elimination of corruption, a census, and organization of truly national political parties. Gowon tackled only parts of the program, with little success. The 1973 census, for example, became the third since 1962 to produce politically unacceptable results. On another occasion, the government carried out a large wage increase in the public sector without foreseeing the inflationary consequences or the tensions that would emerge in the private sector. Gowon's response to his difficulties made things worse: he postponed the return to civilian rule indefinitely. Soon afterward, another military coup toppled his government (July 1975).

The new regime of Brigadier General Murtala Muhammad made a vigorous beginning. He immediately launched a purge of the public services, known as "Operation Deadwoods." Most importantly, he announced a firm date for the restoration of civilian rule—October 1, 1979—and set up a program of preparation, calling for decisions on the creation of new states and the drafting of a new constitution. Murtala Muhammad was assassinated in an unsuccessful coup attempt early in 1976, but his chief of staff assumed his place and carried on with the same program.

Among the changes occurring over the next three years was the increase in the number of states to nineteen. Drafted along U.S. lines, the new constitution provided for a popularly elected president with executive powers, a bicameral federal legislature, and elected state governors and state assemblies. The effort to form political parties of national, rather than regional, scope began under monitorship of a federal commission. Of some fifty attempts, only five new parties passed commission scrutiny. Then, in 1979, Nigeria's 48 million voters elected Shehu Shagari, the candidate of the northern-based National party of Nigeria (NPN), as president of Nigeria's Second Republic.

Shagari began with some important political advantages. The creation of an American-style presidency and federal system greatly reinforced the power of the central government in relation to the states, as had the oil revenues of the 1970s. Regionalism could no longer be the threat it had been under the First Republic. Other problems remained unsolved, however. The parties proved too much like the old regional interests, despite the effort to form national constituencies. Shagari's own NPN was little more than a northern party that agreed to rotate some people from other parts of the country in leadership positions. To heighten the problem, the tendency toward single-party dominance, familiar all across Africa in the 1960s, now asserted itself in Nigeria too. The 47 percent of the vote with which Shagari won re-election in 1983 pointed to blatant manipulation: in a country where the highest estimate of the population was 100 million, and where half the population was below voting age, the list of voters turned out to contain 65 million names!

Economic problems made the political ones worse. Nigeria's oil revenues peaked in 1980, and by 1982 Shagari had to announce an austerity program. In January 1983, the government abruptly expelled non-Nigerian workers, including many Ghanaians whose repatriation caused huge problems for the weak Ghanaian economy. An important factor in worsening economic problems was the gap between agricultural production and food needs. Nigeria now had to import such basic foodstuffs as sugar, rice, cooking oil, fish, and chickens. The questionable presidential election of 1983 occurred amid these problems. Four months later, on December 31, 1983, a coup brought the Second Republic to an end, and restored power to the military.

Once again, military denunciations of civilian corruption and incompetence rang true. Again, it was hard to be sure if the military would do better. And it was becoming hard to tell if military government was the exception in Nigeria or the rule, especially after another coup by generals in August 1985.

South Africa: Inequality, Exploitation, and Isolation

A *pigmentocracy*, shaped by *anglophobia* and *negrophobia*, with *bantustans* scattered about—such are the strange terms made up to describe one of the world's most isolated countries.[1] South Africa experienced remarkable economic growth following World War II. But its political system became more exclusionary than ever as Afrikaners consolidated their dominance over both English-speaking whites and nonwhites. By the early 1980s, the regime had made token concessions, coupled with efforts to bring neighboring black-ruled countries into positions of dependence. South Africa's rulers had clearly not exhausted their ingenuity, but they had limited room for maneuver, if they were to maintain the principle of racial separation.

White Domination, Economic and Political

In recent years, strength and inequality have become more than ever the dominant traits of South Africa's economy. Its minerals remain basic to the country's prosperity, although some mines are playing out. South Africa ranks first in the world in reserves of gold, platinum, chrome, manganese, and vanadium. The country ranks second in reserves of diamonds, and between third and eighth in antimony, asbestos, coal, lead, nickel, phosphate, silver, titanium, and perhaps uranium. The land produces a sizable agricultural surplus for export, although millions remain malnourished in the black reserves. By 1965, the country had become virtually self-sufficient in heavy industry, and manufactured goods accounted for 40 percent of exports. As before World War II, the state continued to control key industries, particularly in energy, one field where South Africa has resource shortages. With no known petroleum resources, the government founded SASOL (South African Coal, Oil and Gas Corporation) in the 1950s to manufacture oil from coal. After the Iranian revolution of 1979 deprived South Africa of its one regular source of oil, efforts began to expand SASOL so that it could supply half of the country's oil needs by 1985. The government also developed a nuclear power industry and began searching for offshore petroleum.

Because of its strong performance in so many sectors, South Africa's overall economic growth averaged nearly 7 per-

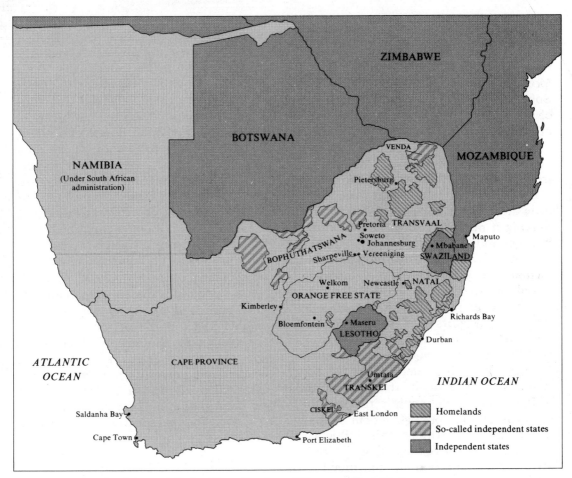

Map 15.3   South Africa, with the Homelands and Surrounding States

cent a year from 1910 to 1974—an extraordinary record. The OPEC oil price
increases and other factors then caused
a crisis. When the United States stopped
buying and selling gold at a fixed $35 per
ounce in 1971, the world price soared,
reaching an all-time high of $875 an
ounce in January 1980. This dramatic
rise in the price of gold was the most
important factor in pulling South Africa
out of its recession of the 1970s. But
drought and long-term commodity price
declines pushed the economy back into
recession by 1983.

One other resource was essential to the
growth of South Africa's economy: nonwhite labor, exploited through bad working conditions and a grossly unequal income distribution. In 1978, for example,
the average wage for nonagricultural
white workers was 588 rand per month
(1 rand being then about U.S. $0.87).
Blacks employed in "white areas" made
only 140 rand. Incomes were far lower
than that in the black "homelands,"
which reserved 13 percent of the country's area for over 70 percent of its population. But South Africa's exploitation

of blacks did not stop at its own frontiers. Historically, the mines employed many migrants from neighboring countries. As long as the Portuguese ruled Mozambique, both South Africa and Southern Rhodesia agreed to remit part of the wages of Mozambican mine workers directly to the colonial government in gold. As the South African economy became more sophisticated, the greatest irony of official attempts to maintain racial separation was that economic growth steadily enlarged labor needs, making it necessary to place nonwhites in more and better jobs.

Politically, South Africa has remained formally a parliamentary democracy, based on the British model. But the country declared itself a republic in 1961, severing its link to the British Commonwealth. Since 1948, moreover, South Africa has been consistently under the rule of the Afrikaner-dominated National party. The apparent consolidation of the single-party republic marked the political triumph of *anglophobia* (dislike of the English). Under this influence, South Africa's move away from British-style parliamentarism has continued.

The character and policies of selected prime ministers illustrate this fact. With the electoral victory of the Nationalist party in 1948, Prime Minister D. F. Malan (1948–1954) formed the first government to consist of Afrikaners only. It drew up laws to systematize racial separation (*apartheid*). The consistency of the governments from then on derived not just from the National party, but also from a complex of other associations formed to further Afrikaner interests. The most important was the Afrikaner *Broederbond* (Brotherhood, founded 1918). All prime ministers since 1948, indeed virtually all Afrikaners in public positions, have been members of this group. The triumph of such interests meant a transition away from a British-derived tradition of procedural restraint to one of Boer authoritarianism.

Prime Minister Hendrik Verwoerd (1958–1966) clearly reflected this transition. A former Nazi sympathizer, he fulfilled the Afrikaner dream of a republic without links to Britain. At the same time his policy of separate development aimed at transforming the native reserves into homelands that would become "independent," theoretically quite separate from the white republic.

The first prime minister to react significantly to the collapse of white rule in neighboring countries was P. W. Botha (1978–). He introduced a new constitution, approved by white voters in November 1983. It made limited political concessions to coloreds and Asians—but not Africans—under a government headed by a powerful presidency, a post assumed by Botha in September 1984. An examination of the apartheid system provides the perspective in which to evaluate these reforms.

Apartheid in Action

Over time, South African racial policy had become rigid. The bases for apartheid were laid before World War II—for example, the Native Land Act of 1913 created the Native Reserves, the Native Urban Areas Act of 1923 segregated black residents of towns, and the Native Representation Act of 1936 removed Africans from the common voter rolls in Cape Province. From 1948 on, more laws followed in rapid succession. The Prohibition of Mixed Marriages Act (1949) forbade future marriages between whites and members of other racial groups. The

Immorality Act of 1957 outlawed sexual relations between whites and nonwhites outside marriage. The Population Registration Act of 1950 required South Africans aged sixteen or over to carry an identity card specifying their race as officially registered. The Group Areas Act of 1950 designated areas for occupancy by specific population groups and controlled interracial property transfers.

Other laws maintained the pass system for black residents—regarded as "temporary sojourners"—in white areas, forbade strikes by certain types of workers, reserved certain jobs for whites, and prohibited registration of racially mixed unions. In 1956, colored residents of Cape Province were taken off the common voters' roll, as the Cape Africans had been twenty years before. There were laws to segregate universities and other public facilities, and to make resistance to apartheid risky. For example, the Suppression of Communism Act (1950) defined "communism" extremely loosely and empowered the minister of justice to punish suspected violators without trial, and without even stating a reason. The Riotous Assemblies Act (1956) and the Sabotage Act (1962) extended police powers considerably.

By 1960, South Africa was more than ever a racially based caste society, or "pigmentocracy." Racial categories—white, colored, Asian, and African—were sealed off from one another biologically, spatially, politically, and—where possible—economically. Because whites denied political participation to the other three categories—all referred to in South Africa as "black"—pigmentocracy also meant *negrophobia* (dislike of blacks). What is more, this system used the forms of parliamentarism and rule of law to create a police state in which the government exercised vast powers without the restraints required to protect human rights and make rule of law a reality.

A new phase in racial policy opened with the declaration of a republic and the plan to consolidate the hundreds of native reserves into ten tribal homelands, or *bantustans*. The consolidation was purely administrative, for the homelands still consisted of scattered parcels of territory. Still, theorists of apartheid argued that just as whites could find fulfillment only in a state under their control, this policy of separate development was the only way for African ethnic groups to find fulfillment. To the outside world, and to liberal South Africans, this was a divide-and-rule strategy designed not only to exclude Africans from citizenship in the republic, but also to fragment them by emphasizing their separate ethnic identities as Zulu, Xhosa, and the like. In 1976, the government began to give "independence" to some homelands. No nation other than South Africa recognized them as independent nations, however, and the Zulu homeland refused to accept this status.

As prime minister (1978–1984) and then president (1984–), P. W. Botha responded to the erosion of white power elsewhere in Africa by readjusting both foreign and domestic policy. Externally, he attempted to establish something like the regional dominance of the United States in Central America. His goal was to have nearby black regimes act as buffers for South Africa, as their colonial predecessors had. Militarily, this required fighting opponents of the South African regime on the territory of the other states, and also supporting movements hostile to unfriendly regimes in those states. For example, South Africa invaded Angola twelve times from 1975 through 1983 and supported an Angolan opposition movement, UNITA. Diplomatically, Botha sought agreements that would keep opponents of the regime, especially the African National Congress, from operating from neighboring countries. By 1984, South Africa had such agreements with several states, including Zimbabwe and Mozambique, and was trying to conclude one with Angola. For an Afro-Marxist state like Mozambique, the inducements to make such an agreement were partly economic—shipment of South African goods through Mozambique's port-capital accounted for a major part of that country's revenues up to 1975. But military considerations also played a role, because each government was to deny bases to movements opposing the other, like the Mozambican opposition operating out of South Africa. Namibia, under South African control since the end of World War I, remained a special case. South Africa was under mounting pressure to give up Namibia, yet profited from holding it and aimed to prevent its passing under control of the South West African People's Organization (SWAPO), the most successful Namibian nationalist movement.

Internally, Botha made certain concessions to nonwhites. For the African majority, concessions were mostly limited to the field of labor relations. In 1979, African and mixed labor unions received official recognition. The African unions then formed their own Federation of South African Trade Unions (FOSATU). Union organization became one of the most important forms of political action among blacks. As the need for skilled African labor grew, Botha also gave greater recognition to Africans as permanent residents of urban areas, by letting them buy their own dwellings, though not the land, in segregated townships. Since the 1960s, a system of local councils existed in nonwhite urban areas. Yet the councils had little credibility, as shown in election turnouts under 10 percent and in violence against elected officeholders.

The two other nonwhite communities, the coloreds and Asians, represented 9 and 3 percent, respectively, of the 1980 population of 27.8 million, compared with 16 and 72 percent for whites and Africans. Botha made political concessions to the two smaller groups through the new constitution that was approved in 1983 and took effect in September 1984. Alongside the white House of Assembly with 178 members, the constitution created a Colored House of Representatives with 85 members, and an Asian House with 45 members. Instead of the prime minister, the constitution provided for an executive president, elected by a white electoral college, and wielding autocratic powers. He would have a President's Council, including twenty white members, ten colored, and five Asian, all elected by their various houses of parliament, plus twenty-five members appointed by the president. Should any of the representative bodies attempt to obstruct a policy, the president could refer it to this council. The official reason for not making similar concessions to Africans was that they had political institutions in the homelands.

The new constitution, another step away from the British parliamentary tradition, made only a guarded attempt at political mobilization of the two minorities that stood between whites and Africans. It also conferred on coloreds and Asians the ambiguous benefit of "eligibility" for military conscription—a significant point for the white military establishment, since the white percentage of the population was declining while the African and colored percentages were increasing. Botha made token cabinet appointments from the two favored minorities. But few Asians and coloreds turned out to vote for their parliamentary representatives, and widespread violence wracked the African communities as the new constitution went into effect in 1984. A year later, violence was becoming endemic among nonwhites, and the white business community showed classic signs of loss of confidence. The Botha government began to speak of further concessions, but its ability to control the course of events was coming into question.

African Responses to Apartheid

By World War II, black South Africans' reactions to white dominance had begun to move beyond their former moderation. The radicalization of the African National Congress (ANC) began during the war, when a new generation of intellectuals became dissatisfied with the established leadership and formed a new pressure group, the ANC Youth League. The leading figures were Anton Lembede, Walter Sisulu, Oliver Tambo, and Nelson Mandela. In 1949, these men won control of the ANC, which elected Sisulu secretary-general and adopted their program of strikes, civil disobedience, and noncooperation. In 1952, they secured the election of President-General Albert Luthuli, who won the Nobel Peace Prize in 1960 for his ANC work. During the 1950s, the ANC still emphasized civil disobedience campaigns in collaboration with Indian, colored and liberal white organizations. The culmination of this phase came at a Congress of the People that adopted the Freedom Charter (1955). Asserting that the "people of South Africa, black and white,"

were "equal, countrymen and brothers," and would work together for democratic change, the charter remains the official ideology of the ANC.

Reactions to the Congress of the People opened a new phase in the history of the African opposition. The government responded by passing more repressive laws, and by arresting 156 people, including leaders of the congress. They were charged with treason on grounds of conspiracy to overthrow the state and replace it with a communist one. All the defendants were later released, but not until 1961 in some cases.

Meanwhile, African activists began to differ among themselves about cooperating with other racial groups and about nonviolence. One group favored a purely African movement that would use any means to assure majority rule. It broke from the ANC and formed the Pan-Africanist Congress (PAC) in 1959. Seeking to retain leadership, the ANC planned a civil disobedience campaign against the pass system for late March 1960. But the PAC jumped in front with a similar campaign beginning a few days earlier. At Sharpeville, near Johannesburg, the police shot at the demonstrators, killing 67 and wounding almost 200. In response to the demonstrations that followed, the government mobilized the armed forces, outlawed both the ANC and the PAC, and jailed some 18,000 Africans amid considerable violence. Now both the ANC and the PAC had to go underground, and even men like Tambo and Mandela concluded that nonviolence—after the response it got at Sharpeville—would not work for their movement.

The ANC then organized an underground group, *Umkhonto we Sizwe* (Spear of the Nation), which carried out its first act of sabotage in December 1961. In 1963, all the ANC leaders but

Tambo, who had gone abroad to found an exile branch, were betrayed and captured. As a result, the ANC became much less active through the late 1960s. An underground branch of the PAC, and a mostly white African Resistance Movement, carried on the sabotage campaign briefly, but were soon suppressed.

When black activism resurfaced inside the country, it focused at first on issues arising from the segregation of higher education. Under the influence of the U.S. civil rights movement, a black consciousness movement emerged to challenge the white liberals' idea of integrating blacks into white society. The slogan of the movement became, "Black man, you're on your own." The government began to crack down on the movement in 1973. But in 1976 the attempt to impose Afrikaans as the language of instruction in the Soweto schools brought out thousands of children to demonstrate, showing that educational issues were not confined to the colleges. When the police shot a student, protests swept the land. The government response left 575 dead, of whom only 5 were white and 134 were younger than eighteen years old. Ruthless repression continued into 1977, leading many activists to join ANC forces abroad. Inside South Africa, organizations that repudiated the regime continued to form. Such were the Soweto Civic Association and the Azanian People's Organization. Indeed, defiance

Mass funeral following riots in Cross Roads, South Africa, 1985.
Mark Peters/Black Star

became the mood of all three subordinate castes.

In the period between the Soweto incident and the 1984 constitution, the struggle against the regime proceeded both inside and outside South Africa. Inside, the African community had some outstanding leaders, who continued to emphasize nonviolence. One of these, the Anglican bishop of Johannesburg, Desmond Tutu, won the 1984 Nobel Peace Prize.

Externally, the exile branch of the ANC remained the main opposition force after Soweto. It conducted military operations from foreign bases, bombing South Africa's main oil-from-coal plant in 1980, a new nuclear plant in 1982, and South African Air Force headquarters in May 1983. Just as the regime used large-scale violence against nonviolent demonstrations at Sharpeville in 1960, it responded disproportionately to the more recent ANC violence. The government retaliated with shootings and letter-bomb assassinations of ANC activists in other countries and with cross-border attacks, including an air strike on the Mozambican capital, with many civilian casualties. The regime also denounced the ANC as communist. This charge was partly propaganda, although frustration was further radicalizing younger black activists.

Inside South Africa, most Africans took little interest in Marxism, and the ANC remained, as it long had been, their preferred movement, As of the mid-1980s, many South Africans, including whites, agreed that in a free election, open to all races, Botha's successor as president would be Nelson Mandela, the ANC leader imprisoned since 1963.

Forty years after World War II, the Republic of South Africa survived as Africa's last settler regime. Factors in its sur-vival included the size of the white community, larger than such communities in other former settler colonies, and the economy's strength. Another factor was the highly developed political and military institutions, which South African whites had controlled ever since the union's formation in 1910. South Africa's army and police forces were larger and better equipped than those of all black African countries combined. The consolidation of apartheid, the policy of homelands or bantustans, and P. W. Botha's combination of constitutional reform and diplomatic-military offensive indicated that the system of white supremacy had an ongoing capacity for development, in its way. Much of the world disapproved of these developments. For example, South Africa has been subject to punitive actions by the United Nations, including a mandatory arms embargo voted in 1977. Pressures from civil rights interests in the United States have led U.S. corporations doing business in South Africa to take steps to improve conditions for their African workers. But implementation of these measures has been inconsistent. And U.S. government policy has wavered, coming back in the 1980s to a combination of verbal denunciation of apartheid with practical support for a conservative, capitalist regime capable of exerting regional hegemony.

As the new constitution took effect in 1984, South Africa appeared strong in many ways. But the government's strengths could not last. The postponement of significant change merely heightened the risk that the majority, when it acquired power, might not show the same forbearance toward whites as in Tanzania or Zimbabwe.

Conclusion

Africa was the last of the continents to be integrated into the European-dominated global pattern of the pre-1914 era. Although Africa was also the last to be formally decolonized, independence came suddenly to most countries, with little or no preparation. As a result, though the political boundaries of the colonial era generally became those of the new states, Africa's nations remained impoverished despite their natural resources, disunited, plagued by corruption, and politically unable to resist military authoritarianism. The oil-related stresses of the 1970s and 1980s seriously affected all African countries, including the few that had oil to export. But the most serious problem was the widespread environmental and agricultural stress resulting from rapid population growth.

The post-1945 period has thus been one of extensive change but little positive development, as Africans themselves have realized. The two largest sub-Saharan economies both illustrate this point—Nigeria with its seeming inability to use its oil income for balanced development, and South Africa with its drastic inequalities. Famine-stricken countries like Ethiopia illustrate the same point even more starkly. In sum, no region has typified the Hungry South more clearly than sub-Saharan Africa. Redressing this situation remains the greatest challenge facing the African societies as they contemplate their future. It is a problem that must also concern the outside world as it contemplates the future of humanity.

Notes

1. Leonard Thompson and Andrew Prior, *South African Politics* (New Haven: Yale University Press, 1982), pp. 17, 131, 166–67, 170.

Suggestions for Further Reading

Achebe, Chinua. *A Man of the People* (1966).

Brown, Lester R., et al. *State of the World: 1985* (1985).

Crowder, Michael. *The Story of Nigeria* (1978).

Curtin, Philip, Steven Feierman, Leonard Thompson, and Jan Vansina. *African History* (1978).

Davenport, T. R. H. *South Africa: A Modern History.* 2d ed. (1978).

Hull, Richard W. *Southern Africa: Civilizations in Turmoil* (1981).

Kirk-Greene, Anthony, and Douglas Rimmer. *Nigeria Since 1970: A Political and Economic Outline* (1981).

Oliver, Roland, and Anthony Atmore. *Africa Since 1800*, 3d ed. (1981).

Rimmer, Douglas. *The Economies of West Africa* (1984).

Thompson, Leonard, and Andrew Prior. *South African Politics* (1982).

Young, Crawford. *Ideology and Development in Africa* (1982).

Newspapers and Periodicals

Africa Report.

Christian Science Monitor.

Current History.

Jeune Afrique (*Young Africa*, French-language weekly published in Paris).

New York Times.

Wall Street Journal.

Chapter *16* ASIAN

RESURGENCE

Some of the most significant developments of post-1945 world history have occurred in Asia. The Middle East has become the center of a major military and political problem, the Arab-Israeli conflict. The transformation of the petroleum industry and a major Islamic resurgence have also brought this region increasingly to the world's attention. India, with roughly one-seventh of the world's population, has become the largest democracy. It has begun to achieve significant economic growth, despite many inequities. China, with about one-fifth of the world's population, has undergone one of the most drastic revolutions of all time and has begun to figure as a potential superpower. Japan, after virtually destroying itself in its bid for empire, has re-emerged as the world's third-largest economy and a part of "the West" in every practical sense. Some experts foresee a Japan-centered East Asian economic complex that may soon excel Western Europe and rival the United States.

This incomplete list of Asian superlatives

implies the agenda for this chapter. To do full justice to this most populous continent, we should have to consider other topics as well—perhaps Indonesia, the world's fifth-most populous nation, with 160 million people; Bangladesh, with its 94 million; Pakistan, with its 87 million; or the 92 million Asian citizens of the Soviet Union. As in Chapter 10, however, the diversity of Asia necessitates an especially selective approach, particularly because Asia's peoples do not even represent a single civilizational tradition. We shall look first at the Middle East and North Africa, an Asian-centered region whose total population approximates that of the United States; then at the world's two most populous countries— one democratic (India) and the other communist (China); and finally at the economic prodigy, Japan. In concluding, we shall assess recent Asian experience with regard to the global pattern of integration.

The Middle East and North Africa: The Struggle for Unity and Development

The political consequences of World War I introduced a new degree of political fragmentation into this region, as we saw in Chapter 10. This fact contradicted the traditional tendency of the region— as of the other major Asian civilizational centers—toward unification in one, or a few, large states. For Muslims, Islam has reinforced this tendency by emphasizing that the unity of the faithful should be a political, and not just a spiritual, reality.

Fragmentation into a number of states has thus greatly complicated the modern history of the Middle East and North Africa. Even more than sub-Saharan Africa, this region displays a tension between the institutional "hardening" of state structures—some of them created by imperialism—and larger, integrative concepts. While struggling with state formation, Middle Eastern peoples have had to sort out inherited concepts of organization—kinship, ethnicity, and religion—and recently acquired concepts— nationalism and secular political ideologies—and have had to try to reach consensus about relationships among them.

It has proved difficult to solve these problems while also achieving goals of political mobilization and economic growth. Material constraints and outside pressures have often added to the difficulty. Into the early postwar years, for example, Turkey maintained its political independence and pursued its policies of national development. But European imperialism still prevented the Arab countries from either following Turkey's path or giving political expression to their cultural unity. As soon as most Arab countries gained independence, they began to think in terms of Arab unity, or pan-Arabism, a drive embodied by Egypt's Nasser. Especially after the petroleum revolution of 1973 furnished surplus resources to use in pursuit of large aspirations, emphasis shifted from Arab unity to Islamic unity. This concept could be pursued through many forms of international action—aid programs, diplomatic collaboration, and Islamic summits—as well as through reform or revolution in specific countries. Sanctioned by tradition, the call to Muslim unity had at least potential appeal to Muslims everywhere, from West Africa to Soviet Central Asia and the Philippines.

Since it has played a major part in the shift of political interest from local nationalism and pan-Arabism to Islamic unity, the transformation of the petro-

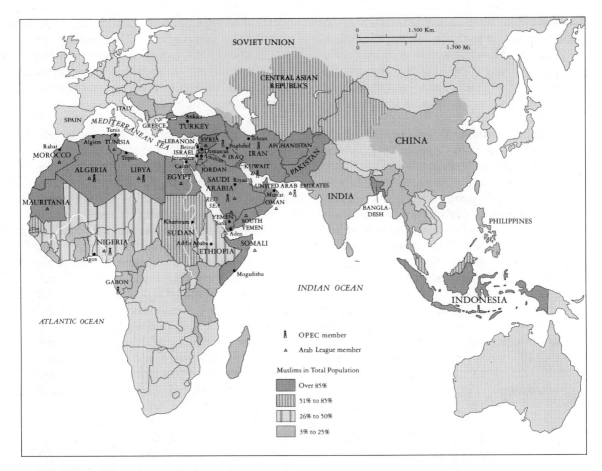

Map 16.1 The Islamic World, c. 1980

leum industry is important to understand. In twentieth-century Asia, this transformation probably ranks as the second most significant economic event after the rise of modern Japan. Yet the Japanese and Middle Eastern situations were fundamentally different. While Japan developed one of the leading industrial economies, the oil-producing countries—as the Mexican and Nigerian cases have shown—experienced a huge export boom based on a single commodity. Except in scale, this resembled a colonial export boom of the old type. In the Mid-

dle East, the results were not equitably distributed, for some countries—including two of the most populous, Egypt and Turkey—were not major oil producers. Because oil is a nonrenewable resource, even the exporting countries' future depends on how long the high income continues, and how well it is used for economic diversification.

Middle Eastern petroleum has been exploited for export since the beginning of the twentieth century, mostly by major international oil companies acting under concessions from the local governments. At first, demand for Middle Eastern oil was low, and the host governments received only about 25 cents (U.S.) per barrel in royalties. Significant change came after World War II. The Marshall Plan for European reconstruction assumed that cheap oil would be available from the Middle East, and that gave the oil states potential leverage over the oil companies. The oil states won agreements for an equal sharing of profits in the early postwar years. Iran made the first attempt at nationalization in 1951. The attempt failed, partly because the producing countries were unorganized. Instead of supporting Iran, the other producers rushed to pick up its share of the market. The companies continued to dominate the industry, and oil prices sometimes fell, even though the major Western economies' consumption roughly tripled between 1945 and 1965.

In 1960, Iraq, Saudi Arabia, Iran, Kuwait, and Venezuela—then the one major Latin America producer—formed the Organization of Petroleum Exporting Countries (OPEC) as a means for concerted action to restore prices. Up to 1973, the cartel's membership grew to include Algeria, Libya, Qatar, the United Arab Emirates, Ecuador, Gabon, Nigeria, and Indonesia, and its accomplishments included nationalization in Libya, Iraq, and Iran. But the gains of 1973 totally outshone earlier ones.

The Arab-Israeli War of 1973 provoked the biggest change in economic relations between the Middle East and the outside world in the 500 years since the voyages of exploration. Although the October War governed the timing of what happened, the underlying causes were OPEC's determination to assume control of production and pricing, and the fact that U.S. oil consumption was growing rapidly while U.S. domestic production was beginning to decline. In 1973, imports accounted for 36 percent of U.S. oil consumption, but by 1977, imports had risen to 48 percent. Because Europe was heavily dependent on OPEC oil and Japan almost entirely so, the growth of U.S. oil imports enabled OPEC to raise prices unilaterally. Angered by Israel's retention of territories occupied in 1967 and by U.S. aid to Israel in the 1973 war, the Arab oil states also decided on a combination of production cuts and embargoes against nations friendly to Israel.

The quadrupling of prices in 1973–1974, with other increases to follow, and the five-month-long embargo jolted the world economy. The price increases also created an unprecedented new flow of wealth. The combined oil revenues of the OPEC nations stood at $22.5 billion in 1973, $90.5 billion in 1974, and $272 billion in 1980.

By then, the price increases had caused global oil consumption to fall. By 1983, the decline in consumption caused the oil price to fall, too. OPEC's ability to set prices, or even to hold together, no longer seemed assured. Oil remains a critical resource ultimately in diminishing supply. But amid the financial crisis of the early 1980s, the future of Middle Eastern oil exporters seemed no more certain than that of their oilless neighbors—especially after the Iranian revolution demonstrated, even more clearly than Mexican or Nigerian experience, that oil wealth alone could not guarantee stability or development.

The waning of the 1970s oil boom provides a good point for comparing the post-1945 experiences of important Middle Eastern countries. We shall consider Iran, a major oil exporter and the scene of an Islamic revolution; then Egypt, under Nasser, the leading example of populist-socialist pan-Arabism; and finally

Israel, the Jewish state and a major factor in recent Middle Eastern history. In the interest of concision, we shall not continue the account of Turkey begun in Chapter 10. With Iran and Egypt, Turkey is one of the largest and most important countries of the region. But its postwar development has continued basically along the course charted in the interwar period without further changes as decisive as those of the Atatürk years.

Iran from Empire to Islamic Revolution

For much of the postwar period, Iran remained an authoritarian monarchy. Few such regimes survived elsewhere. But Iran's government seemed stable largely because of the country's oil wealth. The revolution of 1979 revealed a mortal antagonism between Iranian Islam and the secular-national monarchy, however. Some alarmists then interpreted the shah's fall as the start of a wave of revolution in the Islamic world. In fact, the Iranian revolution was part of a widespread Islamic resurgence, but was primarily rooted in Iranian conditions.

When the British and Soviets occupied Iran in 1941 to use it as an Allied supply route to the USSR, Reza Shah, who had founded the Pahlevi monarchy in 1925, abdicated in favor of his son, Muhammad Reza (1919–1979). It was a long time before the new shah achieved the power he wielded later. First, he and his countrymen had to wait out World War II and—with luck and U.S. help—evade Soviet efforts to divide the country and gain access to Iranian oil. Then, since Iran was formally a parliamentary monarchy under the constitution of 1906 and the politicians had taken the initiative

after Reza Shah had abdicated, the young shah had to regain political initiative from the parliament. The opportunity arose out of a parliament-led effort to nationalize the Iranian oil industry, which the Anglo-Iranian Oil Company (AIOC) controlled under a concession from the government.

To the British and their American allies, the crisis offered a choice like many faced in U.S.–Latin American relations. Nationalization was highly popular in Iran and its champion, Prime Minister Muhammad Mosaddeq, became a hero. Britain and the United States might have chosen to foster democracy in Iran by seeking economic accommodation, if at some cost to Western economic interests. The other possibility was to defend those interests and attack the parliamentary government that challenged them. Britain and the United States chose the latter course. Iranians have never forgotten the CIA-backed coup that toppled Mosaddeq in 1953.

The Western powers then helped the shah form the strong pro-Western regime they preferred. AIOC (later British Petroleum, BP) and other foreign oil interests soon worked out a new agreement. One new prop for the monarchy was the Plan Organization. It was to take charge of further economic development, although its preference for vast projects, the extraterritorial privileges it gave foreign firms, and corruption kept the agency from producing widely felt benefits for Iranians. Economically, oil revenues—which increased from $34 million to $358 million between 1954 and 1960—kept the shah afloat. He also increased his security apparatus, which included both the military forces, equipped with the latest U.S. equipment, and the secret police, known by the Persian acronym

SAVAK. Developed with aid from the CIA and the Israeli intelligence agency Mossad, SAVAK focused on Iranians who opposed the shah. Its abuses helped bring on the revolution of 1979. But the shah used the carrot as well as the stick: the government services became an enormous patronage machine ultimately including over 300,000 civil servants and 400,000 military.

Pro-Western foreign policy, government-controlled economic growth, the security forces, patronage—these were the supports of the throne. For most Iranians, the shah allowed no meaningful political participation. The parliament continued to exist, but the government manipulated elections, chose all candidates, and reorganized "parties" at will. Pushed by U.S. President John F. Kennedy's administration to consolidate the loyalties of the people, the shah enacted a so-called Shah–People Revolution, including land reform, women's suffrage, a literacy campaign, and industrial profit sharing. Because the parliament, many of whose members were large landowners, opposed these policies, the shah suspended the parliament in 1961 and began to rule by decree. The religious leadership also opposed the shah, objecting not so much to specific policies as to the secularism and dictatorial character of the regime. The shah exiled his most vigorous religious opponent, Ayatollah Ruhollah Khomeini, in 1964.

The impact of the land reform told a lot about the shah's goals. The first phase (1962–1963) bore some of the same Kennedy imprint that appeared with the Alliance for Progress in Latin America. In this phase, landlords who owned more than one "village" had to sell their land to the state for resale to their sharecroppers. Later phases, truer to the shah's outlook, attempted to keep change from going too far by asserting the authority of the central government more strongly in the villages, preserving the ownership rights of landlords, and eventually shifting emphasis to a capitalist mechanization of agriculture, rather than land reform. Ultimately, 92 percent of Iran's sharecroppers received some land. But wage laborers, a large part of the rural population, received none. Even those who gained land found themselves more dependent on the central government. In the past they would have blamed the landlords for their problems. Now they blamed the shah.

For years, the growth of oil revenues hid the failures of the Shah–People Revolution, at least from foreigners. Iran, the most populous Middle Eastern oil state, played a leading role in quadrupling oil prices in 1973. Its oil revenues, already $5 billion in 1973–1974, shot to $20 billion in 1975–1976, remaining at about that level until the revolution. The country's population rose about 50 percent in twenty years, reaching 41 million by 1982, but its GNP increased more than tenfold in real terms between 1963 and 1978.

For most Iranians this growth was destructive in many ways. Agriculture represented 27 percent of GNP in 1963, but only 9 percent in 1978, while the contribution of manufacturing remained constant at 13 percent. Rural Iran was in decline, and no significant progress was occurring in industrialization. Growth was confined to the government services and the petroleum sector. The latter accounted for one-third to one-half of GNP through most of the 1970s, while employing less than 1 percent of the labor force.

Such unbalanced growth had high human costs. More and more people poured into the ill–equipped cities—Tehran, for example, had no modern sewerage. Iran's income distribution was one of the most unequal in the world. Conspicuous consumption and corruption blossomed in high places, while the majority had to struggle with inflation rates above 30 percent. How could they express their grievances?

Since 1925, the Pahlevi shahs had modernized Iran in many ways, but denied mass political participation by attacking other power centers in the society, including liberal democrats like Mosaddeq, the radical Left, and even the religious leadership. Power became so concentrated in the shah's hands that ultimately the only way to change government policy was to overthrow his regime.

The only "political" force strong enough to lead a revolution was the religious leadership, which formed the only organized group of national scope. The shah would not tolerate mass political movements, but could not get rid of the religious functionaries, who numbered about 90,000 at the time of the revolution and lived in every city and town, though in few villages. These men were custodians of the religious belief system that offered hope and comfort to Iranians in a way that the shah's secular nationalism could not.

The fact that Iran was the only country officially committed to the Shii branch of Islam, as opposed to the majority Sunni branch, proved particularly significant. Shii concepts of authority, as developed in Iran, make it very difficult to justify a state that does not conform to strict Shii ideals. In a radical departure from historical norms, Ayatollah Khomeini pushed the argument to the limit by insisting that the religious leadership itself should seize executive power. His demand gained in importance from the fact that Iranian Shiism emphasized the duty of the ordinary believer to defer to the most senior experts in Islamic law, known by the title *ayatollah*. Unable to win over the religious functionaries, the shah had attacked them. But they were Iran's mass mobilizers, not he.

What launched Iran's revolution was a combination of socioeconomic stress and the shah's wavering in reaction to criticism—by U.S. President Jimmy Carter among others—of his rights violations. The wavering between concession and repression led to a series of bloody riots and demonstrations. All the political forces the shah had repressed, including liberal democrats and the radical Left as well as the religious leadership, then came out in a common front, and the shah's support vanished. With millions of people in the streets shouting "Death to the Shah" and "Death to America," political mobilization became a fact. The shah fled in January 1979. Khomeini returned from exile on February 1.

Half a decade later, the revolutionary forces had lost their unity, and the religious Right had ousted both the liberals and the radical Left. Many revolutionary changes had occurred, however. In form, the new government was a parliamentary republic under the aribership of a supreme expert on Islamic law. In fact, it was a one-party state dominated by the Islamic Republican party, created after the revolution. The regime was totalitarian: the traditional Islamic concept of *tawhid* (affirming the oneness of God) now also meant political unanimity with no tolerance for dissent. Many women who had begun wearing the all-enveloping black *chador* to express opposition to the shah now found themselves no longer free to set the garment aside. Meanwhile, Iraq's attack on Iran helped Khomeini maintain popular ardor after it might otherwise have waned.

Instead of the shah's pro-Western foreign policy, the Khomeini regime was at least as hostile to the United States as to the Soviet Union. The lengthy detention of U.S. embassy personnel in 1979–1980 in violation of international law dramatized this fact. International law was not Khomeini's kind of law. Iran's foreign policy aimed to maintain independence from the superpowers and to export Islamic revolution, a thrust expressed especially in hostility to Israel and support for Shii minorities in other countries. Differences in doctrine and in organization of the religious leadership of other Islamic lands meant that exporting Iran's revolution would not be easy, although the radicalization of Lebanon's Shii community partly reflected Iranian influence.

The economic policies of the new regime, finally, were not entirely clear. On grounds of Islamic respect for private property, the government had begun in 1983 to back away from land redistribution, which had been proceeding partly through spontaneous land seizures in the countryside. Yet the government had confiscated and redistributed much of the wealth accumulated by beneficiaries of the old order. Efforts continued to create a more egalitarian economic system run according to Islamic criteria. In economics as in other policy fields, the great question was what would happen after the death of the charismatic but aged Khomeini.

Egypt Struggles to Escape Its Poverty

Geographically part of Africa, Egypt has closer historical links with Southwest Asia. Egypt has exerted its greatest influence in recent history as the center of the pan-Arab socialism identified with Gamal Adbel Nasser (properly Abd al-Nasir, 1952–1970). Over time, however, Egypt's policy orientation has shifted. What really governs it is the nation's poverty.

As noted in Chapter 10, Egypt's wartime experience left the old liberal-nationalist leadership and the very idea of parliamentary government in disrepute. Especially after their defeat in the 1948 war against Israel, Egyptians were eager for new political alternatives. The Muslim Brethren, an Islamic fundamentalist group, became increasingly militant. And a group of young officers, including Nasser and Anwar al-Sadat, plotted to overthrow the government. In a bloodless coup on July 23, 1952, they set up a new regime. They installed an older officer, General Muhammad Nagib, as figurehead leader, while they remained in the background as the Revolutionary Command Council (RCC).

The events of July 1952 were not really a revolution. The officers seized power without a clear program or mass following, and experimentation played a large role in shaping Nasser's policies. Yet he had some fixed goals from the beginning: national independence and social justice for people like his postal-worker father, rather than privilege for the old elites and the British. From these goals, important changes followed.

The first few years were mostly a time of consolidation. The RCC abolished the monarchy and the old parties. The most difficult problem turned out to be the

Muslim Brotherhood, a vast movement with many affiliated organizations. It was not destroyed, but outlawed and forced underground. When some Muslim Brethren tried to assassinate Nasser, he took the opportunity to implicate Nagib, who had begun reaching for real power. The ouster of Nagib left Nasser in charge, though he did not assume the title of president until 1956. The power struggle led to the first attempt to organize mass support. Called the Liberation Rally, this was actually an organization to rally support for the regime. Meanwhile, the RCC faced the task of controlling the bureaucracy. They tried to do so by appointing members of their group to head the various ministries—with little coordination. The resulting "bureaucratic feudalism" marked an unwise departure for a regime that would later expand the role of government greatly in the name of "socialism."

The one revolutionary idea of the early years was the land reform law of 1952. Essentially, this limited the amount of land any individual could own to 200 acres. Large estates were to be redistributed to the peasantry in units of 2 to 5 acres. Later laws lowered the ownership limit to 50 acres per person, or 100 acres per nuclear family. In the 2.4 percent of Egypt's land that is cultivable, these laws reduced the amount of land held in estates of over 50 acres to one-sixth, while increasing the proportion of land held by owners of 5 acres or less from one-third to one-half. This change undermined the power of the old elite.

In 1955, Nasser's career entered a new phase that made him the international hero of pan-Arabism. He was already beginning to attract attention as an opponent of Western influence in the Middle East when he received an invitation to a conference of Afro-Asian leaders in Ban-

dung, Indonesia, in April 1955. There he met Yugoslavia's Tito, India's Nehru, and China's Zhou Enlai, who introduced him to the concept of nonalignment. The following September, Nasser applied this lesson by making an arms agreement with Czechoslovakia. Until then, the United States, Britain, and France had monopolized supplying arms to both sides in the Arab-Israeli conflict. This agreement, which brought Egypt Soviet weapons, made it impossible for the Western powers to limit the scope of the Arab-Israeli conflict, marked the beginning of strong Soviet-Arab involvement, and started an arms race in the Middle East.

Rapid developments followed. A new Egyptian constitution established a strong presidential system in 1956 to replace the parliamentary form of government in which a prime minister headed the cabinet. The constitution also committed the state to economic planning and social welfare. And it formally identified Egypt as an Arab nation—an obvious point that had assumed new importance, since most Arab lands were independent and Egypt was bidding for leadership among them. A new effort at mass mobilization, the National Union, replaced the Liberation Rally.

The cutting edge of Egyptian policy remained international. The arms deal heightened Nasser's prestige in the Arab world. British and U.S. offers to help finance the Aswan Dam (see Chapter 1) seemed to confirm that nonalignment could produce advantages from both superpowers. But the United States and Britain soon retracted their offers, resenting Nasser's diplomatic independence. He retaliated by nationalizing the Suez Canal, which was owned by foreign interests, mostly British and French. This move brought France and Britain together with Israel, which was disturbed by Nasser's rise and by Palestinian raids coming from Egyptian-controlled territory. The Suez War of 1956, second round of the Arab-Israeli conflict, followed, as Israel invaded Sinai and Britain and France sent troops to regain control of the canal. Anxious to avoid an international crisis on the eve of a presidential election, the United States joined the Soviet Union in condemning the attack.

Although only outside intervention prevented the loss of Sinai to Israel, Nasser emerged from the conflict looking like a hero to the Arab world. Inside Egypt, he began nationalizing foreign businesses and, by 1960, Egyptian-owned firms as well. The most significant proof of Nasser's enhanced standing was the union of Egypt and Syria in 1958, at Syria's request, to form the United Arab Republic (UAR). At that, the idea of Arab unity seemed to take on the meaning of fusion into a single state. The Syrians soon regretted their request for union, however, for they became virtually an Egyptian colony. Tensions mounted, and the UAR collapsed in 1961.

The demise of the UAR touched off a search for explanations that had a radicalizing effect, pushing Nasser into a new phase of Arab "socialism"—a populist socialism that followed from the land reform, the military relationship with the USSR, and the nationalization ("socialization") of much of the economy. The National Charter (1962) attempted to spell out how Egypt was to combine Islam, Arab nationalism, and socialism. The charter also defined yet another version of the regime's mass movement, to be known as the Arab Socialist Union (ASU). Most large businesses had been nationalized by then. The regime also greatly expanded its welfare policies, providing many new services and subsidies to the public.

Though some Egyptians hailed these changes as a "socialist revolution," the "revolution" had little success. Egypt was becoming a different place, but with so much of the economy nationalized, Egypt's economy could just as well have been described as "state capitalist." The extension of state control, just as Egypt moved beyond import substitution into heavy industry, proved counterproductive. The bureaucracy had grown enormously, partly because the government used it as the employer of last resort for the growing numbers of university graduates. Because of this growth and the lack of coordination that resulted from "bureaucratic feudalism," the government could not direct an efficient industrialization effort. The ASU never became an effective mass political movement, partly because it was a creation of the state. On balance, Nasser's Egypt was another authoritarian regime in which mass participation remained mostly a matter of symbol manipulation by a charismatic leader.

After the breakup of the UAR, moreover, Nasser had to work to maintain his pan-Arab leadership. In 1962, he sent Egyptian troops into a civil war in Yemen. This costly venture antagonized Saudi Arabia, which backed the other side and had close relations with the United States. Israel also remained a chronic concern, for its geographical position seemed to make it a physical barrier to Arab unity.

In 1967, the Israeli question moved abruptly to the forefront. In May, the USSR indicated to Nasser that Israel intended to attack Syria. Nasser began to call up reserves and move forces into Sinai. A UN buffer force had remained there since the 1956 war, but Nasser was now able to negotiate their removal. Beyond that point, Nasser seemed to get swept away by the momentum of events. By the end of May, he had closed the Gulf of Aqaba, Israel's only access by sea to the southern port of Eilat. Nasser verbally escalated the conflict by declaring that the real issue was "the rights of the people of Palestine." Excitement swept the Arab world, and every Arab country promised military support to Egypt. Meanwhile, diplomatic efforts to defuse the crisis proved fruitless. Finally Israel took decisive action by attacking on June 5, 1967. Egypt lost 80 percent of its bombers the first day. By the end of the sixth day, Israel controlled Sinai, the Golan Heights, the West Bank of the Jordan, and Old Jerusalem.[1]

With this catastrophe, Nasser's career entered its final phase (1967–1970). In a moving speech, he announced his intention to leave office. Unable to face defeat without their charismatic leader, Egyptians demonstrated in the streets, forcing him to stay on. Nasser's remaining years were very difficult ones for Egypt, but his sudden death in 1970 aroused even greater emotion than his resignation attempt of 1967.

Nasser's vice president, Anwar al-Sadat, now became the nation's leader. One of the original conspirators of 1952, Sadat had never become well known. Within a year, he proved that he was in control, however, by outmaneuvering serious opposition and placing his antagonists on trial. Although Egypt's problems narrowly limited Sadat's freedom of choice, an era of dramatic changes had begun.

Sadat broke with the USSR and expelled Egypt's Soviet advisers in July 1972. The break expressed long-standing frustration with Soviet interference in Egypt. At first, paradoxically, the rupture increased the flow of military aid, as the Soviets worried about their loss of influence.

In October 1973, Sadat launched a surprise attack on Israel, initiating round four of the Arab-Israeli conflict. The 1967 defeat had been so disastrous, Sadat believed, that something had to be done to restore Arab self-respect. Sadat also wanted to regain Sinai. Setting out to achieve these goals, Sadat avoided mistakes that Nasser made in 1967. Instead of planning for war in a fanfare of publicity and letting Israel take the initiative, Sadat planned secretly, taking only Syria into his confidence. On October 6, 1973, a difficult cross-water attack against Israeli fortifications along the canal and a simultaneous Syrian attack in the Golan Heights inflicted a painful surprise on the Israelis. In this, the war succeeded from the Arab point of view, even though the Israelis would eventually have achieved another lopsided victory had not U.S. Secretary of State Henry Kissinger intervened. Drawing another lesson from 1967, he sought to obtain an early ceasefire and convert the military thrust into a momentum for negotiation. Following the ceasefire, he managed to win some gains with his "step-by-step" peacemaking before it bogged down, as had all previous approaches. Meanwhile in Egypt, Sadat became the "hero of the crossing" (of the canal).

Sadat's next dramatic initiative was to open Egypt to the West. The country's population had grown more than 50 percent between 1952 and 1973 (when it stood at 35 million), and Nasser's state-dominated approach to development had proved woefully inadequate. In a fundamental break with Nasser's Soviet-oriented socialist line, Sadat decided to turn back toward liberalism. He experimented with broader political freedoms and a limited revival of the multiparty system. Economically, he encouraged expansion of the private sector and tried to attract foreign investment.

Sadat's efforts had only limited success. The private-sector share of industrial production increased from 25 percent in 1972 to 30 percent in 1978. By the end of 1979, the government had approved ventures representing $3.6 billion in foreign investment. But the projects were concentrated in tourism and finance. Many never reached implementation because of bureaucratic red tape or the deficiencies of Cairo's communications and transportation systems, which the city's growth had overwhelmed (see Chapter 17).

Egypt's economic situation would have become utterly desperate but for recovery of the Sinai oil fields, tourism, tolls from the reopened Suez Canal, and the emigration of workers and professional personnel to work in oil-rich Arab countries. The most threatening fact was that rapid population growth (45 million people in 1984) was ending Egypt's age-old ability to produce an agricultural surplus.

After World War II, Egypt ceased to be self-sufficient in one foodstuff after another, despite the Aswan Dam. The government's response was to subsidize poor consumers—if necessary, by selling imported foodstuffs for less than they cost to import. With the rapid inflation of the OPEC era, Egyptian public expenditures shot up. But the proportion of public expenditures devoted to subsidies rose faster, from less than 10 percent in 1970 to almost 60 percent in 1980. As balance-of-payments problems wors-

ened, the government turned to international lending agencies, which demanded an end to subsidies. An attempt to terminate several subsidies in January 1977 provoked Egypt's worst riots in sixty years. "Hero of the crossing, where is our breakfast?" the crowds cried. It was time for another dramatic act.

In November, Sadat made a startling journey to Jerusalem to appeal for peace, which he hoped would produce economic relief for Egypt. In his speech to the Israeli Knesset (parliament), Sadat made clear that his conditions included evacuation of the territories Israel had occupied in 1967 and creation of a Palestinian state. He repeated these conditions during the negotiations that led, with the mediation of President Carter, to the Camp David Accords of September 1978 and to the Egyptian-Israeli Peace Treaty of March 26, 1979–Israel's first with any Arab state. The treaty established diplomatic and trade relations between the two countries, allowed Israeli ships to pass through the Suez Canal, and required Israel to return Sinai to Egypt in stages. Under Menachem Begin, however, the Israeli government continued to take hard-line positions about other occupied territories and the Palestinians.

Feeling that Sadat had made a separate peace and sacrificed the Palestinians, most Arab states broke with Egypt and tried to isolate it. Inside Egypt, the hoped-for economic benefits of peace failed to materialize. Again, Sadat's popularity began to slip, and rival ideologies—especially Islamic fundamentalism—gained new followers. Isolated, Sadat drifted into authoritarianism. In September 1981, for example, he arrested 1,500 members of his political opposition. On October 6, 1981, at a celebration of the anniversary of the October War, he was assassinated by Islamic activists. Much lamented in the West, his death was greeted by Arabs with indifference.

Egypt's new president, Husni Mubarak, sought to defuse religious opposition by freeing many imprisoned activists and opening a dialogue between his regime and nonviolent fundamentalists. Today he seems well established in power, and has begun to regain acceptance from other Arab regimes. Yet the hard question remained unsolved: how to achieve the improved living standards central, since 1952, to most Egyptians' concept of democracy.

The State of Israel and Its Search for Security

The Zionist movement that created the State of Israel is unique in the history of nationalism. The movement claimed the ancient homeland of the Jewish people, yet emerged outside that country among Jewish communities scattered across nineteenth-century Europe. At the time, the land the Zionists sought to return to had long-established inhabitants who saw it as rightfully theirs and developed a nationalist movement of their own as Palestinians, in reaction to Zionism. These facts help explain the resultant conflict over nationalist goals. The interference of outside powers complicated things much more.

After World War II, the British faced urgent demands for large-scale immigration of European Jews to Palestine. Sensing that they could not accept these demands and preserve influence in the Arab world, the British announced in 1947 that they would turn their mandate over to the United Nations, which

adopted a complex partition plan. Civil war broke out between Jews and Arabs, with atrocities by both sides, and refugees began fleeing to other Arab lands.

When the British withdrew on May 14, 1948, the Zionist leaders immediately proclaimed the independence of the State of Israel. The proclamation announced the openness of the new state to Jewish immigrants from all over the world and the equality of all citizens without regard to religion, race, or sex. The proclamation offered peace to neighboring states and called on Arabs inside Israel to participate as equal citizens in developing the state. So far, it has proven impossible to fulfill all parts of this vision.

Several Arab states—Egypt, Jordan, Lebanon, Iraq, and Syria—responded by invading Israel. With the Holocaust fresh in their minds and with a small territory and few forces, the Israelis saw the conflict as a life-or-death struggle against a much larger foe. In fact, most Arab states were not yet fully independent, they lacked unity of command, and they did not field even as many soldiers as the Israelis. For the Arabs, the conflict, the first test of a dawning era of independence, ended as "the disaster." Israel won, but got only UN-mediated armistices, without peace treaties or diplomatic recognition from neighboring states. For the first time since antiquity, however, the country had a Jewish majority: Israel's citizenry comprised 650,000 Jews and 165,000 Arabs. About 750,000 Arabs had fled, mostly to the refugee life that fueled later Palestinian militancy.

Within Israel, the years from 1948 to 1977 form a single period of Labor party (Mapai) rule. Founded by a 1929 merger of socialist groups, the party represented much the same ideas as European social

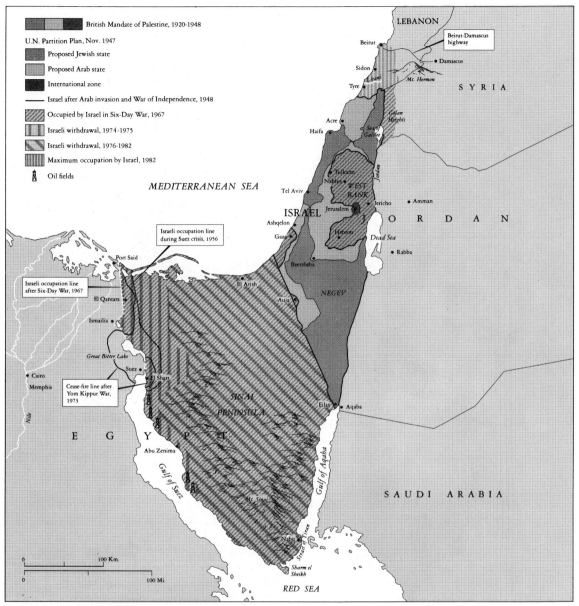

Map 16.2 Israel and Its Neighbors, 1947–1985

Legend:
- British Mandate of Palestine, 1920-1948
- U.N. Partition Plan, Nov. 1947
  - Proposed Jewish state
  - Proposed Arab state
  - International zone
- Israel after Arab invasion and War of Independence, 1948
- Occupied by Israel in Six-Day War, 1967
- Israeli withdrawal, 1974-1975
- Israeli withdrawal, 1976-1982
- Maximum occupation by Israel, 1982
- Oil fields

Map labels: LEBANON, Beirut, Beirut-Damascus highway, Damascus, Sidon, Mt. Hermon, SYRIA, Tyre, Litani, Golan Heights, Acre, Sea of Galilee, Haifa, MEDITERRANEAN SEA, Tel Aviv, Tulkarm, Nablus, WEST BANK, Jordan, Jericho, Amman, JORDAN, ISRAEL, Jerusalem, Ashqelon, Gaza, Hebron, Dead Sea, Rabba, Beersheba, NEGEV, Israeli occupation line during Suez crisis, 1956, Port Said, El Arish, Israeli occupation line after Six-Day War, 1967, El Qantara, Auja, Ismailia, Great Bitter Lake, Cairo, Memphis, Suez, El Shatt, Cease-fire line after Yom Kippur War, 1973, SINAI PENINSULA, Eilat, Aqaba, EGYPT, Nile, Abu Zenima, Gulf of Suez, Mt. Sinai, Gulf of Aqaba, SAUDI ARABIA, Nabq, Strait of Tiran, Sharm el Sheikh, RED SEA

Scale: 0 – 100 Km. / 0 – 100 Mi.

Conclusion of the Egyptian-Israeli Treaty of March 26, 1979: Egyptian President Anwar al-Sadat (left), U.S. President Jimmy Carter (center), and Israeli Prime Minister Menachem Begin.
AP/Wide World Photos

democratic parties. Its leaders were mostly eastern Europeans who had immigrated to Palestine before World War I. The party dominated Israel's great labor federation, the *Histadrut*, and had close ties to an important type of collective agricultural settlement, the *kibbutz*. Kibbutz members played key roles in both agriculture and politics, though they represented only 5 percent of the population in 1948 and less since.

The European origins and socialist ideas of the Labor leadership set the tone for the new state, but its population quickly changed. Mass immigration dou-

bled the Jewish population within three years, first with European survivors of the war, then with Jews from Islamic lands where the new Arab-Israeli conflict was destroying the historical pattern of intercommunal accommodation. After 1951, immigration diminished greatly, but continued with a series of smaller waves. Every Jew's right of migration (*aliya*) to Israel was a matter of basic Zionist commitment.

Questions arose about relations among Jews, as well as between Jews and Arabs. After the 1948–1951 immigration, Jews of African or Asian origin represented a third of Israel's Jewish population, and their rate of increase was almost twice that of the Europeans. The Europeans who dominated the Labor party—people like David Ben-Gurion and Golda Meir—had only so much time to assimilate the later immigrants, or Israel would become "orientalized." The fall of the Labor party in 1977 suggested that this was happening.

A key Zionist goal had always been economic: to create a self-sustaining Jewish community that could become a viable state. After 1948, massive immigration demanded economic development on expanded scale. Development efforts got off to a slow start, yet made great progress through the 1970s. Israel faced huge obstacles to growth. It had little water and few other natural resources. The Zionist mission required permanently high welfare expenditures to attract and retain immigrants. The Arab countries boycotted Israel economically, while the lack of real peace kept defense expenditures high. By the eve of the 1967 war, Israel and its Arab neighbors devoted more of their GNP to defense (11 percent in Israel) than any other countries except the Soviet Union.

Israel's development also benefited, however, from extraordinary positive factors. For its citizens, the "upbuilding of Israel" was a life-or-death matter. They brought to their country high levels of education and skills. Israel's educational institutions soon became better, its irrigated countryside greener, and its industry more highly developed than those of surrounding countries. Israel also enjoyed high investment levels. From 1950 through 1973, annual capital investment equaled an average of 25 percent of GNP—a rate rarely achieved elsewhere. Most of the capital came as aid or loans from the U.S. government, from

reparation payments by the German government, from Jewish communities outside Israel, or from funds that immigrants brought with them. By 1973, Israel had received $18 billion from such sources. The economy had an exceptionally large service sector, and certain industries, such as diamond cutting and armaments, were unusually prominent. For its first quarter-century, Israel achieved an average annual growth rate of 10 percent, fractionally higher than Japan's.

In politics, the strong consensus about defense and the Labor party's control of the government through 1977 created a superficial appearance of simplicity. In fact, the political system was complex. Twenty or more political parties were active. Three clusters of parties were especially important. On the left was a group running from social democratic to Marxist, and dominated by the Labor party. On the right stood a group of nonsocialist, staunchly nationalist parties, the best known being the Freedom (Herut) party, headed by Menachem Begin. It took a militant stand on territorial unification of the historical land of Israel. Although Labor would gladly have accepted diplomatic recognition from the Arabs within the 1949 armistice lines, the Herut party continued to call for a "Greater Israel," including the Kingdom of Jordan as well as the West Bank (biblical Judea and Samaria). The third major group consisted of religious parties that aimed to make Israel a state run according to Jewish law. Because none of these parties ever commanded a majority, Israel always had coalition governments. The religious parties were the favored coalition partners, partly because they would exchange votes on many other issues for support in the religiously defined areas they cared about.

In many ways, the high point of the twenty-nine years of Labor rule was the victory in the Six-Day War of 1967, which gave Israel control of Sinai, the Golan Heights, the Gaza Strip, the West Bank, and the Old City of Jerusalem. The victory improved Israel's strategic position immensely, tripling the amount of land under Israeli control, but shortening Israel's land boundaries by 25 percent. The 1967 war also generated enough support from abroad to touch off an economic boom that lasted into the early 1970s. The Arabs still refused to conclude a peace treaty that recognized Israel's right to exist as a state, however. Later, the realization came that such bitter defeat was no way to induce the Arab states to make concessions. But Israel did not grasp this lesson immediately, and the triumphal mood of 1967 prepared the way for the surprise of October 1973.

The most important question to emerge out of the 1967 war was that of the occupied territories. Sinai meant relatively little to most Israelis. The West Bank meant more, at least to rightists and religious conservatives for whom this was ancient Judea and Samaria. The Golan Heights seemed indispensable for security, and Old Jerusalem meant most of all. The Labor leadership first seemed willing to trade territory for a peace settlement. But soon the territorial issue was eroding Israel's old consensus about defense. Some Israelis thought it in Israel's interest to trade the territories for diplomatic recognition. To hold territories with a large Arab majority could create a demographic danger, especially since the Arab birthrate was higher. Other Israelis found this line of argument unconvincing, holding that the occupied territories provided a buffer that should be consolidated by Jewish settlement, especially in places formerly part of biblical Israel. As this view worked its way into policy in the 1970s, it became clear that ways could be found to restrict Arabs from full participation in the life of the Jewish state. Israeli opponents of the settlement policy pointed out that such methods might turn Israel into another South Africa.[2]

Meanwhile, Palestinians in the occupied territories and in surrounding states were becoming more militant. After the 1967 war, Palestinian activists in exile concluded they would have to regain their homeland by their own efforts, rather than await help from Arab governments. The most important Palestinian organization was *al-Fatah* (Movement for the Liberation of Palestine), headed by Yasir Arafat, who also became the leader in 1968 of the Palestine Liberation Organization (PLO), the Palestinian umbrella organization. Although they sympathized with the Palestinians, Arab governments could not allow guerrillas to operate from bases in their territory without provoking Israeli retaliation. After 1971, Lebanon—least resolute of the Arab governments because of its religiously fragmented society—was the only country adjoining Israel where the Palestinians could operate at all freely. Their increased activism was probably the strongest expression of the global wave of guerrilla violence in the late 1960s. Israelis saw the Palestinians' efforts to regain their homeland as terrorism and viewed Israel's larger-scaled retaliatory operations as legitimate self-defense.

With Palestinian militancy in the background, the October War of 1973 marked the beginning of the end of unbroken Labor rule in Israel. The success of the Arabs' surprise attack raised questions about Israeli military intelligence and preparedness. An official investigation led to the resignation of Prime Minister Golda Meir and Defense Minister Moshe Dayan. The next Labor government, under Yitzhak Rabin, was tainted by scandal. Economic troubles included defense spending that remained above 30 percent of GNP after the war. After rising at an average annual rate of 6 percent in the 1960s, consumer prices rose by 44 percent a year on average in the 1970s. The foreign debt began to swell, and debt service took a fourth of the budget by 1977. Diplomatic support for Israel also weakened after the OPEC shock. The UN and more than a hundred nations recognized the PLO. Inside Israel, Jews of Afro-Asian origin became a majority of the Jewish population in the 1970s. They remembered past inequalities and identified more readily with Begin's simply formulated Greater Israel ideology than with the theories of the Labor party.

The election of May 1977 consequently opened a new political period. The winner was the Likud (Unity) bloc, formed at the initiative of Ariel Sharon, Israel's hero of the 1973 war; the bloc included Begin's Herut party. Begin now became prime minister.

Begin emphasized the Greater Israel theme. After Sadat's trip to Jerusalem and President Carter's mediation efforts, he concluded the Camp David Accords and the Egyptian-Israeli treaty of 1979. This led to the return of Sinai to Egypt, an economic and strategic concession that did not detract from the Greater Israel idea. As for the West Bank, Begin agreed at Camp David to negotiations that would lead to full autonomy for its inhabitants. But he subsequently developed an autonomy plan that offered the Arabs no more than they already had: Israeli military control and sovereignty,

and continued freedom for Israelis to settle there. The founding of settlements did continue. By 1982 the state had acquired control of more than half the land on the West Bank and was making it available for construction of planned communities and new suburbs for Tel Aviv and Jerusalem. Soon, so many Israelis would own property there that it would be politically unthinkable to return this region to Arab control.

The position of the Arabs on the West Bank deteriorated, but the greatest blow to the Palestinians came in Lebanon. After a long series of cross-border exchanges, the Israelis invaded southern Lebanon in 1978 with 20,000 troops. In June 1982, Israel again invaded, pushing all the way to Beirut. Defense Minister Sharon appears to have convinced his government that the invasion would not only protect northern Israel from guerrilla incidents, but also thwart Arab militancy on the West Bank by smashing the PLO center in Beirut. In fact, Arafat and many PLO activists were forced out of Lebanon in August 1982, and he was further challenged by rebellion within al-Fatah a year later.

If this fifth round of the Arab-Israeli conflict inflicted grave blows on the Palestinians, it also was Israel's first defeat. Over two years later, Israel had still not found a way to disengage itself from Lebanon's chaos and had experienced serious morale and discipline problems. Israel suffered many casualties, and some Israeli soldiers began refusing orders to serve. More upsetting were the massacres in September 1982 that the militia of the Maronite Christian Phalange perpetrated in two Palestinian refugee camps in West Beirut, an area under Israeli military control.[3] Israeli commanders claimed they did not know that hundreds of civilians were being massacred, but many Israelis, with long memories of the World War II Holocaust, reacted with revulsion. An official inquiry censured the responsible parties, including Begin and Sharon. Meanwhile, Begin's concentration on his territorial policy had caused him to neglect hard economic questions. Aggravated by the settlement policy and the Lebanese invasion, the inflation rate soared to 800–1,000 percent in 1984.

Begin retired from politics in 1983, and the next general election, in July 1984, reflected the impact of the problems in Israel. Neither Labor nor Likud emerged with enough votes to form a coalition. The result was a government of national unity, based on an unprecedented deal for power sharing: Labor leader Shimon Peres was to be prime minister for two years, followed by Likud leader Yitzhak Shamir for two years. The new government wanted to get out of Lebanon on any terms compatible with Israel's security, to improve the economic situation, to stop the creation of new settlements on the West Bank at least temporarily, and to improve relations with Egypt and other Arab countries.

The future of the Middle East and North Africa in general seemed as uncertain as that of Israel. Clearly the region retained the potential to be one of the world's major scenes of conflict, as it had been through much of the century.

India: Combination of Developed North and Hungry South

India is the second most populous nation in the world, accounting for 740 million of the world's 4.7 billion people in 1983. Like the People's Republic of China, which then had over 1 billion people, India has experienced extensive change since 1945. But the two countries are very different. India is the world's largest democracy, shaped without revolution. Its dominant Hindu tradition has shown a marked capacity to absorb new ideas. China is the largest communist state, created by revolution. Its historically dominant Confucian tradition strongly resisted assimilation of alien ideas. India's democracy, coexisting with the Hindu caste system and tremendous linguistic and religious diversities, tolerates much greater inequality than China does. But India has achieved remarkable development in some respects, with less loss of life than in communist China. Finally, recent strains have moved India away from democracy, while China has begun to liberalize economically, if not to weaken its political authoritarianism. India thus combines traits of both developed North and Hungry South. An examination of the country's development under Prime Minister Jawaharlal Nehru (1947–1964) and during the two premierships of his daughter Indira Gandhi (1966–1977, 1980–1984) will show how this extraordinary pattern took form.

India Under Nehru

The evolutionary character of India's path to independence (see Chapters 4 and 10) found expression in the organization of the Congress party, which was mostly a coalition of elites—merchants, professionals, and landowners. To extend the influence of the party to the grassroots level, its members used traditional social relationships based on caste, clientage, or kinship to mobilize support. With partial exceptions—chiefly Mahatma Gandhi's attempts to improve the status of untouchables and women—the party was thus a system for accommodating, rather than transforming, traditional social relationships. At the same time, economic development formed an important goal of the Congress party, particularly for Nehru and other reformist socialists of its left wing. The key question has remained whether the party could combine development with its accommodative approach to political mobilization.

In the way of the accommodative approach stood huge obstacles to social integration. Even the 1947 partition that created a separate Muslim state, Pakistan, with territories in both west and east (Bengal), left huge problems. Some 10 million people fled and suffered a million fatalities in trying to get to the "right" side of the partition lines. Separatist violence also occurred among the religious and linguistic minorities, such as the Sikhs of the Punjab and the speakers of Dravidian languages in the south. Not all of the 570 princely states wanted to accept the control of the nation in which their territories lay. India used force to establish control over some, and fought Pakistan over Kashmir, which was partitioned. Finally, socioeconomic inequalities, reinforced by the caste system, remained stark. The average Indian was one of the most ill-fed and disease-ridden people on earth, with a life expectancy of only thirty-two years. The population had reached 360 million by 1950 and was increasing by 5 or 6 million a year, more than offsetting gains in food production.

With Nehru (1889–1964) as prime minister, India set about organizing its political and economic life. The constitution of 1950 committed the nation to justice, liberty, equality, and fraternity for all, based on popular sovereignty and universal adult suffrage. Political organization was along mostly British lines, with a president as formal head of state and a prime minister as head of the cabinet. The constitution provided for a federal system; powers were distributed between central and state governments. It also outlawed untouchability—a change easier to make in law than in practice.

Nehru retained power for life. One weakness of India's democracy was, in fact, the preponderance of the Congress party and the strong personalization of leadership within it, starting with Mahatma Gandhi. Most other Indian parties were not national, but represented linguistic or religious minorities. Nehru also acted as foreign minister, and built an international reputation as an advocate of nonalignment.

The Nehru government tackled India's developmental problems with a mixture of reformist socialism, Gandhian idealization of village society, and tolerance for private enterprise. World War II had stimulated industrialization. As part of wartime economic mobilization, the British had also made a sustained commitment to agricultural development following the disastrous Bengal famine of 1943. Nehru attempted to build on this base through centralized planning and state control of major industry. He introduced three five-year plans for 1951–1956, 1965–1961, and 1961–1966. The plans benefited from infusions of foreign aid—over $5 billion for the third plan—and produced limited results.

In agriculture, land reform measures eliminated some abuses, such as large-scale absentee landlordism. Landowning interests had so much political influence, however, that only a small proportion of the land was distributed. Apart from government efforts, Gandhi's foremost disciple, Vinoba Bhave, also persuaded some landowners to give him over a million acres, which he turned over to landless laborers. Otherwise, the government tried to develop agriculture through technological modernization and mobilization strategies that stopped short of structural reform. To make villagers active participants in development, the government created a system of elected local councils (*panchayats*)—eventually over 200,000 of them for some half-million villages. With Ford Foundation aid, the government also began a Community Development and Rural Extension Program to help villagers reclaim land, dig wells, and introduce fertilizer or improved seed.

By the later 1960s, India was making major breakthroughs in food production thanks to what became known as the Green Revolution technique of using improved seed, which required irrigation and large amounts of chemical fertilizer. Yet the strategy was costly, beyond the means of the poorest peasants. It was also vulnerable to increases in the cost of petroleum, which was used to manufacture fertilizers. Inadequate water supplies made it impossible to use this seed in large parts of the country. Agricultural development thus accentuated, rather than reduced, inequality in the countryside, a fact that heightened political tensions.

In industry, too, the Nehru years produced impressive but limited gains. By the end of the third plan period, import substitution was almost complete, thanks to high protective barriers and costly efforts to achieve self-sufficiency even in areas where India could not produce efficiently. Nehru's socialism had begun to give the economy a shape it still retains: extensive state control, especially over foreign firms, and government monopolization of many heavy industries, along with vigorous private enterprise including some enormous industrial empires. Some industrial achievements were spectacular. For example, India produced over 7 million tons of steel in 1966 but, since the economy was too underdeveloped to use it, exported part of this steel to Japan. India's industrialization suffered from the Third World problem that only a small percentage of the populace had enough income to buy many industrial products. Yet in India, even a small percentage amounted to a sizable market.

Major thrusts of social reform under Nehru included women's rights and education. The constitution gave women the vote, and by the late 1950s almost half the eligible women were voting. A series of laws on marriage and inheritance revolutionized women's social status, at least on paper. Some elite women took part in public life, but tokenism remained a problem for both women and Dalits (former untouchables). Most Indian women remained too uneducated or isolated to take advantage of the new laws. The hardships of Indian women led to one of the highest female suicide rates in the world. (During the twentieth century, the female-to-male population ratio declined to 93.5 females for every 100 males in the 1981 census.) Inequities permeated education, too. Higher education expanded greatly during the Nehru years, especially in technical fields—a fact significant for India's economic future. Simultaneously, literacy rose, but stood no higher than 28 percent in 1961 for the whole population—and barely half that for women.

India Under Indira Gandhi

Nehru's death in 1964 opened an interlude of collective leadership that climaxed two years later in a struggle between Morarji Desai and Indira Gandhi, leaders of the right and left wings of the Congress party. Mrs. Gandhi (no relation to Mahatma Gandhi) was the winner—essentially because party leaders thought she would be weaker and more manageable. Over the next three years, electoral support for the Congress party, especially for its right wing, eroded. Mrs. Gandhi became a popular leader, and when Congress tried to "expel" her in 1969, she split the party. Most members followed her into the new Congress (R), or Requisition, party and the left-wing coalition that she built around it. Also felt in the state governments and the countryside, the split in the Congress party struck a blow to the system of accommodative politics.

Prime Minister Gandhi faced serious social and economic problems. A radical separatist rebellion wracked the northeast, and the failure of the monsoon rains threatened famine. Yet economic development continued, with some significant results. The fourth and fifth five-year plans (1969–1974, 1974–1979) produced important gains, although rising prices for oil and grain imports increased India's trade deficits. Land reform initiatives again failed, but the Green Revolution strategies brought production of food grains to 100 million tons in 1968–1969. By then, the average Indian's daily food consumption had passed 2,100 ca-lories, and life expectancy had reached fifty-one years. The government invested increasingly in family planning programs, although gains in life expectancy largely offset the program's impact on total population during the 1970s. Industry reached the point where, by 1975–1976, it produced half of India's exports. Mrs. Gandhi's increasingly socialist emphasis led to bank nationalizations and expansion of government controls over private business. India's first underground nuclear explosion in 1974 and the introduction of satellite television transmission later in the decade indicated the growth of the country's scientific capabilities.

Mrs. Gandhi's political dominance grew through most of the 1970s. In the 1971 general election, her branch of the Congress party won over two-thirds of the seats in the lower legislative house, while the Congress Opposition won only a handful. When Bangladesh broke away from Pakistan in 1971 to form a separate state, the crisis that followed also redounded to her credit. India supported the seceders and won the ensuing war with Pakistan. The breakup of the old Pakistan into two nations increased India's regional dominance. The conjunction of the Sino-Soviet split and the long-standing India-Pakistan hostility also helped move Mrs. Gandhi's regime further to the left. By the early 1970s, Pakistan and the United States were cultivating China, while India and the Soviet Union were drawing closer together, having concluded an alliance shortly before the war with Pakistan.

Her victory against Pakistan gave Mrs. Gandhi momentum to carry through further socializing measures, but economic stress created new challenges to her power from 1973 on. Students and workers demonstrated to protest rapid inflation and corruption in the Congress party. By 1975, a broad coalition of anti-Congress parties called the People's Front (*Janata Morcha*) had formed, and antigovernment violence was occurring. Mrs. Gandhi soon found herself facing a court case on charges of campaign abuses.

She retaliated on June 26, 1975, by having the opposition leadership arrested and by declaring a state of national emergency. She proclaimed a Twenty-Point Program, including social and economic promises especially significant for the rural poor. Some observers thought the emergency provided the strong rule needed to restrain corruption and to slow inflation. But such benefits, felt temporarily in the cities, did not extend to the countryside.

India was suffering from domination not by a single party but by a single individual, Mrs. Gandhi. Her son Sanjay (1947–1980) also emerged in this period as a powerful figure and her presumed successor. He was largely responsible for the abuse of the population policy that led, during the emergency, to the involuntary sterilization of millions of Indian men, mostly from depressed castes. When Mrs. Gandhi terminated the emergency and called for general elections in 1977, India's 200 million voters showed what they thought of corruption, nepotism, and political high-handedness by ending thirty years of Congress party rule and by giving a parliamentary majority to the Janata opposition.

Under the elderly Prime Minister Morarji Desai, the Janata government (1977–1980) proved but an interlude, marked by economic destabilization and rapid loss of confidence in the government. Mrs. Gandhi won re-election to parliament within a year. When the Janata government harassed and briefly jailed her, she became a martyr. The 1980 general election gave her party, now known as Congress-I (for Indira), a two-thirds majority in the lower house and swept her back into office as prime minister.

During her second premiership (1980–1984), India's combination of achievements and problems became more paradoxical than ever. Although the population had doubled since independence to more than 700 million, India at last achieved self-sufficiency in food grains in 1978. It was a precarious achievement. Aside from whether Indian production could keep up with population growth, this was the self-sufficiency of limited demand. Poverty still doomed one-third of the population to chronic hunger, and agricultural modernization depended on strategies beyond the means of most rural Indians. Increasingly intensive exploitation of the land had already led to pollution and environmental degradation—loss of topsoil and deforestation—that raised concern for the future. Finally, the unequal geographic distribution of India's agricultural development raised political questions. The Punjab, where the Green Revolution tripled wheat production during the 1960s, happened to be the center of the Sikhs, one of India's most discontented religious minorities (2 percent of the population).

India's achievement in industry and technology presented a similar paradox. Partly because of its elitist educational policy, the India of 1982 was home to the world's third-largest scientific community—and to half the world's illiterates. India sent up its first communications satellite with an Indian-made launch vehicle in 1980. By 1984, India's first microelectronics plant had opened to produce silicon chips. Due partly to the conservative fiscal management by its civil service—another British relic—India's foreign debt was only about $10 billion in 1980. The ending of grain imports and the beginning of offshore oil production also helped limit debt growth. Oil production reached 340,000 barrels a day in 1982–1983 and was expected to supply all India's needs by 1990. Enthusiasts predicted that India might become a colossus of industry and technology. Others were worried about the effects of government control over, and interference in, the economy. The public-sector share of GDP had risen from 10 percent in 1960 to 21 percent in 1980. This growth was bound to depress productivity in the future.

Politically, too, Mrs. Gandhi faced severe tests. Charges of nepotism and corruption continued, not without reason. After the accidental death of Sanjay Gandhi, another son, Rajiv, emerged as heir apparent. Mrs. Gandhi tried to remove potential rivals from her Congress-I party, and to split opposition parties by bribing the leaders to desert them. She also declared "president's rule" in states controlled by opposition parties, replacing rule by elected state officials with rule from New Delhi. Nevertheless, because most other parties represented local interests, Congress-I remained one of the few national political movements.

Increasingly, Indians demanded political power and improvement in their lives. Women and Dalits campaigned more militantly against their worsening lots. Events in outlying provinces showed the potential for secessions like that of Bangladesh. In 1983, the government was criticized for its handling of Muslim-Hindu violence in the far northeastern state of Assam—reportedly the worst communal violence since 1947. In 1984, faced with a Sikh autonomy movement in the Punjab, the government sent

India's Prime Minister Indira Gandhi, photographed shortly before her assassination in 1984, with her son and successor, Rajiv Gandhi.
UPI/Bettmann Newsphotos

troops into the main Sikh temple at Amritsar. Resentment of this action was widespread, and a Sikh assassin killed Mrs. Gandhi later that year.

With its contrasts of development and underdevelopment, independent India has continued to show a unique capacity to combine seemingly irreconcilable elements. Yet this capacity, as represented in the original accommodative strategy of the Congress party, has not been without limits, as Mrs. Gandhi's assassination showed. Just as rural society needs structural reform for its development, Indian politics needs a new and less elitist approach to mobilization. Given India's caste tradition and population problems, it will not be easy to find ways to spread the political and economic benefits of development more equally. Doing so was surely the greatest challenge facing Rajiv Gandhi as he succeeded his mother as prime minister.

China Under the Communists

In terms of both number of people affected and depth of political, socioeconomic, and cultural change, China since World War II has experienced perhaps the greatest revolution in history. To an exceptional degree, this revolution bears the mark of Mao Zedong (Mao Tse-tung, 1893–1976), although his was never the only influence. In a sense, events since 1945 only continued the immense crisis touched off at the beginning of the twentieth century by the collapse of China's 2,000 year-old synthesis of imperial state and Confucian culture. The crisis was not easy to end.

In the long run, Mao proved more successful in making a revolution than in building a state.[4] Since the Communist triumph in the civil war of 1946–1949, the People's Republic of China (PRC) has evolved through four phases: first, revolution under Communist rule (1949–1953); then the "socialist transformation" (1953–1961), which runs through the Great Leap Forward; next the "second revolution" (1962–1976), which climaxed in the Great Proletarian Cultural Revolution; and finally, the post-Mao period of socialist modernization. China is still a country in transition, but the revolution has clearly created a mass-mobilizing authoritarian state that is economically egalitarian and development-oriented. Behind this abstract summary lies a prodigious human drama.

The First Phase of Communist Rule, 1949–1953

When the Guomindang (GMD) of Chiang Kai-shek and the Chinese Communist party (CCP) formed their second common front in 1937, China became officially united against the Japanese invaders. Inwardly, however, it remained divided by competition between its two nationalist movements. At war's end, the United States, hoping to see China emerge as a great power under the Nationalists, mediated a political agreement between the GMD and the CCP. The agreement collapsed, however, and China lapsed into civil war in 1946. The Nationalists entered the conflict with many advantages, including larger forces (3 million fighters initially) and more foreign aid. But the Communists had a disciplined party, politically indoctrinated military forces (1 million strong), command of guerrilla tactics, and commitment to mobilization of the peasantry. Defeated on the mainland in 1949, Chiang and his supporters retired to the island of Taiwan, which has remained under Nationalist rule as the Republic of China. The CCP, with a 1947 membership of 2.7 million, had won control of a nation of almost 600 million people.

The period between the proclamation of the People's Republic on October 1,

1949 and 1953 represented a consolidation phase. Mao believed that China should have a "democratic revolution" before its "socialist revolution." In this New Democracy phase, a common-front coalition including noncommunists would serve as the initial embodiment of the "people's democratic dictatorship." Private property would survive at first. Already, however, the CCP was restructuring Chinese life in basic ways. It developed a triple organizational base of party, army, and government. The party controlled policymaking and had a hierarchical organization, from the Central Committee under Mao's chairmanship down to village level. To mobilize the populace, the regime created mass organizations for such groups as youth, women, and peasant members of agricultural cooperatives. These movements often had scores of millions of members.

Economically, the Communists had to cope with the damage done by ten years of warfare and rapid inflation. The first task was to restore war-damaged infrastructure and to control inflation by increasing tax receipts and indexing wages to commodity prices. To bring about land reform, cadres (party workers) then went into the villages, arousing the villagers to stage public "trials" of the landlords and redistribute their land. The Communists repeatedly used such procedures, adapted from guerrilla tactics, to mobilize the people for specific objectives. Tens of millions of families acquired land for the first time and became swept up in acts of collective violence that cost millions of lives. In fact, private landownership did not last long; the organization of cooperatives began almost immediately, and full collectivization followed. Unlike Brazil or India, China restructured rural society as it modernized agriculture.

Social and cultural reform began with attacks on the family system idealized in Confucian tradition. The marriage law of 1950 made women and men equal in matters of marriage and property rights. Although Communist society continued to emphasize the family unit in many ways, children were encouraged to denounce their parents as enemies of the revolution, rather than to obey them blindly. Amid the patriotic fervor aroused by China's participation in the Korean War (1951–1953), denunciation of neighbors and relatives crescendoed into a reign of terror. In intellectual life, Mao insisted that literature and art serve as political tools. The Communists also began to make widespread use of thought-reform techniques—called "brainwashing" in Chinese slang—that they had developed to discipline the party. Individuals were drawn into a group where they would be exposed to Mao's thought and excited with a sense of belonging. Intense psychological pressure then created a fear of rejection and humiliation that led them to submit to indoctrination, repudiating other ideas and loyalties. In this way, the Communists replaced old ideas with Mao's new orthodoxy.

Economically, industrialization was a major priority. China's foreign economic relations had previously focused on Japan, Europe, and the United States. After 1950, the Communists turned toward the USSR and began trying to industrialize along Soviet lines, with Soviet technical assistance and loans, which had to be repaid by export of raw materials. The strategy worked none too well, largely because China's economy was much less developed in 1950 than the USSR's had been when Stalin introduced the first five-year plan in 1928, and because China's resources were very different.

The Socialist Transformation, 1953–1961

Like Stalin, Mao concluded that the resources for industrialization must come from agriculture and that collectivization was the way to extract them. The CCP ordered the formation of agricultural producers' cooperatives in 1953, and full collectives in 1955. Farm families gave up their shares in the cooperatives, although they retained small plots for their own use, and became wage laborers. By 1957, Chinese agriculture had been reorganized into about 800,000 collectives, averaging 600–700 people each.

As the collectivization of agriculture progressed, the government began to nationalize business and industry. The first five-year plan, 1953–1957, was a blueprint for heavy industrialization, projecting much slower growth in agriculture and consumer goods. Under the plan, China achieved the fastest industrial growth of any underdeveloped country in Asia.

By 1956, however, rapid collectivization had begun to run into trouble because of peasant reluctance and a shortage of qualified cadres. There was also ideological disagreement within the Central Committee. Mao—ever the enthusiast for revolution—was unhappy at backtracking. Anxious to mobilize China's mostly Western-educated "higher intellectuals" and improve the training and discipline of party cadres, he called for freer criticism of party and government under the classical phrase, "Let a hundred flowers bloom."

At first intellectuals did not respond, but after repeated invitations, they let loose such a torrent of criticism that the government cut it off in mid-1957 with an Antirightist Campaign amounting to a purge. Many intellectuals and cadres were subjected to "downward transfer" to the villages to end their "separation from the masses," and to boost agricultural output. The experience exposed important tensions among the leaders—over the value of "mental" as opposed to "manual" labor, or the importance of expertise as opposed to "redness" (ideological commitment).

Mao's solution to the problem of agricultural production expressed his revolutionary romanticism. China should mobilize the people's energies to make a Great Leap Forward in both industry and agriculture. Industrialization would be decentralized and balanced more evenly with agriculture. The organizational means for such mobilization was the commune, an amalgamation of collectives into units of 20,000 people or more. Each commune would be an administrative, agricultural, and industrial unit. Private plots and most other personal possessions would be taken away. Commune members would be organized into production brigades and teams. They were to work twenty-eight days a month. Children would be cared for in day nurseries, so that women could participate as agricultural and industrial laborers. Nothing better symbolized the Leap than the "battle for steel," the attempt to decentralize iron and steel production in tens of thousands of improvised furnaces scattered about the country.

Mao's approach to building communism turned out to be too long on redness and too short on expertise. The people could not stand the pace demanded of them. For peasants used to performing all the tasks on small holdings, labor in production brigades—performing a single task over a large and unfamiliar area—proved extremely difficult. The decentralization of industry also backfired.

Most products of the "battle for steel" were unusable. Many furnaces dissolved in the rain. In fact, the Leap plunged China into depression. It has been estimated that the Leap's impact on agriculture caused as many as 16 to 30 million additional deaths (2 to 4 percent of the population) between 1958 and 1960. Eventually, the 24,000 large communes were subdivided into 74,000 smaller ones.

How to combine social and economic development remained unclear, and China's leaders were divided as never before. Senior party functionaries with a more practical orientation than Mao—notably Liu Shaoqi (Liu Shao-ch'i), first vice chairman of the Central Committee and Mao's chosen successor, and Deng Xiaoping (Teng Hsiao-p'ing), party general secretary—eased Mao out as chairman of the People's Republic, although he remained party chairman. Gradually, too, they moderated his policies, restoring private peasant plots in 1962.

The Second Revolution, 1962–1976

While Liu and Deng thought the time had come for organization and expertise, Mao thought the party needed to change, either from within or by external force. He tried the first approach in 1962 with a Socialist Education Movement, under which many cadres, teachers, and students were transferred downward to work among the peasants. Mao blamed the disappointing results on sabotage by people like Liu.

By 1965, Mao was ready to try changing the party from without. He launched the Great Proletarian Cultural Revolution to destroy the "four olds" (ideology, thought, customs, and habits) and to transform society, economy, and culture.

This effort was to complete the "transition from socialism to communism." Mao used the media to attack supporters of Liu and Deng. He relied on the army, which had undergone intense political indoctrination under Marshal Lin Biao (Lin Piao), defense minister since 1959. Mao also mobilized youth, forming groups of teenagers into Red Guards—at least 13 million of them by 1966. Mao charged them, in the first of the Cultural Revolution's many wall posters, to "bomb the headquarters" of Liu and Deng. Armed with the little red books of *Quotations from Chairman Mao Zedong*, the Red Guards then bypassed the party and its Youth League to launch a reign of terror across the land. Probably because of Mao's age and infirmity, his wife, Jiang Qing (Chiang Ch'ing) rose to a controlling position in the arts, media, and education. Liu and Deng were attacked as "capitalist roaders," that is, advocates of moving China onto a capitalist road to development, and were toppled from power. Meanwhile, Lin Biao became first vice chairman of the Central Committee and heir-apparent to Mao.

The Cultural Revolution created for young Chinese some of the excitement that the Long March of 1935 had created for their elders. The youth of other countries also noticed: Chairman Mao's mobilization of young people to attack China's political and intellectual leadership helped inspire the global student activism of the late 1960s. In fact, the Red Guard included a variety of interests: children of peasants, who felt they had been denied a fair chance for education and advancement; children of party functionaries, who sought to preserve the advantages they enjoyed; children of former landlords, who joined in attacking government offices and destroying records in hopes of escaping the

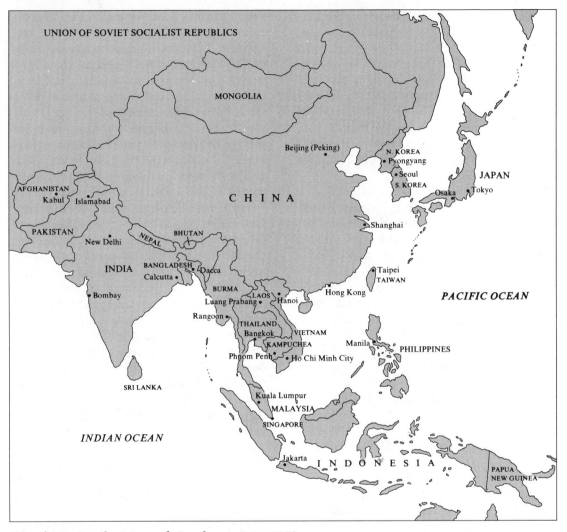

Map 16.3 South Asia and Southeast Asia, 1980s

family taint. Soon, the Red Guards were fighting each other as much as the "four olds." In 1967, even Mao concluded that he must call in the army to restrain the Guards. In 1968, as millions of students followed party cadres in being transferred downward to the communes, the shock troops of the Cultural Revolution suffered the same fate as its enemies.

The Cultural Revolution continued into Mao's last years, producing immense disruption despite some positive gains. Higher education was in disorder for a decade. As Jiang Qing purged "proletarian culture" of foreign and traditional Chinese influences, many artists and writers suffered persecution for being out of step. On the other hand, Mao's effort to close the urban-rural gap led to major improvements in public health. China trained 1.6 million paramedics, or "barefoot doctors," and over 3 million health workers between 1966 and the late 1970s. Remarkably, too, economic growth continued despite the turmoil in party and educational institutions. GNP in 1970 was 40 percent higher than in 1965.

By 1969, efforts were under way to rebuild the party. Signs of policy readjustment also appeared, such as the normalization of relations with the United States during the 1970s and the rehabilitation of Deng Xiaoping in 1973. But confusion lingered at the top. For example, Mao tried to ease out Marshal Lin Biao, whose status as heir-apparent contradicted the principle of party control of the military. According to the official account of what followed, Lin attempted a military coup in 1971, but failed and perished while trying to escape to the Soviet Union. A new purge and another wave of cultural revolution followed to discredit Lin. Jiang Qing and her associates—later derisively known as the Gang of Four—tried to extend the Cultural Revolution. Now she aimed to become her husband's new political heir.

Socialist Modernization

Mao died in 1976, only a few months after Zhou Enlai (Chou En-lai, premier of the PRC since 1949). In the succession struggle, first the Gang of Four was toppled by an opposing coalition in 1976. Then a shake-out followed among the groups that composed the coalition. In the meantime, the end of the Cultural Revolution was officially declared in 1977. By 1980–1981, China's most important leader was Deng Xiaoping, vice chairman of the party. A veteran of the Long March, Deng was in his late seventies. He tried to prepare for an orderly succession by placing his protégés Zhao Ziyang (Chao Tzu-yang) and Hu Yaobang (Hu Yao-pang) in the offices of premier and party chairman, respectively.

Deng had opposed Mao at the time of the Great Leap and fallen victim to the Cultural Revolution. His triumph marked a retreat from Mao's idea of permanent revolution. Deng spoke of a New Long March to achieve goals first defined by Zhou Enlai as the Four Modernizations—in agriculture, industry, science, and defense. A new willingness to criticize Mao's legacy replaced the Mao personality cult. This shift climaxed with the trial of the Gang of Four in 1980–1981 on a long list of charges stemming from the excesses of the Cultural Revolution. Jiang Qing's defiant claims that she acted only on Mao's orders turned the proceeding into a virtual trial of her late husband.

Several years later, the ultimate direction of socialist modernization is still not fully clear, but some dimensions of change are evident. Perhaps most significant is the shift away from a state-controlled command economy. Instead, government uses controls like taxation, credit, and dominance of key industries to regulate the economy, but otherwise allows market forces considerable free play. Perhaps Mao was right in calling Deng a "capitalist roader." After 1978, the government also dismantled collectivized agriculture. Landownership remained collective, but family holdings were restored on long-term leases, and new incentives for productivity produced dramatic increases.

Many industrial enterprises are now expected to operate as competitive independent entities on a profit-and-loss basis. A small-scale private business sector has also been allowed to develop.

Contemporary Chinese life: women pick up children from a state-run nursery school. China has been remarkably successful in improving living conditions for its billion people, and now seeks to limit population growth through a policy of one child per family.
Magnus Vassal/Liaison

Reasoning that the stress on heavy industry had limited industrialization by stunting internal demand, the government has put greater emphasis on consumer goods. The government has ended consumer subsidies, but also adopted a new income policy aimed at increasing disposable income. Largely to gain access to up-to-date technologies, China again has expanded its foreign trade, especially with Japan. As the economic policies of the two countries appear to converge, it seems possible that both

might become leading members in a future East Asian center of economic productivity.

The changes under Deng were not solely economic. The new orientation to business has required a new emphasis on law and regularity, which has led to developments in law and justice. With 40 million members in 1984, the CCP still monopolizes political life, having little or no tolerance for dissent. But now individuals can occupy themselves with nonpolitical pursuits. In keeping with the Four Modernizations theme, Deng has begun to rehabilitate mental labor, pointing to the need for scientists and technicians. The universities have resumed normal operations, although the 300,000 students who can be admitted at a time, and the few thousands sent abroad, are not enough for a country of China's size. Cultural life has become freer. Even Confucian ethics, which Mao vigorously attacked, again has become the object of official interest.

The change most noted in the outside world has been in population policy. Earlier efforts to formulate such a policy foundered against peasant attitudes and Mao's belief that population was not a problem in a communist society because more people meant more workers. In 1979, the PRC became the first country to launch a campaign to limit the number of children to one per family. Massive government pressure reduced the population growth rate to 1.2 percent in 1983, compared with about 3 percent twenty years earlier.

With the transition from Mao to Deng, the PRC has moved past its revolutionary phase. Some of Mao's policies were extremely brutal and of doubtful benefit. Perhaps permanent revolution was not really a good idea. Yet comparison with India suggests that China has gained more from revolution than India has from its reformist approach. Between 1949 and 1979, China's population doubled, but agricultural production multiplied 2.4 times, light industrial production 20 times, and heavy industrial production 90 times. With this growth came major improvements in quality of life. For example, while Chinese and Indian life expectancies were virtually the same in 1960 (41–43 years), the gap widened by 1981 to 67 years in China against India's 52. In addition, China's estimated adult literacy rate rose by over half in twenty years to reach 69 percent in 1982, while India's increased to only 36 percent.

China is not as free as India and, although it became a nuclear power in 1964, probably cannot match India's scientific and technological successes. Yet China has achieved impressive growth, and has done a better job than India in equalizing access to its benefits. At a time when India's democracy seems in jeopardy, the Deng government's socialist modernization program represents a significant effort to achieve both more freedom and greater economic growth. In attempting to combine development and social justice in a poor country, China has done a better job.

Japan: Re-emergence of the East Asian Challenger

When U.S. atomic bombs destroyed Hiroshima and Nagasaki in August 1945, Japan's phenomenal rise seemed all undone. The war left 2 million Japanese dead, 40 percent of Japan's urban areas destroyed, industry smashed, and agriculture in decline. But Japan rose again to become a major world power. The postwar U.S. occupation played a part in this revival, but the qualities of the Japanese people were more important. By 1970, Japan had the third-largest GNP in the world, after the United States and the USSR, and its developmental pattern made it a potential model for other states. For a country 10 percent smaller than California, with no significant natural resources but with a population of 120 million in 1983, this was an unparalleled achievement.

Reconstruction Under U.S. Occupation

Japan's postwar reconstruction began under the nominally Allied, but in fact U.S., occupation. Many changes made during the occupation had a lasting positive effect on Japan, partly because they coincided with an emerging Japanese consensus on the priority of reconstruction, democratization, and demilitarization. Political reform began with the prosecution of top war leaders. The emperor renounced the divine status that had been attibuted to him, and a new constitution went into effect in 1947. This document transferred sovereignty from the emperor to the people, expressed Japan's renunciation "forever" of war, reorganized the government along the lines of a British-style cabinet system, and guaranteed "fundamental human rights" to all. Further social reforms spelled out full legal equality for women, extended the number of years of compulsory schooling, and tried to make higher education less elitist.

Like the New Deal in the United States, the occupation gave many Japanese an increased stake in Japan's emerging postwar order. One important reform was the breakup of the great *zaibatsu* firms that had dominated the prewar economy. Though some old company names survived, business and industry assumed new organizational forms. The occupation authorities also brought labor legislation up to international standards and encouraged unionization, regarding it as a part of democratization.

In the agricultural sector, a land reform program virtually eliminated absentee landlords and reduced the proportion of tenant-operated farms to under 10 percent. The average farm size was henceforth only 2.5 acres. Yet the reform created a more egalitarian rural society, and technical improvements eventually made the small farms highly efficient. Together with the land reform, tax reforms gave Japan one of the most equitable income distributions in the world—an important factor in assuring the demand needed to stimulate economic recovery.

After the occupation ended in 1952, Japan continued to depend on the United States for both aid and defense. A bilateral security pact provided for maintenance of U.S. bases in Japan, and most Japanese remained opposed to large-scale rearmament. The low level of military spending became a major factor in spurring Japan's economic growth.

The Emergence of an Economic Superpower

As Japan entered its postoccupation era, economic change became—even more conspicuously than in other countries—the driving force in its development. Recovery at first was painful. The label "Made in Occupied Japan" had meant flimsiness and garish design. But that soon began to change. In 1952, the government pledged to double GNP in a decade. In fact, growth proved even faster than that, as GNP regained its prewar levels in 1955. In 1960, Prime Minister Hayato Ikeda planned to double income again in ten years. This time, the goal was passed in seven years. Until the early 1970s, Japan's real growth, net of inflation, was close to 10 percent a year. At the time, only Israel was growing faster, by a fraction of a point.

The global growth of the first postwar quarter-century probably benefited Japan more than any other country.

Growth became a virtual religion. The Japanese followed GNP statistics almost like sports scores. They were especially proud of international recognitions of Japan's re-emergence, from the 1964 Olympics held in Tokyo to the Nobel Prizes awarded to Japanese scientists. By the end of the 1960s, Japan was beginning to run trade surpluses, and its productive capacity had become almost as great as that of all the rest of Asia.

Dependent on imports for most foodstuffs and almost all energy and raw materials, Japan suffered several shocks in the 1970s, but responded well to these challenges. Tensions in U.S.-Japanese relations had been building since the late 1950s, as the volume of Japanese exports to the United States grew, while U.S. exporters had difficulty gaining access to Japanese markets. Faced with serious balance-of-payments problems partly because of the Vietnam War, the United States imposed a 10 percent surcharge on imports in 1971 and suspended the convertibility of the dollar into gold. Earlier the United States had also surprised the Japanese by announcing that President Nixon would visit the People's Republic of China, reversing U.S. policy. The Japanese had been led to expect that the United States would confer with Tokyo before taking such a step. Frictions over trade continued. For example, fearing a shortage, the United States placed an embargo on soybean exports in 1973, but forgot that soybeans were a major protein source for the Japanese.

The oil shock that followed the Arab-Israeli War of October 1973 hit Japan even harder. Dependent on imported petroleum for nearly three-fourths of its energy, Japan was more threatened by the oil embargo than any other country. The short-term effects of higher oil prices included negative trade balances and an inflation rate that reached 20 percent in 1974. The average rate of growth in Japan's GNP also fell to 5 percent per year for the 1970s.

The Japanese responded creatively to this new phase in their economic development. They searched for alternative sources of energy. By design, they began to move away from heavy industries like steel and shipbuilding, which had eclipsed the light industries of the early postwar years, toward a new generation of "knowledge industries." These would require less energy, labor, and raw materials, and would take advantage of Japan's high levels of skill and technology. A further reason for Japan's move away from heavy industry was that other East Asian economies, such as Taiwan and South Korea, were now developing heavy industry and resented Japanese domination of their markets. Perhaps the most important consideration, however, was the Japanese desire to move beyond the importing and refining of technologies developed elsewhere and to pioneer new technologies that Japan could export to earn royalties. Quadrupling the sums spent on research and development, Japan was able to become a technology exporter by the end of the 1970s.

Japan has probably adjusted more successfully than any other highly developed country to the new era of scarcity. In fiscal 1983, an exceptional year even for Japan, it had a foreign trade surplus of $35 billion and a long-term investment deficit—indicating Japanese investment abroad—of $21 billion. Overall growth fell to 3 or 4 percent per year. Such a drop was inevitable, however, because a large economy cannot maintain the rapid percentage increases that are possible when growth is measured against a very small base.

The Japan of the 1980s is a mature economy, not without certain limitations. More than any other country's, Japan's is a global economy, dependent on worldwide markets, both for its imports of food, energy, and raw materials and for sales of its products. Its high-performing export industries cluster in a few sectors—steel, automobiles, machine tools, and electronics. By the early 1980s Japan established a lead in certain technologies, such as robotics, fiber optics, and the most widely used types of random access computer memory chips. It made a huge commitment to research, illustrated by the creation of a new city for research at Tsukuba. Japanese science and technology still lacked the breadth that might be necessary to achieve clear leadership. For example, in the early 1980s while pushing to develop supercomputers, Japan still depended on communications satellite technologies that it had to import in "black boxes," without the technical information needed for repairs. Yet Japan's economy—in ruins less than forty years before—then outperformed the other highly developed economies by almost every indicator.

Tsukuba Science City, Japan. This overview of the futuristic city suggests the magnitude of Japan's determination to lead in scientific and technical research.
Kaku Kurita/Gamma

Major Factors in Japan's Success

How has Japan achieved so much economically? Many factors have played a part. The land reform and income equalization measures of the occupation helped by stimulating agriculture and raising internal demand. So did the practice of limiting defense spending to 1 percent of GNP—a rate that nonetheless gave Japan the eighth-largest military budget of the world by the late 1970s. But some of the most important factors lie in the world of business and in government-business relations.

Commercial organization has made a major difference in Japan's growth. In place of the old zaibatsu firms, consisting of a complex of interests dominating a single industry and controlled by a holding company, large-scale organizations known as *keiretsu*, or "business groups," emerged by the 1960s. These organizations grouped firms in different industries around a large bank or industrial firm. Benefiting from lack of U.S.-style antitrust laws, the business groups could be extremely large. A key part of the group, the general trading company, conducted the group's foreign trade. Bigger than most U.S. export-import firms, the trading companies benefited from economies of scale and could maintain large expert staffs. Because the business groups tended to raise capital from internal sources rather than by selling shares, they could plow much of their profits back into their enterprises instead of paying dividends to shareholders, as most U.S. corporations must. Having interests in a variety of industries also made it easier for the business groups to shift investment from fields where growth had slowed to others that offered better future prospects.

Japanese labor relations, too, contributed to business success. The unions were typically company unions, less militant than the industrywide unions found in other industrial countries. Japanese corporate culture was typically less top-heavy than in other countries, and less likely to segregate managers from workers. It also emphasized team spirit and corporate loyalty, qualities deeply rooted in Japanese society.

Since the nineteenth century, government has played a major role in Japan's economic development, though government has been smaller than in other industrial countries. In 1980, government officials formed only 1.7 percent of the working population in Japan, against 2.3 in the United States. Government revenues were also low—22 percent of GNP in Japan in 1977, against 30 percent in the United States and 38 percent in West Germany. Even so, partly because expenditures for defense and welfare were low, more of Japan's government revenues went for purposes that contributed to economic development, such as public works.

Fiscal conservatism enabled the government to maintain balanced budgets through 1976. After that, expansion of welfare spending without correspondingly increased revenue produced an internal debt of $425 billion by 1983—roughly 60 percent as much debt per capita as in the United States at the time. An important consequence of conservative government finance was that Japan consistently maintained a savings rate among the highest in the world—25–33 percent of GNP through the mid-1970s, declining to about 17 percent in the early 1980s. Inducements to save included both low public welfare spending and tax incentives, such as tax exemption for interest on postal savings accounts.

Special government agencies played a key role in stimulating the economy. The most important of these was the Ministry of International Trade and Industry (MITI). Japan's economic support for scientific research began to approach the levels found in most highly developed countries only in the late 1960s. This was especially true for basic research, which tackles new problems for the advancement of science, without immediate regard to practical applications and economic benefits. Basic research ultimately does more to advance both science and industry, but research aimed at particular practical applications can produce huge economic benefits. Overall, Japan has emphasized applied research even more than basic. MITI played a key role, in collaboration with the large business groups, in sponsoring applied research programs. In addition, MITI provided leadership in phasing out industries in which Japan could no longer compete effectively—such as the energy-intensive aluminum industry after the escalation in oil prices.

Japan's industry-government collaboration has been original as well as effective. Because the relationship was collaborative and MITI-sponsored projects always preserved the principle of competition among participating firms, Japan's method has differed fundamentally from a communist economy, which eliminates competition for profits. The Japanese method also differs from conventional Western ideas of free enterprise in that government helps chart the course of growth and innovation rather than leaving the economy to itself or intervening only to regulate it. Japan's technological mastery and its ability to adjust to the shocks of the 1970s speak well for its approach to government-industry relations.

Japanese Society and Economic Growth

Japan's postwar economic growth depended most of all on its people, the country's one abundant resource. After the war, the Japanese faced daunting problems—food shortages, runaway inflation, unemployment, repatriation of 6 million Japanese from overseas, and then a baby boom (1946–1948). But the same qualities that underlay Japan's earlier accomplishments helped make possible a new era of rapid growth.

With growth, certain social traits persisted. These included strong family ties and a strong sense of group solidarity recalling that of village life. Many Japanese assumed that their commitment to their employers was for life, although in fact only a third of Japan's workers worked in large firms that guaranteed them employment throughout their careers. Tradition also affected the lives of Japanese women, despite legal equality; most of those who worked when young withdrew into family life after marriage. Their potential to contribute to the economy remained Japan's greatest untapped resource, though in the 1970s and 1980s, more older women returned to the work place, where they found unequal wages and conditions. An emphasis on education was another strong tradition. Examination pressures produced occasional student violence against teachers or even suicide. Finally, while traditional arts and crafts were being lost in some Asian societies, the Japanese retained theirs, enriching their industries with distinctive standards of design and workmanship.

In time, kimonos and scroll paintings became affordable luxuries for a people among whom, by the 1960s, 80 to 90 percent thought of themselves as middle class. Japanese men aspired to the image of the white-collar "salary man" employed by a large corporation. Population growth had leveled off to about 1 percent per year. Low growth created a labor shortage, for Japan did not import workers as many other industrial countries did. Rising wages provided an impetus for the shift toward the knowledge industries and increased use of automation and robotics.

Meanwhile, urbanization progressed. The rural population fell to 19 percent of the total in 1970, down from 50 percent in the 1930s. Many rural Japanese combined work in town with cultivation of their tiny farms. As the cities grew, the largest grew the fastest. The population of Tokyo reached 8 million in the 1960s and 17 million by 1984, when it was the world's largest city.

The reduction in Japan's birthrate had occurred voluntarily and reflected the shift in attitudes that has accompanied urbanization and achievement of middle-class status the world over. People came to prefer having only a few children so that family resources could be concentrated on their education and advantageous placement in society. In Japan, this shift in attitudes led to an increase in the number of students going on to high school, from about 60 percent in 1960 to over 90 percent in 1983. Over the same period, the percentage in higher education rose from 20 to 28 percent for men and—a much stronger increase—from 14 to 32 percent for women.

Japan's rapid social change had some troublesome side effects, especially in the more difficult economic environment of the 1970s and 1980s. Inevitably crowded—half of the population lived in just 2 percent of the land area—the Japanese remained poorly housed by European or American standards. Yet housing costs were much higher in relation to salaries than in the United States or Europe. As in Third World supermetropolises, many workers spent as much as four hours a day commuting. Park lands and public facilities of all types were in short supply. Industrial pollution was also a severe problem, at least until stringent controls took effect in the 1970s.

Urbanization and other factors took their toll on the extended family. By the early 1980s, nuclear families (not including grandparents) accounted for 60 percent of Japan's 36 million households. But the need for family support remained strong, particularly because public spending on welfare was relatively low. (At 1980 rates, deductions from workers' wages for income tax and social security added up to 32 percent of GNP in Japan, compared with 38 percent in the United States, 51 percent in West Germany, and 64 percent in Sweden.) Many workers had company health and retirement plans, and the government began to broaden health-care coverage and provide free medical care for the aged by 1973. The government expanded benefits by deficit financing, however, and demographic trends threatened the stability of the benefit programs because the percentage of the population aged 65 or over was growing, at a rate faster than that in the United States, Britain, France, or West Germany.

Rapid change and increasing isolation of the individual produced displays of alienation especially among the young. Leftist university students attracted international attention in 1960 with their demonstrations—in which many other Japanese joined—against ratification of the new U.S.-Japanese security treaty. In 1968, student violence flared again, primarily directed against the poorly financed and ill-equipped universities. Other issues—such as the Vietnam War and the U.S. bases in Japan—were additional irritants. A radical fringe group, the Japanese Red Army, remained active in international terrorism into the 1980s. By the early 1980s, a variety of observers sensed that alienation was becoming more general in Japanese society. The work force, consisting largely of people born since World War II, lacked the work ethic that had fired their parents.

Even in Japan, prosperity had its perils. A tide of consumerism had been rising in Japanese society since the 1950s. The salary men of the 1980s displayed less organizational loyalty than had the preceding generation, and were more eager for such benefits as the five-day work week, which less than 10 percent of the workforce then enjoyed. Old values will no doubt still shape Japan's responses to future challenges. Yet change is also at work, giving Japan the familiar traits of a postindustrial society.

Consensual Politics amid Affluence

Japan's economic development influenced its political evolution as well as its social history. The early postwar years produced many political movements, but by the mid-1950s, these had sorted themselves into what has been called a one-and-a-half-party system. The Liberal Democratic party (LDP), made up of five conservative factions, has dominated every government since it coalesced in 1955. The next-largest party is the Japan Socialist party (JSP), but its vote has been consistently smaller, partly because the Left is split among four different parties. Japan has not had a leftist prime minister since 1947–1948.

As the economy grew, the Marxist-inspired slogans of the Left seemed increasingly irrelevant to most Japanese. Growth thus reinforced political consensus. The issues that excited most interest were economic, whether they were domestic questions like pollution control, which enabled leftist parties to win local elections in large urban areas, or international questions like trade relations.

In a period of general consensus, the LDP succumbed to the temptations of long tenure in office. In 1975–1976, for example, Prime Minister Kakuei Tanaka and others were implicated in scandals, including the taking of bribes from the Lockheed Corporation. Tanaka's conviction in 1983 appears to have been a factor in the relatively poor LDP showing in elections that fall. Still, Prime Minister Yasuhiro Nakasone, head of the smallest LDP faction and indebted for his position to Tanaka, appeared to be in a strong position. In addition to internal measures aimed at educational reform and debt reduction, his government announced policies designed to ease import restrictions, facilitate export of advanced technologies, increase foreign aid, and begin to increase defense spending, while reaffirming Japan's pro-Western policy orientation. Most Japanese now saw themselves as part of the West, and Nakasone was anxious to show that he was not just a "transistor salesman," as France's President De Gaulle had called another Japanese prime minister twenty years earlier.

Japan's place in the world has concerned foreigners as well as Japanese. Some observers see Japan as the leading member of an emerging East Asian concentration of political and economic power that also includes Taiwan, South Korea, Hong Kong, Singapore, and potentially North Korea and China.[5] Another, not incompatible, view emphasizes that the Pacific rim is becoming as important in world affairs as the Atlantic rim previously was. Since 1975, the value of U.S. trade across the Pacific indeed has exceeded the value of U.S. trade across the Atlantic. Japan's postwar resurgence and its extraordinarily farflung economic interests clearly illustrate the tightening of global interdependence.

Conclusion: Asian Challenges

Since World War II, major Asian societies, far more than those in other parts of the Third World, have found ways to challenge the global pattern of political and economic relations that emerged from World War II. In the future, one or more Asian powers may again rival the greatest found elsewhere. Important elements of such a transformation are in place. Completion of such a shift would not be extraordinary, for throughout most of history, the great Asian civilizations have been more brilliant than that of the West.

Economically subjugated and politically fragmented by European expansion, the Middle East and North Africa has found in petroleum a means to reverse 500 years of dependence. The Islamic resurgence suggests that cultural as well as economic and political dependence has ended. Instead of modeling themselves on the West as liberal modernizers used to do, the peoples of the region seem increasingly to want to use their new wealth and power to combine the practical benefits of modernity with the values that mean most to them as Muslims. Because the oil revolution does not assure all-round economic development, it is unclear where recent events will lead. But the region—especially Iran—has entered a new era, both in its internal history and in its relations with the rest of the world.

India is in a more problematical position. The decline of democratic institutions under Indira Gandhi's rule and the inequitable distribution of the benefits of economic growth indicate a need for fundamental structural change. Especially in a country with strongly inegalitarian traditions, the reformist path of development has its dangers. But India has changed a great deal since independence. The challenge for future leaders will be not just to increase India's resemblances to the developed nations, but also to enable more Indians to benefit from them.

The greatest transformation has occurred in East Asia. Japan has become a dominant economic power. China has gone through a revolution so drastic that Mao must be recognized, with Confucius, as one of the most influential figures in Chinese history. China has moved beyond dependence on either the Soviet Union or the West. Since 1976, China has also moved beyond Mao's radicalism to unlock its economic potential as never before.

If China's economic growth remains strong and ideological differences with Japan continue to narrow, the resurgence of Japan may prove to be just the first step toward formation of a new East Asian center of economic productivity. Whatever happens, the post-1945 history of East Asia has tightened the bonds of global interdependence and changed the list of major powers.

Notes

1. Nadav Safran, *Israel: The Embattled Ally* (Cambridge, Mass.: Harvard University Press, 1981), pp. 381–413.
2. Meron Benvenisti, *The West Bank Data Project: A Survey of Israel's Policies* (Washington, D.C.: American Enterprise Institute, 1984), pp. x, 69.
3. Ze'ev Schiff and Ehud Ya'ari, *Israel's Lebanon War* (New York: Simon and Schuster, 1984), pp. 250–285.
4. Immanuel C. Y. Hsü., *The Rise of Modern China*, 3d ed. (New York: Oxford, 1983), p. 780.
5. Roy Hofheinz, Jr., and Kent E. Calder, *The Eastasia Edge* (New York: Basic Books), 1982.

Suggestions for Further Reading

Middle East and North Africa

Aroian, Lois, and Richard P. Mitchell, *The Modern Middle East and North Africa* (1984).

Bakhash, Shaul, *The Reign of the Ayatollahs: Iran and the Islamic Revolution* (1984).

Grose, Peter, *A Changing Israel* (1985).

Hopwood, Derek, *Egypt: Politics and Society, 1945–1981* (1982).

Isaac, Rael Jean, *Party and Politics in Israel: Three Visions of a Jewish State* (1981).

Katouzian, Homa, *The Political Economy of Modern Iran, 1926–1979* (1981).

Keddie, Nikki, *Roots of Revolution: An Interpretive History of Modern Iran* (1981).

Lustick, Ian, *Arabs in the Jewish State* (1980).

Safran, Nadav, *Israel: The Embattled Ally* (1981).

Said, Edward W., *The Question of Palestine* (1980).

Vatikiotis, P. J., *Egypt: From Muhammad Ali to Sadat*, 2d ed. (1980).

Waterbury, John, *The Egypt of Nasser and Sadat: The Political Economy of Two Regimes* (1983).

India

Brown, Judith, *Modern India: The Origins of an Asian Democracy* (1985).

Frankel, Francine R., *India's Political Economy, 1947–1977* (1977).

Kumar, Dharma, ed., *The Cambridge Economic History of India*, Vol. 2, *c. 1757–c. 1970* (1983).

Wolpert, Stanley, *A New History of India*, 2d ed. (1982).

China

Fairbank, John, *The United States and China*, 4th ed. (1980).

Fairbank, John K., Edwin O. Reischauer, and Albert M. Craig, *East Asia: Tradition and Transformation* (1978).

Hsü, Immanuel C. Y., *Modern China*, 3d ed. (1983).

Kraus, Willy, *Economic Development and Social Change in the People's Republic of China*, trans. E. M. Holz (1982).

Spence, Jonathan D., *The Gate of Heavenly Peace: The Chinese and Their Revolution, 1895–1980* (1981).

Japan

Burks, Ardath W., *Japan: Profile of a Postindustrial Power* (1981).

Duus, Peter, *The Rise of Modern Japan* (1976).

Hofheinz, Roy, Jr., and Kent Calder, *The Eastasia Edge* (1982).

Look Japan (Tokyo).

Reischauer, Edwin, O., *Japan: The Story of a Nation*, 3d ed. (1981).

Part **6**

THE
WORLD
TODAY

Chapter 17

AFFLUENT NORTH AND HUNGRY SOUTH: A CONTEMPORARY PHOTOGRAPHIC ESSAY

I n Chapter 2 we visited a European capital and a colonial village, symbols of the two poles of human experience under the European-dominated world system of 1914. Now we shall make similar visits to places that symbolize the poles of the world's experience today.

Dramatic change in the political map of the world since 1914 has replaced the European empires with some 170 supposedly sovereign nations. Economically, however, the world is still divided into two parts. The Affluent North (Canada, the United States, Europe, the Soviet Union, Japan, Australia, and New Zealand) has one-quarter of the world's population, but earns three-quarters of its income, primarily because the North includes 90 percent of world industry. The rest of the world makes up the Hungry South. To reflect the realities of the 1980s, this photographic essay will visit representative environments in the Affluent North and Hungry South.

Both these environments are giant cities of the kind sometimes called supermetropolises or megalopolises. The modern processes of urbanization that had already given Europe its Berlins and North America its Chicagos by 1914 have since swept the world. Today, eleven of the world's twenty largest cities are found in the Hungry South, and the number is expected to rise to thirteen by 1990. Cairo vividly illustrates the problems of these megalopolises, as this chapter will reveal. Because the United States exerts vast influence over both the Affluent North and the Hungry South, however, we shall visit a U.S. city first. We have chosen Los Angeles as a symbol of the most recent problems and accomplishments of the developed world.

Los Angeles: Modern Megalopolis

Like Berlin on the eve of World War I, Los Angeles—"LA"—has been transfigured by explosive growth in less than two generations. Because of the city's importance as a staging point for the Pacific campaigns of World War II, federal government expenditures in LA increased fiftyfold between 1940 and 1945. In the postwar years, this impetus made Los Angeles, like Berlin, a center of innovation—producer of the new technologies of the knowledge explosion.

Los Angeles' society is made of layers sharply differentiated by wealth. Because of its sprawling geography shaped by the automobile, rich and poor meet far less often than did their counterparts in 1914 Berlin.

Although in many respects it embodied the Western orientation to change, Berlin also harked back to the traditions of the Prussian past. But Los Angeles, critics have charged, is so obsessed with the present and the future that it regards the past with contempt. Idealizing progress through technological innovation, LA until recently demolished most of its few historic buildings. If the city's architecture reflects continual and uncontrolled improvisation, that is partly because LA lacks Berlin's effective city government. The Los Angeles charter, dating from the beginning of the century, was deliberately designed to keep all authority weak, in keeping with a basic American mistrust of governmental power. Tasks assumed by the municipality in Berlin were left to the individual in LA. Only recently, for example, has Los Angeles outlawed the individual backyard incinerators in which its citizens used to burn their rubbish as they pleased, regardless of pollution.

The political ideal of LA is radically different from the socialism of most 1914 Berliners. Mass mobilization in LA has paradoxically produced a political outlook that stresses the rights of the individual over those of the community. This idealization of individualism, some critics contend, compounds the psychological stresses of a population composed of uprooted strangers. A large number of cults invented by spiritual entrepreneurs prey on the loneliness of newcomers to LA.

Other observers consider the array of LA religious experiences a virtue—an illustration of the city's vibrant variety—rather than a drawback. Like Berlin in 1914, LA in the 1980s has a controversial reputation. The restless, impermanent quality of its life seems exhilarating to some, disturbing to others. In the boom years of the 1950s and 1960s, LA came to symbolize the future to Americans. Its changing fortunes in the 1970s and 1980s symbolize the crucial dilemmas of the Affluent North at the end of the twentieth century.

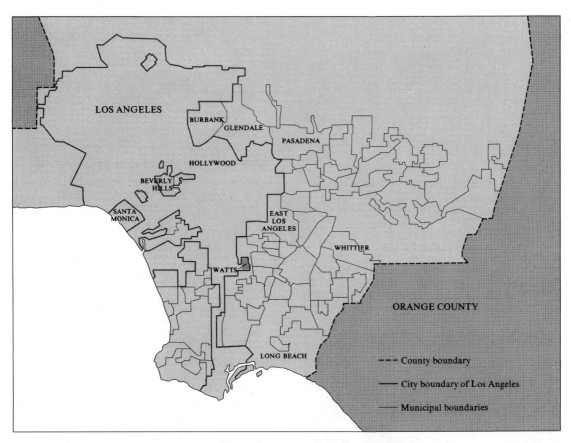

Map 17.1 Contemporary Los Angeles and Surrounding Communities

Technology and the LA Economy

In 1980, Los Angeles with a population of 11,496,206 was the seventh-largest metropolitan area in the world, surpassed only by Tokyo-Yokohama (the world's largest), New York, and London in the Affluent North; and Mexico City, São Paulo (Brazil), and Shanghai in the Hungry South.

Los Angeles is a creation of twentieth-century technology. It was no small achievement to build a supermetropolis in a sunny, but otherwise inhospitable, environment where the accessibility of beaches and mountains is counterbal-

anced by a near absence of usable water. LA's prodigious growth between 1900 and 1940 (1,600 percent) would have been impossible without the construction of a 233-mile-long aqueduct, 53 miles of it in tunnel, to bring water from the mountains to the arid plain on which the city lies.

But it was the technology of the post-1945 knowledge explosion that made LA a megalopolis. The decades of cold war boom transformed it from a remote provincial city into a center of the world economy. Jet aircraft shrank the distance between the U.S. West Coast and the eastern power centers to a few hours. In the years of bipolar confrontation, the armaments race flooded the Southern California aeronautical industry with orders. Filling the aerospace needs of the warfare state, 10,000–12,000 firms—some with famous names like Hughes Aircraft, Litton Industries, and Ramo-Wooldridge—helped make LA the United States' second industrial center by the 1960s. LA was also the home of half the Americans employed in the film and television industries.

A Society of Immigrants

As employment opportunities beckoned, newcomers from the Northeast and Midwest flocked to LA, overwhelming any feeble efforts to create an orderly plan for the development of the mushrooming region. Because of the dispersion of its population, critics derided Los Angeles as "a collection of suburbs in search of a city," lacking the central amenities (first-class orchestras, theaters, and museums, for example) typical of close-knit, long-established communities with elite traditions of culture. The massive invasion of newcomers, coinciding with the nationwide American flight to the suburbs, did little to change this situation. Angelenos (as LA's inhabitants are called) wanted to be their own landlords and chauffeurs. These preferences precluded the kind of high-density, vertical development characteristic of the older great cities of the Western world like Berlin and New York. For a time in the 1960s when it was welcoming a thousand newcomers a day, Los Angeles had the highest growth rate of any city in the Affluent North. Ranchers and orange-growers of the region, watching land prices increase by a third in a year, sold off their holdings, which were instantly transformed into sprawling subdivisions of standardized houses. At one point, 260 acres of Southern California farm or wild land were being "urbanized" every day, providing LA with the highest proportion of privately owned, single-family dwellings in the world.

Downtown Los Angeles in the 1980s. After decades of sprawling outwards, the center city has begun to rise skyward with the construction of office towers overlooking the freeway.
UPI/Bettmann Newsphotos

Rush hour on an LA freeway. The stalled traffic reflects a paradox. LA was built to accommodate vehicles that allowed drivers freedom to go wherever they liked in high-speed privacy, unlike public transportation. The result of all these individual choices when everyone is using the same route, however, is chaos.
Earl Young/Robert Harding Picture Library

During the boom years, LA confirmed its reputation as a new and distinctive kind of twentieth-century urban landscape. Stretching seventy miles from one end to the other, reaching into five counties and including some eighty other muncipalities around the central city, Greater Los Angeles had a population density only a quarter that of cities like New York, which had developed in the era of the pedestrian and the street railway. LA was the city that taught Americans how to live much of their life in their automobiles. Its most eye-catching constructions were not the ornamental buildings on which earlier cities had prided themselves, but the arteries of transportation: the freeways. Until environmentalists got it changed in 1965, the law required that these giant ribbons of concrete be built by "the most direct route." In the process, the homes of approximately a quarter-million people were destroyed—a striking testimony to the relative value of mobility and permanence in LA.

The choice of the name freeway was not accidental. The central value of the LA lifestyle was individual satisfaction through material consumption of the products of technology, with a minimum of social organization and control. The freeway was conceived as the high road to this goal, an ideal toward which mass societies of the developed world had been steadily moving in the twentieth century.

Angelenos might travel fifty or sixty miles to work over the freeway, shaving or dictating letters or listening to an inspirational tape as they drove. They moved at the level of the rooftops, unaware of communities of fellow Angelenos whose conditions and backgrounds were utterly different from their own. Neither necessity nor any ethic inherent in the nature of LA compelled an interest in these communities. Many freeway travelers had other concerns. Often they were absorbed in white-collar, high-technology jobs requiring expertise of which they were proud—for example, perfecting an inertial guidance system for jet fighters. Or they might work for the RAND Corporation, the Air Force–financed "think tank" that employed physical and social scientists to prepare cold war strategies. From this exacting post-industrial work, these Angelenos returned home to a subdivision full of people quite like themselves. In the evening they watched standardized mass entertainment on television, including crime thrillers—most of them made in LA and even set there, so that the obligatory car-chase hurtled through LA's characteristic landscape. On weekends Angelenos entertained friends at cookouts at the backyard barbecue pit, or attached their boat or skis to the car for a trip to the beach or the mountains.

Critics from an older tradition often satirized this pleasant lifestyle, along with LA's propensity for religious cults and oddly shaped restaurants. Though the economic center of the United States was rapidly moving westward toward them, many Angelenos reacted to such criticism with the defensiveness of Middle Americans faced with East Coast snobbery. A great majority of white, non-Hispanic Angelenos *were* transplanted Midwesterners, drawn by the double lure of perpetual sunshine and opportunity.

Politics: Home Base of Nixon and Reagan

The fact that so many found opportunity in LA explains much about the region's politics. White middle-class Angelenos tended to be fervent believers in individualism and "free enterprise," attributing their own success to these systems of social and economic organization. They were suspicious of government, especially the federal government—even though in the 1960s a third of LA's employment was sustained directly by federal dollars, and much more of it indirectly. Most Angelenos did not see any analogies between the defense contracts that gave them jobs and the government's welfare subsidies to the poor. They supported politicians who set the American agenda by championing a stronger military and repudiating the domestic generosity of the New Deal "guarantor state." Two such politicians became president of the United States. Richard Nixon grew up in the suburbs of Los Angeles. Ronald Reagan, whose roots were in small-town Illinois, took the earliest steps of his political career in the Hollywood movie industry before becoming a conservative spokesman as the host of television programs sponsored by General Electric.

The careers of these self-made men were larger-than-life versions of typical

Hot-dog vendor's vehicle in Los Angeles. In a city like Los Angeles, lacking any established tradition of design, there is no reason for an entrepreneur not to have a truck that looks like the product being sold.
Michael Abramson/Liaison

LA success stories. The Los Angeles of the boom years during the 1950s and 1960s marked the fulfillment of the American dream. Since the foundation of their country, Americans had been pushing ever westward in search of more privacy, more elbow room, more success, and more money. By 1900 the frontier was closed—the Pacific had been reached. Yet in their suburban houses and automobiles, Angelenos of the boom years could still believe that despite the interdependent organization of postindustrial society, they were as independent as nineteenth-century frontiersmen.

Watts, 1965

Black Angelenos had not shared in this fulfillment of the American dream. On a hot summer night in August 1965, white police officers arrested a black motorist in the heart of Watts, the vast ghetto that stretches south from the center of LA. The resulting confrontation eventually escalated into a six-day riot, quelled only by sending in nearly 14,000 troops. The death toll rose to 34, most of them poor and black, an indication that the rioters were not as well armed as those who repressed them. The 1,000 injured included 136 firemen hurt while battling some 600 separate blazes, sometimes under sniper attack. Two hundred buildings were totally destroyed, for a total property loss of over $40 million.

The riots of 1965 provoked a short-lived interest in sociological analysis of Watts, until then just another of those anonymous communities beside the freeways. LA's blacks lived in bungalows on palm-decorated streets, but Watts was as much a ghetto as New York's South Bronx. Studies found that LA had a higher degree of racial segregation than any other American city except Chicago and Cleveland. The 21-year-old driver whose arrest had touched off the riot was typical of thousands of young people in Watts. Born in Oklahoma, a high school dropout, he worked part-time at a gas station. (He had held only one full-time job, for five months at the age of 19.) Though many blacks, like whites, had migrated to LA in search of opportunities, they were frequently disappointed. In Watts, half the children came from broken homes, and half the population lived on public assistance. In a city with the highest per capita automobile ownership in the world, relatively few people owned cars, though the nearest jobs (like the nearest hospital) were ten miles away.

Twenty years after the riots of 1965, the prospects of Watts have hardly changed. Indeed, not all of the burned-out buildings have been replaced. American society has moved on from its brief anxiety about impending racial civil war. Nevertheless, the riots may have marked a turning point in the history of LA by drawing attention to some consequences of undirected growth. Similarly, as the 1970s forced Americans to recognize that the world had only a finite supply of natural resources, the energy-intensive freewheeling LA lifestyle lost some of its appeal. Californians consumed an average of 533 gallons of gas annually (compared with 349 for New Yorkers). LA was the most extreme example of a way of life in which Americans, 6 percent of the world's population, consumed a third of its resources. Many people now saw LA as a warning rather than as a promise for the future.

Frontier of the Hungry South in the 1980s

The 1980s have brought startling demographic changes to LA. The city has now become the United States' open door to the Third World, not only Latin America but the entire Pacific rim of Asian nations. In this respect, too, it remains to be seen whether LA is a promise for the future, or a warning.

In 1984, Los Angeles, the heart of a sprawling supermetropolis, became the second largest U.S. city. Demographers calculated that the gain of 150,000 people, which enabled LA to exceed Chicago's population, would not have occurred without the massive Hispanic and Asian influx. In fact, without these new arrivals the city proper would have lost 200,000 people as white Angelenos, like their middle-class counterparts elsewhere, continued their flight to the suburbs in the 1970s. That decade saw an increase of one-third in the population of Orange County, a bastion of political conservatism southeast of LA, where average household income was $43,000, compared with $15,000 in the city and $19,000 in the suburbs as a whole. Court-enforced busing, intended to diminish racial segregation in LA schools, actually had the opposite effect as white Angelenos moved beyond its reach.

Whites represented only 21 percent of the city's population in the early 1980s, down from 54 percent in the early 1960s. Newcomers of Hispanic and Asian origin took their places and spread out into Los Angeles County as well. In 1960, only one in nine county residents was Hispanic, and Asians represented less than 1 percent of the total. By the 1980s the county was nearly one-third Hispanic and 10 percent Asian. White Angelenos were a minority like everyone else. Since blacks constituted almost 20 percent of the population, LA could now be called the first Third World city in the United States, because a majority of its population was of African, Asian, or Latin American descent.

By eliminating quotas based on country of origin, President Johnson's Great Society legislation of 1965 reopened to immigrants the gates that Americans had closed in the 1920s. The new Angelenos came from everywhere in Asia and Latin America. The Iranian contingent grew from 20,000 in 1970 to 200,000 in 1983, the Koreans from 9,000 to 150,000. These and many other newcomers, in the tradition of nineteenth-century immigrants of European stock, were fleeing

Angelenos watching New Year's Day parade in Chinatown. Each ethnic group has tried to preserve something of its own tradition even in this most change-oriented of modern cities.
Eric Sander/Gamma Liaison

"The world's largest group photo." Fifteen thousand Angelenos crowd a freeway ramp to be in the photo welcoming the Olympic Games in 1984. Such harmless but meaningless nonevents are characteristic of the age of visual mass-media.
AP/Wide World Photos

political disorder or misrule in their homelands. (Salvadoran Angelenos, fewer than 2,000 in 1970, numbered 200,000 in 1983.) Other sizable LA ethnic communities included Armenians, Filipinos, and Arab-Americans, each numbering over 100,000. At Hollywood High School, which in the 1950s enrolled the children of movie stars, 70 percent of the students now are immigrants who speak 32 different languages. Only two-thirds of them have command of English.

Mexicans make up the largest contingent of newcomers. Ironically, they could be said to be resettling their own country, for LA had been part of Mexico until

seized by an American army in 1846. Four-fifths of LA's Hispanic population— over 2 million people—are of Mexican origin. Their numbers reflect the fact that LA lies not far north of the world's longest and most easily traversed border between the Affluent North and the Hungry South. In 1983, with Mexican unemployment officially estimated at 36 percent—and in reality perhaps higher— U.S. authorities arrested a half-million immigrants who had illegally crossed the sixty-six-mile-long border between San Diego County and Mexico. Most illegal immigrants, of course, are not apprehended. Their arrival put considerable strain on LA's social services. Ten percent of the babies born in Los Angeles County were the children of illegal aliens, mostly Mexican. In 1984, almost two-thirds of the kindergartners in the Los Angeles school district were Hispanic speakers, many with little command of English.

Like education, employment for this tide of newcomers represents a critical problem for LA. As has the rest of the United States, LA has shifted rapidly into the postindustrial age. Despite its image as a city of unusual occupations like moviemaking, LA at the end of World War II had a substantial industrial base, including nine automobile plants turning out 650,000 cars annually. By the 1980s, LA's share of smokestack America had waned, leaving only one automobile plant struggling to stay open. Even the aerospace industry slumped, with the rest of the U.S. economy, in the 1970s.

LA is the principal broker of the United States' rapidly growing Pacific trade, which in the 1980s has outstripped trans-Atlantic trade. This growing business may compensate for the decline of industry. Yet even LA's remarkable assortment of some hundred institutions of higher education may not be enough to train unskilled immigrants for postindustrial occupations.

Angelenos themselves were not necessarily willing to spend for such community purposes. Californians in the 1980s seemed to have lost some of their exuberant confidence in a future of unlimited growth. Rebellions against the state's tax structure reduced revenue so much that it became necessary to revoke the generous policy of providing free higher education at a whole range of public institutions. In a 1982 referendum California voters rejected plans to build a "peripheral canal" to divert Northern California water to Southern California. The lukewarm support of Southern Californians was not enough to overcome the expected opposition of Northern Californians. Although the plan was designed to benefit their region, many Angelenos evidently concluded that more water would only foster further cancerous urban growth.

For newer Angelenos however, such growth might spell opportunity. Their feelings on this issue were not easily ascertained, for they were startlingly underrepresented politically. LA elected a black mayor, Tom Bradley, in 1973, and in 1983 he presided over the two-hundredth anniversary of the city's foundation. But he was widely criticized as being the front man for wealthy "Anglo" (white) families that were still said to dominate the city's politics from their exclusive, racially segregated downtown clubs. In 1984, no Angeleno of Hispanic or Asian background held major elective office, though the city had Spanish- and Chinese-language television channels.

Historically, immigrants to the older cities of the East had found their political voice by providing blocs of votes to politicians in return for specific favors to their community. It was not clear whether such a system of machine politics could be created in the Californian atmosphere of loose party affiliations in dispersed suburbs. Without some such form of political integration, however, a collection of ethnic communities that barely recognized each other's existence could scarcely be expected to solve LA's growing problems, which ranged from deteriorating roads and buildings to high unemployment and violent crime in Watts and East Los Angeles (the Mexican-American stronghold).

East Los Angeles is a reminder that the

realities of the Third World—overpopulation, unemployment, poverty, dependency—that seem remote to most Americans are to be found right on their doorstep. Most of LA's recent immigrants have revived the dream of success of earlier immigrants who became middle-class Americans. Having escaped from Vietnam or rural Mexico, many will doubtless raise a family and make a success in business. Nevertheless, a thoughtful visitor to LA today must wonder how long and under what conditions the Affluent North can remain an island of plenty in a sea of poverty. In areas of LA where Asian and Hispanic immigrants have settled, the sights and sounds of other cultures suggest a Third World supermetropolis. One could almost be 1,900 miles away in Mexico City, destined to be the world's largest city by the end of the century—or even in Cairo, projected to rise from seventeenth in 1980 to thirteenth in rank by 1990 when it will be larger than London, Paris, or the Osaka-Kobe urban complex in Japan.

Cairo: The Urbanization of Poverty

If the village was the representative environment in the colonial world of 1914, the most distinctive environment of the Third World today is the megalopolis. In many Third World countries, especially the poorest, most of the population is still rural. Yet from Mexico to South Africa to the Philippines, social and economic forces are pulling people from the remotest locales to the cities. Grandchildren of many people who lived in the Egyptian village of Dinshawai in 1906 today live in Cairo. Their experiences

have many distinctively Egyptian facets, but also others with counterparts all across the Third World.

Cairo, Third World Megalopolis

By Middle Eastern standards, Cairo is not an old city. It is barely over 1,000 years old, although it has grown to incorporate earlier settlements. Only recently has Cairo become a supermetropolis. When the British occupied Egypt in 1882, Cairo's population was only about 400,000. With twentieth-century improvements in public health and the migration from the countryside, growth became rapid. By 1920, the city's population had reached 800,000; by 1950, 2.3 million; by 1960, 3.5 million. The estimate for 1983 was 14 million. In fact, no one knows the current population of the city exactly. To anyone who has been there, 14 million does not seem incredible.

Since the 1960s, Cairo's population density has reportedly risen as high as 250,000 people per square mile in some areas. Much housing in poorer neighborhoods is not over three or four stories high, and Cairo—like other cities in poor countries—has few of the parks and open spaces that grace Paris or Washington. In poor neighborhoods, living quarters with as little as 1.4 square yards per person have been reported. For some Cairenes, then, the world of "standing room only" is already here. Some do not occupy any space at all permanently but only rent a nook for part of the day.

Cairo's many neighborhoods and districts fall into four general categories.[1] Districts of the same type are not necessarily located together. The oldest districts are *medieval* (or older). These include the central districts on the site

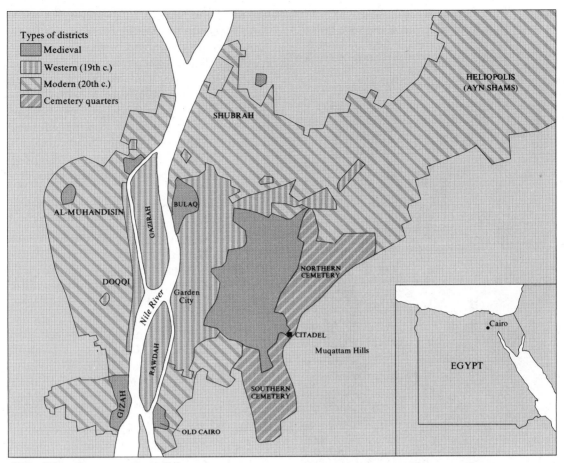

Map 17.2 Contemporary Cairo

where Cairo proper was founded, together with several originally separate settlements: the southern district of Old Cairo, or Fustat, which goes back at least to Roman times, and the former villages of Bulaq and Gizah. The medieval districts include Cairo's greatest architectural monuments, its old-fashioned bazaar, and the homes of many of the city's poor. Some live in buildings constructed during the Middle Ages. But much of the housing is newer, and more being built.

Another type of district is the *western* or European-style quarters of the nineteenth century. The most important dis-

trict of this type, on the east bank of the Nile, is still the city's center. The present riverbank was developed only in the nineteenth century, as drainage work and the building of embankments made new land available. On the east bank, near Liberation Square, are located many of today's government buildings, embassies, luxury hotels, international businesses, and some of the most luxurious housing. Especially elegant is the area just south of Liberation Square known as Garden City, with its winding streets, European-style apartment houses, and opulent villas. The develop-

Yellow Lane, a side street in medieval Cairo, 1983. A woman wears the robe (*milayah*) that urban women in general used to wear in public to conceal their persons and clothing.
C. V. Findley

ment of the islands in the Nile, Rawdah and Gazirah, and of the river's west bank began as an extension of the nineteenth-century European district on the east side of the Nile. The recurrent attempt to imitate European and especially Parisian urban-design concepts justifies the name *western* for the nineteenth-century districts. The echoes of Paris have all been overwhelmed, however, by the poverty and congestion of the modern megalopolis.

Outward from the center and especially northward toward the Nile Delta is the *modern* or twentieth-century part of Cairo. Here are many of the most prosperous districts. Ayn Shams, also known as Heliopolis, is noted for its luxurious private houses and apartment buildings. Farther out from the center of the city, the buildings become taller, bigger, and more ultramodern. On the west bank of the Nile, areas like al-Muhandisin show a similar pattern of growth to the north and west. The architecture is no longer distinctive, as in the medieval quarters or the Paris-inspired sections, but rather a Third World adaptation of contemporary international styles. The city has grown so rapidly in the twentieth century that one occasionally finds former villages, with their narrow lanes and mud brick houses, engulfed in the urban tide.

Not many Cairenes can afford to live in places like Garden City or Ayn Shams. In recent years, many could not find a place even in the shabby medieval quarters. Their solution to the problem of housing is distinctive to Cairo, yet in a larger sense is only a variant of the shantytowns found around other Third World cities.

Between the eastern edge of the city and the Muqattam Hills lie extensive *cemeteries*. Fine mosques and mausoleums

Qait Bay Cemetery in Cairo looking toward Muqattam Hills. The building on the corner and the one to its right are characteristic family mausoleums, with plaques over the doors naming the families to whom they belong.
C. V. Findley

built by rulers of past centuries stand alongside the burial places of contemporary Cairo families. In simplest form, the burial places consist of lots enclosed by a wall about the height of a one-story house, with a gate opening onto the street. Inside is a courtyard with one or two rooms or simply a shed to give shelter from the sun. Burials occur in the courtyard or in an undeground vault. Some of the grander tombs resemble the houses their occupants enjoyed in life, with resident caretakers, elegant reception rooms for mourners, and separate marble crypts for men and women—sug-

gesting an attitude toward death that may have come down from ancient Egypt.

In recent decades, poor migrants began to move into the cemeteries as squatters. As the city became more congested, the silent streets lined with walls and gates must have made the cemeteries look like uninhabited residential areas. Gradually, new construction began to go up. Today, the Qait Bay Cemetery includes apartment buildings up to seven stories high, a garage for auto repair, and a workshop making cafe tables—to name a few of the buildings. In some places, new construction has covered up all signs of the cemetery.

The first settlers in the cemeteries had to do without such utilities as electricity and water, but gradually the authorities responded to the "urbanization" of these areas. Today, around Qait Bay are found schools, electricity, signs of some kind of water supply, and a police station. On the other hand, urban services, which are inadequate throughout the city, are not good here. We notice puddles of standing water—it might be sewage—extending the width of a busy lane. Living among burial places inevitably suggests public health dangers. But observers agree that the cemetery quarters are more pleasant and less crowded than Cairo's slums.

Life in Cairo's cemeteries, as in the shantytowns of other Third World super-metropolises, is depressing in many ways. But it also illustrates the determination of the human spirit. A visit to the Qait Bay cemetery quarter early on a June evening revealed an irresistible gaiety about the place. Because it was Ramadan, pious Muslims were obliged to fast from sunup to sundown each day. From the top of the minaret of the mosque-mausoleum of Sultan Qait Bay, an observer could sense the holiday mood that emerged as the heat faded and the sixteen-hour fast approached its end.* Clothes, placed to dry on tomb-

_____

* Ramadan is the ninth month of the Islamic religious calendar. This is a lunar calendar, with twelve months averaging 29.5 days each, rather than a solar calendar (like the commonly used Gregorian calendar). Thus, there is no fixed relation between months in the Islamic calendar and the seasons. Each year, Ramadan begins eleven days earlier than in the previous solar year. As a result, the sunup-to-sundown fast varies in length over the years, much shorter in winter than in summer.

stones, flapped in the breeze. There was laughter and animated conversation in the streets. A woman was tending goats and chickens on the roof of a four-story apartment house. Other rooftops displayed similar attempts to re-create something of the village environment high above the cemetery's lanes. Children were flying kites. From an upper window of a seven-story apartment house, two boys lowered a basket on a rope, yelled their mother's order to the grocer below, and hauled the basket up after he had filled it. Lights, strung between the minarets of mosques for the festive month, now flickered on. And everyone listened for the signal that the time had come to begin the evening meal.

Social Fabric of the City

The social world of contemporary Cairo differs in many ways from the kinship society of the village as we saw it in Dinshawai in Chapter 2. Although individual neighborhoods may preserve a villagelike cohesiveness and homogeneity, the city as a whole contains great diversity. Cairo is the focus of urban migration within Egypt and exerts an international attraction as the greatest metropolis of the Arab world. As a result, the city contains a populace with broad variations in speech, dress, and skin color. Cairo possesses a wide range of religious institutions: the innumerable mosques and shrines of the Muslim majority, a large number of Coptic churches and fewer churches for many other Christian sects, and still a few synagogues, although most Jews had left Egypt by 1956.

An unskilled villager, driven to the great city by economic necessity, would have considerable difficulty adapting to the new environment with its incredible congestion and unfamiliar sights and sounds. But village and city are alike in their rapid population growth. The towns and villages of the Nile Delta, like Cairo, all seem in the 1980s to be doubling and tripling in size, gobbling up scarce cultivable land. In place of the mud brick of earlier times, the new buildings have a modern type of construction, framed and floored in reinforced concrete and walled in baked brick covered with stucco—a building technique common in Cairo, too. Egypt's urbanization focuses on Cairo but makes itself felt everywhere.

Cairo society contrasts with that of the village, however, in the strongly marked differentiation between the poor and what we may loosely call the middle class. Village society also has its economic inequalities, but they are more apt to be bridged by extended kinship connections among people at different income levels. In Cairo, such connections less often remain intact. In the city, upward mobility is possible in principle, and religious values encourage equality among Muslims. But inequality is still real enough.

The gap between poor and middle class shows in many ways. Cairo's poor often still dress like villagers, whereas the middle class wear either Western dress or the distinctive new "Islamic dress." Members of the middle class differ from the poor in education and often in the value they attach to it. Partly for this reason, there are class differences in speech. In their leisure activities, the poor are more apt to maintain the traditional segregation of the sexes—the women visit each other at home and the men congregate in teahouses. The more affluent enjoy a greater range of amuse-

A crowded street in Cairo. The contrast between the village dress of the man in the foreground and the Western dress of the men behind him is a common expression of the city's diversity.
Sahm Doherty/Liaison

ments, often in mixed company. Ultimately, the most extensive class-related differences are ones of values. The middle class, for example, is increasingly willing to see women work outside the home, while many of the poor still see this as disgraceful, even if unavoidable.

Urbanization has exposed Egyptians to a more complex and stratified social environment than they knew in the village, but few of them have experienced the "liberation" of the individual or the mobilization into social organizations and movements that are so conspicuous

Contrasting dress of Egyptian women. Today many Cairo women find that Islamic dress helps them assert their values and their respectability as they move into the public life of the congested city.
Sahm Doherty/Liaison

in the more affluent parts of Los Angeles. This is one more dimension of inequality between rich and poor parts of Cairo, like the contrast between Beverly Hills and Watts in LA. In affluent Cairo families, both men and women can continue their education through the university; enter the professions, business, or government service; and affiliate with a variety of political, social, or cultural movements. At the same time, paradoxically, studies of political leaders suggest that they and their families do better than the poor in maintaining the social cohesion and mutual support of the extended kin group after the move into the city. Perhaps it is really maintenance of

these traits over generations that enables such people to become political leaders.[2] Finally, Egypt has had a feminist movement ever since a handful of patrician ladies flung aside their veils to participate in nationalist agitation following World War I. In the Cairo of the 1980s, women from prosperous families have achieved considerable visibility in fields such as telecommunications, tourism, education, the arts, medicine, and even politics.

The poor face much less satisfactory conditions. One study showed that in the late 1960s and early 1970s, most of those studied were living as nuclear, rather than extended, families with six, seven, or more children crowded into a tiny apartment, which might lack running water or electricity, or both. Other relatives might also live in the city, but they could rely on one another much less than they had in the village. Although crumbling somewhat under pressure, social discipline nonetheless remained far stronger than in many poor neighborhoods of American cities. A visitor who would not feel safe at all in Watts could walk through Bulaq without fear, although children might make fun of foreigners. An unaccompanied woman in Western dress would encounter offensive behavior from men. By conservative Islamic standards, respectable women do not appear in public with more than their face and hands showing and preferably should be accompanied by a male relative. A foreign woman who wanted to visit Bulaq could avoid annoyance by observing these conventions—however much she might wish to see them changed. For a poor woman of Cairo, the main cost of these conventions is that her sphere of acquaintance (all female, except for relatives) and her range of movement tend to be confined to her immediate neighborhood, where she and her family are known.

Perhaps the harshest effect of poverty is that it hinders fulfillment of idealized sex roles for those who still value most the traditional, highly differentiated role concepts. The poor commonly think of the father as the family bread winner, who should not only provide adequately but also show his love for his wife and daughters by gifts of gold jewelry. The wife should be a homemaker and mother, finding fulfillment through her husband and children. She and her daughters should lead an irreproachable life that will maintain the family honor. Custom and religious practice add other requirements: offering hospitality to friends and visitors; providing for the feast at the end of Ramadan, when gifts of new clothing should be given; and arranging the exchanges of property that should accompany a marriage. Inability to meet these cultural claims exposes one's inadequacies to the view of others. Poverty makes it impossible for men and women to fulfill their expectations of themselves. Some poor families manage to overcome these problems. Yet rarely does a poor family make its way into the middle class.

Economic Life of the City

An unskilled migrant from Dinshawai faces bleak economic prospects in Cairo. A man can look for a low-level factory job or construction work. Many find marginal subsistence as street vendors and the like. Men and women both take jobs as domestic servants. Almost inevitably, their income barely covers their families' routine expenses, even assuming the government's consumer subsidies, with nothing left for needs created by illness, the children's schooling, or special occasions.

Even education will not necessarily enable a young person to escape from poverty, given the effects of Nasser's populist socialist policies. In 1963, the government recognized the principle of open admission to the universities, and in the following year it acknowledged a responsibility to hire any university graduate. A drastic overloading of both universities and government services has ensued. Academic standards have sagged, and government payrolls have expanded to encompass one-third of the work force. The results include extreme underemployment of most officials and low salaries, so that the vast majority—despite their degrees—cannot earn enough to keep above the poverty line. Many hold two jobs. The OPEC era has also made possible a large "labor emigration." Both university graduates and laborers go to work for a time in more affluent Arab countries where they can earn ten times as much as at home.

Cairo's economy today shows the effects of economic policy changes since 1952, compounded by Third World superurbanization. Many Cairenes remember the last days of the old landowning elites, whose survivors still occupy some shuttered mansions in Garden City or Zamalek. Many more Cairenes lived through the socializing reforms that peaked in the early 1960s. Most experienced Sadat's "opening" to the West.

Although economic policy changes created serious dangers for those who could not adjust, they offered opportunities to the middle class—a term that covers a wide range. Even under Nasser, the well connected could prosper in politics, administration, the professions, and various fields of business and industry, often by serving as subcontractors for state enterprises. As in other countries with weak business and industrial sectors, real estate and construction remained favored investment fields, especially as urban growth accelerated.

The government attempted to regulate real estate development by controlling the supply of materials during the socialist period, by requiring government approval of construction plans, and by rent control. But Cairenes developed ingenious means to subvert the controls: a black market in building materials, alteration of approved plans during construction, and rent-gouging devices. The housing shortage became so acute that young couples, unable to find apart-ments, began to marry secretly—an almost unthinkable step in a country with a strong tradition of familial control over marriage. Efforts to create housing by adding more stories to existing structures sometimes led to the collapse of buildings and loss of life.

Today many of Cairo's gravest economic problems result from the impact of population growth on its urban facilities. In Los Angeles, comparable problems are minor by comparison. Cairo's urban sprawl combines with much higher population densities. Although the government does what it can to upgrade roads and bridges, Cairo is hardly a freeway city. But it has enough motor vehicles that the traffic jams seem to last all day. Burning low-grade gasoline and subject to no emissions controls, the cars and buses produce clouds of exhaust that blend overhead with the black smoke from the incineration of garbage on the city outskirts and with airborne dust from the desert, causing a thick pall over the city. Cairo's growth has overwhelmed not only its roads, but all its urban utilities. Water and sewerage are inadequate. The telephone and postal systems are in a state of virtual collapse. The buses are usually so full that men and boys hang on the outside. Efforts begun in the early 1980s to build a subway system ran into serious problems because underground cables and pipes proved far more numerous than expected. Despite its vitality, the city faces the threat of "thrombosis" due to superurbanization amid acute poverty.

Political Mobilization Without Participation?

Politically, Cairo is the most important city of the Arab world. The Arab League headquarters building on Liberation Square continues to symbolize this fact, although the organization's actual headquarters moved to Tunis in 1979 when almost all member states opposed Egypt's peace with Israel. The importance of the Egyptian state in the city's life finds expression in the many government agencies, including the immense administrative complex also located on Liberation Square. For most Cairenes, however, political mobilization remains as incomplete as Egypt's economic development. Despite experiments in mass political organization, such as Nasser's Arab Socialist Union, the post-1952 regimes have generally represented a type of pharaonic democracy in which a charismatic leader solicits cheers more often than ballots from the citizenry. Although Egypt may be moving toward greater democratization, the authoritarian note has remained strong until recently.

Poor Cairenes have indeed turned out in mass at moments of crisis, for example, to demonstrate support for Nasser or opposition to Sadat's attempts to cancel consumer subsidies. Otherwise, political cynicism and noninvolvement have been more typical attitudes. Even though Nasser's Arab Socialist Union had an office in every district of the city, many Cairenes saw it as an "organ of acclaim" for the government, staffed by workers who did not care about their constituents or who were corrupt.[3] Some Cairenes even said that things had been better under the British. Such statements hint at the "old person's view of history," the notion that time brings only decline. But the city was less crowded and better serviced before 1952.

In the 1980s, alienation has found an outlet increasingly in the Islamic fundamentalist movements. Their leaders typically are bright young men of village

Cairo Smog. This view from the Nile (lower left) to the Pyramids, faintly visible a few miles away, illustrates Cairo's modern growth, along with its severe air pollution.
C. V. Findley

or small-town background (including sons of migrants to the city); they have studied to qualify for prestigious professions like engineering only to find their prospects limited to dead-end government jobs at about $65 per month. The movements mobilize such people into cells known significantly as "families." The Islamic ideology of the movements readily provides the basis for a critique of the existing order. If the movements triumphed, would the ideology solve Egypt's problems?[4]

Cairo as a Center of Intellectual and Spiritual Life

Culturally and spiritually, Cairo stands at the opposite end of a continuum from villages like Dinshawai. Historically, villages and country towns were the centers of popular religion and folk culture. The strict Islam of the religious scholars and the learned literary culture were urban products, although city and village each displayed some of the cultural traits more typical of the other. The contrast to the village is particularly marked in the case of Cairo, for it is the leading cultural center of the entire Arab world, stretching from the Atlantic shores of North Africa to Arabia and Iraq. Cairo's influence as a center of Islamic religious learning stretches farther—to the outermost limits of the Islamic world.

Evidences of Cairo's cultural pre-eminence abound. The city houses the al-Azhar mosque university, one of the foremost centers of Islamic studies. Cairo was an early center of Arabic journalism and still is one of the most important. Since the Nasser period, it has become a center of the electronic media also. Cairo has been home to a large share of the great Arab thinkers and writers of the last century and a half. Some were natives of the city, some were drawn from Egypt's villages, and many came from other Arab lands. One of the most distinguished contemporary novelists, Naguib Mahfouz, has written extensively about the life of the city; his *Midaq Alley* depicts the impact of World War II on ordinary people in the medieval part of Cairo. In modern times, Cairo's literary culture has become largely secularized, adding an Islamic-secular tension to the historical popular-learned tension.

The Islamic religious life of the great city displays the same mixture of elements found in a Delta village eighty years earlier, but with much more emphasis on the strict Islam of the learned. The steady influx of villagers helps to perpetuate forms of popular religious practice that are familiar to them. The healing ceremonies of the *zar* cult, discussed in Chapter 2, have their urban practitioners and followers even now. Though they have been attacked by both secular-minded modernizers and advocates of strict Islam, the saint cults and mystical orders are also living realities of the contemporary city, if less so than in the past. Closer to strict Islam, the devotion of Cairenes to the Prophet Muhammad and his immediate family is one of the hallmarks of the city's religious life, as shown by the prominence of shrines dedicated to members of the Prophet's family. Finally, the strict Islam of the religious scholars and pious activists has become increasingly influential in recent years.

The exponents of the strict Islam of Qur'an and religious law are a varied group, and their influence has wavered considerably over the last century and a half. For a long time, Western expansion seemed to erode their influence, although some people always looked to Islam for a way to overcome the Western threat. For people like these, part of the problem was that pure Islam had become deeply mired in the superstition and mysticism that we saw in Dinshawai at the beginning of this century. From the late nineteenth century on, religious activists taught that God meant for Muslims to flourish in this world and the next, and that a return to strict Islam and a revitalization of religious thought to address the problems of a new era would help liberate Muslims from foreign domination. In the post-1945 era of independence and especially after the OPEC oil revolution of the 1970s, experience seemed to confirm these arguments, and Islamic activism became more influential in Cairo and across the Islamic world.

As Islamic activism extended its scope, leadership passed out of the hands of the "established" religious leaders, who are found in institutions like al-Azhar. Instead, Islamic activism became a mass phenomenon, such as political life as narrowly defined had not produced. Episodes involving militant fundamentalists, like the assassination of Sadat in 1981, illustrate this point. Evidence of the change over the past few years can be seen on Cairo streets. One sees many people whose conservative style of dress advertises their Islamic commitment: bearded men, and women whose clothing leaves only their faces and hands visible.

The situation of these women merits examination. Some are daughters or granddaughters of women who cast off an older style of Islamic dress in the interest of achieving greater independence. Today's young women begin at a level of independence their mothers had to fight for, and seek to combine these gains with a renewed expression of their Islamic identity. Nothing could be more typical of contemporary Third World cultures than the desire to combine the advantages of modernity with inherited values.

Conclusion

While it was difficult in 1914 to imagine environments more dissimilar than a great European capital and a colonial village, our comparison of Los Angeles and Cairo shows more resemblances between contemporary supermetropolises of Affluent North and Hungry South. Both Los Angeles and Cairo are products of growth processes of national and even international scope. Both cities are socially highly differentiated. Los Angeles has a greater variety of ethnic groups, many of them recent migrants from the Hungry South, but both cities display marked socioeconomic inequalities. Both cities are major political centers, though their characteristic forms of political mobilization are different. Cairo offers its citizens fewer channels for effective political participation than LA, but Watts residents and poor Cairenes probably have much the same feeling about the responsiveness of the political system under which they live. Culturally, both cities exert an international influence. The contrast between secularism and religiosity, which was so marked in Chapter 2, seems less striking in the 1980s. Los Angeles and Cairo differ most in their economic life, although even here they are perhaps closer together than were Berlin and Dinshawai. Although both cities suffer from overcrowding and pollution, Los Angeles' problems are those of the postindustrial society, while Cairo's are those of perhaps worsening underdevelopment. Overall, our visits to these two great cities suggest that the tightening of global integration has significantly narrowed differences between dominant and dependent societies in the late twentieth century.

Notes

1. Based on Janet-Abu Lughod, *Cairo: 1001 Years of the City Victorious* (Princeton: Princeton University Press, 1971), pp. 171–180.
2. Robert Springborg, *Family, Power, and Politics in Egypt: Sayed Bey Marei—His Clan, Clients, and Cohorts* (Philadelphia: University of Pennsylvania Press, 1982).
3. Unni Wikan, *Life Among the Poor in Cairo*, trans. Ann Henning (London: Tavistock Publications, 1980), pp. 161–163.
4. Sana Hasan, "Egypt's Angry Islamic Militants," *New York Times Magazine*, November 20, 1983, pp. 137–147.

Suggestions for Further Reading

Los Angeles

Brodsley, David, *L.A. Freeway: An Appreciative Essay* (1982).
Cohen, Jerry, and William S. Murphy, *Burn, Baby, Burn: The Watts Riot* (1966).
"The New Ellis Island," *Newsweek*, June 13, 1983.
Rand, Christopher, *Los Angeles* (1967).
Rolle, Andrew, *Los Angeles: From Pueblo to City of the Future* (1981).

Cairo

Abu-Lughod, Janet, *Cairo: 1001 Years of the City Victorious* (1971).
Rugh, Andrea, *Coping with Poverty in a Cairo Community* (1979).
Springborg, Robert, *Family, Power, and Politics in Egypt: Sayed Bey Marei—His Clan, Clients, and Cohorts* (1982).
Waterbury, John, *The Egypt of Nasser and Sadat: The Political Economy of Two Regimes* (1983).
Wikan, Unni, *Life Among the Poor in Cairo*, trans. Ann Henning (1980).
———, "Living Conditions Among Cairo's Poor: A View from Below," *Middle East Journal*, 39, No. 1 (1985), 7–26.

Chapter *18*

A WORLD OF INTERDEPENDENCE AMID SCARCITY

The preceding comparison of contemporary Los Angeles and Cairo illustrates the growing integration and interdependence of the world in which we live. Similarly, both cities' situations—Cairo's poverty and Los Angeles' water problems and air pollution—indicate how growing human numbers strain our earthly habitat. With these facts in mind, this book concludes with an examination of the forces shaping the global pattern now and for the foreseeable future. The central question of this inquiry is whether human beings can direct these forces for their own good. By investigating problems of population, food and energy, economic development, transnational integration, and technology and nuclear weapons, together with possible solutions, this chapter attempts to answer that question.

Population

Discussion of global interdependence amid scarcity must begin with *demography*, the study of population. This idea is not new. In his *Essay on Population* (1798), Thomas Malthus pointed out that although humanity's means of subsistence could only grow by arithmetic increments, unchecked population growth would compound itself in a geometric progression. Strictly speaking, arithmetic progression means addition of a fixed factor $(2 + 2 = 4, 4 + 2 = 6, 6 + 2 = 8)$. Geometric progression means multiplication by a fixed factor $(2 \times 2 = 4, 4 \times 2 = 8, 8 \times 2 = 16)$, the result being a much faster increase.

Malthus's idea that unchecked population growth would outstrip increases in food supply has exerted a lasting influence. For a long time, however, exceptional increases in the means of human subsistence postponed major crisis. The opening of new continents and improvements in agricultural yield expanded food supplies enormously. As a result, many doubted Malthus's logic. In the late twentieth century, however, there are no more continents left to open, the world population is six times higher than in Malthus's day, and the latest technologies prove often to have undesirable side effects. Malthusian logic again haunts us. With many of the world's peoples living in poverty, and starvation threatening almost half the countries in Africa in the mid-1980s, population growth is a major problem.

The twentieth century exemplifies the geometric population growth that Malthus dreaded. In the year 1500, the population of the world was about 600 million and was increasing slowly. Birth and death rates were both high, and plague, famine, or war periodically wiped out whatever growth occurred. In the eighteenth century, the number of people began to rise. In nineteenth-cen-

tury Europe, economic growth associated with the Industrial Revolution led to declines in death rates, followed later by drops in birthrates. Until the two rates regained equilibrium at a lower level, population grew very rapidly. To demographers, Western Europe's experience became the classic example of the *demographic transition*. There, the shift from high birth and death rates to low ones was associated with the rise of the urban middle class, whose attitudes toward children were very different from those of their peasant grandparents.

In the twentieth century, public health has improved around the world, increasing life expectancy almost everywhere. In some places, such as Japan, economic growth has recreated something like the European demographic transition, including drops in the birthrate. But living standards in most poor nations have not improved greatly, and their birthrates remain high. In some Third World countries, the increased availability of contraception and the spread of middle-class values are leading to reductions in family size even without substantial increases in income. This fact suggests that if the world could support present population trends long enough, it might achieve a new equilibrium eventually, much as nineteenth-century Europe did. Meanwhile, the world's population is growing faster than ever in history.

The world population of the mid-1980s is growing by almost 80 million people each year, over 70 million of them in the developing countries. In Europe, a dozen countries—Austria, Belgium, Denmark, East Germany, Hungary, Italy, Luxembourg, Norway, Sweden, Switzerland, the United Kingdom, and West Germany—have achieved zero population growth: the numbers of births and

Ambuya Nemuzukuru Centre, Zimbabwe, 1984. "Educate a Woman, You Educate a Nation": the clinic teaches child spacing, along with prenatal, infant, and child care. *The Rev. Margaret B. Gunness*

deaths each year are essentially equal. In most developing countries, in contrast, population growth is still rapid, and because a large part of the population has not yet entered the child-bearing years, population growth will inevitably continue long into the future. To judge solely from demographic data, global population appears likely to rise from 4.7 billion in 1983 to 9.8 billion by 2050 and to stabilize at more than 11 billion around the year 2150.

Could the earth support a population that large? Today Bangladesh, one of the poorest nations, has 97 million people in an area slightly smaller than Wisconsin. If Bangladesh's problems were magnified to global scale and population growth continued at present rates, the world would surely encounter the natural obstacles that Malthus identified: famine, pestilence, and war. Death rates would again soar past birthrates for a

time, causing the pattern that demographers call "dismal peaks." The only alternative to such a tragic outcome would be for the world's societies to find ways to bring population back into line with food supplies. By pressuring families to limit themselves to one child each, the Chinese authorities have shown one way to do this. Most societies will have to rely on less high-pressure methods of population control, such as mass education, extension of family planning services to the village level, or offering tax advantages to families with no more than a certain number of children. Fortunately, many of the world's religions—including Islam and Buddhism—do not oppose birth control. But experience seems to show that population control strategies will not work well unless the initiative seems to come from within the society itself. In Third World environments, efforts by international agencies to play a direct role are vulnerable to attack as "imperialist" efforts to "sterilize the nation" and make it easy to dominate. But many Third World governments lack China's capability to organize nationwide family planning services. In such societies, what is to keep Malthusian catastrophe from doing the work people cannot do for themselves?

Food and Energy

The population problem is one of food and natural resources as well as human numbers. When population issues are considered in their ecological setting, the key question becomes the "sustainability" of a given population in a finite world. The oil problems that ended a quarter-century of rapid growth in the

1970s and the African famines of the 1970s and 1980s have forced us to look at the question of sustainability. In fact, many other resource problems also illustrate the theme of interdependence amid scarcity. The United States, for example, is dependent on foreign sources for many minerals, including aluminum, chromium, cobalt, copper, manganese, and tin. A full discussion would have to consider all such resources. But because the needs for food and energy are most pressing on a global scale, this discussion is limited to those topics. In examining them, we shall look for ways to achieve the sustainability on which human survival depends.[1]

Food for the Billions?

Some discussions of the food problem mistakenly attempt to isolate it from population and resource questions. Such presentations tend to make the world food problem look like one of distribution, rather than one of supply. In this view, the needed response to the African famines of the 1980s appears to be a more efficient redistribution of agricultural surpluses from regions like North America. In fact, such measures would provide no more than short-term relief and leave Africa's demographic and agricultural problems of sustainability untouched.

Other analyses of the food problem make implausible assumptions in order to argue the possibility of expanding food production to keep pace with population growth. One study has argued that food production could be increased thirtyfold—assuming no limits on resources like fertilizer, labor, and agricultural skills, no damage to crops, and no use of agricultural land for other pur-

poses. As any farmer knows, these are unrealistic assumptions. Unless we can develop productivity-enhancement techniques less dependent on petroleum than the Green Revolution strategies of the 1960s, even the more modest goal of tripling agricultural productivity is doubtful, particularly on the world scale.[2] The historical record can help us get a more realistic sense of the food problem. To simplify the discussion, we shall focus on grains. (See Table 18.1.)

Until the late 1930s, Western Europe was the only major world region that was not self-sufficient in grain, and Latin America was the largest grain exporter. After World War II as population growth accelerated, the number of grain exporters declined, while grain exports of the United States and Canada mounted sharply because of improvements in productivity. By the 1970s, only a handful of countries could be counted on to export grain: the United States, Canada, Australia, Argentina, and France. The United States and Canada together accounted for over 70 percent of exports. Those two countries were leading world suppliers of feed grains and soybeans, as well as wheat. In fact, the world's grain dependency was even more concentrated on one region than its oil dependency. In 1982, the United States provided 55 percent of global grain exports, while Saudi Arabia, the largest oil exporter, accounted for 32 percent of oil exports. Because the United States and Canada are subject to the same climatic fluctuations, the world's grain dependency is narrowly focused, indeed.

To understand the problem of sustainability in food production, we must recognize how population growth stresses agricultural productivity. New roads and buildings reduce croplands. But a greater limit on food production is the

Table 18.1 World Grain Production, 1950–1983 (millions of metric tons)[a]

Region	1950[b]	1960	1970	1980	1983[c]
North America	+23	+39	+56	+131	+122
Latin America	+ 1	0	+ 4	− 10	− 3
Western Europe	−22	−25	−30	− 16	+ 2
E. Europe and Soviet Union	0	0	0	− 46	− 39
Africa	0	− 2	− 5	− 15	− 20
Asia	− 6	−17	−37	− 63	− 71
Australia and New Zealand	+ 3	+ 6	+12	+ 19	+ 9

[a] Plus sign indicates net exports; minus sign, net imports.
[b] Average for 1948–1952.
[c] Preliminary.

Source: Lester R. Brown et al., *State of the World, 1984: A Worldwatch Institute Report on Progress Toward a Sustainable Society* (New York: W. W. Norton & Company, 1984), p. 183. Figures from United Nations Food and Agriculture Organization, *Production Yearbook* (Rome: various years); U.S. Department of Agriculture, *Foreign Agriculture Circular*, August 1983; author's estimates.

"population-land-fertilizer link."[3] Increased use of chemical fertilizers has made possible great increases in food production. Yet there is a point of diminishing returns. In the 1970s, for example, the increase in oil and natural gas prices led to rises in fertilizer prices, for fertilizer manufacture requires much oil and gas. Even without that, there would have been the greater long-run problem that the productivity of agricultural land will not increase indefinitely in proportion to the amount of chemical fertilizer applied. Chemical fertilizers add chiefly nitrogen, phosphate, and potash to the soil. But soil fertility also depends on other things, such as trace minerals and organic matter, which intensive cultivation depletes and chemical fertilizers cannot replace. In terms of worldwide averages, an additional ton of fertilizer made it possible during the 1950s to grow another 11.5 tons of grain. By the 1970s, another ton of fertilizer would produce only 5.8 additional tons of grain. Ultimately, it is not possible to substitute fertilizer for cropland.

What is happening to the croplands of the world? As noted in Chapter 15, excessive cultivation, grazing, and woodcutting and inadequate water supplies appear to be the major causes of the famine and drought that have produced tragic and perhaps irreversible consequences in Africa. Even the naturally better-watered parts of tropical Africa have suffered from overcultivation.

Other continents have comparable problems. In many places, farmers have intensified cultivation and extended it into marginal lands, improving yields in the short run but creating long-term risks of soil degradation. The problem has many dimensions. In mountainous regions from Japan to the Andes, the extension of cultivation has historically depended on the painstaking building of terraces. In recent years, growing food needs have led to cultivation of slopes without proper terracing. The result is erosion and a growing danger of landslides. Even in less difficult environments, other dangers have arisen from neglect of fallowing and crop rotation patterns formerly used to restore fertility. U.S. farmers have increasingly planted their lands in crops like corn or soybeans, relying on fertilizers to replace the nitrogen once supplied by periodic planting of legumes, even though research has shown that the new practice may increase erosion to dangerous levels. Meanwhile, expansion of the areas cultivated has increased the risk of wind erosion in many parts of the United States and in other countries. It is estimated that the Soviet Union abandons 1.2 million acres of cropland every year because of wind erosion.

Deforestation worsens soil problems in many areas. In the Hungry South of the early 1980s, over 28 million acres of tropical forest and open woodland were cleared each year, even though the soils underneath were often unsuited for cultivation. In the Affluent North, acid rain from industrial pollution was the main threat. All told, the threat to the world's forests appeared very grave. Deforestation compounds the threat of soil erosion from unsound agricultural practices and, by increasing the runoff rate for rainwater, increases the danger of flooding. As of 1983, it was estimated that the world lost 23 billion tons of soil from its croplands each year.

Enough information is available about sound cultivation and reforestation practice to make it possible, in theory, to correct most of the problems discussed here. With time, new techniques and crop strains improved by genetic engineering may also help. But can the information and new techniques be applied in time? And can they keep food production abreast of population growth?

Energy, Nonrenewable and Renewable

OPEC may have done the world a favor by increasing the price of oil, for the shocks of the 1970s may have driven home an awareness that the world has only a finite amount of oil. For the quarter-century preceding the oil embargo of 1973, the price of oil had been kept low, while world oil consumption had more than quintupled, to 20 billion barrels in 1973. Petroleum and related products had become the basis for much of the world's transportation, heating, and electric-power generation. Because they were produced in such quantities, by-products of the refining process had become the basic raw material for much of the chemical industry, even where other materials could have served as well. Plastics, synthetic fibers, and even fertilizers were manufactured from petroleum derivatives.

One way to measure oil dependency is to compute the number of barrels of oil required to produce $1,000 of world GNP each year. Reckoning GNP in 1980 dollars, that figure stood as low as 1.33 barrels in 1950, then peaked at 2.27 in 1973 before beginning an irregular fall that again brought the figure below 2.0 from 1981 on. During the third quarter of the century, then, the world consumed ever-larger amounts of oil and relied on oil for more uses. Of course, there were gross regional disparities. In 1973, for example, it required 5.11 barrels of oil to produce $1,000 in GNP in the United States, but it only took 1.04 barrels in China.

People could not go on forever using a nonrenewable resource without regard to the risk of depletion. The high consumption levels of the developed economies and the concentration of much of the world's oil resources in a handful of culturally similar Middle Eastern states made OPEC possible. A variety of factors, including conservation, the shift to alternative forms of energy, and global recession, then began to lower world oil consumption from 1979 on. A few years later, oil prices also began to fall.

The oil crisis was not over, however. At 1983 production levels, the world's proven oil reserves would be depleted in 37 years. Its recoverable reserves, which could be extracted by more costly techniques, would last 114 years at the same rate of production. Still more oil could theoretically be extracted from tar sands and shale deposits at far higher prices. Each new year of oil exploration reduced the likelihood that new reserves could be found in quantities that would fundamentally alter this picture. There were ways, such as gasification of coal, to produce petroleum substitutes. But the age of oil was passing. The age of cheap oil ended in 1973.

What energy alternatives lie before us for the foreseeable future? The world has many times more coal than oil, enough to last for centuries at present rates of consumption. Ultimately, however, coal too is a nonrenewable resource. Moreover, its use presents significant problems: air pollution and acid rain. Oxides of sulfur and nitrogen, released into the atmosphere by coal burning, combine with water to form acids that fall to the earth with the rain. If acidity becomes high enough, it can destroy wildlife and trees and can cause lasting soil damage.

In an era when people look to advanced technologies to solve problems, another common assumption has been that nuclear power would help relieve energy needs. Ten years after the oil boycott, the record of nuclear power has shown what disappointments could follow from regarding technology as a genie able to solve all problems by magic. What has most clouded the future of nuclear power is not so much environmental worries, though they are well grounded, as economics.

In the United States, construction costs for nuclear power plants are at least twice as high as those for coal-powered generating plants of the same capacity. At U.S. prices, electricity generated from nuclear power costs about 65 percent more than electricity generated from coal, and 25 percent more than electricity generated from petroleum. Between 1975 and 1983, plans for the construction of eighty-seven nuclear plants were canceled in the United States.[4]

The experience of most other developed countries appears similar. West Germany had the largest nuclear program in Europe into the late 1970s, but after 1975 ordered only one more plant. The country also developed a vigorous antinuclear movement. Soviet data indicates that nuclear power plants cost up to twice as much to build as coal plants in that country too. Among the developed economies, only France and Japan have clear ongoing commitments to nuclear power. Both plan to use this method to meet half or more of their needs within a decade or two. Their programs continue more because better alternatives to petroleum imports are lacking than because nuclear power is cost effective. In the Third World, only a handful of countries have nuclear power plants. Most cannot bear the costs of nuclear power generation, even if they have the expertise.

The most promising alternatives to petroleum are the various renewable energy sources, which often have the advantage of being technologically simple. One renewable energy source already finding some use is *biomass conversion*—energy derived from plants. The homeliest example is wood-burning. Wood never ceased being a major source of heat for cooking in the Third World and has recently made a comeback for heating in parts of the United States and Europe.

Other biomass processes use crops or plant wastes either for producing inflammable pellets or for converting chemically into ethyl alcohol or methane gas. The Brazilian program for producing fuel alcohol from sugar cane relies on such a process. However, most countries that are not self-sufficient in food will probably conclude that cropland has more important uses than energy generation. In time, bioengineering may make it possible to get through this bottleneck by using genetically modified micro-organisms to produce biomass or even petroleum-like substances.

No renewable energy source has captured popular awareness more than solar energy. This is already in wide use in some countries, like Israel, for hot-water heating. Another promising application of solar energy is the use of photovoltaic cells, made of silicon, which produce electricity when light strikes them. Originally developed for the U.S. space program, the first cells were extremely expensive; by the mid-1980s, their cost had fallen sharply enough to make them marketable in such applications as solar calculators. Further reductions would be needed to make the cells cost competitive with other forms of electricity generation in large-scale applications. But the cells are already the preferred electricity source for remote locations and may soon replace the diesel generators widely used in the Third World. The cells are expected to be cost competitive in most parts of the world by the 1990s. Some day, houses equipped with arrays

High technology and hand labor in India. Workers with hoes move earth near a nuclear power plant site. This picture sums up the unevenness of a major Third World country's developmental record.
Henri Cartier-Bresson/Magnum

of cells may become their own major providers of electricity, and even sell excess power to the local utility company, without pollution or hazardous side effects.

A successful adjustment to the passing of the petroleum age will certainly mean a greater reliance on these and other renewable energy sources. Such an adjustment will probably also mean reliance on a greater number of energy sources and on technologies simpler and less costly to apply than those of nuclear power generation. Diversification and increased use of nondepletable energy sources, especially solar energy, will create more possibilities to serve the energy needs of large populations. The possibilities are not unlimited, however. Where could we put enough solar cell arrays to produce electricity for 11 billion people?

Wherever we look, questions of food and resources reinforce the impression of interdependence amid scarcity. New technologies may eventually push back some of the limits discussed here. If a sustainable equilibrium between population and environment could be restored, global interdependence might even lessen as major regions regained greater self-sufficiency in food, energy, and other resources. Unless population growth can be restrained, however, the basic logic of vastly increased human numbers straining the resources of a finite environment will dominate our future. The declining living standards and environmental degradation of the Hungry South today show that the crisis of sustainability is real and will not be solved quickly.

Alternative Strategies of Economic Development

The issue of living standards in poor nations raises broader questions about economic development and the forms of global integration. This section will compare strategies of economic development in the Affluent North and the Hungry South. The next section reviews the question of international integration, especially as it relates to economic interdependence. In these discussions, the prime interest lies not so much in the developmental strategies of individual governments, as in the inequalities in the global distribution of population and wealth, as shown in Maps 18.1 and 18.2, and in possible ways of reducing these disparities while promoting development.

Developmental Strategies of the Affluent North

In the Affluent North, three general types of economic development strategies require consideration. The first strategy is that of the capitalist welfare economies of Western Europe and North America. Countries like the United States, Britain, and Germany developed through a process of industrialization according to the free enterprise philosophy of nineteenth-century liberal economics. Over time, these nations introduced a variety of social safeguards, such as those pioneered in Germany in the late nineteenth century, developed in the United States with the New Deal, and widely applied in Europe after World War II. By the 1980s, all these economies displayed problems symptomatic of postindustrial societies: obsolescence of industrial plant, falling productivity, high unemployment, inability to compete with imports from Japan or Third World countries, demands for protection against such imports, high government welfare expenditures, and threatening deficits.

In the United States and Britain, governmental responses to these problems in the early 1980s suggested a desire to return to an earlier era of free enterprise. In fact, however, the role of the guarantor state had become too great to permit any fundamental retreat. For example, any suggestion of reducing Social Security benefits in the United States would provoke an uproar. Protectionism was not the answer either. High tariffs had brought international trade to a standstill during the Great Depression. In the 1980s, one of every six industrial jobs in the United States depended on exports to the Third World, and debt repayment by countries like Brazil and Mexico hinged on their earning foreign currency by exporting. Was there not some better way to stimulate investment and increase productivity again?

The communist countries certainly could not provide an answer. They presented an even less satisfactory aspect, except where they had deviated from strict communist theory—as in Hungary, Rumania, and China—by making concessions to individual initiative. In the Soviet Union, the 1984 grain harvest fell short of plan targets for the sixth year in a row. To import grain, the Soviets relied heavily on foreign currency earnings from exports of petroleum products. In the early 1980s, however, the USSR suffered both from declining oil prices and from an apparent inability to increase oil production further. The greatest need of the Soviet economy was to improve productivity, but this is extremely difficult to do in a centrally controlled economy that does not acknowledge individual incentives and cannot respond flexibly to changing conditions.

In response to these problems, Soviet economists and bureaucrats were beginning to allow such experiments as paying workers according to their production. Compared with China's, the experiments seemed modest—as was perhaps inevitable in a country that had to consider its image as the flagship of Marxism-Leninism. The Soviet economy was still powerful. Although it could not maintain—let alone improve—living standards, it supported an impressive defense establishment and space program. Nonetheless, many foreign observers saw the USSR as a less successful state-dominated variant of the capitalist economies of the Affluent North. All were trying to achieve the same goals of growth through industry and technology.

As of the 1980s, the most successful development strategy in the Affluent North was Japan's hybrid approach. In some respects, such as government finance and welfare spending, Japan was closer than any European or North American economy to the liberal capitalist tradition of the nineteenth century. Of course, even in Japan, rising demand for social benefits had produced a substantial internal government debt by the 1980s. On a per capita basis, Japan's debt was then 60 percent of the very high U.S. level. Japan too appeared headed for the problems of the guarantor state.

What seemed more significant, however, was Japan's distinctive pattern of relations between government and industry, particularly the collaborative relationship between the Ministry of International Trade and Industry (MITI) and the major business groups. This government-industry symbiosis had emerged organically from Japan's modern development—the first signs had appeared during the Meiji period. Thus, it was not likely that other governments could simply copy the Japanese approach. Indeed, some of them were still stronger than Japan in important respects, such as basic science. Nevertheless, the Japanese example fascinated observers in the United States. Democrats traditionally thought of government's role as regulating the economy, whereas Republicans demanded a decrease in the economic role of government. But Japan presented an alternative model of *government leadership* in economic development. This policy had proved highly successful in

POPULATION

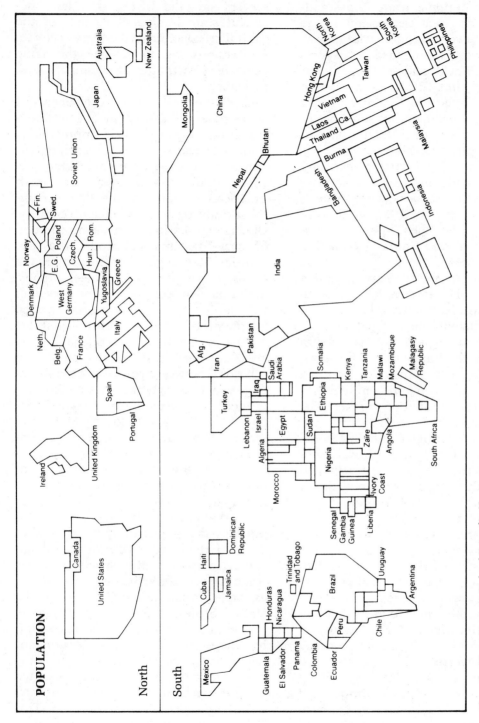

North

South

Charts by Marta Norman, Richard Tringali—NEWSWEEK

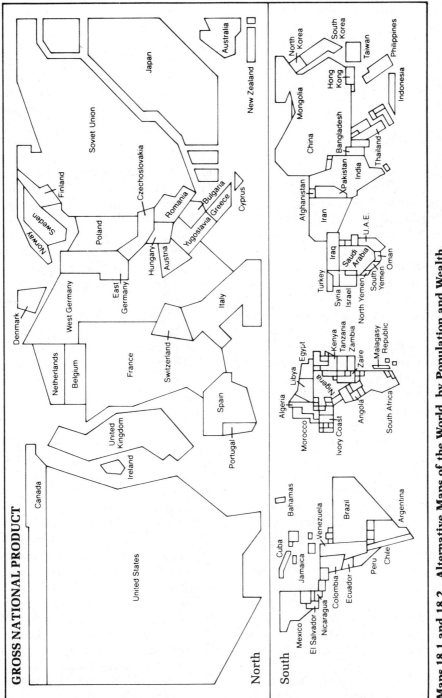

Maps 18.1 and 18.2   Alternative Maps of the World, by Population and Wealth.

Measured by gross national product, the Northern Hemisphere controls the bulk of the earth's wealth. Measured by population, on the other hand, the South contains masses of peoples whose economic problems multiply with high birth rates. (*Newsweek*, October 26, 1981, p. 104. Copyright 1981, by Newsweek, Inc. All rights Reserved. Reprinted by Permission.)

the one affluent nation most dependent on other economies for both raw materials and markets.

Developmental Strategies of the Hungry South

In the Hungry South, since the national economies are far more at the mercy of external forces than are those of the Affluent North, it is more difficult to think in terms of national development strategies. Nevertheless, it makes some sense to look at these economies at the national level. This is how Third World policy makers have to begin, as they confront the limited resources at their disposal.

A classic economic argument states that each economy should maximize its *comparative advantage* by concentrating on the production processes in which its efficiency, relative to other producers, is greatest. In the 1980s, conservative economists again repeated this counsel to Third World governments. In crudest form, this argument means continued reliance on exports of agricultural products and minerals—for example, the Ivory Coast should concentrate on cocoa exports, and Nigeria on oil. The argument points toward industrialization primarily in the limited sense that a poor country can exploit the comparative advantage of cheap labor to develop labor-intensive industries. For most small countries, however, the comparative advantage argument will continue to mean neocolonial economic dependency because of their limited resources and capabilities.

Social issues also bear on economic development. As we have noted, failure to restructure a historically inequitable agrarian economy will hinder economic development. The persistence of the hacienda system in Latin America or the caste system in India tends to limit the productivity of the agricultural sector and its ability to provide capital for investment, qualified workers for industry, or a market for industrial products. Because their country has a history of abundant land and a comparatively open rural society (except for slavery and its aftereffects), Americans have often misunderstood such problems. They tend to think that the universal key to agricultural development lies in the technical improvements that have done so much to increase U.S. agricultural productivity. In much of the Hungry South, however, attempts to develop agriculture by technical means without changing its socioeconomic bases cannot produce balanced development.

Of course, the leaders of most Third World nations are beneficiaries of the very social order that needs changing. This is why fundamental change in social structure usually comes only with social revolution, as in the USSR, Cuba, and China. Yet successful social revolutions are rare. Even a successful one is no guarantee of industrialization or extensive economic development, as Cuba's experience illustrates.

In an exceptional case, a Third World country may be able to bring about the needed changes in social structure without the violence of full-scale social revolution. Japan, for example, underwent its social restructuring in two stages. First—and not without some violence— the Meiji Restoration (1868) eliminated the old warrior class and its privileges. Later, the land reform enacted under the U.S. occupation after World War II almost eliminated absentee landlordism and tenant farming. Then, war and defeat, rather than revolution, provided the impetus for social restructuring.

Third World efforts at industrialization have typically begun with import substitution behind high protective barriers. Runaway protectionism and the virtual collapse of international trade during the 1930s helped launch industries in many places. In countries where rural society had not been appropriately restructured, that fact exerted an ongoing drag on industrialization. But most Third World countries that we have examined achieved a fair measure of industrialization by the 1960s, at least in light consumer goods for the domestic market.

Ultimately, import-substitution industrialization reaches limits, as seen in Latin America. It then becomes necessary to shift to an export orientation. Because other countries also want to penetrate export markets, such an orientation implies moving away from protectionism toward free trade. But it is dangerous for a small developing country to try to compete unprotected in international trade with the world's greatest economies. Up to a point, such a country can exploit its comparative advantage in cheap labor by developing labor-intensive export industries. This advantage may prove short-lived, however. Either development will lead to rising wage demands, as happened in postwar Japan, or the advantage will pass to multinational corporations that move in to exploit it, as hundreds of U.S. corporations have done by locating plants in Mexico or the Caribbean. In the long run, the most fruitful export strategy for an industrializing country is to identify specific product lines in which it can compete and for which it can become internationally known. Often, the shortest route to this goal is to acquire a competitive position in processing goods previously exported as raw materials. If more countries followed this route, many petroleum products—from motor oil to fertilizers—might eventually be marked "made in Saudi Arabia," and premium brands of cocoa would be "made in the Ivory Coast," rather than in Holland.

Such an export strategy would still be difficult for very small countries. They could probably succeed, if at all, only by performing unique combinations of services. The role of banking in Switzerland's economic performance is perhaps the best model for this kind of development. Lebanon was a kind of Switzerland for the Arab world until the civil war broke out in 1975. Hong Kong and Singapore are East Asian Switzerlands, with their own combinations of service industries, trade, and manufacturing.

Third World countries that cannot develop distinctive and competitive export lines or a unique service role are probably doomed to neocolonial subordination, unless a major restructuring of international economic relations occurs. The success stories of Third World industrialization are rare. Even partial successes, like Brazil or South Korea, are few.

Third World nations thus face distinctive economic problems and cannot simply mimic the developmental strategies of the most highly developed economies. The economic problems that confront Third World nations at the national level, moreover, are not the only ones. For national economies are not discrete entities but rather parts of a tightening pattern of integration in which inequalities of size and resources remain critically significant. To complete this survey of development issues, we must therefore look beyond the national level to consider transnational integration.

Transnational Integration and Economic Relations

Long before the modern nation-state emerged, integrative processes already operated among the world's states and societies. Long-distance trade and the spread of major religions are forms of "transnational" integration that occurred in ancient times. In this century, transnational integration has intensified and taken a greater variety of forms. Not all of these forms are economic, but many of the most important are.

Existing Forms of Transnational Integration, with Economic Examples

In terms of purpose or form of organization, processes of transnational integration vary enormously. Some have little or no formal organization, like fads in European tourism. Others are organized informally, like the pattern that brings Algerians from a certain village to a certain town in France to work in a certain factory. Often, however, transnational integration occurs through formal organizations.[5]

There are several types of such formal organizations. One of the categories consists of intergovernmental organizations, whose members are national governments. There were 49 such organizations in 1914 and over 300 in the 1970s. Examples include the UN and the North Atlantic Treaty Organization (NATO). A second category, much larger than the first, consists of associations whose members are other organizations. This category includes the Red Cross and some fraternal organizations, like Rotary International. Multinational corporations are commonly a variety of this type of organization. Finally, there are transnational associations of individuals. Some religious organizations are organized in this way, and so might be an international association of scientists.

A most important question about transnational integrative processes is whether they reinforce or diminish the effects of the division of the world into nation-states. So far, the evidence points toward reinforcement as the answer. The UN Security Council provides a good example. In it, five large countries, including the United States and the Soviet Union, enjoy permanent membership and veto power, while ten less powerful countries hold rotating memberships with no veto. International economic relations offer many other examples of how transnational integration reinforces the inequities of the state system.

Multinational corporations are a case in point. Although they operate across national borders, these corporations typically are based in one of the affluent nations. Some corporations are bigger than most national economies: the sales of the Exxon Corporation exceed the GNP of all but fifteen of the world's nations. As we have seen, transnational corporations transfer capital from the Hungry South to the Affluent North. They reinforce a "vertical" division of labor that assigns unskilled functions to the Hungry South, while sophisticated functions are performed either by citizens of the affluent nations or by educated people from poor countries, many of whom migrate to wealthy countries. This is the brain drain that has made university faculties in the United States, for example, so international. In industries like oil, multinational corporations rely on capital-intensive and technologically advanced production processes that split the economies of developing countries into sectors of low and high productivity, as happened in Nigeria and Iran. The industries in the high-productivity sector normally create too few jobs to relieve local unemployment. These firms also import their advanced technologies. This process is commonly referred to as transfer of technology, but it actually retards or blocks the development of technology or research skills in the developing countries. Many corporations produce things that the local population either does not need or cannot afford— soft drinks, tobacco products, or luxury hotels. Finally, these corporations recruit members of local elites with a vested interest in maximizing inequality. On balance, the corporations do more to compound the problem of international inequity than to promote Third World development.[6]

Similar criticisms apply to the international financial institutions created after World War II to prevent a recurrence of the economic crisis conditions of the Depression. As in the Latin American cases discussed in Chapter 14, the International Monetary Fund has routinely prescribed economic stabilization programs that impose severe hardship on the populations of developing countries. These programs also call for increasing exports so as to increase foreign exchange earnings. There is an element of paradox in urging this point on country after country, however. All nations, including the affluent, aim to increase their exports. Obviously not all of them can achieve positive foreign trade balances at the same time.

Comparable problems surround the International Bank for Reconstruction and Development, known as the World Bank. For example, the bank played an important role in Chilean affairs by cut-ting off all aid to the Allende government (1971–1973), and then by restoring aid, at a 50 percent higher level, to the Pinochet regime.[7] The consequences for the Chilean economy have been mentioned in Chapter 14. In the economic sphere as elsewhere, existing patterns of international integration all too clearly reinforce the inequities of the state system.

Transnational Economic Integration as It Might Be

Today the world faces a pressing need to diminish its existing economic inequities and foster economic development in the Hungry South so as to achieve regional sustainability. What would a more equitable international order look like? One answer to this question—there could be many others—appears in a report produced by an international commission led by Willy Brandt, former chancellor of the Federal Republic of Germany.[8]

The recommendations of the report are too detailed to list fully, but a few examples will suggest one way to restructure international economic relations. The report recommends at least doubling the funds at the disposal of the International Monetary Fund and restructuring its stabilization programs to emphasize improvements in output, employment, and income distribution in the countries needing assistance, rather than devaluation and restraint of demand. Such an approach might simultaneously improve living standards in Third World debtor countries and restore their international credit. Third World countries would also benefit from the recommended elimination of barriers to importation of their products, including processed goods, into developed countries. Other financial proposals include the creation of a fund to guarantee loans by private lenders, so protecting international banks against default by debtor countries, and an increase in international aid to 0.7 percent of GNP of the donor nations—a goal set over a decade earlier but not reached more than halfway by the 1970s.

The Brandt Commission also made recommendations on food and energy. It called for poor countries to prepare national food strategies and regional plans to prevent environmental disaster. And it urged increased energy production in developing countries and international dialogue to assure oil supplies for the poorest of them. In general, the report called for more North-South negotiation through organizations like the United Nations Council on Trade and Development and more cooperation among Third World nations, for example, by the creation of a Third World Bank.

At the heart of such recommendations stands a critical question: can the North-South inequality be eliminated, or even reduced significantly, without depriving the North of the privileged way of life that it takes for granted? In recent years, the widening of the developmental gap between rich and poor countries has attracted increasing attention. Must this widening continue, raising the risk of a world economy so polarized that it may collapse?

To assume the worst, fortunately, is not always realistic. So far, people have done very little to redress global inequity. Historically, the affluent guarantor states have succeeded in reducing economic inequities among their citizens and thus preventing social and political tensions from becoming unmanageable. Internationally, something of the concern for the disadvantaged that appeared in Roosevelt's New Deal might help forestall more serious world economic crisis and foster the development of the poor nations. Implementing proposals like those of the Brandt Commission might stimulate the global economy by increasing purchasing power around the world.

Many proposals that have been made for redressing existing inequities are remarkably modest. The Brandt Commission recommended a level of foreign aid equivalent to less than 1 percent of the GNP of the affluent nations—hardly a heroic sacrifice. Similarly, proposals to broaden the resources at the disposal of international lending agencies and to introduce guarantees into their lending procedures are far from revolutionary. But such measures might help stave off the bankruptcies and international debt repudiations that could accompany revolutions in Third World countries or crises in international economic relations.

So little has been done to create a more equitable global order that ample scope remains for reformist efforts to make a difference. People in the Affluent North, especially, need only vision and motivation to make such efforts. Unfortunately, those who benefit from an inequitable socioeconomic order seldom develop such vision and motivation before it is too late. Will people be different in the global village of the twenty-first century, threatened not only by economic inequities but also by nuclear war?

Science and Security for the Nuclear Civilization

Things used to be much simpler. Statesmen believed that to preserve the peace, they had to be prepared for war. Cannons were "the final argument of kings," and war was a continuation of politics by other means, as strategist Karl von Clausewitz put it. Only a minority of pacifists questioned that the relationship between military preparedness and security was positive. Science and technology had destructive uses, but their greatest application was in understanding the universe and creating the prosperity that military preparedness would protect. In sum, science meant progress. As a part of the patriotism inculcated through mass education, citizens of the various nations associated these ideas with the moral rectitude they saw in their leaders and their nations.

Little of this simplistic outlook has survived since World War II. Science and technology have continued to make important advances.[9] The introduction of oral contraceptives in 1960 played a revolutionary part in giving women control of their reproductive capacity. The development of digital computers launched a revolution in information processing. Today its effects appear at every level from preschool education to the frontiers of research. Lasers (an acronym for "light amplification by stimulated emission of radiation") have captured the popular imagination as "death rays," but have found their major applications in fiber optics, surgery, and precise measurement of time and distance. Probably the most revolutionary scientific breakthrough of this period was James Watson and Francis Crick's discovery in 1953 of the double-helix structure of deoxyribonucleic acid (DNA), the substance that transmits the genetic information of living cells. Their work opened the field of molecular biology, as well as the applied field of genetic engineering.

But we can no longer confidently identify science and technology with progress. Today we live in a "nuclear civilization" that has stood many old simplicities on their heads.[10] With the nuclear weapons now in existence, it is not clear that military preparedness leads to peace. If cannons were the final arguments of kings, nuclear weapons could be the final arguments, in a different sense, for all humanity. Whether the idea of moral right can be associated with any use of these weapons is a grave question. Ever since World War II, moreover, military uses and military sponsorship of research have increasingly become the driving forces in the development of science and technology. The military emphasis of research magnifies what has been called the "technological imperative." If the technology to develop a new weapon becomes available, then with disturbing frequency the weapon is developed whether or not policy demands this effort. The best way to illustrate these problems is to survey the nuclear arms race and its implications, not just for the United States, the Soviet Union, and their allies, but for the whole world.

Global Militarization

Today's nuclear civilization has developed in the midst of a dramatic global militarization. Before World War II, military spending absorbed less than 1 percent of gross world product. In 1983, the figure stood around 6 percent. Just between 1973 and 1983, world military spending rose from $474 billion to $663 billion. In the United States of the mid-1980s, debates over how to reduce budget deficits drew attention to the size of military spending, which amounted to 6 percent of GNP. The Soviet Union presented a starker picture of an economy drained by military spending—10 percent of GNP—among other problems. Militarily strong, the USSR had paradoxically become dependent on the United States for imported grain and for such advanced technologies as it could pirate.

The U.S.-Soviet rivalry is at the heart of the military spending increase, but it is a global phenomenon with serious developmental costs. The United States and Soviet Union have the world's largest GNPs. When military spending claims the same share or more of a poor country's GNP, the developmental costs can become tragic. Countries that have matched or exceeded U.S. military expenditures, expressed as a percentage of GNP at 1980 rates, include Vietnam, China, Ethiopia, Zimbabwe, Egypt, Jordan, Syria, and Israel. Most Western European nations have spent smaller percentages than the United States, and the Japanese rate of 0.9 percent, lowest of any large nation, has helped to strengthen that country's economy.

Has the world gained security from this arms spending? Some people argue that preparedness has deterred nuclear attack—so far. But the historical association between arms build-ups and eventual outbreak of war is very strong.[11] By the 1980s, some 50,000 nuclear weapons had been manufactured; 98 percent of them are in the United States and the Soviet Union. What would happen if they were used?

Effects of a Nuclear Explosion

A nuclear explosion has several distinct effects, and a large number of explosions would create added complications.[12] Detonating a nuclear warhead produces pressures millions of times greater than normal atmospheric pressure and releases high-energy radiation, mostly gamma rays. This initial nuclear radiation is the first destructive effect of the explosion. Moving through the air, the gamma rays generate a second destructive effect, the electromagnetic pulse, which induces a destructive voltage surge through electrical conductors. The nuclear reactions that follow detonation culminate in the formation of a fireball, which releases the third destructive effect: the thermal pulse, a wave of intense light and heat. If the fireball touches ground, it vaporizes or incinerates most of what it touches. The fireball expands, releasing a fourth effect: the blast wave, which can destroy all but the strongest structures. From a ground burst, the fireball will rise and condense water from the air to form a mushroom cloud. From that cloud comes the fifth destructive effect: radioactive fallout, much of which returns to earth soon after the blast in the form of ash.

One "medium-sized" nuclear weapon —a one-megaton bomb, equivalent to the explosive power of a million tons of TNT—would produce enough initial nuclear radiation to kill unprotected people over 6 square miles. The damage done by the electromagnetic pulse would depend on the altitude of the burst. For a blast near the earth's surface, the pulse would affect about the same area as the direct blast. In contrast, one high-yield warhead detonated over Nebraska could produce a pulse that would burn out many kinds of circuitry throughout most of the continental United States. A one-megaton bomb would produce a ten-second thermal pulse that would cause second-degree burns to exposed people over 280 square miles, and a blast wave that would destroy buildings over 64 square miles. The lethal fallout range from a one-megaton weapon would depend on whether it exploded on the ground or in the air. The weather would also have an influence. On average, a ground burst of such a weapon would contaminate more than 1,000 square miles with enough radiation to kill half the able-bodied young adults in a short time.

It is highly unlikely that only one nuclear weapon would be exploded in a conflict. To imagine a large-scale nuclear war, we cannot simply multiply the effects just discussed. If, say, 10,000 megatons were exploded over a large part of the earth's surface, three other direct effects would be predictable. Explosions above a certain size would produce delayed fallout that does not fall to ground nearby, but rises into the stratosphere, circles the globe, and gradually falls back to earth worldwide. Another likely global effect would be a change in climate: ground bursts would throw up so much dust that it would block the sunlight and cause a cooling of the earth's surface. This "nuclear winter" could have a catastrophic effect on most forms of life. The third predicted global effect is partial destruction of the stratospheric ozone layer, which shields the earth from lethal amounts of ultraviolet radiation. This effect might well destroy many plant and animal species and make it impossible for surviving human beings to venture out into the sunlight without special protection.

A nuclear explosion would also have dire secondary effects. The destruction of medical facilities and personnel would greatly increase the number of fatalities. Epidemics would soon ravage those who survived the blasts. Food supplies would be so disrupted that people would die from starvation and probably from fighting over food. Communications and transport facilities would be badly damaged. Nor could such consequences be quickly overcome. Even without a nuclear winter, many more people would undoubtedly die during the seasonal winter following the blasts. In the extreme case, civilization would collapse, human beings might be exterminated, and the world might become only a "republic of insects and grass." Such are the maximum dimensions of interdependence in the nuclear civilization.

Nuclear Weapons and Their Uses—or Nonuses

To prevent nuclear destruction, we must understand the nuclear arms race and find ways to control or eliminate it. The nuclear arms race is not a single contest, but a number of races with a variety of criteria by which to measure which nation is ahead. To illustrate this point, let us begin with a distinction—whose significance we shall later question—between *strategic* and *theater* weapons. In U.S. usage, *strategic weapons* are those that could be launched from the United States or its submarines and hit the Soviet Union, or vice versa. *Theater weapons* have shorter ranges, down to the so-called battlefield weapons.

The strategic nuclear capabilities of the United States and the Soviet Union today have three modes of deployment—the strategic triad.[13] The three sides of the triad are intercontinental ballistic missiles (ICBMs), submarine-launched ballistic missiles (SLBMs), and strategic bombers. Figure 18.1 compares U.S. and Soviet forces in terms of the number of launchers, number of warheads, destructive force of the warheads, and launcher payload.

As the figure shows, which nation is

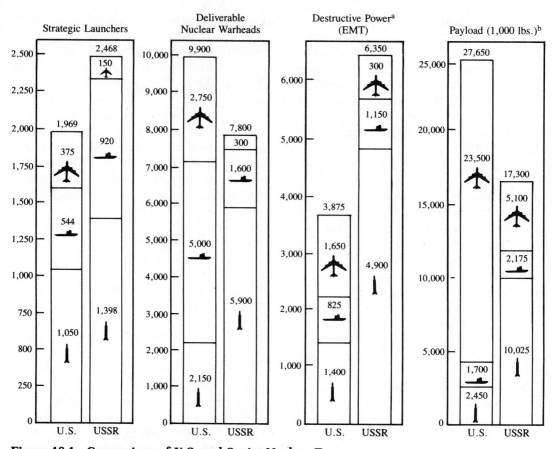

Figure 18.1 Comparison of U.S. and Soviet Nuclear Forces
Source: The Harvard Nuclear Study Group, (Albert Carnesale, Paul Doty, Stanley Hoffmann, et al.), *Living with Nuclear Weapons* (Cambridge, Mass.: Harvard University Press, 1983), p. 120. Reprinted with permission.

[a] Because the destruction that nuclear weapons cause is not directly proportional to their size, destructive power is measured not in megatons, but in equivalent megatons (EMT), a measure proportional to the area warheads destroy when used on "soft" targets like cities.
[b] Payload is the weight of the warheads and guidance systems that one side can launch toward the other.

ahead in the strategic arms race depends partly on which race we look at. The perceived interests of each superpower also will affect its interpretation of the differences that appear in the figure. Moreover, the arms race has qualitative dimensions absent from a figure like this one. In ICBMs, for example, the Soviets have marked quantitative superiority.

But U.S. ICBMs have the advantage in qualities like accuracy. Since the early 1970s, the development of multiple warheads and improvements in accuracy have made qualitative issues the key questions of the ICBM race. The greatest of these questions is the survivability of each side's missiles in the event of a surprise attack by the other side. In the

United States in the 1970s and 1980s, the debate surrounding the controversial MX missile, which was to be highly accurate and carry a number of powerful warheads, largely focused on ways to deploy it so as to maximize its chances of surviving surprise attack. The debate suggests that the numerical Soviet lead in ICBMs may be deceptive and that ICBMs are no longer the most important leg of the strategic triad, for their survivability now appears less and less assured.

Figure 18.1 also shows sharp U.S.-Soviet differences in the other two legs of the triad, bombers and submarines. In bombers, the United States has the advantage both quantitatively and in qualitative dimensions like range and speed. Only the Soviets have made a major commitment to air defense, but their defensive capabilities do not appear strong enough to deprive the U.S. bomber forces of their deterrent value. Despite the superiority of its forces, the United States has continued costly efforts to develop and deploy improved bombers, cruise missiles (essentially unmanned aircraft to deliver nuclear warheads), the "stealth" technology (which would enable bombers to escape radar detection by minimizing their reflection of microwaves and equipping them with electronic countermeasures), and the airborne warning and control system (AWACS, specially equipped planes to detect hostile aircraft, including low-flying ones that would escape detection by ground radar).

The third leg of the triad, submarine-launched ballistic missiles, is of special importance to the United States. The Soviet Union has almost twice as many SLBM submarines as the United States, but the U.S. submarines are equipped with more than three times as many nu-

clear missiles as the Soviets'. Moreover, because SLBM technology has developed more rapidly than that of antisubmarine warfare, the United States has relied increasingly on its nuclear-powered and nuclear-armed submarines to compensate for the growing doubts about ICBM survivability. The SLBM leg of the triad is considered invulnerable to surprise attack, and is expected to remain so well into the future. The U.S. advantage in submarines is magnified by readier access to the open seas. Even so, U.S. efforts to upgrade submarine capabilities, such as the development of the technologically advanced Trident submarine, have continued, perhaps partly because of rivalry between the navy and other armed services and partly because of the technological imperative.

Before evaluating the overall evidence on the strategic triad, we should note that it has an added dimension, as theater weapons systems do also, in what U.S. military experts call C^3I—command, control, communications, and intelligence. No system of nuclear weapons can be any better than the equipment that enables the people in charge of it to perform the C^3I functions. Such equipment is highly vulnerable to nuclear attack. The electromagnetic pulse could wreak devastation in the electronic circuitry on which the equipment depends. The United States has begun major efforts to make command and control systems less vulnerable. Doubts remain, however, because the effects of the electromagnetic pulse are not yet well understood.

Overall, our assessment of the strategic arms race will depend in part on how we look at the data. Those who focus on numbers of warheads, destructive power, and antibomber defenses can make a case that the Soviets are in the lead. The Reagan administration has taken this view. But because industry is more concentrated in the Soviet Union than in the United States, it is not clear that the United States "needs" as many warheads as the USSR. Many U.S. experts also question Soviet superiority on the grounds that the United States has maintained a persistent technological lead and that the greater accuracy of U.S. delivery systems compensates for the greater destructive power of Soviet warheads.

The more important question may be how to keep the superpowers from using their nuclear weapons. Conventional thinking on this question holds that the value of nuclear weapons lies not in use, but in deterring nuclear attack by an adversary. The best way to achieve deterrence, in this view, is to have an assured second-strike capability. This means that even if a nation suffered a massive nuclear attack, it would be able to counterattack and inflict intolerable damage on its assailant. Calculations about "how much is enough" probably explain why the United States has not developed larger forces than it has. It is estimated that U.S. capabilities exceed minimum unacceptable damage levels for the Soviet Union 20 times over, and Soviet capabilities exceed the corresponding damage level for the United States 30 times. These numbers are *overkill* factors. The difference between being able to "kill" an opponent twenty times or thirty is difficult to appreciate, unless one imagines enduring a first strike so massive that it would take such overkill capabilities to have anything left for the assured second strike, should anyone be left to push the button.

When all parties to a nuclear arms race have an assured second-strike capability, the result is *mutual assured destruction*, commonly abbreviated as MAD. One of the most disconcerting features of the nuclear civilization is that since the Soviets acquired an assured second-strike capability in the 1960s, the prevention of nuclear war has hinged on MAD.

The way in which people perceive MAD is vitally affected by issues pertaining not only to strategic nuclear weapons but also to theater weapons, above all those stationed in Europe. However we evaluate the balance of forces at the strategic level, the Soviets have a decided superiority at the theater level in Europe.

In terms of numbers, Warsaw Pact forces, both conventional and nuclear, are superior to those of NATO—although qualitative factors, like the reliability of troops from Poland or Czechoslovakia, could make a difference if war broke out. The disparity stems in part from decisions that Western European governments made in the 1950s to rely less on conventional forces and more on nuclear weapons. This strategy made it possible to minimize government spending on defense—in 1980 the percentage of GNP spent on the military was scarcely higher in France or the Federal Republic of Germany than in neutral Sweden. Once adopted, this policy became practically impossible to change, even though the NATO nuclear weapons led to mounting fears that Europe would become a nuclear battleground for the superpowers.

These fears have found vigorous expression in the protests of the mid-1980s against the deployment of U.S.-made Pershing II ballistic missiles and ground-launched cruise missiles in several European countries. U.S. TV audiences could not afford to watch news of the demonstrations disinterestedly, however, for the Soviet Union responded to the deployment of the new NATO warheads by announcing that their use would bring Soviet nuclear retaliation directly against the United States. Nuclear weapons differ in size and range, but the idea they can be used at theater level without escalation to strategic level is probably an illusion.

Thus, we come back to the idea of deterrence as the value of nuclear weapons, the concept of mutual assured destruction, and the question of whether there are ways to create a more stable situation. A number of ideas are under discussion. Some focus primarily on defense against nuclear attack, others on peacemaking and arms control.

Defense Against Nuclear Attack

To date, no sure defense against nuclear attack exists. The Soviet Union, Switzerland, and—reportedly—the People's Republic of China have extensive civil defense programs designed to protect the civilian population from the effects of nuclear attack. But it is doubtful that these programs would prove very effective in the event of nuclear war. Estimates of the costs of building effective shelters against a nuclear blast ran to $1,000 a person in the United States in the early 1980s—at which rate it would cost about $2.5 billion to shelter 1 percent of the U.S. population. Evacuation of civilians, another possibility, takes time. In case of attack, the Soviet Union is unlikely to have the several days' notice that its evacuation plans require. For reasons like this, U.S. planners have generally not put much faith in civil defense.

The alternative to civil defense is *ballistic missile defense* (BMD), an active military defense that would destroy approaching missiles. In the 1950s and 1960s, the United States had a program of this kind, but sacrificed it in the SALT I (Strategic Arms Limitation Talks) agreements of 1972. The SALT I agreements included an ABM (antiballistic missile) treaty limiting deployment of defensive missiles. At the time, many experts doubted that an ABM defense system, which would require a complex interworking of radars and missiles, could be effective under attack. Such a system would be highly vulnerable to countermeasures designed to confuse or destroy its radars, or to overload the system by launching many projectiles simultaneously. On the offensive side, one reason for U.S. willingness to limit deployment of ABM defenses in the early 1970s was the development of multiple independently targetable re-entry vehicles (MIRVs), which would enable a single attacking missile to carry a number of warheads aimed at different targets. In fact, MIRVs were developed as a way to overwhelm antimissile defenses.

The idea of a ballistic missile defense resurfaced in the United States during the Reagan administration in a form known officially as the Strategic Defense Initiative, but popularly referred to as the Star Wars Defense. Instead of relying on defensive missiles, this system would rely on particle beams and lasers to destroy attacking missiles. This concept immediately raised great controversy. Experts disagreed over whether the dollar cost of such a defense would be scores of billions or hundreds of billions, over its technical feasibility, over the vulnerability of the satellite battle stations to cheaper and simpler countermeasures, and over the effectiveness of such a complex system under combat conditions. Enthusiasts of the Strategic Defense Initiative argued that it would have a stabilizing effect on the superpower rivalry by ending dependence on MAD and making it possible to eliminate nuclear weapons entirely through negotiated agreements. Opponents of the plan countered that the Soviets would see it as another escalation of the arms race and would invest heavily in measures to defeat it, such as cruise missiles or depressed-trajectory missiles. In 1985, as the U.S. Congress debated funding for Star Wars research, it remained unclear whether an effective defense against nuclear attack is possible, and at what cost.[14]

Peacemaking and Arms Control

The lack of clear defensive alternatives to MAD illustrates a point discussed earlier: that the advent of nuclear civilization calls in question the historical relationship between preparedness and security. If there is no sure defense, the only ways of escaping the uncertainties of MAD lie among strategies aimed at peace and arms control.

One strategy, a nuclear freeze, arises from the idea that MAD, in its way, is not so bad. The concept is that the superpowers should bilaterally freeze testing, production, and deployment of nuclear weapons systems.[15] A key issue of debate has been whether it would be possible to verify the freeze. Its supporters have argued that a freeze would be easier to verify than a more complex agreement like the SALT II Treaty of 1979. Although that agreement was never ratified by the U.S. Senate, it presumably would not have been negotiated if available monitoring techniques—seismic stations, invitational on-site inspections, satellite reconnaissance, electronic listening posts—were inadequate for verification.

The freeze proposal accepted nuclear weapons as a reality and sought, in effect, to make the nuclear balance of terror into a source of stability by stopping further innovations that would open new rounds in the arms race. The freeze proposal attracted great popular attention and became an issue in the 1984 U.S. presidential campaign.

Official approaches to arms control have been quite different from the freeze, however. Recent decades have witnessed a number of arms control agreements. Multilateral agreements have prohibited deployment of nuclear weapons in the Antarctic, on the sea bed, in Latin America, and in outer space. The Nuclear Nonproliferation Treaty (1968) prohibited signatory states that did not have nuclear weapons from acquiring them. As of 1981, 120 governments had adhered to the treaty—not enough to keep nuclear proliferation from being a very big problem. One of the most important multilateral agreements was the Limited Test Ban Treaty (1963), prohibiting nuclear testing in the atmosphere, in space, and under water. Only underground testing remained possible. This treaty is also significant as an instance of governmental response to popular pressure, roused by fears of nuclear fallout from atmospheric testing.

The United States and the Soviet Union have also reached several important bilateral agreements. Among these are the Hot Line Agreement (1963), establishing radio (later satellite) links between the superpowers for emergency communications, and the SALT I Treaty (1972). It limited numbers of ICBMs and SLBMs for five years and prohibited deployment of antiballistic missiles by each superpower to two sites (the limit was lowered to one in 1976). Two more recent bilateral agreements were not ratified by the U.S. Senate. The first, the Threshold Nuclear Test-Ban Treaty (1974), was intended to limit even underground tests to nuclear devices with yields of less than 150 kilotons (0.15 megatons). The SALT II Treaty (1979) would have placed carefully defined qualitative and quantitative limits on strategic weapons and limited some technologies, such as the MIRVing of warheads. Although the Senate did not approve the SALT II Treaty—because of widespread reservations about specific provisions and such other current issues as the Soviet invasion of Afghanistan—the terms of the agreement have been observed in practice.

Five years after SALT II, the net momentum has been away from arms control. Nonetheless, in June 1982, the Soviet Union took the important step of declaring that it would not be the first to use nuclear weapons. The United States has refused to take the same step, on the grounds that NATO plans for the defense of Europe require the threat of first use of theater nuclear weapons. The U.S. failure to make a commitment that would be so desirable in larger perspective underscores the need to find other solutions to the problem of European defense.

What more could be done to ease the uncertainties of MAD? The military institutions of the United States and the Soviet Union have been described as the "most powerful and . . . expensive institutions ever created."[16] But the sums spent on arms control are only an infinitesimal fraction of those spent on defense. The problem of protecting the world from nuclear holocaust is surely one that will occupy government leaders for a long time to come, if there is peace to pursue it. No simple solution is possible. But we can review here a few suggestions that have been made about how to approach the problem.

Many observers feel that the world situation of the late twentieth century is more like that of 1914 than like that of 1939. The threat to peace is not an aggressor out for aggrandizement at the cost of war, but rather a global pattern with many danger points from which conflict could spread. To prevent this from happening, some analysts emphasize the need for international authorities with enough power over national governments to play an effective role in conflict control. However desirable, such authorities do not exist now and are not likely to emerge in the foreseeable future. Although processes of transnational integration—such as creation of treaty systems—will play a major role, the governments of the world and their citizens must find a way to save themselves, if they can. Economics may push them in the right direction. As we have seen, the Soviet Union is a military colossus strapped to an economy with massive problems, including dependence on its major enemy for grain. At the same time, the Star Wars concept presents the United States with a shopping list that it may not be able to afford.

The superpowers have already initiated some efforts to make MAD safer and to reduce overall arms levels. The United States has instituted elaborate failsafe procedures to prevent accidental weapon launchings, though doubts always remain about such systems. The hot line for emergency communications is in place. The Soviet Union, but not the United States, has made a declaration of "no first use." Each side has elaborate surveillance capabilities, using reconnaissance satellites and other means to monitor the military activities and treaty-compliance of the other. Among other possible steps, specific types of equipment or strategies could be prohibited by agreement. Freezes could be negotiated—if not on all new nuclear weapons, then on specific types.

All such efforts require a greater and continuous commitment to arms control negotiations. To date, recurrent problems have characterized such negotiations. Some agreements have not gone far enough—for example, the unratified 1974 agreement limiting nuclear testing to devices of no more than 150 kilotons. Existing technology would have made it possible to monitor compliance with a ban on tests one-tenth as large. Other agreements, like the complicated SALT II agreements, have seemed almost more difficult to negotiate than they were worth. Yet it might be possible to define goals for negotiation more simply. Goals that have been suggested include complete denuclearization of central and northern Europe, a complete ban on nuclear testing, or an across-the-board reduction of 50 percent in the superpowers' nuclear arsenals.[17] A vital principle to remember is that the most desirable outcome in the "game" of nuclear deterrence is not a win for one side or the other, but a draw.

The obstacles to reversing the momentum of the arms race are massive. The defense establishments of both superpowers represent huge vested interests, committed to increasing the resources at their disposal. Even more serious is the technological imperative and the fact that military applications have become perhaps the most important driving force in technological development. History is full of technological advances that stimulated the arms race. The miniaturization of computers, for example, made possible the development of navigational systems for the cruise and Pershing II missiles. The Star Wars concept requires a veritable symphony of military applications of advanced technologies—lasers, particle beams, computers—all orchestrated against incoming nuclear warheads. As the Atmospheric Test Ban Treaty showed, however, concerned public opinion can be effective in the face of institutional and technological imperatives. It will certainly be active in future, at least in Western Europe, North America, and Japan. In terms of containing the bureaucratic momentum and technological imperatives, it would be highly desirable for this movement of opinion to become a major international force for such concrete goals as a total ban on testing of nuclear weapons.

Proliferation

The technological imperative does not apply only to the superpowers. A great danger of the nuclear civilization is proliferation—the spread of nuclear weapons to other nations or even to terrorist groups. In the early 1980s, six countries clearly possessed nuclear weapons, or the capacity to produce them: the United States, the Soviet Union, Britain, France, the People's Republic of China, and India. Many people believed that South Africa and Israel also had the capability to make such weapons and might even have stockpiled nuclear weapons without testing them. Other countries that worried proliferation experts were Argentina (where funding for the program was sharply cut after the return to civilian government in 1983), Iraq (at least until the Israelis bombed a major reactor site in 1981), Libya, Pakistan, South Korea, and Taiwan.

Despite efforts to raise barriers against proliferation—chiefly the Nonproliferation Treaty and the International Atomic Energy Agency (IAEA), which monitors compliance with it—access to the required technology and materials is not easy to control. In the United States, university undergraduates have designed nuclear weapons, using only publicly available information. Their designs were primitive ones that would not have stood up well in production. But the radioactive materials used in bomb construction are widely accessible as by-products of nuclear power generation. By the end of 1982, thirty-six countries had nuclear power plants either in operation or under construction, including all the actual and potential weapons-possessor states named above except Israel.[18]

Events in Pakistan have illustrated how readily a country can circumvent attempts at proliferation control. With one nuclear power reactor, one research reactor, limited industrial capabilities, and a good supply of highly skilled personnel (including expatriates employed in other countries), Pakistan acquired the capability to enrich uranium to the high level of fissionable content required for weapons production. Apparently, secret centrifuge technology was stolen from a uranium-enrichment plant in the Netherlands and then necessary equipment acquired through Pakistanis in other countries. As the project director said, "Such an achievement by our team in a country where no basic infrastructure is available, where we cannot make a good bicycle or even a grinding machine, speaks [for] itself."[19] Present estimates of the cost to produce a nuclear bomb in the Indian subcontinent range as low as $30,000.

While the attention of the world remains riveted on the superpower arms race, it is equally likely that the next to use nuclear weapons might be rival states of the Third World or even terrorists. These dangers are particularly disturbing because the potential for nuclear conflict in these settings has not acquired even the degree of stabilization offered by MAD. Nor is concerned public opinion likely to play an effective restraining role in the Third World.

Any serious effort to assure the survival of nuclear civilization must take the control of proliferation as one of its urgent goals. No international body is now powerful enough to prevent the development of nuclear weapons in countries that have not previously had them. To some extent, the superpowers can lead by example, by showing their own seriousness about arms control and by moving away from war-fighting doctrines that treat nuclear weapons more or less like conventional ones. Another useful approach would be to work for further agreements creating regional nuclear-free zones, as the Tlatelolco Treaty (1967) did in principle for Latin America—though Argentina and Cuba did not ratify the treaty. India and Pakistan would certainly both be better off if they forgot about developing nuclear weapons, directed their resources to basic developmental needs, and declared the Indian subcontinent a "no explosion" zone. It would be desirable for others to emulate the Israeli declaration that they will not be the first to introduce nuclear weapons into the Middle East. As for the terrorist threat, it remains to be seen whether any antiterrorist and antiproliferation strategy can eliminate this risk.

There is no way we can return to the simpler time when the relationship between technology and progress appeared more straightforward and when weapons seemed to have a clear-cut defensive value. There is no "technological fix" for the present problem—no next discovery that will, like some wonder drug that conquers a disease, make the problem go away. All people in all nations face this threat together. Unless we all realize and act in our common interest, the nuclear problem may become the ultimate one of human interdependence.

Conclusion: Sustainability or Self-destruction—Toward a New World Order?

Are the world's peoples moving in any conscious and concerted way toward the creation of a rationally structured global order? World history shows that there is always a global pattern of interrelatedness, changing over time. When stresses build to an intolerable level, they produce the kind of global crises—two vast wars and a crushing depression—that destroyed the world of 1914. The twentieth century is unique only in the sense that modern science and technology have raised unprecedented questions about the sustainability and the potential for self-destruction of the world's societies.

Today more than ever, what is lacking is not awareness of problems and alternatives. We know about the extraordinary growth of twentieth century populations and the imbalance in distribution of the world's wealth among its peoples. The need to restore balance between human societies and their earthly environment with its finite resources has also become clear—the global village, like the villages of long ago, must live in harmony with nature. Comparison of different economic development strategies yields basic conclusions about which ones have worked best. Meanwhile. the

thought of 50,000 nuclear weapons scattered across North America, Europe, and the Soviet Union reminds us of the most threatening problem of all. The world is increasingly integrated, but we have not yet managed transnational integrative processes effectively to overcome economic inequity or the threat of nuclear annihilation.

All these problems have identifiable solutions, or at least strategies for coping. There are strategies for slowing population growth; for moving us toward regional sustainability in food, energy, and other resources; for stimulating development in the Hungry South by reducing inequities among major regions of the world; and for diminishing the nuclear danger by negotiating limits on the superpower arms race and proliferation. None of these strategies is simple or easy, especially because successful implementation depends on a reformulation of values. We must learn to identify ourselves as members of a global community, not a village or a nation, and to work for goals like those discussed here. If we cannot comprehend our common human interests and endeavor to seek solutions, then the world of interdependence amid scarcity will lurch toward a new configuration, shaped perhaps by human and environmental catastrophe, perhaps by the awesome force of nuclear conflict.

Notes

1. This discussion largely follows Lester R. Brown et al., *State of the World, 1984: A Worldwatch Institute Report on Progress Toward a Sustainable Society* (New York: W. W. Norton, 1984), in which "sustaina-

bility" is a central concept. See also Lester R. Brown et al., *State of the World, 1985* (New York: W. W. Norton, 1985).

2. Donella Meadows, John Richardson, and Gerhart Bruckman, *Groping in the Dark: The First Decade of Global Modelling* (New York: John Wiley, 1982), pp. 54–55, 93.

3. Brown et al., *State of the World, 1984*, p. 178.

4. Ibid., p. 123.

5. Johan Galtung, *The True Worlds: A Transnational Perspective* (New York: Free Press, 1980), pp. 305–316.

6. Ibid., pp. 312–315.

7. Leften Stavrianos, *Global Rift: The Third World Comes of Age* (New York: William Morrow, 1981), pp. 474–475.

8. Brandt Commission (Willy Brandt et al.), *Common Crisis, North-South: Cooperation for World Recovery* (Cambridge, Mass.: MIT Press, 1983), pp. 152–159.

9. George A. Miller et al., "20 Discoveries That Changed Our Lives," *Science84*, 5 (November 1984), 127–138, 149–155.

10. Dietrich Schroeer, *Science, Technology and the Nuclear Arms Race* (New York: John Wiley, 1984), p. 217. Except as otherwise noted, the discussion of nuclear issues follows Schroeer.

11. Bruce Russett, *The Prisoners of Insecurity: Nuclear Deterrence, the Arms Race, and Arms Control* (New York: Freeman, 1983), pp. 60–61.

12. This account of a nuclear blast follows Jonathan Schell, *The Fate of the Earth* (New York: Avon Books, 1982), pp. 1 ("A Republic of Insects and Grass"), 17–26.

13. Harvard Nuclear Study Group (Albert Carnesale et al.), *Living with Nuclear Weapons* (New York: Bantam Books, 1983), pp. 119–131.

14. Union of Concerned Scientists (Kurt Gottfried et al.), "Reagan's Star Wars," *New York Review of Books*, April 26, 1984, pp. 47–52; Zbigniew Brzezinski, Robert Jastrow, and Max M. Kampelman, "Defense in Space Is Not 'Star Wars,'" *New York Times Magazine*, January 27, 1985, pp. 28–51; George W. Ball, "The War for Star Wars," *New York Review of Books*, April 11, 1985, pp. 38–44.

15. Randall Forsberg, "A Bilateral Nuclear-Weapon Freeze," *Scientific American*, 247 (November 1982), 52–61.

16. Harvard Study Group, *Living with Nuclear Weapons*, p. 193.

17. George F. Kennan, *The Nuclear Delusion: Soviet-American Relations in the Atomic Age* (New York: Pantheon Books, 1982), pp. 175–207.

18. Christopher Chant and Ian Hogg, *Nuclear War in the 1980's?* (New York: Harper and Row, 1983), pp. 56–63.

19. John J. Fialka, "How Pakistan Secured U.S. Devices in Canada to Make Atomic Arms," *Wall Street Journal*, November 26, 1984, p. 1, quoting Abdul Qadir Khan in the Pakistani *Defence Journal*.

Suggestions for Further Reading

Brandt Commission (Willy Brandt et al.), *Common Crisis, North-South Cooperation for World Recovery* (1983).

Brown, Lester R., et al., *State of the World, 1984: A Worldwatch Institute Re-*

port on *Progress Toward a Sustainable Society* (1984).

———, *State of the World, 1985: A Worldwatch Institute Report on Progress Toward a Sustainable Society* (1985).

Calder, Nigel, *Nuclear Nightmares: An Investigation into Possible Wars* (1981).

Chant, Christopher, and Ian Hogg, *Nuclear War in the 1980's?* (1983).

Galtung, Johan, *The True Worlds: A Transnational Perspective* (1980).

Harvard Nuclear Study Group (Albert Carnesale et al.), *Living with Nuclear Weapons* (1983).

Kennan, George F., *The Nuclear Delusion: Soviet American Relations in the Atomic Age* (1982).

Kidron, Michael, and Ronald Segal, *The New State of the World Atlas* (1984).

Lewis, John P., and Valeriana Kallab, eds., *U.S. Foreign Policy and the Third World: Agenda, 1983* (1983).

McNeill, William H., *The Pursuit of Power: Technology, Armed Force and Society Since A.D. 1000* (1982).

Meadows, Donella, John Richardson, and Gerhart Bruckmann, *Groping in the Dark: The First Decade of Global Modelling* (1982).

Miller, George A., et al., "20 Discoveries That Changed Our Lives," *Science84*, 5 (November 1984); published by the American Association for the Advancement of Science, Washington, D.C.

Russett, Bruce, *The Prisoners of Insecurity: Nuclear Deterrence, the Arms Race, and Arms Control* (1983).

Schell, Jonathan, *The Fate of the Earth* (1982).

Schroeer, Dietrich, *Science, Technology, and the Nuclear Arms Race* (1984).

Stavrianos, L. S., *Global Rift: The Third World Comes of Age* (1981).

Union of Concerned Scientists, *The Fallacy of Star Wars: Why Space Weapons Can't Protect Us* (1985).

World Development Report, 1985 (World Bank, 1985).

World Tables, 3d ed., 2 vols. (World Bank, 1983).

Newspapers and Periodicals

Christian Science Monitor.
New York Review of Books.
New York Times.
Wall Street Journal.

Index

Aba Women's War, 218
Absolute monarchy, 9
Absolutism, liberalism and, 10
Abstract expressionism, 168
Achebe, Chinua, 390
Adenauer, Konrad, 320
Afghanistan, 310, 313
Africa: colonialism in, 7, 211 (map), 212–214; colonies, German, 31, 33, 65, 77; common traits among countries of, 207–208; diversity of, 204–207; economic and ecological problems, 383–387, 386 (fig.); foreign intervention in, 391–392; Great Depression and, 119; independence movements, 379–382, 381 (map); integration into Europe-centered pattern, 208–212; international politics after World War I, 77; Nigeria, 214–219, 392–398, 393 (map), 395 (fig.); political evolution, 387–388; population explosion, 382–383; South Africa, 219–226, 398–405, 399 (map), 404; starvation in, 477; after World War II, 280. See also North Africa
African National Congress, 234, 402, 403–404, 405
Afro-Marxism, 388–389, 391
Agrarian reform: in Brazil, 362; in China, 433; in Cuba, 370, 371; in Egypt, 416; in India, 427–429; in Iran, 413, 415; in Japan, 256, 440; in Latin America, 184, 200, 348; in Mexico, 99, 195, 197; in Nicaragua, 374. See also Landownership
Agrarian societies, 13, 14
Agribusiness, 322

Agriculture: in Africa, 205, 213, 384–387, 386 (fig.); in Argentina, 356; in Brazil, 191, 194, 363; in China, 247, 433, 434, 435; in Depression, 119, 120, 126; in Egypt, 51; in Germany, 33, 144, 145; global issues, 479–481, 480 (fig.); in India, 427–428, 430; in Iran, 413; Italian Fascism and, 138; labor force after World War I, 73; in Japan, 440; in Latin America, 200, 346, 348; in Mexico, 366; in Nigeria, 396; rural vs. urban environment, 35; in Russia before revolution, 24, 90; shifts to service sector occupations, 322; in South Africa, 398; technology and, 24; in United States, 325, 339; in USSR, 96, 307; workforce of, industrialization and, 21; after World War I, 116
Aguyi-Ironsi, J. T., 394
Ahimsa (nonviolence), 102
Aid programs: in India, 427; in Latin America, 352; military aid to African countries, 391
Alemán, Miguel, 365
Alfonsín, Raúl, 359–360
Algeria, 12, 210, 281, 320; colonial rule after World War I, 76; French possession of, 236; independence of, 379; urban growth, 383
Ali Jinnah, Muhammad, 231, 232
Al Kata'ib, 152
Allende, Salvador, 349, 353, 354
Alliance for Progress, 352, 373
Alliances, causes of World War I, 58, 59, 60, 62–63
Allies, 260. See also World War II; specific countries

Alsace, 69
Al-Sadat, Anwar, 43, 415, 418–420
Amin, Idi, 388
Amritsar massacres, 77, 431
Andropov, Yuri, 307–308
Anglo-Boer War, 221
Angola, 380, 384, 389, 391, 401
Anthropology, 164–166
Apartheid, 224, 400–405
Appeasement, 148, 149–150
Arab-Israeli conflict, 408, 411, 417, 422; in 1967, 418; in 1973, 418; nuclear alert during, 310
Arab nationalism: Islamic activism in 1970s and 1980s, 408, 409, 420, 473; U.S. support of, in 1956, 295
Arab Revolt, 239
Arabs: definitions, 234n; fascism, 152; and Israel, 424; in Israel, 420; Palestinian, 240; Pan-Arabism, 409, 411, 415, 416; Zionism and, 239
Arab Socialist Union, 417
Arab states: and Israel, 420; and Sadat, 419
Arafat, Yasir, 424, 425
Architecture, 170–171
Arévalo, Juan, 355
Argentina: Alfonsín government, 359–360; between wars, 187–190; charismatic leaders, 199–201; democracy and development, 355–360; democratic politics in, 184; dirty war, 359; food exports, 479; foreign debt of, 350; military authoritarian governments in, 351; neocolonial militarism in, 358–359; nuclear capability of, 502; Peronist defeat, 357–358; urbanization in, 347

Aristocracy, 33, 75
Armenians, 238
Armistice, 70
Arms build up, *see* Militarism and military governments
Arms control, *see* Disarmament
Arms embargo, of South Africa, 405
Arms industry: in Brazil, 363; military industrial complex, 265, 319
Arms race, 296; beginnings of, 293; as cause of World War I, 62; Cuban missile crisis, 296–298; Soviet ICBMs, 306
Art: African, 207–208, 208 (fig.); in nineteenth century, 156–157; after World War I, 74, 166–170, 167 (fig.), 169 (fig.)
Asia, 437 (map); China, 243–254, 432–439, 438 (fig.); colonialism in, 7; comparison of countries, 254–256; in Depression, 119; end of World War II in, 274, 276; independence of colonial countries, 381 (map); India, 229–234, 233 (fig.), 255, 426–432, 431 (fig.); international politics after World War I, 77; Japan, 243–254, 439–447, 442 (fig.); Middle East, 234–242, 237 (fig.); North Africa, 234–242; Pacific theater of World War II, 275 (map). *See also* Middle East; North Africa; *specific countries*
Aswan Dam, 24–25, 416, 419
Atatürk (Mustafa Kemal), 68, 240–242, 241 (fig.), 255
Atlantic Charter, 267, 280
Atomic physics, 159–161, 282
Atomic weapons, *see* Nuclear weapons and technology
Auden, W. H., 155
Australia, 292; food exports, 479; Japanese bombing of, 267; after World War I, 77; in World War I, 82, 84
Austria: German annexation of, 147; Hitler's plans for, 145; neutralization of, 294; Triple Alliance, 60; Wilson's Fourteen Point proposal, 75; zero population growth in, 477
Austro-Hungarian Empire, 6, 7, 75; causes of World War I, 58, 59–60; division of, after World War I, 77–78

Authoritarianism: in Argentina, 189, 190; in Brazil, 193–194; in culturally conservative societies, 14; in Egypt under Sadat, 419; in Latin America, 351, 354; of mass societies, 20–23; of Sandinista regime, 375; varieties of, 132–135
Authoritarian monarchy, 14
Authority: in culturally conservative societies, 14; forms of, in national states, 9; of kaiser, 40; Nazi *Führerprinzip*, 144; of ruler, sources of, 14; World War I and, 72, 75
Auyama, Chief, 217 (fig.)
Axis Powers: defeat of, 272–276; defined, 260; homefronts of, 260–261; Mediterranean campaigns of, 263–264
Ayatollah, 414
Azikiwe, Nnamdi, 219, 393, 394

Balance of payments: in Egypt under Sadat, 419; in Japan, 441; Latin American, 349–350. *See also* Debt
Balance of power, 265–266; and Gandhi's movement, 88; after World War I, 82; after World War II, 276–280, 279 (map). *See also* United States–Soviet relations
Balance of trade, Latin American, 349–350
Baldwin, Stanley, 111, 123
Balewa, Abubakar Tafawa, 394
Balfour Declaration, 238, 239
Bandung Conference, 313
Bangladesh, 409, 429, 478
Bantustans, 398, 401, 405
Basutoland, 221
Batista, Fulgencio, 368–369, 370
Battle of Britain, 262–263
Battle of Marne, 66
Bauhaus, 171
Bay of Pigs, 297, 371
Bechuanaland, 221
Beckman, Max, 168, 169 (fig.)
Begin, Menachem, 419, 423, 426
Belgian Congo, 210, 213, 379
Belgium, 210; African decolonization, 379; in Common Market, 298; empire of, 7; fascism in, 150; Germany and, in World War I, 62, 66,

69; Germany and, in World War II, 262; Wilson's Fourteen Point proposal, 75; zero population growth in, 477
Benelux countries, 290
Ben-Gurion, David, 423
Benin, Marxism in, 389
Berlin, 290, 296, 452
Berlin, in 1914: as imperial capital, 31–33, 32 (fig.); mass politics, 39–41, 40 (fig.); political system, historical consequences of, 41; population growth of, 32 (fig.); social change in, 33–36, 13 (fig.), 35 (fig.); social classes in, 36–39, 37 (fig.), 39 (fig.); vs. village life in Dinshawai, 54
Bernays, Martha, 161 (fig.)
Bethe, Hans, 160
Bhave, Vinoba, 428
Biafran Civil War, 394–396, 395 (fig.)
Big Three, 79
Biomass conversion, 482–483
Bishop, Maurice, 312
Bismarck, Otto von, 22
Blacks, 318; economic and social protests of, 325–327, 335; Great Society and, 331–332; in Latin America, 180; Reagan policies and, 339; unemployment among, in 1980s, 335; unemployment among, in postwar period, 325–326; Watts riots, 457–458; after World War I, 73. *See also* South Africa
Blitzkreig, 261, 262, 263
Blum, Léon, 122, 124, 338
Boers, 219, 220, 400
Boer war, 221
Bokassa, Jean Bedel, 388
Bolivia, 186, 351
Bolsheviks, 58; Entente treaty publication by, 74; and Provisional Government, 92; second revolution of 1917, 92–94; Stalin's purges, 96. *See also* Revolution, Russian
Bosnian Crisis of 1908–1909, 62
Botha, Louis, 222
Botha, P. W., 400, 401, 402, 405
Botswana, 221
Boxer Uprising, 244, 245
Bradley, Tom, 461
Brandt, Willy, 300, 308, 334
Brazil, 11, 179, 182 (fig.), 348 (fig.); charismatic leaders, 199–201; civilian rule, return

to, 363–364; democratic politics in, 184; export products, 183; fascism in, 151–152; foreign debt of, 350; Great Depression in, 120; independence of, 190–194; literacy in, 347; military authoritarian governments in, 351; military phase, 362–363; neocolonialism, 349; racial composition of, 180; Second Republic of, 360–362; urbanization in, 348 (fig.)

Brest-Litovsk, Treaty of, 70, 93

Breton, André, 169

Breuer, Josef, 162

Breznev, Leonid, 307–308

Britain, see Great Britain

Britain, Battle of, 262–263

British East India Company, 229–230

Brussels Pact, 290, 292

Bulgaria, 68, 309

Bureaucracy: in Argentina, Perón and, 357; in Chile, 353; in Egypt, 417; in Germany, Weimar Republic, 140-141; Reagan policies and, 340; in Russia, in World War I, 91; in USSR, 307; Weber on, 172

Bureaucratic feudalism, 416, 417

Bureaucratization: of Communist party, in 1920s, 95; computers and, 321–322; urbanization and, 35; after World War I, 71–72

Burma, 265, 280

Business: in China under Mao, 434; and Italian Fascism, 137, 138; in Nazi Germany, 144, 145

Business organization, 8, 9; in Japan, 443; multinational corporations, 12; before World War I, 71–72; World War I and, 75

Cairo: districts of, 463–466, 463 (map); economic life of, 466–469, 467 (fig.); growth of, 462–466, 463 (map); intellectual and spiritual life, 471–472; political participation and mobilization, 470–471; social composition of, 466–469, 467 (fig.)

Calles, Plutarco, 197–198

Camara, Helder, 362

Cambodia, 304

Cameroon, 210, 214, 384

Camp David Accords, 419, 422 (fig.), 425

Canada, 273, 292, 479

Cape Colony, 220, 224

Capital: for investment in Israel, 423; in Latin American economies, 348; Stalin's Five-Year Plan, 96

Capitalism: growth orientation, 19; Latin American colonialism, 180; and rise of West, 8–9; values for survival, 26

Cárdenas, Lázaro, 184, 198–199, 200, 364, 365

Caribbean nations, 186

Carranza, Venustiano, 196, 197

Cartels, 72. See also Organization of Petroleum Exporting Countries

Carter, Jimmy, 324, 333, 425; Camp David Peace Accords, 419, 422 (fig.); and détente, 309–310; human rights policy, 374; and Iran, 414; Iranian hostage crisis, 311; Latin American policy of, 353

Castro, Fidel, 349, 351, 369–373, 370 (fig.); Bay of Pigs invasion, 297; and Sandinistas, 374

Castro, Raul, 369, 370

Caudillo politics, 184, 186, 187, 200

CCP, see Chinese Communist Party

Censorship, 69, 71

Central African Republic, 388

Central Intelligence Agency (CIA), 375; Bay of Pigs invasion, 297; Chile, overthrow of Allende, 354; formation of, 292; and Radio Free Europe, 295; and SAVAK, 413

Central Powers, 65–66, 82. See also specific countries

Césaire, Aimé, 388

Ceylon, 267

Cézanne, Paul, 166

Chagall, Marc, 168

Chamberlain, Neville, 147 (fig.), 148, 149–150, 262

Change-oriented societies, 16–20; in Germany in 1914, 33; values for survival, 26. See also Postindustrial society

Charismatic leaders, 172, 199–201, 415–418

Chiang Ch'ing, see Jiang Qing

Chiang Kai-shek, 24, 105, 106, 246 (fig.), 274, 277, 292, 293, 432

Chiefship, 205, 212, 217, 218

Chile, 349, 352; in Depression, 119; fascism in, 151; foreign debt of, 350; military governments in, 351; U.S. foreign policy, 352–355

China, 14, 313, 447; communist rule, first phase, 432–433; cultural conservatism in, 13; De Gaulle's recognition of, 300; détente and, 305–306, 306 (fig.); economic development in, 485; emperors as source of authority, 14; family planning in, 478; family in, 14; Japanese aggression, 247–249, 248 (fig.), 249 (map), 259, 265; and Korean War, 292; as mass society, authoritarian, 23; military spending in, 494; Nationalists vs. Communists, 245–247; nuclear capability of, 502; Opium War, 243; Qing dynasty, 244–245; revolution of 1911, 87; second revolution, 435–437; socialist modernization, 437–439, 438 (fig.); socialist transformation, 434–435; Soviet postwar demands, 277–278; television in, 324; and West, 243; in world affairs, 447. See also Mao Zedong; Revolution, Chinese

Chinese Communist party (CCP), 245–249, 254

Chinese Nationalists, 88. See also Guomindang

Chou En-lai, see Zhou Enlai

Christians: African sects, 213; Coptic, 45; group identification, 15. See also Roman Catholic Church

Churchill, Winston, 320; and Atlantic Charter, 267; Battle of Britain, 262–263; and British National Service Act of 1941, 268; concessions to Stalin, 273; home front activities, 268; invasion of Russia after World War I, 94; in 1930s, 149; opposition to Hitler, 266; postwar political defeat of, 281; and Soviets, 264; at Yalta conference, 277–280, 278 (fig.)

Civil rights movement, 326–327, 326 (fig.), 330, 332

Clan, 15

Class structure: in Brazil, 194; Indian caste system, 101, 102, 103; Latin American colonialism, 180; Marxist philosophy, 10; in Russia before revolution, 89. *See also* Middle class; Peasants; Social classes; Working class

Clemenceau, Georges, 71, 79–80, 82, 111

Coal, 482

Codreanu, Corneliu, 151

Cold war, 288, 289–293, 291 (map), 319–325

Colonialism, 12; in Africa, 208–214; in Cuba, 368; German, 30–31, 32, 65; Great Depression and, 112; issues after World War I, 76–77; Latin America, 179, 181–184; nationalism before World War I, 63; in 1914, 6–7; technological status of colonial countries, 24; Wilson's Fourteen Point proposal, 75; after World War II, 261, 280; values for survival, 26. *See also* Africa; Latin America; Imperialism; Neocolonialism; Village life, in Dinshawai

"Coloreds," in South Africa, 402

Columbus, Christopher, 8

Comintern, 122

Commerce: innovations in Middle Ages, 8; in ninteenth-century liberalism, 9–10; in seventeenth century, 9. *See also* Business organization; Trade

Common Market, 298–299

Commonwealth of Nations, 391

Communalism, 15, 388

Communications: in Africa, 384; and economic integration, 14, 19, 21; and power, in 1980s, 12. *See also* Mass media

Communism: alternatives to, 122; attitudes toward, in 1920s, 110–111; in France, Popular Front, 124, 125; in Germany, 142; and Nazi rise, 143; and rise of Fascism, 137; "War Communism," 93, 94; and Weimar Republic, 140, 141. *See also* Bolsheviks;

Revolution(s); *specific revolutions*

Comparative advantage, 488

Computer revolution, 321–322

Concentration camps, 143, 221

Conflict: in culturally conservative societies, 16, 49. *See also* Politics; Rebellion; Resistance; Social change

Confucius, 13–16

Conscription, 63

Conservatism, cultural, *see* Culturally conservative societies

Conservatives/conservatism, 124n; in Argentina, 188; in Britain, 111, 123; in Chile, 353; and fascism, 150–151; Islamic activism, 420, 473; and Nazi support, 142–143; and New Deal, 127; in 1970s, 317, 333; nnieteenth-century liberalism and, 10; after World War II, 319, 320. *See also* Fascism

Constitutions: Egyptian, 416; Ghanian, 387; in Cuba, 372; Mexican, 99; Russian (before revolution), 91; South African, 400, 402–403

Constitutional monarchy, 9

Containment policy, 289, 293–298

Coolidge, Calvin, 118

Coptic Christians, 45

Corporations: and Depression, 116, 117; in Nazi Germany, 144, 145; after World War I, 75. *See also* Multinational corporations; Neocolonialism

Corporatism, 137

Corruption: in Africa, 384, 390; in Iran, 414; in Mexico, 367; in Nigeria, 394, 396, 398

Costa Rica, 347, 374

Counterrevolution, in Russia, 95

Coups, 18; African, 387–388; in Argentina, 358; in Brazil, 194, 362; in Cuba, 368; in Nigeria, 394, 397, 398. *See also* Militarism and military governments

Credit-Anstalt, 113, 118

Credit structure: and Depression, 111–112, 115–116. *See also* Debt

Crick, Francis, 493

Cromer, Lord, 43, 44

Cuba, 310, 313, 349; and Angolan civil war, 380, 382; and

Grenada, 312; infant mortality rates, 347; revolution in, 367–373, 369 (fig.); and Sandinistas, 374; U.S. rule of, 186

Cuban missile crisis, 288, 296–298, 371

Cubism, 166, 171

Cultural dependency, 7

Culturally conservative societies, 13–16; confrontation with change-oriented societies, 20; values for survival, 26. *See also* Village life, in Dinshawai

Cultural nationalism, Brazilian, 192

Cultural relativism, 164–166

Culture, 112; and African political divisions, 389–390; change-oriented societies, institutions of, 17; television and, 323–325; values for survival, 26. *See also* Intellectual life between world wars

"Culture of poverty," 330

Cyprus, 236, 238

Czechoslovakia, 300; communist coup in, 290; in détente period, 309; Egyptian arms sales, 416; Hitler's plans for, 145, 147; Munich agreement, 147–148, 147 (fig.), 149

Czechs, after World War I, 77–78

Dadaism, 74, 170

da Gama, Vasco, 8

Dali, Salvador, 170, 170 (fig.)

dan Fodio, Usman, 215

Darwin, Charles, 63

Darwinian view, 156

Darwinism, Social, 145, 184

Dayan Moshe, 425

D-day, 273

Death squads, in Brazil, 362

Debs, Eugene, 112

Debt: in Argentina, Alfonsín and, 360; in Argentina, Perón and, 356; and Depression, 111–112; by France, 338; global issues, 491, 492; Latin American, 349–350, 375; U.S. government, deficit spending by, 127, 340; World War I and, 72

Debt servitude, 181, 368

Decolonialization, 11

Defense: armaments as, before World War I, 64; in Israel, 423, 425. *See also* Arms race;

Militarism and military governments
Deficit spending, 127, 340
Deflation, 122
Deforestation, 430, 481
De Gaulle, Charles, 262, 288, 320; exile of, 262, 267, 274; opposition to U.S. leadership, 299–300; protest movements and, 325; provisional government of, 281–282; return to France of, 274
Democracy: in Argentina, 359–360; culturally conservative societies as, 14; in Latin America, 352; liberal, 389; mass-oriented societies, 20–23; participatory, 14; socialism and, 112
Democratic party, liberalism of, 10
Democratic Revolution, 9–10
Democratic socialism, 10
Demographics: African, 383; global patterns, 476–478; in Latin America, 346–347; population, 476–478
Demographic transition, 477
Deng Xiaoping (Teng Hsiao-p'ing), 435, 437, 438, 439
Denmark, 122, 292, 298, 477
Dependency: aid programs and, 352; cultural, 7; vs. economic integration, 12
Depression, see Great Depression
Desai, Morarji, 429, 430
Desaparecidos, 359
d'Estaing, Giscard, 332, 337, 338
Détente, 305–312; Carter years, 309–310; confrontation, return to, 311–312; defined, 305; for Europeans, 308–309; making of, 305–306; Persian Gulf and, 310–311; Soviet concerns, 306–308; U.S. economy, 308
Deterrence: before World War I, 64; mutually assured destruction, 313, 498, 500
Development: in Arentina, 359–360; in Brazil, 194; in Israel, 423; in Latin America, 184, 186, 200; in Mexico, 199; in Turkey, 242. See also Africa; Asia; Development, economic; Industrialization; Latin America
Development, economic, 19; alternative strategies of,

484–489, 486–487 (fig.); in Brazil, 194; in India, 429; in Japan, 441–442, 443; labor sources for, 21; in Latin America, 347–350, 348 (fig.), 354, 355, 375; in Mexico, 199; in Nigeria, 217, 392, 393; and population growth, 25–26
Dialectical materialism, 161
Díaz, Porfirio, 98, 101, 195, 196
Díaz Ordaz, Gustavo, 365
Dictatorships: fascist, 150–151; by Russian Commuist party, 95; U.S. sponsored, 186. See also Authoritarianism; Militarism and military governments
Diem, Ngo Dinh, 302, 304
Dinshawai, see Village life, in Dinshawai
Disarmament: arms control, 500–502; cold war and, 296; after World War I, 146. See also Arms control
Dissent: in Iran, 414; in mass society, 21–22, 23; protest movements in 1960s and 1970s, 318, 325–331; See also Rebellion
Divine right monarchy, 40
Doe, Samuel K., 388
Dominican Republic, 186, 352
Domino theory, 302, 313
Dong, Pham Van, 303
Dostoevski, Feodor, 75
Draft, 327
Drought, 195, 384–387, 386 (fig.)
Duchamp, Marcel, 167
Dulles, John Foster, 289, 293
Duma, 91–92, 94
Dutch East Indies, 8, 265
Dyer, Reginald, 77

East, 6
East Germany, 308, 477
Eastman, George, 33
Ecology, see Environmental/ecological issues
Economic growth: in Africa, 383–387, 386 (fig.); in Argentina, 360; in Brazil, 363; capitalist orientation, 19; in change-oriented societies, 19; and demographic transition, 477; in Cuba, 372; in Iran, 413; in Japan, 440–447; in Mexico, 365–367; in 1960s and 1970s, 335; in South Africa, 398–399, 400; values for

survival, 26; and world domination in 1914, 10; after World War II, 320–321
Economic integration, 12, 14, 19, 21, 317; European Economic Community, 298–299
Economic policy, 72; of Cuba, 371; in Iran, 414, 415. See also Government; Guarantor state; Liberalism, economic; Marxism; Welfare state
Economic powers, before World War I, 71–72
Economics/economic conditions, 333, 424; in African colonies, 213; in African nations, 382; in Argentina, 355–357, 358; in Brazil, 361, in change-oriented societies, 18–19; colonial dependency, 7, 12; in colonial village, 50–52; in culturally conservative societies, 13, 14–15; De Gaulle's policy, 299–300; and détente, 306–308; in Germany in 1914, 30, 41; in Germany, Nazification of, 144; Great Society, 330–331; and fascism, 133–134; in India, 427, 431; in Israel, 423, 424; Italian Fascism and, 138; in Japan, 444–446; in Latin America, 181–184, 186, 199, 347, 355; nineteenth-century liberalism, 9–10; in Los Angeles, 453–454; Marshall Plan, 290; Marxist philosophy, 10; and rise of West, 8–9; in Soviet Union, 96, 307; stagflation, 333–337; transnational integration, 490–492; in Turkey, 242; values for survival, 26; after World War I, 72–74; after World War II, 261, 281–282. See also Agrarian reform; Agriculture; Development, economic; Guarantor state; Industrialization; Inflation; Revolution(s); Unemployment; Welfare state
Economy: colonial, 7; national, 14
Ecuador, 350
Eddington, Arthur, 160
Education: in Berlin, in 1914, 33–34, 41; in change-oriented societies, 17; colonialism and, 217; in colonial villages, 49; compulsory, 63; and disappearance of folk

Education (*continued*)
culture, 171; in Cuba, 372; in India, 428–430; in Israel, 423; in Japan, 444; in Latin America, 200; in Nigeria, 392–393; in nineteenth century, 156–157; after Russian Revolution, 93; in Turkey, 241. *See also* Literacy
EEC, *see* European Economic Community
Egypt, 210, 410, 415–420; Aswan Dam, 24–25; British occupation of, 236; fascism in, 152; independence movements, 238–239; and Israel, 420; Italian invasion of, 263; military spending in, 494; urban growth, 383; after World War I, 76, 77, 238. *See also* Cairo; Village life, in Dinshawai
Egyptian-Israeli Peace Treaty, 419, 422 (fig.), 425
Einstein, Albert, 157, 158–161, 162, 167, 174
Eisenhower, Dwight D., 319, 320; cold war policy of, 293; and Cuba, 297; Latin American policy of, 352; support of Nasser, 295
Elections: in Argentina, 357; in Brazil, 191, 194, 364; in mass societies, 22, 23; in Mexico, 195, 364–365, 367; in Nigeria, 394
Electronics industry, 363, 430
Electronics technology, 321–322
El Salvador, 347
Embargoes: of Cuba, 297, 371; of Japan, 265; oil, 411; of South Africa, 405
Empires: in 1914, 6–7; after World War II, 280. *See also* Austro-Hungarian Empire; Colonialism; Imperialism; Neoimperialism
Employment: in Nazi Germany, 144; after World War I, 73. *See also* Unemployment
Energy: global issues, 481–484; South Africa, resources of, 398. *See also* Oil prices, Oil supplies
Energy crisis, 336
England, *see* Great Britain
Entente powers, 65–66, 74
Environment, urban vs. rural, 35
Environmental/ecological is-

sues: in Africa, 384–387; air pollution, 25, 470, 482; Aswan Dam, 25; in Cairo, 470; deforestation, 430, 481; drought, 195, 384–387, 386 (fig.); global issues, 492; Great Society programs, 330; in India, 430; soil fertility and erosion, 120, 430, 480, 481; technology and, 23–26; values for survival, 26
Estancias, 181
Ethiopia, 205, 207, 209; British defense of, 272; famine in, 385–387, 386 (fig.); invasion of, 140, 210, 212, 213, 214, 259; Marxism in, 389; military spending in, 494; Soviets in, 391; urban growth, 383
Ethnic groups: and African political divisions, 389–390; in Austria-Hungary, 59–60, 61 (fig.); in Los Angeles, 458–462; in Nigeria, 393; in South Africa, 401. *See also* Race issues
Europe: alliances of, in 1914, 60; cold war era, 319–325; détente and, 308–309; great powers in 1914, 6–7; integration of, 298–299; Marshall Plan, 290; rise of West, 7–10; after World War II, 317, 318, 319–320
European Economic Community (EEC), 298–299, 336
Évolués, 212
Exports: of African colonies, 213; of Argentina, 187; of Brazil, 191–192, 363; of Cuba, 367, 372; in Depression, 119; of Egypt, 51; of Japan, 442; of Latin America, 347; of Nigeria, 396; of Russia, before revolution, 90; of South Africa, 398; third world economic development, 489. *See also* Trade
Expressionism, 168
Extraterritoriality, 235, 239, 244

Fair Deal, 319, 330
Falkland War, 359
Family: in culturally conservative societies, 14–16; in colonial villages, 48–49; in Japan, 445
Family planning, 429, 439, 478, 478 (fig.)

Famine: in Africa, 384–387, 386, 477 (fig.), 479; global issues, 477; in India, 429; and population control, 23; in Russia, 90
Far East, 6
Fascism: appeal of, 152–153; authoritarianism, varieties of, 132–135; in Brazil, 151–152, 193–194; economic and social changes contributing to, 133–135; European movements, 150–151; ideology, sources of, 132–133; in Italy, 135–140; in Lebanon, 152; mass electorate and, 157. *See also* Fascism, German
Fascism, German, 142–150; Hitler's design, 145–146; lessons of history, 149–150; Nazi society and economy, 143–145; Versailles Treaty, destruction of, 146–149; Weimar Republic, weakness of, 140–142; World War I aftermath, 142–143; World War II, causes of, 145–150
Fazendas, 181
Federalism, 9, 184
Federal Republic of Germany, 290. *See also* West Germany
Fellahin, 50, 53
Ferdinand, Archduke Franz, 57, 58
Fermi, Enrico, 160
Ferraro, Geraldine M., 340
Feuds, 16, 49
Flores Magón brothers, 195, 196
Foch, Ferdinand, 70, 82
Folk cultures, 171
Food imports: Mexican, 195; Nigerian, 398
Food production: global issues, 479–481, 480 (fig.), 492; in India, 428, 430; in Mexico, 366. *See also* Agriculture
Ford, Gerald R., 333
Foreign aid, *see* Aid programs
Foreign debt: of Argentina, 356, 360; of Brazil, 361, 363; global issues, 491, 492; in Latin America, 349–350, 352, 375; Lenin's repudiation of, 93; of Mexico, 366. *See also* Debt
Foreign investment: in Africa, 391; in Argentina, 358; in Brazil, 361–362, 363; in Mexico, 195, 366; World War I and, 72. *See also* Nationalization of foreign interests

Foreign policy: German, 60, 146; Soviet, Comintern and, 105; United States, 265–267, 302, 369; Wilson's Fourteen Point proposal, 75–76. *See also* Balance of power; Central Intelligence Agency; Latin America; United States–Soviet relations

Foreign trade, *see* Trade

Fourteen Points, 75–76

France: absolute monarchy of, 9; African interests of, 391; anticommunist attitudes in 1919, 110–111; Atlantic Charter, 280–281; Brussels Pact, 290; colonialism of, in Africa, 210, 212, 379; colonialism of, in Middle East, 152, 236; in Common Market, 298; De Gaulle withdrawal from NATO, 299; democratic socialism in, 112; in détente period, 308; Egyptian arms sales, 416; fascism in, 150; food exports, 479; Franco-Prussian War, 30; as great power, 6; and Hitler's military build-up, 146; invasion of Russia after World War I, 94; Mitterrand in, 337–339; and Nasser's seizure of Suez Canal, 295; nuclear capability of, 502; revolution in, 9; Paris peace conference position, 79–80, 82; Rights of Man, 22; socialism in 1930s, 122, 123–125; support of racial equality after World War I, 77; television in, 324; Treaty of Sèvres and, 238; treaty with Czechoslovakia, 147; Triple Entente, 60; U.S. credit arrangements in 1920s, 118; and Versailles Treaty, 58, 82; and Vietnam, 301–302; women's liberation in, 332–333; women's suffrage in, 73, 317; after World War I, 76–77; and World War I, 58, 62, 66, 69–70, 79; after World War II, 280, 281, 320, 323; and World War II, 261–262, 267

Franco, Francisco, 132, 138, 264

Franco-Prussian War of 1870, 30

Freedom, 16, 17

Free enterprise, global issues, 484

Free market economy, 330

Free trade: British, 117; Hawley-Smoot Tarriff Act, 118; in India, 230; and Latin American economies, 182; in Nigeria, 217; in nineteenth century, 9–10

Frei, Eduardo, 353, 354

FRELIMO, 380

Freud, Sigmund, 157, 161–164, 161 (fig.), 174

Frondizi, Arturo, 358

Gallipoli, Battle of, 68

Gambia, 218, 379

Gandhi, Indira, 429–432, 431 (fig.), 447

Gandhi, Kasturbai, 102

Gandhi, Mohandas, 97, 108, 255, 326, 427; British cotton boycott, 119 (fig.), 120; Churchill and, 262–263; ideology of, 88; independence movement, 231–234, 233 (map); mass mobilization by, 101–103; South African years, 224, 225

Gandhi, Rajiv, 431, 431 (fig.), 432

Gandhi, Sanjay, 430, 431

Gaza Strip, 424

Gemayel, Pierre, 152

Genealogy, 15–16

German Democratic Republic, 290. *See also* East Germany

German East Africa, 210

Germany, 209, 334; anticommunist attitudes in 1920s, 111; Brest-Litovsk Treaty, 70; colonialism of, in Africa, 210, 214; credit arrangements in 1920s, 118; domination of Eastern European countries by, 78; economic crisis of 1970s in, 336; as great power, 6; lessons of history, 149–150; political climate, postwar, 320; postwar partition of, 289, 290; and Russian Revolution, 92; socialists and communists in 1930s, 122; social welfare legislation in, 22; student protest in, 327; technological achievements, 24; television in, 324; Triple Alliance, 60; Versailles Treaty conditions, 79–84; war socialism in, 72; women's suffrage in, 73; and World War I, 58, 62, 69, 74; and World War II, 145–150, 261–262, 272–274. *See also* Berlin, in 1914; Fascism, German; Hitler, Adolph; World War II

Ghana, 210, 218, 398; government in, 387–388; independence of, 379

Giroud, Françoise, 332

Global economy, 317, 334, 476; and exports, 336; Japan in, 442; world depression, 113–114. *See also* Interdependence

Global interdependence: change-oriented societies, 16–20; culturally conservative societies, 13–16; mass-oriented societies, 20–23; world trade, 11

Global patterns: classification of societies, 4–6; of 1914, 6–7; from 1914 to 1980s, 10–12; television and, 324–325. *See also* Interdependence

Global power: U.S. ascent to, 283; after World War II, 276–280, 279 (map)

GMD, *see* Guomindang

Goebbels, Joseph, 144

Golan Heights, 418

Gold, 209, 221, 223, 300, 398, 399

Gold Coast, 210, 218, 379

Goldie, George, 216

Gold standard, 111, 118

Gomulka, Wladyslaw, 295

Goulart, João, 360, 361–362

Government: African political evolution, 387–391; in Argentina, Perón and, 356; Bolshevik experiment, 85; in colonial villages, 48, 49–50; in economic development, 485, 488; fascism and, 153; in India under Indira Gandhi, 429, 431; in India under Nehru, 427; and Japanese economy, 443, 444; in Latin America, economic policy and, 348, 350–351; liberalism, nineteenth-century, 9–10; in Mexico, one-party rule, 364–365; in Nazi Germany, 144; participation in, in culturally conservative societies, 14; pastoralism and, 205; urbanization and, 33–34; World War I and, 71–72, 75; World War II and, 261, 268. *See also* Guarantor state; Political authority; Political systems; Politics; Welfare state

Gowon, Yakubu, 395, 396, 397
Grand Alliance, 260, 267, 268, 273
Grau San Martín, Ramón, 368, 369
Great Britain: African interests of, 391; anticommunist attitudes in 1920s, 111; Balfour Declaration, 238; Battle of Britain, 262–263; Bill of Rights, 22; Brussels Pact, 290; Chinese trade of, 243–244; in cold war, 289, 295; colonialism of, in Africa, 210, 215–225; colonialism of, in India, 119 (fig.), 120; colonialism of, in Middle East, 236; in Common Market, 298; credit arrangements in 1920s, 118; democratic socialism in, 112; in détente period, 308; and Egypt, 42–43, 416; Falkland War, 359; gold standard, 111; Great Depression, in, 117–118; as great power, 6; and Hitler's military build-up, 146; invasion of Russia after World War I, 94; and Iran, 412; and Israel, 420; Latin American interests, 183; monarchy of, 14, 17; Munich agreement, 147 (fig.), 147–148, 149; Suez Canal seizure, 295; nuclear capability of, 502; as pluralistic society, 22; postwar society, 281; socialism in 1930s, 123; social welfare legislation in, 22; Thatcher election, 333; Treaty of Sèvres and, 238; Triple Entente, 60; Versailles Treaty, 58, 79–80, 82; women's suffrage in, 73; after World War I, 76–77; and World War I, 62, 65, 69, 74, 79–80; after World War II, 250–251; and World War II, 261, 263, 267–268, 272–273; zero population growth in, 477. See also specific colonies; World War I; World War II
Great Depression: and African colonies, 213; in Argentina, 189–190; in Brazil, 192; conditions leading to, 111–112; in Cuba, 368; in developing world, 118–120; economic flaws, 116–117; liberalism, failure of, 120–122; and Fascism, 133; in France, 123–

125; guarantor state, global trends toward, 128–129; in Great Britain, 123; in Italy, 138; in Japan, 253; and Japanese invasion of China, 265; in Latin America, 199–200; Latin American exports during, 183; mass production and underconsumption, 116–117; in Mexico, 197–199; New Deal, 125–128; origins of, 115–118; socialism, 122; spread of, 117–118; USSR during, 96; Wall Street crash, 113–116
Great powers: defined, 6; Japan as, 252–253; in 1914, 6, 7; in 1980s, 12; United States as, 283
Great Society, 330–331, 335, 459
Greece, 263, 289, 298
"Green" party, 334
Green Revolution, 428, 429, 430, 479
Grenada, 311–312
Gross national product (GNP): in Africa, 385; defined, 383n; oil consumption for, 481; Soviet, in 1970s, 307
Growth, economic, see Economic growth
Guarantor state, 128–129, 318, 336, 456; Britain as, 334; in France in 1980s, 338; global issues, 484; Great Society, 330–331; postindustrial, 317; after World War II, 319, 320
Guatemala, 180, 347
Guevara, Ernesto "Che," 351, 370, 371
Guinea, 379
Guinea-Bissau, 380
Guomindang (GMD) (Kuomintang), 105, 107, 108, 245–248, 432; and Chinese resistance to foreign ideas, 254; Japanese invasion and, 248–249

Hacienda system, 181, 186, 195, 196, 200
Haiti, 186, 347
Hapsburgs, 60, 70, 111
Harding, Warren, 82, 111
Heisenberg, Werner, 159
Helsinki treaty, 309
Hertzog, J. B. M., 222, 223, 224, 225
Herzl, Theodor, 239
Himmler, Heinrich, 271

Hindenberg, Paul von, 142
Hiroshima, 276, 282
Hitler, Adolph, 74, 131, 133, 135; and atomic weapons development, 160; and Comintern policies, 124; death of, 274; domination of Eastern European countries by, 78; Enabling Act, 143; factions in government, 144; and Freud, 163; Holocaust, 271–272, 272 (fig.); homefront mobilization, 270; invasion of Poland, 259–260; and modern art, 171; Munich agreement, 147–148, 147 (fig.), 149; phony war, 261–262; policies of, 270–271; rise of, 141–142; Versailles Treaty, destruction of, 146–149; World War I and, 58
Ho Chi Minh, 280, 301–303, 304, 351
Holland, see Netherlands, The
Honduras, 347, 352
Hong Kong, 265, 447, 489
Hoover, Herbert, 113, 121
Huerta, Victoriano, 196
Human rights, 353, 359, 362, 374
Hungary: anticommunist attitudes in 1920s, 111; economic development in, 485; fascism in, 150; rebellion against Soviets in 1956, 295; after World War I, 77–78; zero population growth in, 477

Iceland, 292
Ideology: as cause of war, 58; Chinese Communist party, 254; fascism and, 153; in Latin America, 184; political, in change-oriented societies, 18; of resistance, 12; and revolution, 108; rise of Fascism, 134; U.S.-Soviet confrontations, 287; values for survival, 26. See also Free trade; Liberalism; Liberalism, economic; Marxism; United States–Soviet relations
Ikeda, Hayato, 440
Illegal immigration, 347, 460–461
Illia, Arturo, 358
Imperialism: causes of World War I, 58, 59–60; Chinese,

103–107; neoimperialism, 12; in 1914, 6–7; nineteenth-century, 9; socialist, 391. *See also* Africa; Colonialism; Latin America; Neoimperialism

Imports: food, 195, 398; in Latin America, 200, 201, 346, 347; In Mexico, 195, 197; in Nigeria, 398. *See also* Trade

Import-substitution, 375, 489; in Africa, 384; in Latin America, 348, 349, 350, 354; political effects of, 351

Impressionists, 166

Income, *see* Wages

Income distribution: in Africa, 384; in Argentina, 357; in Iran, 414; in Mexico, 367; New Deal and, 128

Independence movements: in Argentina, 187; in Cuba, 367–368; in India, 231–234, 233 (map); in Latin America between wars, 182, 186. *See also* Nationalism; *specific countries*

India, 65, 118, 230–234, 447; Amritsar massacres, 77, 431; British East India Company, 229–230; British product boycotts, 119 (fig.), 120; and China, 254, 255; colonial rule after World War I, 76, 77; depression in, 120; under Indira Gandhi, 429–432, 431 (fig.); and Mohandas Gandhi, 108, 231–234, 232 (fig.); national identity, 255; under Nehru, 426–429; nuclear capability of, 502; partition of, 233 (map); self-rule, progress toward, 230–234; in World War I, 82, 84

Individual, the: in change-oriented societies, 19; in colonial villages, 47–48; in culturally conservative societies, 14, 15, 16; human rights issues, 184; in Japan, 445; in mass societies, 22, 23; urbanization and, in Berlin 1914, 33–34; values for survival, 26

Individualism, 452, 456

Indochina: independence of, 379; Japanese seizure of, 265; after World War II, 280, 281. *See also* Vietnam

Indonesia, 8, 280

Industrial economies: and power, 9, 10; production, after World War I, 111

Industrialization: in Africa, 384; in Argentina, 189, 356–357; in Brazil, 191, 194; in China after Mao, 438; in China under Mao, 432, 433, 434; in Egypt, 417; in Germany, 33, 36–37; global issues, 484; in India, 103, 427, 428, 430; in Iran, 413; labor sources for, 21; in Latin America, 183, 184, 200, 347, 348; and population growth, 25–26; in Russia, 24, 90, 97; in South Africa, 222; Stalin's Five-Year Plan, 96; third world, 488–489; In Turkey, 242; in United States in World War II, 282. *See also* Development

Industrial Revolution, 6–7, 9, 23

Industrial workers: in Nazi Germany, 144; proletariat, 133; Russian, 96; after World War I, 73. *See also* Labor force; Working class

Industry: African colonies, 213; in Brazil, 361; in China, 434; global competition in 1960s and 1970s, 334; in Japan, 441; in Nazi Germany, 144; in South Africa, 398; war-related technological advances, 282

Inflation: in Argentina, 356, 360; in Brazil, 363; in France in 1980s, 338; in Germany's Weimar Republic, 141; in Iran, 414; in Mexico, 366, 367; stagflation, 333–337; in United States, 331, 339; after World War I, 72, 73–74; after World War II, 319

Inönü, Ismet, 241 (fig.), 242

Integralistas, 133, 151–152

Integration, *see* Economic integration; Global economy; Interdependence

Intellectual life between world wars, 74; age of uncertainty, 172–174; art and architecture, 166–171; cultural relativism, 164–166; Einstein, 157, 158–161; Freud, 157, 161–164; mass culture, emergence of, 171–172; nineteenth century and, 156–157

Intellectuals: in British Labour party, 123; in China under Mao, 434; in Latin America, 184

Intellectual tradition, 14

Interdependence, 317; defense against nuclear attack, 499–500; economic development, 484–489, 487 (map); energy, 481–484; food, 478–481; militarization, global, 493–494; nuclear explosion, effects of, 494–495; nuclear weapons, 495–499, 495 (fig.), 502–504; peacemaking and arms control, 500–502; population, 476–478, 486 (map); transnational integration and economic relations, 490–492. *See also* Cairo; Los Angeles

International Bank for Reconstruction and Development, 491

International finance, after World War I, 111–112

Internationalism, before World War I, 63–64

International Monetary Fund, 283, 349, 491

International relations: in Cuba, 372; in Latin America, 184–186; in 1914, 59; Wilson's Fourteen Point proposal, 75–76; before World War I, 64. *See also* Foreign policy; United States–Soviet relations

International terrorism, 446

Interventionism, 186, 369

Investment: and the Great Depression, 116, 117; Italian Fascism and, 138; in Latin America, 349; stock market collapse, 115–116. *See also* Foreign investment; Nationalization of foreign interests

Iran, 12, 18, 234n, 235, 411, 459, 491; European colonial interests in, 236, 238; hostage crisis, 311, 333; as mass society, authoritarian, 23; in 1970s, 309; postwar period, 412–415; revolution of 1905–1911, 87; and Soviet cold war policies, 289

Iraq, 12, 152, 411, 420, 502

Ireland, 85, 298. *See also* Great Britain

Iron Curtain, 294

Ironsi, J. T. Aguyi, 394

Islam, 14; in Africa, 206, 207; Crusades and, 7–8; defined, 49n, 234n; formal, 52; Pan-

Islam (*continued*)
Arabism, 409, 411, 415, 416; Shiism, 414; in Turkey, 255. *See also* Middle East
Islamic activism, 408, 409, 420, 473
Islamic civilization, extraterritoriality policy, 235
Islamic Republican party, 414
Isolationism, U.S., 82
Israel, 42, 420–426, 421 (map), 422 (fig.); assignment of, after World War I, 238; Egyptian war with, 415; military spending in, 494; and Nasser's seizure of Suez Canal, 295; nuclear capability of, 502. *See also* Arab-Israeli conflict
Israeli intelligence, and SAVAK, 413
Italy, 209; in Common Market, 298; empire of, 7; Ethiopian invasion, 210, 212, 213, 214, 259; Fascism in, 135–140; in NATO, 292; at Paris Peace conference, 77, 79, 82; and World War I, 60, 68, 69; and World War II, 263, 272–273; zero population growth in, 477
Ivory Coast, 383, 391, 488–489

Jabavu, John, 224
Jackson, Jesse, 340
Jameson, Leander Starr, 221
Japan, 118, 313, 410; vs. China, 254–255; China, invasion of, 247–249, 248 (fig.), 249 (map), 259; and China, during World War I, 245; Chinese territorial claims, 105; consensual politics and affluence, 446–447; economic growth of, 444–446, 485, 488; factors in success, 442–444; great power status, 249–252; vs. India, 255; Meiji Restoration, 250–252; military spending in, 494; modernization of, 255; monarchy of, 17; in 1914, 7; Pearl Harbor, 260; racial equality proposal after World War I, 77; and Russia, postwar invasion of, 94; Russo-Japanese War, 90; student protest in, 327; as superpower, 440–442, 442 (fig.); trade with United States, 244; vs. Turkey, 255;

U.S. occupation of, 292, 440; Western contacts, limitation of, 243; between world wars, 77, 253–254, 256; and World War II, 264–265, 266 (fig.), 274–276, 276 (fig.)
Jaruzelski, Wojciech, 309
Jazz, 172
Jerusalem, 424
Jews: anti-Semitism, Hitler's exploitation of, 141; in Berlin in 1914, 37–38; Holocaust, 271–272, 272 (fig.). *See also* Arab-Israeli conflict; Israel; Zionism
Jiang Jieshi, *see* Chiang Kaishek
Jiang Qing (Chiang Ch'ing), 436, 437
Jinnah, Muhammad Ali, 231, 232
Johnson, Lyndon B.: Great Society of, 330–331; Latin American policy of, 352; protest movements and, 325, 330; and Vietnam, 302–303
Joint-stock company, 9
Jordan, 238, 420, 494
Juaréz, Benito, 135

Kádár, János, 295
Kafka, Franz, 174
Kaiser, 39–40, 41, 70
Kampuchea, 304
Kandinski, Vasili, 168
Kapp, Wolfgang, 140
Kashmir, 427
Kemal, Mustafa, *see* Atatürk
Kennedy, John F., 324; and Berlin, 296; Cuban missile crisis, 288, 296–297; and Iran, 413; Latin American policy of, 352; and Vietnam, 302
Kent State University, 327
Kenyatta, Jomo, 380
Keynes, John Maynard, 127
Khan, Reza, 238
Khomeini, Ayatollah Ruhollah, 413
Khomeini regime, 414–415
Khrushchev, Nikita, 293–298, 294 (fig.); and Berlin, 296; Cuban missile crisis, 296–297
King, Martin Luther, Jr., 234, 326–327, 326 (fig.), 340
Kin groups: and African politics, 389–390; in African societies, 206, 207; in colonial villages, 45, 47–48; in cultur-

ally conservative societies, 14–16; kinsmen as wealth, 51
Kinship communalism, 388
Kissinger, Henry, 305, 418
Knesset, Israeli, 419
Knowledge explosion, 321–322
Knowledge industries, in Japan, 441–442
Koran, 49, 52n
Koreans, in Los Angeles, 459
Korean war, 292–293, 433
Kubitschek, Juscelino, 360, 361, 362
Kulaks, 96
Kuomintang, *see* Guomindang
Kurds, 238
Kuwait, 411

Labor force: in African colonies, 213; in Argentina, 190, 360; in Cuba, 372; and Great Depression, 116, 117, 121 (map); global pool of, 317; in Japan, 443; New Deal legislation concerning, 127, 128; sources of, for economic development, 21; in underdeveloped countries, 318; after World War I, 72, 73–74. *See also* Industrial workers; Union(s); Wages
Landownership: in China after Mao, 437; in Cuba, 368; in Latin America, 181; in Russia before revolution, 89. *See also* Agrarian reform
Laos, 304
Latin America, 184 (map): Argentina, 186–190, 187 (fig.), 355–360, 356 (fig.); Brazil, 190–194, 193 (fig.), 360–364; charismatic leaders, compared, 199–201; Chile, 352–355; colonialism in, 7; continental overview, 180–186, 346; Cuba, 367–373, 369–370 (fig.); in Great Depression, 119; economic development, 347–350, 348 (fig.); economies of, 181–184; fascism in, 151–152; immigrants from, 458–462; international politics after World War I, 77; Mexico, 195–199, 198 (fig.), 364–367; Nicaragua, 373–375; Paris peace conference representation, 79; politics, socioeconomic stress and, 350–351; politics and international relations, 184, 185

(fig.), 186; societies of, 180–181; struggle for independence and development, 186. *See also specific countries*
League of Nations, 80, 146, 186; African mandates, 210; condemnation of Japanese invasion of China, 253, 265; limitations of, 82; and Ottoman Empire, 238; Wilson's proposal of, 75–76
Lebanon, 17, 489; assignment of, after World War I, 238; fascism in, 152, 153; and Israel, 420; Palestinians in, 425; Reagan administration policy and, 311
Left, 124n; in Brazil, 362; and fascism, 132–133, 152; in Iran, 414; in Latin America, 351; New, 127–128; New Deal, 112, 125–129. *See also* Liberalism; Marxism; Socialism; Union(s)
Le May, Curtis, 274
Lembede, Anton, 403
Lend Lease Act, 267
Lenin, V. I., 58, 70, 85, 91–95, 93 (fig.), 168; assessment of role of, 96–97; changes instituted by, 93; Marxism, adaptation of, 88. *See also* Marxism-Leninism
Lesotho, 221
Liberalism, 18; in Argentina, 188; global issues, 484; Marxist philosophy, 10; New Deal, 127; nineteenth-century, 9–10, 156–157; old vs. new, 10; "savage," 338; and workers' benefits, 39
Liberalism, economic: failure of, 120–122; global issues, 484; in postindustrial society, 318
Liberia, 209, 388
Libertarian political systems, 20–23
Libido, 163
Libya, 12, 42, 502
Li Dazhao, 105
Life expectancy: in China, 439; in colonial villages, 47, 48; and demographic transition, 477; in India, 429; and kin group size, 15; technology and, 23–24
Lin Biao (Lin Piao), 437
Lister, Joseph, 41
Li Ta-chao, 105
Literacy: colonialism and, 217;

in Cuba, 371; in India, 428–429, 430; in Iran, 413; in Russia before revolution, 89; Sandinistas and, 374. *See also* Education
Liu Shaoqi (Liu Shao-ch'i), 435
Living standards: in Argentina, 357; in Brazil, 363; and demographic transition, 477; in Germany, prewar, 36, 37 (fig.), 38 (fig.)
Lloyd George, David, 68 (fig.), 71, 79–80, 81
Local economies, 14–15
López Mateos, Adolfo, 365
Lorraine, 69
Los Angeles, 452–453 (map); demographics, 458–462; economy of, 453–454; ethnic groups in, 458–462; growth of, 452, 454, 454 (fig.); migration to, 454–456; politics, 456–457; transportation, 455–456, 455 (fig.); Watts, 457–458
Louis XIV, 9
Ludendorff, Erich, 70
Lugard, Frederick, 216, 217, 218
Lunacharski, Anatoli, 168
Luther, Martin, 9
Luthuli, Albert, 403
Luxembourg, 2909, 298, 477

MacArthur, Douglas, 292
MacDonald, Ramsey, 123
McGovern, George, 333
Machado regime, in Cuba, 368
MAD, *see* Mutually assured destruction
Madagascar, Marxism in, 389
Madero, Francisco, 195, 196, 199
Mafia, 138
Magritte, René, 173 (fig.)
Malan , Daniel, 223, 224, 400
Malawi, 380
Malaya, 265, 280
Malinowski, Bronislaw, 164–166
Malthus, Thomas, 477, 478
Manchuria: Japanese invasion of, 247–249, 248 (fig.), 259; Soviet invasion of, 276
Mandates, 76–77, 239
Mandela, Nelson, 403, 405
Mao Zedong (Mao Tse-tung), 88, 98, 351, 447; anti-Soviet attitudes, 300; Chinese Revolution, 103–107, 106 (fig.); Cultural Revolution, 435–

437; democratic revolution of, 433; industrialization by, 434; on mass mobilization and military struggle, 247; successor of, 435
Markets, colonies as, 51–52
Maronite Christian Phalange, 425
Maronite Christians, 152
Marshall, George, 290
Marshall Plan, 290, 411
Marx, Karl, 10, 123
Marxism, 18, 88; and Chinese Revolution, 105, 106, 107; Depression and, 121–122; Einsteinian physics and, 161; and German welfare state in 1914, 39; in Latin America, 351; and rise of Fascism, 133; Russian Revolution and, 95. *See also* Socialism
Marxism-Leninism, 88; in Africa, 388–389; of Castro, 371; in Ethiopia, 385; exportation of, 98, 103–107; Mao's adaptation of, 88, 103–107
Mass culture: emergence of, 171–172; and art, 157
Mass education, *see* Education
Mass media, 171; Berlin, 1914, 34–35; censorship during World War I, 69, 71; and civil rights movement, 326; and mass society, 21–22; mobilization of public opinion for World War I, 63–64; and power, in 1980s, 12; Radio Free Europe, 295
Mass mobilization, 452; in Argentina, 189; causes of World War I, 60, 62–63; in Chile, 353; China vs. India, 254–255; in Cuba, 371, 372; in Egypt, 471–472; in India, 101–103, 428; in Latin America, 199, 200, 201; Mao Zedong on, 247; in Nicaragua, 373, 374; vs. revolution, 97–107; for World War I, media and, 63–64. *See also* Political mobilization
Mass politics, 18, 157; fascism and, 153; German, 39–41; in Latin America, 184
Mass production, and Depression, 116, 117
Mass society: authoritarian, 22–23; pluralistic, 22; political participation in, 333; rise of, 20–23
Mateos, Adolfo López, 365

Matteotti, Giacomo, 137
Mau Mau rebellion, 380
Medicaid, 330
Medicare, 330, 335
Meiji Restoration, 250–252, 488
Meir, Golda, 423, 425
Mensheviks, 92
Mercantilism, 181–183
Metropolis, 36
Mexicans, in Los Angeles, 460–461
Mexico, 411; agriculture in, 348; charismatic leaders, 199–201; democratic politics in, 184; economic shifts, 365–367; fascism in, 151; foreign debt of, 350; German activity in, during World War I, 69; "Great Rebellion," 195–199; Indians of, 180; infant mortality rates, 347; literacy in, 347; revolution in, 87, 97, 98–101; and Sandinistas, 374; single-party regime, 364–365; urbanization in, 347
Michels, Robert, 172
Middle class: in Argentina, 359; in Berlin in 1914, 36-39, 37 (fig.), 39 (fig.); and British Labour Party, 123; Marxist philosophy, 10; Nazi votes from, 142–143; and rise of fascism, 133
Middle East, 6, 8, 409–426, 410 (map): Egypt, 236, 237, 238–239, 415–420; European dominance in, 235–237, 236 (map); fascism in, 152, 153; independence movements, 236–242; Iran, 412–415; Israel, 420–426, 421 (map), 422 (fig.); Ottoman Empire, succession to, 238; Palestine, 239–240; petroleum and, 12; political fragmentation of, 236–242; Turkey, 240–242, 241 (fig.); after World War I, 77. See also specific countries
Mies van der Rohe, Ludwig, 171
Militarism and military governments: in Argentina, 358–359; in Brazil, 362–363; as cause of World War I, 62, 64–65; in Chile, 355; consolidation of German state, 30; and economic recovery in Nazi Germany, 144; German, in 1914, 33; Japanese, 253–

254, 264; in Latin America, 351, 354, 355, 375; of Lebanese Phalange, 152; in mass society, 22; in Middle Ages, 7–8; in Paraguay, 351; and relationship between strong and weak powers, 11; Shiite Muslims, 415; U.S. Latin American policy, 352, 355. See also Coups
Militarization: of African politics, 387–388; global, 493–494; by Hitler, 146; of Mexican politics, 98
Military: aid to African countries, 391; in Argentina, 189–190, 357; in Chile, 353; in Cuba, and overthrow of Machado regime, 368; in Iran, 412; in Latin America, 184; mobilization, Mao on, 247; service, universal, 63; technological developments, 282. See also Coups
Minorities: in Israel, 421, 423; in mass societies, authoritarian, 23; Russian, 89. See also Blacks; Ethnic groups; Palestinians
Missionaries, 7, 213, 216, 217
Mitterrand, François, 318, 337–339, 341, 342
Mobutu, Joseph, 379–380, 388
Molecular psychology, 163–164
Monarchy: authoritarian, 14; German, 40; symbolic bases, 17; types of, 9
Monet, Claude, 166
Monroe Doctrine, 183
Montagu, Edwin Samuel, 230
Morocco, 210, 383
Mosaddeq, Muhammad, 412, 414
Moslems, see Islam; Muslims
Movies, 171
Mozambique, 400; independence of, 380; Marxism in, 389; and socialist imperialists, 391; South Africa and, 402; USSR and, 391
Mubarak, Husni, 420
Mugabe, Robert, 380, 389
Mughal Empire, 229
Muhammad, Murtala, 397
Muhammad Reza, 412
Multinational corporations, 12; European fears about, 334; global issues, 490–492; Latin American neocolonialism, 349; price setting by, 340; after World War II, 323

Multinational states, 85. See also Colonialism; Empires; Imperialism
Munch, Edvard, 168
Munich agreement, 147–148, 147 (fig.), 149
Muslim Brethren, 415, 416
Muslims: common religious bond among, 49; Crusades and, 7–8; defined, 49n, 234n; extraterritoriality policy, 235; group identification, 15; in India, conflict with Hindus, 234, 255, 431; in Lebanon, 152; Pan-Arabism, 409, 411, 415, 416; in Russia, 6; in Syria, 152. See also Arabs; Islam
Mussolini, Benito, 74, 131, 133, 136 (fig.), 142; anti-Semitic laws, 160; defeat of, 272–273; foundation of Fascism by, 135–136; invasion of Ethiopia, 138, 140, 213, 214; policies of, 137–138; political rise of, 136–137
Mutually assured destruction (MAD), 313, 498, 500

Nagasaki, 276
Nagib, Muhammad, 415, 416
Nagy, Imre, 295
Nakasone, Yasuhiro, 446
Namibia, 210, 382, 402
Napoleonic wars, 190
Nasser, Gamel Abdul, 24, 239, 242, 409, 411; policies of, 415–417; Suez Canal seizure, 295
Natal, 224
National Autonomist party, 188
National debt, see Debt
National economy, 14, 21
National interest, as cause of World War I, 62
Nationalism: Arab, 417; in Argentina, Perón and, 357; in Brazil, 192; Chinese, 107; Japanese, 253–254; mobilization of public opinion for war, 63–64; in Nigeria, 218–219; in 1914, 6; in 1980s, 11; and World War I, 58–59. See also Independence movements
Nationalists, Chinese, 88. See also Guomindang
Nationality, defined, 6
Nationalization of foreign interests: in Argentina, 189,

356; in Chile, 353; in China, 245; in Egypt, 417; in India, 429; by Lenin, 93; in Mexico, 199

National Socialism, *see* Nazis

Nation-states: Germany, unification of, 30; in 1914, 6; in rise of West, 8–9

NATO, *see* North Atlantic Treaty Organization

Natural resources: in Argentina, 187; competition for, 12, 63; South African, 398. *See also* Interdependence

Naval powers, 6, 62, 65

Nazis, 135, 143; and Freud, 163; Hitler's infiltration of, 141; society and economy, 143–145; sources of votes, 142–143. *See also* Germany; Hitler, Adolph

Nazi-Soviet pact, 149

Negritude, 388

Negrophobia, 401

Nehru, Jawaharlal, 234, 426–429

Neocolonialism, 12, 351; in Argentina, 358–359; in Brazil, 362–363; in Latin America, 183–184, 186, 349, 354, 375; political effects of, 351; values for survival, 26; after World War II, 323. *See also* Africa; Latin America

Neoliberalism, 340, 341

Netherlands, The, 7, 8; Brussels Pact, 290; colonies after World War II, 280; in Common Market, 298; federal union in, 9; German invasion of, 262

Neves, Tancredo, 364

New Deal, 112, 125–129

New Left, 127–128

Newton, Isaac, 156

New Zealand, 292

Nicaragua, 349; coffee exports, 347; Reagan administration policy and, 311; Sandinista Revolution, 373–375; U.S. rule of, 186

Nicholas II, 62, 64, 90, 91

Nigeria, 210, 411, 491; Biafran Civil War/Second Republic, 394–398, 395 (fig.); British rule, 214–216; development of, 216–218; First Republic of, 392–394; GNP of, 385; independence of, 379; nationalism, rise of, 218–219; oil exportation by, 384; regions

of, 393 (map); urban growth, 383

Nineteenth-century world, 156–157

Nixon, Richard M., 324, 331, 333, 456; and Allende, 354; and détente, 305, 306 (fig.); in Japan, 441; Latin American policy of, 352–353; nuclear alert called by, 310; and Vietnam, 303–304

Nkomo, Joshua, 389

Nkrumah, Kwame, 379, 382, 387, 388

Nonviolence (*ahimsa*), 101–103, 326–327

North Africa: European dominance in, 235–236; German campaigns of World War II, 263; German occupation of, 267; independence struggles in, 236, 238–239; Ottoman Empire, succession to, 238–239

North Atlantic Treaty Organization (NATO), 498; creation of, 292; De Gaulle withdrawal of France from, 299; Soviet response to, 294

North Korea, 313, 447

Norway: German occupation of, 261–262; in NATO, 292; socialism in, 122; zero population growth in, 477

Nuclear weapons and technology: alert during Arab-Israeli war, 310; arms control, 500–502; arms race, 26, 296; Cuban missile crisis, 296–298; defense, 499–500; development of, 261, 282; global militarization, 493–494; and great powers, 12; in India, 429; nuclear explosion, effects of, 494–495; policies, 495–499; proliferation, 502–504; Soviet development of, 293; theoretical basis of, 159–161; and U.S. cold war strategy, 292; U.S. use of, on Japan, 260, 276

Nuremberg Laws, 271

Nyasaland, 380

Nyerere, Julius, 380, 388

OAS, *see* Organization of American States

Obregón, Álvaro, 99, 197

Oil companies: in Angola, 389; in Latin America, 199; in Mexico, 197

Oil prices: and African economies, 384; and Brazilian economy, 363; increases in 1970s, 12, 336, 350; and Japanese economy, 441; and Latin American economies, 355

Oil-producing countries: Brazil, 361, 363; Iran, 412, 413; Latin American, 199; Mexico, 366; Nigeria, 396; political and economic changes in, 409–412. *See also* Organization of Petroleum Exporting Countries

Oil supplies: crisis, 310–311, 336; global issues, 481–484

One-party governments: in Ghana, 387; in Mexico, 364–365

OPEC, *see* Organization of Petroleum Exporting Countries

Operation Overlord, 273–274

Operation Torch, 267

Opium War, First, 243

Organization of American States (OAS), 352, 382

Organization of Petroleum Exporting Countries (OPEC), 313, 318, 481; formation of, 411; and Israel, 425; oil prices, 310–311, 336, 350

Ortega, Daniel, 370 (fig.), 375

Ortega y Gassett, José, 172

Ottoman Empire, 42; division of territories of after World War I, 236; entry into World War I, 65; revolution in, 87; territory of, 235; trade in, 235–236; Turkish Republic from, 240; and Wilson's Fourteen Points, 75

Pahlevi dynasty, of Iran, 238

Pakistan, 427; formation of, 234; hostility with India, 429–430; nuclear capability of, 502, 503; and partition, 233 (map)

Palestine, 65, 85, 239–240, 418, 420, 422

Palestine Liberation Oranization (PLO), 424, 425

Palestinians, 420, 424, 425; independence movements, 240; massacre of, 425–426; Sadat and, 419

Palmer raids, 110

Palm oil, 216

Pan-Africanism, 382, 388

Panama, 186, 347, 374

Pan American Union, 186
Pan-Arabism, 409, 411, 415, 416
Pankhurst, Emmeline, 73
Paraguay, 351
Pareto, Vilfredo, 172
Paris Peace Conference, 186; and Chinese national interests, 246; Japanese territorial claims, 105. *See also* Versailles Treaty
Parks, Rosa, 326
Parliamentary democracy: socialism and, 112; South Africa as, 400
Parliamentary systems: and rise of Fascism, 133; after World War I, 71
Parliaments, 9; British, in seventeenth century, 9; German (Reichstag), 39, 40–41, 142, 143; Iranian, 413; Israeli, 419; Italian, 137; Russian (Duma), 91–92, 94; South African, 222
Pastoralism, 205
Patriotism, 63–64, 91
Peacemaking: global issues, 500–502; after World War I, 75–84. *See also* Disarmament; Versailles Treaty
Peace movement, 325
Pearl Harbor, 265
Peasants: in Brazil, 360; in China, 105, 107; in Japan, 256; in Latin America, 96, 181, 200, 348; in Mexico, 98–99, 100; in Russia before revolution, 89, 90; Stalin's Five-Year Plan, 96
People's Republic of China, *see* China
Peres, Shimon, 426
Perón, Eva Duarte, 190, 357
Perón, Isabel, 359
Perón, Juan, 184, 190, 199, 200, 351, 358–359, 360; economic policies of, 355–357
Peronistas, 357–358
Perry, Matthew, 244, 249
Persian Gulf, and U.S.-Soviet relations, 310–311
Peru, 180, 184, 350
Pétain, Phillipe, 262, 281
Phalange, 133, 152, 153, 425
Philippines, 265, 280, 292
Phony war, 261–262
Physics, 156, 157, 158–161
Picasso, Pablo, 166–167, 167 (fig.), 171
Pigmentocracy, 401

Pinochet, Augusto, 354
Planck, Max, 158, 159
PLO, *see* Palestine Liberation Organization
Pluralistic societies, mass, 22
Poincaré, Raymond, 111
Point Four Program, 352
Poland: German invasion of 1930s, 148, 149; Hitler's plans for, 145; invasion of, 259–260; Jewish extermination in, 271; Khrushchev's policy toward, 295; Paris peace conference decisions, 80–81; postwar territorial adjustment, 273; Solidarity movement in, 309; Wilson's Fourteen Point proposal, 75; after World War II, 277; in World War II, 261
Political action committee, 333
Political authority: in culturally conservative societies, 14; in Japan, 255; of monarchs, sources of, 14; popular sovereignty, 18, 20–23; World War I and, 75. *See also* Authority; Sovereignty
Political mobilization, 360; in Africa, 214, 383; in Brazil, 193–194, 362; in Chile, 353; in Cuba, 368; in Egypt, 50; in India, 120, 427; in Latin America, 354; in mass society, 21–22; in Mexico, 199; of South African blacks, 225. *See also* Arab nationalism; Independence movements; Mass mobilization
Political systems: in change-oriented societies, 17, 18; in colonial countries, 7; in culturally conservative societies, 14, 48, 49, 205, 207; innovations in Middle Ages, 8; Marxist philosophy, 10; in mass-oriented societies, 20–23; postindustrial, 317; in rise of West, 9–10; after World War I, 71, 74. *See also* Communism; Democracy; Fascism; Marxism; Marxism-Leninism; Socialism; Sovereignty
Politics: in Africa, 382, 384, 387–391; in Argentina, 188, 356, 357, 359; in Asia, 254–255; conflict in 1960s, 325–331, 339; conformity in 1950s, 319; conservatism in

1970s, 334; in Cuba, 372; in Germany, 39–41, 142–150; in Iran, 413; in Israel, 423; in Japan, 255, 440, 446–447; in Latin America, 184–186, 350–351; in Los Angeles, 461; mass, 21–22; in Mexico, 364–365; in Nigeria, 217; Russian before Revolution, 89; in Turkey, 241–242; Wilson's Fourteen Point proposal, 75–76. *See also* Fascism, German; Independence movements; Rebellion; Resistance; Revolution(s); *specific countries*
Popular culture, 171
Popular mobilization, *see* Mass mobilization; Political mobilization
Population growth, 486 (map); in Africa, 382; Aswan Dam project and, 25; in China, 439; as environmental threat, 25–26; global issues, 476–478; in India, 120; in Latin America, 346–347; in Mexico, 366
Population shifts, to suburbs, 322–323. *See also* Urbanization
Populism: in Argentina, 357; in Brazil, 193–194
Portugal: African colonial rule, 212; African decolonization, 379, 380; and Brazil, 190; in Common Market, 298; dictatorships, collapse of, 317; empire of, 7; explorations in Middle Ages, 8; Latin American colonies, 180, 182; in NATO, 292
Portuguese Guinea, 380
Positivism, 184
Postindustrial society: authority, re-establishment of, 331–337; black rebellion, 325–327, 326 (fig.); change, acceleration in, 320–321; cold war era, 319–325; collapse of authority in 1960s, 325; computer revolution, 321–322; France under Mitterrand, 337–339; political direction, search for, 333–337; problems in 1980s, 337; rebellion of young, 327–330, 329 (fig.); stagflation in, 333–337; suburbs, flight to, 322–323; television, 323–325; in United States, 339–340; wel-

fare state, 330–331; women's liberation, 331–333

Poverty: in India, 430; in United States, 339. See also Africa; Asia; Colonialism; Imperialism; Latin America; Revolution(s); Social issues; Unemployment

Power: government, Bolshevik experiment, 85; redistribution of, in Mexico, 100; resources and, 12; after World War I, 75, 77. See also Authority; Balance of power; Political authority; Revolution(s)

Princip, Gavrilo, 57, 58, 59 (fig.), 60

Private property, in China, 433

Private sector: in China after Mao, 437–438; in Egypt, 419; in India, 428, 429

Progress, idea of, 74, 85

Proletariat, 133. See also Industrial workers; Labor force; Working class

Propaganda: anticommunist, 110–111; in mass societies, 23; Nazi, 144; in Russia before revolution, 90; and World War I, 63–64, 74. See also Mass media

Protectionism, 489; global issues, 484; in India, 428; in Latin America, 201

Protest movements, 318, 325–331. See also Rebellion; Resistance; Student protests

Provisional Government, Russian, 91–92, 94

Prussia, 30, 39, 75

Psychology, 161–164, 161 (fig.)

Public health: Aswan Dam project and, 25; in change-oriented societies, 17; in colonial countries, 7, 47; in Cuba in early 1900s, 368; and demographic transition, 477; in Germany, 41; improvements in early twentieth century, 33–34; Indian populations, decimation of, 180; internationalism in, 63; Sandinistas and, 374; war-related technological advances, 282

Public opinion: in mass societies, 21–22; in Russia before revolution, 89; and World War I, 63–64, 74–75. See also Propaganda

Public spending: in Japan, 443, 445; in Egypt, 51, 419. See also Guarantor state; Welfare state

Qing dynasty, 244–245

Quinine, 216

Qur'an (Koran), 49, 52

Qur'an schools, 47

Rabin, Yitzhak, 425

Race issues: German attitudes in 1914, 30–31, 32; Hitler's policies, 270–272, 272 (fig.); in international politics after World War I, 77; in Latin America, 180–181; in Soviet Union, 391; in United States, 325–327; in Versailles Treaty, 77, 253; Watts riots, 457–458. See also Blacks; Ethnic groups; South Africa

Radicalization, of South African blacks, 225

Radicals: in Argentina, 188–189; in British Labour party, 123; in Latin America, 351; left, origin of term, 124n

Radio, 34, 171

Radioactivity, 160

Radio Free Europe, 295

Ramadan, 466

Ramirez, Sergio, 370 (fig.)

Rand Rebellion, 223

Rasputin, Grigori, 91

Rathenau, Walter, 72

Rawlings, Jerry, 388

Reagan, Ronald W., 289, 318, 324, 333, 341, 456; domestic policies of, 339–340; foreign policy of, 311–312

Rebellion: in India, 429; in Mexico, 195–199; rise of Fascism as, 134; in Russia before revolution, 89. See also Resistance

Red Scare, 110

Reformation, 9

Reich, German, 30

Reichstag, 39, 40–41, 142, 143

Relativism, cultural, 164–166

Relativity theory, 159–161

Religion: of Boers, 219: in change-oriented societies, 17; changes in values, 174; in colonial Egypt, 52–53; in culturally conservative societies, 15, 48, 49; in Germany, 41; and Islamic revolution, 414, 415; of Lebanese minorities, 152; and Middle East

conflicts, 236, 239; Reformation, 9; in Russia before revolution, 89; and sovereignty, 18; values for survival, 26. See also Islam; Missionaries; Roman Catholic Church

Remarque, Erich Maria, 74

Renaissance, 9

Republican party, 10. See also Conservatives/conservatism; Right

Resistance: ideology of, 12; nonviolent, 101–103, 326–327; passive, 102; in Russia before revolution, 89; in United States, 325–331. See also Rebellion

Revolution(s), 18, 165, 488; Cuban, 367–373, 369 (fig.); Cultural, 435–437; Egyptian, 239; Fascism as, 132–133, 135; in Germany, 140; Iranian, 310–311; Islamic, 414, 415; vs. mass mobilization, 97–107; Mexican, 97, 98–101, 195–199; pluralism and, 22; Sandinista, 349, 373–375; Shah-People, 413. See also Fascism; Revolution, Chinese; Revolution, Russian

Revolution, Chinese, 18, 103–107, 106 (fig.); phases of, 432–439; against Qing Dynasty, 245; vs. Russian Revolution, 103–107

Revolution, Russian, 58; artists serving, 168; attitudes toward, in 1920s, 110–111; vs. Chinese Revolution, 103–107, 106 (fig.); historic roles of Lenin and Stalin, 96–97; vs. Indian independence movement, 101–103; invasion, civil war and new economic policy, 94–95; and Lenin, 91–97; vs. mass mobilization, 97–107; vs. Mexican Revolution, 98–101; of 1905, 90; vs. other revolutions, 107–108; politics before, 89; provisional government, 91–92; second Revolution of 1917, 92–94; socialism in one country doctrine, 95–96; society before, 89; and Stalin, 95–97; tsarist Russia, 89–91; Western ideas, 89–91; World War I and, 69–70. See also Russia; Union of Soviet Socialist Republics

Reza Khan, 238

Reza Shah, Muhammad, 238, 242, 310–311, 412
Rhineland, 81
Rhodes, Cecil, 221
Rhodesia, 221, 380, 392, 400
Right, 124n; elements of, in Fascism, 132–133; in Iran, 414; in Japan, 253–254; religious, 414. *See also* Conservatives/conservatism
Rights: human, 353, 359, 362, 374; in mass societies, authoritarian, 23; political, bases for, 22
Right-to-work laws, 319
Rio Pact, 352
Rivera, Diego, 197, 198 (fig.)
Rogers, Will, 111
Roman Catholic Church: in Argentina, 357; and Fascism in Germany, 142; and Fascism in Italy, 137, 138; in Latin America, 184, 351; in Mexico, 197, 200
Roman Empire, 7
Roosevelt, Franklin Delano, 112; and Atlantic Charter, 267, 280; compromises with Stalin, 273; Fair Employment Practices Commission of, 282; Good Neighbor Policy, 186; isolationist foreign policy of, 265–267; and Japan, trade embargoes against, 265; and Lend-Lease Act, 267; New Deal of, 125–129; Yalta Conference, 277–280, 278 (fig.)
Rumania, 150, 485
Rural population shifts, 322. *See also* Urbanization
Russia: Bosnian Crisis of, 62; empire of, 7; as great power, 6; invasion of, after World War I, 94; of Lenin, 91–95; revolution in, 18; early technological status, 24; Triple Entente, 60; tsarist, end of, 89–91; and Wilson's Fourteen Point proposal, 75; and World War I, 58, 65–66, 68, 69–70, 91. *See also* Revolution, Russian; Union of Soviet Socialist Republics
Russian Revolution, *see* Revolution, Russian
Russo-Japanese War, 90

Sadat, Anwar, 43, 242, 415, 418–420
Salazar, Oliveira, 132, 138

Salgado, Plinio, 151
SALT I, 308, 499, 500
SALT II, 310, 501
Sandinista Revolution, 349, 373–375
Sandino, Augusto, 373, 374
San Martín, Ramón Grau, 368, 369
Santayana, George, 27
Satyagraha, 102
Saudi Arabia, 12, 411, 417
SAVAK, 413
Scandinavia, socialism in, 122
Scarcity, interdependence amid, 12
Schlieffen, Alfred von, 64
Schmidt, Helmut, 334
Schönberg, Arnold, 172
Science: in Berlin in 1914, 36; government policies in World War I, 72; intellectual life between wars, 156, 157, 158–161; nineteenth century, 156–157. *See also* Technology
Scientific Revolution, 9, 23, 158
Secret police, Iranian (SAVAK), 413
Securities and Exchange Commission (SEC), 127
Segregation, 325–327. *See also* South Africa
Seko, Mobutu Sese, 388
Senegal, 213
Senghor, Leopold, 388
Sepoy Mutiny, 230
Serbia, 57, 60
Serbs, 65
Service sector, 322; in Israel, 423; new jobs in, 339; and political attitudes of workers, 336–337; in third world, 489
Sevrès, Treaty of, 77, 238
Sex discrimination, 332
Sex roles: in culturally conservative societies, 14; in Latin America, 181; in mass societies, pluralistic, 22. *See also* Women's rights
Shagari, Shehu, 397
Shah of Iran, *see* Reza Khan; Reza Shah, Muhammad
Shah-People Revolution, 413
Shaka, 220
Shamir, Yitzhak, 426
Sharon, Ariel, 425, 426
Shiism, 414
Siam, 119
Sierra Leone, 209, 210, 218, 379

Sikhs, 427, 430, 431
Sinai, 424
Singapore, 265, 447, 489
Single-party regimes, *see* One-party governments
Siqueiros, David Alfaro, 197
Sisulu, Walter, 403
Six-Day War, 418, 424
Slavery, 22; African export of, 208; in African societies, 206; in Brazil, 191; in Latin America, 181
Slave trade, 213, 215
Slavs, 145
Slovaks, 77–78
Smuts, Jan, 222, 224, 225
Smuts-Hertzog fusion government, 223
Social change: in Asian countries, 254–255; and Fascism, 133–134; in Germany in 1914, 30; in India, 428; in Japan, 445; in Turkey, 241–242; after World War I, 72, 73
Social classes: in Berlin in 1914, 36–39, 37 (fig.), 39 (fig.); and Fascism, 133, 134; in Latin America, 346; in Russia before revolution, 89; after World War I, 75. *See also* Class structure; Middle class; Peasants; Working class
Social Darwinism, 145, 184
Social integration: in Latin America, 346; values for survival, 26
Socialism: in Africa, 388–389; Arab, 417; in Britain, 123; in Chile, 353; in Cuba, 368, 369; democratic vs. Marxist, 10; Depression and, 122–125; and Fascism, 137; in France, 123–125, 338; in Germany, 39, 140, 142, 143; in Latin America, 349, 351; need for, 112; New Deal as, 125, 126, 127, 128; pan-Arab, 415; political effects of, 351; Swedish, defeat of, 334; "war," 72. *See also* Left; Marxism
Social issues: in Africa, 382; and economic development, 488; in Latin America, 346–347, 350–351, 354; in Nigeria, 392, 393; and World War I, 64, 74
Socialist imperialists, 391
Social organization: of African societies, 206, 207; in

change-oriented societies, 17, 19; in colonial villages, 47; in culturally conservative societies, 14, 15–16, 205; World War I and, 72–74
Social planners, 330
Social policy, of Cuba, 371
Social Security, 335
Social welfare, in mass societies, 22. *See also* Guarantor state
Society: agrarian, 13–14; classifications, 4–6; German, Nazification of, 144; in Japan, 444–446; in Mexico, 99; post-industrial, 317; Russian, before revolution, 89; village, 47–49; after World War I, 75; after World War II, 261, 281–282. *See also* Change-oriented societies; Culturally conservative societies
Sociology, development of, 172
Soil fertility, 120, 430, 480, 481
Solar energy, 483
Somalia, 205, 389
Somme, Battle of The, 66
Somoza, Anastasio, 186, 373–374
Somoza, Anastasio, Jr., 374
South Africa, 85, 219–225; African mandates, 210; and Angolan civil war, 380, 382; apartheid, 400–405; black activism in, 403–405; economic and political domination by whites, 398–400; GNP of, 385; homelands, 399 (map); nonwhite responses, 224–225; nuclear capability of, 502; perspective on, 225–226; Union of, 221–224; urban growth, 383
Southeast Asia, 437 (map)
Southern Rhodesia, *see* Rhodesia
South Korea, 11, 441, 447, 502
South Slavs, 57, 58, 59, 60; Russia and, 62; after World War I, 77–78
South-West Africa, 210, 214
South-West African People's Organization (SWAPO), 382, 402
Sovereignty: in change-oriented societies, 18; popular, 18, 20–23; sources of authority for, 14
Soviets (councils), 92, 94
Spain: in Common Market, 298; dictatorships, collapse

of, 317; empire of, 7; explorations in Middle Ages, 8; Islamic rule of, 8; Latin American colonies, 180, 182
Spheres of influence, 244
Spiritual life: in colonial village, 52–53; World War I and, 74–75
Stagflation, 333–337
Stalin, Joseph, 78, 85, 93 (fig.), 95–97; and art, 168, 171; assessment of, 96–97; Berlin blockade, 290; and Chinese Revolution, 105; cold war policies, 290; concessions to, 273; effects of policies, 293; European Communist party policies, 124; and German invasion of USSR, 264; Khrushchev's denunciation of, 294; Nazi-Soviet Pact, 260, 264; at Yalta conference, 277–280, 278 (fig.)
Standard of living, *see* Living standards
Starvation, *see* Famine
Star Wars Defense, 499–500
Stateless societies, 205, 207
Strategic Arms Limitations Talks (SALT I and II), 308, 310, 499, 500, 501
Strategic Defense Initiative, 499–500
Strategic weapons, 495
Strikes: in Chile, 354; in Latin America, 199; in Mexico, 99, 195, 197; after World War I, 73, 110; of U.S. air controllers, 340
Strong-man regimes, U.S. sponsored, 292. *See also* Military governments
Student groups, in Brazil, 362
Student Nonviolent Coordinating Committee, 327
Student protests: in Argentina, 359; in Brazil, 362; in Japan, 445; in United States, 327–330
Submarine warfare, 65, 69; and nuclear weapons, 495–497
Suburbs, 322–323, 335
Suez Canal, 416, 417, 419
Suez War, 417
Suffrage: in France, 317; in Germany, 40; in Japan, 253; in mass societies, pluralistic, 22; in Mexico, 99; in South Africa, 400; in Turkey, 241. *See also* Women's suffrage

Summit conferences, 294, 297
Sunbelt, 319
Sun Yat-sen (Sun Yixuan), 88, 245, 246 (fig.)
Superpowers, *see* United States–Soviet relations
Superurbanization, 348, 349 (fig.); in Latin America, 354; in Nigeria, 393. *See also* Cairo; Los Angeles
Surrealism, 169–170
Swaziland, 221
Sweden, 122, 334, 347, 447
Switzerland, 477, 489
Symbols, 17, 23
Syria: assignment of, after World War I, 238; fascism in, 152; formation of United Arab Republic, 417; French mandate, 77; and Israel, 418, 420; Lebanon as part of, 152; military spending in, 494

Taft-Hartley Law, 319
Taiping Rebellion, 244
Taiwan, 292, 293, 432; and Japan, 441; nuclear capability of, 502; in world affairs, 447
Tambo, Oliver, 403
Tanaka, Kakuei, 446
Tanganyika, 210, 380
Tanzania, 210, 380, 388
Tariffs, 118, 184, 200
Taxes: in African colonies, 213; in Latin America, 184; World War I and, 72
Tax incentives, in Japan, 443
Technological unemployment, 116
Technology, 321; World War II, 318; benefits of, 23–26; in Berlin in 1914, 36; in change-oriented societies, 16–20; computer revolution, 321–322; and employment level, 320–321; government policies in World War I, 72; great powers and, 12; in India, 430; in Japan, 441–442, 444; and Latin American economies, 348–349; and Los Angeles economy, 453–454; in Middle Ages, 8; political, 333; postindustrial society, 317; in rise of West, 8–9; television, 323–325; war and, 85; after World War II, 282. *See also* Electronics industry; Electronics technology; Nuclear weapons and technology; Postindustrial society

Telegraph, 34
Television, 12, 323–325, 326
Teng Hsiao-p'ing, *see* Deng
  Xiaoping
Terrazas-Creel, 181
Terrorism, 15 (fig.), 446
Thatcher, Margaret, 341, 342
Theory of Special Relativity,
  158–159
Third Reich, 143, 144
Third World, 281; economic
  development, 488; economic
  position of, 19; immigrants
  in Los Angeles, 458–462. *See
  also* Africa; Asia; Latin
  America
Thoreau, Henry David, 102
Three People's Resistance, 247
Tito, Marshal (Josip Broz),
  294–295
Togo, Heihachiro, 90, 210, 214
Tolstoy, Leo, 102
Touré, Sékou, 379
Trade: African, 208, 209, 213;
  in Argentina, 187; chartered
  companies, 229; in China,
  243–244; in Depression, 118,
  119–120; European Eco-
  nomic Community, 298–299;
  extraterritoriality policy,
  235; global issues, 11, 484–
  485; Hawley-Smoot Tariff
  Act, 118; in Cuba, 372; in India, 230; innovations in Middle Ages, 8; in Japan, 244; in
  Latin America, 347; and
  Latin American economies,
  181–183; Nigerian, 215–216,
  396; in nineteenth-century
  liberalism, 9–10; in Ottoman
  Empire, 235–236; in South
  Africa, 398; transnational
  global integration, 490–492.
  See also Embargoes; Exports; Free trade
Trade balance: Brazilian, 363;
  Japanese, 441; Latin American, 349–350; Mexican, 367
Trade unions, *see* Union(s)
Tradition-oriented societies,
  see Culturally conservative
  societies
Transnational integration: European Economic Commu-
  nity, 298–299; global issues,
  490–492. *See also* Interdependence; Multinational
  corporations
Transportation: in Africa, 384;
  and disappearance of folk
  culture, 171; and economic

integration, 14, 19, 21; early
  improvements in, 33; in Los
  Angeles, 455–456, 455 (fig.);
  nationalization of Chinese
  railways, 245; Nazi construc-
  tion of superhighways, 144;
  and power, in 1980s, 12; in
  Russia, 89, 91
Transvaal, 221
Treaties: unequal treaty sys-
  tem, 243, 244; after World
  War I, 74, 77–84. *See also
  specific treaties*
Trench warfare, 66, 68
Tribal groups, 15, 389–390
Triple Alliance, 60
Triple Entente, 60
Truman, Harry S, 289, 319;
  cold war policies, 289–290;
  and Korean War, 292; Latin
  American policy of, 352
Truman Doctrine, 290
Tunisia, 210, 236
Turkey, 42, 65, 66, 409, 410,
  412; independence move-
  ments, 240–242, 241 (fig.);
  modernization of, 255;
  Treaty of Sèvres and, 238;
  and U.S. cold war policies,
  289
Turks, defined, 234n
Tutu, Desmond, 405

UAR, *see* United Arab Republic
Uganda, 380, 388
Ulyanov, Vladimir Ilyich, *see*
  Lenin
UN, *see* United Nations
Uncertainty principle, 159
Unconscious, the, 156
Underconsumption, and
  Depression, 116, 117
Underdeveloped countries, 4;
  Depression in, 114–115. *See
  also* Third World
Unemployment: in Britain in
  1930s, 123; in France in
  1980s, 338; in Great Depres-
  sion, 112, 113, 121 (map),
  126; in Grenada, 312; in Ja-
  pan, 444; in Nazi Germany,
  144; Reagan policies and,
  339; technological, 116; in
  United States in 1980s, 335
Unequal treaty system, 243,
  244
Union Monetaire Ouest-Afri-
  caine (UMOA), 382
Union(s), 127; in Argentina,
  190, 360; in Brazil, 194; and

British Labour party, 123; in
  Chile, 353; in Germany, 39,
  144; internationalism in, 63;
  Italian Fascism and, 137; in
  Japan, 440, 443; in Mexico,
  99, 199; in Poland, 309; in
  Russia, 90, 96; in South Africa, 402; weakening of, in
  1980s, 337; World War I, 73;
  after World War II, 319
Union of Soviet Socialist Republics (USSR), 85, 417; Afghanistan invasion by, 310;
  and African independence
  movements, 310; African interests, 391; and Angolan
  civil war, 380, 382; and
  Arab-Israeli war, 309–310;
  art in, 168; and Atlantic
  Charter, 280; and China, 300,
  305–306; control of European communist parties,
  122; Cuba and, 297, 371,
  372; Cuban missile crisis,
  296–298; détente, 306–310,
  311, 313–314; domination of
  Eastern European countries
  by, 78, 280; and East Berlin,
  296; economic development
  in, 485; economy of, 306–
  308; Egypt and, 417, 418; in
  European Security Conference, 308–309; and India,
  429; international relations
  after 1945, 286–289; and
  Iran, 412; Iron Curtain control, 294–296, 309; and Korean War, 292; in Manchuria, 276; as mass society,
  authoritarian, 23; military
  spending, 494; North Vietnam, aid to, 304; and nuclear disarmament, 294, 296;
  nuclear weapons development by, 292, 293, 306, 494–
  500, 496 (fig.); pact with Hitler, 149; Paris peace conference position, 80; postwar
  alignments of, 291 (map);
  postwar technology, 282;
  SALT talks, 308; of Stalin,
  95–97; Stalingrad, Battle of,
  268; as superpower, 281,
  283; treaty with Czechoslovakia, 147; Warsaw Pact,
  294; and World War II, 264,
  268, 279 (map). *See also* Revolution, Russian; Russia;
  United States–Soviet
  relations
UNITA, 401

United Arab Republic (UAR), 417

United Kingdom, *see* Great Britain

United Nations (UN): Arab-Israeli conflict, 417, 420; foundation of, 283; and Korean War, 292; Palestine settlement (Israel), 240; recognition of Palestine Liberation Organization, 425; and South African policies, 405

United States: and Afghanistan, 310; African interests in, 391–392; and Angolan civil war, 380, 382; anticommunist attitudes in 1920s, 110; atomic bombing of Japan, 276 (fig.); Bill of Rights, 22; and Brazilian coup, 362; CIA, 292; China, relations with, 305; cold war, 289–293, 319–325; and Cuba, 296–298, 367–368; and De Gaulle, 299–300; détente, 306–310, 311, 313–314; domination of means of transport and communication, 12; and Egypt, 416, 417; in European Security Conference, 308–309; food exports, 479; and Grenada, 311–312; infant mortality rates, 347; international relations after 1945, 286–289; invasion of Russia after World War I, 94; and Iran, 309, 310–311, 412–413; isolationism of, 265–267; and Japan, 244, 260, 440, 445–446; Korean War, 292; and Latin America, 186, 369; and Lebanon, 311; and Mexico, 100, 101, 197; Monroe Doctrine, 183; multipolarity and, 299; in NATO, 292; and Nicaragua, 311; in 1914, 7; and nuclear disarmament, 294, 296; nuclear weapons development, 292, 293; Pacific theater, 275, 276; Paris peace conference, 79–80; Pearl Harbor, 265, 267; postwar alignments of, 291 (map); Reagan administration policies, 339–340; SALT talks, 308, 310; and spread of Depression, 118; as superpower, 281, 283; and Taiwan, aid to, 293; technology, 282–283; Versailles Treaty, 58, 82; and Vietnam, 300–

305, 301 (fig.); women's liberation in, 331–332, 333; women's suffrage in, 73; and World War I, 69–70, 79; and World War II, 267, 273, 275. *See also* Central Intelligence Agency; Foreign Policy; Latin America; United States–Soviet relations

United States–Soviet relations: Berlin, 296; Carter administration, 309–310; challenges to bipolarity, 298–305; China and, 300, 305–306, 306 (fig.); cold war, 289–293, 291 (map); confrontation, return to, 311–312; Cuban missile crisis, 296–298; De Gaulle and, 299–300; Eastern Europe, Soviets in, 294–296; economic factors, 308; Europe, integration of, 298–299; interpreting, 287–289; Iranian Revolution, 310–311; Khrushchev, containment of, 293–298; and Latin America, 52; and military spending, 494; Persian Gulf, 310–311; and power distribution, 287; Vietnam, 300–305, 301 (fig.). *See also* Détente; Nuclear weapons and technology

Urbanization: in Africa, 383; in Brazil, 194, 348 (fig.); in Cuba, 368; and disappearance of folk culture, 171; in Germany, 33; industrialization and, 25–26; in Japan, 445; in Latin America, 347; in Mexico, 366; in Middle Ages, 8; in Nigeria, 396; in Russia before revolution, 90; in Soviet Union, 307. *See also* Berlin, in 1914; Cairo; Los Angeles

Urban societies, 335

Uruguay, 184, 351

Valorization, 191, 192

Values: and African politics, 390; in change-oriented societies, 17, 18; in culturally conservative societies, 13; in Germany in 1914, 41; mass education and, 63; rise of Fascism, 134; science and technology, optimism about, 24; for survival, 26–27, 499–504; World War I and, 74–75

Vargas, Getúlio, 151, 184, 192–

194, 193 (fig.), 199, 200, 351, 360, 361

Venezuela, 350, 374, 411

Verdun, Battle of, 66

Versailles Treaty, 58, 76, 301; conditions of, 79–84; Hitler's destruction of, 146–149; Japanese-sponsored clause on racial equality, 253; and rise of Fascism, 135; and Weimar Republic, 140–142

Verwoerd, Hendrik, 400

Vichy government, 267, 281

Victoria, queen of England, 230

Vietnam, 12, 288, 300–305, 301 (fig.); military spending in, 494

Vietnam War, 325, 327, 331, 446

Villa, Pancho, 99

Village life, in Dinshawai: vs. Berlin, 54; British Army incident, 42–44, 43 (fig.), 44 (fig.); economics, 50, 50 (fig.), 52; kinship system, 49–50; religion and spirituality, 52–53; society, 47–49, 47 (fig.); village structure, 44–46, 45 (fig.), 46 (fig.)

Violence, 400–405; in African cities, 383; in Argentina, 359; of Fascists, 133, 134, 136–147; in Germany, 142; terrorism, 15 (fig.), 446

Vital interest, as cause of World War I, 62

von Schlieffen, Alfred, 64

Wage controls, after World War I, 110

Wages: in African colonies, 213; in Argentina, 357, 358, 360; in Brazil, 362; in Chile, 353; in Cuba, 368, 371; and Depression, 116, 117; in Latin America, 349; in South Africa, 399

Wagner Act, 127

Wales, *see* Great Britain

Wall Street crash, 112, 113–116

War, causes of, 58, 62

War Communism, 93, 94

Warrant chiefs, 212, 217, 218

Warsaw Ghetto, 271

Warsaw Pact, 294, 498

War socialism, 72

Watergate, 333

Watson, James, 493

Watt, James, 41

Watts, 457–458
Wealth, distribution of, *see* Agrarian reform; Income distribution; Landownership; Natural resources
Weber, Max, 172
Weimar Republic, 81–82, 140–143. *See also* Germany
Welfare: in Egypt, 417; in Japan, 445. *See also* Guarantor state
Welfare state, 281–282; German, 39; global issues, 484. *See also* Guarantor state
West Bank, 424, 425
Western civilization: nineteenth-century views, 156; rise of, 7–10; Russia and, before revolution, 89–91
West Germany (Federal Republic of Germany), 294; in cold war, 290; in détente period, 308; rearming of, 292; zero population growth in, 477. *See also* Germany
Wilhelm II, 40
Wilson, H. L., 196
Wilson, Woodrow, 110, 111, 186, 196; Fourteen Points of, 75–76; Paris peace conference decisions of, 79–80, 81; recognition of Carranza, 196
Wittgenstein, Ludwig, 173
Women: in Cairo, 473; in colonial villages, 47; in Japan, 444; in labor force, during world wars, 73, 331
Women's liberation movement, 331–333
Women's rights: in Cuba, 372; in India, 428, 429; in mass societies, pluralistic, 22
Women's suffrage, 73; in France, 317; in Iran, 413; in Japan, 253; in Turkey, 241
Workers: in African colonies, 213; Italian Fascism and, 138; in Japan, 445; in mass societies, pluralistic, 22. *See also* Industrial workers
Working class: in Argentina, 357; in Berlin, 38–39; Marxist philosophy, 10; in Nazi

Germany, 142, 144; political conservatism of, 337; and rise of Fascism, 133; in Russia before revolution, 90; in USSR, 96
World Bank, 283, 491
World Court, 63
World domination, in 1914, 10
World economy: global interdependency, 11, 318; Latin American economies, 183. *See also* Global economy; Global interdependence; Interdependence
World Missionary Congress, 63
World War I: alliances and mobilization, 60, 62–63; Austro-Hungarian Empire and, 59–60; boundaries after, 83 (map); colonial issues, 76–77; economic and social effects, 72–74; Entente vs. Central Powers, 65–66; ideologies, 58–59; militarism, 64–65; nationalism and interdependence, 63–64; peace treaties, 77–84; psychological impact of, 74–75; and role of government, 71–72; and Russia, 69–70, 91; U.S. entry into, 69–70; western front, 66, 68–69; Wilson's Fourteen Points, 75–76
World War II: in Africa, 213–214; Allied mobilization, 268, 270; Axis defeat, 272–276; Battle of Britain, 262–263; Brazil in, 194; and Chamberlain's policy, 149; China in, 107; divisions after, 276–281; fall of France, 261–262; Egyptian independence, 239; European empires, end of, 280–281; European theater, 269 (map); German preparation for, 145–150; Hitler's design for aggression, 145–146; Hitler's European empire, 270–271; Holocaust, 271–272, 272 (fig.); homefronts, 268–272; India in, 232, 427; Japanese invasion of Manchuria, 247–249,

248 (fig.); Japan-U.S. conflict, 264–267; Latin America in, 183; Mediterranean campaigns, 263–264; Operation Barbarossa, 264; Pacific theater, 275 (map); Pearl Harbor, 265; phony war, 261–262; postwar influences of, 281–282; South Africa in, 222; start of, 259–261; turning points, 267–268; U.S. dominance after, 282–283; USSR western border changes, 279 (map); Yalta Conference, 277–280, 278 (fig.)

Xuma, Alfred, 225

Yalta Conference, 276–280, 279 (map)
Yemen, and Egypt under Nasser, 417
Yrigoyen, Hipólito, 188, 189, 195, 199, 360
Yuan Shikai (Yüan Shih-k'ai), 245
Yugoslavia, 78, 263

Zahran, 44
Zaire, 210, 379, 388, 392
Zambia, 221, 380
Zanzibar, 380
Zapata, Emiliano, 99, 196, 197, 199
Zar, 53
Zelaya, José Santos, 373
Zero population growth, 478
Zhou Enlai (Chou En-lai), 104–105, 246, 306 (fig.), 437
Zimbabwe, 221; family planning in, 478; Marxism in, 389; military spending in, 494; South Africa and, 402; Zimbabwe African Nationalist Union (ZANU), 380, 389; Zimbabwe African People's Union (ZAPU), 380, 389
Zionism, 38, 420, 422, 423; Balfour Declaration, 238; and Palestine, 239–240
Zulus, 206, 219–220